RELIVE PATRIOTS HISTORY
SIX-TIME WORLD CHAMPIONS

To Lori,
To a totally passionate
fan of the Patriots!
Go PATS!
Bob Hyldburg
Patriots Historian!

Hyldburg Publishing
Woburn, Massachusetts

2020

xo A ♡
Andrew
Orel

Merry Christmas
Law!
I still owe ya
a Pats game!

Hyldburg Publishing
HistorianBob@hotmail.com

ISBN: 978-0-9969921-2-1

Printed in the United States of America
King Printing Inc., 181 Industrial Avenue East, Lowell, MA 01852

DEDICATION

To the Holy Spirit
for giving me the gifts of
Passion, Persistency and Faith.

Thanks to my most awesome
and loving wife Millie
for her unconditional love.

TABLE OF CONTENTS

FOREWORD

Bill Belichick has won six Super Bowls and wide acclaim as possibly the greatest coach in NFL history but when it comes to attention to detail he ranks a distant second to Bob Hyldburg in the long history of the New England Patriots.

The first time I met Bob, he had my number. Actually, he had some obscure numbers for me that illuminated a moment in Patriots' history. Little did I know then that this would become a regular occurrence I would come to look forward to with great anticipation.

Hyldburg is the master of the odd moment and a historian without peer. If there is an arcane statistic or an esoteric incident in Patriot history, Bob not only has the story he has the story behind that story and the significance behind the most seemingly insignificant acts in the 60-year history of the NFL's winningest and most controversial franchise.

Fortunately for the rest of us, Bob has decided to again share his vast knowledge of the moments and the minutiae every Patriot fan worth his salt needs to know in his new book, *Relive Patriots History: Six-Time World Champions!* It is as much a must-read for Patriots' fans as Josh McDaniels' playbook is for Patriots' quarterbacks—and much more entertaining.

It is a perfect compendium to Bob's 5.4-pound tome, *Total Patriots: The Definitive Encyclopedia of the World-Class Franchise,* published in 2009. That book was considered the ultimate source for insanely detailed statistics and tales both tall and small covering the franchise's first 50 years. Now Bob, The Stat Man, as Hyldburg is known around the press box, has taken an updated deeper dive into the team's past and present in *Relive Patriots History.*

If you want to win a trivia contest, be considered the most knowledgeable Patriots' fan on your block or just care to know something unique about every player in team history, this book has to be in your library.

Did you know, for example, that the greatest birthday gift Bill Belichick ever received was the one he gave himself when he drafted an obscure sixth round draft choice named Tom Brady on April 16, 2000, Belichick's 48th birthday? Bob knew.

Who knew the Patriots played a HOME game at Jack Murphy Stadium in San Diego, nearly 3,000 miles from Massachusetts, on October 8, 1967?

Why? Because the Red Sox were playing a World Series game at Fenway Park that day so the Patriots' home field was not available. You can win a lot of trivia contests with that pearl from this gem of a book.

Relive Patriots History is a treasure trove of such odd moments backed by a staggering statistical depth. Ever wonder, for example, how many Patriots' quarterbacks completed a pass on their birthday? Bob did and he found them for you.

Do you have a vague recollection of the top five games played by the Patriots in various forms of extreme weather from foggiest to snowiest to windiest to wettest to coldest (with and without wind chill factored in to be precise) to hottest? *Relive Patriots History* fills you in on the details from the most sweltering to the most frigid.

Bob Hyldburg invested more than 20,000 hours of research over the past 25 years in a far from trivial pursuit of these stories and stats, an obsession that began with his desire to list the uniform number of every player who ever wore the Patriots' colors. During that quest he found a staggering amount of untold stories and odd categories of numbers. Thus, was laid the foundation for *Relive Patriots History!'*

Not only does this book contain recollections of the biggest wins of every Patriots head coach, but also entries ranging from topics like the top nine 'Did That Really Happen Offensive Plays?' to the top 10 'Most Bizarre Plays On A Punt.' Of all the information packed inside, my favorite is this gem: "A list of every reception of a pass thrown by a left-handed Patriots wide receiver" (hint they all happened in 1979).

Bob Hyldburg's *Relive Patriots History'* goes deeper than Randy Moss, hits the mark as accurately as Tom Brady, and is more fun than a barrel of Gronks. You can't call yourself a true Patriots fan if you don't have this insanely detailed, quirky compilation on your bookshelf. It's the perfect gift for the fan who has everything, because until you have this book you won't know everything about the NFL's greatest dynasty. Fortunately, Bob Hyldburg does and he's going to do for his readers what he did so many times for me. He's going to pass on his knowledge.

~ Ron Borges

ACKNOWLEDGEMENTS

Thanks for the encouragement from my sisters Darlene, Sherry, and Bonnie and her family; my Mom and her husband Jack; my son AJ and his wife Krista; and all of my cousins and extended family across the globe.

Kudos to the amazing cover art by my dear friend Paul Murphy AKA Paul D'Angelo.

Many of these obscure facts would not have been uncovered without the access to material provided by Richard Johnson and The Sports Museum, archives from the *Boston Globe* and the *Patriots Ledger* newspapers and the Media Relations Staff of the New England Patriots.

Thanks a million to Steve Burton, Dan Roche, Aaron Salkin, Sean Glennon, Bryan Morry, Ron Borges, Karen Guregian, Steve Buckley, Steve Sanchez, Glen Farley and Upton Bell.

Couldn't have done this project without my friend Phil Castinetti at *Sportsworld USA*.

Huge thanks to Rick Gonsalves for providing me with the information on every holder of the Patriots.

My TKE Fraternity brothers Max, Helmut, Patrick, Mike, Sean, Zink, Zoo, Bailey and Jack.

Tremendous accolades to Robin Wrighton. Her expertise in designing the book, cover, and patience editing this massive amount of information was stupendous. Her incredible assistance and support was off the charts.

Appreciate the meaningful connection and friendship from: David Chapin and his family, Joanne and Lenny Hensas, Keith "The Silver Bullet" Birchall, Scott Holt, Todd King, Harry Skigis, Kevin Karlson, Pete McKenzie and Heather Ford, Brendan Kirby, Gene Lavanchy, Steve Sweeney, Joey 'Voices' Noone, Mikey Adams, Tyler Gates, David Black, Nick "Fitzy" Stevens, Ryan Fine, Rick Pike, Frank Failla, Kurt Krause, Bob Cofrancesco, Frank Walsh, Mike Wigdor, Kevin Tocci, Keith Hayes, Christopher Cooney, Kevin Tame, Jayne Ross, Maria Alaina Paradise, Anne Stone, Marian Muse, Yuki Henry, Judy Ryan, Robert Hayes, John Sapochetti, Dan Saltzman, Joe Gill, Shaun L. Kelly, Bill White, Todd Orsatti, Joe O'Hara, Scott Bilotta, Dennis Gero, Gregory Nitikin, Harvey McCarthy, Chris Porter, Steven Parmenter, John Graham, George Brew, Jeffrey Fuller, Andy Gresh, Jerry Thornton, John Molori, Chris Fleser, Bob Elliot, David and Lauren Biller, David Bowen, Joe Murray, Mike 'Sarge' Riley, Toucher and Rich, Hank Morse, Robin Dirocco, Nina Cook, Belinda Wolf, Donna Spigarolo, Pam Dockx, Jeanne Dooley, Mary Tonks, Ginger Betty, Michael Bevilacqua, Ian Abreu, Kevin Willett, Mark Berger, Bob Salvas, Michael Vickery, Dan Curran, Joe LoRusso, Dennis Mcelhiney, Corey Briggs, Scott Prusak and Russell Baxter.

Truly appreciate Stacey James for giving me the opportunity to work for the National Football League for every Patriots Home Game from 2005-2018.

INTRODUCTION

Can you believe that the New England Patriots have won 6 World Championships? As the last team to join the newly formed American Football League in 1959 it is still hard to believe how dominant the Patriots have been since winning their 1st World Championship in 2002.

On November 19, 1959, the 8th and final franchise of the newly formed American Football League was awarded to Boston. A few months later the team held a public naming contest. Many names were suggested such as the Beaneaters, Beantowners, Braves, Bulls, Colonials, Hubs, Minutemen, Musketeers, Patriots, Pilgrims, Puritans and Revolutionaries. And after reviewing numerous essays to choose between the Minutemen and Patriots, it was decided that the Patriots would be the most appropriate name for this franchise.

During the 11-year run of the Boston Patriots, from 1960-70, they won only 1 playoff game. After moving to a new stadium in Foxboro in 1971 they changed their name to the New England Patriots and yet the losing continued. During the 1970s they played in 2 playoff games and lost them both. Not a great start for their first twenty years of playing professional football.

In the 1980s they had some success with Head Coach Raymond Berry and became the 1st NFL Wild Card Team to win 3 consecutive road playoff games and play in the Super Bowl. Alas they were crushed by Da' Bears 46-10 in Super Bowl XX.

Even though they only won 1 game in 1990 and just 2 games in 1992, they did manage to participate in 6 playoff games and make it back to the Super Bowl in the 1990s. Unfortunately, they lost that Championship Game by 2 touchdowns to the Green Packers.

A few very significant events happened during the 4th decade of this franchise. On January 21, 1993, they hired Bill Parcells and almost immediately things started to change for the better. One year later, Robert K. Kraft became the fourth owner of the team and finally fans had hope that someday the Patriots might become a Championship Team.

At the beginning of the 20th century, the Patriots made two of the most important decisions ever made by any NFL franchise. On January 27, 2000, Bill Belchick was hired as their Patriots 14th Head Coach and on his April 16, 2000, (Bill's 48th birthday) Tom Brady was drafted to play QB for the Patriots. The Greatest Coach and Greatest QB in Pro Football History.

Here is the collaboration of insane stats of everyone who has played for this team since their first regular season game on September 9, 1960. We certainly hope you enjoy reviewing and reliving some of these crazy and certainly memorable moments.

~ Bob Hyldburg

CHAPTER 1

EVERY RADIO AND TELEVISION ANNOUNCER AND COLOR COMMENTATOR

THE BOSTON / NEW ENGLAND PATRIOTS RADIO PLAY BY PLAY AND COLOR COMMENTATORS

Years	Play by Play	Color Commentator	Radio Station
1960-64	Bob Gallagher	Fred Cusick	WEEI 590 AM
1965	Bob Gallagher	Ned Martin	WEEI 590 AM
1966-70	James "Bob" Starr	Gil Santos	WBZ 1030 AM
1971	Gil Santos	John Carlson	WBZ 1030 AM
1972-78	Gil Santos	Gino Cappelletti	WBZ 1030 AM
1979	Gil Santos	Jon Morris	WBZ 1030 AM
1980-86	John Carlson	Jon Morris	WEEI 590 AM
1987	Curt Gowdy	Jon Morris	WHDH 850 AM
1988-90	Dale Arnold	Gino Cappelletti	WHDH 850 AM
1991-94	Gil Santos	Gino Cappelletti	WBZ 1030 AM
1995-2000	Gil Santos	Gino Cappelletti	WBCN 104.1 FM
2001	Gil Santos	Pete Brock (1st 8 games)	WBCN 104.1 FM
2001-08	Gil Santos	Gino Cappelletti	WBCN 104.1 FM
2009-11	Gil Santos	Gino Cappelletti	WBZ 98.5 FM
2012	Gil Santos	Scott Zolak	WBZ 98.5 FM
2013--	Bob Socci	Scott Zolak	WBZ 98.5 FM

Official Home Offices of the Boston/New England Patriots

1960-63: **520 Commonwealth Ave,** Boston 7 Phone COngress 2-1776
1964-65: **522 Commonwealth Ave,** Boston 15 Phone #262-1776
1966-71: **78 Landsdowne Street,** Fenway Park Boston, MA 02115
August 1971 to May 1983: **Schaefer Stadium,** Rte 1 Foxboro MA 02035 Phone #617-262-1776
May 1983 to May 1990: **Sullivan Stadium,** Route 1 Foxboro, MA 02035
May 1990 to May 2002: **Foxboro Stadium,** Rte 1 Foxboro, MA 02035 Toll Free 1-800-543-1776
May 2002 to August 2002: **CMGI Field,** Route 1 Foxboro, MA 02035
August 2002 to Present: **Gillette Stadium,** One Patriot Place Foxboro, MA 02035 508-384-4203

Location and Dates of the Home Games for the Boston Patriots

Boston University Field (7 games in 1960, 7 games in 1961 and 6 games in 1962)
Harvard Stadium (Sept. 16, 1962 and 7 games in 1970)
Boston College Alumni Stadium (Sept. 8, 1963, Oct. 15, 1967 and 7 games in 1969)
Fenway Park (6 games in 1963; 7 games in 1964, 1965, 1966; 5 games in 1967; and 6 games in 1968)
Jack Murphy Stadium in San Diego, CA on Oct. 8, 1967 (the Red Sox were in the 1967 World Series)
Legion Field in Birmingham, AL on Sept. 22, 1968 (the college home field of Joe Namath)

From 1963-68, Fenway Park was the Patriots Home Field except for Red Sox Home Games

PATRIOTS GAMES THAT WERE BROADCAST ON NATIONAL TELEVSION

Boston Patriots Games on ABC TV

Friday Night Games

Beat the Buffalo Bills 21-10 (Curt Gowdy and Paul Christman) on 11-23-62
Beat Houston 25-24 (Charlie Jones and George Ratterman) on 11-06-64 *(Cappelletti kicked GW FG)*

Only Boston Patriots Game That Was Played on Saturday Night and on ABC TV

Beat the NY Titans 28-24 (Jim Simpson and Frank Leahy) on 09-17-60 *(First Win in Team History)*

Boston Patriots Games on ABC TV from 1960-64

Sunday Afternoon Games

Lost 31-24 to the Denver Broncos (Jack Buck and Elmer Angsman) on 10-23-60
Lost 38-14 to the Buffalo Bills (Bob Wolff) on 12-04-60
Lost 37-21 to the Houston Oilers (Les Keiter and Elmer Angsman) on 12-18-60

Lost 37-30 to the New York Titans (Charlie Jones) on 10-01-61
Beat the Dallas Texans 18-17 (Charlie Jones) on 10-29-61 *(Parilli and Songin alternated plays at QB)*
Shutout the San Diego Chargers 41-0 (Bob Neal and Elmer Angsman) on 12-17-61

Beat the Houston Oilers 34-21 (Charlie Jones and George Ratterman) on 09-16-62
Beat the Broncos 33-29 (Curt Gowdy and Paul Christman) on 11-11-62
Beat the San Diego Chargers 20-14 (Curt Gowdy and Paul Christman) on 12-09-62

Beat the New York Jets 38-14 (Curt Gowdy and Paul Christman) on 09-08-63
Beat the Oakland Raiders 20-14 (Jack Buck and George Ratterman) on 09-22-63
Lost 7-6 to the San Diego Chargers (Jack Buck and George Ratterman) on 11-10-63
Tied the Kansas City Chiefs 24-24 (Charlie Jones) on 11-17-63
Beat Buffalo 26-8 in **AFL Divisional Playoff** (Jack Buck and George Ratterman) on 12-28-63
Lost 51-10 to San Diego in **AFL Championship** (Curt Gowdy and Paul Christman) on 01-05-64

Beat Oakland 17-14 (Charlie Jones and George Ratterman) on 09-13-64
Beat San Diego 33-28 (Charlie Jones and George Ratterman) on 09-20-64
Beat the Jets 26-10 (Curt Gowdy and Paul Christman) on 09-27-64
Destroyed Denver 39-10 (Charlie Jones and George Ratterman) on 10-04-64
Beat Buffalo 36-28 (Charlie Brockman and Elmer Angsman) on 11-15-64
Lost 24-14 to Buffalo (Curt Gowdy and Paul Christman) on 12-20-64

Boston Patriots Games Played on Saturday Afternoon on NBC TV for 1966-67

Lost 38-28 to the Jets (Jim Simpson and Elmer Angsman) on 12-17-66
Lost 44-16 to Buffalo (Curt Gowdy and Paul Christman) on 12-09-67

Boston Patriots Games on Sunday Afternoon on NBC TV from 1965-70

Lost 31-10 to the Houston Oilers (Curt Gowdy and Paul Christman) on 09-19-65
Lost 27-10 to the Kansas City Chiefs (Bill O'Donnell and Elmer Angsman) on 10-03-65
Tied the San Diego Chargers 13-13 (Herb Carneal and Andy Robustelli) on 10-17-65
Lost 30-21 to the Oakland Raiders (Herb Carneal and Andy Robustelli) on 10-24-65
Beat San Diego 22-6 (Charlie Jones and George Ratterman) on 10-31-65
Lost to Buffalo 23-7 (Herb Carneal and Andy Robustelli) on 11-07-65
Lost to the Jets 30-20 (Curt Gowdy and Paul Christman) on 11-14-65
Tied the Chiefs 10-10 (Herb Carneal and Andy Robustelli) on 11-21-65
Beat the Jets 27-23 (Curt Gowdy and Paul Christman) on 11-28-65
Beat Denver 28-20 (Bill O'Donnell and Elmer Angsman) on 12-12-65
Humbled Houston 42-14 (Curt Gowdy and Paul Christman) on 12-18-65 *(Cappelletti scored 28 pts)*

Beat Denver 24-10 (Jim Simpson and Elmer Angsman) on 09-18-66
Tied the Jets 24-24 (Curt Gowdy and Paul Christman) on 10-02-66
Lost 17-10 to Denver (Jim Simpson and Elmer Angsman) on 11-06-66
Beat Miami 20-14 (Jim Simpson and Elmer Angsman) on 11-27-66
Beat Buffalo 14-3 (Jim Simpson and Elmer Angsman) on 12-04-66 (Cover of *Sports Illustrated*)
Humiliated Houston 38-14 (Jim Simpson and Elmer Angsman) on 12-11-66

Lost 26-21 to Denver (Curt Gowdy and Paul Christman) on 09-03-67
Shutout Buffalo 23-0 (Charlie Jones and George Ratterman) on 09-24-67
Lost 27-6 to Houston (Curt Gowdy and Paul Christman) on 11-26-67
Lost 41-32 to Miami (Curt Gowdy and Paul Christman) on 12-17-67

Beat Buffalo 16-7 (Charlie Jones and Al DeRogatis) on 09-08-68
Lost 47-31 to the Jets (Charlie Jones) on 09-22-68
Beat Denver 20-17 (Charlie Jones) on 09-29-68
Lost 41-10 to the Oakland Raiders (Charlie Jones and Al DeRogatis) on 10-06-68
Beat Buffalo 23-6 (Charlie Jones) on 10-20-68
Beat the Bengals 33-14 (Jim Simpson and Elmer Angsman) on 12-01-68
Lost 45-17 to Houston (Charlie Jones and George Ratterman) on 12-15-68

Beat Miami 38-23 in Tampa (Charlie Jones and Al DeRogatis) on 11-30-69
Beat Miami 27-14 (Jim Simpson and Al DeRogatis) on 09-20-70
Lost 14-6 to the Baltimore Colts (Jay Randolph and Johnny Morris) on 10-04-70
Lost 23-10 to the Chiefs (Charlie Jones and Kyle Rote) on 10-11-70
Lost 27-3 to the Baltimore Colts (Bill O'Donnell and Dave Kocourek) on 10-25-70
Lost 45-10 to Buffalo (Bill Enis and Dave Kocourek) on 11-01-70
Lost 31-0 to the St. Louis Cardinals (Jay Randolph and Gordie Soltau) on 11-08-70
Lost 16-14 to San Diego (Ross Porter and Willie Davis) on 11-15-70
Beat Buffalo 14-10 (Charlie Jones and George Ratterman) on 11-29-70
Lost 37-20 to Miami (Jim Simpson and Al DeRogatis) on 12-06-70
Lost 45-7 to Cincinnati (Bill Enis and Johnny Morris) on 12-20-70

Only Boston Patriots Games on CBS TV

Lost 16-0 to the NY Giants (Jack Whitaker and Tom Brookshier) on 10-18-70
Lost 35-14 to the Minnesota Vikings (Lindsey Nelson and Don Perkins) on 12-13-70

New England Patriots Games on NBC TV from 1971-74

Beat the Oakland Raiders 20-6 (Charlie Jones and George Ratterman) on 09-19-71
Lost 23-3 to Baltimore (Charlie Jones and Al DeRogatis) on 10-03-71
Lost 41-3 to Miami (Bill Enis and George Ratterman) on 10-17-71
Lost 44-21 to the Cowboys (Jay Randolph and Dave Kocourek) on 10-24-71
Lost 27-10 to San Francisco (Ross Porter and Johnny Morris) on 10-31-71
Beat Houston 28-20 (Bill Enis and Dave Kocourek) on 11-07-71
Beat Buffalo 38-33 (Jay Randolph and Paul Maguire) on 11-14-71
Lost 27-7 to Cleveland (Bill O'Donnell and Johnny Morris) on 11-21-71
Lost 27-20 to Buffalo (Bill Enis and Dave Kocourek) on 11-28-71
Beat Miami 34-13 (Bill Enis and Dave Kocourek) on 12-05-71
Lost 13-6 to the Jets (Bill Enis and Dave Kocourek) on 12-12-71
Beat Baltimore 21-17 (Jim Simpson and Kyle Rote) on 12-19-71

Lost 31-7 to the Bengals (Jay Randolph and Willie Davis) on 09-17-72
Beat Atlanta 21-20 (Don Criqui and Irv Cross) on 09-24-72
Lost 38-14 to Buffalo (Ken Coleman and Paul Maguire) on 10-08-72
Lost 33-3 to Pittsburgh (Jay Randolph and Alan Miller) on 10-22-72
Lost 34-10 to the Jets (Jim Simpson and Kyle Rote) on 10-29-72
Lost 52-0 to Miami (Jay Randolph and Dave Kocourek) on 11-12-72
Lost 27-24 to Buffalo (Ross Porter and Dave Kocourek) on 11-19-72
Lost 31-0 to Baltimore (Ken Coleman and Dave Kocourek) on 11-26-72
Lost 37-21 to Miami (Jim Simpson and Kyle Rote) on 12-03-72
Beat the Saints 17-10 (Jay Randolph and Dave Kocourek) on 12-10-72
Lost 45-21 to the Broncos (Charlie Jones and George Ratterman) on 12-17-72

Lost 31-13 to Buffalo (Jay Randolph and Dave Kocourek) on 09-16-73
Lost 10-7 to the Chiefs (Jay Randolph and Paul Maguire) on 09-23-73
Lost 44-23 to Miami (Jay Randolph and Paul Maguire) on 09-30-73
Beat Baltimore 24-16 (Bill O'Donnell and Dave Kocourek) on 10-07-73
Lost 9-7 to the Jets (Charlie Jones and Sam De Luca) on 10-14-73
Beat the Bears 13-10 (Ken Coleman and Sam DeLuca) on 10-21-73
Lost 30-14 to Miami (Jay Randolph and Paul Maguire) on 10-28-73
Lost 24-23 to Philadelphia (Bill Enis and Paul Maguire) on 11-04-73
Lost 33-13 to the Jets (Jim Simpson and Kyle Rote) on 11-11-73
Shutout Houston 32-0 (Bill Enis and Dave Kocourek) on 11-25-73
Beat San Diego 30-14 (Ross Porter and Willie Davis) on 12-02-73
Lost 37-13 to Buffalo (Jay Randolph and Alan Miller) on 12-09-73
Lost 18-13 to Baltimore (Jay Randolph and Paul Maguire) on 12-16-73

Beat Miami 34-24 (Bill O'Donnell and Sam De Luca) on 09-15-74
Beat the Giants 28-20 (Bill O'Donnell and Johnny Morris) on 09-22-74
Blasted Baltimore 42-3 (Charlie Jones and John Brodie) on 10-06-74
Shutout the Jets 24-0 (Charlie Jones and John Brodie) on 10-13-74
Lost 30-28 to Buffalo (Jim Simpson and John Brodie) on 10-20-74
Beat the Vikings 17-14 (Jim Simpson and John Brodie) on 10-27-74 *(Windsor with GW TD)*
Lost 29-28 to Buffalo (Curt Gowdy, Don Meredith and Al DeRogatis) on 11-03-74
Lost 21-14 to Cleveland (Bill O'Donnell and Johnny Morris) on 11-10-74
Lost 21-16 to the Jets (Jim Simpson and John Brodie) on 11-17-74
Beat Baltimore 27-17 (Jay Randolph and Paul Maguire) on 11-24-74
Lost 41-26 to the Oakland Raiders (Bill O'Donnell and Johnny Morris) on 12-01-74
Lost 21-17 to Pittsburgh (Charlie Jones and Sam De Luca) on 12-08-74
Lost 34-27 to Miami (Charlie Jones and Sam De Luca) on 12-15-74

Games on NBC TV from 1975-78

Lost 7-0 the Houston Oilers (Ross Porter and Willie Davis) on 09-21-75
Lost 22-14 to Miami (Jim Simpson and John Brodie) on 09-28-75
Lost 36-7 to the Jets (Charlie Jones and Al DeRogatis) on 10-05-75
Lost 27-10 to the Bengals (Bill O'Donnell and Sam De Luca) on 10-12-75
Beat Baltimore 21-10 (Bill O'Donnell and Sam De Luca) on 10-19-75
Lost 24-17 to St. Louis (Ross Porter and Willie Davis) on 11-02-75
Beat San Diego 33-19 (Ross Porter and Willie Davis) on 11-09-75
Lost 45-31 to Buffalo (Charlie Jones and Sam De Luca) on 11-23-75
Lost 30-28 to the Jets (Jim Simpson and John Brodie) on 12-07-75
Lost 34-14 to Buffalo (Jim Simpson and Al DeRogatis) on 12-14-75
Lost 34-21 to Baltimore (Curt Gowdy and Al DeRogatis) on 12-21-75

Lost 27-13 to Baltimore (Jay Randolph and Floyd Little) on 09-12-76
Beat Miami 30-14 (Charlie Jones and Sam De Luca) on 09-19-76
Beat Pittsburgh 30-27 (Jim Simpson and John Brodie) on 10-03-76
Ransacked the Raiders 48-17 (Curt Gowdy and John Brodie) on 10-03-76
Lost 30-10 to the Lions (Jim Simpson and John Brodie) on 10-10-76
Beat Buffalo 26-22 (Tim Ryan and Lionel Aldridge) on 10-24-76
Lost 10-3 to Miami (Jack Buck and Paul Maguire) on 10-31-76
Beat Buffalo 20-10 (Charlie Jones and Sam De Luca) on 11-07-76
Beat Baltimore 21-14 (Jack Buck and Len Dawson) on 11-14-76
Beat the Jets 38-24 (Jim Simpson and Len Dawson) on 11-21-76 *(Team Record 10 takeaways)*
Ran over Denver 38-14 (Jim Simpson and John Brodie) on 11-28-76 *(Team Record 332 yards rushing)*
Beat the Buccaneers 31-14 (Charlie Jones and Sam De Luca) on 12-12-76
Lost 24-21 to Oakland in **Divisional Game** (Curt Gowdy and Don Meredith) on 12-18-76

Beat Kansas City 21-17 (Charlie Jones and Len Dawson) on 09-18-77
Lost 30-27 to the Jets (Charlie Jones and Len Dawson) on 10-02-77
Shutout Seattle 31-0 (Dick Stockton and Lionel Aldridge) on 10-09-77
Beat San Diego 24-20 (Jay Randolph and Len Dawson) on 10-16-77
Beat Baltimore 17-3 (Curt Gowdy and John Brodie) on 10-23-77
Beat the Jets 24-13 (Jim Simpson and Merlin Olsen) on 10-30-77
Lost 24-14 to Buffalo (Charlie Jones and Andy Russell) on 11-06-77
Lost 17-5 to Miami (Dick Stockton and Mike Haffner) on 11-13-77
Beat Buffalo 20-7 (Jim Simpson and Merlin Olsen) on 11-20-77
Beat Atlanta 16-10 (Charlie Jones and Andy Russell) on 12-04-77
Beat Miami 14-10 (Jim Simpson and Merlin Olsen) on 12-11-77
Lost 30-24 to Baltimore (Dick Enberg and Merlin Olsen) on 12-18-77

Beat St. Louis 16-6 (Dick Enberg and Merlin Olsen) on 09-10-78
Beat San Diego 28-23 (Charlie Jones and Len Dawson) on 10-01-78
Beat the Bengals 10-3 (Sam Nover and Bob Trumpy) on 10-15-78
Beat Miami 33-24 (Dick Enberg and Merlin Olsen) on 10-22-78
Smoked the Jets 55-21 (Dick Enberg and Merlin Olsen) on 10-29-78
Beat Buffalo 14-10 (Sam Nover and Len Dawson) on 11-05-78
Beat the Jets 19-17 (Jay Randolph and Bob Trumpy) on 11-12-78
Beat Baltimore 35-14 (Jim Simpson and Paul Warfield) on 11-26-78
Lost 17-10 to Dallas (Dick Enberg and Merlin Olsen) on 12-03-78
Beat Buffalo 26-24 (Sam Nover and Mike Haffner) on 12-10-78
Lost 31-14 to the Oilers in **Divisional Game** (Charlie Jones and Len Dawson) on 12-31-78

Games on NBC TV from 1979-82

Blasted the Jets 56-3 (Charlie Jones and Len Dawson) on 09-09-79 (*McDonough/Clayborn scuffle*)
Beat the Bengals 20-14 (Merle Harmon and George Kunz) on 09-16-79
Beat San Diego 27-21 (Dick Enberg and Merlin Olsen) on 09-23-79 (*Fans rejected new logo*)
Beat the Bears 27-7 (Dick Enberg and Merlin Olsen) on 10-14-79
Beat Miami 28-13 (Don Criqui and John Brodie) on 10-21-79
Lost 31-26 to Baltimore (Sam Nover and Bob Trumpy) on 10-28-79
Beat Buffalo 26-6 (Sam Nover and Bob Trumpy) on 11-04-79
Got crushed 45-10 by the Broncos (Dick Enberg and Merlin Olsen) on 11-11-79
Crushed the Colts 50-21 (Jay Randolph and Paul Maguire) on 11-18-79
Lost 16-13 in OT to Buffalo (Jay Randolph and Paul Maguire) on 11-25-79
Lost 27-26 to the Jets (Marv Albert and Mike Haffner) on 12-09-79

Beat Cleveland 34-17 (Sam Nover and Bob Trumpy) on 09-07-80
Beat Seattle 37-31 (Bob Costas and Len Dawson) on 09-21-80
Beat the Jets 21-11 (Marv Albert and Dave Rowe) on 10-05-80
Beat Baltimore 37-21 (Jay Randolph and Gene Washington) on 10-19-80
Lost 31-13 to Buffalo (Charlie Jones and Len Dawson) on 10-26-80
Beat the Jets 34-21 (Sam Nover and Bob Trumpy) on 11-02-80
Beat Baltimore 47-21 (Jay Randolph and Dave Rowe) on 11-23-80
Lost 21-17 to San Francisco (Sam Nover and Bob Trumpy) on 11-30-80
Beat Buffalo 24-2 (Bob Costas and Gene Washington) on 12-14-80
Beat New Orleans 38-27 (Merle Harmon and Bob Trumpy) on 12-21-80

Lost 29-28 to Baltimore (Phil Stone and Gene Washington) on 09-06-81
Loat 13-3 to Philadelphia (Dick Enberg and John Brodie) on 09-13-81
Lost 27-21 in OT to the Steelers (Bob Costas and Bob Trumpy) on 09-27-81
Beat Kansas City 33-17 (Don Criqui and John Brodie) on 10-04-81
Lost 28-24 to the Jets (Charlie Jones and Len Dawson) on 10-11-81
Beat the Oilers 38-10 (Jay Randolph and Mike Haffner) on 10-18-81
Lost 24-22 to the Redskins (Bob Costas and Bob Trumpy) on 10-25-81
Lost 27-17 to Oakland (Merle Harmon and George Kunz) on 11-01-81
Lost 17-6 to the Jets (Marv Albert and Jim Turner) on 11-15-81
Lost 20-17 to Buffalo (Phil Stone and Mike Haffner) on 11-22-81
Lost 24-14 to Miami (Charlie Jones and Len Dawson) on 12-06-81
Lost 19-10 to Buffalo (Sam Nover and Dave Rowe) on 12-13-81
Lost 23-21 to the Baltimore Colts (Sam Nover and Dave Rowe) on 12-20-81

Beat the Baltimore Colts 24-13 (Bob Costas and Bob Griese) on 09-12-82
Lost 31-7 to the Jets (Bob Costas and Bob Trumpy) on 09-19-82
Lost 10-7 to Cleveland (Merle Harmon and Jim Turner) on 11-21-82
Beat Houston 29-21 (Jay Randolph and Bob Griese) on 11-28-82
Lost 26-13 to Chicago (Merle Harmon and Jim Turner) on 12-05-82
Shutout Miami 3-0 (Jay Randolph and Bob Griese) on 12-12-82 (*Snow Plow Game*)
Shutout Seattle 16-0 (Jay Randolph and Gene Washington) on 12-19-82
Lost 37-14 to Pittsburgh (Bob Costas and Bob Trumpy) on 12-26-82
Beat Buffalo 30-19 (Jay Randolph and Bob Griese) on 01-02-83
Lost 28-13 to Miami in **1st Round Playoff Game** (Bob Costas and Bob Trumpy) on 01-08-83

7 NFL Games were cancelled during the 1982 season because of the NFL Players Strike

Games on NBC TV from 1983-85

Lost 29-23 in OT to Baltimore (Don Criqui and Jim Turner) on 09-04-83
Lost 34-24 to Miami (Charlie Jones and Bob Griese) on 09-11-83
Beat the Jets 23-13 (Bob Costas and Bob Trumpy) on 09-18-83
Beat Pittsburgh 28-23 (Dick Enberg and Merlin Olsen) on 09-25-83
Lost 12-7 to the Baltimore Colts (Phil Stone and John Brodie) on 10-09-83
Beat San Diego 37-21 (Don Criqui and Jim Turner) on 10-16-83
Shutout Buffalo 31-0 (Charlie Jones and Bob Griese) on 10-23-83
Lost 24-13 to Atlanta (Don Criqui and Gene Washington) on 10-30-83
Beat Buffalo 21-7 (Don Criqui and Gene Washington) on 11-06-83
Beat Miami 17-6 (Bob Costas and Bob Trumpy) on 11-13-83
Lost 20-0 to Cleveland (Phil Stone and Reggie Rucker) on 11-20-83
Lost 26-3 to the Jets (Marv Albert and John Brodie) on 11-27-83
Shutout the Saints 7-0 (Jim Kelly and John Dockery) on 12-04-83
Beat the LA Rams 21-7 (Marv Albert and John Brodie) on 12-11-83
Lost 24-6 to Seattle (Charlie Jones and Bob Griese) on 12-18-83

Beat Buffalo 21-17 (Jay Randolph and Gene Washington) on 09-02-84
Lost 28-7 to Miami (Jay Randolph and Bob Griese) on 09-09-84
Smoked Seattle 38-23 (Don Criqui and Bob Trumpy) on 09-16-84
Beat the Jets 28-21 (Marv Albert and John Brodie) on 09-30-84
Barely beat the Browns 17-16 (Todd Donoho and Reggie Rucker) on 10-07-84
Beat the Bengals 20-10 (Todd Donoho and Gene Washington) on 10-14-84
Lost 44-24 to Miami (Charlie Jones and Bob Griese) on 10-21-84
Beat the Jets 30-20 (Marv Albert and John Brodie) on 10-28-84
Lost 26-19 to Denver (Don Criqui and Bob Trumpy) on 11-04-84
Buffaloed the Bills 38-10 (Dick Enberg and Merlin Olsen) on 11-11-84
Crushed the Colts 50-17 (Charlie Jones and Bob Griese) on 11-18-84
Lost 20-17 to the Cowboys (Dick Enberg and Merlin Olsen) on Thanksgiving on 11-22-84
Lost 27-17 to the Eagles (Phil Stone and Dave Rowe) on 12-09-84
Beat Indianapolis 16-10 (Len Berman and Gene Washington) on 12-16-84

Beat Green Bay 26-20 (Jim Hill and John Dockery) on 09-08-85
Lost 20-7 to the Bears (Don Criqui and Bob Trumpy) on 09-15-85
Beat Buffalo 17-14 (Bob Lobel and Dave Rowe) on 09-22-85
Lost 35-20 to the LA Raiders (Marv Albert and Bob Griese) on 09-29-85
Lost 24-20 to Cleveland (Phil Stone and Bob Kutchenberg) on 10-06-85
Beat Buffalo 14-3 (Len Berman and Bob Kutchenberg) on 10-13-85
Beat the Jets 20-13 (Marv Albert and Bob Griese) on 10-20-85 *(Game Winning TD Run by Grogan)*
Beat Tampa Bay 32-14 (Len Berman and Bob Kutchenberg) on 10-27-85
Beat Miami 17-13 (Jay Randolph and Bob Griese) on 11-03-85
Beat Indianapolis 34-15 (Charlie Jones and Sam Rutigliano) on 11-10-85
Beat Seattle 20-13 (Dick Enberg and Merlin Olsen) on 11-17-85
Lost 16-13 in OT to the Jets (Charlie Jones and Merlin Olsen) on 11-24-85
Beat the Colts 38-31 (Len Berman and Bob Kutchenberg) on 12-01-85
Beat the Bengals 34-23 (Phil Stone and Sam Rutigliano) on 12-22-85
Beat the Jets 26-14 in **Wild Card Game** (Marv Albert and Bob Griese) on 12-28-85
Beat the LA Raiders 27-20 in **Divisional Playoff** (Dick Enberg and Merlin Olsen) on 01-05-86
Beat the Dolphins 31-14 in **AFC Championship** (Dick Enberg and Merlin Olsen) on 01-12-86

Games on NBC TV from 1986-89

Beat Indianapolis 33-3 (Bob Lobel and Reggie Rucker) on 09-07-86
Lost 38-31 to Seattle (Tom Davis and Dave Rowe) on 09-21-86
Lost 27-20 to Denver (Dick Enberg and Merlin Olsen) on 09-28-86
Beat Miami 34-7 (Dick Enberg and Merlin Olsen) on 10-05-86
Lost 31-24 to the Jets (Marv Albert and Bob Griese) on 10-12-86
Shutout the Steelers 34-0 (Don Criqui and Bob Trumpy) on 10-19-86
Beat Buffalo 23-3 (Len Berman and Sam Rutigliano) on 10-26-86
Beat the Colts 30-21 (Tom Hammond and Bob Griese) on 11-09-86
Barely beat the Rams 30-28 (Dick Enberg and Merlin Olsen) on 11-16-86 *(Hail Mary TD Pass)*
Beat Buffalo 22-19 (Marv Albert and Bob Griese) on 11-23-86
Barely beat the Saints 21-20 (Len Berman and Sam Rutigliano) on 11-30-86
Lost 31-7 to the Bengals (Marv Albert and Bob Griese) on 12-07-86
Lost 22-17 to Denver in **Divisional Playoff** (Dick Enberg and Merlin Olsen) on 01-04-87

Beat Miami 28-21 (Don Criqui and Bob Trumpy) on 09-13-87
Lost 20-10 to Cleveland (Don Criqui and Bob Trumpy) on 10-04-87 *(Strike Game #1)*
Beat Buffalo 14-7 (Charlie Jones and Jimmy Cefalo) on 10-11-87 *(Strike Game #2)*
Beat Houston 21-7 (Mel Proctor and Reggie Rucker) on 10-18-87 *(Strike Game #3)*
Lost 30-16 to Indianapolis (Kevin Slaten and Reggie Rucker) on 10-25-87
Beat the LA Raiders 26-23 (Don Criqui and Bob Trumpy) on 11-01-87
Shutout the Colts 24-0 (Don Criqui and Bob Trumpy) on 11-22-87
Lost 31-20 to Denver (Dick Enberg and Merlin Olsen) on 12-06-87
Beat the Jets 42-20 (Marv Albert and Joe Namath) on 12-13-87
Beat Buffalo 13-7 (Jay Randolph and Reggie Rucker) on 12-20-87

Beat the Jets 28-3 (Marv Albert and Joe Namath) on 09-04-88
Lost 36-6 to the Vikings (Jim Donovan and Reggie Rucker) on 09-11-88
Lost 16-14 to Buffalo (Mel Proctor and Jon Morris) on 09-18-88
Lost 31-6 to Houston (Mel Proctor and Jerry Kramer) on 09-25-88
Beat Indianapolis 21-17 (Steve Grad and Jon Morris) on 10-02-88 *(Ickey Balookey crowd reaction)*
Lost 45-3 to the Packers with (Curt Gowdy and Jerry Kramer) on 10-09-88
Beat the Bengals 27-21 (Don Criqui and Bob Trumpy) on 10-16-88
Lost 23-20 to Buffalo (Tom Hammond and Jon Morris) on 10-23-88
Beat Miami 21-10 (Marv Albert and Paul Maguire) on 11-06-88
Beat the Jets 14-13 (Marv Albert and Paul Maguire) on 11-13-88
Lost 24-21 to the Colts (Charlie Jones and Jon Morris) on 11-27-88
Beat Seattle 13-7 (Don Criqui and Bob Trumpy) on 12-04-88
Lost 21-10 to the Broncos (Dick Enberg and Merlin Olsen) on 12-17-88

Beat the Jets 27-24 (Marv Albert and Bob Trumpy) on 09-10-89
Lost 24-10 to Miami (Joel Meyers and Paul Maguire) on 09-17-89
Lost 24-3 to Seattle (Don Criqui and Ahmad Rashad) on 09-24-89
Beat Houston 23-13 (Jim Donovan and Jimmy Cefalo) on 10-08-89
Lost 16-15 to Atlanta (Jim Donovan and Jimmy Cefalo) on 10-15-89
Lost 37-20 to the 49ers (Dick Enberg and Bill Walsh) on 10-22-89 *(Earthquake moved game to Palo Alto)*
Beat the Colts 23-20 in OT (Marv Albert and Bob Trumpy) on 10-29-89
Lost to the Jets 27-26 (Don Criqui and Ahmad Rashad) on 11-05-89
Beat the Bills 33-24 (Charlie Jones and Merlin Olsen) on 11-19-89
Lost 24-21 to the LA Raiders (Tom Hammond and Joe Namath) on 11-26-89
Beat the Colts 22-16 (Tom Hammond and Joe Namath) on 12-03-89
Lost 28-10 to the Steelers (Jim Donovan and Jimmy Cefalo) on 12-17-89

Games on NBC TV from 1990-92

Lost 27-24 to Miami (Tom Hammond and Joe Namath) on 09-09-90
Beat Indianapolis 16-14 (Don Cruqui and Bob Trumpy) on 09-16-90
Lost 41-7 to Cincinnati (Don Criqui and Bob Trumpy) on 09-23-90
Lost 37-13 to the Jets (Tom Hammond and Joe Namath) on 09-30-90 *(Uniform #73 was retired)*
Lost 33-20 to Seattle (Don Criqui and Bob Trumpy) on 10-07-90
Lost 27-10 to Buffalo (Don Criqui and Bob Trumpy) on 10-28-90
Lost 48-20 to Philadelphia (Joel Meyers and Ahmad Rashad) on 11-04-90
Lost 13-10 to Indianapolis (Tom Hammond and Joe Namath) on 11-11-90
Lost 14-0 to Buffalo (Jim Donovan and Bob Trumpy) on 11-18-90
Lost 37-7 to Kansas City (Joel Meyers and Ahmad Rashad) on 12-02-90
Lost 24-3 to Pittsburgh (Tom Hammond and Joe Namath) on 12-09-90
Lost 42-7 to the Jets (Don Criqui and Bob Trumpy) on 12-23-90

Beat the Colts 16-7 (Kevin Harlan and Joe Namath) on 09-01-91
Lost 20-0 to Cleveland (Jim Donovan and Beasley Reece) on 09-08-91
Lost 20-6 to Pittsburgh (Joel Meyers and Dan Hampton) on 09-15-91
Beat Houston 24-20 (Mel Proctor and Jim Laslavic) on 09-22-91
Lost 24-10 to Phoenix (Don Criqui and Todd Christensen) on 09-29-91
Lost 20-10 to Miami (Don Criqui and Bob Trumpy) on 10-06-91
Lost 9-6 to Denver (Kevin Harlan and Joe Namath) on 10-27-91
Lost 22-17 to Buffalo (Joel Meyers and Dan Hampton) on 11-03-91
Lost 28-21 to the Jets (Don Criqui and Ahmad Rashad) on 11-17-91
Beat Buffalo 16-13 (Jim Donovan and Beasley Reece) on 11-24-91 *(Steve Grogan Tribute)*
Lost 20-3 to Denver (Charlie Jones and Todd Christensen) on 12-01-91
Beat Indianapolis 23-17 in OT (Jim Donovan and Beasley Reece) on 12-08-91 *(Timpson with GW TD)*
Beat the Jets 6-3 (Tom Hammond and Joe Namath) on 12-15-91
Lost 29-7 to Cincinnati (Joel Meyers and Dan Hampton) on 12-22-91

Lost 14-0 to the LA Rams (Joey Meyers and Beasley Reece) on 09-13-92
Lost 10-6 to Seattle (Tom Hammond and Cris Collinsworth) on 09-20-92
Lost 41-7 to Buffalo (Don Criqui and Paul Maguire) on 09-27-92
Lost 38-17 to Miami (Dan Hicks and Dan Hampton) on 10-18-92
Lost 19-17 to Cleveland (Dan Hicks and Dan Hampton) on 10-25-92
Lost 16-7 to Buffalo (Don Criqui and Paul Maguire) on 11-01-92
Beat Indianapolis 37-34 in OT (Don Criqui and Paul Maguire) on 11-15-92 *(The legend of Zo)*
Beat the Jets 24-3 (Jim Lampley and Ahmad Rashad) on 11-22-92
Lost 34-0 to Atlanta (Jim Lampley and Ahmad Rashad) on 11-29-92
Lost 6-0 to Indianapolis (Dan Hicks and Dan Hampton) on 12-06-92
Lost 27-20 to Kansas City (Don Criqui and Paul Maguire) on 12-13-92
Lost 20-10 to Cincinnati (Joel Meyers and Beasley Reece) on 12-20-92
Lost 16-13 to Miami in OT (Jim Donovan and Dan Hampton) on 12-27-92

BONUS TRIVIA

Patriots Retired Uniform #s

#20	Gino Cappelletti	#78	Bruce Armstrong
#40	Mike Haynes	#79	Jim Lee Hunt
#57	Steve Nelson	#89	Bob Dee
#73	John Hannah		

Games on NBC TV from 1993-95

Lost 38-14 to Buffalo (Tom Hammond and Cris Collinsworth) on 09-05-93
Lost 17-14 to Seattle (Don Criqui and Beasley Reece) on 09-19-93
Beat Phoenix 23-21 (Don Criqui and Beasley Reece) on 10-10-93
Lost 28-14 to Houston (Charlie Jones and Todd Christensen) on 10-17-93
Lost 10-9 to Seattle (Dan Hicks and Dan Hampton) on 10-24-93
Lost 9-6 to Indianapolis (Don Criqui and Beasley Reece) on 10-31-93
Lost 13-10 in OT to Buffalo (Don Criqui and Beasley Reece) on 11-07-93
Lost 17-13 to Miami (Marv Albert and Paul Maguire) on 11-21-93
Lost 6-0 to the Jets (Don Criqui and Paul Maguire) on 11-28-93
Lost 17-14 to Pittsburgh (Don Criqui and Beasley Reece) on 12-05-93
Beat Cincinnati 7-2 (Drew Goodman and Cris Collinsworth) on 12-12-93
Beat Cleveland 20-17 (Don Criqui and Beasley Reece) on 12-19-93
Shutout Indianapolis 38-0 (Drew Goodman and Beasley Reece) on 12-26-93
Beat Miami 33-27 in OT (Don Criqui and Beasley Reece) on 01-02-94 *(Timpson with GW TD)*

Lost 39-35 to Miami (Jim Lampley and Todd Christensen) on 09-04-94
Lost 38-35 to Buffalo (Don Criqui and Beasley Reece) on 09-11-94
Beat the Bengals 31-28 (Tom Hammond and Cris Collinsworth) on 09-18-94
Beat Detroit 23-17 (Marv Albert and Paul Maguire) on 09-25-94
Lost 21-17 to the Rams (Marv Albert and Paul Maguire) on 10-09-94
Lost 24-17 to the Jets (Charlie Jones and Randy Cross) on 10-16-94
Lost 23-3 to Miami (Jim Lampley and Todd Christensen) on 10-30-94
Lost 13-6 to Cleveland (Tom Hammond and Cris Collinsworth) on 11-06-94
Beat San Diego 23-17 (Don Criqui and Beasley Reece) on 11-20-94
Beat the Jets 24-13 (Marv Albert and Paul Maguire) on 12-04-94
Beat the Colts 28-13 (Don Criqui and Beasley Reece) on 12-11-94
Beat Buffalo 41-17 (Marv Albert and Paul Maguire) on 12-18-94
Beat Chicago 13-3 (Marv Albert and Paul Maguire) on 12-24-94
Lost 20-13 to the Browns in **Wild Card Game** (Dick Enberg and Bob Trumpy) on 01-01-95

Barely beat the Browns 17-14 (Dick Enberg, Paul Maguire and Phil Simms) on 09-03-95
Lost 20-3 to Miami (Marv Albert and Cris Collinsworth) on 09-10-95
Lost 28-3 to the 49ers (Dick Enberg, Paul Maguire and Phil Simms) on 09-17-95
Lost 30-17 to Atlanta (Marv Albert and Cris Collinsworth) on 10-01-95
Lost 31-26 to the Chiefs (Dick Enberg, Pual Maguire and Phil Simms) on 10-15-95
Beat the Jets 20-7 (Don Criqui and Beasley Reece) on 11-05-95
Beat the Dolphins 34-17 (Marv Albert and Cris Collinsworth) on 11-12-95
Lost 24-10 to the Colts (Don Criqui and Beasley Reece) on 11-19-95
Beat Buffalo 35-25 (Tom Hammond and Cris Collinsworth) on 11-26-95
Barely beat the Jets 31-28 (Dan Hicks and Bob Trumpy) on 12-10-95
Lost 41-27 to the Steelers (Tom Hammond and Bob Trumpy) on 12-16-95

Games on NBC TV from 1996-97

Lost 24-10 to the Dolphins (Dick Enberg and Paul Maguire) on 09-01-96
Lost 17-10 to Buffalo (Don Criqui and Beasley Reece) on 09-08-96
Beat Jacksonville 28-25 in OT (Marv Albert and Sam Wyche) on 09-22-96
Beat the Ravens 46-38 (Don Criqui and Beasley Reece) on 10-06-96
Beat the Colts 27-9 (Tom Hammond and Bob Trumpy) On 10-20-96
Beat the Dolphins 42-23 (Dick Enberg, Paul Maguire and Phil Simms) on 11-03-96
Beat the Jets 31-27 (Marv Albert and Sam Wyche) on 11-10-96
Lost 34-8 to Denver (Dick Enberg, Paul Maguire and Phil Simms) on 11-17-96
Beat the Colts 27-13 (Tom Hammond and Bob Trumpy) on 11-24-96
Beat the Jets 34-10 (Marv Albert and Sm Wyche) on 12-08-96
Lost 12-6 to the Dallas Cowboys (Marv Albert, Randy Cross and Sam Wyche) on 12-15-96
Narrowly defeated the Giants 23-22 (Dick Enberg, Paul Maguire and Phil Simms) on 12-21-96
Beat the Steelers 28-3 in **Divisional Playoff** (Marv Albert and Sam Wyche) on 01-05-97
Beat the Jaguars 20-6 in **AFC Championship** (Dick Enberrg, Paul Maguire and Phil Simms) on 01-12-97

Smoked San Diego 41-7 (Marv Albert and Randy Cross) on 08-31-97
Beat the Colts 31-6 (Dan Hicks and Bob Trumpy) on 09-07-97
Beat Buffalo 33-6 (Tom Hammond, Randy Cross and Jim Kelly) on 10-12-97
Lost 24-19 to the Jets (Mike Breen and James Lofton) on 10-19-97
Lost 23-18 to Minnesota (Dick Enberg and Phil Simms) on 11-02-97
Beat Buffalo 31-10 (Dick Enberg, Paul Maguire and Phil Simms) on 11-09-97
Defeated the Dolphins 27-24 (Tom Hammond and Randy Cross) on 11-23-97
Defeated the Colts 20-17 (Mike Breen and James Lofton) on 11-30-97
Beat the Jaguars 26-20 (Tom Hammond and Randy Cross) on 12-07-97
Lost 24-21 in OT to Pittsburgh (Dick Enberg, Paul Maguire and Phil Simms) on Saturday on 12-13-97
Beat Miami 17-3 in **Wild Card** (Dick Enberg, Paul Maguire and Phil Simms) on 12-28-97
Lost 7-6 to the Steelers in **Divisional Playoff** (Tom Hammond and Randy Cross) on 01-03-98

Super Bowl XLVI

Lost 21-17 to the NY Giants in **Super Bowl XLVI** (Al Michaels and Cris Collinsworth) on 02-05-12

BONUS FUN FACTS

Former Patriots Players Who Have Been Radio Color Commentators for Patriots Games

Pete Brock, Gino Cappelletti, Jon Morris and Scott Zolak

Former Patriots Players Who Have Been TV Color Commentators for Patriots Games

Dennis Byrd, Nick Buoniconti, Craig James, Trevor Mattich, Jon Morris, Reggie Rucker and Dave Rowe

Games That Were Moved to Another Date or Location During the Season

September 16, 1960 game was moved to Sept 17th due to a Yankees/Orioles Game at Yankee Stadium
October 20, 1961 game was moved to Oct 22nd because of a potential hurricane that never arrived
October 26, 1969 Home Game vs the Jets was moved to BC on Oct 5th because of World Series
October 22, 1989 game was moved to Stanford Stadium because of the San Francisco Earthquake
September 6, 1992 game was moved to October 18, 1992 because of Hurricane Andrew in Florida
September 16, 2001 game was moved to Jan 6, 2002 because of terrorist attacks on September 11th

Games on CBS TV from 1971-93

Lost 34-7 to Detroit (Jack Drees and George Connor) on 09-26-71
Shutout the Jets 20-0 (Don Criqui and Irv Cross) on 10-10-71

Barely beat Washington 24-23 (Jack Whitaker and Jim Morse) on 10-01-72
Lost 41-13 to the Jets (Jack Whitaker and Tucker Fredrickson) on 10-15-72

Beat Green Bay 33-24 (Jack Whitaker and Tom Brookshier) on 11-18-73
Beat the Los Angeles Rams 20-14 (Frank Glieber and Wayne Walker) on 09-29-74

Beat San Francisco 24-16 (Al Michaels and Wayne Walker) on 10-26-75
Lost 34-31 to the Cowboys (Pat Summerall and Tom Brookshier) on 11-16-75

Smashed the Saints 27-6 (Bob Costas and Tom Matte) on 12-05-76
Beat the Eagles 14-6 (Don Criqui and Nick Buoniconti) on 11-27-77

Lost 16-14 to the Redskins (Frank Glieber and Sonny Jurgensen) on 09-03-78
Beat the Eagles 24-14 (Gary Bender and Hank Stram) on 10-08-78 *(Nellie with 3 fumble recoveries)*

Beat Detroit 24-17 (Dick Stockton and Roman Gabriel) on 10-07-79
Beat Minnesota 27-23 (Curt Gowdy and Hank Stram) on 12-16-79

Lost 37-21 to the Atlanta Falcons (Gary Bender and John Madden) on 09-14-80
Lost 17-14 to the LA Rams (Pat Summerall and Tom Brookshier) on 11-16-80

Lost 27-20 to the St. Louis Cardinals (Jim Kelly and John Dockery) on 11-29-81
Lost 33-13 to the 49ers (Dick Stockton and Wayne Walker) on 10-02-83
Shutout the Saints 7-0 (Jim Kelly and John Dockery) on 12-04-83

Lost 26-10 to the Redskins (Frank Glieber and Dick Vermeil) on 09-23-84
Lost 33-10 to the Cardinals (Frank Glieber and Dick Vermeil) on 12-02-84

Beat Green Bay 26-20 (Jim Hill and John Dockery) on 09-08-85
Beat Detroit 23-6 (Jim Hill and John Dockery) on 12-08-85

Beat Atlanta 25-17 (Tim Ryan and Terry Bradshaw) on 11-02-86
Lost 29-24 to the 49ers (Dick Stockton and Dan Dierdorf) on 12-14-86
Lost 23-17 in OT to the Cowboys (Tim Ryan and Joe Theismann) on 11-15-87
Lost 34-31 in OT to the Eagles (Dick Stockton and Terry Bradshaw) on 11-29-87

Beat the Bears 30-7 (Tim Brant and Hank Stram) on 10-30-88
Beat Tampa Bay 10-7 in OT ((Tim Brant and Hank Stram) on 12-11-88

Lost 28-24 to the Saints (Dick Stockton and Dan Fouts) on 11-12-89
Lost 24-20 to the LA Rams (Tim Brant and Dan Jiggetts) on 12-24-89
Lost 25-10 to the Redskins (Dick Stockton and Merlin Olsen) on 12-15-90
Lost 13-10 to the Giants (James Brown and Randy Cross) on 12-30-90

Beat Minnesota 26-23 in OT (Jim Nantz and Hank Stram) on 10-20-91

Lost 24-12 to the 49ers (James Brown and John Robinson) on 10-11-92
Lost 31-14 to the Saints (Sean McDonough and Hank Stram) on 11-08-92

Lost 19-16 in OT to the Lions (James Brown and Dennis Byrd) on 09-12-93

Games on CBS TV from 1998-2001

Beat Tennessee 27-16 (Gus Johnson and Steve Tasker) on 09-20-98
Beat the Saints 30-27 (Kevin Harlan and Sam Wyche) on 10-04-98
Beat the Chiefs 40-10 (Greg Gumbel and Phil Simms) on 10-11-98
Lost 12-9 in OT to Miami (Verne Lundquist and Randy Cross) on 10-25-98
Beat Indianapolis 21-16 (Don Criqui and Beasley Reece) on 11-01-98
Lost 13-10 to Buffalo (Greg Gumbel and Phil Simms) on 11-15-98
Beat Buffalo 25-21 (Verne Lundquist and Randy Cross) on 11-29-98 *(Coates with TD on last play)*
Beat the Steelers 23-9 (Verne Lundquist and Randy Cross) on 12-06-98
Lost 32-18 to St. Louis (Don Criqui and Beasley Reece) on 12-13-98
Lost 31-10 to the Jets (Greg Gumbel and Phil Simms) on 12-27-98
Lost 25-10 to Jacksonville in **Wild Card Game** (Greg Gumbel and Phil Simms) on 01-03-99

Beat Indianapolis 31-28 (Gus Johnson and Brent Jones) on 09-19-99
Barely beat the Broncos 24-23 (Verne Lundquist and Dan Dierdorf) on 10-24-99
Beat Arizona 27-3 (Kevin Harlan and Sam Wyche) on 10-31-99
Lost 17-7 to Buffalo (Verne Lundquist and Dan Dierdorf) on 11-28-99
Lost 20-15 to the Colts (Greg Gumbel and Phil Simms) on 12-12-99
Lost 24-9 to the Eagles (Gus Johnson and Brent Jones) on 12-19-99
Lost 13-10 in OT to Buffalo (Verne Lundquist and Dan Dierdorf) on 12-26-99

Lost 10-3 to Miami (Dick Enberg and Dan Dierdorf) on 09-24-00
Beat the Broncos 28-19 (Greg Gumbel and Phil Simms) on 10-01-00
Beat the Colts 24-16 (Kevin Harlan and Daryl Johnston) on 10-08-00
Lost 34-17 to the Jets (Greg Gumbel and Phil Simms) on 10-15-00
Lost 30-23 to the Colts (Gus Johnson and Brent Jones) on 10-22-00
Lost 16-13 in OT to Buffalo (Don Criqui and Steve Tasker) on 11-05-00
Lost 19-11 to Cleveland (Ian Eagle and Mark May) on 11-12-00
Beat the Bengals 16-13 (Craig Bolerjack and Charles Mann) on 11-19-00
Lost 34-9 to Detroit on Thursday Night (Greg Gumbel and Phil Simms) on 11-23-00
Lost 24-17 to the Bears (Kevin Harlan and Daryl Johnston) on 12-10-00
Lost 27-24 to Miami (Kevin Harlan and Daryl Johnston) on 12-24-00

Lost 23-17 to the Bengals (Gus Johnson and Brent Jones) on 09-09-01
Lost 10-3 to the Jets with (Dick Enberg and Dan Dierdorf) on 09-23-01 *(Bledsoe injured/Brady took over)*
Crushed the Colts 44-13 (Gus Johnson and Brent Jones) on 09-30-01 *(Bruce Armstrong Tribute)*
Lost 30-10 to the Dolphins (Gus Johnson and Brent Jones) on 10-07-01
Beat San Diego 29-26 in OT (Ian Eagle and Solomon Wilcots) on 10-14-01
Beat the Colts 38-17 (Ian Eagle and Solomon Wilcots) on 10-21-01
Lost 31-20 to Denver (Don Criqui and Steve Tasker) on 10-28-01
Beat Atlanta 24-10 (Craig Bolerjack and Trevor Matich) on 11-04-01
Beat Buffalo 21-11 (Gus Johnson and Brent Jones) on 11-11-01
Barely beat the Jets 17-16 (Gus Johnson and Brent Jones) on 12-02-01
Beat Cleveland 27-16 (Gus Johnson and Brent Jones) on 12-09-01
Beat Buffalo 12-9 in OT (Don Criqui and Steve Tasker) on 12-16-01
Beat Miami 20-13 (Greg Gumbel and Phil Simms) on Saturday on 12-22-01
Pasted the Panthers 38-6 (Kevin Harlan and Craig James) on 01-06-02
Beat the Raiders 16-13 in OT, in **Divisional Playoff** (Greg Gumbel and Phil Simms) on 01-19-02
Beat Pittsburgh 24-17 in **AFC Championship** (Greg Gumbel and Phil Simms) on 01-27-02

Games on CBS TV from 2002-05

Blasted the Jets 44-7 (Dick Enberg and Dan Dierdorf) on 09-15-02
Beat Kansas City 41-38 in OT (Dick Enberg and Dan Dierdorf) on 09-22-02
Lost 21-14 to San Diego (Greg Gumbel and Phil Simms) on 09-29-02
Lost 26-13 to Miami (Greg Gumbel and Phil Simms) on 10-06-02
Lost 24-16 to Denver (Greg Gumbel and Phil Simms) on 10-27-02
Blasted Buffalo 38-7 (Greg Gumbel and Phil Simms) on 11-03-02
Barely beat the Bears 33-30 (Kevin Harlan and Randy Cross) on 11-10-02
Beat Detroit 20-12 on Thanksgiving (Greg Gumbel and Phil Simms) on 11-28-02
Beat Buffalo 27-17 (Greg Gumbel and Phil Simms) on 12-08-02
Beat Miami 27-24 in OT (Greg Gumbel and Phil Simms) on 12-29-02

Lost 31-0 to Buffalo Bills (Verne Lundquist and Dan Dierdorf) on 09-07-03
Beat the Eagles 31-10 (Greg Gumbel and Phil Simms) on 09-14-03
Beat the Jets 23-16 (Verne Lundquist and Dan Dierdorf) on 09-21-03
Lost 20-17 to Washington (Greg Gumbel and Phil Simms) on 09-28-03
Beat Tennessee 38-30 (Gus Johnson and Brent Jones) on 10-05-03
Beat Miami 19-13 in OT (Dick Enberg and Dan Dierdorf) on 10-19-03 *(Troy Brown 82 yd GW TD)*
Beat Cleveland 9-3 (Dick Enberg and Dan Dierdorf) on 10-26-03
Beat Houston 23-20 in OT (Kevin Harlan and Randy Cross) on 11-23-03
Beat Indianapolis 38-34 (Greg Gumbel and Phil Simms) on 11-30-03
Shutout Miami 12-0 (Kevin Harlan and Randy Cross) on 12-07-03 *(Bruschi's TD dance on his knees)*
Beat Jacksonville 27-13 (Greg Gumbel and Phil Simms) on 12-14-03
Shutout Buffalo 31-0 on Saturday (Dick Enberg and Dan Dierdorf) on 12-27-03
Beat Tennessee 17-14 in **Divisional Playoff** (Greg Gumbel and Phil Simms) on 01-10-04
Beat the Colts 24-14 in **AFC Championship** (Greg Gumbel and Phil Simms) on 01-18-04
Beat the Panthers 32-29 in **Super Bowl XXXVIII** (Greg Gumbel and Phil Simms) on 02-01-04

Beat Arizona 23-12 (Don Criqui and Steve Tasker) on 09-19-04
Beat Buffalo 31-17 (Jim Nantz and Phil Simms) on 10-03-04
Beat Miami 24-10 (Dick Enberg and Dan Dierdorf) on 10-10-04
Beat the Jets 13-7 (Jim Nantz and Phil Simms) on 10-24-04 *(NFL Record 21st consecutive victory)*
Lost 34-20 to the Steelers (Jim Nantz and Phil Simms) on 10-31-04
Beat the Rams 40-22 (Jim Nantz and Phil Simms) on 11-07-04
Beat Baltimore 24-3 (Jim Nantz and Phil Simms) on 11-28-04
Crushed Cleveland 42-15 (Kevin Harlan and Randy Cross) on 12-05-04
Beat the Bengals 35-28 (Dick Enberg and Dan Dierdorf) on 12-12-04
Beat the Jets 23-7 (Jim Nantz and Phil Simms) on 12-26-04
Crushed the Colts 20-3 in **Divisional Playoff** (Jim Nantz and Phil Simms) on 01-16-05
Pummeled Pittsburgh 41-27 in **AFC Championship** (Jim Nantz and Phil Simms) on 01-23-05

Lost 27-17 to Carolina (Dick Enberg and Dan Dierdorf) on 09-18-05
Beat Pittsburgh 23-20 (Jim Nantz and Phil Simms) on 09-25-05
Lost 41-17 to San Diego (Jim Nantz and Phil Simms) on 10-02-05
Beat Atlanta 31-28 (Jim Nantz and Phil Simms) on 10-09-05
Lost 28-20 to Denver (Jim Nantz and Phil Simms) on 10-16-05
Beat Miami 23-16 (Jim Nantz and Phil Simms) on 11-13-05
Lost 26-16 to Kansas City (Dick Enberg and Rich Gannon) on 11-27-05
Beat the Jets 16-3 (Kevin Harlan and Randy Cross) on 12-04-05
Beat Buffalo 35-7 (Kevin Harlan and Randy Cross) on 12-11-05
Lost 28-26 to Miami (Kevin Harlan and Randy Cross) on 01-01-06 *(Flutie Drop Kick)*
Lost 27-13 to Denver in **Divisional Playoff** (Jim Nantz and Phil Simms) on 01-14-06

Games on CBS TV from 2006-09

Beat Buffalo 19-17 (Jim Nantz and Phil Simms) on 09-10-06 (*B-2 Stealth Bomber Flyover*)
Beat the Jets 24-17 (Dick Enberg and Randy Cross) on 09-17-06
Beat the Bengals 38-13 (Jim Nantz and Phil Simms) on 10-01-06
Beat Miami 20-10 (Greg Gumbel and Dan Dierdorf) on 10-08-06
Beat Buffalo 28-6 (Greg Gumbel and Dan Dierdorf) on 10-22-06
Lost 17-14 to the Jets (Jim Nantz and Phil Simms) on 11-12-06
Shutout Green Bay 35-0 (Greg Gumbel and Dan Dierdorf) on 11-19-06
Lost 21-0 to Miami (Dick Enberg and Randy Cross) on 12-10-06
Beat Houston 40-7 (Kevin Harlan and Rich Gannon) on 12-17-06
Beat Jacksonville 24-21 (Greg Gumbel and Dan Dierdorf) on 12-24-06
Beat Tennessee 40-23 (Dick Enberg and Randy Cross) on 12-31-06
Beat the Jets 37-16 in **Wild Card Game** (Jim Nantz and Phil Simms) on 01-07-07
Barely beat the Chargers 24-21 in **Divisional Playoff** (Jim Nantz and Phil Simms) on 01-14-07
Lost 38-34 to the Colts in **AFC Championship** (Jim Nantz and Phil Simms) on 01-21-07

Defeated the Jets 38-14 (Jim Nantz and Phil Simms) on 09-09-07
Blasted the Bills 38-7 (Kevin Harlan and Rich Gannon) on 09-23-07
Defeated Cleveland 34-17 (Greg Gumbel and Dan Dierdorf) on 10-07-07
Destroyed Dallas 48-27 (Jim Nantz and Phil Simms) on 10-14-07
Defeated the Dolphins 49-28 (Greg Gumbel and Dan Dierdorf) on 10-21-07
Beat the Colts 24-20 (Jim Nantz and Phil Simms) on 11-04-07
Defeated Pittsburgh 34-13 (Jim Nantz and Phil Simms) on 12-09-07
Beat the Jets 20-10 (Jim Nantz and Phil Simms) on 12-16-07
Beat Miami 28-7 (Jim Nantz and Phil Simms) on 12-23-07 (*2007 World Series Tribute*)
Beat Jacksonville 31-20 in **Divisional Playoff** (Jim Nantz and Phil Simms) on 01-12-08
Beat San Diego 24-21 in **AFC Championship** (Jim Nantz and Phil Simms) on 01-20-08

Beat the Chiefs 17-10 (Greg Gumbel and Dan Dierdorf) on 09-07-08
Beat the Jets 19-10 (Jim Nantz and Phil Simms) on 09-14-08
Lost 38-13 to Miami (Ian Eagle and Solomon Wilcots) on 09-21-08
Beat the 49ers 30-21 (Dick Enberg, Randy Cross and Dan Fouts) on 10-05-08
Beat Buffalo 20-10 (Dick Enberg and Randy Cross) on 11-09-08 (*Blackhawk Helicopters Flyover*)
Beat Miami 48-28 (Greg Gumbel and Dan Dierdorf) on 11-23-08
Beat Seattle 24-21 (Dick Enberg and Randy Cross) on 12-07-08
Beat Oakland 49-26 (Kevin Harlan and Rich Gannon) on 12-14-08
Shutout Buffalo 13-0 (Greg Gumbel and Dan Dierdorf) on 12-28-08

Lost 16-9 to the Jets (Greg Gumbel and Dan Dierdorf) on 09-20-09
Beat Baltimore 27-21 (Jim Nantz and Phil Simms) on 10-04-09
Lost 20-17 in OT to Denver (Jim Nantz and Phil Simms) on 10-11-09
Toasted the Titans 59-0 (Jim Nantz and Phil Simms) on 10-18-09 (*Brady 5 TDs in 2nd Qtr*)
Torched Tampa 35-7 in London (Jim Nantz and Phil Simms) on 10-25-09
Beat Miami 27-17 (Greg Gumbel and Dan Dierdorf) on 11-08-09
Beat the Jets 31-14 (Jim Nantz and Phil Simms) on 11-22-09
Lost 22-21 to Miami (Jim Nantz and Phil Simms) on 12-06-09
Beat Buffalo 17-10 (Greg Gumbel and Dan Dierdorf) on 12-20-09
Beat Jacksonville 35-7 (Kevin Harlan and Solomon Wilcots) on 12-27-09
Lost 34-27 to the Texans (Kevin Harlan and Solomon Wilcots) on 01-03-10
Lost 33-14 to the Ravens in **Wild Card Game** (Jim Nantz and Phil Simms) on 01-10-10

Games on CBS TV from 2010-13

Beat the Bengals 38-24 (Jim Nantz and Phil Simms) on 09-12-10 (*F-15 Flyover*)
Lost 28-14 to the Jets (Jim Nantz and Phil Simms) on 09-19-10
Beat Buffalo 38-30 (Kevin Harlan and Solomon Wilcots) on 09-26-10
Beat Baltimore 23-20 in OT (Jim Nantz and Phil Simms) on 10-17-10
Beat San Diego 23-20 (Jim Nantz and Phil Simms) on 10-24-10
Lost 34-14 to the Browns (Bill Macatee and Rich Gannon) on 11-07-10
Beat Indianapolis 31-28 (Jim Nantz and Phil Simms) on 11-21-10
Beat Detroit 45-24 (Jim Nantz and Phil Simms) on 11-25-10
Beat Chicago 36-7 (Jim Nantz and Phil Simms) on 12-12-10
Beat Buffalo 34-3 (Kevin Harlan and Solomon Wilcots) on 12-26-10
Beat Miami 38-7 (Bill Macatee and Rich Gannon) on 01-02-11
Lost 28-21 to the Jets in **Divisional Playoff** (Jim Nantz and Phil Simms) on 01-16-11

Beat SD 35-21 (Jim Nantz and Phil Simms) on 09-18-11 (*Drew Bledsoe and Jon Morris Tribute*)
Lost 34-31 to Buffalo (Marv Albert and Rich Gannon) on 09-25-11
Beat the Jets 30-21 (Marv Albert and Rich Gannon) on 10-09-11 (*2011 Stanley Cup Tribute*)
Beat the Colts 31-24 (Marv Albert and Rich Gannon) on 12-04-11
Beat Washington 34-27 (Greg Gumbel and Dan Dierdorf) on 12-11-11
Defeated Denver 45-10 **Divisional Playoff** (Jim Nantz and Phil Simms) on 01-14-12
Barely beat Baltimore 23-20 in **AFC Championship** (Jim Nantz and Phil Simms) on 01-22-12

Beat Tennessee 34-13 (Jim Nantz and Phil Simms) on 09-09-12
Buried the Bills 52-28 (Greg Gumbel and Dan Dierdorf) on 09-30-12
Beat the Broncos 31-21 (Jim Nantz and Phil Simms) on 10-07-12
Lost 24-23 to Seattle (Ian Eagle and Dan Fouts) on 10-14-12
Beat the Jets 29-26 in OT (Jim Nantz and Phil Simms) on 10-21-12
Destroyed the Rams 45-7 (Jim Nantz and Phil Simms) on 10-28-12
Beat Buffalo 37-31 (Ian Eagle and Dan Fouts) on 11-11-12 (*Kevin Faulk Tribute and C5 Flyover*)
Crushed the Colts 59-24 (Jim Nantz and Phil Simms) on 11-18-12
Beat Miami 23-16 (Greg Gumbel and Dan Dierdorf) on 12-02-12
Beat Jacksonville 23-16 (Kevin Harlan and Solomon Wilcots) on 12-23-12
Shutout Miami 28-0 (Jim Nantz and Phil Simms) on 12-30-12 (*Gino Cappelletti and Gil Santos Tribute*)
Beat Houston 41-28 in **Divisional Playoff** (Jim Nantz and Phil Simms) on 01-13-13
Lost 28-13 to the Ravens in **AFC Championship** (Jim Nantz and Phil Simms) on 01-20-13

Barely beat Buffalo 23-21 (Greg Gumbel and Dan Dierdorf) on 09-08-13
Lost 13-6 to the Bengals (Greg Gumbel and Dan Dierdorf) on 10-06-13
Lost 30-27 to the Jets in OT (Greg Gumbel and Dan Dierdorf) on 10-20-13
Beat Miami 27-17 (Jim Nantz and Phil Simms) on 10-27-13
Smoked the Steelers 55-31 (Jim Nantz and Phil Simms) on 11-03-13 (*2013 World Series Tribute*)
Beat Houston 34-31 (Greg Gumbel and Dan Dierdorf) on 12-01-13
Barely beat the Browns 27-26 (Don Criqui and Steve Tasker) on 12-08-13
Lost 24-20 to Miami (Jim Nantz and Phil Simms) on 12-15-13
Blasted Baltimore 41-7 (Jim Nantz and Phil Simms) on 12-22-13
Beat Buffalo 34-20 (Ian Eagle and Dan Fouts) on 12-29-13
Beat Indy 43-22 in **Divisional Playoff** (Greg Gumbel and Dan Dierdorf) on 01-11-14
Lost 26-16 to Denver in **AFC Championship** (Jim Nantz and Phil Simms) on 01-19-14

Games on CBS TV from 2014-17

Lost 33-20 to Miami (Greg Gumbel and Trent Green) on 09-07-14
Beat Minnesota 30-7 (Ian Eagle and Dan Fouts) on 09-14-14
Beat the Raiders 16-9 (Greg Gumbel and Trent Green) on 09-21-14
Beat Denver 43-21 (Jim Nantz and Phil Simms) on 11-02-14 (*3 Time Super Bowl Champs Tribute*)
Lost 26-21 to Green Bay (Jim Nantz and Phil Simms) on 11-30-14
Beat Miami 41-13 (Ian Eagle and Dan Fouts) on 12-14-14
Barely beat the Jets 17-16 (Spero Dedes and Solomon Wilcots) on 12-21-14
Lost 17-9 to Buffalo (Spero Dedes and Solomon Wilcots) on 12-28-14
Deflated the Colts 45-7 in **AFC Championship** Game (Jim Nantz and Phil Simms) on 01-18-15

Beat the Bills 40-32 (Kevin Harlan and Rich Gannon) on 09-20-15
Jolted the Jaguars 51-17 (Kevin Harlan and Rich Gannon) on 09-27-15
Destroyed Dallas 30-6 (Jim Nantz and Phil Simms) on 10-11-15
Beat the Jets 30-23 (Ian Eagle and Dan Fouts) on 10-25-15

Beat Miami 31-24 (Greg Gumbel and Trent Green) on 09-18-16 (*F-15 Flyover*)
Beat the Browns 33-13 (Greg Gumbel and Trent Green) on 10-09-16
Beat the Bengals 35-17 (Ian Eagle and Dan Fouts) on 10-16-16
Beat the Steelers 27-16 (Jim Nantz and Phil Simms) on 10-23-
Beat the Eagles 41-25 (Ian Eagle and Dan Fouts) on 10-30-16
Beat the 49ers 30-17 (Greg Gumbel and Trent Green) on 11-20-16
Beat the Jets 22-17 (Greg Gumbel and Trent Green) on 11-27-16
Beat the Broncos 16-3 (Jim Nantz and Phil Simms) on 12-18-16
Blasted the Jets 41-3 (Ian Eagle and Dan Fouts) on 12-24-16
Mashed Miami 35-14 (Ian Eagle and Dan Fouts) on 01-01-17
Toasted the Texans 34-16 in **Divisional Playoff** (Jim Nantz and Phil Simms) on 01-14-17
Smoked the Steelers 36-17 in **AFC Championship** (Jim Nantz and Phil Simms) on 01-22-17

Beat the Saints 36-20 (Jim Nantz and Tony Romo) on 09-17-17
Beat the Texans 36-33 (Ian Eagle and Dan Fouts) on 09-24-17 (*Raymond Clayborn Tribute*)
Beat the Jets 24-17 (Ian Eagle and Dan Fouts) on 10-15-17
Beat the Chargers 21-13 (Ian Eagle and Dan Fouts) on 10-29-17
Beat the Raiders 33-8 (Jim Nantz and Tony Romo) on 11-19-17
Beat the Dolphins 35-17 (Ian Eagle and Dan Fouts) on 11-26-17
Beat the Bills 23-3 (Jim Nantz and Tony Romo) on 12-03-17
Beat the Steelers 27-24 (Jim Nantz and Tony Romo) on 12-17-17
Beat the Bills 37-16 (Jim Nantz and Tony Romo) on 12-24-17
Beat the Jets 26-6 (Jim Nantz and Tony Romo) on 12-31-17
Beat the Titans 35-14 in **Divisional Playoff** (Jim Nantz and Tony Romo) on 01-13-18
Beat the Jaguars 24-20 in **AFC Championship** (Jim Nantz and Tony Romo) on 01-21-18

BONUS TRIVIA

Former Patriots Players Who Have Also Coached for the Patriots

Don Blackmon, Fred Bruney, Corwin Brown and Troy Brown,
Gino Cappelletti, Don Davis, Ray Hamilton, Harold Jackson,
Eddie Khayat, Rommie Loudd, Jerod Mayo, Guy Morriss,
Steve Nelson, Babe Parilli, Jesse Richardson, Ray Ventrone and Tom Yewcic

Games on CBS TV from 2018-19

Beat the Texans 27-20 (Jim Nantz and Tony Romo) on 09-09-18 (*F-15 Flyover*)
Lost 31-20 to the Jaguars (Jim Nantz and Tony Romo) on 09-16-18
Beat Miami 38-7 (Kevin Harlan and Rich Gannon) on 09-30-18
Beat the Bears 38-31 (Ian Eagle and Dan Fouts) on 10-21-18
Lost 34-10 to the Titans (Ian Eagle and Dan Fouts) on 11-11-18
Defeated the Jets 27-13 (Ian Eagle and Dan Fouts) on 11-25-18
Lost 34-33 "in the Miracle Game" in Miami (Ian Eagle and Dan Fouts) on 12-09-18
Lost 17-10 to the Steelers (Jim Nantz and Tony Romo) on 12-16-18
Beat Buffalo 24-12 (Greg Gumbel, Trent Green and Bruce Arians) on 12-23-18
Defeated the Jets 38-3 (Ian Eagle and Dan Fouts) on 12-30-18
Beat the LA Chargers 41-28 in **Divisional Playoff** (Jim Nantz and Tony Romo) on 01-13-19
Beat the Chiefs 37-31 in OT in **AFC Championship** (Jim Nantz and Tony Romo) on 01-20-19
Beat the LA Rams 13-3 in **Super Bowl** (Jim Nantz and Tony Romo) on 02-03-19

Shutout Miami 43-0 (Ian Eagle and Dan Fouts) on 09-15-19
Beat the Jets 30-14 (Kevin Harlan and Rich Gannon) on 09-22-19 (*Ty Law Tribute*)
Beat the Bills 16-10 (Ian Eagle and Dan Fouts) on 09-29-19
Roughed up the Redskins 33-7 (Greg Gumbel and Trent Green) on 10-06-19
Beat the Browns 27-13 (Jim Nantz and Tony Romo) on 10-27-19
Beat the Eagles 17-10 (Jim Nantz and Tony Romo) on 11-17-79
Lost 23-16 to Kansas City (Jim Nantz and Tony Romo) on 12-08-19
Beat the Bengals 34-13 (Andrew Catalon and James Lofton) on 12-15-19
Lost 27-24 to Miami (Greg Gumbel and Trent Green) on 12-29-19
Lost 20-13 to Tennessee in **Wild Card Game** (Jim Nantz and Tony Romo) on 01-04-20

BONUS FUN TRIVIA

Animal Nicknames

Bat	Rick Sanford	Pound Puppy	Ted Johnson
Big Dog	Leon Gray	Roadrunner	Carl Garrett
Black Unicorn	Martellus Bennett	Seabass	Sebastian Vollmer
Boss Hog	Ty Warren	Spider	Don Webb
Bull	John Bramlett	Squirrel	Julian Edelman and Kelley Washington
Cat	Mike Ballou	Sugar Bear	Ray Hamilton
Dancing Bear	Chris Canty	Tasmanian	James Develin
Fred Dog	Fred Sturt	The Falcon	Jim Boudreaux
Gator	Don Blackmon	The Rabbit	Randy Vataha
Hawk	Mike Hawkins	The Mole	Mel West
Hog	John Hannah	Thumper	Rick Cash
Moose	Eddie Ray	Ox	Garin Veris

Games on Fox TV from 1994-2019

Beat Green Bay 17-16 (Kevin Harlan and Jerry Glanville) on 10-02-94
Beat Minnesota 26-20 in OT (Kevin Harlan and Jerry Glanville) on 11-13-94 *(K. Turner with GW TD)*

Lost 20-17 in OT to Carolina (Kevin Harlan and Jerry Glanville) on 10-29-95
Lost 31-17 to the Saints (Kevin Harlan and Jerry Glanville) on 12-03-95

Lost 41-10 to Atlanta (Sam Rosen and Jerry Glanville) on 11-08-98
Beat the 49ers 24-21 (Sam Rosen and Jerry Glanville) on 12-20-98

Lost 21-16 to Tampa (Ron Pitts and Ray Bentley) on 09-03-00
Lost 21-13 to Minnesota (Sam Rosen and Bill Maas) on 09-17-00

Beat the Saints 34-17 (Sam Rosen and Bill Maas and Levan Reid) on 11-25-01
Beat the Rams 20-17 in **Super Bowl XXXVI** (Pat Summerall and John Madden) on 02-03-02

Lost to Green Bay 28-10 (Dick Stockton, Cris Collinsworth and Troy Aikman) on 10-13-02
Beat Minnesota 24-17 (Kenny Albert and Tim Green) on 11-24-02

Beat the Giants 17-6 (Kenny Albert and Daryl Johnston) on 10-12-03

Beat Seattle 30-20 (Dick Stockton, Cris Collinsworth and Troy Aikman) on 10-17-04
Beat San Francisco 21-7 (Curt Menefee, Tim Green and Butch Stearns) on 01-02-05

Beat New Orleans 24-17 (Ron Pitts, Tim Ryan and Butch Stearns) on 11-20-05

Beat Chicago 17-13 (Joe Buck and Troy Aikman) on 11-26-06
Beat Detroit 28-21 (Matt Vasgersian and JC Pearson) on 12-03-06

Routed the Redskins 52-7 (Kenny Albert and Daryl Johnston) on 10-28-07

Beat the Rams 23-16 (Chris Rose and J.C. Pearson) on 10-26-08
Destroyed Arizona 47-7 (Kenny Albert and Daryl Johnston) on 12-21-08

Beat Atlanta 26-10 (Joe Buck and Troy Aikman) on 09-27-09
Beat Carolina 20-10 (Kenny Albert and Daryl Johnston) on 12-13-09

Beat Minnesota 28-18 (Tom Brennaman and Troy Aikman) on 10-31-10

Lost 20-18 to Arizona (Dick Stockton and John Lynch) on 09-16-12 *(Troy Brown Tribute)*

Beat Tampa 23-3 (Kevin Burkhardt and John Lynch) on 09-22-13
Beat the Saints 30-27 (Thom Brennaman and Troy Aikman) on 10-13-13

Beat Buffalo 37-22 (Kenny Albert and Daryl Johnston) on 10-12-14
Buried the Bears 51-23 (Sam Rosen and John Lynch) 10-26-14
Defeated Detroit 34-9 (Joe Buck and Troy Aikman) on 11-23-14 *(F-15 Flyover)*

Beat the Rams 26-10 (Kevin Burkhardt and John Lynch) on 12-04-16 *(2001 Champs Team Tribute)*

Lost 33-30 to Carolina (Joe Buck and Troy Aikman) on 10-01-17

Beat the Vikings 24-10 (Joe Buck and Troy Aikman) on 12-02-18
Beat the Cowboys 13-9 (Joe Buck and Troy Aikman) on 11-24-19

Only Boston Patriots Game on Saturday Afternoon on ABC TV

Beat Buffalo 26-8 in AFL **Divisional Playoff** (Jack Buck and George Ratterman) on 12-28-63

Saturday Afternoon Games on NBC TV

Lost 38-28 to the Jets (Jim Simpson and Elmer Angsman) on 12-17-66
Lost 44-16 to Buffalo (Curt Gowdy and Paul Christman) on 12-09-67
Lost 24-21 to Oakland in **Divisional Playoff** (Curt Gowdy and Don Meredith) on 12-18-76
Lost 28-13 to Miami in **1st Round Playoff** (Bob Costas, Bob Trumpy and Bob Griese) on 01-08-83
Beat the Jets 26-14 in **Wild Card Game** (Marv Albert and Bob Griese) on 12-28-85
Lost 41-27 to the Steelers (Tom Hammond and Bob Trumpy) on 12-16-95
Lost 7-6 to Pittsburgh in **Divisional Playoff** (Tom Hammond and Randy Cross) on 01-03-98

Only Saturday Afternoon Game on FOX TV

Shutout Tampa Bay 28-0 (Dick Stockton and Daryl Johnston) on 12-17-05

Saturday Afternoon Games on CBS TV

Lost 25-10 to Washington (Dick Stockton and Merlin Olsen) on 12-15-90
Shutout Buffalo 31-0 (Dick Enberg and Dan Dierdorf) on 12-27-03
Beat Buffalo 24-17 (Greg Gumbel and Trent Green) on 12-21-19

Only Saturday Afternoon Game on the NFL TV Network

Beat Buffalo 24-17 (Mike Tirico and Kurt Warner) on 12-21-19

Saturday Afternoon/Night Games on NBC TV

Lost 41-34 to the 49ers (Al Michaels and Cris Collinsworth) on 12-16-12
Beat Baltimore 35-31 in **Divisional Playoff** (Al Michaels and Cris Collinsworth) on 01-10-15

Saturday Night Games on ABC TV

Boston Patriots beat NY Titans 28-24 on the last play (Jim Simpson and Frank Leahy) on 09-17-60
Beat Jacksonville 28-3 in **Wild Card Game** (Al Michaels and John Madden) on 01-07-06

Only Saturday Night Game on ESPN/WCVB TV

Beat the Jets 21-16 (Mike Patrick, Joe Theismann and Paul Maguire) on 12-20-03

Saturday Afternoon/Night Games on CBS TV

Lost 27-13 to Denver in **Divisional Playoff** (Jim Nantz and Phil Simms) on 01-14-06
Beat Oakland 16-13 in OT, in **Divisional Playoff** (Greg Gumbel and Phil Simms) on 01-19-02
Beat Tennessee 17-14 in **Divisional Playoff** (Greg Gumbel and Phil Simms) on 01-10-04
Lost 27-13 to Denver in **Divisional Playoff** (Jim Nantz and Phil Simms) on 01-14-06
Beat Jacksonville 31-20 in **Divisional Playoff** (Jim Nantz and Phil Simms) on 01-12-08
Blasted the Broncos 45-10 in **Divisional Playoff** (Jim Nantz and Phil Simms) on 01-14-12
Crushed the Colts 43-22 in **Divisional Playoff** (Greg Gumbel and Dan Dierdorf) on 01-11-14
Beat the Chiefs 27-20 in **Divisional Playoff** (Ian Eagle and Dan Fouts) on 01-16-16
Beat Houston 34-16 in **Divisional Playoff** (Jim Nantz and Phil Simms) on 01-14-17
Toasted Tennessee 35-14 in **Divisional Playoff** (Jim Nantz and Tony Romo) on 01-13-18
Lost 20-13 to Tennessee in **Wild Card Game** (Jim Nantz and Tony Romo) on 01-04-20

Sunday Night Football Games on TNT from 1992-97

Lost 30-21 to the Jets (Gary Bender and Pat Haden) on 10-04-92
Lost 45-7 to the Jets (Gary Bender and Pat Haden) on 09-26-93
Lost 37-3 to the Broncos (Verne Lundquist and Pat Haden) on 10-08-95
Beat Buffalo 28-25 (Verne Lundquist and Pat Haden) on 10-27-96
Beat the Jets 27-24 in OT (Verne Lundquist, Pat Haden and Mark May) on 09-14-97

Only Sunday Night Football Game on ABC TV

Beat the Raiders 21-14 in Oakland (Frank Gifford, Howard Cosell and Don Meredith) on 09-24-78

Sunday Night Football Games on ESPN TV from 1987-2005

Lost 17-10 to the NY Giants (Mike Patrick and Roy Firestone) on 11-08-87
Beat Miami 6-3 (Mike Patrick and Joe Theismann) on 11-20-88
Lost 31-10 to the Dolphins (Mike Patrick and Joe Theismann) on 12-10-89

Lost 30-20 to the Dolphins (Mike Patrick and Joe Theismann) on 11-10-91

Beat the Colts 12-10 (Mike Patrick, Joe Theismann and Paul Maguire) on 11-27-94
Lost 10-7 to the Colts (Mike Patrick, Joe Theismann and Paul Maguire) on 12-23-95
Crushed the Chargers 45-7 (Mike Patrick, Joe Theismann and Paul Maguire) on 12-01-96

Beat Indianapolis 29-6 (Mike Patrick, Joe Theismann and Paul Maguire) on 09-15-98
Beat the NY Giants 16-14 (Mike Patrick, Joe Theismann and Paul Maguire) on 09-26-99
Beat Dallas 13-6 (Mike Patrick, Joe Theismann and Paul Maguire) on 12-05-99

Lost 24-17 to the St. Louis Rams (Mike Patrick, Joe Theismann and Paul Maguire) on 11-18-01

Lost 27-20 to the Raiders (Mike Patrick, Joe Theismann and Paul Maguire) on 11-17-02
Lost 30-17 to the Jets 30-17 (Mike Patrick, Joe Theismann and Paul Maguire) on 12-22-02

Shutout Dallas 12-0 (Mike Patrick, Joe Theismann and Paul Maguire) on 11-16-03

Beat Buffalo 29-6 (M. Patrick, J. Theismann and P. Maguire) on 11-14-04 (*2004 World Series Tribute*)

Beat Buffalo 21-16 (Mike Patrick, Joe Theismann and Paul Maguire) on 10-30-05

DO YOU REMEMBER ANY OF THESE NICKNAMES?

Behemoth	Ike Lassiter	Gentle Giant	Shelby Jordan
Big Bo	Jim Nance	Hard Hittin New Britain	Tebucky Jones
Big Country	Max Lane	Harry the Thump	Harry Crumb
Big Jess	Jesse Richardson	Little Big Man	Dave Meggett
Big Mac	Willie McGinest	Mini	Mack Herron
Big Red	Ed Philpott	Plugger	Tom Addison
Big Sey	Richard Seymour	The Big Nuge	Dave Nugent
Big Twan	Antowain Smith	The Hitman	Rodney Harrison
Blount Force Trauma	LeGarrette Blount	The Undertaker	Vincent Brown
Boston Strong Boy	Lennie St. Jean	Too Strong	Greg Boyd

Sunday Night Games on NBC TV from 2006-2019

Lost 17-7 to the Broncos (Al Michaels and John Madden) on 09-24-06
Lost 27-20 to the Colts (Al Michaels and John Madden) on 11-05-06

Beat the San Diego Chargers 38-14 (Al Michaels and John Madden) on 09-16-07
Destroyed Buffalo 56-10 (Al Michaels and John Madden) on 11-18-07
Beat Philadelphia 31-28 (Al Michaels and John Madden) on 11-25-07

Lost 30-10 to the Chargers (Al Michaels and John Madden) on 10-12-08
Lost 18-15 to the Colts (Al Michaels and John Madden) on 11-02-08

Lost 35-34 to the Colts "4th and 2" (Al Michaels and Cris Collinsworth) on 11-15-09

Beat Pittsburgh 39-26 (Al Michaels and Cris Collinsworth) on 11-14-10
Beat Green Bay 31-27 (Al Michaels and Cris Collinsworth) on 12-19-10

Grounded the Jets 37-16 (Al Michaels and Cris Collinsworth) on 11-13-11

Lost 31-30 to the Ravens (Al Michaels and Cris Collinsworth) on 09-23-12
Lost 41-34 to 49ers (A. Michaels and C. Collinsworth) on 12-16-12 (*Curtis Martin and Mike Haynes Tribute*)

Beat the Falcons 30-23 (Al Michaels and Cris Collinsworth) on 09-29-13
Beat Denver 34-31 in OT (Al Michaels and Cris Collinsworth) on 11-24-13

Beat the Bengals 43-17 (Al Michaels and Cris Collinsworth) on 10-05-14
Crushed the Colts 42-20 (Al Michaels and Cris Collinsworth) on 11-16-14
Defeated San Diego 23-14 (Al Michaels and Cris Collinsworth) on 12-07-14

Beat the Colts 34-27 (Al Michaels and Cris Collinsworth) on 10-18-15 (*Bizarre Colts 4th down play*)
Lost 30-24 in OT to the Broncos (Al Michaels and Cris Collinsworth) on 11-29-15
Beat Houston 27-6 (Al Michaels and Cris Collinsworth) on 12-13-15

Defeated Arizona 23-21 in Home Opener (Al Michaels and Cris Collinsworth) on 09-11-16
Lost 31-24 to Seattle (Al Michaels and Cris Collinsworth) on 11-13-16

Beat Atlanta 23-7 (A. Michaels and C. Collinsworth) on 10-22-17 (*Hannah, Haynes and Tippett Tribute*)
Beat the Broncos 41-16 (Al Michaels and Cris Collinsworth) on 11-12-17

Lost to the Lions 26-10 (Al Michaels and Cris Collinsworth) on 09-23-18
Barely beat the Chiefs 43-40 (Al Michaels and Cris Collinsworth) on 10-14-18
Beat Green Bay 31-17 (A. Michaels and C. Collinsworth) on 11-04-18 (*2018 World Series Tribute*)

Smoked the Steelers 33-3 (Al Michaels and Cris Collinsworth) on 09-08-19 (*2018 Champs Tribute*)
Lost 37-20 to the Ravens (Al Michaels and Cris Collinsworth) on 11-03-19
Lost 28-22 to the Texans (Al Michaels and Cris Collinsworth) on 12-01-19

Monday Night Football Games on ABC TV from 1972-2005

Lost 24-17 to the Colts (F. Gifford, H. Cosell and D. Meredith) on 11-06-72 (*Jumpin' Joe Gerlach*)

Lost 20-7 to the Dolphins (Frank Gifford, Howard Cosell and Alex Karras) on 12-01-75

Grounded the Jets 41-7 (Frank Gifford, Howard Cosell and Alex Karras) on 10-18-76

Lost 30-27 in OT to the Browns (Frank Gifford, Howard Cosell and Don Meredith) on 09-26-77

Lost 34-27 to Baltimore in the rain (Frank Gifford, Howard Cosell and Don Meredith) on 09-18-78
Lost 23-3 to Miami (Frank Gifford, Howard Cosell and Don Meredith) on 12-18-78

Lost 16-13 in OT to the Steelers (F. Gifford, H. Cosell and D. Meredith) on 09-03-79 (*Stingley Ovation*)
Lost 27-14 to the Packers (Frank Gifford, Howard Cosell and Don Meredith) on 10-01-79

Beat Denver 23-14 (Frank Gifford, Howard Cosell and Don Meredith) on 09-29-80
Lost 38-34 to the Houston Oilers (Frank Gifford, Howard Cosell and Don Meredith) on 11-10-80
Lost 16-13 in OT to Miami (Frank Gifford, Howard Cosell and Don Meredith) on 12-08-80

Lost 35-21 to the Cowboys 35-21 (Frank Gifford, Howard Cosell and Don Meredith) on 09-21-81

Lost 30-27 to the Dolphins 30-27 (Frank Gifford, Joe Namath and OJ Simpson) on 12-16-85

Finally beat the Dolphins 34-27 in Miami (Al Michaels and Frank Gifford) on 12-22-86

Lost 43-24 to the NY Jets 43-24 (Al Michaels, Frank Gifford and Dan Dierdorf) on 09-21-87
Beat Miami 24-10 (Al Michaels, Frank Gifford and Dan Dierdorf) on 12-28-87

Beat Buffalo 27-14 (Al Michaels, Frank Gifford and and Dan Dierdorf) on 10-23-95
Lost 34-13 to the Broncos (Al Michaels, Frank Gifford and Dan Dierdorf) on 10-06-97
Beat Miami 14-12 (Al Michaels, Frank Gifford and Dan Dierdorf) on 12-22-97

Lost 27-21 to Denver (Al Michaels, Dan Dierdorf and Boomer Esiason) on 09-07-98
Lost 24-14 to the Jets (Al Michaels, Dan Dierdorf and Boomer Esiason) on 10-19-98
Beat Miami 26-23 (Al Michaels, Dan Dierdorf and Boomer Esiason) on 11-23-98 (*Drew broke his finger*)

Lost 24-17 to the Jets (Al Michaels and Boomer Esiason) on 11-15-99

Lost 20-19 to the Jets (Al Michaels, Dan Fouts and Dennis Miller) on 09-11-00
Beat Kansas City 30-24 (Al Michaels, Dan Fouts and Dennis Miller) on 12-04-00

Beat Pittsburgh 30-14 (Al Michaels and John Madden) on 09-09-02 (*2001 Champs Tribute*)
Lost 24-7 to Tennessee (Al Michaels and John Madden) on 12-16-02

Bear the Broncos 30-26 in Denver (Al Michaels and John Madden) on 11-03-03 (*Deliberate Safety*)

Beat Kansas City 27-19 (Al Michaels and John Madden) on 11-22-04
Lost 29-28 to Miami (Al Michaels and John Madden) on 12-20-04

Lost 40-21 to the Colts (Al Michaels and John Madden) on 11-07-05
Beat the Jets 31-21 (Al Michaels and John Madden) on 12-26-05

Monday Night TV Football Games on ESPN from 2006-19

Beat the Minnesota Vikings 31-7 (Mike Tirico and Tony Kornheiser) on 10-30-06

Blasted the Bengals 34-13 (Mike Tirico, Ron Jaworski and Tony Kornheiser) on 10-01-07
Barely beat Baltimore 27-24 (Mike Tirico, Ron Jaworski and Tony Kornheiser) on 12-03-07

Blasted the Broncos 41-7 (M. Tirico, R. Jaworski and T. Kornheiser) on 10-20-08 (*Andre Tippett Night*)

Beat Buffalo 25-24 (Mike Tirico, Ron Jaworski and Jon Gruden) on 09-14-09 (*50th Year Team Tribute*)
Lost 38-17 to the Saints (Mike Tirico, Ron Jaworski and Jon Gruden) on 11-30-09

Beat Miami 41-14 (Mike Tirico, Ron Jaworski and Jon Gruden) on 10-04-10 (*Scored TDs 5 ways*)
Blasted the Jets 45-3 (Mike Tirico, Ron Jaworski and Jon Gruden) on 12-06-10 (*Tedy Bruschi Tribute*)

Flew by Miami 38-24 (Mike Tirico and Jon Gruden) on 09-12-11 (*Team Record 516 yards passing*)
Crushed the Chiefs 34-3 (Mike Tirico and Jon Gruden) on 11-21-11

Humbled Houston 42-14 (Mike Tirico and Jon Gruden) on 12-10-12 (*Matt Light Tribute*)

Lost 24-20 to the Panthers (Mike Tirico and Jon Gruden) on 11-18-13

Lost to the Chiefs 41-14 (Mike Tirico and Jon Gruden) on 09-29-14

Beat Buffalo 20-13 (Mike Tirico and Jon Gruden) on 11-23-15

Beat Baltimore 30-23 (Sean McDonough and Jon Gruden) on 12-12-16

Lost 27-20 to Miami (Sean McDonough and Jon Gruden) on 12-11-17

Beat Buffalo 25-6 (Joe Tessitore, Jason Witten and Booger McFarland) on 10-29-18

Shutout the Jets 33-0 (Joe Tessitore and Booger McFarland) on 10-21-19

MORE FUN NICKNAMES

Food Related Nicknames

Bake	Robert Turner
Cornflakes	Corwin Brown
Juice	Olrick Johnson
Kool Aid	Laurence Maroney
Pickles	Jim Lee Hunt
Pineapple	John Simerson
The Whopper	Ron Berger
Sugar Bear	Ray Hamilton

TV Related Nicknames

Banacek	Jess Phillips
Harpo	Bob Gladieux
Hollywood	Harold Jackson
Hollywood	Larry Whigham
Rambo	Johnny Rembert
Spanky	Billy Neighbors
Tarzan	Tom Beer
Tonto	Chuck Shonta
Whimpy	Dwight Wheeler

Thursday Night Games on ABC TV from 1979-2005

Lost 39-24 to Miami (Frank Gifford, Howard Cosell, Don Meredith and Fran Tarkenton) on 11-29-79
Beat the Jets 20-6 (Al Michaels, Frank Gifford and OJ Simpson) on 09-11-86
Beat the Colts 27-24 (Al Michaels and John Madden) on 09-09-04 (*2003 Champs Tribute*)
Beat Oakland 30-20 (Al Michaels and John Madden) on 09-08-05 (*2004 Champs Tribute*)

Thursday Night Games on the NFL Network and CBS TV from 2007-18

Beat the New York Giants 38-35 (Bryant Gumbel and Cris Collinsworth) on 12-29-07
Lost 34-31 in OT to the Jets (Bob Papa and Cris Collinsworth) on 11-13-08
Beat the Jets 13-10 (Brad Nessler and Mike Mayock) on 09-12-13
Barely beat the Jets 27-25 (Jim Nantz and Phil Simms) on 10-16-14 (*Ty Law Tribute*)
Mashed Miami 36-7 (Jim Nantz and Phil Simms) on 10-29-15 (*Willie McGinest Tribute*)
Shutout Houston 27-0 (Jim Nantz and Phil Simms) on 09-22-16
Beat Tampa 19-14 (Jim Nantz and Tony Romo) on 10-05-17
Beat Indianapolis 38-24 (Joe Buck and Troy Aikman) on 10-04-18

Only Thursday Night Game on the NFL TV Network and FOX TV

Beat the New York Giants 35-14 (Joe Buck and Troy Aikman) on 10-10-19

Thanksgiving Games That Were Broadcast on Numerous TV Stations

Lost 20-17 to Dallas (Dick Enberg and Merlin Olsen) on **NBC TV** on 11-22-84
Beat Detroit 20-12 (Greg Gumbel and Phil Simms) on **CBS TV** on 11-28-02
Beat Detroit 45-24 (Jim Nantz and Phil Simms) on **CBS TV** on 11-25-10
Belted the Jets 49-19 (Al Michaels and Cris Collinsworth) on **NBC TV** on 11-22-12

Thursday Night Games on NBC TV

Blasted the Jets 49-19 on Thanksgiving (Al Michaels and Cris Collinsworth) on 11-22-12
Beat the Steelers 28-21 (Al Michaels and Cris Collinsworth) on 09-10-15 (*2014 Champs Tribute*)
Lost 42-27 to the Chiefs (Al Michaels and Cris Collinsworth) on 09-07-17 (*2016 Champs Tribute*)

Only Thursday Night Game on TNT

Lost 17-10 to Miami (Skip Caray and Pat Haden) on 10-18-90

Thursday Night Games on FOX TV

Beat the Colts 38-24 (Joe Buck and Troy Aikman on 10-04-18
Beat the NY Giants 35-14 (Joe Buck and Troy Aikman) on 10-10-19

Outcome, Opponent, Score, TV Announcers and Date of Every Patriots Super Bowl Game

Lost to Da' Bears 46-10 (Dick Enberg, Merlin Olsen and Bob Griese) on 01-26-86
Lost to the Packers 35-21 (Pat Summerall and John Madden) on 01-26-97
Beat the St. Louis Rams 20-17 (Pat Summerall and John Madden) on 02-03-02
Beat the Panthers 32-29 (Greg Gumbel and Phil Simms) on 02-01-04
Beat the Eagles 24-21 (Joe Buck, Troy Aikman and Cris Collinsworth) on 02-06-05
Lost to the New York Giants 17-14 (Joe Buck and Troy Aikman) on 02-03-08
Lost to the New York Giants 21-17 (Al Michaels and Cris Collonsworth) on 02-05-12
Beat the Seahawks 28-24 (Al Michaels and Cris Collinsworth) on 02-01-15
Beat the Falcons 34-28 in OT (Joe Buck and Troy Aikman) on 02-05-17
Lost to the Eagles 41-33 (Al Michaels and Cris Collinsworth) on 02-04-18
Beat the Los Angeles Rams 13-3 (Jim Nantz and Tony Romo) on 02-03-19

CHAPTER 2

HEAD COACHES, EXTREME WEATHER GAMES AND OTHER FUN FACTS

EVERY PATRIOTS HEAD COACH AND HIS MOST MEMORABLE VICTORY

Lou Saban (1960-61)
Beat the New York Titans 28-24 (on the last play of the game) at the Polo Grounds on 09-17-60

Mike Holovak (1961-68)
Beat the Buffalo Bills 14-3 in "The Game" at Fenway Park on 12-04-66 (*Made cover of Sports Illustrated*)

Clive Rush (1969-70)
Beat the Miami Dolphins 27-14 (Bob Gladieux Game) at Harvard Stadium on 09-20-70

John Mazur (1970-72)
Beat the Baltimore Colts 21-17 (Upton Bell Game) at Memorial Stadium on 12-19-71

John "Phil" Bengston (1972)
Beat the New Orleans Saints 17-10 on 12-10-72

Charles "Chuck" Fairbanks (1973-78)
Destroyed the Oakland Raiders 48-17 at Schaefer Stadium on 10-18-76

Ron Erhardt (1979-81)
Blasted the New York Jets 56-3 (Will McDonough/Ray Clayborn Fight) at Schaefer Stadium on 09-09-79

Ron Meyer (1982-84)
Beat the Miami Dolphins 3-0 (Snow Brush/Mark Henderson) at Schaefer Stadium on 12-12-82

Raymond Berry (1984-89)
Beat the Miami "Squish the Fish" Dolphins 31-14 to win AFC Championship at the Orange Bowl
        on 01-12-86

Rod Rust (1990)
Beat the Indianapolis Colts 16-14 (Steve Grogan's last game as PATS QB) at the Hoosier Dome
        on 09-16-90

Dick MacPherson (1991-92)
Beat the Vikings 26-23 in OT (Jason Staurovsky kicked 42 yard FG with no time left in OT) on 10-20-91

Dante Scarnecchia (1992)
Defeated the Indianapolis Colts 37-34 in OT (Zolak was AFC Player/Week) at the Hoosier Dome
        on 11-15-92

Duane "Bill" Parcells (1993-96)
Defeated the Minnesota Vikings 26-20 in OT (after trailing 20-0) at Foxboro Stadium on 11-13-94

Pete Carroll (1997-99)
Beat the 49ers 24-21 (Scott Zolak vs Steve Young) at Foxboro Stadium on 12-20-98

Bill Belichick (2000+)
Beat the Atlanta Falcons 34-28 in OT (after trailing 28-3) in **Super Bowl LI** on 02-05-17

Top 5 Foggiest Games

Heavy Fog during their 33-13 loss to the 49ers at Sullivan Stadium 10-02-83
Thick Fog during their 28-14 loss to the Oilers at Foxboro Stadium on 10-17-93
Heavy Fog during their 28-3 **Divisional** win vs the Steelers at Foxboro on 01-05-97
100% Humidity and Fog in their 23-7 win over the Falcons at Gillette Stadium on 10-22-17
1st half of Heavy Fog in their 20-13 **Wild Card** loss to the Titans at Gillette on 01-04-20

Top 5 Games with the Heaviest Rain

Downpour of rain in their 34-27 loss to the Baltimore Colts at Schaefer Stadium on 09-18-78
Torrential Rain in the 1st half of their 14-13 win over the Jets at Giants Stadium on 11-13-88
Heavy Rain in their 6-0 loss to the Jets at Foxboro Stadium on 11-28-93
Heavy Rain in their 24-3 rout of the Baltimore Ravens at Gillette Stadium on 11-28-04
Monsoon of Rain in their 13-6 loss to the Bengals at Paul Brown Stadium on 10-06-13

Top 5 Snowiest Games

3-5 inches of snow during the game in their 16-13 OT **Playoff** win vs Oak at Foxboro on 01-19-02
Snow in their 31-0 win over the Bills at Gillette Stadium on 12-27-03
Snow in their 24-14 **AFC Championship** win vs the Colts at Gillette on 01-18-04
Snow in their 47-7 rout of the Cardinals at Gillette Stadium on 12-21-08
Snow in their 36-7 rout of the Bears at Soldier Field on 12-12-10

Top 5 Coldest Games (without the Wind Chill Factor)

4 degrees in their 17-14 **Divisional Playoff** win vs the Titans at Gillette Stadium on 01-10-04
5 degrees in their 28-10 loss to the Steelers at 3 Rivers Stadium on 12-17-89
9 degrees in their 45-3 loss to the Chiefs at Municipal Stadium on 12-14-63
11 degrees in their 41-27 **AFC Championship** win over the Steelers at Heinz Field on 01-23-05
13 degrees in their 26-6 win over the Jets at Gillette Stadium on 12-31-17

Top 5 Coldest Games (with the Wind Chill Factor)

-10 degrees Wind Chill Factor in their 17-14 **Divisional** win vs the Titans at Gillette on 01-10-04
-3 degrees Wind Chill Factor in their 28-10 loss to the Steelers at 3 Rivers Stadium on 12-17-89
-3 degrees Wind Chill Factor in their 14-10 win over the Dolphins at Schaefer Stadium on 12-11-77
-2 degrees Wind Chill Factor in their 26-6 win over the Jets at Gillette Stadium on 12-31-17
-2 degrees Wind Chill Factor in their 38-0 shutout of the Colts at Foxboro Stadium on 12-26-93

Top 6 Windiest Games

Wind gusts of up to 68 MPH during their 6-0 loss to the Jets at Foxboro Stadium on 11-28-93
Wind gusts of up to 55 MPH during their 13-0 win vs Buffalo at Ralph Wilson Stadium on 12-28-08
Wind gusts of up to 43 MPH during their 38-0 shutout of the Colts at Foxboro Stadium on 12-26-93
Winds gusts of more than 40 MPH in their 13-10 OT win vs the Bills at Ralph Wilson Stadium on 12-17-00
Wind gusts of up to 40 MPH in their 13-7 win over Buffalo at Ralph Wilson Stadium on 12-20-87
Wind gusts of up to 40 MPH during their 13-6 loss to the Browns at Municipal Stadium on 11-06-94

Top 6 Warmest Weather Games

97 degrees in their 31-20 game at the Jaguars at TIAA Bank Stadium in Jacksonville on 09-16-18
94 degrees in their 24-10 loss to Phoenix at Sun Devil Stadium in Tempe, Arizona on 09-29-91
94 degrees in their 23-12 win over the Cardinals at Sun Devil Stadium in Tempe, Arizona on 09-19-04
94 degrees in their 33-20 loss to the Dolphins at Hard Rock Stadium in Miami, Florida on 09-07-14
90 degrees in their 27-17 loss to the Panthers at Bank of America Stadium in North Carolina on 09-18-05
90 degrees in their 19-10 win over the Jets at Giants Stadium in New Jersey on 09-14-08

Opening Day 1970

On September 20, 1970, about an hour before game time, team owner Billy Sullivan refused to renegotiate the contract of John Charles and Larry Carwell, so he released them. Thinking quickly, they called John Outlaw, who was recently cut from the team, at his apartment in Milton. They told him to go to Curry College, put on his uniform and drive to Harvard Stadium as the game was about to begin.

Unfortunately, when John Outlaw arrived at the parking lot in Cambridge, the gate security didn't allow him to enter the stadium. He pleaded with them emphatically stating that he was a last-minute replacement and not only needed a parking spot but entrance to the locker room. A few minutes later, one of the Patriots coaches noticed John's dilemma and he was granted permission to park his car and play in the game.

The Patriots still had one more position to fill though, so they called another former player Bob Gladieux, but he was not at his South End apartment. On Friday, the day Bob was released, they gave him two complimentary tickets to this game, so perhaps Bob might already be in the stands.

Bob Gladieux, who had played for the Patriots in 1969 and was very disappointed that he was cut from the team, was told to stay in the Boston area for a while. After being released from the team on Friday, he went on a 3-day partying binge. He was drinking Schlitz beer and port wine and eating hot dogs and burgers with his friends in the tailgating section of Harvard Stadium prior to this game.

As Bob was entering the stadium, he noticed that the coaches of the Boston Patriots were very close to the seats in the stadium. Not wanting to be recognized in the (unhealthy) condition he was in, he bent down and crawled on his hands and knees until he had a clear path to go underneath the stadium to get out of their viewpoint. Meanwhile, the team owner of the Patriots, Billy Sullivan, decided to make an announcement over the intercom, "If Bob Gladieux was in the stands, could he please report to the Patriots locker room." Bob was shocked to hear his name over the loudspeaker so he took a few seconds to gather his thoughts. "What do I have to lose? Maybe something

happened in the locker room and they want to resign me to a contract? Even though I might not have had the proper pre-game nutrition, I could always use the money."

So, he reported to the locker room, signed the contract and was told he would be on the opening kickoff of this game. The Patriots lost the toss of the coin and had to kickoff. As he was running down the field he was hoping he wouldn't make contact with anyone and disperse his pre-game fluids and food on the field. With this thought in mind he ran for an empty area of the field trying to run out of bounds and avoid any contact. Meanwhile, Jack Scott took Gino Cappelletti's kickoff and instead of following behind his blockers, he ran for this same area of the field and bumped into Bob Gladiuex. The public address announcer declared "Tackle made by #24 Bob Gladieux on the Dolphins 34 yard line. That was a 25-yard kickoff return by Jake Scott." Bob threw up later in this game and played two more years for the Patriots.

The Snow Brush Game

On December 12, 1982, the New England Patriots defeated the Dolphins 3-0 on a sleet and snow-covered field. Because of the poor field conditions the Official enacted the Emergency Ground Rule, which allowed them to call time out so a portion of the field could be cleared by the Ground Crew. Mark Henderson, who was a convicted burglar on a work release program from the local MCI-Norfolk Prison, was assigned the duty of driving a John Deere Model 314 Sweeper tractor across the field numerous times throughout this game.

Both teams were able to move the ball on the ground, as Miami had 176 yards rushing and the Patriots ran for 199 yards. Mark Van Eeghen ran for 100 yards and Mosi "the Samoan Snowman" Tatupu ran for an additional 81 yards for the Patriots.

Patriots Kicker John Smith fell on the ice while attempting an 18-yard field goal that deflected off the helmet of Patriots Offensive lineman Bob Cryder, in the 2nd Qtr and Dolphins Kicker Ove Johansson's 45-yard FGA was blocked by Julius Adams in the 3rd Qtr.

With about 5 minutes left in the game, the Patriots were in position to try another field goal attempt when Steve Grogan suggested to Head Coach Ron

Meyer that Mark Henderson might be able to use the snow tractor to clear a spot for John Smith before his 33-yard field goal attempt. During the time out, Mark Henderson drove his tractor on the field, and rather than continue on a straight path along the 30-yard line stripe, he drove to the spot where John Smith stood, which would allow him to get substantially better footing for his field goal attempt.

Needless to say, Don Shula and the rest of the Dolphins were furious that this was allowed to happen. The Officials decided that if the Dolphins had the chance to kick a field goal with the remaining time left in the game, they would have allowed the snow tractor to clear a path for their kicker. Interceptions by Don Blackmon and Roland James on the last two drives by the Dolphins prevented that situation from arising though.

When the game had concluded, Mark Henderson's tractor stalled on the field as he was attempting to put it away, which allowed all of the reporters to surround him. When the Miami reporters asked if Mark knew that Don Shula was on the NFL Rule Committee and what he did was against the rules he replied "What is he going to do, throw me in jail?"

These interviews delayed his departure so Patriots Head Coach Ron Meyer had to call the prison to explain why Mark was going to be arriving after his required time of 6 PM. Mark received a game ball for this game was released from prison a few months later and has had an exemplary life since.

This John Deere Tractor is displayed on the ceiling, suspended by heavy duty wires, at the Patriots Hall of Fame.

Do You Remember This Football Folly Moment by John Tarver?

Patriots RB John Tarver, while running backward, (for a 14 yard loss) tossed the ball over his head, into the end zone, from the 1 yard line, while trying to avoid getting tackled in the Patriots 41-16 loss to Oakland Raiders on December 1, 1974. He thought by throwing the ball out of the end zone his team would get the ball back at the 20 yard line. The referee blew the whistle just prior to his faux pas and gave him forward progress on the 1 yard line.

Top 9 "Did That Really Happen?" Offensive Plays by the Patriots

Larry Garron's lateral to QB Babe Parilli, who advanced it 9 yards, in their 34-21 win on 09-16-62
John Tarver throwing the ball over his head from the 1 yard line into the end zone vs the Raiders on 12-01-74
Jim Plunkett handing off to Tackle Tom Neville, who was then tackled for an 8 yard loss, on 10-03-71
Doug Flutie's lateral to Reggie Dupard on 4th + 1, for a 7 yard gain, in their 31-10 loss to Buffalo on 10-01-89
Hugh Millen's 18 yard run lateral to Irving Fryar, who advanced it 8 more yards, on 10-04-92
Leonard Russell advancing Vincent Brisby's fumble 22 yards in the overtime period on 01-02-94
Max Lane advancing Troy Brown's 5 yard reception fumble an additional 30 yards on 10-15-95
Wes Welker's recovery on Tom Brady's fumbled lateral in their 31-28 win over the Colts on 11-21-10
Julian Edelman's reception of a pass that deflected off Falcons DB Robert Alford in **SB** win on 02-05-17

Most Memorable and Bizarre Plays on a Punt

Chuck Shonta returning a poor snap to the Titans Punter 52 yards for a TD on the last play on 09-17-60
LeRoy Moore recovering an end zone punt, that deflected off the goal line cross bar back for a TD on 11-17-61
Punter Eddie Hare throwing a 4 yard pass to Mosi Tatupu in their 28-13 win over the Dolphins on 10-21-79
Don Westbrook tackling Brent McClanahan on a fake punt in their 27-23 win on 12-16-79
Bryan Wagner's end zone punt hit the backside of a teammate and was recovered for a TD on 09-15-91
Lonie Paxton deliberately hiking the ball out of the end zone for a safety in their 30-26 win on 11-03-03
Aqib Talib trying to advance Julian Edelman's fumbled punt return lateral in their 30-27 win on 10-13-13
Tom Brady's 32 yard pooched punt, on 3rd down, in their 34-20 win over the Bills on 12-29-13
Brandon Bolden tackling Colt Anderson on a bizarre formation fake punt play in their 34-27 win on 10-18-15
Brandon King tackling Travis Benjamin on his -8 yard punt return for a safety in their 21-13 win on 10-29-17
Nate Ebner's 14 yard run on a fake punt play in their 35-17 win over the Dolphins on 11-26-17

Three Memorable Moments Involving a Fan on the Last Play of the Game

Bob Dee bear-hugged a kid who was on the field trying to get a live fumble in the end zone on 10-28-60
A man snuck onto the field and disrupted the last play saving their 28-21 win vs Dallas on 11-03-61
A fan picked up John Huarte's incomplete pass and ran to the exit doors at Fenway Park on 10-23-66
Joyous Fans charged the field at Fenway Park with 5 seconds left in their 33-14 win on 12-01-68

Alphabetical List of Everyone Who Played in Just One Regular Season Game for the Patriots

Kamar Aiken, Darren Anderson, Glenn Antrum, Jack Atchason, Ricky Atkinson, Kole Ayi, Mel Baker, Brooks Barnard, Frank Bianchini, Joe Biscaha, OJ Brigance, Antonio Brown, Wilbert Brown, Travaris Cadet, Rico Clark, Thomas Clayton, Pat Coleman, Tom Condon, Korey Cunningham, Kevin Donnalley, Kai Forbath, Tony Gaiter, Leonard Hankerson, Raymont Harris, James Harrison, Jeremy Hill, Kevin Hunt, Damarius Johnson, Rufus Johnson, Dan Kecman, Ethan Kelley, Ishmaa'ily Kitchen, Merv Krakau, Harvey Langi, Bill Larson, Jamie Lawson, Louis Leonard, Steve Maneri, Riley McCarron, Terrell McClain, Don McComb, Sean McDermott, Dewey McDonald, Emanuel McNeil, Rashad Moore, Marques Murrell, Andre Neblett, Jeff Paulk, Willis Perkins, Clay Pickering, Lousaka Polite, Tom Porell, Andre President, Kenny Price, Ray Ratkowski, Al Romine, Greg Salas, Terdell Sands, Eric Schubert, Walter Scott, Peter Shorts, Alex Silvestro, Kendall Simmons, Eric Stokes, Gene Taylor, Greg Taylor, Ross Tucker, Darren Twombly, Todd Whitten, Brian Williams, Darrell Wilson, David Wilson and Kellen Winslow II.

Played in Just Regular Season Game and Was a Member of a Championship Team for the Patriots

Kole Ayi, Brooks Barnard, Wilbert Brown, Jeremy Hill, Ethan Kelley, Steve Maneri, Riley McCarron and Sean McDermott only played in 1 regular season game and yet were a member of a Championship Team.

Offensive Players Who Have Played on the Defensive Side of the Ball for the Patriots

Larry Garron played in 3 games as a defensive back in 1960
Gino Cappelletti had 4 interceptions as a defensive back in 1960
Walter Beach was a running back who was used as a defensive back during the 1961 season
TE Tom Stephens was used as a DB and had an 22 yard return of a pass by Dick Wood on 09-08-63
Punter Tom Janik was used a DB and had an 8 yard return of a pass by Greg Cook on 11-16-69
Randy Vataha was used as a safety in their final series during their 30-27 win over the Steelers on 09-26-76
Randy Moss intercepted Kyle Orton's Hail Mary Pass on 10-11-09
Troy Brown intercepted passes by Drew Bledsoe, Luke McCown and Jon Kitna during the 2004 season
Christian Fauria was used as an extra defensive back in 3 games in 2004
Bam Childress had 3 receptions for 32 yards as a WR and made 4 tackles as a DB on 01-01-06
Julian Edelman played in 8 games as a DB in 2011 and made a tackle on QB Vince Young on 11-27-11
Matthew Slater played in 3 games as a defensive back in 2011
Rob Gronkowski was a safety on 10-16-11, 10-30-11, 09-24-17, 12-09-18 and in 1 Playoff Game on 01-10-15
Josh Gordon was used as a Defensive Back for 3 plays in their 38-31 win over the Bears on 10-21-18
John Tanner played Tight End, Defensive End and Linebacker over the 1973-74 seasons

Offensive Linemen Who Have Played on the Defensive Line for the Patriots

Houston Antwine was an offensive guard in 1961 before becoming a 6 time AFL All Star Defensive Tackle
Jim Boudreaux was an offensive tackle and a defensive end over the 1966-68 seasons
Johnny Cagle was an offensive guard, a defensive lineman and a linebacker during the 1969 season
Walt Cudzik was a center and played linebacker & kicked off occasionally for the Patriots from 1960-63
Steve DeOssie was a linebacker on goal line situations
Tom Funchess was an offensive tackle who played as a DE in their 23-10 loss to the Chiefs on 10-11-70
Chris Gannon was a long snapper who started in 2 games as a defensive end over the 1990-93 seasons
Milt Graham was an offensive lineman and a defensive lineman over the 1961-63 seasons
Halvor Hagen was an offensive guard and recorded 1 sack as a Defensive End on 11-12-72
Harry Jagielski was an offensive lineman and a defensive lineman over the 1960-61 seasons
Dick Klein was an offensive lineman and a defensive lineman over the 1961-62 seasons
Tom Neville was an offensive tackle and had 7 tackles as a DT in their 24-10 loss to Oakland on 10-08-65
Tony Sardisco was an offensive guard and a defensive end over the 1960-62 seasons
Lennie St. Jean was an AFL All Star Guard in 1966 and he had 5.5 sacks as a DE over the 1964-65 seasons
JR Williamson was an offensive center and a linebacker over the 1968-71 seasons

Defensive Players Who Have Been Used on the Offensive Team

Defensive Linemen Henry Thomas, Dan Klecko and Richard Seymour were used at Full Back
Linebackers Bryan Cox, Junior Seau and Elandon Roberts were used at Full Back
Defensive backs Gino Cappelletti, Chuck Shonta, Don Webb, Terrell Buckley were used as Wide Receivers
Linebackers Mike Vrabel and John Tanner were used as Tight Ends

SPECIAL TEAM PLAYERS WHO HAVE CONTRIBUTED ON OFFENSE

Patriot Kickers Who Have Had at Least One Pass Reception

Offensive Lineman Walt Cudzik attempted a 48 yard field goal and caught a deflected pass
Offensive Lineman Justin Canale kicked off in 54 games and caught a deflected pass
Gino Cappelletti kicked 176 FGs, 342 PATs and caught 292 passes for 4,589 yards and 42 TDs

Everyone Who Has Returned a Free Kick and Completed a Pass for the Patriots

Dave Meggett returned a free kick on 10-27-96 and completed a 35 yard TD pass on 11-23-97
Kevin Faulk returned a free kick on 09-10-06 and completed 2 passes for 23 yards
Danny Amendola returned a free kick on 10-29-17 and completed a 36 yard pass on 12-06-15
Julian Edelman has returned 3 free kicks and completed 5 passes for 141 yards + 2 TDs (Incl. Playoffs)

Every Special Team Player Who Has Worn at Least Two Uniform #s for the Patriots

Walter Beach	#26 and #41	Mike Cloud	#21 and #34
Mel Black	#94 and #51	Larry Garron	#46 and #40
Deion Branch	#83 and #84	Cyrus Jones	#26 and #41
Troy Brown	#86 and #80	Maugaula Tuitele	#96, #47 and #59
Hubie Bryant	#45 and #84	Dekoda Watson	#53 and #52
Patrick Chung	#25 and #23		

CHAPTER 3

MEMORABLE RUSHING, PASSING AND RECEIVING MOMENTS

Only Player Who Has Run for a TD on the 1st Offensive Play of the Game

Sam Cunningham ran for a 75 yard TD on the 1st play in their 30-28 loss to Buffalo on 10-20-74

Chronological List of Every Patriots QB Who Has Run for a Game Winning Touchdown

Babe Parilli ran for a game winning 7 yard TD to defeat the Broncos 28-24 on 12-03-61
Jim Plunkett ran for a game winning 5 yard TD to defeat the Bears 13-10 on 10-21-73
Steve Grogan ran for a game winning 10 yard TD to defeat the Bills 26-22 on 10-24-76
Steve Grogan ran for a 3 yard TD to defeat the Baltimore Colts 21-14 on 11-14-76
Steve Grogan ran for a 4 yard TD to defeat the San Diego Chargers 28-23 on 10-01-78
Steve Grogan ran for a game winning 3 yard TD to defeat the Jets 20-13 on 10-20-85
Steve Grogan ran for a game winning 1 yard TD to defeat the Dolphins 17-13 on 11-03-85
Bob Bleier ran for a game winning 1 yard TD to defeat the Bills 14-7 on 10-11-87
Doug Flutie ran a naked bootleg 13 yard TD to defeat the Indianapolis Colts 21-17 on 10-02-88
Hugh Millen ran for a game winning 2 yard TD to defeat the Bills 16-13 on 11-24-91

Chronological List of Patriots RBs Who Have Run for the Game Winning Touchdown

Jim Crawford ran for a game winning 1 yard TD to defeat San Diego 24-20 on 10-19-62
JD Garrett ran for a game winning 1 yard TD to beat the Chiefs 31-24 on 12-06-64
Carl Garrett ran for a game winning 12 yard TD to defeat the Falcons 21-20 on 09-24-72
Jess Phillips ran for a game winning 11 yard TD to defeat the Chiefs 21-17 on 09-18-77
Sam Cunningham dove 1 yard for the game winning TD to defeat the Raiders 21-14 on 09-24-78
Sam Cunningham ran 3 yards for the game winning TD to defeat the Bengals 10-3 on 10-15-78
Horace Ivory ran for a game winning 5 yard TD to defeat the Bills 14-10 on 11-05-78
Tony Collins ran for a game winning 3 yard TD to defeat the Saints 7-0 on 12-04-83
Tony Collins ran for a game winning 2 yard TD to defeat the Browns 17-16 on 10-07-84
Reggie Dupard ran for a game winning 4 yard TD to defeat the Jets 27-24 on 09-10-89
John Stephens ran for a 10 yard TD to defeat the Indianapolis Colts 22-16 on 12-03-89
Leonard Russell ran for a 4 yard TD to defeat the Browns 20-17 on 12-19-93
Curtis Martin ran for a game winning 1 yard TD to beat the Browns 17-14 on 9-03-95
Curtis Martin ran for a game winning 1 yard TD to defeat the Jets 31-28 on 12-10-95
Dave Meggett ran for a game winning 5 yard TD to beat the Dolphins 14-12 on 12-22-97
Terry Allen ran for a game winning 3 yard TD to defeat the Cowboys 13-6 on 12-05-99
Sammy Morris ran for a game winning 1 yard TD to defeat Seattle 24-21 on 12-07-08

Everyone Who Has Run for a Touchdown to Win a Playoff Game in Overtime

James White ran for a 2 yard TD to beat the Falcons in OT 34-28, to win the **Super Bowl** on 02-05-17
Rex Burkhead ran a 2 yard TD to beat the Chiefs in OT 37-31, to win the **AFC Championship** on 01-20-19

Every Running Back of the Patriots Who Was Named the *AFC Offensive Player of the Week*

Curtis Martin had 35 carries for 166 yards + 2 TDs in their 20-7 victory over the Jets on 11-05-95
Curtis Martin had 27 carries for 148 yards and caught a 2 point pass from Drew Bledsoe on 11-26-95
LeGarrette Blount had 24 carries for 189 yards + 2 TDs in their 34-20 win over Buffalo on 12-29-13
Jonas Gray had 37 carries for 201 yards + 4 TDs in their 42-20 rout of the Indianapolis Colts on 11-16-14
Dion Lewis had 24 carries for 129 yards + 1 TD and 5 receptions for 24 yards + 1 TD on 12-24-17

Most Yards Rushing/Game	Most Yards Rushing/Season	Most Yards Rushing/Career
212 yards by Tony Collins	1,635 yards by Corey Dillon	5,453 yards by Sam Cunningham
208 yards by Jim Nance	1,487 yards by Curtis Martin	5,323 yards by Jim Nance
201 yards by Jonas Gray	1,458 yards by Jim Nance	4,648 yards by Tony Collins
199 yards by Curtis Martin	1,263 yards by Stevan Ridley	3,799 yards by Curtis Martin
196 yards by Robert Edwards	1,227 yards by Craig James	3,607 yards by Kevin Faulk

Longest Run by Every Patriots Quarterback

46 yards by Tom Yewcic in their 14-10 loss to the Broncos on 09-29-63

41 yard TD run by Steve Grogan in their 41-7 rout of the Jets on 10-18-76

41 yards by Steve Grogan in their 31-0 shutout of the Seahawks on 10-09-77

37 yards by Jim Plunkett in their 41-26 loss to the Oakland Raiders on 12-01-74

32 yard TD run by Babe Parilli in their 34-21 victory over the Houston Oilers on 09-16-62

26 yards by Tony Eason in their 30-28 comeback win over the LA Rams on 11-16-86

26 yards by Hugh Millen in their 14-0 loss to the Los Angeles Rams on 09-13-92

26 yards by Hugh Millen in their 30-21 loss to the Jets on 10-04-92

25 yards by Drew Bledsoe in their 13-10 OT loss to the Bills on 12-26-99

23 yards by Tommy Hodson in their 42-7 loss to the Jets on 12-23-90

23 yard TD run by Jacoby Brissett in their 27-0 shutout of Houston on 09-22-16

22 yards by Matt Cavanaugh in their 24-2 victory over the Bills on 12-14-80

22 yards by Doug Flutie in their 31-10 loss to the Bills on 10-01-89

22 yards by Tom Brady in their 38-13 win over the Bengals on 10-01-06

21 yards by Tom Greene in their 13-0 loss to the Bills on 09-23-60

21 yards by Mike Taliaferro in their 23-6 victory over the Bills on 10-20-68

20 yards by Butch Songin in their 37-21 loss to the Houston Oilers 37-21 on 12-18-60

20 yards by Brian Hoyer in their 35-7 rout of the Buccaneers on 10-25-09

19 yards by Tom Ramsey in their 31-20 loss to the Broncos on 12-06-87

19 yards by Scott Zolak in their 6-0 loss to the Indianapolis Colts on 12-06-92

19 yards by Matt Cassel in their 34-31 OT loss to the Jets on 11-13-08

17 yards by Eddie Wilson in their 30-21 loss to the Oakland Raiders on 10-24-65

17 yards by Tom Sherman in their 34-10 loss to the Dolphins on 11-24-68

14 yards by Joe Kapp in their 16-0 loss to the Giants on 10-18-70

13 yards by John Huarte in their 20-14 victory over the Dolphins on 11-27-66

13 yards by Scott Secules in their 13-10 OT loss to the Bills on 11-07-93

11 yards by Brian Dowling, on 4th + 10, in their 45-21 loss to the Broncos on 12-17-72

11 yards by Marc Wilson in their 28-10 loss to the Steelers on 12-17-89

10 yards by Don Trull, on 4th + 4, in their 29-24 loss to the Jets on 11-19-67

10 yards by Jimmy Garoppolo in their 23-21 win over Arizona on 09-11-16

7 yards by Jeff Carlson in their 20-10 loss to the Bengals on 12-20-92

5 yards by Harvey White in their 35-0 shutout of the Los Angeles Chargers on 10-08-60

4 yards by Damon Huard, on 4th + 1, in their 33-30 victory over the Bears on 11-10-02

3 yards by Rohan Davey in their 21-7 win over the 49ers on 01-02-05

2 yards by Neil Graff in their 7-0 loss to the Houston Oilers on 09-21-75

2 yards by Michael Bishop in their 20-19 loss to the Jets on 09-11-00

1 yard TD run by Bob Bleier in their 14-7 victory over the Bills on 10-11-87

Kim Hammond ran for a 2 point conversion in their 28-18 loss to San Diego on 12-07-69

Alphabetical List of the Longest Run by Every Patriots Receiver Who Ran for at Least 20 Yards

Troy Brown's longest run was for 35 yards in their 21-16 loss to Tampa on 09-03-00
Julian Edelman's longest run was for 47 yards in their 59-24 rout of the Colts on 11-18-12
Irving Fryar's longest run was for 31 yards in their 34-7 rout of the Dolphins on 10-05-86
Terry Glenn's longest run was for 35 yards in their 30-24 win over the Chiefs on 12-04-00
David Patten's longest run was a 29 yard TD in their 38-17 rout of the Colts on 10-21-01
Darryl Stingley's longest run was a 34 yard TD, on his birthday, in their 21-17 win over KS on 09-18-77
Brandon Tate's longest run was for 22 yards in their 23-20 OT win vs the Ravens on 10-17-10
Randy Vataha's longest run was for 24 yards in their 27-17 win over the Baltimore Colts on 11-24-74
Wes Welker's longest run was for 27 yards in their 34-13 rout of the Bengals on 10-01-07

10 Longest Runs for a TD by a Patriots Running Back

85 yard TD by Larry Garron in their 52-21 rout of the Bills on 10-22-61
80 yard TD by Carl Garrett in their 17-16 loss to the Dolphins on 11-09-69
78 yard TD by Curtis Martin in their 28-3 **Divisional** win over the Steelers on 01-05-97
75 yard TD by Sam Cunningham, on their 1st play, in their 29-28 loss to Buffalo on 10-20-74
73 yard TD by LeGarrette Blount in their 43-22 **Divisional** rout of the Colts on 01-11-14
71 yard TD by Claude King in their 41-16 rout of the Broncos on 09-21-62
70 yard TD by Curtis Martin in their 31-3 rout of the Bears on 09-21-97
69 yard TD by Andy Johnson in their 31-14 victory over Tampa Bay on 12-12-76
67 yard TD by Larry Garron in their 23-21 win over the Bills on 09-23-61
66 yard TD by Andy Johnson in their 21-10 win over the Baltimore Colts on 10-19-75

10 Longest Runs from Scrimmage by a Patriots RB That Did Not Result in a TD

77 yard run by Ron Burton in their 31-24 loss to the Broncos on 10-23-60
77 yard run by Robert Weathers in their 29-23 OT loss to the Baltimore Colts on 09-04-83
74 yard run by Don Calhoun in their 16-6 win over the St. Louis Cardinals on 09-10-78
73 yard run by Craig James in their 33-10 loss to the St. Louis Cardinals on 12-02-84
71 yard run by Sedrick Shaw in their 31-10 loss to the Jets on 12-27-98
58 yard run by JD Garrett in their 39-10 rout of the Broncos on 10-04-64
57 yard run by Curtis Martin in their 27-22 loss to the Redskins on 10-13-96
55 yard run by Mosi Tatupu in their 17-6 win over the Dolphins on 11-13-83
55 yard run by Sammy Morris in their 35-7 rout of the Jaguars on 12-27-09
54 yard run by Larry Garron in their 24-21 victory over the Oakland Raiders on 10-30-66
54 yard run by Jim Nance in their 24-21 victory over the Oakland Raiders on 10-30-66
54 yard run by Don Calhoun in their 21-14 win over the Baltimore Colts on 11-14-76
54 yard run by Tony Collins in their 24-13 victory over the Baltimore Colts on 09-12-82

Every Patriots Punter Who Has Run for a 1st Down on a 4th Down Play in a Regular Season Game

Tom Yewcic ran 20 yards, on 4th & 4, in their 26-16 victory over the Oakland Raiders on 10-26-62
Pat Studstill ran 11 yards, on 4th & 3, in their 27-24 loss to the Bills on 11-19-72
Lee Johnson ran 13 yards, on 4th & 3, in their 17-7 loss to the Bills on 11-28-99

Only Patriots Quarterback Who Has Run for a 1st Down on a Fake Punt Play in a Regular Season Game

Damon Huard, on a fake punt, ran 4 yards, on 4th & 1, in their 33-30 win over the Bears on 11-10-02

Every Patriots Player Who Has Run with a Lateral from a Teammate on a 4th Down Play

Gino Cappelletti lost 6 yards after getting a lateral from Ross O'Hanley on a bad field goal snap on 10-16-60
Tony Franklin lost 5 yards after getting a lateral from Tony Eason after a poor field goal snap on 11-17-85
Reggie Dupard ran for a gain of 7 yards with a lateral from Doug Flutie, on a 4th & 1 play, on 10-01-89

Only Patriots Field Goal Holder Who Has Run for a 1st Down

Field Goal Holder Scott Zolak ran 8 yards, on 4th + 2, in their 31-17 loss to the Saints on 12-03-95

Progression of the Most Yards Rushing by a Patriots Quarterback in a Regular Season Game

2 yards rushing by Butch Songin in their 13-10 loss to the Broncos on 09-09-60
33 yards rushing by Tom Greene in their 13-0 loss to the Bills on 09-23-60
46 yards rushing by Babe Parilli in their 35-21 win over the Oakland Raiders on 12-09-61
90 yards rushing by Tom Yewcic in their 24-17 victory over the New York Titans on 11-30-62
96 yards rushing by Babe Parilli in their 25-24 victory over the Houston Oilers on 11-06-64
103 yards rushing by Steve Grogan in their 41-7 rout of the Jets on 10-18-76

MEMORABLE PASSES

Only Player Who Has Thrown a Touchdown Pass on the 1st Offensive Play of the Game

Doug Flutie threw an 80 yard TD pass to Irving Fryar, on the 1st play, in their 30-7 win on 10-30-88

Every QB Who Has Thrown a TD Pass on the Patriots 1st Offensive Play in a Game

Mike Taliaferro tossed a 34 yard TD pass to Charley Frazier on their 1st play in their 35-21 win on 11-23-69
Steve Grogan tossed a 34 yard TD pass to Sam Cunningham on their 1st play in their 30-14 loss on 10-28-73
Doug Flutie tossed an 80 yard TD pass to Irving Fryar on the 1st play, in their 30-7 win on 10-30-88
Tom Brady tossed a 35 yard TD pass to David Givens on their 1st play in their 21-16 win on 12-20-03

Every Patriots Player Who Has Completed a Left-Handed Pass in a Game

RB Bob Gladieux tossed a 48 yard pass to Hubie Bryant in their 28-20 win over Houston on 11-07-71
WR Don Westbrook tossed a 28 yard pass to Russ Francis in their 24-17 win over the Lions on 10-07-79
WR Don Westbrook tossed a 24 yard pass to Don Hasselbeck on their 27-23 win over the Vikings on 12-16-79
QB Jeff Carlson tossed a 6 yard TD pass to Kevin Turner in their 27-20 loss to the Chiefs on 12-13-92
Jeff Carlson completed a 10 yard pass to John Stephens and a 40 yard pass to Irving Fryar on 12-13-92
Jeff Carlson had completions of 12 yds + 19 yds to Marv Cook and 1 yd and 8 yds to Jon Vaughn on 12-20-92
Jeff Carlson tossed 8 yds to Greg McMurtry, 5 yds to Irving Fryar + 5 yds to John Stephens on 12-20-92
Jeff Carlson tossed 16 yards to Ben Coates and 11 yards to Marv Cook in their 16-13 OT loss on 12-27-92
Jeff Carlson completed a 33 yard pass to Greg McMurtry and a 22 yard pass to Irving Fryar on 12-27-92
Jeff Carlson tossed 12 yards to Irving Fryar and 4 yards, 7 yards and 11 yards to Michael Timpson on 12-27-92

Every Patriots Punter Who Has Completed a Pass in a Game

Eddie Hare completed a 4 yard pass to Mosi Tatupu in their 28-13 win over Miami on 10-21-79
Shawn McCarthy completed an 11 yard pass to Ben Coates in their 16-13 win over Buffalo on 11-24-91
Lee Johnson tossed an 18 yard pass to Eric Bjornson for a 1st down in their 24-16 win vs the Colts on 10-08-00

Every Patriots Kicker Who Has Completed a Pass in a Game

Gino Cappelletti tossed a 27 yard TD pass to Larry Garron in their 37-30 loss to the NY Titans on 10-01-61
Adam Vinatieri completed a 4 yard TD pass to Troy Brown in their 40-22 win over the Rams on 11-07-04

Every Patriots Wide Receiver Who Has Completed a Pass in a Game

Don Westbrook tossed a 28 yard pass to Russ Francis in their 24-17 win over the Lions on 10-07-79
Don Westbrook completed a 24 yard pass to Don Hasselbeck in their 27-23 win vs the Vikings on 12-16-79
Harold Jackson tossed a 23 yard pass to Russ Francis in their 34-21 win over the Jets on 11-02-80
Harold Jackson tossed a 12 yard pass to Russ Francis in their 16-13 OT loss to the Dolphins on 12-08-80
David Patten completed a 60 yard TD pass to Troy Brown in their 38-17 rout of the Colts on 10-21-01
Julian Edelman tossed a 51 yard TD pass to Danny Amendola in their 35-31 **Divisional** win on 01-10-15
Danny Amendola tossed a 36 yard pass to Tom Brady in their 35-28 loss to the Eagles on 12-06-15
Danny Amendola completed a 20 yard pass to Dion Lewis in their 24-20 **Divisional** win on 01-21-18
Julian Edelman tossed a 37 yard pass to James White in their 31-17 win vs GB on 11-04-18
Julian Edelman completed a 6 yard pass to Tom Brady in their 34-10 loss to the Titans on 11-11-18
Julian Edelman threw a 32 yard pass to James White in their 33-3 rout of the Steelers on 09-19-19
Julian Edelman tossed a 15 yard TD pass to Phillip Dorsett in their 17-10 win vs Philly on 11-17-19

Most Yards Passing for Every Patriots QB Who Has Thrown for More Than 400 Yards in a Game

517 yards passing by Tom Brady in their 38-24 win over the Dolphins 09-12-11
426 yards passing by Drew Bledsoe in their 26-20 OT win vs the Vikings on 11-13-94
422 yards passing by Babe Parilli in their 43-43 tie with the Raiders on 10-16-64
415 yards passing by Matt Cassel in their 48-28 rout of the Dolphins on 11-23-08
414 yards passing by Tony Eason in their 38-31 loss to the Seahawks on 9-21-86
402 yards passing by Tom Ramsey in their 34-31 OT loss to the Eagles on 11-29-87
401 yards passing by Steve Grogan in their 31-24 loss to the Jets on 10-12-86

Every Patriots Running Back Who Has Thrown a Half-Back Option TD Pass in a Game

Dick Christy threw a 10 yard TD pass to Tom Stephens in their 38-21 win over the NY Titans on 11-11-60
Dick Christy threw a 10 yard TD pass to Tom Stephens in their 42-14 rout of Dallas Texans on 11-18-60
Tom Yewcic threw an 18 yard TD pass to Jim Colclough in their 45-17 rout of the Broncos on 09-16-61
Andy Johnson threw an 8 yard TD pass to Mosi Tatupu in their 29-28 loss to Baltimore Colts on 09-06-81
Andy Johnson threw a 66 yard TD pass to Stanley Morgan in their 33-17 win over the Chiefs on 10-04-81
Andy Johnson threw a 28 yard TD pass to Stanley Morgan in their 38-10 rout of the Oilers on 10-18-81
Andy Johnson threw a 56 yard TD pass to Stanley Morgan in their 20-17 loss to the Bills on 11-22-81
Craig James threw a 5 yard TD pass to Tony Collins in their 17-14 victory over the Bills on 09-22-85
Craig James threw an 11 yard TD pass to Tony Collins in their 32-14 win over the Buccaneers on 10-27-85
Craig James threw a 10 yard TD pass to Tony Collins in their 20-6 victory over the Jets on 09-11-86
Mosi Tatupu threw a 15 yard TD pass to Tony Collins in their 26-23 victory over the LA Raiders on 11-01-87
Jon Vaughn threw a left handed 13 yard TD pass to Marv Cook in their 24-20 win over the Oilers on 09-22-91
Dave Meggett threw a 35 yard TD pass to Troy Brown in their 27-24 win over the Dolphins on 11-23-97

Every Patriots QB Who Has Thrown a TD Pass on the Last Play of a Regulation Game

Babe Parilli threw a 25 yard TD to Bobby Leo in their 44-16 loss to Buffalo on 12-09-67
Jim Plunkett threw a 10 yard TD pass to Bob Windsor to defeat the Vikings 17-14 on 10-27-74
Steve Grogan threw a 13 yard TD pass to Carlos Pennywell in their 39-24 loss to Miami on 11-29-79
Tony Eason threw a 10 yard TD pass to Irving Fryar in their 27-20 loss to Denver on 09-28-86
Tony Eason threw a 25 yard Hail Mary pass to Irving Fryar to defeat the LA Rams 30-28 on 11-16-86
Tony Eason threw a 10 yard TD pass to Hart Lee Dykes in the 24-10 loss to Miami on 09-17-89
Hugh Millen threw a 34 yard TD pass to Greg McMurtry to defeat Houston 24-20 on 09-22-91
Hugh Millen threw a 2 yard TD pass to Ben Coates in their 23-17 OT win vs the Colts on 12-08-91
Drew Bledsoe threw a 1 yard TD pass to Ben Coates to defeat the Bills 25-21 on 11-29-98

Every Quarterback Who Has Thrown an Overtime Game Winning Touchdown Pass

Hugh Millen threw 45 yard TD pass to Michael Timpson to defeat the Colts 23-17 in OT on 12-08-91
Drew Bledsoe threw a 36 yard TD pass to Michael Timpson to beat Miami 33-27 in OT on 01-02-94
Drew Bledsoe threw a 14 yard TD pass to Kevin Turner to defeat the Vikings 26-20 in OT on 11-13-94
Tom Brady tossed an 82 yard TD pass to Troy Brown to beat Miami 19-13 in OT on 10-19-03

Every Patriots Quarterback Who Has Completed a Touchdown Pass On His Birthday

Jim Plunkett threw 2 TD passes to Randy Vataha, on his 24th birthday, in the 34-13 win vs Miami on 12-05-71
Doug Flutie threw a 12 yd TD pass to Irving Fryar, on his 26th birthday, in the 23-20 loss to Bills on 10-23-88

Every Patriots Quarterback Who Has Completed a Pass on His Birthday

Jim Plunkett was 16-23 for 233 yards & 2 TDs on his 24th birthday in the 34-13 win over Miami on 12-05-71
Doug Flutie was 5-16 for 58 yards & 1 TD on his 26th birthday in the 23-20 loss to the Bills on 10-23-88
Scott Zolak was 5-10 for 65 yards on his 25th birthday in the 27-20 loss to the Chiefs on 12-13-92

College QBs Who Played a Different Offensive Position for the Patriots

WR Gino Cappelletti was the QB for the Minnesota Golden Gophers
WR Steven Burks was a QB for the Arkansas State Indians
RB Andy Johnson played QB for the Georgia Bulldogs
WR Marlin Briscoe was the QB for the University of Nebraska Omaha Mavericks
WR Stephen Starring was a QB for the McNeese State Cowboys
WR Bert Emanuel played QB for the Rice Owls
WR Julian Edelman was the QB for the Kent State Golden Flash
WR Jakobi Myers was a QB for the North Carolina State Wolfpack
TE Derrick Ramsey played QB for the Kentucky Wildcats

College QBs Who Played as a Defensive Back for the Patriots

Gino Cappelletti, Daryl Johnson, Greg Boyd, Jack Mildren and Julian Edelman

Most Yards Passing/Game	Most Yards Passing/Season	Most Career Yards Passing
517 yards by Tom Brady	5,235 by Tom Brady (2011)	74,571 yards by Tom Brady
466 yards by Tom Brady	4,827 by Tom Brady (2012)	29,657 yards by Drew Bledsoe
447 yards by Tom Brady	4,806 by Tom Brady (2007)	26,886 yards by Steve Grogan
443 yards by Tom Brady	4,770 by Tom Brady (2015)	16,747 yards by Babe Parilli
432 yards by Tom Brady	4,577 by Tom Brady (2017)	10,732 yards by Tony Eason

Some of the Passing Stats of Every Patriots QB Who Was Named
AFL/AFC Offensive Player of the Week

Butch Songin had 182 yards passing + 1 TD in their 35-0 shutout of the LA Chargers on 10-08-60

Babe Parilli had 250 yards passing + 3 TDs in their 35-17 win over the San Diego Chargers on 10-23-66

Babe Parilli had 281 yards passing + 5 TDs in their 41-10 rout of the Dolphins on 10-15-67

Tony Eason had 126 yards passing + 2 TDs in their 38-23 comeback win over Seattle on 09-16-84

Tony Eason had 375 yards passing + 2 TDs in their 30-28 last second win over the LA Rams on 11-16-86

Doug Flutie had 132 yards passing + 1 TD and ran for the GW TD in their 21-17 win vs the Colts on 10-02-88

Scott Zolak had 261 yards passing + 2 TDs in their 37-34 OT win vs the Colts on 11-15-92

Drew Bledsoe had 334 yards passing + 2 TDs in their 17-16 last second comeback win vs GB on 10-02-94

Drew Bledsoe had 426 yards passing + 3 TDs in their epic 26-20 OT win vs the Vikings on 11-13-94

Drew Bledsoe had 310 yard passing, 4 TDs and 2 Two-point passes in their 46-38 win on 10-06-96

Drew Bledsoe had 423 yards passing + 2 TDs in their 26-23 victory over Miami on 11-23-98

Drew Bledsoe had 299 yards passing + 4 TDs in their 31-28 win over the Colts on 09-19-99

Drew Bledsoe had 271 yards passing + 4 TDs in their 28-19 victory over the Broncos on 10-01-00

Tom Brady had 364 yards passing + 2 TDs in their comeback 29-26 OT win vs SD on 10-14-01

Tom Brady had 258 yards passing + 4 TDs in their 34-17 win over the Saints on 11-25-01

Tom Brady had 294 yards passing + 3 TDs in their 30-14 win over Pittsburgh on 09-09-02

Tom Brady had 265 yards passing + 3 TDs in their 38-7 rout of the Bills on 11-03-02

Tom Brady had 350 yards passing + 3 TDs in their 30-26 comeback win over Denver on 11-03-03

Tom Brady had 204 yards passing + 4 TDs in their 31-0 shutout of Buffalo on 12-27-03

Tom Brady had 350 yards passing + 3 TDs in their 31-28 win over Atlanta on 10-09-05

Tom Brady had 311 yards passing + 4 TDs in their 38-7 rout of Buffalo on 09-23-07

Tom Brady had 388 yards passing + 5 TDs in their 48-27 rout of Dallas on 10-14-07

Tom Brady had 354 yards passing + 6 TDs in their 49-28 rout of Miami on 10-21-07

Tom Brady had 399 yards passing + 4 TDs in their 34-13 rout of Pittsburgh on 12-09-07

Tom Brady had 356 yards passing + 2 TDs in their 38-35 win over the Giants on 12-29-07

Matt Cassel had 185 yards passing + 3 TDs in their 41-7 rout of the Broncos on 10-20-08

Matt Cassel had 415 yards passing + 3 TDs in their 48-28 rout of the Dolphins on 11-23-08

Tom Brady had 378 yards passing + 2 TDs in their 25-24 win over Buffalo on 09-14-09

Tom Brady had 380 yards passing + 6 TDs in their 59-0 shutout of the Titans on 10-18-09

Tom Brady had 267 yards passing + 4 TDs in their 35-7 rout of the Jaguars on 12-27-09

Tom Brady had 341 yards passing + 4 TDs in their 45-24 rout of the Lions on 11-25-10

Tom Brady had 326 yards passing + 4 TDs in their 45-3 rout of the Jets on 12-06-10

Tom Brady had 517 yards passing + 4 TDs in their 38-24 win over Miami on 09-12-11

Tom Brady had 423 yards passing + 3 TDs in their 35-21 win over San Diego on 09-18-11

Tom Brady had 304 yards passing + 1 TD in their 27-24 win over Miami on 12-24-11

Tom Brady had 340 yards passing + 3 TDs in their 52-28 rout of Buffalo on 09-30-12

Tom Brady had 304 yards passing + 4 TDs in their 45-7 win over the St, Louis Rams on 10-28-12

Tom Brady had 296 yards passing + 4 TDs in their 42-14 rout of the Texans on 12-10-12

Tom Brady had 344 yards passing + 3 TDs in their 34-31 OT win vs the Broncos on 11-24-13

Tom Brady had 356 yards passing + 4 TDs in their 36-7 rout of Miami on 10-29-15

Tom Brady had 406 yards passing + 3 TDs in their 33-13 rout of Cleveland on 10-09-16

Tom Brady had 280 yards passing + 4 TDs in their 30-17 win over the 49ers on 11-20-16

Tom Brady had 447 yards passing + 3 TDs in their 36-20 win over the Saints on 09-17-17

Tom Brady had 378 yards passing + 5 TDs in their 36-33 win over the Houston Texans on 09-24-17

Tom Brady had 266 yards passing + 3 TDs in their 41-16 rout of the Broncos on 11-12-17

MEMORABLE RECEPTIONS

Every Receiver of the Patriots Who Was Named the *AFL/AFC Offensive Player of the Week*

Ron Sellers caught 4 passes for 124 yards + 2 TDs in their 24-0 shutout of Houston on 11-02-69
Irving Fryar caught 6 passes for 134 yards + 1 TD (50 yard TD) in their 16-13 win over Buffalo on 11-24-91
Terry Glenn had 13 receptions for 214 yards in their 19-7 win over the Browns on 10-03-99
David Patten ran for a 29 yd TD, caught a 91 yd TD, threw a 60 yd TD and caught a 6 yd TD pass on 10-21-01
Randy Moss caught 9 passes for 145 yards + 1 TD in their 24-20 win over the Colts on 11-04-07
Randy Moss caught 10 passes for 128 yards + 4 TDs (3 TDs in the 2nd Qtr) in their 56-10 rout on 11-18-07
Julian Edelman had 8 receptions for 151 yards and 1 TD and caught a 2 point pass in 35-14 win on 01-01-17

Every Tight End of the Patriots Who Was Named the *AFC Offensive Player of the Week*

Marv Cook had 10 receptions for 99 yards + 1 TD in their 24-20 victory over Houston on 09-22-91
Daniel Graham had 7 receptions for 110 yards in their 9-3 win over the Browns on 10-26-03
Rob Gronkowski had 6 receptions for 160 yards + 2 TDs in their 34-27 win over the Redskins on 12-11-11
Rob Gronkowski had 9 receptions for 168 yards and caught a 2 point pass in their 27-24 win on 12-17-17

Everyone Who Has Caught an Overtime Game Winning Touchdown Pass

Michael Timpson hauled in a 45 yard TD pass from Hugh Millen to defeat the Colts on 12-08-91
Michael Timpson hauled in a 36 yard TD pass from Drew Bledsoe to defeat the Miami on 01-02-94
Kevin Turner grabbed a 14 yard TD pass from Drew Bledsoe to defeat the Vikings on 11-13-94
Troy Brown caught an 82 yard touchdown pass from Tom Brady to defeat the Dolphins on 10-19-03

Every Patriots Wide Receiver Who Has Caught a 4th Qtr Game Winning TD Pass

Jim Colclough caught a 78 yard TD pass from Tom Yewcic to beat the NY Titans on 11-30-62
Jim Colclough caught a 56 yard TD pass from Babe Parilli to defeat the Raiders on 10-11-63
Stephen Starring caught a 76 yard TD from Steve Grogan to stifle the Steelers on 09-25-83
Irving Fryar caught a 13 yard TD from Steve Grogan to defeat the Seattle Seahawks on 11-17-85
Irving Fryar caught a 25 yard TD pass from Tony Eason to beat the LA Rams on 11-16-86
Stanley Morgan caught an 30 yard TD from Steve Grogan to defeat the Dolphins on 12-22-86
Greg McMurtry caught a 34 yard TD from Hugh Millen to oust the Oilers on 09-22-91
Shawn Jefferson caught a 25 yard TD pass from Drew Bledsoe to defeat the Dolphins on 11-23-98
David Patten caught a 20 yard TD pass from Tom Brady to beat the Bears on 11-10-02
David Givens caught an 18 yard TD pass from Tom Brady to beat the Broncos on 11-03-03
Jabar Gaffney caught an 8 yard TD pass from Tom Brady to defeat the Ravens on 12-03-07
Kembrell Thompkins caught a 17 yard TD pass from Tom Brady to defeat the Saints on 10-13-13
Danny Amendola caught a 1 yard TD pass from Tom Brady to beat the Browns on 12-08-13
Brandin Cooks caught a 25 yard TD pass from Tom Brady to beat the Texans on 09-24-17

Every Patriots Tight End who has caught a 4th Qtr Game Winning Touchdown Pass

Tony Romeo caught a 4th down 2 yard TD pass from Babe Parilli to defeat the Jets on 11-28-65
Bob Windsor caught a 10 yard TD pass from Jim Plunkett to defeat the Vikings on 10-27-74
Don Hasselbeck caught a 4 yard TD pass from Steve Grogan to beat San Diego on 10-16-77
Don Hasselbeck caught a 16 yard TD pass from Steve Grogan to slay the Seahawks on 09-21-80
Greg Baty caught a 13 yard TD pass from Tony Eason to defeat the Bills on 11-23-86
Ben Coates caught a 4th down 13 yard TD pass from Drew Blesdoe to defeat the Giants on 12-21-96
Benjamin Watson caught a 16 yard TD pass from Tom Brady to beat the Bills on 09-14-09
Aaron Hernandez caught an 8 yard TD pass from Tom Brady to crush the Cowboys on 10-16-11

Every Patriots Running Back Who Has Caught a Game Winning Touchdown Pass

Josh Ashton caught a game winning 24 yard TD to defeat the Redskins on 10-01-72
Keith Byars caught a game winning 2 yard TD pass to defeat the Jets on 11-10-96

Everyone Who Has Caught a Touchdown Pass and a 2 Point Pass in the Same Game

Jim Colclough caught a 36 yard TD and a 2 point pass from Babe Parilli in the 43-43 Tie on 10-16-64
Ben Coates caught a 1 yard TD pass and a 2 point pass from Drew Bledsoe in the 46-38 win on 10-06-96
Reche Caldwell caught a 15 yard TD and a 2 point pass from Tom Brady in their 17-14 loss on 11-12-06
Julian Edelman caught a 2 yard TD pass and a 2 point pass from Tom Brady in their 27-26 win on 12-08-13
Julian Edelman caught a 77 yard TD pass and a 2 point pass from Tom Brady in their 35-14 rout on 01-01-17
Danny Amendola caught a 6 yard TD and a 2 point pass from Tom Brady in their 34-28 OT win on 02-05-17

Everyone Who Has Caught a Touchdown Pass on His Birthday

Andy Johnson caught a 10 yard TD pass on his 24th birthday in the 41-7 rout of the Jets on 10-18-76
Darryl Stingley caught a 21 yard TD pass on his 26th birthday in the 21-17 win over the Chiefs on 09-18-77
Irving Fryar caught a 10 yd TD pass on his 24th birthday in the 27-20 loss to the Broncos on 09-28-86

Only Player Who Caught 2 TD Passes on the Day After His Birthday

Randy Vataha caught a 26 yard TD pass & a 25 yard TD pass on the day after his 23rd birthday on 12-05-71

Progression of the Longest Reception by a Patriots Player in a Regular Season Game

1 yard reception by Jim Colclough in their 13-10 loss to the Broncos on 09-09-60
6 yard reception by Jim Colclough in their 13-10 loss to the Broncos on 09-09-60
13 yard reception by Oscar Lofton in their 13-10 loss to the Broncos on 09-09-60
17 yard reception by Oscar Lofton in their 13-10 loss to the Broncos on 09-09-60
19 yard reception by Jim Colclough in their 13-10 loss to the Broncos on 09-09-60
40 yard reception by Jim Crawford in their 13-10 loss to the Broncos on 09-09-60
78 yard reception by Billy Wells in their 35-0 shutout of the Los Angeles Chargers on 10-08-60
78 yard TD reception by Jim Colclough in their 24-17 victory over the New York Titans on 11-30-62
80 yard TD reception by Art Graham in their 37-17 victory over the Houston Oilers on 11-29-64
87 yard TD reception by Jim Whalen in their 48-14 loss to the Jets on 10-27-68
88 yard TD reception by Randy Vataha in their 21-17 victory over the Baltimore Colts on 12-19-71
90 yard TD reception by Craig James in their 20-7 loss to the Bears on 09-15-85
91 yard TD reception by David Patten in their 38-17 victory over the Indianapolis Colts on 10-21-01
99 yard TD reception by Wes Welker in their 38-24 win over the Dolphins on 09-12-11

10 Longest Receptions by the Patriots That Did Not Result in a TD

82 yard combined pass reception/lateral by Kevin Turner and Leonard Russell on 10-10-93
78 yard reception by Billy Wells in their 35-0 shutout of the Los Angeles Chargers on 10-08-60
77 yard reception by Ron Sellers in their 27-23 loss to the Houston Oilers on 12-14-69
76 yard reception by Steve Burks in their 34-31 loss to the Cowboys on 11-16-75
76 yard reception by Shawn Jefferson in their 23-18 loss to the Vikings on 11-02-97
73 yard reception by Deion Branch in their **27-13 Divisional Playoff** loss to Denver on 01-14-06
72 yard reception by Vincent Brisby in their 30-17 loss to the Falcons on 10-01-95
71 yard reception by Stanley Morgan in their 21-17 loss to the 49ers on 11-30-80
68 yard reception by Darryl Stingley in their 17-3 win over the Colts on 10-23-77
68 yard reception by James White in their 20-10 loss to the Dolphins on 01-03-16

A Few Memorable Receptions on the Patriots 1ˢᵗ Offensive Play of the Game

Charley Frazier caught a 34 yard TD pass from Mike Taliaferro on the 1ˢᵗ play on 11-23-69
Sam Cunningham caught a 34 yard TD pass from Steve Grogan on their 1ˢᵗ play on 10-28-73
Sam Cunningham ran for a 75 yard TD on the 1ˢᵗ play of the game, in their 29-28 loss to Buffalo on 10-20-74
Steve Grogan catch his own pass, deflected by Lucius Sanford, on the 1ˢᵗ play, on 11-06-83
Irving Fryar caught an 80 yard TD pass from Doug Flutie on the 1ˢᵗ play of the game on 10-30-88

Did You Know that Former Patriots TE Russ Francis Once Landed the BZ Copter on the 50 Yard Line at Schaefer Stadium?

Russ was piloting the 'Green Machine" WBZ helicopter high above Greater Boston during one of Joe Green's morning traffic reports. After they finished Russ flew the helicopter to Schaefer Stadium. On the way back Russ noticed that their was snow on the field, so rather than land the helicopter in the parking lot, he hovered over the field and manuevered the helicopter to blow the snow off the field, and then landed it on the 50 yard line.

Every Patriots Lineman Who Has Caught a Pass

Walt Cudzik caught an 11 yard pass from Butch Songin in their 45-16 loss to the LA Chargers on 10-28-60
Justin Canale caught a pass from Tom Sherman for no gain in their 27-17 loss to the SD Chargers on 11-10-68
Pete Brock caught a 6 yard touchdown pass from Steve Grogan in their 38-24 win over the Jets on 11-21-76
Brian Holloway grabbed a 5 yard pass from Steve Grogan in their 34-7 win over the Dolphins on 10-05-86
Sean Farrell cradled a 4 yard pass from Doug Flutie in their 13-7 victory over the Seahawks on 12-04-88
Joe Andruzzi snared a deflected pass on the line of scrimmage in their 38-34 win over the Colts on 11-30-03
Dan Klecko had 3 receptions for 18 yards during the 2004 season
Tom Ashworth caught a 1 yard TD pass from Tom Brady in their 28-0 shutout of Tampa on 12-17-05
Logan Mankins caught a pass from Tom Brady for a 9 yard loss in their 34-13 rout of the Bengals on 10-01-07
Nate Solder caught a 16 yard TD from Tom Brady in their **45-7 Championship** rout of the Colts on 01-18-15

Every Patriots Quarterback Who Has Caught a Pass in a Regular Season Game

Steve Grogan caught a 16 yard pass from Andy Johnson in their 29-28 loss to the Baltimore Colts on 09-06-81
Matt Cavanaugh caught an 8 yard pass from Andy Johnson in their 27-21 loss to the Steelers on 09-27-81
Steve Grogan caught a 9 yard pass from Andy Johnson in their 27-17 loss to the Raiders on 11-01-81
Steve Grogan caught a deflected pass for an 8 yard loss, on 1ˢᵗ play, in their 21-7 win vs Buffalo on 11-06-83
Tommy Hodson caught a deflected pass for a 6 yard loss in their 30-17 loss to Miami on 10-18-92
Drew Bledsoe caught a deflected pass for a 9 yard loss in their 41-27 loss to the Steelers on 12-16-95
Tom Brady cradled a 23 yard pass from Kevin Faulk in their 20-13 victory over Miami on 12-22-01
Tom Brady caught a 36 yard pass from Danny Amendola in their 35-28 loss to the Eagles on 12-06-15
Jimmy Garoppolo caught his own deflected pass for a 3 yard gain in their 23-21 win vs AR on 09-11-16
Tom Brady caught a 6 yard pass from Julian Edelman in their 34-10 loss to Tennessee on 11-11-18

Every Reception of a Pass Thrown by a Left-Handed Patriots Running Back

Hubie Bryant had a 48 yard reception of Bob Gladieux's left handed pass in their 28-20 win on 11-07-71
Marv Cook had a 13 yard TD reception of Jon Vaughn's left handed pass in their 24-20 win on 09-22-91

Every Reception of a Pass Thrown by a Left-Handed Patriots Wide Receiver

Russ Francis had a 28 yard reception of Don Westbrook's left handed pass in their 24-17 win on 10-07-79
Don Hasselbeck had a 24 yard reception of Don Westbrook's left handed pass in their 27-23 win on 12-16-79

Only TD Reception of a Left-Handed Pass Thrown by a Patriots QB

Kevin Turner had a 6 yard TD reception of Jeff Carlson's left handed pass in their 27-20 loss on 12-13-92

Every Non QB Who Caught a Pass and Was Also Sacked Trying to Attempt a Pass for the Patriots

Carl Garrett had 5 receptions for 92 yds and was sacked by Jack Ham in their 33-3 loss to Pitt on 10-22-72
Marlin Briscoe caught a 13 yard pass and was sacked by Lawrence Billers in 41-7 win vs the Jets on 10-18-76

Only QB Who Was Intercepted by the Patriots and Later Became a Receiver for the Patriots

Broncos QB Marlin Briscoe was intercepted by Patriots DB Leroy Mitchell on 11-03-68 and he caught 10 passes for 136 yards and 1 TD as a Wide Receiver for the Patriots in 1976

The Five Times the Patriots Had at Least Two Receivers with 10 or more Receptions in a Game

Leroy Thompson had 11, Michael Timpson and Ben Coates had 10 in their OT win vs Minn on 11-13-94
Wes Welker and Randy Moss had 12 receptions in their win 25-24 over Buffalo on 09-14-09
Aaron Hernandez and Brandon Lloyd had 10 receptions in their 41-34 loss to SF on 12-16-12
Julian Edelman had 13 catches and Danny Amendola had 10 in their 24-20 loss to Miami on 12-15-13
Julian Edelman and Mohamed Sanu had 10 receptions in their 37-20 loss to the Ravens on 11-03-19

Touchdown Reception on a Pass That Deflected Off the Knee of a Defensive Player

Troy Brown caught Tom Brady's pass, that deflected on Ashley Ambrose's knee, for a 44 yd TD on 11-04-01

Offensive Players Who Have Caught a Pass That Deflected Off a Teammate

Irving Fryar caught a game winning 25 yard TD pass that was tipped to him by Stanley Morgan on 11-16-86
J. Wiggins caught a 4 yard pass as he was going out of bounds, that deflected off David Patten, on 01-19-02
Julian Edelman's 12 yard reception of a pass, that deflected off Gronk, with 1:08 left on 01-16-16

Top 5 Yards Receiving in a Game by a Patriots Tight End

168 yards receiving by Rob Gronkowski in their 27-24 win vs Pittsburgh on 12-17-17
162 yards receiving by Rob Gronkowski in their 35-17 win vs Cincinnati on 10-16-16
161 yards receiving by Ben Coates in their 39-35 loss to Miami on 09-04-94
160 yards receiving by Rob Gronkowski in their 34-27 win vs Washington on 12-11-11
149 yards by Tony Romeo in their 24-24 tie with Kansas City on 11-17-63

Top 5 Yards Receiving in a Game by a Patriots Running Back

153 yards receiving by Shane Vereen in their 27-26 comeback win over the Browns on 12-08-13
124 yards receiving by Dick Christy in their 34-28 win over Oakland on 11-04-60
120 yards receiving by Larry Garron in their 26-8 **Playoff** win vs Buffalo on 12-28-63
115 yards by James White in their 35-28 loss to Philadelphia on 12-06-15
113 yards by Larry Garron in their 38-14 rout of Houston on 12-11-66

Most Yards Receiving/Game	Most Yards Receiving/Season	Most Yards Receiving in a Career
217 yards by Wes Welker	1,569 by Wes Welker ('11)	10,352 yards by Stanley Morgan
214 yards by Terry Glenn	1,493 by Randy Moss ('07)	7,861 yards by Rob Gronkowski
193 yards by Terry Glenn	1,491 by Stanley Morgan ('86)	7,459 yards by Wes Welker
192 yards by Wes Welker	1,354 by Wes Welker ('12)	6,507 yards by Julian Edelman
190 yards by Brandon Lloyd	1,348 by Wes Welker ('09)	6,366 yards by Troy Brown

Only Double Lateral Following a Pass Reception

Ron Burton advanced Gino Cappelletti's lateral 7 yards, after Gino's advancement of 14 yards on 10-16-64

Longest Combination of Fumbles and Laterals Following a Pass Reception

Tom Brady completed a pass of 7 yards to Julian Edelman on the last play of the game. Since the Patriots were trailing by 3 points to the Dolphins, Julian attempted to lateral it back and his lateral was ruled a fumble. Tom Brady recovered that fumble on the initial line of scrimmage, and then Tom lateraled it to James White who lost 2 yards and then lateraled it to Joe Thuney. Joe was able to advance it 1 yard before he fumbled it. Tom Brady recovered this fumble as well as then he lateraled it to Benjamin Watson who lost 1 yard before lateralling it back to Julian Edelman, who then lateraled it back to Joe Thuney. Joe advanced it another 2 yards before lateralling it to Mohamed Sanu, who then lost 4 yards before lateraling it to James White. James was able to advance it 2 yards and then he fumbled and Miami recovered the fumble ending the game on 12-29-19.

Every Running Back Who Has Lateraled the Ball Back to the QB Which Resulted in a TD Pass

Mosi Tatupu lateraled to Tony Eason, who then threw a 42 yard TD pass to Stephen Starring on 10-07-84
Mosi Tatupu lateraled to Steve Grogan, who then threw a 28 yard TD pass to Greg Hawthorne on 11-03-85
Mosi Tatupu lateraled to Tony Eason, who then threw a 45 yard TD pass to Stanley Morgan on 01-04-87
Mosi Tatupu lateraled to Steve Grogan, who then threw a 55 yard TD pass to Stanley Morgan on 10-22-89
Ben Jarvus Green Ellis tossed back Tom Brady's lateral and Tom then threw a 40 yard TD pass on 10-18-09
Dion Lewis lateraled to Tom Brady, who then threw a 34 yard TD pass to Chris Hogan on 01-22-17

Every Wide Receiver Who Has Lateraled the Ball Back to the QB on a Successful Pass Completion

Randy Moss tossed back Tom Brady's lateral and Tom then threw a 56 TD pass on 12-09-07
Julian Edelman took a lateral from Tom Brady and then threw a 51 yard TD pass on 01-10-15
Danny Amendola took a lateral from Tom Brady and then threw a 20 yard pass to Dion Lewis on 01-21-18
Julian Edelman took a Tom Brady lateral and tossed a 37 yard pass to James White on 11-04-18
Julian Edelman took a Tom Brady lateral and tossed a 32 yard pass to a James White on 09-08-19
Julian Edelman took a Tom Brady lateral and threw a 15 yard TD pass to Phillip Dorsett on 11-17-19

Everyone Who Has Lateraled the Ball Following a Run from Scrimmage

Larry Garron was stopped at the line so he lateraled it to Babe Parilli, who advanced it 9 yards, on 09-16-62
Doug Flutie ran for a 7 yard gain and then lateraled it to Reggie Dupard, who ran for no gain, on 10-01-89
Hugh Millen ran for an 18 yard gain and lateraled to Irving Fryar, who advanced it 8 more yards, on 10-04-92

A Few Other Memorable Laterals from a Patriots QB

Jim Whalen received a lateral from Tom Sherman but was stopped for no gain in their 33-14 win on 12-01-68
Sam Cunningham ran for a 31 yard TD on a lateral from Jim Plunkett in their 29-28 loss on 11-03-74
Tony Collins took QB Stephen Starring's lateral and ran for a 14 yard gain in their 38-31 win on 12-01-85
Rob Gronkowski took Tom Brady's lateral and ran for a 2 yard TD in their 31-24 win on 12-04-11

Every Defensive Player Who Has Returned a Lateral by an Opposing Player

Ed Philpott returned Babe Parilli's backward lateral 10 yards for a TD in 47-31 loss to the Jets on 09-22-68
Ed Weisacosky returned Steve Harkey's backward lateral 3 yards in their 34-10 loss to the Jets on 10-29-72
Vince Wilfork returned Chad Pennington's backward lateral 31 yards in 37-16 **Wild Card** win on 01-07-07

Every Receiver Who Has Lateraled the Ball to a Teammate Following His Pass Reception

Joe Johnson caught a pass and then lateraled it to Dick Christy, who advanced it 5 yards, on 11-18-60
Jim Colclough caught 37 yard pass and lateraled to Gino Cappellettti, who advanced it 14 yards, on 10-16-64
Willie Scott caught an 8 yard pass and lateraled to Craig James, who advanced it 20 more yards, on 09-18-88
Cedric Jones caught an 11 yard pass and lateraled to Stanley Morgan, who ran 7 more yards, on 12-11-88
Eric Sievers caught a 5 yard pass and his lateraled fumble was recovered by John Stephens on 10-18-90
Kevin Turner caught a 13 yard pass and lateraled to Leonard Russell, who ran for 69 more yards, on 10-10-93
Wes Welker caught a 26 yard pass and lateraled to Randy Moss, who advanced it 11 more yards, on 09-23-07

Every Defensive Player Who Has Recovered a Lateral Fumble by an Opposing Player

Larry Eisenhauer recovered Gene Mingo lateral fumble in their 45-17 rout of Denver on 09-16-61
Bob Dee recovered Lee Grosscup's lateral fumble in their 43-14 rout of the NY Titans on 10-06-62
Steve Zabel recovered Bill Troup's bad lateral,that was juggled and fumbled by Ron Lee, on 09-18-78
Eugene Wilson recovered Antwann Randle El's lateral fumble in 23-20 win vs the Steelers on 09-25-05

Only Player to Recover a Fumbled Return of an Advancement of an Interception Return Lateral

Bob Cryder recovered K. Williams' 18 yard lateral return fumble after J. Kearney's 5 yard int on 10-09-83

Only Player to Force a Lateral Fumble Which Resulted in Safety

Dont'a Hightower forced Cody Kessler's lateraled fumble, which resulted in a safety on 10-09-16

Only Time a Patriots Running Back Lateraled to Another Patriots Running Back

Kevin Turner caught a 13 yard pass and tossed it to Leonard Russell, who ran for another 69 yards on 10-10-93

Patriots Wide Receivers Who Have Lateraled the Ball to Another Patriots Wide Receiver

J. Colclough caught a 37 yard pass and tossed it to G. Cappelletti, who advanced it 14 yards on 10-16-64
Cedric Jones caught an 11 yard pass and tossed it to Stanley Morgan, who advanced it 7 yards on 12-11-88
Wes Welker caught a 26 yard pass and lateraled it to Randy Moss, who advanced it 11 yards on 09-23-07

Everyone Who Was Involved in a Defensive Fumble Recovery and Subsequently Lateraled it to a Teammate

Jim Cheyunski returned Bob Davis' fumble 3 yards + lateraled to John Bramlett for 17 more yds on 12-14-69
Ed Williams recovered Sammy Winder's fumble and lateraled to Jim Bowman, for 8 more yards on 12-06-87
Anthony Pleasant returned D. McNabb's fumble 6 yards + lateraled to W. McGinest, for 20 yards on 09-14-03

Every Patriots Defensive Back Who Has Lateraled His Interception Return to a Teammate

Gino Cappelletti lateraled his 20 yard interception return to Clyde Washington, for 1 more yard on 10-28-60
Myron Guyton lateraled his interception of Jim Harbaugh to Ricky Reynolds, for 2 more yards on 11-19-95

Every Patriots Linebacker Who Has Lateraled His Interception Return to a Teammate

Rod Shoate lateraled his interception of Joe Ferguson to Rick Sanford, for 27 more yards on 11-04-79
Steve Nelson lateraled his interception of Cliff Stoudt to Clayton Weishuhn, for a 27 yard TD on 09-25-83
Johnny Rembert lateraled his 37 yard interception return to Andre Tippett, for 27 more yards on 10-26-86
Jamie Collins lateraled his interception of Geno Smith to Brandon Browner, for 2 more yards on 12-21-14

Every Lateral on a Fake Extra Point Attempt

Fred Bruney took the snap and lateraled it to Gino Cappelletti, who ran for 2 points on 10-16-60
Fred Bruney took the snap and lateraled it to Gino Cappelletti, who ran for 2 points on 11-18-60
Fred Bruney took the snap and lateraled it to Gino Cappelletti, who ran for 2 points on 12-18-60

Every Lateral on a Field Goal Attempt

Ross O'Hanley lateraled a bad snap to Gino Cappelletti, who ran for a 6 yard loss, in 27-14 loss on 10-16-60
Tony Eason lateraled a bad snap to Tony Franklin, who ran for a 5 yard loss, in their 20-13 win on 11-17-85

Everyone Who Has Returned a Lateral Following a Blocked Field Goal Attempt for a TD

John Zamberlin lateraled to Mike Haynes who took it 65 yards for a TD in their 21-11 win on 10-05-80
Troy Brown ran 11 yards + tossed it to Antwan Harris who took it 49 yards for a TD on 01-27-02

Only Player Who Has Been Part of a Lateraled Play on Defense, Offensive and on Special Teams

DB Gino Cappelletti in 1960, WR Gino Cappelletti in 1964 and Kicker Gino Cappelletti in 1960

Every Offensive Lineman Who Was Involved with a Lateraled Kickoff Return

John Simerson received Jack Hill's kickoff and lateraled to Larry Garron for more 26 yards on 09-16-61
Charlie Long received Mack Yoho's kickoff and lateraled to Mel West for 14 more yards on 09-23-61
Bob Yates received Jim Norton's free kick and tossed it to Bob Suci for 21 more yards on 12-08-63
Bob Yates received Jack Spikes' kickoff and lateraled it to Bob Suci for 22 more yards on 12-14-63
Lennie St. Jean tossed Tom Dempsey's kickoff to Mack Herron, who advanced it 30 yards on 11-04-73

Every Defensive Lineman Who Was Involved with a Lateraled Kickoff Return

Bob Dee received Mack Yoho's kickoff and lateraled to Dick Christy, for 19 more yards, on 12-04-60
Bob Dee received Mack Yoho's kickoff and lateraled it to Jim Crawford, for 6 more yards, on 11-23-62
Jim Lee Hunt received Mike Mercer's kickoff and tossed it to JD Garrett, for 24 more yards, on 10-16-64

Every Linebacker Who Was Involved with a Lateraled Kickoff Return

Rommie Loudd tossed Cotton Davidson's kickoff to Larry Garron, for 36 more yards, on 10-26-62
Marty Schottenheimer tossed Pete Gogolak's kickoff to Odell Lawson, for 17 more yards, on 10-18-70

Only Patriots Tight End Who Was Involved in a Lateral Kickoff Return

Tom Beer received Jim O'Brien's kickoff and lateraled it to Carl Garrett, for 21 more yards, on 10-25-70
Tom Beer received Grant Guthrie's kickoff and lateraled it to Carl Garrett, for 15 more yards, on 11-01-70
Tom Beer received another Grant Guthrie kickoff and tossed it to Carl Garrett, for 27 more yards, on 11-01-70

Only Time a Patriots Running Back Lateraled a Kickoff Return to Another Running Back

Dion Lewis returned J. Elliott's kickoff 3 yards and tossed it to Rex Burkhead, who lost 1 yard, on 02-14-18

Only Patriot Who Has Recovered His Teammates Lateral Fumble on a Punt Return

Aqib Talib recovered Julian Edelman's punt return lateral fumble in their 30-27 win vs the Saints on 10-13-13

Only Time Two Players Where Involved with a Lateral on a Free Kick Return

Bob Yates received Jacky Lee's free kick and lateraled to Bob Suci, for 21 more yards, on 12-14-63

Only Patriots Running Back Who Has Received a Lateral and Has Lateraled the Ball to a Teammate

Larry Garron advanced a kickoff return lateral from John Simerson on 09-16-61 and from Rommie Loudd on 10-26-62 and tossed a lateral back to QB Babe Parilli, who advanced it 9 yards, on 09-16-02

Patriot Linebackers Who Have Lateraled the Ball to Another Patriots Linebacker

Jim Cheyunski lateraled to John Bramlett for 17 more yards in their 27-23 loss on 12-14-69
Steve Nelson lateraled to Clayton Weishuhn for a 27 yard TD in their 28-23 win on 09-25-83
Johnny Rembert lateraled to Andre Tippett for 32 more yards in their 23-3 win on 10-26-86

Most Laterals by Two Players in a Game

2: Tom Beer lateraled 2 kickoff returns to Carl Garrett in their 45-10 loss to the Bills on 11-01-70
2: Reggie Rucker ran for a 1 yard loss and for no gain on laterals from Jim Plunkett in 30-14 loss on 10-28-73
2: Irving ran for a 10 yard gain and a 5 yard gain on laterals from Steve Grogan in their 42-20 win on 12-13-87

Most Times One Player Was Involved in a Lateral During a Season (1960)

5: Gino Cappelletti received 3 from Fred Bruney, 1 from Ross O'Hanley and lateraled to Clyde Washington

Most Times One Player Was Involved in a Lateral During His Career

7: Gino Cappelletti received 5 laterals and tossed back two laterals

Uniform # of Every Patriots QB

#2	Doug Flutie and Brian Hoyer
#6	Rohan Davey
#7	John Huarte, Hugh Millen, Michael Bishop, Matt Gutierrez and Jacoby Brissett
#8	Brian Hoyer
#10	Harvey White, Don Trull, Tom Flick, Bob Bleier, Scott Secules and Jimmy Garopollo
#11	Butch Songin, Joe Kapp, Dick Shiner, Tony Eason and Drew Bledsoe
#12	Don Allard, Eddie Wilson, Matt Cavanaugh, Tom Ramsey and Tom Brady
#13	Tommy Hodson
#14	Tom Greene, Tom Yewcic, Tom Sherman, Brian Dowling, Steve Grogan and Vinny Testaverde
#15	Tom Dimitroff, Babe Parilli, Jim Corcoran, Kim Hammond, Neil Graff, Todd Whitten, Marc Wilson and Ryan Mallett
#16	Jim Plunkett, Scott Zolak and Matt Cassel
#17	Mike Taliaferro, Tom Owen, Jeff Carlson and John Friesz
#19	Mike Kerrigan, Tom Tupa and Damon Huard
#81	Stephen Starring

Every RB, WR and TE Who Has Worn Two Uniform #s for the Patriots

Running Backs	Uniform #s
Walter Beach	#26 and #41
Mike Cloud	#21 and #34
Larry Garron	#46 and #40
Bruce Hansen	#24 and #35
Michael LeBlanc	#40 and #27

Wide Receivers	Uniform #s	Tight Ends	Uniform #s
Troy Brown	#86 and #80	Greg Baty	#48 and #85
Hubie Bryant	#45 and #84	Fred Baxter	#49 and #84
Deion Branch	#83 and #84	Barry Brown	#66 and #86
Preston Brown	#87 and #81	Al Chandler	#87 and #82
Dennis Gadbois	#82 and #48	Marv Cook	#46 and #85
Dietrich Jells	#18 and #83	Russ Francis	#81 and #49
Tony Simmons	#15 and #81	Aaron Hernandez	#85 and #81
Michael Timpson	#45 and #83	Lovett Purnell	#48 and #85
Donte' Stallworth	#18 and #19	Jermaine Wiggins	#49 and #85

Every Defensive Lineman Who Has Worn Two Uniform #s for the Patriots

Defensive Linemen	Uniform #s	Defensive Linemen	Uniform #s
Julius Adams	#85 and #69	Sealver Siliga	#71 and #96
Jim Boudreaux	#78 and #64	Fred Smerlas	#66 and #76
Ron Brace	#92 and #97	Garin Veris	#60 and #90
Andre Carter	#93 and #96	Gerard Warren	#92 and #98
Landon Cohen	#66 and #98	Dennis Wirgowski	#85 and #70
Dominique Easley	#74 and #99	Mel Witt	#70 and #71
Eric Moore	#98 and #92		

Every Offensive Lineman Has Worn Two Uniform #s for the Patriots

Offensive Linemen	Uniform #s	Offensive Linemen	Uniform #s
Jim Boudreaux	#78 and #64	Greg Robinson	#61 and #68
Walt Cudzik	#56 and #54	Greg Robinson-Randall	#77 and #64
Steve DeOssie	#50 and #99	Danny Villa	#73 and #75
Shelby Jordan	#63 and #74	Dave Watson	#67 and #62

CHAPTER 4

MEMORABLE DEFENSIVE PLAYERS AND PLAYS

Every Patriots Linebacker Who Was Named the *AFL Defensive Player of the Week*

Nick Buoniconti tackled RB Roy Hopkins for a safety to end the half and had 1 sack on 11-05-67
Nick Buoniconti intercepted Dan Darragh 3 times in their 23-6 win over the Bills on 10-20-68
Jim Cheyunski fell on a fumble and had a 37 yard interception return in their 25-14 win on 11-16-69

Every Patriots Linebacker Who Was Named The *NFL Defensive Player of the Week*

Steve Kiner held Earl Campbell to 2.7 yds per carry and had key interception late in the game on 11-07-71
Jim Cheyunski had 18 tackles in their 21-20 win over the Falcons on 09-24-72
Tedy Bruschi forced a fumble and recovered 2 fumbles in their 20-3 **Divisional** win on 01-16-05

Every Patriots Linebacker Who Was Named the *AFC Defensive Player of the Week*

Andre Tippett sacked Ken O'Brien 3 times and stuffed the Jets running attack in their 20-13 win on 10-20-85
Andre Tippett sacked Brent Pease 3 times and blocked a FGA that was returned for a TD on 10-18-87
Johnny Rembert made a tackle on the first 3 plays and had 16 total tackles in their 21-10 win on 11-06-88
Chris Slade had 12 tackles and sacked Vinny Testaverde in their 17-14 win over Cleveland on 09-03-95
Willie McGinest had 2 sacks and forced a fumble in their 27-9 win over the Indianapolis Colts on 10-20-96
Willie McGinest recovered a strip sack fumble in the end zone for a TD in their 45-7 rout of SD on 12-01-96
Willie McGinest had 2 sacks and recovered Tom Tupa's fumble for a TD in their 30-28 win on 09-12-99
Ted Johnson sacked Tony Banks twice and his 2nd sack was returned for a TD in their 20-3 rout on 01-20-00
Tedy Bruschi sacked Donovan McNabb and returned an interception 18 yards for a TD on 09-14-03
Tedy Bruschi had 9 tackles and returned an interception 5 yards for a TD in their 12-0 win on 12-07-03
Willie McGinest had 11 tackles, 1.5 sacks and 1 interception in their 21-16 victory over the Jets on 12-20-03
Tedy Bruschi forced Drew Bledsoe's fumble that was returned 68 yards for a TD on 10-03-04
Tedy Bruschi had 16 tackles and forced a fumble in the 4th Qtr of the 21-7 win over the 49ers on 01-02-05
Tedy Bruschi had 7 tackles in his 1st game back after suffering stroke in 21-16 win vs Buffalo on 10-30-05
Mike Vrabel strip sacked Jason Campbell 3 times in their 52-7 rout of the Redskins on 10-28-07
Dont'a Hightower sacked Andy Dalton for a safety and shared in another sack in their 35-17 rout on 10-16-16
Kyle Van Noy had 2 sacks and 2 forced fumbles in their 16-10 win over Buffalo on 09-29-19

Every Patriots Defensive Lineman Who Was the *AFL Defensive Player of the Week*

Larry Eisenhauer led the Patriots defense in their 23-0 shutout of the Bills on 09-24-67
Houston Antwine sacked Dan Darragh 3 times in their 16-7 win over Buffalo on 09-08-68

Every Patriots Defensive Lineman Who Was Named the *NFL Defensive Player of the Week*

Ron Berger had 3 sacks of Bob Griese in their 27-14 win over the Dolphins on 09-20-70
Julius Adams: Miami only had 41% completion and held Kiick and Morris to 23 yds rushing on 12-05-71

Every Patriots Defensive Lineman Who Was Named the *AFC Defensive Player of the Week*

Brent Williams recorded 2 sacks in their 33-24 victory over the Bills on 11-19-89
Chad Eaton sacked Kordell Stewart 3 times in their 23-9 win over the Steelers on 12-06-98
Jarvis Green had a strip sack and 2 additional sacks in their 38-13 rout of the Bengals on 10-01-06
Andre Carter sacked Mark Sanchez 4 times in their 37-16 rout of the Jets on 11-13-11
Chandler Jones sacked Matt Cassel twice and had blocked a FGA and returned it for a TD on 09-14-14

Every Patriot Defensive Lineman Who Was Named the *AFC Defensive Player of the Month*

Garin Veris had a sack in 5 straight games & forced a fumble for the game winning TD in November 1986
Willie McGinest had 4 sacks and returned a pass 46 yards for a touchdown during the month of October 1996

Every Patriot Linebacker Who Was Named the *AFC Defensive Player of the Month*

Chris Slade had 4 sacks and forced 2 fumbles during the month of September 1997
Mike Vrabel had 4 sacks, 2 forced fumbles, an interception and a fumble recovery in December 2003

Every Patriot Defensive Back Who Has Been Named the *AFC Defensive Player of the Month*

Eugene Wilson (Sept 2004), Devin McCourty (Sept 2019) and Stephon Gilmore (Oct 2019)

INTERCEPTIONS

Chronological List of Every Patriots DB Who Was Named the *AFC Defensive Player of the Week*

Ronnie Lippett had 2 interceptions of Joe Ferguson in their 38-10 rout of the Bills on 11-11-84
Fred Marion had a 36 yard interception return (Mike Pagel) and a 9 yard fumble return on 11-10-85
Ronnie Lippett had 2 interceptions of Dan Marino in their 34-7 rout of the Dolphins on 10-05-86
Fred Marion intercepted pass by Boomer Esiason in the end zone and returned a fumble 8 yards on 10-16-88
Larry Whigham intercepted Dan Marino twice, returning 1 pass for a 60 yard TD, in 27-24 win on 11-23-97
Lawyer Milloy returned 2 interceptions of Peyton Manning 24 yards, in their 21-16 win on 11-01-98
Willie Clay's interception of Steve Young set up the game winning FG in their 24-21 win on 12-20-98
Lawyer Milloy had 14 tackles, 1 forced fumble and had a 2 yard interception return on 11-19-00
Rodney Harrison had 7 tackles, along with a sack and then a strip sack of Josh McCown, on 09-19-04
Asante Samuel returned 3 interceptions of Rex Grossman 26 yards and had 8 tackles on 11-26-06
Asante Samuel intercepted A.J. Feeley *twice*, returning 1 pass for a 40 yard TD, in their 31-28 win on 11-25-07
Brandon Meriweather returned 2 passes by Josh Johnson 70 yards for 1 TD (a 39 yard TD) on 10-25-09
Leigh Bodden returned 3 passes by Mark Sanchez 60 yards for a 1 TD (a 53 yard TD) on 11-22-09
James Sanders returned a pass by Ben Roethlisberger 32 yards for a TD in their 39-26 win on 11-14-10

10 Longest Interception Returns for a TD

100 yard TD by Jimmy Hitchcock, of a pass by Dan Marino, in their 27-24 win over Miami on 11-23-97
99 yard TD by Rick Sanford, of a pass by Jim McMahon, in their 26-13 loss to the Bears on 12-05-82
98 yard TD by Bob Suci, of a pass by George Blanda, in their 45-3 rout of the Houston Oilers on 11-01-63
91 yard TD by Darius Butler, of a pass by Matt Schaub, in their 34-27 loss to the Houston Texans on 01-03-10
90 yard TD by Victor Green, of a pass by Vinny Testaverde, in their 44-7 rout of the Jets on 09-15-02
87 yard TD by Rodney Harrison, (Ben Roethlisberger) in their 41-27 **Championship** win vs Pitt on 01-23-05
87 yard TD by Alfonzo Dennard, of a pass by Andrew Luck, in their 59-24 rout of the Colts on 11-18-12
84 yard TD by Devin McCourty of a pass by Derek Anderson in their 25-6 rout of Buffalo on 10-29-18
82 yard TD by Chris Singleton, of a pass by Jeff George, in their 37-34 OT win vs the Colts on 11-15-92
79 yard TD by Logan Ryan, of a pass by Geno Smith, in their 30-27 OT loss to the Jets on 10-20-13

10 Longest Interception Returns That Were Not Returned for a TD

87 yard return by Ron Hall, of a pass by John McCormick, in their 24-10 win over Denver on 09-18-66
85 yard return by Ray Clayborn, of Paul McDonald's pass on the last play, in their 17-16 win on 10-07-84
83 yard return by Fred Marion, of a pass by Dave Krieg, in their 20-13 win over Seattle on 11-17-85
73 yard return by Ronnie Lippett, of a pass by Dan Marino, in their 27-24 loss to Miami on 09-09-90
72 yard return by Art McMahon, of a pass by John Huarte, in their 23-10 loss to Kansas City on 10-11-70
70 yard return by Ellis Hobbs, of a pass by Brooks Bollinger, in their 31-7 win vs Minnesota on 10-30-06
62 yard return by Bob Suci, of a pass by Don Breaux, in their 40-21 victory over Denver on 10-18-63
61 yard return by Ross O'Hanley, of a pass by Tom Flores, in their 20-14 win over Oakland on 10-11-63
60 yard return by Devin McCourty, of a pass by Matt Cassel, in their 30-7 rout of Minnesota on 09-14-14
60 yard return by Duron Harmon, of a pass by Ryan Tannehill, in their 41-13 rout of Miami on 12-14-14

Uniform #s of Offensive Players Who Have Been Utilized in the Defensive Backfield

#10   Josh Gordon
#11   Julian Edelman
#13   Bam Childress
#18   Randy Vataha and Matthew Slater
#20   Gino Cappelletti
#40   Larry Garron
#80   Troy Brown
#81   Randy Moss
#87   Rob Gronkowski
#88   Christian Fauria

Do You Remember Any of These Interceptions from a Teammates Pass Deflection?

Steve Kiner's interception, of a pass tipped by Dave Rowe, in their 21-17 win over the Colts on 12-19-71
Steve King's 9 yard return, of a pass tipped by Ron Bolton, in their 24-0 shutout of the Jets on 10-13-74
Fred Marion's interception in the end zone, of a pass tipped by Ray Clayborn, in their 27-21 win on 10-16-88
Chris Slade's interception, of a pass tipped by Ty Law, in their 30-28 victory over the Jets on 09-12-99
Ty Law's interception, of a pass tipped by Ferric Collons, in their 27-3 rout of Arizona on 10-31-99
Ty Law's interception, of a pass tipped by Ted Johnson, in their 24-16 victory over the Colts on 10-08-00
Roman Phifer's interception, of a pass tipped by Terrell Buckley, in their 44-13 rout of the Colts on 09-30-01
Tedy Bruschi's 48 yard TD return, deflected off Lawyer Milloy's foot, in their 27-20 loss to Oak on 11-17-02
Rodney Harrison's interception, tipped by Richard Seymour, in their 17-6 win over the Giants on 10-12-03
Tyrone Poole's interception, of a pass tipped by Richard Seymour, in their 17-6 win vs the Giants on 10-12-03
Willie McGinest's 27 yard interception return, of a pass tipped by Richard Seymour, on 10-17-04
James Sanders 39 yard TD return of a pass, tipped by Tedy Bruschi, in their 35-7 rout of Buffalo on 12-11-05

A Few Interceptions by a Player Who Tipped the Ball to Themselves

Willie McGinest tipped a pass by Chad Pennington to himself and took it 15 yards for a TD on 12-20-03
Roosevelt Colvin tipped a pass by Philip Rivers to himself, in their 24-21 **Divisional** win over SD on 01-14-06
Richard Seymour tipped a pass by David Carr to himself, in their 40-7 rout of the Houston Texans on 12-17-06
Vince Wilfork tipped a pass by Philip Rivers to himself and returned it 28 yards in their 35-21 win on 09-18-11

Every Patriots Defensive Lineman Who Had an Interception in a Regular Season Game

Bob Dee had a 14 yard return of a pass by Babe Parilli in their 27-14 loss to the Raiders on 10-14-60
Jim Lee Hunt had a 78 yard TD return of a pass by Jacky Lee in their 45-3 rout of Houston on 11-01-63
Larry Eisenhauer intercepted Jack Kemp in their 17-7 victory over Buffalo on 12-01-63
Houston Antwine had a 2 yard return of a pass by Jacky Lee in their 28-20 win over Denver on 12-12-65
Mel Witt had a 4 yard TD return of a pass by Joe Namath in their 47-31 loss to the Jets on 09-22-68
Mark Buben had a 49 yard return of a pass by Bill Kenney in their 33-17 win over the Chiefs on 10-04-81
Willie McGinest had a 46 yard TD return of a pass Jim Kelly in their 28-25 win over Buffalo on 10-27-96
Henry Thomas had a 24 yard TD return of a pass by Danny Wuerffel in their 30-27 win vs NO on 10-04-98
Anthony Pleasant intercepted Aaron Brooks in their 34-17 victory over the Saints on 11-25-01
Anthony Pleasant intercepted Tim Couch in their 27-16 victory over Cleveland on 12-09-01
Bobby Hamilton intercepted Joey Harrington in their 20-12 win over Detroit on 11-28-02
Richard Seymour had a 6 yard return of a pass by Drew Bledsoe in their 27-17 win over Buffalo on 12-08-02
Vince Wilfork had a 28 yard return of a pass by Philip Rivers in their 35-21 win over SD on 09-18-11
Vince Wilfork had a 19 yard return of a pass by Jason Campbell in their 31-19 win over Oakland on 10-02-11
Dominique Easley intercepted Matt Cassel in their 30-7 rout of the Vikings on 09-14-14
Vince Wilfork had a 1 yard return of a pass by David Carr in their 16-9 win over Oakland on 09-21-14
Chandler Jones intercepted Brock Osweiler in their 30-24 OT loss to the Broncos on 11-29-15
Lawrence Guy had a 5 yard return of a pass by Baker Mayfield in their 27-13 win over Cleveland on 10-27-19

Every Interception by a Patriots Defensive Back Who Was Also Used as a WR in the Same Season

Gino Cappelletti intercepted 3 passes by Tom Flores in their 27-14 loss to the Raiders on 10-16-60
Gino Cappelletti had a 20 yard return of a pass by Bob Laraba in their 45-16 loss to the Chargers on 10-28-60
Chuck Shonta had a 12 yard return of a pass by Cotton Davidson in their 28-21 win over Dallas on 11-03-61
Terrell Buckley had a 52 yard return of a pass by Kurt Warner in their 24-17 loss to the Rams on 11-18-01
Terrell Buckley intercepted Vinny Testaverde to help seal their 17-16 win over the Jets on 12-02-01
Terrell Buckley had a 24 yard return of a pass by Tim Couch in their 27-16 win over the Browns on 12-09-01
Troy Brown had a 17 yard return of a pass by Drew Bledsoe in their 29-6 rout of Buffalo on 11-14-04
Troy Brown intercepted Luke McCown in their 42-15 rout of the Browns on 12-05-04
Troy Brown had a 5 yard return of a pass by Jon Kitna in their 35-28 win over the Bengals on 12-12-04
Randy Moss caught Kyle Orton's Hail Mary pass to end the half in their 20-17 OT loss to Denver on 10-11-09

Linebackers Who Have Intercepted a Pass Late in the 4th Qtr to Help Seal a Patriots Win

Steve Nelson intercepted a pass by Dan Fouts, on the 2 yard line, to help seal their 27-21 win on 09-23-79
Don Blackmon intercepted a pass by David Woodley, on the 10 yard line, in their 3-0 win on 12-12-82
Tedy Bruschi intercepted a pass by Chad Pennington, with 15 ticks left, to preserve 24-17 win on 09-17-06
Mike Vrabel returned a Jon Kitna pass 1 yard, with 2 minutes left, to help seal their 28-21 win on 12-03-06

Every Patriots Player with Three Interceptions of a QB in a Game

Gino Cappelletti intercepted 3 passes by Tom Flores in their 27-14 loss to the Raiders on 10-16-60
Ross O'Hanley intercepted 3 passes by George Blanda in their 21-17 loss to Houston on 11-18-62
Nick Buoniconti intercepted 3 passes by Dan Darragh in their 23-6 win over Buffalo on 10-20-68
Roland James intercepted Joe Ferguson 3 times in the 3rd Qtr of their 31-0 shutout of Buffalo on 10-23-83
Ty Law intercepted Peyton Manning 3 times in their 24-14 Championship win vs the Colts on 01-18-04
Asante Samuel intercepted Rex Grossman 3 times in their 17-13 win over Chicago on 11-26-06
Leigh Bodden intercepted Mark Sanchez 3 times in their 31-14 rout of the Jets on 11-22-09

Every Patriots Player with Three Interceptions of Different QBs in a Game

Ron Hall intercepted Tobin Rote twice and John Hadl once in their 33-28 win vs SD on 09-20-64
Mike Haynes intercepted Joe Namath twice and Richard Todd once in their 38-24 win on 10-18-76

Here are a Few Interceptions by the Patriots on the Last Play of the Game

Bob Geddes returned a pass by Norm Snead 3 yards in their 28-20 win over the Giants on 09-22-74
Dick Conn had a 24 yard return of a pass by Ken Stabler in their 21-14 win over the Raiders on 09-24-78
Roland James intercepted a pass by David Woodley, on the last play, in their 3-0 win over Miami on 12-12-82
Raymond Clayborn had an 85 yard return of a pass by Paul McDonald in 17-16 win vs Cleveland on 10-07-84
Jim Bowman intercepted a pass by Boomer Esiason in their 27-21 win over the Bengals on 10-16-88
Eugene Wilson intercepted a pass by Aaron Brooks in the end zone in 24-17 win vs the Saints on 11-20-05
Patrick Chung intercepted a pass by Chad Henne in their 23-16 win over the Jaguars on 12-23-12
Duron Harmon intercepted a pass by Ben Roethlisberger in the end zone, on a fake spike play, on 12-17-17

Every Patriots Player Who Has Intercepted a Pass in a Championship Playoff Game

Fred Marion had a 21 yard return of a pass by Dan Marino in their 31-14 win vs Miami on 01-12-86
Raymond Clayborn intercepted a pass by Dan Marino, on 4th + goal, in the end zone, in 31-14 win on 01-12-86
Willie Clay intercepted a pass by Mark Brunell in the end zone, in their 20-6 vs the Jaguars on 01-12-97
Tedy Bruschi had a 12 yard return of a pass by Mark Brunell in their 20-6 win vs Jacksonville on 01-12-97
Terrell Buckley intercepted a pass by Kordell Stewart to end the 1st half in their 24-17 win on 01-27-02
Tebucky Jones had a 19 yard return of a pass by Kordell Stewart in their 24-17 win vs Pittsburgh on 01-27-02
Lawyer Milloy had an 11 yard return of a pass by Kordell Stewart to help seal their 24-17 win on 01-27-02
Rodney Harrison intercepted a pass by Peyton Manning in the end zone, in their 24-14 win on 01-18-04
Ty Law returned a pass by Peyton Manning 6 yards in the 2nd Qtr of their 24-14 win vs the Colts on 01-18-04
Ty Law intercepted another pass by Peyton Manning, in the 3rd Qtr, during their 24-14 win on 01-18-04
Ty Law returned a pass by Peyton Manning 20 yards in the 4th Qtr of their 24-14 win vs the Colts on 01-18-04
Eugene Wilson intercepted a pass by Ben Roethlisberger on the 3rd play in their 41-27 win on 01-23-05
Rodney Harrison returned a pass by Ben Roethlisberger 87 yards for a TD in their 41-27 win on 01-23-05
Eugene Wilson intercepted another pass by Ben Roethlisberger in their 41-27 win vs Pittsburgh on 01-23-05
Asante Samuel returned a pass by Peyton Manning 39 yards for a TD in their 38-34 loss on 01-21-07
Asante Samuel returned a pass by Philip Rivers 10 yards in their 21-12 win vs San Diego on 01-20-08
Ellis Hobbs lost 3 yards returning a pass by Philip Rivers in their 21-12 win over the Chargers on 01-20-08
Brandon Spikes intercepted a pass by Joe Flacco in their 23-20 win vs the Ravens on 01-22-12
Darrelle Revis returned a pass by Andrew Luck 30 yards in their 45-7 rout over the Colts on 01-18-15

Every Patriots Player Who Has Intercepted a Pass in a Super Bowl Game

Ty Law returned a pass by Kurt Warner 47 yards for a TD in their 20-17 win vs the Rams on 02-03-02
Otis Smith returned a pass by Kurt Warner 30 yards in their 20-17 win vs the Rams on 02-03-02
Rodney Harrison lost 1 yard returning a pass by Donovan McNabb in their 24-21 win vs Philly on 02-06-05
Tedy Bruschi intercepted a pass by Donovan McNabb in their 24-21 win vs the Eagles on 02-06-05
Rodney Harrison returned a pass by Donovan McNabb 6 yards to seal 24-21 win vs the Eagles on 02-06-05
Ellis Hobbs returned a pass by Eli Manning 23 yards in their 17-14 loss to the Giants on 02-03-08
Malcolm Butler intercepted a Russell Wilson pass on the 1 yard line to seal their 28-24 win on 02-01-15
Duron Harmon returned a pass by Nick Foles 8 yards in their 41-33 loss to the Eagles on 02-04-18
Stephon Gilmore intercepted a pass by Jared Goff in their 13-3 win over the Rams on 02-03-19

<u>Chronological List of Everyone Who Has Recovered an Opposing Player's Interception Return Fumble</u>

Jim Crawford recovered Eddie Bell's 8 yard interception return fumble in their 28-24 win vs NY on 09-17-60

Babe Parilli recovered Daniard Paulson's 11 yard int return fumble in their 30-20 loss to NY on 11-14-65

Carl Garrett recovered Jim Kearney's interception fumble in their 23-10 loss to the Chiefs on 10-11-70

Carl Garrett recovered John Pitts' 11 yard interception return fumble in their 45-10 loss to Buffalo on 11-01-70

Craig James recovered Leroy Irvin's 23 yard interception fumble in their 30-28 win vs the Rams on 11-16-86

Bethel Johnson recovered Eric Brown's 5 yard int return fumble in 23-20 OT win vs Houston on 11-23-03

Reche Caldwell recovered Marlon McCree's 3 yard int return fumble in their **Playoff** win vs SD on 01-14-06

<u>A Few Memorable Defensive Plays in Patriots History</u>

Jim Lee Hunt out running everyone during his 78 yard interception return for a TD, on 11-01-63

Shelby Jordan's game saving tackle of Bob Horn's 30 yard interception return, in their 27-21 win on 09-23-79

Rod Shoate lateraling his interception return to Rick Sanford, who advanced it 27 yards, on 11-04-79

Steve Nelson's 6 yard int return + lateral to Clayton Weishuhn, who took it 27 yards for a TD, on 09-25-83

Tedy Bruschi's 48 interception return for a TD in their 27-20 loss to Oakland on 11-17-02

Willie McGinest's goal line stop of Edgerrin James with 11 seconds left in their 38-34 win on 11-30-03

Troy Brown's 17 yard return of a pass by his former QB Drew Bledsoe in their 29-6 win on 11-14-04

Vince Wilfork's 31 yard return of Chad Pennington's lateral in their 37-16 **Wild Card** win on 01-07-07

DB Julian Edelman tackling Vince Young, at the end of his 7 yard run, in their 38-20 win on 11-27-11

Steve Gregory's 32 yard TD return of Mark Sanchez's "Butt Fumble" in their 49-19 rout on 11-22-12

Malcolm Butler's interception of a pass by Russell Wilson to seal their 28-24 **Super Bowl** win on 02-01-15

<u>Games That the Patriots Won Because the Opposing Team's Kicker Missed a Field Goal Late in the Game</u>

George Fleming missed a 60 yard game tying FG on last play in PATS 20-17 win vs Oakland on 11-17-61

Bill Bell missed a 10 yard FG on the last play in the Patriots 21-20 win over Atlanta on 09-24-72

Curt Knight missed a 50 yard FG on the last play in the Patriots 24-23 win over Washington on 10-01-72

Roy Gerela missed a 48 yard FG on the last play in the Patriots 30-27 win vs the Steelers on 09-26-76

Pat Leahy missed a 33 yard FG on the last play in the Patriots 19-17 win over the Jets on 11-19-78

Jason Elam missed a 59 yard FG late in the 4th Qtr of the PATS 24-23 win over Denver on 10-24-99

Mike Vanderjagt missed a 48 yard FG with 24 seconds left in the PATS 27-24 win vs Indy on 09-09-04

Kris Brown's 50 yard FGA hit the right upright in the PATS 23-20 victory over San Diego on 10-24-10

Billy Cundiff missed a 32 yard game tying FG in the PATS 23-20 **Championship** win vs Balt on 01-22-12

Billy Cundiff missed a 58 yard FG on the last play in the PATS 27-26 comeback win vs Clev on 12-08-13

Chandler Catanzaro missed a 47 yard FG on the last play in the PATS 23-21 win vs Arizona on 09-11-16

<u>Only Time the Patriots Had a Roughing the Kicker Penalty on a Successful Field Goal That Worked in Their Favor</u>

The Redskins accepted Ron Bolton's penalty only to have Curt Knight miss on a shorter FGA on 10-01-72

<u>Only Time That a Penalty Denied a TD Pass Because the Patriots Had an Illegal Receiver Down Field</u>

Brian Dowling took a bad snap on a 21 yard FGA + tossed a TD pass but a penalty voided play on 12-10-72

SACKS

First Patriots Player to Sack the Quarterback in a Regular Season Game

Bob Dee sacked Frank Tripucka in their 13-10 loss to the Broncos on 09-09-60

First Patriots Player to Sack a Quarterback in a Playoff Game

Jack Rudolph had 2 sacks (Jack Kemp, Daryle Lamonica) in their 26-8 **Divisional** win vs Buffalo on 12-28-63

Every Patriots Linebacker Who Has Tackled the Quarterback in the End Zone for a Safety

Jack Rudolph sacked Jacky Lee for a safety in their 46-28 win over the Houston Oilers on 12-08-63
Jack Rudolph sacked Jacky Lee for a safety in their 12-7 win over the Broncos on 11-20-64
Steve Kiner sacked Dan Pastorini for a safety in their 32-0 shutout of the Houston Oilers on 11-25-73
Don Blackmon sacked Lynn Dickey for a safety in their 26-20 win over the Packers on 09-08-85
Don Blackmon sacked Steve DeBerg for a safety in their 32-14 win over the Buccaneers on 10-27-85
Larry McGrew strip sacked Jim Kelly for a safety in their 22-19 win over Buffalo on 11-23-86
Dont'a Hightower sacked Andy Dalton for a safety in their 35-17 win over the Bengals on 10-16-16
Eric Lee sacked Bryce Petty for a safety in their 26-6 rout of the Jets on 12-31-17

Only Patriot Nose Tackle Who Has Tackled the Quarterback in the End Zone for a Safety

Richard Bishop tackled Bob Griese for a safety in their 33-24 victory over the Dolphins on 10-22-78

Every Patriot Defensive End Who Has Tackled the Quarterback in the End Zone for a Safety

Jim Lee Hunt sacked Jack Kemp for a safety in their 44-16 loss to the Bills on 12-09-67
George Crump sacked Archie Manning for a safety in their 29-21 win vs the Houston Oilers on 11-28-82

Only Time That Two Defensive Players of the Patriots Were Credited with a Sack for a Safety

Jarvis Green & Mike Vrabel sacked Jay Fiedler for a safety in their 12-0 shutout of Miami on 12-07-03

Only Game That a Player Forced a Fumble and it Went Out of the End Zone for a Safety

Larry McGrew strip sacked Jim Kelly and the ball went out of the end zone in their 22-19 win on 11-23-86

Most Sacks in a Regular Season Game	Most Sacks/Season	Most Sacks/Career
4 sacks by Julius Adams (12-04-77)	18.5 by Andre Tippett	100 by Andre Tippett
4 sacks by Tony McGee (11-16-78)	16.5 by Andre Tippett	79.5 by Julius Adams
4 sacks by Mike Hawkins (09-09-79)	12.5 by Andre Tippett	78 by Willie McGinest
4 sacks by Andre Carter (11-13-11)	12.5 by Mike Vrabel	70 by Tony McGee
3.5 sacks by Andre Tippett (10-26-86)	12.5 by Chandler Jones	54 by Ray Hamilton
3.5 sacks by Chris Slade (11-20-94)		

Everyone Who Has Recorded a Sack in a Super Bowl Game

Dennis Owens sacked Jim McMahon in their 46-10 loss to Da' Bears on 01-26-86
Dennis Owens sacked William Perry in their 46-10 loss to Da' Bears on 01-26-86
Ben Thomas sacked Steve Fuller in their 46-10 loss to Da' Bears on 01-26-86
Otis Smith sacked Brett Favre in their 35-21 loss to the Packers on 01-26-97
Tedy Bruschi sacked Brett Favre *twice* in their 35-21 loss to the Packers on 01-26-97
Ferric Collons sacked Brett Favre in their 35-21 loss to the Packers on 01-26-97
Willie McGinest sacked Brett Favre in their 35-21 loss to the Packers on 01-26-97
Richard Seymour sacked Kurt Warner in their 20-17 win over the St. Louis Rams on 02-03-02
Bobby Hamilton sacked Kurt Warner in their 20-17 victory over the St. Louis Rams on 02-03-02
Willie McGinest sacked Kurt Warner in their 20-17 win over the St. Louis Rams on 02-03-02
Willie McGinest sacked Jake Delhomme in their 32-29 win over the Panthers on 02-01-04
Mike Vrabel sacked Jake Delhomme *twice* in their 32-29 victory over the Panthers on 02-01-04
Rodney Harrison sacked Jake Delhomme in their 32-29 win over the Panthers on 02-01-04
Richard Seymour sacked Donovan McNabb in their 24-21 win over the Eagles on 02-06-05
Tedy Bruschi sacked Donovan McNabb in their 24-21 win over the Eagles on 02-06-05
Mike Vrabel sacked Donovan McNabb in their 24-21 win over the Eagles on 02-06-05
Rodney Harrison sacked Donovan McNabb in their 24-21 win over the Eagles on 02-06-05
Jarvis Green sacked Eli Manning in their 17-14 loss to the Giants on 02-03-08
Adalius Thomas sacked Eli Manning *twice* in their 17-14 loss to the Giants on 02-03-08
Mark Anderson had 1.5 sacks of Eli Manning in their 21-17 loss to the Giants on 02-05-12
Rob Ninkovich shared in a sack of Eli Manning in their 21-17 loss to the Giants on 02-05-12
Brandon Deaderick sacked Eli Manning in their 21-17 loss to the Giants on 02-05-12
Chandler Jones sacked Russell Wilson in their 28-24 win over the Seahawks on 02-01-15
Rob Ninkovich sacked Russell Wilson in their 28-24 victory over the Seahawks on 02-01-15
Darrelle Revis sacked Russell Wilson in their 28-24 win over the Seahawks on 02-01-15
Jabaal Sheard shared in a sack of Matt Ryan in their 34-28 OT win over Atlanta on 02-05-17
Alan Branch shared in a sack of Matt Ryan in their 34-28 OT win over Atlanta on 02-05-17
Kyle Van Noy shared in a sack of Matt Ryan in their 34-28 OT win over Atlanta on 02-05-17
Dont'a Hightower strip sacked Matt Ryan in their 34-28 OT win over the Falcons on 02-05-17
Trey Flowers sacked Matt Ryan *2.5 times* in their 34-28 OT win over the Falcons on 02-05-17
Dont'a Hightower sacked Jared Goff twice in their 13-3 victory over the LA Rams on 02-03-19

Most Sacks in a Playoff Game

4.5 sacks by Willie McGinest (01-07-06)
3 sacks by Julius Adams (12-18-76)
3 sacks by Garin Veris (12-28-85)
3 sacks by Willie McGinest (01-10-04)
2.5 sacks by Jarvis Green on (01-18-04)
2.5 sacks by Trey Flowers (02-05-17)

Most Career Sacks in the Playoffs

16 sacks by Willie McGinest
7 sacks by Mike Vrabel
6 sacks by Rob Ninkovich
5 sacks by Jarvis Green
4.5 by Tedy Bruschi and Richard Seymour

FUMBLES

10 Longest Defensive Fumble Returns for a TD

68 yard TD by Richard Seymour, of a fumble by Drew Bledsoe, in their 31-17 win over Buffalo on 10-03-04
49 yard TD by Don Webb, of Johnny Robinson's fumble, in 18-17 win vs the Dallas Texans on 10-29-61
46 yard TD by Kyle Van Noy, of a fumble by Sam Darnold, in their 38-3 rout of the Jets on 12-30-18
45 yard TD by Brent Williams, of Dave Krieg's fumble, in their 33-20 loss to Seattle on 10-07-90
41 yard TD by Randall Gay, of a fumble by William Green, in their 42-15 rout of the Browns on 12-05-04
38 yard TD by Matt Chatham, of Tiki Barber's fumble, in their 17-6 victory over the Giants on 10-12-03
35 yard TD by Ellis Hobbs, of a fumble by Dwayne Wright, in their 56-10 rout of the Bills on 11-18-07
35 yard TD by Gary Guyton, of a fumble by Johnny Knox, in their 36-7 win over the Bears on 12-12-10
32 yard TD by Daryl Johnson, of Hoyle Granger's fumble, in their 24-0 shutout of the Oilers on 11-02-69
32 yard TD by Steve Gregory, of Mark Sanchez's butt fumble, in their 49-19 rout of the Jets on 11-22-12

10 Longest Fumble Returns That Were Not Returned for a TD

69 yard return by Shea McClellin, of a fumble by Damien Williams, in 35-14 rout of Miami on 01-01-17
63 yard return by Rob Ninkovich, of a fumble by Philip Rivers, in their 23-20 win vs SD on 10-24-10
51 yard return by Jim Lee Hunt, of a fumble by Don Trull, in their 45-17 loss to the Oilers on 12-15-68
50 yard return by Dick Felt, of a fumble by Johnny Olszewski in their 41-16 rout Denver on 09-21-62
47 yard return by Don Blackmon, of Earl Campbell's fumble, in their 29-21 win vs Houston on 11-28-82
31 yard return by Mark Buben, of a fumble by Bert Jones, in their 29-28 loss to the Colts on 09-04-83
31 yard return by Mike Jones, of a fumble by Kent Graham, in their 31-0 win vs Arizona on 09-15-96
31 yard return by Vince Wilfork, of a fumble by Chad Pennington, in their 37-16 **Wild Card** win on 01-07-07
30 yard return by Bob Dee, of a fumble by Warren Rabb, in their 52-21 rout of the Bills on 10-22-61
27 yard return by Johnny Rembert, of a fumble by Jim Kelly, in their 33-24 win vs Buffalo on 11-19-89

Longest Fumble Returns by the Patriots in a Playoff Game

47 yard TD by Otis Smith, of James Stewart's fumble, in their 20-6 **Championship** win on 01-12-97
31 yards by Vince Wilfork, of Chad Pennington's lateral fumble, in their 37-16 **Wild Card** win on 01-07-07
21 yards by Rick Sanford, of Andra Franklin's fumble, in their 28-13 **Playoff** loss to Miami on 01-08-83
15 yard TD by Johnny Rembert of Johnny Hector's KR fumble, in their 26-14 **Wild Card** win on 12-28-85
15 yards by Terrell Buckley, of Ricky Proehl's fumble, in their 20-17 **Super Bowl** on 02-03-02

Chronological List of Everyone Who Has Returned a Fumble by a Running Back for a TD

Don Webb returned Johnny Robinson's fumble 49 yards for a TD in their 18-17 win over Dallas on 10-29-61
Nick Buoniconti returned Bill Tobin's fumble 7 yards for a TD in their 46-28 win over Houston on 12-08-63
Jim Lee Hunt returned Darrell Lester's fumble 5 yards for a TD in their 17-10 loss to Denver on 11-06-66
Darryl Johnson returned Hoyle Granger's fumble 32 yards for a TD in their 17-16 loss to Miami on 11-02-69
Vincent Brown returned a fumble by Thurman Thomas 25 yards for a TD in their 16-7 loss on 11-01-92
Tim Goad returned Christian Okoye's fumble on the 1st play, 19 yds for a TD, in their 27-20 loss on 12-13-92
Ricky Reynolds returned Carwell Gardner's fumble 25 yds for a TD in their 41-17 rout of Buffalo on 12-18-94
Otis Smith returned Jonathan Stewart's fumble 47 yards for a TD in 20-6 **Championship** win on 01-12-97
Matt Chatham returned Tiki Barber's fumble 38 yards for a TD in their 17-6 win vs the Giants on 10-12-03
Ellis Hobbs returned Dwayne Wright's airborne fumble 35 yards for a TD in their 56-10 rout on 11-18-07
Kyle Van Noy returned Jon Hilliman's fumble 22 yards for a TD in their 35-14 win vs the Giants on 10-10-19

Everyone Who Has Returned an Opponent's Fumbled Punt Return for a TD

Tom Stephens returned Paul Lowe's fumble 10 yards for a TD in their 38-27 loss to San Diego on 10-07-61
Corwin Brown returned Bryan Still's fumble 42 yards for a TD in their 45-7 rout of San Diego on 12-01-96

Everyone Who Has Recovered a Fumbled Kickoff Return in the End Zone for a TD

Johnny Rembert recovered Clarence Weathers' fumble in the end zone in their 24-20 loss on 10-06-85
Jim Bowman recovered Sam Seale's kickoff return fumble for a TD in 27-20 **Divisional** win on 01-05-86

Everyone Who Has Recovered a Teammate's Fumble in the End Zone for a TD

Cedric Jones recovered Mosi Tatupu's fumble in the end zone for a TD in their 27-17 loss on 12-09-84
John Stephens recovered Robert Perryman's fumble in the end zone for a TD in their 27-21 win on 10-16-88
Brandon Lloyd recovered Danny Woodhead's fumble in the end zone for a TD in 42-14 rout on 12-10-12
Freddie Childress recovered a fumbled snap in the end zone for a TD in their 26-23 OT win on 10-20-91

Only Patriots Defensive Player Who Has Recovered an Opponent's Bad Snap in the End Zone for a TD

Akiem Hicks recovered Gino Gradkowski's bad snap in the end zone for a TD in their 33-16 win on 12-20-15

Everyone Who Has Returned Fumble by a QB for a Touchdown

Ray Hamilton returned Jim Hart's fumbled snap 23 yards for a TD in their 24-17 loss to St. Louis on 11-02-75
Brent Williams returned Dave Wilson's fumble 21 yards in their 21-20 victory over the Saints on 11-30-86
Brent Williams returned Garin Veris' strip sack of Dave Krieg 45 yds for a TD in their 33-20 loss on 10-07-90
Chris Slade returned Willie McGinest's strip sack of Jim Kelly 27 yds for a TD in their 35-25 win on 11-26-95
Chad Eaton returned Ted Johnson's strip sack of Tony Banks 23 yards for a TD in their 20-3 win on 01-02-00
Tebucky Jones returned his strip sack of Vinny Testaverde 24 yards for a TD in their 44-7 rout on 09-15-02
Richard Seymour returned Tedy Bruschi's 4th down strip sack of Drew Bledsoe 68 yds for a TD on 10-03-04
Rosevelt Colvin returned Mike Vrabel's strip sack of Jason Campbell 11 yards for a TD on 10-28-07
Dont'a Hightower returned Chandler Jones' strip sack of Jake Locker 6 yds for TD in 34-13 win on 09-09-12
Steve Gregory returned Mark Sanchez's butt fumble 32 yards for a TD in their 49-19 rout on 11-22-12
Rob Ninkovich returned Zach Moore's strip sack of Jay Cutler 15 yards for a TD in 51-23 rout on 10-26-14
Jamie Collins returned Jabaal Sheard's sack of Ryan Fitzpatrick 14 yds for a TD in 26-20 OT loss on 12-27-15
Kyle Van Noy returned Adam Butler's strip sack of San Darnold 46 yards for a TD in 38-3 rout on 12-30-18

Everyone Who Has Recovered a Fumble by a QB in the End Zone for a TD

John Hannah recovered Jim Plunkett's fumble in the end zone for a TD in their 34-27 loss on 12-15-74
Johnny Rembert recovered Gary Hogenboom's fumble in the end zone for a TD in their 33-3 rout on 09-07-86
Willie McGinest recovered Stan Humphries fumble in the end zone for a TD in their 45-7 rout on 12-01-96
Willie McGinest recovered Tom Tupa's fumble in the end zone for a TD in their 30-28 victory on 09-12-99
Jarvis Green recovered Kyle Boller's fumble in the end zone for a TD in their 24-3 rout on 11-28-04
Logan Mankins recovered Tom Brady's fumble for a TD in their 38-34 **Championship** loss on 01-21-07
Vince Wilfork recovered Rex Grossman's fumble in the end zone for a TD in their 34-27 win on 12-11-11
Chandler Jones recovered Marcus Mariota's fumble in the end zone for a TD in their 33-16 win on 12-20-15

10 Longest Offensive Fumble Advancements That Were Not Advanced for a TD

30 yard advancement by Max Lane, of Troy Brown's 5 yard reception fumble, in their 31-26 loss on 10-15-95
22 yards by Leonard Russell, of Vincent Brisby's fumble in Overtime, in their 33-27 OT win vs on 01-02-94
20 yard advancement by Stanley Morgan, on a fumble by Tony Collins, in their 30-0 loss on 11-20-83
14 yard advancement by Darryl Stingley, of Sam Cunningham's fumble, in their 22-14 loss on 09-28-75
12 yard advancement by Jay Cunningham, of Tom Hennessey's fumble, in their 31-10 loss on 09-19-65
12 yard advancement by Shelby Jordan, of Jim Plunkett's fumble, in their 34-31 loss to Dallas on 11-16-75
11 yard advancement by Pat Studstill of a poor snap, for a 1st down, in their 27-24 loss to the Bills on 11-19-72
10 yard advancement by Jim Colclough, of Billy Lott's fumble, in their 23-21 win over Buffalo on 09-23-61
9 yard advancement by Chris Canty of a fumble by Derrick Cullors in their 14-12 win over Miami on 12-22-97
8 yard advancement by Stephen Starring of a fumble by Tony Collins in their 38-23 win on 09-16-84
8 yard advancement by Reche Caldwell, of Benjamin Watson's fumble, in their 17-13 win on 11-26-06
8 yard advancement by Julian Edelman, of his own fumbled punt return, in their 31-24 win on 12-04-11
8 yard advancement by Julian Edelman, of his own fumbled punt return, in their 34-31 OT win on 11-24-13

Every Patriots Player Who Has Advanced a Fumble by a Patriots Receiver

Leonard Russell advanced Vincent Brisby's OT fumble 22 yards in their 33-27 OT win on 01-02-94
Max Lane advanced Troy Brown's fumble 30 yards in their 31-26 loss to the Chiefs on 10-15-95
Reche Caldwell advanced Benjamin Watson's fumble 8 yards in their 17-13 win over the Bears on 11-26-06

Every Offensive Lineman Who Has Advanced a Fumble By a Patriots QB

Shelby Jordan advanced Jim Plunkett's fumble 12 yards in their 34 -31 loss to the Cowboys on 11-16-75
Bruce Armstrong advanced Marc Wilson's fumble 4 yards in their 17-10 loss to Miami on 10-18-90
Joe Andruzzi advanced Drew Bledsoe's fumble 2 yards in their 10-3 loss to Miami on 09-24-00

Every Patriots Running Back Who Has Advanced a Fumble by a Patriots QB

Jack Maitland advanced Jim Plunkett's 4th down fumble 3 yards, for a 1st down, in their 13-6 loss on 12-12-71
John Stephens advanced Doug Flutie's fumble 4 yards in their 45-3 loss to the Packers on 10-09-88
Kevin Turner advanced Scott Secules' fumble 6 yards in their 28-14 loss to Houston on 10-17-93
Marc Edwards advanced Tom Brady's fumble 2 yards in their 29-26 OT win vs the Chargers on 10-14-01

Chronological List of Patriots Who Have Advanced a Fumble by a Patriots RB

Jim Colclough advanced Billy Lott's fumble 20 yards in their 23-21 win over the Bills on 09-23-61
Babe Parilli advanced Larry Garron's fumble 1 yard for a TD in 28-21 win over the Dallas Texans on 11-03-61
Charlie Long advanced Ron Burton's fumble 2 yards in their 27-7 loss to the Dallas Texans on 10-12-62
Gino Cappelletti advanced Ron Burton's fumble 4 yards in their 12-7 win over the Broncos on 11-20-64
Randy Vataha advanced Mack Herron's fumble 46 yards for a TD in 24-16 win over the Colts on 10-07-73
Darryl Stingley advanced Sam Cunningham's fumble 14 yards in their 22-14 loss to the Miami on 09-28-75
Leon Gray advanced Don Calhoun's fumble 4 yards in their 30-28 loss to the Jets on 12-07-75
Steve Grogan advanced Don Calhoun's fumble 6 yards for a TD in their 41-7 rout of the Jets on 10-18-76
Stanley Morgan advanced Don Calhoun's fumble 3 yards in their 37-31 win over the Seahawks on 09-21-80
Stanley Morgan advanced a fumble by Tony Collins 20 yards in their 30-0 loss to the Browns on 11-20-83
Stephen Starring advanced a fumble by Tony Collins 8 yards in their 38-23 win over Seattle on 09-16-84

Every Patriots Defensive Player Who Has Recovered a Lateraled Fumble by a Receiver

Larry Eisenhauer recovered Gene Mingo's lateraled fumble, after his 2 yard catch, on 09-16-61
Eugene Wilson recovered Antwann Randle El's lateraled fumble, after his 49 yard catch, on 09-25-05

Every Offensive Fumble Recovery by a Patriot in a Championship Playoff Game or Super Bowl Game

Tony Romeo recovered Babe Parilli's fumble in their 56-10 AFL Championship loss to SD on 01-05-64
Dave Meggett recovered Drew Bledsoe's fumble in their 20-6 Championship win vs the Jaguars on 01-12-97
Logan Mankins fell on Tom Brady's fumble in the end zone for a TD in their 38-34 loss to Indy on 01-21-07
David Andrews recovered Tom Brady's fumble in their 13-3 **Super Bowl** win over the LA Rams on 02-03-19

Every Special Team Fumble Recovery by the Patriots in an AFC Championship Playoff Game

Greg Hawthorne recovered Lorenzo Hampton's fumbled kickoff return in their 31-14 vs Miami on 01-12-86
Mike Bartrum recovered Chris Hudson's fumbled punt return in their 20-6 win vs the Jaguars on 01-12-97

Only Special Team Fumble Recovery by the Patriots in a Super Bowl Game

Troy Brown recovered his own fumbled punt return in their 32-29 **Super Bowl** win on 02-01-04

Two Patriots Linebackers Who Have Ripped the Ball Out of a Running Back's Hands

Andre Tippett stole the ball from Eric Dickerson in their 21-7 win over the Rams on 12-11-83
Tedy Bruschi stole the ball from Dominic Rhodes in their 20-3 **Playoff** win over the Colts on 01-16-05

Every Defensive Fumble Recovery by the Patriots in a Super Bowl Game

Larry McGrew recovered Walter Payton's fumble in their 46-10 loss to Da' Bears on 01-26-86
Raymond Clayborn recovered Matt Suhey's fumble in their 46-10 loss to Da' Bears on 01-26-86
Terrell Buckley returned Ricky Proehl's fumble 15 yards in their 20-17 win over the Rams on 02-03-02
Richard Seymour recovered Jake Delhomme's fumble in their 32-29 win over Carolina on 02-01-04
Eugene Wilson recovered L.J. Smith's fumble in their 24-21 win vs the Eagles on 02-05-06
Alan Branch recovered Dont'a Hightower's strip sack of Matt Ryan in 34-28 OT win vs Atlanta on 02-05-17

Patriot Players Who Have Forced a Fumble on a Kickoff Return That Resulted in a TD by the Patriots

Mosi Tatupu forced Nesby Glasgow's fumble that Rick Sanford took for a TD in their 47-21 win on 11-23-80
Rod McSwain forced Joe Carter's fumble that Cedric Jones returned for a TD in their 30-27 loss on 12-16-85
Johnny Rembert forced Johnny Hector's fumble and returned it himself for a TD in **Playoff** win on 12-28-85
Mosi Tatupu forced Sam Seale's fumble that Jim Bowman fell on for a TD in their **Playoff** win on 01-05-86
Devin McCourty forced Joe McKnight's fumble that Julian Edelman took for a TD in 49-19 rout on 11-22-12

Everyone Who Forced a Fumble on the Opening Kickoff That Was Recovered by the Patriots

Mosi Tatupu forced Reggie Smith's fumble that was recovered by Prentice McCray on 09-14-80
Raymond Clayborn forced George Wonsley's fumble that was recovered by Mosi Tatupu on 10-25-81
Michael Timpson forced Terrance Mathis' fumble that was recovered by Todd Collins on 10-04-92
Larry Whigham forced Karl Williams' fumble that was recovered by Kato Serwanga on 09-03-00
Eric Alexander forced Chris Carr's fumble that was recovered by Brandon McGowan on 10-04-09

Other Patriot Players Who Have Recovered an Opponent's Fumble of the Opening Kickoff

Billy Lott fell on Elbert Dubenion's fumble of the opening kickoff in their 26-8 **Playoff** win on 12-28-63
White Graves recovered Joe Beauchamp's fumble of the opening kickoff in their 35-17 win on 10-23-66

Other Patriot Players Who Have Forced Fumbles That Were Returned for a TD by the Patriots

John Bramlett forced Hoyle Granger's fumble that Daryl Johnson returned for a TD on 11-02-69
Dwayne Sabb forced Thomas Thomas' fumble that Vincent Brown returned for a TD on 11-01-92
Maurice Hurst forced Christian Okoye's fumble that Tim Goad returned on the 1st play for a TD on 12-13-92
Mike Pitts forced Cardwell Gardner's fumble that Ricky Reynolds returned for a TD on 12-18-94
Chris Slade forced James Stewart's fumble that Otis Smith returned for a TD in **Playoff** win on 01-12-97
Tyrone Poole forced Tiki Barber's fumble that Matt Chatham returned for a TD on 10-12-03
Richard Seymour forced William Green's fumble that Randall Gay returned for a TD on 12-05-04
Devin McCourty forced Johnny Knox's fumble that Gary Guyton returned for a TD on 12-12-10

Only Patriot Who Has Recovered a Fumbled Kickoff Return for a TD

Jim Bowman recovered Sam Seale's KR fumble for a TD in their 27-20 **Playoff** win vs LA on 01-05-86

Only Patriot Who Has Returned an Opponent's Fumbled Kickoff Return But Did Not Score a TD

Steve Schubert returned Charley Leigh's fumbled KR 13 yards in their 34-24 win vs Miami on 09-15-74

Chronological List of Every Patriot Who Has Returned an Opponent's Fumbled Kickoff Return for a TD

Allan Clark took Kim Anderson's fumble 15 yards for a TD in their 47-21 rout of the Colts on 11-23-80
Rick Sanford returned Nesby Glasgow's fumble 22 yards for a TD in their 47-21 rout of the Colts on 11-23-80
Cedric Jones returned Joe Carter's fumble 15 yards for a TD in their 30-27 loss to Miami on 12-16-85
Johnny Rembert took Johnny Hector's fumble 15 yds for a TD in 26-14 **Playoff** win vs the Jets on 12-28-85
Julian Edelman returned Joe McKnight's fumble 22 yards for a TD in their 49-19 rout of the Jets on 11-22-12
Kyle Arrington returned Brandon Tate's fumble 9 yards for a TD in 43-17 rout of the Bengals on 10-05-14

Every Patriots Player Who Has Recovered a Teammate's Interception Return Fumble

Clyde Washington recovered Bob Dee's interception return fumble in their 27-14 loss on 10-16-60
Fred Marion recovered Ronnie Lippett's interception return fumble in their 16-10 win on 12-16-84
Steve Nelson fell on Garin Veris' interception return fumble in their 26-14 **Playoff** win on 12-28-85
Ricky Reynolds recovered Larry Whigham's interception return fumble in their 41-17 win on 12-18-94
Matt Stevens recovered Tedy Bruschi's interception return fumble in their 31-20 loss on 10-28-01
James Sanders fell on Ellis Hobbs' interception return fumble in their 21-12 **Playoff** win on 01-20-08

SAFETIES

Everyone Who Has Tackled a Running Back for a Safety

Nick Buoniconti tackled RB Roy Hopkins for a safety in their 18-7 win vs the Oilers on 11-05-67
Doug Satcher tackled RB Paul Robinson for a safety in their 33-14 win vs the Bengals on 12-01-68
Daryl Johnson tackled RB Jess Phillips for a safety in their 25-14 win over the Bengals on 11-16-69
Roland James tackled RB Frank Middleton for safety in their 38-10 rout of the Bills on 11-18-84
Malcom Brown tackled RB Ken Dixon for a safety in their 30-23 win over the Ravens on 12-12-16

Every Special Team Player Who Has Tackled the Punt Returner for a Safety

Jay Cunningham tackled Les "Speedy" Duncan for a safety in their 22-6 win vs SD on 10-31-65
Ezell Jones tackled Mercury Morris for a safety in their 38-23 win vs Miami on 11-30-69
Brandon King tackled Punt Returner Travis Benjamin for a safety in 21-13 win over SD on 10-29-17

Chronological List of Everyone Who Has Recorded a Safety for the Patriots

Jack Rudolph sacked Jacky Lee for a safety in their 46-28 win over the Houston Oilers on 12-08-63
Jack Rudolph sacked Jacky Lee for a safety in their 12-7 victory over the Broncos on 11-20-64
Jay Cunningham tackled Punt Returner "Speedy" Duncan for a safety in their 22-6 win over SD on 10-31-65
Nick Buoniconti tackled RB Roy Hopkins for a safety in their 18-7 win over the Houston Oilers on 11-05-67
Jim Lee Hunt sacked Jack Kemp for a safety in their 44-16 loss to the Bills on 12-09-67
Doug Satcher tackled RB Paul Robinson for a safety in their 33-14 victory over the Bengals on 12-01-68
Daryl Johnson tackled RB Jess Phillips for a safety in their 25-14 win over the Bengals on 11-16-69
Ezell Jones tackled Punt Returner Mercury Morris for a safety in their 38-23 victory over Miami on 11-30-69
Steve Kiner sacked Dan Pastorini for a safety in their 32-0 shutout of the Houston Oilers on 11-25-73
Raymond Clayborn forced Punter Mike Michel out of the end zone for a safety on 11-13-77
Richard Bishop sacked Bob Griese for a safety in their 33-24 victory over the Dolphins on 10-22-78
Tim Fox forced Punter Rusty Jackson out of the end zone for a safety in their 26-24 win on 12-10-78
George Crump forced Archie Manning to ground the ball for a safety in their 29-21 win on 11-28-82
Roland James tackled RB Frank Middleton for safety in their 38-10 rout of the Bills on 11-18-84
Don Blackmon sacked Lynn Dickey for a safety in their 26-20 win over the Packers on 09-08-85
Don Blackmon sacked Steve DeBerg for a safety in their 32-14 win over the Tampa on 10-27-85
Larry McGrew strip sacked Jim Kelly for a safety on the 2nd play of their 22-19 win vs Buffalo on 11-23-86
Mike Jones forced Jim Kelly to ground the ball for a safety in their 28-25 win over Buffalo on 10-27-96
Henry Thomas forced Neil O'Donnell to ground the ball for a safety in their 24-19 loss to the Jets on 10-19-97
Jarvis Green and Mike Vrabel shared in a sack of Jay Fiedler for a safety in their 12-0 shutout on 12-07-03
Ty Warren sacked JP Losman for a safety and the final points scored in their 19-17 win on 09-10-06
Dont'a Hightower forced Cody Kessler's lateral into the end zone for a safety in their 33-13 win on 10-09-16
Dont'a Hightower sacked Andy Dalton for a safety in their 35-17 win over the Bengals on 10-16-16
Malcom Brown tackled RB Ken Dixon for a safety in their 30-23 win over the Ravens on 12-12-16
Brandon King tackled Punt Returner Travis Benjamin for a safety in their 21-13 win over SD on 10-29-17
Eric Lee sacked Bryce Petty for safety in their 26-6 rout of the Jets on 12-31-17

Everyone Who Has Sacked the Quarterback for a Safety

Jack Rudolph sacked Jacky Lee for a safety in their 46-28 win over the Oilers on 12-08-63
Jack Rudolph sacked Jacky Lee for a safety in their 12-7 victory over the Broncos on 11-20-64
Jim Lee Hunt sacked Jack Kemp for a safety in their 44-16 loss to the Bills on 12-09-67
Steve Kiner sacked Dan Pastorini for a safety in their 32-0 shutout of the Oilers on 11-25-73
Richard Bishop sacked Bob Griese for a safety in their 33-24 victory over the Dolphins on 10-22-78
Don Blackmon sacked Lynn Dickey for a safety in their 26-20 win over the Packers on 09-08-85
Don Blackmon sacked Steve DeBerg for a safety in their 32-14 win over the Tampa on 10-27-85
Larry McGrew strip sacked Jim Kelly for a safety in their 22-19 win vs Buffalo on 11-23-86
Jarvis Green and Mike Vrabel shared in a sack of Jay Fiedler in their 12-0 shutout on 12-07-03
Ty Warren sacked JP Losman for a safety and the final points scored in their 19-17 win on 09-10-06
Dont'a Hightower forced Cody Kessler's lateral for a safety in their 33-13 win on 10-09-16
Dont'a Hightower sacked Andy Dalton for a safety in their 35-17 win over the Bengals on 10-16-16
Eric Lee sacked Bryce Petty for safety in their 26-6 rout of the Jets on 12-31-17

Everyone Who Has Forced the QB into an Intentional Grounding Penalty for a Safety

George Crump forced Archie Manning's penalty in their 29-21 win vs Houston on 11-28-82
Mike Jones forced Jim Kelly's grounding penalty for a safety in 28-25 win vs Buffalo on 10-27-96
Henry Thomas forced Neil O'Donnell's penalty for a safety in 24-19 loss to the Jets on 10-19-97

Every Special Team Player Who Has Forced the Punter Out of the End Zone for a Safety

Raymond Clayborn forced Punter Mike Michel out of the end zone for a safety on 11-13-77
Tim Fox forced Rusty Jackson out of the end zone for a safety in their 26-24 win on 12-10-78

Chronological List of Everyone Who Has Returned a Free Kick Following a Patriots Safety

Bob Yates caught Jim Norton's free punt and lateraled to Bob Suci for a 21 yard gain on 12-08-63
JD Garrett returned Jim Fraser's free punt 12 yards in their 12-7 win against Denver on 11-20-64
Jim Nance returned Rick Redman's free punt 16 yards in their 22-6 win over San Diego on 10-31-65
Bob Cappadona caught Jim Norton's free punt for no gain in their 18-7 win vs Houston on 11-05-67
Jay Cunningham returned Paul Maguire's free punt 10 yards in their 44-16 loss to the Bills on 12-09-67
Willie Porter returned Rex Keeling's free punt 17 yards in their 33-14 win over the Bengals on 12-01-68
Clarence Scott returned Dale Livingston's free punt 12 yards in their 25-14 win over the Bengals on 11-16-69
Aaron Marsh returned Larry Seiple's free punt 9 yards in their 38-23 victory over Miami on 11-30-69
Mack Herron returned Skip Butler's free punt 11 yards in their 32-0 shutout of Houston on 11-25-73
Mike Hawkins returned the free punt by George Roberts for no gain in 33-24 win over Miami on 10-22-78
Stanley Morgan returned Rusty Jackson's free punt 17 yards in their 26-24 win over Buffalo on 12-10-78
Ricky Smith returned Cliff Parsley's free punt 19 yards in their 29-21 win over Houston on 11-28-82
Irving Fryar returned Rohn Stark's free punt 18 yards in their 50-17 rout of the Colts on 11-18-84
Irving Fryar returned Joe Prokop's free punt 24 yards in their 26-20 win over Green Bay on 09-08-85
Irving Fryar returned Frank Garcia's free punt 16 yards in their 32-14 win over Tampa on 10-27-85
Irving Fryar returned John Kidd's free punt 16 yards in their 22-19 victory over Buffalo on 11-23-86
Dave Meggett returned Chris Mohr's free punt 16 yards in their 28-25 win over Buffalo on 10-27-96
Dave Meggett returned John Hall's free punt 21 yards in their 24-19 loss to the Jets on 10-19-97
Bethel Johnson had a fair catch of Matt Turk's free punt in their 12-0 shutout of Miami on 12-07-03
Troy Brown returned Hunter Smith's free punt 16 yards in their 24-14 **Championship** win on 01-18-04
Kevin Faulk returned Brian Moorman's free punt 23 yards in their 19-17 win over Buffalo on 09-10-06
Julian Edelman returned Britton Colquitt's free punt 9 yards in their 33-13 win over the Browns on 10-09-16
Julian Edelman returned Kevin Huber's free punt 16 yards in their 35-167 win over the Bengals on 10-16-16
Julian Edelman returned Sam Koch's free punt 19 yards in their 30-23 win over the Ravens on 12-12-16
Danny Amendola returned Drew Kaser's free punt 16 yards in 21-13 win over the LA Chargers on 10-29-17
Patrick Chung returned the free punt by Lac Edwards 4 yards in their 26-6 win over the Jets on 12-31-17

Only Patriots Player Who Caught a Free Kick (Following a Fair Catch on a Kickoff) in a Game

Roland James caught Raul Allegre's 61 yard free kick in their 50-17 rout of the Colts on 11-18-84

Mike "Super Foot" Walker

In the spring of 1971, "The Sports Huddle" radio show wanted to help the Patriots find a kicker to replace Gino Cappelletti, who was nearing the end of his career. They held a "Super Foot" kicking contest in the United Kingdom. After eight weeks of tryouts throughout Scotland and England, it was narrowed down to twelve men who kicked three field goals from various distances at Upper Hyeford, a Royal Air Force Base in Oxfordshire, England. In the end, Mike Walker, a 21 year old bricklayer and English soccer player, who made 2-of-3 field goal attempts from 55 yards, emerged as the winner. Even though he did not make the final Patriots roster in 1971, he was invited back in 1972 and was the Patriots kicker to start the 1972 season. Walker played in just eight games for the Patriots in 1972 because he injured his thigh, ending his kicking career.

Uniform #s of Defensive Backs

#21   Bob Suci, Jay Cunningham, Tom Janik, Joe Blahak, Sindey Brown, Erroll Tucker, Mickey Washington, Reyna Thompson, Ricky Reynolds, Steve Israel, Randall Gay, Deltha O'Neal, Ras-I Dowling, Malcolm Butler and Duron Harmon

#22   Phil Clark, Sandy Durko, Dick Conn, Keith Lee, Eugene Profit, Ricky Atkinson, Eric Coleman, Rod Smith, Terrance Shaw, Terrell Buckley, Asante Samuel, Terrence Wheatley and Justin Coleman

#23   Ron Hall, Daryl Johnson, George Hoey, Kevin Donnalley, Rod McSwain, Rod Smith, Terry Ray, Terry Billups, Antwan Harris, Omare Lowe, Duane Starks, Willie Andrews, Jason Webster, Shawn Mayer, Leigh Bodden, Nate Jones, Marquis Cole and Patrick Chung

#24   Mel West, Dick Felt, Bob Howard, Ty Law, Michael Stone, Mel Mitchell, Jonathan Wilhite, Kyle Arrington, Darrelle Revis, Rashaan Melvin, Bradley Fletcher, Cyrus Jones and Stephon Gilmore

#25   Ross O'Hanley, John Charles, Rickie Harris, John Sanders, Rick Sanford, Vencie Glenn, Tony Zackery, Darren Anderson, Larry Whigham, Leonard Myers, Arturo Freeman, Artrell Hawkins, Patrick Chung, Kyle Arrington, Tarell Brown and Eric Rowe

#26   Walter Beach, Clarence Scott, Raymond Clayborn, David Key, David Wilson, Jerome Henderson, Chris Canty, Matt Stevens, Eugene Wilson, Phillip Adams, Derrick Martin and Logan Ryan

#27   Willie Porter, Randy Beverly, Ron Bolton, Doug Beaudoin, Ricky Smith, Howard Feggins, Junior Robinson, David Pool, Darryl Wren, Mike McGruder, Terrell Buckley, Victor Green, Ellis Hobbs, Kyle Arrington, Antwan Molden, Tavon Wilson and J.C. Jackson

#28   Dave Cloutier, Art McMahon, Dave Mason, Bill Currier, Jim Bowman, David Hendley, Dion Lambert, Antwain Spann, Darius Butler and Steve Gregory

#29   Honor Jackson, Greg Boyd, Durwood Keeton, Willie Germany, Darrell Fullington, Myron Guyton, Hakim Akbar, Chris Hayes, Aric Morris, Earthwind Moreland, Guss Scott, Chidi Iwuoma, Eddie Jackson, Lewis Sanders, Tony Carter, Shawn Springs, Sterling Moore and Johnson Bademosi

#30   Tom Hennessy, Corwin Brown, Je'Rod Cherry, Chad Scott, Brandon McGowan, Josh Barrett, Duron Harmon and Jason McCourty

#31   Clyde Washington, Fred Marion, Jon Sawyer, Jimmy Hitchcock, Kato Serwanga, Ben Kelly, Hank Poteat, Antwain Spann, Brandon Meriweather, Sergio Brown, Aqib Talib, Dewey McDonald and Jonathan Jones

#32   Willie Clay, Hank Poteat, Rashad Baker and Devin McCourty

#33   Fred Bruney and Joejuan Williams

#34   Bobby Towns, Chuck Shonta, Prentice McCray, Tebucky Jones, Chris Atkins and Leonard Johnson

#35   Mike Richardson, Ross Ventrone and Keion Crossen

#36   Brian Hutson, Jerome Henderson, Lawyer Milloy, James Sanders, Kanorris Davis and Brandon King

#37   Willie Osley, Maurice Hurst, Jimmy Hitchcock, Rodney Harrison, Alfonzo Denard and Jordan Richards

#38   Ellis Johnson, Don Martin, Roland James, Perry Williams, Adrian White, Steve Lofton, Antonio Langham, Tyrone Poole, Ray Mickens, Sergio Brown and Bret Lockett

#39   Perry Pruett, Shawn Mayer and Brandon Browner

#40   Chuck Shonta, Larry Garron, Dave McCurry, Mike Haynes, Tim Hauck, Harry Colon and Carlos Yancy

#41   Walter Beach, Leroy Mitchell, Larry Carwell, Ken Pope, Darryl Holmes, Tim Gordon, Eddie Cade, Tony George, Raymond Ventrone, Cyrus Jones, Malcolm Williams and Justin Green

#42   Bob Soltis, Don Webb, Ronnie Lippett, Ron Shegog, Harlon Barnett, Chris Carter and Dexter Reid

#43   Jay Cunningham, Irvin Mallory, Ernest Gibson, Duffy Cobbs, Rodney Rice, Vernon Lewis, James Ihedigbo and Nate Ebner

#44   White Graves, John Outlaw and Jarrad Page

#45   Tom Stephens, Jack Mildren, Joe Peterson and Otis Smith

#46   Leroy Phelps, Bob Soltis, Al Romine, Paul Gipson and Mark Washington

#47   Billy Johnson, Jim Massey, Darrell Wilson, Paul Dombrowski and Roger Brown

#48   Don Webb, Tim Fox and Randy Robbins

#49   Ralph Anderson

#51   Don Davis

Uniform #s of Linebackers

#44   Jonathan Freeny

#47   Rob Holmberg

#48   Tully Banta-Cain

#49   Dick Blanchard, Eric Alexander and Vince Redd

#50   Jim Cheyunski, Edgar Chandler, Sam Hunt, Larry McGrew, Ilia Jarostchuk, Steve DeOssie,
       Bobby Abrams, Rob Holmberg, Mike Vrabel, Rob Ninkovich, Nicholas Grisby and Chase Winovich

#51   Frank Robotti, Don McKinnon, Jim Fraser, Mike Ballou, Randy Edmunds, Ron Acks,
       Kent Carter, Maury Damkroger, Donnie Thomas, Bob Golic, Brian Ingram, Mel Black,
       Bruce Scholtz, Eugene Lockhart, David White, Bernard Russ, Olrick Johnson, Bryan Cox,
       Don Davis, Jerod Mayo, Barkevious Mingo, Trevor Reilly and John Simon

#52   Phil Bennett, Ed Meixler, Ed Philpott, Ron Kadziel, Steve King, Johnny Rembert, Jerry McCabe,
       David Bavarro, Ted Johnson, Monty Beisel, Eric Alexander, Dane Fletcher, Akeem Ayers,
       Jonathan Casillas, Eric Martin and Elandon Roberts

#53   Tom Addison, Freed Whittingham, Dennis Coleman, John Tanner, Jim Romaniszyn, Merv Krakau,
       Bill Mathews, Clayton Weishuhn, Randy Sealby, Tom Benson, Richard Tarditts, Chris Slade,
       Larry Izzo, Jeff Tarpinian, Ja'Gared Davis, Eric Martin, Darius Fleming and Kyle Van Noy

#54   Bill Brown, Mike Dukes, Ed Koontz, Marty Schottenheimer, Gail Clark, Steve Zabel,
       John Zamberlin, John Gillen, Ed Williams, Greg Moore, Todd Collins, Alcides Catanho,
       Tedy Bruschi and Dont'a Hightower

#55   Lonnie Farmer, J.R. Williamson, Ralph Cindrich, Will Foster, Kevin Reilly, Ray Costict,
       Don Blackmon, Joe McHale, Chris Singleton, Willie McGinest, Junior Seau, Derrick Burgess,
       Brandon Spikes, Deontae Skinner, Jonathan Freeny, Cassius Marsh and Eric Lee

#56   Rod Shoate and Andre Tippett

#57   John Bramlett, Steve Kiner and Steve Nelson

#58   Doug Satcher, Terrence Cooks, Richard Harvey, Rob McGovern, Marty Moore, Matt Chatham,
       Pierre Woods, Tracy White, Steve Beauharnais, Darius Fleming, Jonathan Bostic and Shea McClellin

#59   Brian Stenger, Bob Geddes, Pete Barnes, Mike Hawkins, Tim Golden, Steve Doig, Randy Sealby,
       Vincent Brown, Todd Collins, Andy Katzenmoyer, O.J. Brigance, Roosevelt Colvin, Gary Guyton,
       Mike Rivera, Bobby Carpenter, Chris White, Rufus Johnson and Marquis Flowers

#60   Rommie Loudd

#66   Ed Weiascosky

#80   Jack Rudolph

#85   Nick Buoniconti

#90   George Webster, Marty Moore and Niko Koutouvides

#91   Rogers Alexander, Eric Napolski, Orlando Lowry, Jeff Kopp and Jamie Collins

#92   Geneo Grissom and James Harrison

#93   Tim Jordan, Monty Brown, Shawn Stuckey, Antico Dalton and Marques Murrell

#94   Mel Black and David Ward

#95   Ed Reynolds, Frank Sacco, Dwayne Sabb, Roman Phifer, Tully Banta-Cain, Roosevelt Colvin,
       and Shawn Crable

#96   Adalius Thomas

#99   David Howard, Jason Carthen, Steve DeOssie and Vernon Crawford

CHAPTER 5

MEMORABLE SPECIAL TEAM PLAYERS AND PLAYS

Alphabetical List of Every Long Snapper of the Patriots

Danny Aiken was the long snapper for Zoltan Mesko, Ryan Allen and Stephen Gostkowski

Mike Bartrum was the long snapper for Tom Tupa

Pete Brock was the long snapper for Rich Camarillo, Luke Prestridge, Mike Hubach, Ken Hartley, John Smith, Fred Steinfort, and Tony Franklin

Joe Cardona was the long snapper for Stephen Gostkowski, Mike Nugent, Kai Forbath, Nick Folk, Ryan Allen and Jake Bailey

Freddie Childress was the long snapper for Charlie Baumann on 11-10-91

Marv Cook was the long snapper for Shawn McCarthy and Mike Saxon from 1992-93

Jeff Dellenbach was the long snapper for Tom Tupa and Adam Vinatieri

Steve DeOssie was the long snapper for Matt Bahr and Pat O'Neill

Chris Gannon was the long snapper for Shawn McCarthy, Mike Saxon and Scott Sisson

Tim Goad was the long snapper for Charlie Baumann, Jason Staurovsky and Shawn McCarthy

Jake Ingram for Steven Gostkowski, Chris Hanson, Zoltan Mesko and for Wes Welker (on 11-07-10)

Todd Jones was the long snapper for Scott Sisson for his 2 extra points on 12-05-93

Matt Katula was the long snapper for Zoltan Mesko and Shayne Graham

Brian Kinchen was the long snapper for Ken Walter and Adam Vinatieri for 5 games in 2003

Dan Koppen was the long snapper on Tom Brady's 36 yard punt on 12-27-03

Jon Morris was the LS for Gino Cappelletti, Tom Yewcic, Jim Fraser, Terry Swanson, Bob Scarpitto, Tom Janik, Charlie Gogolak, Mike Walker, Bruce Barnes, Jeff White, Dave Chapple and John Smith

Guy Morriss was the long snapper for Rich Camarillo, Alan Herline, Tony Franklin and Eric Schubert

Rob Ninkovich was the long snapper for Stephen Gostkowski and Ryan Allen on 11-30-14

Lonie Paxton was the LS for Adam Vinatieri, Stephen Gostkowski, Doug Flutie, Lee Johnson, Chris Hanson, Todd Sauerbrun, Ken Walter, Josh Miller, Matt Cassel and Brooks Barnard

Gregg Rakoczy was the long snapper for Shawn McCarthy and Charlie Baumann

Danny Villa hiked for Bryan Wagner, Shawn McCarthy, Charlie Baumann and Jason Staurovsky

Ryan Wendell was the long snapper on Tom Brady's 32 yard punt on 12-29-13

Jim Whalen was the long snapper for Gino Cappelletti, Tom Yewcic and Eddie Wilson from 1964-66

Dwight Wheeler was the long snapper for Fred Steinfort, Tony Zendejas and Rich Camarillo

Dennis Wirgowski was the long snapper for Pat Studstill and Mike Walker on 09-17-72

Uniform #s of Every Long Snapper

#46	Brian Kinchen	#66	Jefff Dellenbach and Lonie Paxton
#47	Jake Ingram	#67	Dan Koppen
#48	Matt Katula and Danny Aiken	#70	Dennis Wirgowski
#49	Joe Cardona	#71	Gregg Rakoczy
#50	Steve DeOssie and Rob Ninkovich	#72	Tim Goad
#56	Jon Morris	#74	Chris Gannon
#58	Pete Brock	#75	Guy Morriss and Danny Villa
#61	Freddie Childress	#82	Jim Whalen
#62	Dwight Wheeler and Ryan Wendell	#85	Marv Cook
#63	Todd Jones	#86	Mike Bartrum

Alphabetical List of Every Holder of the Patriots

Ryan Allen (#6) was the holder for Stephen Gostkowski from 2013-18

Jake Bailey (#7) was the holder for Stephen Gostkowski, Mike Nugent, Kai Forbath and Nick Folk

Bob Bleier (#10) was the holder for Tony Franklin on 10-18-87

Fred Bruney (#33) was the holder for Gino Cappelletti in 1960

Matt Cassel (#16) was the holder for Stephen Gostkowski

Matt Cavanaugh (#12) was the holder for John Smith, Rex Robinson and Dan Miller

Dick Conn (#22) was the holder for David Posey in 1978 and for Steve Zabel's extra point on 12-12-76

Brian Dowling (#14) was the holder for Mike Walker, Charlie Gogolak, Jeff White and Bill Bell

Tony Eason (#11) was the holder for Tony Franklin and Fred Steinfort

Tom Flick (#10) was the holder for John Smith

Neil Graff (#15) was the holder for John Smith

Steve Grogan (#14) was the holder for John Smith in 1975

Damon Huard (#19) was the holder for Adam Vinatieri

Tom Janik (#21) was the holder for Gino Cappelletti and Charlie Gogolak from 1970-71

Lee Johnson (#10) was the holder for Adam Vinatieri from 1999-2001

Zoltan Mesko (#14) was the holder for Shayne Graham, Stephen Gostkowski and Wes Welker

Josh Miller (#8) was the holder for Adam Vinatieri from 2004-06

Ross O'Hanley (#25) was the holder for Gino Cappelletti on his 22 yard FGA on 10-16-60

Babe Parilli (#15) was the holder for Gino Cappelletti from 1961-67

Mike Patrick (#2) was the holder for John Smith from 1976-78

Tom Reynolds (#21) was the holder for Charlie Gogolak in 1972

Mike Saxon (#4) was the holder for Scott Sisson on 11-07-93

Scott Secules (#10) was the holder for Scott Sisson in 1993

Tom Sherman (#14) was the holder for Gino Cappelletti in 1968

Mike Taliaferro (#17) was the holder for Gino Cappelletti in 1969

Tom Tupa (#19) was the holder for Adam Vinatieri

Ken Walter (#13) was the holder for Adam Vinatieri from 2001-03

Ken Walter (#15) was the holder for Stephen Gostkowski in 2006

Marc Wilson (#15) was the holder for Jason Staurovsky and Greg Davis in 1989

Tom Yewcic (#14) was the holder for Gino Cappelletti in 1962

Scott Zolak (#16) was the holder for Matt Bahr from 1994-95

Long Snapper Brian Kinchen

In December of 2003, Brian Kinchen was teaching a bible class for 7th grade students at Parkview Baptist School, in Baton Rouge, when he received a phone call from the New England Patriots. Their long snappers Sean McDermott and Lonie Paxton were both injured and they needed someone to be their long snapper for the last two games of the season and the playoffs. Even though Brian was 38 years old, he had 13 years experience as a long snapper in the NFL and spent five years with the Cleveland Browns, when Bill Belichick was their head coach. He had also worked with Patriots Holder Ken Walter in Carolina. It had been three years since Brian had played in the NFL, but he was encouraged when one of his students exclaimed, "The Patriots 12-2, the best team in football and they are going to win the Super Bowl." Brian made the team and practiced like crazy, snapping footballs while in full uniform hundreds of times into a pillow in his hotel room. As much as he practiced, he still made a few bad snaps in some of the Patriots Playoff Games. To make matters even more tense, he cut his thumb with a steak knife, requiring three stiches, at the Patriots Pre-Game Dinner the night before the Super Bowl. But when it mattered most Brian delivered a perfect snap to Ken Walter on Adam Vinatieri's game winning 41 yard field goal in their 32-29 win over the Panthers on February 1, 2004. He did his job for their 2003 World Championship Team.

<u>Every Special Team Player (Non-Kicker or Punter) Who Was the *AFC Special Team Player of the Week*</u>

Dave Meggett had a 60 yard punt return for a TD in the 4th Qtr of their 23-22 comeback win on 12-21-96
Larry Whigham tackled Punter Bryan Barker on the 4 yard line in their 20-6 **Divisional** win on 01-12-97
Chad Eaton blocked 2 field goals in their 13-10 OT win vs the Bills on 12-17-00
Larry Izzo had 5 solo special team tackles in their 41-38 OT win over the Chiefs on 09-22-02
Richard Seymour blocked a potential GW 35 yard FGA by Olinda Mare in their 19-13 OT win on 10-19-03
Bethel Johnson returned a kickoff 92 yards for a TD in their 38-34 win over the Colts on 11-03-03
Doug Flutie dropped kicked an extra point with about 6 minutes left in their 28-26 loss to Miami on 01-01-06
Laurence Maroney had a 77 yard kickoff return in their 31-7 rout of the Vikings on 10-30-06
Ellis Hobbs returned a kickoff 108 yards for a TD in their 38-14 rout of the Jets on 09-09-07
Ellis Hobbs returned a kickoff 95 yards for a TD in their 49-26 rout of the Raiders on 12-14-08
Dan Connolly had a 71 yard kickoff return in their 31-27 win over the Packers on 12-10-10
Julian Edelman returned a punt 72 yards for a TD in their 34-3 rout of the Chiefs on 11-21-11
Devin McCourty returned a kickoff 104 yards for a TD in their 29-26 OT win over the Jets on 10-21-12
Chris Jones blocked a potential game winning field goal attempt in their 27-25 win over the Jets on 10-16-14
Julian Edelman returned a punt 84 yards for a TD in their 43-21 rout of the Broncos on 11-02-14
Dion Lewis returned a kickoff 103 yards for a TD in their 41-16 rout of the Broncos on 11-12-17
Dont'a Hightower blocked a punt that was returned for a TD by Kyle Van Noy in their 38-31 win on 10-21-18
Matthew Slater blocked a punt that was recovered by Nate Ebner in their 13-9 win vs Dallas on 11-24-19

KICKING

<u>Every Patriots Kicker who was named the *AFC Special Team Player of the Week*</u>

Matt Bahr kicked a 55 yard field goal to end the 1st half in their 34-17 win over the Dolphins on 11-12-95
Adam Vinatieri kicked 5 FG's, including a 40 yarder, to beat the Jaguars 28-25 in Overtime on 09-22-96
Adam Vinatieri kicked 4 field goals, including 1 from 52 yards, in their 33-6 win over Buffalo on 10-12-97
Adam Vinatieri kicked 3 FG's, including a game winning 27 yard FG to beat the Saints 30-27 on 10-04-98
Adam Vinatieri kicked 4 field goals to help defeat the Dolphins 26-23 on 11-23-98
Adam Vinatieri kicked a 25 yard FG to tie the game & a 23 yard FG to beat the Bills 12-9 in OT on 12-16-01
Adam Vinatieri kicked 4 FG's; a 43 yard FG with 1:14 left, and the GW 35 yard FG in OT on 12-29-02
Adam Vinatieri kicked 4 FG's and tossed a 4th down 4 yd TD pass to Troy Brown in 40-22 win on 11-07-04
Adam Vinatieri kicked 2 FG's, including a 43 yard FG, on 3rd down, with 5 seconds left, on 09-25-05
Stephen Gostkowski kicked 4 FG's in their 27-17 win over the Dolphins on 11-08-09
Stephen Gostkowski kicked 3 FG's in their 30-23 victory over the Jets on 10-25-15
Stephen Gostkowski kicked 2 FG's, including one from 54 yds on the last play, in their 27-26 win on 11-15-15
Stephen Gostkowski kicked 3 FG's in their 23-21 win over the Arizona Cardinals on 09-11-16
Stephen Gostkowski kicked 4 FG's in their 26-10 win over the Los Angeles Rams on 12-04-16
Stephen Gostkowski kicked 4 FG's, including a career long 62 yard field goal, in their 33-8 win on 11-19-17

<u>Everyone Who Has Kicked a PAT to Tie the Game and Force the Overtime Period</u>

John Smith kicked a PAT with 29 seconds left in their 27-21 OT loss to Pittsburgh on 09-27-81
Tony Franklin kicked a PAT with 65 ticks left in their 34-31 OT loss to the Eagles on 11-29-87
Jason Staurovsky kicked a PAT to tie the game in the 10-7 OT win vs the Buccaneers on 12-11-88
Charlie Baumann kicked a PAT with 7 ticks left in their 23-17 OT win vs the Colts on 12-08-91
Scott Sisson kicked a PAT with 12 seconds left to tie the game in their 19-16 OT loss to the Lions on 09-12-93
Matt Bahr kicked a PAT with 52 seconds left in their 20-17 OT loss to Carolina on 10-29-95
Adam Vinatieri kicked a PAT in the 4th Qtr to tie the game in their 13-10 OT win vs the Bills on 12-17-00

Everyone Who Has Kicked the Game Winning Extra Point in a Regular Season Game

Mike Walker kicked the extra point to defeat the Atlanta Falcons 21-20 on 09-24-72
Charlie Gogolak kicked the extra point to defeat the Redskins 24-23 on 10-01-72
Tony Franklin kicked the extra point to defeat the Browns 17-16 on 10-07-84
Tony Franklin kicked the extra point to defeat the Saints 21-20 on 11-30-86
Jason Staurovsky kicked the extra point to defeat the Jets 14-13 on 11-13-88
Adam Vinatieri kicked the extra point to defeat the Broncos 24-23 on 10-24-99

Only Patriot Who Has Kicked the Game Winning FG on the Next to Last Play of a Playoff Game

Adam Vinatieri kicked a 41 yard FG, with 4 tics left, to defeat Carolina 32-29 in **Super Bowl** on 02-01-04

Everyone Who Has Kicked a Game Winning Field Goal on the Last Play of a Game

Gino Cappelletti kicked a 41 yard field goal to defeat the Houston Oilers 25-24 on 11-06-64
Matt Bahr kicked a 33 yard field goal to defeat the Packers 17-16 on 10-02-94
Adam Vinatieri kicked a 27 yard field goal to defeat the Saints 30-27 on 10-04-98
Adam Vinatieri kicked a 35 yard field goal to defeat the 49ers 24-21 on 12-20-98
Adam Vinatieri kicked a 48 yard FG to defeat the St. Louis Rams 20-17 in **Super Bowl** on 02-03-02
Stephen Gostkowski booted a 35 yard field goal to defeat the Bills 23-21 on 09-08-13
Stephen Gostkowski kicked a 54 yard field goal to defeat the Giants 27-26 on 11-15-15

Everyone Who Has Kicked the Overtime Game Winning Field Goal

Jason Staurovsky kicked a 27 yard field goal to defeat the Buccaneers 10-7 on 12-11-88
Greg Davis kicked a 51 yard field goal to defeat the Indianapolis Colts 23-20 on 10-29-89
Jason Staurovsky kicked a 42 yard field goal to defeat the Vikings 26-23 on 10-20-91
Charlie Baumann kicked an 18 yard FG to defeat the Indianapolis Colts 37-34 on 11-15-92
Adam Vinatieri kicked a 40 yard field goal to defeat the Jaguars 28-25 on 09-22-96
Adam Vinatieri booted a 34 yard field goal to defeat the Jets 27-24 on 09-14-97
Adam Vinatieri kicked a 22 yard field goal to defeat the Bengals 16-13 on 11-19-00
Adam Vinatieri kicked a 24 yard field goal to defeat the Bills 13-10 on 12-17-00
Adam Vinatieri kicked a 44 yard field goal to defeat the San Diego Chargers 29-26 on 10-14-01
Adam Vinatieri kicked a 23 yard field goal to defeat the Bills 12-9 on 12-16-01
Adam Vinatieri kicked a 23 yard FG to defeat the Raiders 16-13 in OT in **Divisional** win on 01-19-02
Adam Vinatieri kicked a 35 yard field goal to defeat the Chiefs 41-38 on 09-22-02
Adam Vinatieri booted a 35 yard field goal to defeat the Dolphins 27-24 on 12-29-02
Adam Vinatieri kicked a 28 yard field goal to defeat the Houston Texans 23-20 on 11-23-03
Stephen Gostkowski booted a 35 yard field goal to defeat the Baltimore Ravens 23-20 on 10-17-10
Stephen Gostkowski kicked a 48 yard field goal to defeat the Jets 29-26 on 10-21-12
Stephen Gostkowski kicked a 31 yd FG to beat Denver 34-31 in their biggest comeback on 11-24-13

Everyone Who Has Kicked a Field Goal on His Birthday

Tony Franklin kicked a 28 yard & a 40 yard FG on his 28th birthday in the 50-17 rout of Colts on 11-18-84
Greg Davis kicked 3 FG's (47 yds, 48 yds and an OT GW 51 yard FG) on his 34th birthday on 10-29-89
Adam Vinatieri kicked a 22 yard FG, on his 25th birthday, in their 17-3 **Wild Card** win vs Miami on 12-28-97

Everyone Who Has Kicked an Extra Point on His Birthday

Tony Franklin kicked 6 extra points on his 28th birthday in their 50-17 rout of the Colts on 11-18-84
Greg Davis kicked 2 extra points on his 34th birthday in their 23-20 OT win vs the Colts on 10-29-89
Adam Vinatieri kicked 2 extra points on his 25th birthday in their 17-3 **Wild Card** win vs Miami on 12-28-97

Only Player Who Has Kicked Four FGs and Completed a TD Pass in the Same Game

Adam Vinatieri kicked 4 field goals, 4 extra points and tossed a 4 yard TD pass to Troy Brown on 11-07-04

Only Player Who Has Kicked a FG and Completed a 2 Point Pass in the Same Game

Gino Cappelletti kicked 2 field goals and threw a 2 point pass to Jim Crawford on 10-08-60

Only Patriot Who Has Kicked Three FGs, Thrown a TD Pass and Caught a TD Pass in the Same Game

Gino Cappelletti kicked 3 FGs + 3 PATs, threw a 27 yard TD pass and caught a 32 yard TD on 10-01-61

Only Player Who Has Kicked a FG and Run for a 2 Point Conversion in the Same Game for the Patriots

Adam Vinatieri kicked a 44 yard field goal & ran for a 2 point conversion in the game played on 11-29-98

Only Patriot Who Has Kicked a FG That Deflected Off the Camera Positioned Inside the Goal Post

Adam Vinatieri's 52 yard FG hit the camera inside the goal post in their 29-6 win over the Colts on 09-13-98

Only Patriot Who Has Kicked a FG for the Only Points Scored in the Game

John Smith kicked a 23 yard field goal to beat the Dolphins 3-0 at Schaefer Stadium on 12-12-82

Only Patriot Who Kicked Four PATs, Caught Three TD Passes and Ran for a 2 Point Play in the Same Game

Gino Cappelletti scored 24 points in their 36-28 win over the 1964 AFL Champion Bills on 11-15-64

Only Patriots Kicker Who Has Recovered a Fumble on a Kickoff Return

Stephen Gostkowski recovered Leodis McKelvin's kickoff return fumble in their 25-24 win on 09-14-09

Every Patriots Onside Kick That Has Been Recovered by the Patriots

Gino Cappelletti's onside kick was recovered by Jim Lee Hunt in their 26-10 *victory* over the Jets on 09-27-64
Justin Canale's onside kick was recovered by Billy Johnson in their 29-24 loss to the Jets on 11-19-67
Gino Cappelletti's onside kick was recovered by Carl Garrett in their 38-23 loss to the Raiders on 09-28-69
Charlie Gogolak's onside kick was recovered by Clarence Scott in their 35-14 loss to Minnesota on 12-13-70
Charlie Gogolak's onside kick was recovered by Clarence Scott in their 24-17 loss to Baltimore on 11-06-72
Jeff White's onside kick was recovered by Claxton Welch in their 33-13 loss to the Jets on 11-11-73
John Smith's onside kick was recovered by Don Westbrook in their 34-27 loss to the Colts on 09-18-78
Mike Hubach's onside kick was recovered by Mosi Tatupu in their 38-34 loss to the Oilers on 11-10-80
Jason Staurovsky's onside kick was recovered by Hart Lee Dykes in their 28-24 loss to the Saints on 11-12-89
Scott Sisson's onside kick was recovered by Darryl Wren in their 29-14 loss to the Houston Oilers on 10-17-93
Matt Bahr's onside kick was recovered by Corwin Brown in their 20-13 **Wild Card** loss on 01-01-95
Stephen Gostkowski's onside kick was recovered by Kyle Arrington in their 27-26 *comeback win* on 12-08-13
Stephen Gostkowski's onside kick was recovered by Jonathan Freeny in their 27-10 win vs Wash on 11-08-15
Stephen Gostkowski's onside kick was recovered by Rashaan Melvin in their 35-28 loss to Philly on 12-06-15

Other Players Who Have Attempted an Onside Kick for the Patriots

Fred Bruney attempted an onside kick in their 28-24 last second win over the NY Titans on 09-17-60
Nate Ebner attempted an onside kick in their 35-28 loss to the Eagles on 12-06-15

Positional Players Who Have Kicked Off for the Patriots

Center Bob Yates kicked off in 55 regular season games in a 2 playoff games over the 1960-65 seasons
Guard Justin Canale kicked off in 54 games for the Boston Patriots over the 1965-68 seasons
Defensive End Dennis Wirgowski kicked off for the Boston Patriots in 2 games (on 09-27-70 and 10-04-70)
Wide Receiver Wes Welker had a 45 yard kickoff in their 34-14 loss to the Browns on 11-07-10

Only Patriots Linebacker Who Has Kicked an Extra Point in a Game

Linebacker Steve Zabel kicked an extra point in their 31-14 win over Tampa on 12-12-76

Only Patriots Wide Receiver Who Has Kicked an Extra Point in a Game

WR Wes Welker kicked an extra point in their 34-14 loss to the Browns on 11-07-10

Uniform #s of Every Kicker

#1	John Smith, Eric Schubert and Tony Franklin
#2	Jeff White, Joaquin Zendejas, Doug Flutie, Mike Nugent and Kai Forbath, Nick Folk
#3	Matt Bahr and Stephen Gostkowski
#4	Jason Staurovsky and Adam Vinatieri
#5	Shayne Graham, Pat O'Neill, Fred Steinfort and Greg Davis
#6	Danny Miller and Mike Hubach
#7	Nick Lowery, Rex Robinson, Teddy Garcia and Charlie Gogolak and Jake Bailey
#8	Charlie Baumann and Bill Bell
#9	David Posey and Scott Sisson
#20	Gino Cappelletti
#33	Fred Bruney
#43	Nate Ebner
#50	Bob Yates
#54	Steve Zabel
#63	Justin Canale
#70	Dennis Wirgowski
#83	Wes Welker

Every Patriots Punter Who Was Named the *AFC Special Team Player of the Week*

Mike Saxon had 3 punts downed inside the 20 in their 23-21 win vs Phoenix on 10-10-93
Pat O'Neill had a 67 yard punt and 3 punts for 143 yards in their 41-17 rout of the Bills on 12-18-94
Tom Tupa had a 62 yard punt and 4 punts for 201 yards in their 28-25 win over the Bills on 10-27-96
Ken Walter had 2 punts inside the 20 yard line in their 20-13 win over the Dolphins on 12-22-01
Chris Hanson had 3 punts for 135 yards in very windy conditions in their 13-0 shutout of Buffalo on 12-28-08
Ryan Allen had 5 punts for 260 yards in their 23-14 win over the San Diego Chargers on 12-07-14
Ryan Allen had 7 punts for 333 yards in their 27-0 shutout of the Houston Texans on 09-22-16
Jake Bailey had 7 punts for 310 yards and 5 inside the 20 yard line in their 30-14 win over the Jets on 09-22-19
Jake Bailey had 8 punts for 381 yards, and 3 inside the 10, in their 17-10 win over the Eagles on 11-17-19

Alphabetical Listing of the Career Longest Punt by Every Patriots Punter

Ryan Allen had two 67 yard punts (in their win on 11-02-14 and in their win on 09-10-15)

Matt Bahr pooched a punt 29 yards in their 27-14 victory over the Bills on 10-23-95

Jake Bailey had two 65 yard punts (in their win on 11-24-19 and in their win on 12-15-19)

Brooks Barnard punted the football 49 yards in their 12-0 shutout of the Dolphins on 12-07-03

Bruce Barnes punted the football 53 yards in their 13-10 victory over the Bears on 10-21-73

Tom Brady had a 48 yard punt in their 45-10 **Divisional** rout of the Broncos on 01-14-12

Rich Camarillo punted the football 76 yards in their 31-7 loss to the Jets on 09-19-82

Matt Cassel had a 57 yard punt, on 3rd down, in their 13-0 shutout of the Bills on 12-28-08

Dave Chapple punted the football 57 yards in their 34-27 loss to the Dolphins on 12-15-74

Jeff Feagles punted the football 74 yards in their 21-17 win over the Colts on 10-02-88

Jim Fraser punted the football 68 yards in their 24-10 victory over the Broncos on 09-18-66

Tom Greene had two 66 yard punts (in their loss on 10-16-60 and in their loss on 10-28-60)

Brian Hansen had a 69 yard punt in their 37-13 loss to the Jets on 09-30-90

Chris Hanson had a 70 yard punt in their 17-10 win over the Chiefs on 09-07-08

Eddie Hare punted the football 58 yards in their 16-13 Overtime loss to the Steelers on 09-03-79

Ken Hartley punted the football 41 yards in their 28-24 loss to the Jets on 10-11-81

Alan Herline had a 50 yard punt in their 14-7 victory over the Bills on 10-11-87

Mike Hubach punted the football 69 yards in their 34-0 shutout of the Dolphins on 10-12-80

Tom Janik punted the football 58 yards in their 24-21 loss to the Cowboys on 10-24-71

Lee Johnson had a 76 yard punt in their 23-17 loss to the Bengals on 09-09-01

Shawn McCarthy punted the football 93 yards in their 22-17 loss to the Bills on 11-03-91

Zoltan Mesko had two 65 yard punts (in their loss on 10-17-10 and in their win on 12-24-11)

Josh Miller punted the football 69 yards in their 35-28 victory over the Bengals on 12-12-04

Pat O'Neill had 67 yard punt in their 41-17 victory over the Bills on 12-18-94

Babe Parilli punted the football 45 yards in their 24-14 loss to the Bills on 12-20-64

Mike Patrick had a 64 yard punt in their 30-24 loss to the Baltimore Colts on 12-18-77

Luke Prestridge punted the football 89 yards in their 44-24 loss to the Dolphins on 10-21-84

Todd Sauerbrun had a 58 yard punt in their 40-23 win over Tennessee on 12-31-06

Mike Saxon punted the football 59 yards in their 17-13 loss to the Dolphins on 11-21-93

Bob Scarpitto punted the football 87 yards in their 20-17 victory over the Broncos on 09-29-68

Pat Studstill had a 57 yard punt in their 21-20 win over the Atlanta Falcons on 09-24-72

Terry Swanson punted the football 62 yards in their 23-0 shutout of the Bills on 09-24-67

Tom Tupa punted the football 73 yards in their 34-13 loss to the Broncos on 10-06-97

Adam Vinatieri pooched a punt 33 yards in their 27-16 victory over the Browns on 12-09-01

Bryan Wagner had 57 yard punt in their 10-7 loss to the Indianapolis Colts on 12-23-95

Ken Walter had a 58 yard punt in their 21-11 victory over the Bills on 11-11-01

Clyde Washington had a 48 yard punt in their 24-10 loss to the Houston Oilers on 11-25-60

Jeff White punted the football 51 yards in their 30-14 loss to the Dolphins on 10-28-73

Eddie Wilson had a 49 yard punt in their 13-13 Tie with the San Diego Chargers on 10-17-65

Jerrel Wilson punted the football 57 yards in their 17-10 loss to the Cowboys on 12-03-78

Tom Yewcic punted the football 70 yards in their 27-23 win over the Jets on 11-28-65

Only Time That a Patriots Penalty on a Punt Resulted in a TD for the Patriots

Al Crow's 46 yard punt, on 4th and 9 from his own 4 yard line, was returned 38 yards by Ron Burton, but was nullified by an offside penalty on the Patriots. The Raiders accepted the penalty and on the next play Al's punt from the end zone hit the goal line cross bar and deflected back into the end zone (the goal posts were located on the goal line until 1974). Patriots Defensive End LeRoy Moore fell on the loose ball in the end zone for a TD and were the last points scored in the Patriots 20-17 win vs Oakland on 11-17-61.

Every Patriots Punter Who Had the Longest Punt in the NFL During the Season

Rich Camarillo had the longest punt in the NFL of 75 yards in their 27-17 loss to the Raiders on 11-01-81
Rich Camarillo had the longest punt in the NFL of 70 yards in their 7-0 shutout of the Saints on 12-04-83
Luke Prestridge had the longest punt in the NFL of 89 yards in their 44-24 loss to Miami on 10-21-84
Rich Camarillo had the longest punt in the NFL of 75 yards in their 20-7 loss to the Bears on 09-15-85
Jeff Feagles had the longest punt in the NFL of 74 yards in their 21-17 win over the Colts on 10-02-88
Shawn McCarthy had the longest punt in the NFL of 93 yards in their 22-17 loss to Buffalo on 11-03-91

Progression of the Longest Punt by a Patriots Punter in a Regular Season Game

44 yard punt by Tom Greene in their 13-10 loss to the Broncos on 09-09-60
50 yard punt by Tom Greene in their 13-10 loss to the Broncos on 09-09-60
66 yard punt by Tom Greene in their 27-14 loss to the Oakland Raiders on 10-16-60
66 yard punt by Tom Greene in their 45-16 loss to the Los Angeles Chargers on 10-28-60
70 yard punt by Tom Yewcic in their 27-23 victory over the Jets on 11-28-65
87 yard punt by Bob Scarpitto in their 20-17 victory over the Broncos on 09-29-68
89 yard punt by Luke Prestridge in their 44-24 loss to the Dolphins on 10-21-84
93 yard punt by Shawn McCarthy in their 22-17 loss to the Bills on 11-03-91

Progression of the Longest Punt by a Patriots Punter in a Playoff Game

20 yard punt by Tom Yewcic in their 26-8 AFL **Divisional** victory over the Bills on 12-28-63
46 yard punt by Tom Yewcic in their 26-8 AFL **Divisional** victory over the Bills on 12-28-63
68 yard punt by Tom Yewcic in their 51-10 AFL Championship loss to the San Diego on 01-05-64

Chronological List of Every Patriots Punter Who Has Punted the Football at Least 70 Yards

Tom Yewcic punted it 70 yards, to the 10 yard line, in their 27-23 win over the Jets on 11-28-65
Bob Scarpitto punted it 87 yards, to the 3 yard line, in their 20-17 win over the Broncos on 09-29-68
Rich Camarillo punted it 75 yards, to the 5 yard line, in their 27-17 loss to the Raiders on 11-01-81
Rich Camarillo punted it 72 yards, for a touchback, in their 20-17 loss to the Bills on 11-22-81
Rich Camarillo punted it 76 yards, for a touchback, in their 31-7 loss to the Jets on 09-19-82
Rich Camarillo punted it 70 yards, to the 8 yard line, in their 7-0 shutout of the Saints on 12-04-83
Luke Prestridge punted it 89 yards, for a touchback, in their 44-24 loss to the Dolphins on 10-21-84
Luke Prestridge punted it 82 yards, to the 1 yard line, in their 30-20 victory over the Jets on 10-28-84
Rich Camarillo punted it 75 yards, for a touchback, in their 20-7 loss to the Bears on 09-15-85
Rich Camarillo punted it 74 yards, to the 8 yard line, in their 16-13 Overtime loss to the Jets on 11-24-85
Rich Camarillo punted it 73 yards, for a touchback, in their 28-21 win over the Dolphins on 09-13-87
Jeff Feagles punted it 74 yards, for a touchback, in their 21-17 victory over the Indianapolis Colts on 10-02-88
Shawn McCarthy punted it 93 yards, to the 1 yard line, in their 22-17 loss to the Bills on 11-03-91
Tom Tupa punted it 73 yards, to the 3 yard line, in their 34-13 loss to the Broncos on 10-06-97
Lee Johnson punted it 76 yards, for a touchback, in their 23-17 loss to the Bengals on 09-09-01
Chris Hanson punted it 70 yards, to the 9 yard line, in their 17-10 win over the Chiefs on 09-07-08

Every Free Kick After a Safety by a Patriots Punter in a Playoff Game

Rich Camarillo booted a 56 yard free kick after a Bears safety in their 46-10 **Super Bowl** loss on 01-26-86
Rich Camarillo booted an 11 yard onside free kick after a Denver safety in 22-17 **Divisional** loss on 01-04-87
Zoltan Mesko booted a 62 yard free kick after a Giants safety in their 21-17 **Super Bowl** loss on 02-05-12
Ryan Allen booted a 68 yard free kick after a Colts safety in their 43-22 **Divisional** win on 01-11-14

Two Most Recent Times a Punt by a Patriots Punter Helped Set Up a 2 Point Safety by the Patriots

Tom Tupa's 51 yard punt was downed on the 1 yard line in their 28-25 win over the Bills on 10-27-96
Tom Brady's 36 yard punt was downed on the 1 yard line in their 12-0 shutout of Miami on 12-07-03

Shortest Punt by a Patriots Punter (it was not blocked or deflected)

Jeff White's punt of negative 7 yards was recovered by the Patriots on Miami's 3 yard line on 10-28-73

Chronological List of Players Who Have Downed a Patriots Punt on the 1 Yard Line

Paul Dombroski downed Luke Prestridge's 82 yard punt, on 1 yd line, in 30-20 win vs the Jets on 10-28-84
Tony Zackery downed Shawn McCarthy's 93 yd punt, on 1 yd line, in their 22-17 loss to Buffalo on 11-03-91
Todd Rucci downed Pat O'Neill's 30 yard fake field goal punt in their 24-13 win vs the Jets on 12-04-94
Larry Whigham downed Tom Tupa's 51 yard punt on the 1 yard line in their 28-25 win vs Buffalo on 10-27-96
Lonie Paxton downed Adam Vinatieri's 33 yd punt on 1 yard line in their 27-16 win vs Cleveland on 12-09-01
David Givens downed Tom Brady's 36 yard punt on the 1 yard line in their 12-0 shutout of Miami on 12-07-03
Nicholas Grisby downed Ryan Allen's punt, tapped back by J. Jones and R. Burkhead, in 17-10 loss on 12-16-18
Jonathan Jones downed Jake Bailey's punt, tapped by Matt Slater, in their 30-14 win vs the Jets on 09-22-19

Only Patriots Punter Who Has Tackled the Son of a Former Patriots Player on a Punt Return

Rich Camarillo tackled Scott Schwedes (son of Ger Schwedes) on his 31 yard punt return on 09-13-87

Everyone Who Has Punted on 3rd Down

Matt Cassel's 57 yard punt, on 3rd + 8, was downed on 2 yard line, in their 13-0 win vs Buffalo on 12-28-08
Chris Hanson had a 41 yard punt, on 3rd + 3, in windy conditions, in their 13-0 win vs Buffalo on 12-28-08
Tom Brady's 48 yard punt, on 3rd + 10, was downed on the 10 yard line, in 45-10 **Divisional** win on 01-14-12
Tom Brady's 32 yard punt, on 3rd + 32, was caught by Jim Leonhard, in 34-20 win vs Buffalo on 12-29-13

Chronological List of Everyone Who Has Recovered or Returned a Blocked Punt for a TD

LeRoy Moore recovered an end zone punt that was deflected back into the end zone for a TD on 11-17-61
Don Webb returned a blocked punt 20 yards for a TD in their 41-0 shutout of the Chargers on 12-17-61
JD Garrett recovered a blocked punt in the end zone for a TD in their 41-32 loss to Miami on 12-17-67
Roland Moss returned a blocked punt 10 yards for a TD in their 38-33 win over Buffalo on 11-14-71
Will Foster recovered a blocked punt in the end zone for a TD in their 9-7 loss to the Jets on 10-14-73
Rick Sanford returned a blocked punt 8 yards for a TD in their 50-21 rout of the Colts on 11-18-79
Rodney McSwain returned a blocked punt 31 yards for a TD in their 30-28 win over the LA Rams on 11-16-86
Mosi Tatupu returned a blocked punt 17 yards for a TD in their 21-20 win over the Saints on 11-30-86
Willie Scott returned a blocked punt 3 yards for a TD in their 24-0 shutout of the Colts on 11-22-87
Tedy Bruschi returned a blocked punt 4 yards for a TD in their 46-38 win over the Ravens on 10-06-96
Ramon Humber returned a blocked punt 6 yards in their 34-33 loss to the Dolphins on 12-09-18
Kyle Van Noy returned a blocked punt 29 yards for a TD in their 38-31 win over the Bears on 10-21-18
Matthew Slater returned a blocked punt 11 yards for a TD in their 16-10 win over the Bills on 09-29-19
Chase Winovich returned a blocked punt 6 yards for a TD in their 35-14 win vs the Giants on 10-10-19

Uniform #s of Every Punter

#2	Pat Studstill, Jeff White and Mike Patrick
#3	Bruce Barnes, Rich Camarillo and Matt Bahr
#4	Jerrel Wilson and Adam Vinatieri
#5	Pat O'Neill
#6	Mike Hubach, Alan Herline, Jeff Feagles, Chris Hanson and Ryan Allen
#7	Ken Hartley, Mike Saxon and Jake Bailey
#8	Eddie Hare, Bryan Wagner, Brooks Barnard and Josh Miller
#9	Bryan Wagner
#10	Dave Chapple, Brian Hansen and Lee Johnson
#11	Shawn McCarthy
#12	Eddie Wilson and Tom Brady
#13	Ken Walter
#14	Tom Greene, Tom Yewcic and Zoltan Mesko
#15	Babe Parilli and Ken Walter
#16	Matt Cassel
#17	Luke Prestridge
#18	Todd Sauerbrun
#19	Tom Tupa
#21	Tom Janik
#31	Clyde Washington
#36	Terry Swanson
#46	Bob Scarpitto
#51	Jim Fraser

Only Patriots Player with Three Defensive Fumble Recoveries in a Game

Steve Nelson recovered fumbles by Wilbert Montgomery, Ron Jaworski and Keith Kreple on 10-08-78

Only Patriots Player with Two Defensive and One Special Team Fumble Recoveries in a Game

Roland James recovered fumbles by Eric Dickerson, Mike Barber and Rick Sanford on 12-11-83

Only Patriots Player with Two Defensive and One Offensive Fumble Recovery in a Game

Ricky Reynolds recovered fumbles by Carwell Gardner, Andre Reed and Larry Whigham on 12-18-94

Fumble Recoveries in a Season

5 by Bob Dee (1961)
4 by Jack Rudolph (1960)
4 by Jim Lee Hunt (1968)
4 by Tim Fox (1976)
4 by Steve Nelson (1978)
4 by Roland James (1983)
4 by Andre Tippett (1983 & 1985)
4 by Brent Williams (1986)
4 by Ronnie Lippett and Fred Marion (1990)
4 by Rob Ninkovich and Vince Wilfork (2012)

Fumble Recoveries in a Career

19 by Andre Tippett
16 by Steve Nelson
15 by Willie McGinest
14 by Ray Hamilton
14 by Rob Ninkovich

Chronological List of Everyone Who Has Blocked or Deflected a Punt for the Patriots

Abe Cohen blocked a punt by George Herring in their 31-24 loss to the Broncos on 10-23-60
Dick Klein blocked a punt by Billy Atkins in their 52-21 rout of the Bills on 10-22-61
Dick Klein blocked a punt by Jerry Burch in their 35-21 win over the Raiders on 12-09-61
Don Webb blocked a punt by Paul Maguire + took it 20 yds for a TD, in 41-0 shutout of SD on 12-17-61
Jack Rudolph blocked a punt by Curley Johnson in their 31-24 loss to the Jets on 10-05-63
Bob Dee blocked a punt by Jim Fraser in their 39-10 rout of the Broncos on 10-04-64
White Graves blocked a punt by Bob Scarpitto in their 17-10 loss to the Broncos on 11-06-66
Bobby Nichols blocked a punt by Larry Seiple (recovered for a TD) in their 41-32 loss to Miami on 12-17-67
Ezell Jones blocked a punt by Larry Seiple in their 38-23 win over the Dolphins on 11-30-69
Roland Moss blocked a punt by Spike Jones and took it 10 yards for TD, in 38-33 win vs Buffalo on 11-14-71
Willie Banks blocked a punt by Julian Fagan (recovered for a TD) in their 9-7 loss to the Jets on 10-14-73
John Sanders blocked a punt by Larry Seiple in their 22-14 loss to the Dolphins on 09-28-75
Don Westbrook partially blocked a punt by Chuck Ramsey in their 56-3 rout of the Jets on 09-09-79
Rick Sanford blocked a punt by Bucky Dilt and took it 8 yds for a TD, in their 50-21 rout of Indy on 11-18-79
Larry McGrew blocked a punt by Harry Newsome in their 34-0 shutout of the Steelers on 10-19-86
Rod McSwain blocked a punt by Dale Hatcher and took it 31 yds for a TD, in 30-28 win vs Rams on 11-16-86
Eugene Profit blocked a punt by Brian Hansen, (17 yd TD return) in their 21-20 win vs the Saints on 11-30-86
Willie Scott blocked a punt by Rohn Stark and took it 3 yds for TD, in their 24-0 shutout of Colts on 11-22-87
Eugene Profit blocked a punt by John Teltschik in their 34-31 Overtime loss to the Eagles on 11-29-87
Maurice Hurst blocked a punt by Dan Stryzinski in their 24-3 loss to the Steelers on 12-09-90
Larry Whigham deflected a 17 yard punt by Jeff Feagles in their 31-0 shutout of the Cardinals on 09-15-96
Larry Whigham blocked a punt by Greg Montgomery, (4 yd TD return) in their 46-38 win vs Balt on 10-06-96
Larry Whigham deflected a 13 yard punt by Mark Royals in their 30-27 win over the Saints on 10-04-98
Larry Whigham blocked a punt by Sean Landeta in their 24-9 loss to the Eagles on 12-19-99
Kelley Washington blocked a punt by Ben Graham in their 20-10 win over the Jets on 12-16-07
Patrick Chung blocked a punt by Brandon Fields in their 41-14 rout of the Dolphins on 10-04-10
Brandon Bolden blocked a punt by Mike Scifres in their 23-14 win over the San Diego Chargers on 12-07-14
Rex Burkhead blocked a punt by Riley Dixon in their 41-14 rout of the Broncos on 11-12-17
Patrick Chung blocked a punt by Brandon Fields in their 41-14 rout of Miami on 11-26-17
Jeremy Hill partially blocked a punt by Daniel Trevor in their 27-20 win over Houston on 09-09-18
Dont'a Hightower blocked a punt by Pat O'Donnell, (29 yd TD return) in 38-31 win vs Chicago on 10-21-18
Albert McClellan blocked a punt by Matt Haack in their 34-33 loss to the Dolphins on 12-09-18
Albert McClellan deflected a 2 yard punt by Matt Haack in their 34-33 loss to the Dolphins on 12-09-18
J.C. Jackson blocked a punt by Corey Bojorquez, (11 yard TD return) in their 16-10 win vs Buffalo on 09-29-19
Brandon Bolden blocked a punt by Riley Dixon (6 yd TD return) in their 35-14 rout of the Giants on 10-10-19
Matthew Slater blocked a punt by Chris Jones in their 13-9 win over Dallas on 11-12-19
Nate Ebner blocked a punt by Dustin Colquitt in their 23-16 loss to the Chiefs on 12-08-19

EXTRA POINTS

10 Most Memorable Plays on a Patriots Extra Point Attempt

K Gino Cappelletti tossed a 2 point pass to Jim Crawford in their 35-0 shutout of the Chargers on 10-08-60
Offensive Lineman Justin Canale kicked an extra point in their 18-7 victory over the Oilers on 11-05-67
John Smith kicked an extra point from the 39 yard line, after numerous penalties, in 17-14 win on 10-27-74
LB Steve Zabel replaced John Smith at the last second and kicked an extra point in win vs Tampa on 12-12-76
Adam Vinatieri ran for 2 points because the Bills defense was not on the field on 11-29-98
Adam Vinatieri tossed a 4 yard TD pass to Troy Brown in their 40-22 rout of the Rams on 11-07-04
Doug Flutie drop kicked an extra point in their 28-26 loss to the Dolphins on 01-01-06
WR Wes Welker kicked an extra point in their 34-14 loss to the Browns on 11-07-10
Rob Gronkowski broke his forearm while blocking on an extra point attempt in their 59-24 rout on 11-18-12
Jamie Collins jumped over long snapper Matt Overton and blocked Adam Vinatieri's PAT on 10-18-15

Chronological List of Everyone Who Has Blocked an Extra Point Attempt

Tom Addison blocked an extra point attempt by Gene Mingo in their 31-24 loss to Denver on 10-23-60
Dick Felt blocked an extra point attempt by Fletcher Smith in their 43-24 loss to the Chiefs on 09-25-66
Nick Buoniconti blocked another extra point attempt by Fletcher Smith in their 43-24 loss to KS on 09-25-66
John Charles blocked an extra point attempt by Gary Kroner in their 26-21 loss to Denver on 09-03-67
Ed Philpott blocked an extra point attempt by Jim Turner in their 29-24 loss to the Jets on 11-19-67
John Bramlett blocked an extra point attempt by Karl Kresmer in their 38-23 win over Miami on 11-30-69
Willie Osley blocked an extra point attempt by John Leypoldt in their 30-28 loss to Buffalo on 10-20-74
Julius Adams blocked an extra point attempt by John Leypoldt in their 29-28 loss to Buffalo on 11-03-74
Donnell Smith blocked an extra point attempt by Roy Gerela in their 21-17 loss to the Steelers on 12-08-74
John Sanders blocked an extra point attempt by Pat Leahy in their 36-7 loss to the Jets on 10-05-75
John Sanders blocked an extra point attempt by Steve Mike-Mayer in their 24-16 win vs SF on 10-26-75
Jerry Patton blocked an extra point attempt by John Leypoldt in their 34-14 loss to Buffalo on 12-14-75
Tim Fox blocked an extra point attempt by Chester Marcol in their 27-14 loss to Green Bay on 10-01-79
Ronnie Lippett blocked an extra point attempt by Pat Leahy in their 23-13 win over the Jets on 09-18-83
Steve Nelson blocked an extra point attempt by Uwe Von Schamann in their 44-24 loss to Miami on 10-21-84
Steve Nelson blocked an extra point attempt by Neil O'Donoghue in their 33-10 loss to St. Louis on 12-02-84
Don Blackmon blocked an extra point attempt by Al Del Greco in their 26-20 win over Green Bay on 09-08-85
Garin Veris blocked an extra point attempt by Scott Norwood in their 22-17 loss to Buffalo on 11-03-91
Troy Barnett blocked an extra point attempt by Doug Christie in their 35-25 win over Buffalo on 11-26-95
Tebucky Jones blocked an extra point attempt by Olindo Mare in their 26-13 loss to Miami on 10-06-02
Vince Wilfork blocked an extra point attempt by Sebastian Janikowski in their 49-26 win vs Oak on 12-14-08
Jamie Collins jumped over LS and blocked Adam Vinatieri's PAT attempt in their 34-27 win on 10-18-15
Shea McClellin blocked an extra point attempt by Steven Hauschka in their 31-24 loss to Seattle on 11-13-16

A Few Memorable Missed Extra Points by the Patriots

Adam Vinatieri had trouble with the Militia's Men's TD Celebration smoke and missed a PAT on 11-16-03
Stephen Gostkowski's extra point hit the goal post in their 34-28 OT **Super Bowl** win vs Atlanta on 02-05-17
Stephen Gostkowski's extra point attempt hit the right goal post in their 36-20 win vs the Saints on 09-17-17

Most Field Goals in a Game

6 by Gino Cappelletti
5 by Stephen Gostkowski
5 by Adam Vinatieri
5 by Adam Vinatieri
5 by Jason Staurovsky

Most Field Goals in a Season

38 by Stephen Gostkowski
37 by Stephen Gostkowski
36 by Stephen Gostkowski
35 by Stephen Gostkowski
33 by Stephen Gostkowski

Most Field Goals in a Career

374 FGs by Stephen Gostkowski
263 FGs by Adam Vinatieri
176 FGs by Gino Cappelletti
128 FGs by John Smith
93 FGs by Tony Franklin

Three Patriots Players Who Have Won a National Punt, Pass and Competition

Hart Lee Dykes, Shawn McCarthy and Tom Tupa

BLOCKED FIELD GOAL ATTEMPTS

Chronological List of Patriots Player Who Has Blocked a Field Goal Attempt

Harry Jacobs blocked a 35 yard FGA by Ben Agajanian in their 45-16 loss to the LA Chargers on 10-28-60
Bob Dee blocked a 37 yard FGA by Gene Mingo in their 41-16 rout of the Broncos on 09-21-62
George Pyne blocked a 30 yard FGA by Pete Gogolak in their 24-7 loss to the Bills on 09-11-65
Nick Buoniconti blocked a 36 yard FGA by George Blanda in their 31-10 loss to the Oilers on 09-19-65
Larry Eisenhauer blocked a 35 yard FGA by Herb Travenio in their 22-6 win over the SD on 10-31-65
John Charles blocked a 47 yard FGA by Mike Mercer in their 16-7 victory over Buffalo on 09-08-68
Ron Hall blocked Tommy Booker's potential game winning 28 yd FGA in their 10-10 with KS on 11-21-65
Nick Buoniconti blocked a 40 yard FGA by John Wittenborn in their 16-0 loss to the Oilers on 10-13-68
John Charles blocked a 25 yard FGA by John Wittenborn in their 16-0 loss to the Houston Oilers on 10-13-68
Larry Carwell blocked a 51 yard FGA by Horst Mulmann and returned it 45 yards for a TD on 09-17-72
Ron Bolton blocked a 32 yard FGA by Bill Bell in their 21-20 victory over Atlanta on 09-24-72
Rick Cash blocked a 48 yard FGA by Garo Yepremian in their 52-0 loss to the Dolphins on 11-12-72
Steve Kiner blocked a 39 yard FGA by Jan Stenerud in their 10-7 loss to the Chiefs on 09-23-73
Art Moore blocked a 43 yard FGA by Skip Butler in their 32-0 shutout of the Oilers on 11-25-73
Art Moore blocked a 47 yard FGA by Dennis Partee in their 30-14 win over San Diego on 12-02-73
Art Moore blocked a 41 yard FGA by David Ray in their 20-14 win over the LA Rams on 09-29-74
Ray Hamilton blocked a yard FGA by Jim Bakken in their 24-17 loss to St. Louis on 11-02-75
Pete Cusick blocked a 48 yard FGA and a 46 yard FGA by Pat Leahy in their 30-28 loss the Jets on 12-07-75
Mel Lunsford blocked a 39 yard FGA by Don Cockroft in their 30-27 OT loss to the Browns on 09-26-77
Julius Adams blocked a field goal attempt by Pat Leahy in their 30-27 loss to the Jets on 10-02-77
Ray Hamilton blocked a 19 yard FGA by Ove Johansson in their 14-6 victory over the Eagles on 11-27-77
Steve Nelson blocked a 49 yard FGA by Pat Leahy in their 21-11 win over the Jets on 10-05-80
Richard Bishop blocked a 40 yard FGA by Mark Moseley in their 24-22 loss to the Redskins on 10-25-81
Julius Adams blocked a field goal attempt by Ove Johansson in their 3-0 win over the Dolphins on 12-12-82
Lester Williams blocked a 52 yard FGA by Norm Johnson in their 16-0 shutout of Seattle on 12-19-82
Julius Adams blocked a field goal attempt by Raul Allegre in their 16-10 victory over the Colts on 12-16-84
Ken Sims blocked a 40 yard FGA by Al DelGrecoo in their 26-20 win over Green Bay on 09-08-85
Don Blackmon blocked a 53 yard FGA by Mick Luckhurst in their 25-17 victory over Atlanta on 11-02-86
A. Tippett blocked a 48 yard FGA by Tony Zendejas (returned for TD) in 21-7 win vs Houston on 10-18-87
Darryl Holmes blocked a 23 yard FGA by Mike Cofer in their 37-20 loss to the 49ers on 10-22-89
Ken Sims blocked a 45 yard FGA by Mike Cofer in their 37-20 loss to the 49ers on 10-22-89
Brent Williams blocked a 48 yard FGA by Dean Biasucci in their 16-7 win over the Colts on 09-01-91
Troy Barnett blocked a 38 yard FGA by Kevin Butler in their 13-3 victory over the Bears on 12-24-94
Mike Pitts blocked a 50 yard FGA by Matt Stover in their 20-13 **Wild Card** loss to Cleveland on 01-01-95
Troy Barnett blocked a 54 yard FGA by Pete Stonyanovich in their 20-3 loss to Miami on 09-10-95

More Blocked Field Goal Attempts

Mike Jones blocked a potential GW 29 yard FGA by John Hall, in their 27-24 OT win vs the Jets on 09-14-97
Chad Eaton blocked a 38 yard FGA by John Hall in their 24-14 loss to the Jets on 10-19-98
Ferric Collons blocked a 47 yard FGA by Morton Anderson in their 41-10 loss to Atlanta on 11-08-98
Chad Eaton blocked a 23 yard FGA by Steve Christie in their 13-10 OT win vs the Bills on 12-17-00
Chad Eaton blocked a 30 yard FGA by Steve Christie in their 13-10 OT win vs the Bills on 12-17-00
Brandon Mitchell blocked a 46 yard FGA by Mike Vanderjagt in their 38-17 win over the Colts on 10-21-01
Richard Seymour blocked a 43 yard FGA by John Carney in their 34-17 win over the Saints on 11-25-01
Brandon Mitchell blocked Kris Brown's 34 yd FGA in their 24-17 **Championship** win on 01-27-02
Richard Seymour blocked a 49 yard FGA by Sebastian Janikowski in their 27-20 loss to Oakland on 11-17-02
Richard Seymour blocked a 43 yard FGA by Gary Anderson in their 24-17 win over the Vikings on 11-24-02
Dan Klecko blocked a 48 yard FGA by John Hall in their 20-17 loss to the Redskins on 09-28-03
R. Seymour blocked a 35 yd FGA by Olindo Mare, which forced OT, in 19-13 OT win vs Miami on 10-19-03
R. Seymour blocked a 31 yd FGA by Gary Anderson in their 17-14 **Divisional** win vs Tenn on 01-10-04
Richard Seymour blocked a 45 yard FGA by Robbie Gould in their 17-13 win over the Bears on 11-26-06
Patrick Chung blocked a 53 yard FGA by Dan Carpenter in their 41-14 rout of Miami on 10-04-10
Chandler Jones blocked a 48 yd FGA by Blair Walsh and took it 58 yards for a TD, in 30-7 win on 09-14-14
Chris Jones blocked a potential game winning 58 yd FGA by Nick Folk in 27-25 win vs the Jets on 10-16-14
Jamie Collins blocked a 41 yd FGA by Caleb Sturgis (returned for a TD) in 41-13 rout of Miami on 12-14-14
Vince Wilfork tipped a 52 yard FGA by Nick Folk in their 17-16 win over the Jets on 12-21-14
Alan Branch blocked a 54 yard FGA by Nick Folk in their 22-17 victory over the Jets on 11-27-16
Shea McClellin jumped over LS and blocked Justin Tucker's 34 yd FGA in 30-23 win vs Balt on 12-12-16
Cassius Marsh blocked a 37 yard FGA by Matt Bryant in their 23-7 victory over Atlanta on 10-22-17
Lawrence Guy blocked a 51 yard FGA by Nick Novak in their 21-13 win over the LA Chargers on 10-29-17

Chronological List of Everyone Who Has Returned a Blocked Field Goal Attempt

Bob Suci returned a blocked field goal 5 yards in their 28-21 loss to the Bills on 10-26-63
Larry Carwell returned a blocked field goal 45 yards for a TD in their 31-7 loss to Cincy on 09-17-72
Don Martin returned a blocked field goal 35 yards in their 32-0 shutout of Houston on 11-25-73
John Zamberlin and Mike Haynes returned blocked FG 65 yds for a TD in 21-11 win vs the Jets on 10-05-80
Roland James returned a blocked field goal 26 yards in their 16-10 victory over the Colts on 12-16-84
Raymond Clayborn returned a blocked FG 71 yards for a TD in their 21-7 win vs Cleveland on 10-18-87
Vernon Lewis returned a blocked field goal 3 yards in their 13-3 win over the Bears on 12-24-94
Leonard Myers returned a blocked field goal 25 yards in their 38-17 rout of the Colts on 10-21-01
Troy Brown and Antwann Harris returned a blocked FG for a TD in 24-17 **Championship** win on 01-27-02
Troy Brown returned a blocked field goal 6 yards in their 19-13 OT win vs the Dolphins on 10-19-03
Kyle Arrington returned a blocked FG 35 yards for a TD in their 41-14 rout of Miami on 10-04-10
Chandler Jones returned a blocked field goal 58 yards for a TD in their 30-7 rout of Minn on 09-14-14
Kyle Arrington returned a blocked field goal 62 yards for a TD in their 41-13 rout of Miami on 12-14-14
Dont'a Hightower returned a blocked field goal 6 yards in their 22-17 win over the Jets on 11-27-16

Most Memorable Moments of an Opponent's Missed, Mishandled or Blocked Field Goal Attempt

Ron Burton returned Gene Mingo's missed field goal attempt 91 yards for a TD in their 33-29 win on 11-11-62
Ron Hall blocked a 28 yard FGA with 26 seconds left in their 10-10 tie with the Chiefs on 11-21-65
Larry Carwell blocked Horst Muhlmann's 51 yard FGA and returned it 45 yards for a TD on 09-17-72
John Zamberlin's lateraled to Mike Haynes who took a blocked FGA 65 yards for a TD on 10-05-80
Mike Jones blocked a 29 yard FGA with 16 seconds left in their 27-24 OT win on 09-14-97
Chad Eaton blocked a 30 yard field goal attempt in Overtime in their 13-10 OT win on 12-17-00
Antwan Harris advanced Troy Brown's lateral 49 yds for a TD in their 24-17 **Championship** win on 01-27-02
Richard Seymour blocked a 35 yard FGA in their 19-13 OT win vs the Dolphins on 10-19-03
Richard Seymour blocked a 31 yard FGA in their 17-14 **Divisional** win vs Tennessee on 01-10-04
Nate Ebner recovered John Denny's bad snap that deflected off the facemask of Brandon Fields on 12-15-13
Shea McClellin jumped over the Ravens offensive line and blocked Justin Tucker's 34 yard FGA on 12-12-16

10 Most Memorable Field Goals by a Patriots Kicker

Gino Cappelletti kicked a game winning 41 yd FG on last play of their 25-24 win vs Houston on 11-06-64
David Posey's Game Winning AFC East clinching 21 yard FG in their 26-24 win vs Buffalo on 12-10-78
John Smith used the path cleared by Mark Henderson to kick a 33 yard FG in 3-0 win vs Miami on 12-12-82
Charlie Baumann's 44 yard FG on the last play to force OT in their 37-34 win over the Colts on 11-15-92
Adam Vinatieri's 52 yd FG hit the camera positioned inside the goal post in their win vs the Colts on 09-13-98
Adam Vinatieri's 44 yard Overtime Game Winning field goal in their 29-26 OT win vs SD on 10-14-01
Adam Vinatieri's 45 yard game tying FG in the snow in their 16-13 OT **Divisional** win on 01-19-02
Adam Vinatieri's 23 yard Game Winning FG to beat the Raiders 16-13 in OT in **Divisional** Game on 01-19-02
Adam Vinatieri's Game Winning 48 yard FG on the last play in their 20-17 **Super Bowl** win on 02-03-02
Adam Vinatieri's Game Winning 41 yard FG on the last play of their 32-29 **Super Bowl** win on 02-01-04

A Few Field Goal Attempts by the Patriots That Hit the Cross Bar

Matt Bahr's 19 yard FGA hit the left post and was no good in their 34-17 win over Miami on 11-12-95
Adam Vinatieri's 45 yard FGA hit the right post and his 47 yard FGA hit the left post, no good, on 09-08-96
Adam Vinatieri's 43 yard FGA hit the right post and was no good in 27-22 loss to the Redskins on 10-13-96
Adam Vinatieri's potential GW 32 yard FGA bounced off the right goal post in their 16-14 loss on 10-10-99
Adam Vinatieri's 31 yard FGA deflected off the post and was good in their 41-27 Playoff win on 01-23-05

The Shortest Players Who Have Played for the Patriots

Height Player

5'5"   Mack Herron
5'7"   Wayne Coffey, Pat Coleman, Dave Meggett and Jamie Morris
5'8"   Frank Bianchini, Tim Dwight, Kevin Faulk, Tony Franklin, Tony Gaiter, Chidi Iwuoma,
        Damaris Johnson, Dion Lewis, Ray Mickens, Tyrone Poole, Rodney Rice, Eric Schubert,
        Greg Taylor, Erroll Tucker, Ross Ventrone, Leon Washington and Amos Zereoue

The Tallest Players Who Have Played for the Patriots

Height Player

6'8"   Ron Berger, Wesley Britt, Trent Brown, Scott Rehberg, Peter Shorts, Nate Solder
        and Sebastian Vollmer

Alphabetical List of Everyone's Longest Field Goal in a Game for the Patriots

Matt Bahr kicked a 55 yard field goal in their 34-17 victory over Miami on 11-12-95
Charlie Baumann kicked a 46 yard field goal in their 16-13 win over Buffalo on 11-24-91
Bill Bell kicked a 36 yard field goal in their 44-23 loss to Miami on 09-30-73
Gino Cappelletti kicked a 53 yard field goal in their 27-23 win over the Jets on 11-28-65
Greg Davis kicked a 52 yard field goal for the 1st point scored in their 16-15 loss to the Falcons on 10-15-89
Nick Folk kicked a 51 yard field goal in their 24-17 victory over the Bills on 12-21-19
Kai Forbath kicked a 23 yard field goal in their 28-22 loss to the Texans on 12-01-19
Tony Franklin kicked a barefooted 50 yard field goal in their 31-14 win over Tampa on 10-27-85
Tony Franklin kicked a barefooted 50 yard field goal in their 23-6 win over the Lions on 12-08-85
Teddy Garcia kicked a 50 yard field goal in their 36-6 loss to the Vikings on 09-11-88
Charlie Gogolak kicked a 51 yard field goal in their 41-3 loss to the Dolphins on 10-17-71
Stephen Gostkowski kicked a 62 yard field goal in their 33-8 win over the Raiders on 11-19-17
Shayne Graham kicked a 41 yard field goal in their 45-3 rout of the Jets on 12-06-10
Mike Nugent kicked a 37 yard field goal in their 44-7 rout of the Redskins on 10-06-19
Danny Miller kicked a 25 yard field goal in their 29-21 win over the Houston Oilers on 11-28-82
David Posey kicked a 47 yard field goal in their 19-17 victory over the Jets on 11-19-78
Rex Robinson kicked a 24 yard field goal in their 24-13 win over the Baltimore Colts on 09-12-82
Eric Schubert kicked a 23 yard field goal in their 20-10 loss to the Browns on 10-04-87
Scott Sisson kicked a 40 yard field goal in their 9-6 loss to the Indianapolis Colts on 10-31-93
Scott Sisson kicked a 40 yard field goal in their 17-13 loss to the Dolphins on 11-21-93
John Smith kicked a 50 yard field goal in their 33-17 win over the Chiefs on 10-04-81
Jason Staurovsky kicked a 53 yard field goal in their 33-20 loss to the Seahawks on 10-07-90
Fred Steinfort kicked a 35 yard field goal in their 37-21 win over the San Diego Chargers on 10-16-83
Adam Vinatieri kicked a 57 yard field goal in their 33-30 comeback win over the Bears on 11-10-02
Mike "Superfoot" Walker kicked a 36 yard field goal in their 27-24 loss to the Bills on 11-19-72
Mike "Superfoot" Walker kicked a 36 yard field goal in their 17-10 win over the Saints on 12-10-72
Jeff White kicked a 48 yard field goal in their 32-0 shutout of the Houston Oilers on 11-25-73

Every Patriots Kicker Who Has Kicked Exactly Five Field Goals in a Game

Jason Staurovsky kicked 5 field goals in their 22-16 win over the Indianapolis Colts on 12-03-89
Adam Vinatieri kicked 5 field goals in their 28-25 Overtime win vs the Jaguars in 09-22-96
Adam Vinatieri kicked 5 field goals in their 29-6 rout of the Bills on 11-14-04
Stephen Gostlowski kicked 5 field goals in their 43-17 rout of the Bengals on 10-05-14

Only Patriot Who Has Kicked Six Field Goals for the Patriots in a Game

Gino Cappelletti kicked 6 field goals in their 39-10 rout of the Broncos on 10-04-64

Every Patriot Player Who Has Returned a Missed Field Goal Attempt

Ross O'Hanley had a 14 yard return of Larry Barnes missed FGA in their 27-14 loss to OAK on 10-16-60
Ross O'Hanley had a 2 yard return of Gene Mingo's missed FGA in their 45-17 rout of Denver on 09-16-61
Ron Burton returned Gene Mingo's missed FGA 91 yards for a TD in their 33-29 win vs Denver on 11-11-62
Ross O'Hanley had a 6 yard return of Dick Guesman's missed FGA in their 38-14 rout of the Jets on 09-08-63
Ron Burton returned Dick Guesman's missed FGA 18 yards in their 12-7 win over Denver on 11-20-64
Ron Burton returned Herb Travenio's missed FGA 19 yards in their 13-13 tie with San Diego on 10-17-65
Billy Johnson had a 13 yd return of Wayne Walker's missed FGA in their 45-17 loss to Houston on 12-15-68
Tim Fox had a 7 yd return of Fred Steinfort's missed 73 yard FGA in their 24-14 win vs Denver on 09-29-80

KICKOFF RETURNS

Every Patriots Kickoff Returnman Who Was Named the *AFC Special Team Player of the Week*

Bethel Johnson returned a kickoff 92 yards for a TD in their 38-34 win over the Colts on 11-03-03
Laurence Maroney had a 77 yard kickoff return in their 31-7 rout of the Vikings on 10-30-06
Ellis Hobbs returned a kickoff 108 yards for a TD in their 38-14 rout of the Jets on 09-09-07
Ellis Hobbs returned a kickoff 95 yards for a TD in their 49-26 rout of the Raiders on 12-14-08
Dan Connolly had a 71 yard kickoff return in their 31-27 win over the Packers on 12-10-10
Devin McCourty returned a kickoff 104 yards for a TD in their 29-26 OT win vs the Jets on 10-21-12
Dion Lewis returned a kickoff 103 yards for a TD in their 41-16 rout of the Broncos on 11-12-17

Chronological List of Every Patriot Who Has Returned a Kickoff for a TD

Larry Garron returned a kickoff 89 yards for a TD in their 31-31 tie with the Houston Oilers on 10-13-61
Ron Burton had a 91 yard kickoff return for a TD in their 28-21 win over the Dallas Texans on 11-03-61
Larry Garron returned a kickoff 95 yards for a TD in their 28-28 win over Buffalo on 11-03-62
Mack Herron had a 92 yard return for a TD in their 30-14 win over the San Diego Chargers on 12-02-73
Allen Carter returned the opening kickoff 99 yards for a TD in their 34-21 loss to the Colts on 12-21-75
Raymond Clayborn returned a kickoff 100 yards for a TD in their 30-27 loss to the Jets on 10-02-77
Raymond Clayborn returned a kickoff 93 yards for a TD in their 24-14 loss to the Bills on 11-06-77
Raymond Clayborn had a 101 yard kickoff return for a TD in their 30-24 loss to the Colts on 12-18-77
Horace Ivory had a 98 yard kickoff return for a TD in their 37-21 win over the Baltimore Colts on 10-19-80
Ricky Smith returned a kickoff 98 yards for a TD in their 31-7 loss to the Jets on 09-19-82
Sammy Martin returned the opening kickoff 95 yards for a TD in their 24-21 loss to the Colts on 11-27-88
Jon Vaughn returned a kickoff 99 yards for a TD in their 24-10 loss to the Phoenix Cardinals on 09-29-91
Jon Vaughn had a 100 yard kickoff return for a TD in their 20-10 loss to the Bengals on 12-20-92
Derrick Cullors had an 86 yard kickoff return for a TD in their 31-10 victory over Buffalo on 11-09-97
Kevin Faulk returned a kickoff 86 yards for a TD in their 27-20 loss to Oakland on 11-17-02
Kevin Faulk returned a kickoff 87 yards for a TD in their 30-17 loss to the Jets on 12-22-02
Bethel Johnson returned a kickoff 92 yards for a TD in their 38-34 win over the Colts on 11-30-03
Bethel Johnson returned the opening kickoff 93 yards for a TD in their 42-15 rout of the Browns on 12-05-04
Ellis Hobbs had a 93 yard kickoff return for a TD in their 40-7 rout of Houston on 12-17-06
Ellis Hobbs returned a kickoff 108 yards for a TD in their 38-14 blowout of the Jets on 09-09-07
Willie Andrews returned a kickoff 77 yards for a TD in their 49-28 rout of the Dolphins on 10-21-07
Ellis Hobbs had a 95 yard kickoff return for a TD in their 49-26 rout of the Raiders on 12-14-08
Brandon Tate returned a kickoff 97 yards for a TD in their 38-24 win over the Bengals on 09-12-10
Brandon Tate had a 103 yard kickoff return for a TD in their 41-14 rout of the Dolphins on 10-04-10
Devin McCourty had a 104 yard kickoff return for a TD in their 29-26 OT win vs the Jets on 10-21-12
LeGarrette Blount returned a kickoff 83 yards for a TD in their 34-20 win over Buffalo on 12-29-13
Dion Lewis returned a kickoff 98 yards for a TD in their 34-16 **Divisional** win over the Texans on 01-14-17
Cordarelle Patterson returned a kickoff 95 yards for a TD in their 38-31 win over the Bears on 10-21-18

10 Longest Kickoff Returns That Were Not Returned for a TD

95 yard kickoff return by Kevin Faulk in their 24-17 loss to the Jets on 11-15-99
83 yard kickoff return by LaGarrette Blount in their 34-20 win over the Bills on 12-29-13
81 yard kickoff return by Danny Amendola in their 34-9 rout of the Lions on 11-23-14
80 yard kickoff return by Ellis Hobbs in their 38-34 **Championship** loss to the Colts on 01-21-07
77 yard kickoff return by Laurence Maroney in their 31-7 rout of the Vikings on 10-30-06
75 yard kickoff return by Keyshawn Martin in their 33-16 triumph over the Titans on 12-20-15
73 yard kickoff return of the 2nd half kickoff by Danny Amendola in their 41-25 win over Buffalo on 10-30-16
71 yard kickoff return by Jess Phillips in their 26-22 victory over the Bills on 10-24-76
71 yard kickoff return Dan Connolly in their 31-27 win over the Packers on 12-19-10
68 yard kickoff return by Derrick Cullors in their 27-21 loss to the Broncos on 09-07-98

10 Longest Kickoff Returns by a Patriots Player in a Super Bowl Game

43 yard kickoff return by Laurence Maroney in their 17-14 **Super Bowl** loss to the Giants on 02-03-08
38 yard kickoff return by Cordarrelle Patterson in their 13-3 **Super Bowl** win over the LA Rams on 02-03-19
36 yard kickoff return by Stephen Starring in their 46-10 **Super Bowl** loss to the Bears on 01-26-86
35 yard kickoff return by Patrick Pass in their 20-17 **Super Bowl** win over the St. Louis Rams on 02-03-02
31 yard kickoff return by Julian Edelman in their 21-17 **Super Bowl** loss to the Giants on 02-05-12
29 yard kickoff return by Patrick Pass in their 20-17 **Super Bowl** win over the St. Louis Rams on 02-03-02
29 yard kickoff return by Bethel Johnson in their 32-29 **Super Bowl** win over the Panthers on 02-01-04
26 yard kickoff return by Dave Meggett in their 35-21 **Super Bowl** loss to the Packers on 01-26-97
25 yard kickoff return by Stephen Starring in their 46-10 **Super Bowl** loss to the Bears on 01-26-86
25 yard kickoff return by Dion Lewis in their 41-33 **Super Bowl** loss to the Eagles on 02-04-18

Every Patriots Player Who Has Recovered a Short Kickoff by a Teammate

Steven Hawkins recovered a short kickoff by Matt Bahr in their 21-17 loss to the Raiders on 10-09-94
Tully Banta Cain recovered a short kickoff by Adam Vinatieri in their 23-7 win vs the Jets on 12-26-04

Chronological List of Every Patriot Who Has Advanced a Kickoff Return Fumble

Ron Burton advanced his own fumble 91 yards for a TD in their 33-29 win vs Denver on 11-11-62
Tom Stephens advanced his own fumble 6 yards in their 20-0 loss to Oakland on 12-16-62
Larry Garron advanced Bob Suci's kickoff return fumble 2 yards in their 46-28 win over Houston on 12-08-63
RC Gamble advanced his own fumble 2 yards in their 48-14 loss to the Jets on 10-27-68
Marvin Allen advanced Jamie Morris' kickoff return fumble 3 yards in their 37-7 loss to KS on 12-02-90
Jon Vaughn advanced his own fumble 100 yards for a TD in their 20-10 loss to Cincy on 12-20-92
Troy Brown advanced Dave Meggett's KR fumble 75 yards for a TD in 31-28 win vs the Jets on 12-10-95
Chris Canty advanced Derrick Cullors' KR fumble 9 yards in their 14-12 win vs Miami on 12-22-97

10 Most Obscure Plays on a Kickoff

Ron Berger holds the Team Record for the longest kickoff return by a DL of 20 yards on 10-19-69
Bob Gladieux made a tackle on the opening kickoff in the Patriots 27-14 win over Miami on 09-20-70
Adam Vinatieri caught Hershell Walker from behind on his 70 yard KR in 12-6 loss to Dallas on 12-15-96
Ben Coates holds the Team Record for the longest kickoff return by a TE of 20 yards on 12-07-97
Tully Banta Cain's recovery of a short kickoff by Adam Vinatieri in their 23-7 win over the Jets on 12-26-04
Stephen Gostkowski recovered Leondis McKelvin's 4th Qtr fumbled KR to set up the GW score on 09-14-09
Wes Welker's 45 yard kickoff in their 34-14 loss to the Browns on 11-07-10
Dan Connolly holds Team Record for longest return by an Offensive Lineman of 71 yds on 12-19-10
Kyle Arrington recovered S. Gostkowski's onside kick to set up last second GW TD on 12-08-13
Nate Ebner's onside kick attempt in their 35-28 loss to the Philadelphia Eagles on 12-16-15

Most Kickoff Return Yards/Game | Most Kickoff Yards/Season | Most Kickoff Return Yards/Career

Most Kickoff Return Yards/Game	Most Kickoff Yards/Season	Most Kickoff Return Yards/Career
237 by Ellis Hobbs	1,281 by Ellis Hobbs (2008)	4,098 yards by Kevin Faulk
220 by Kevin Faulk	1,092 by Mack Herron (1973)	2,913 yards by Ellis Hobbs
206 by Allen Carter	1,085 by Derrick Cullors (1998)	2,561 yards by Dave Meggett
201 by Deion Branch	1,057 by Brandon Tate (2010)	2,557 yards by Bethel Johnson
175 by Carl Garrett	1,016 by Bethel Johnson (2004)	2,299 yards by Larry Garron

ONSIDE KICKS

Chronological List of Every Patriot Who Has Recovered an Onside Kick by His Teammate

Jim Lee Hunt recovered Gino Cappelletti's onside kick in their 26-10 win over the Jets on 09-27-64
Billy Johnson recovered Justin Canale's onside kick in their 29-24 loss to the Jets on 11-19-67
Carl Garrett recovered Gino Cappelletti's onside kick in their 38-23 loss to the Oakland Raiders on 09-28-69
Clarence Scott recovered Charlie Gogolak's onside kick in their 35-14 loss to the Vikings on 12-13-70
Clarence Scott recovered Charlie Gogolak's onside kick in their 24-17 loss to the Baltimore Colts on 11-06-72
Claxton Welch recovered Jeff White's onside kick in their 33-13 loss to the Jets on 11-11-73
Don Westbrook recovered John Smith's onside kick in their 34-27 loss to the Baltimore Colts on 09-18-78
Mosi Tatupu recovered Mike Hubach's onside kick in their 38-34 loss to the Houston Oilers on 11-10-80
Hart Lee Dykes recovered Jason Staurovsky's onside kick in their 28-24 loss to the Saints on 11-12-89
Darryl Wren recovered Scott Sisson's onside kick in their 28-14 loss to the Houston Oilers on 10-17-93
Corwin Brown recovered Matt Bahr's onside kick in their 20-13 **Wild Card** loss to Cleveland on 01-01-95
Kyle Arrington recovered Stephen Gostkowski's 4th Qtr onside kick in 27-26 win vs Cleveland on 12-08-13
Jonathan Freeny recovered Stephen Gostkowski's onside kick in their 27-10 win over Washington on 11-08-15
Rashaan Melvin recovered Stephen Gostkowski's onside kick in their 35-28 loss to the Eagles on 12-06-15

Every Patriots Running Back Who Has Recovered an Opponent's Onside Kick

Ger Schwedes recovered Gene Mingo's onside kick in their 28-24 victory over the Broncos on 12-03-61
Andy Johnson recovered Steve Mike Mayer's onside kick in their 24-16 win over the 49ers on 10-26-75
Andy Johnson recovered Chris Bahr's onside kick in their 20-14 victory over the Bengals on 09-16-79
Andy Johnson recovered Don Cockroft's onside kick in their 34-17 win over the Browns on 09-07-80
Mosi Tatupu recovered Al Del Greco's onside kick in their 26-20 victory over the Packers on 09-08-85
Craig James recovered Raul Allegre's onside kick in their 38-31 win over the Colts on 12-01-85
Keith Byars recovered Steve Christie's onside kick in their 28-25 victory over the Bills on 10-27-96

Every Offensive Lineman of the Patriots Who Has Recovered an Opponent's Onside Kick

Walt Cudzik recovered Billy Atkins' onside kick in their 23-21 victory over the Bills on 09-23-61
Dave Watson recovered Mike Mercer's onside kick in their 17-14 win over the Oakland Raiders on 09-13-64
Bob Yates recovered Mike Mercer's onside kick in their 43-43 Tie with the Oakland Raiders on 10-16-64
John Hannah recovered John Leypoldt's onside kick in their 37-13 loss to the Bills on 12-09-73

Every Wide Receiver of the Patriots Who Has Recovered an Opponent's Onside Kick

Darryl Stingley recovered Rolf Bernirscke's onside kick in their 24-20 win over the Chargers on 10-16-77
Steve Burks recovered Ove Johansson's onside kick in their 14-6 victory over the Eagles on 11-27-77
Carlos Pennywell recovered Don Cockroft's onside kick in their 34-17 win over the Browns on 09-07-80
Cedric Jones recovered Pat Leahy's onside kick in their 14-13 victory over the Jets on 11-13-88
Troy Brown recovered an onside kick by Mike Hollis in their 26-20 win over the Jaguars on 12-07-97
Fred Coleman recovered Olindo Mare's onside kick in their 20-13 victory over the Dolphins on 12-22-01

Every Patriots Tight End Who Has Recovered an Opponent's Onside Kick

Ben Coates recovered Chris Gardocki's onside kick in their 20-17 victory over the Colts on 11-30-97
Ben Coates returned Mike Hollis' onside kick 20 yards in their 26-20 win over the Jaguars on 12-07-97
Ben Coates recovered Brad Daluiso's onside kick in their 16-14 victory over the Giants on 09-26-99
Eric Bjornson recovered Danny Knight's onside kick in their 24-16 win over the Colts on 10-08-00
Christian Fauria recovered Craig Hentrich's onside kick in their 38-30 victory over Tennessee on 10-05-03
Ben Watson returned Mike Nugent's onside kick 1 yard in their 31-21 win over the Jets on 12-26-05
Christian Fauria recovered Mike Vanderjagt's onside kick in 24-14 **Championship** win vs Indy on 01-18-04
Christian Fauria recovered Jeff Reed's onside kick in their 41-27 **Championship** win vs Pitt on 01-23-05
Christian Fauria recovered David Akers' onside kick in their 24-21 **Super Bowl** win vs Philly on 02-06-05

Only Defensive Lineman of the Patriots Who Has Recovered an Opponent's Onside Kick Attempt

Bob Dee recovered George Blair's onside kick in their 33-28 win over the Chargers on 09-20-64

Every Patriots Defensive Back Who Has Recovered an Opponent's Onside Kick

Tom Stephens recovered George Blair's onside kick in their 33-28 win over the Chargers on 09-20-64
Billy Johnson recovered Gary Kroner's onside kick in their 17-10 loss to the Broncos on 11-06-66
Tom Janik recovered John Leypoldt's onside kick in their 38-33 victory over the Bills on 11-14-71
Don Webb recovered Jim O'Brien's onside kick in their 21-17 win over the Baltimore Colts on 12-19-71
Sandy Durko recovered Garo Yepremian's onside kick in their 34-24 win over the Dolphins on 09-15-74
Jim Bowman recovered Morton Andersen's onside kick in their 21-20 win over the Saints on 11-30-86
Ronnie Lippett recovered Dean Biasucci's onside kick in their 16-14 win over the Colts on 09-16-90
Myron Guyton recovered Doug Pelfrey's onside kick in their 31-28 win over Cincinnati on 09-18-94
Corwin Brown recovered Matt Stover's onside kick in their 46-38 win over the Ravens on 10-06-96

Every Patriots Linebacker Who Has Recovered an Opponent's Onside Kick

Harry Jacobs recovered Jim Fraser's onside kick in their 33-29 victory over the Broncos on 11-11-62
Jim Cheyunski recovered George Blanda's onside kick in their 41-10 loss to the Oakland Raiders on 10-06-68
Barry Brown recovered Grant Guthrie's onside kick in their 14-10 win over Buffalo on 11-29-70
Steve Zabel recovered Tom Dempsey's onside kick in their 14-10 victory over the Bills on 11-05-78
Mike Vrabel recovered an onside kick by Jake Arians in their 21-11 victory over the Bills on 11-11-01
Larry Izzo recovered Seth Marler's onside kick in their 27-13 win over the Jaguars on 12-14-03
Larry Izzo fell on the onside kick by Lawrence Tynes in their 26-16 loss to the Chiefs on 11-27-05

Every Patriots Tight End Who Has Recovered a Short Kickoff by the Opponent's Kicker

Bob Windsor recovered George Hunt's short kickoff in their 24-16 win over Baltimore on 10-07-73
John Burke fell on Nick Lowery's short kickoff in their 24-13 win over the Jets on 12-04-94

Every Offensive Lineman of the Patriots Who Has Recovered a Squibbed Kickoff

Don Oakes recovered Dick Guesman's squibbed kickoff in their 12-7 win over the Broncos on 11-20-64
Justin Canale recovered Herb Travenio's squibbed kickoff in their 13-13 Tie with the Chargers on 10-17-65
Justin Canale recovered Herb Travenio's squibbed kickoff in their 22-6 win over the Chargers on 10-31-65
Dwight Wheeler recovered Mark Moseley's squibbed kickoff in their 16-14 loss to the Redskins on 09-03-78

Every Defensive Lineman of the Patriots Who Has Recovered an Opponent's Squibbed Kickoff

George Pyne recovered Jim Fraser's squibbed kickoff in their 27-17 loss to the Chiefs on 10-03-65
Donnell Smith recovered George Jakowenko's short kickoff in their 41-26 loss to the Raiders on 12-01-74
Ray Hamilton recovered Nick Mike-Mayer's squibbed kickoff in their 20-17 loss to the Bills on 11-22-81
Bobby Hamilton recovered Paul Edinger's squibbed kickoff in their 24-17 loss to the Bears on 12-10-00

Every Patriots Linebacker Who Has Recovered a Squibbed Kickoff in a Regular Season Game

Jack Rudolph returned Gary Korner's opening kickoff 4 yards in their 27-10 loss to Denver on 09-24-65
John Tanner recovered Garo Yepremian's squibbed kickoff in their 34-27 loss to Miami on 12-15-74
Bill Matthews recovered Nick Mike-Mayer's squibbed kickoff in their 19-10 loss to the Bills on 12-13-81
Johnny Rembert recovered David Treadwell's squibbed kickoff in their 20-3 loss to the Broncos on 12-01-91
George Webster recovered Ray Guy's squibbed kickoff in their 24-21 **Divisional** loss to Oakland on 12-18-76

PUNT RETURNS

Every Punt Returner of the Patriots Who Was Named the *AFC Special Team Player of the Week*

Dave Meggett had a 60 yard punt return for a TD in their 23-22 comeback win vs the Giants on 12-21-96
Julian Edelman had a 72 yard punt return for a TD in their 34-3 rout of the Chiefs on 11-21-11
Julian Edelman had an 84 yard punt return for a TD in their 43-21 rout of the Broncos on 11-02-14

Chronological List of Every Patriot Who Has Returned a Punt for a TD

Mike Haynes returned a punt by Marv Bateman 89 yards for a TD in their 20-10 win over Buffalo on 11-07-76
Mike Haynes returned a punt by Billy Van Heusen 62 yards for a TD in their 38-14 rout Denver on 11-28-76
Stanley Morgan returned a punt by Bucky Dilts 80 yards for a TD in their 50-21 rout of the Colts on 11-18-79
Roland James returned a punt Chuck Ramsey 75 yards for a TD in their 34-21 win over the Jets on 11-02-80
Irving Fryar returned a punt by John Kidd 85 yards for a TD in their 17-14 win over Buffalo on 09-22-85
Irving Fryar returned a punt by Rohn Stark 77 yards for a TD in their 34-15 rout of the Colts on 11-10-85
Irving Fryar returned a punt by Rick Donnelly 59 yards for a TD in their 25-17 win over Atlanta on 11-02-86
Dave Meggett returned a punt by Mike Horan 60 yds for a TD in their 23-22 win over the Giants on 12-21-96
Troy Brown returned a punt by Mark Royals 66 yards for a TD in their 21-16 loss to Tampa Bay on 09-03-00
Troy Brown returned a punt by Chris Gardocki 85 yards for a TD in their 27-16 win vs Cleveland on 12-09-01
Troy Brown returned a punt by Todd Sauerbrun 68 yards for a TD in their 38-6 rout of Carolina on 01-06-02
Troy Brown returned a punt by Josh Miller 55 yards for a TD in 24-17 **Championship** win vs Pitt on 01-27-02
Julian Edelman returned a punt by Brandon Fields 94 yards for a TD in their 38-7 rout of Miami on 01-02-11
Julian Edelman returned a punt by Dustin Colquit 72 yards for a TD in their 34-3 rout of KS on 11-21-11
Julian Edelman returned a punt Pat McAfee 68 yards for a TD in their 59-24 rout of the Colts on 11-18-12
Julian Edelman returned a punt Britton Colquit 84 yards for a TD in their 43-21 rout of Denver on 11-02-14

10 Longest Punt Returns by the Patriots That Were Not Returned for a TD

82 yard punt return by Danny Amendola, in their 27-26 win over the Giants on 11-15-15
69 yard punt return by Wes Welker, in their 35-34 loss to the Colts on 11-15-09
66 yard punt return by Mack Herron, in their 42-3 rout of the Colts on 10-06-74
62 yard punt return by Ron Burton, in their 27-15 loss to the Oilers on 11-12-61
62 yard punt return by Carl Garrett, in the 31-21 loss to the Jets on 09-27-70
55 yard punt return by Ricky Smith, in their 29-23 OT loss to the Colts on 09-04-83
55 yard punt return by Irving Fryar, in their 38-23 win over the Seahawks on 09-16-84
54 yard punt return by Mack Herron, in their 24-16 victory over the Colts on 10-07-73
53 yard punt return by Stanley Morgan, in their 20-7 win over the Bills on 11-20-77
52 yard punt return by Billy Johnson, in their 16-7 win over the Oilers on 11-05-67

Most Punt Return Yards/Game	Most Punt Return Yards/Season	Most Punt Return Yards/Career
156 by Mike Haynes	608 yards by Mike Haynes (1976)	2,625 yards by Troy Brown
133 by Irving Fryar	588 yards by Dave Meggett (1996)	2,055 yards by Irving Fryar
133 by Stanley Morgan	520 yards by Irving Fryar (1985)	1,986 yards by Julian Edelman
126 by Billy Johnson	517 yards by Mack Herron (1974)	1,438 yards by Dave Meggett
117 by Julian Edelman	504 yards by Troy Brown (2000)	1,185 yards by Wes Welker

Longest Punt Return by Every Patriot Player in a Super Bowl Game

28 yard punt return by Troy Brown, in their 32-29 **Super Bowl** win over the Panthers on 02-01-04
26 yard punt return by Julian Edelman, in their 34-28 OT **Super Bowl** win over the Falcons on 02-05-17
20 yard punt return by Dave Meggett, in their 35-21 **Super Bowl** loss to the Packers on 01-26-97
15 yard punt return by Wes Welker, in their 17-14 **Super Bowl** loss to the Giants on 02-03-08
14 yard punt return by Bethel Johnson, in their 24-21 **Super Bowl** win over the Eagles on 02-06-05
12 yard punt return by Irving Fryar, in their 46-10 **Super Bowl** loss to the Bears on 01-26-86
2 yard punt return by Deion Branch, in their 32-29 **Super Bowl** win over Carolina on 02-01-04
-1 yard punt return by Patrick Chung, in their 34-28 OT **Super Bowl** win over the Falcons on 02-05-17

Ron Burton Community Service Award

This Award honors the player who best displays his commitment to helping others in the community

2003	Joe Andruzzi	2012	Zoltan Mesko
2004	Troy Brown	2013	Matthew Slater
2005	Matt Light	2014	Devin McCourty
2006	Jarvis Green	2015	Nate Solder
2007	Ty Warren	2016	Rob Gronkowski
2008	Larry Izzo	2017	Jordan Richards
2009	Kevin Faulk	2018	Joe Cardona
2010	Vince Wilfork	2019	Kyle Van Noy
2011	Jerod Mayo		

Chapter 6

MEMORABLE SCORING PLAYS

Everyone Who Has Scored a TD on the 1st Play of the Game

Charley Frazier caught a 34 yard TD pass from Mike Taliaferro on the Patriots 1st play on 11-23-69
Sam Cunningham caught a 34 yard TD pass from Steve Grogan on the Patriots 1st play on 10-28-73
Sam Cunningham dashed 75 yards for a touchdown on the 1st play of the game on 10-20-74
Allen Carter returned the opening kickoff 99 yards for a touchdown on 12-21-75
Irving Fryar caught an 80 yard TD pass from Doug Flutie on the 1st play of the game on 10-30-88
Sammy Martin returned the opening kickoff 95 yards for a touchdown on 11-27-88
Tim Goad returned Christian Okoye's fumble 19 yards for a TD, on the 1st play of the game, on 12-13-92
David Givens caught a 35 yard TD pass from Tom Brady on the Patriots 1st play on 12-20-03
Bethel Johnson returned the opening kickoff 93 yards for a touchdown on 12-05-04

Everyone Who Has Scored a TD on the Last Play of the Game

Chuck Shonta returned a poor snap to the Titans Punter 52 yards for the game winning TD on 09-17-60
Bob Windsor caught a 10 yard TD pass from Jim Plunkett for the game winning TD on 10-27-74
Carlos Pennywell caught a 13 yard TD pass from Steve Grogan on the last play on 11-29-79
Irving Fryar caught a 10 yard TD pass from Tony Eason on the last play on 09-28-86
Irving Fryar caught a 25 yard GW TD pass from Tony Eason, tipped by Stanley Morgan, on 11-16-86
Hart Lee Dykes caught a 10 yard TD pass from Tony Eason on the last play on 09-17-89
Greg McMurtry caught a 34 yard game winning TD pass from Hugh Millen on 09-22-91
Ben Coates caught a 2 yard TD pass from Hugh Millen on the last play for force Overtime on 12-08-91
Michael Timpson caught a 45 yard game winning TD pass from Hugh Millen in Overtime on 12-08-91
Michael Timpson caught a 36 yard game winning TD pass from Drew Bledsoe in Overtime on 01-02-94
Kevin Turner caught a 14 yard TD game winning TD pass from Drew Bledsoe in Overtime on 11-13-94
Ben Coates caught a 1 yard game winning TD pass from Drew Bledsoe on 11-29-98
James White ran for a 2 yard **Super Bowl** game winning TD in Overtime on 02-05-17
Rex Burkhead ran for a 2 yard **AFC Championship** game winning TD in Overtime on 01-20-19

Only Patriot Wide Receiver Who Has Run for a TD and Caught a Touchdown Pass on His Birthday

Darryl Stingley ran for a 34 yard TD and caught a 21 yard TD on his 26th birthday in 21-17 win on 09-18-77

Only Patriot Running Back Who Has Run for a Touchdown and Caught a TD Pass on His Birthday

Andy Johnson ran for a 4 yard TD and caught a 10 yard TD on his 24th birthday in the 41-7 rout on 10-18-76

Only Patriot Who Has Run for a TD, Caught a TD Pass and Thrown a TD Pass in the Same Game

David Patten ran for a 29 yard TD, caught a 2 TD passes & threw a 60 yard TD in the 38-17 win on 10-21-01

Only Patriot Who Has Caught Two TDs, Ran for a TD and Caught a 2 Point Pass in the Same Game

Curtis Martin caught a 13 yard TD + a 7 yard TD pass, ran for a 1 yard TD + caught a 2 point pass on 09-15-96

Only Patriot Who Has Run for Two TDs, Caught a TD Pass and Run for a 2 Point Conversion in a Game

James White ran for 2 TDs, caught a 5 yard TD pass and ran for 2 points in their 34-28 OT win on 02-05-17

Only Patriot Who Has Caught Three TD Passes and a 2 Point Conversion Pass in the Same Game

Gino Cappelletti caught 3 TD passes & a 2 point conversion pass in the 36-28 win over the Bills on 11-15-64

Chronological List of Everyone Who Has Scored 20 or More Points Scored in a Game

Gino Cappelletti scored 20 points in the 26-16 victory over the Oakland Raiders on 10-26-62
Gino Cappelletti scored 22 points in the 40-21 victory over the Broncos on 10-18-63
Gino Cappelletti scored 21 points in the 33-28 victory over the San Diego Chargers on 09-20-64
Gino Cappelletti scored 21 points in the 39-10 rout of the Broncos on 10-04-64
Gino Cappelletti scored 24 points in the 36-28 win over the Bills on 11-15-64
Gino Cappelletti scored 20 points in the 22-6 victory over the San Diego Chargers on 10-31-65
Gino Cappelletti scored 28 points in the 42-14 rout of the Houston Oilers on 12-18-65
Gino Cappelletti scored 21 points in the 27-21 victory over the Houston Oilers on 11-13-66
Curtis Martin scored 20 points in the 31-0 shutout of the Arizona Cardinals on 09-15-96
Randy Moss scored 24 points in their 56-10 rout of the Bills on 11-08-07
LaGarrette Blount scored 24 points in their 43-22 **Divisional** rout of the Colts on 01-11-14
Jonas Gray scored 24 points in their 42-20 rout of the Indianapolis Colts on 11-16-14
James White scored 20 points in their 34-28 OT **Super Bowl** win over the Falcons on 02-05-17

Chronological List of Everyone Who Scored at Least 33% of the Team's Total Points Scored in a Season

Year	% Pts Scored	Player
1961	35.6%	Gino Cappelletti
1962	37.0%	Gino Cappelletti
1963	34.6%	Gino Cappelletti
1964	42.5%	Gino Cappelletti (AFL League MVP and Player of the Year)
1965	54.1%	Gino Cappelletti
1966	37.8%	Gino Cappelletti
1967	33.9%	Gino Cappelletti
1968	36.2%	Gino Cappelletti
1986	33.9%	Tony Franklin
1994	33.3%	Matt Bahr
1998	37.7%	Adam Vinatieri
1999	35.8%	Adam Vinatieri
2000	38.4%	Adam Vinatieri
2013	36.1%	Stephen Gostkowski
2014	33.3%	Stephen Gostkowski
2017	34.1%	Stephen Gostkowski

Every Patriots Player Who Has Led the League in Total Points Scored in a Regular Season

Gino Cappelletti led the AFL and the NFL with 147 points scored in 1961
Gino Cappelletti led the AFL and the NFL with 113 points scored in 1963
Gino Cappelletti led the AFL and the NFL with 155 points scored in 1964 (AFL Record)
Gino Cappelletti led the AFL and tied with Gale Sayers for the NFL lead with 132 points scored in 1965
Gino Cappelletti led the AFL and the NFL with 119 points scored in 1966
John Smith was the NFL Scoring Leader with 115 points scored in 1979
John Smith was the NFL Scoring Leader with 129 points scored in 1980
Tony Franklin was the NFL Scoring Leader with 140 points scored in 1986
Adam Vinatieri was the NFL Scoring Leader with 141 points scored in their 2004 Championship Season
Stephen Gostkowski was the NFL Scoring Leader with 148 points in 2008
Stephen Gostkowski was the NFL Scoring Leader with 153 points scored in 2012
Stephen Gostkowski was the NFL Scoring leader with 158 points scored in 2013
Stephen Gostkowski was the NFL Scoring Leader with 156 points scored in their 2014 Championship Season
Stephen Gostkowski was the NFL Scoring Leader 151 points scored in 2015

Everyone Who Has Scored at Least 12 Touchdowns in a Season

23 TDs were scored through the air by Randy Moss during their undefeated 2007 regular season
18 TDs were scored on the ground by LeGarrette Blount during their 2016 Championship Season
18 TDs were scored by Rob Gronkowski (17 receiving and 1 rushing) during the 2011 season
17 TDs were scored by Curtis Martin (14 rushing and 3 receiving) during the 1996 season
15 TDs were scored by Curtis Martin (14 rushing and 1 receiving) during the 1995 season
13 TDs were scored on the ground by BenJarvus Green Ellis during the 2010 season
13 TDs were scored through the air by Randy Moss during the 2009 season
13 TDs were scored on the ground by Corey Dillon during the 2006 season
13 TDs were scored by Corey Dillon (12 rushing and 1 receiving) during the 2005 season
13 TDs were scored by Corey Dillon (12 rushing and 1 receiving) in their 2004 Championship Season
13 TDs were scored by Steve Grogan (12 rushing and 1 fumble advancement) in the 1976 season
13 TDs were scored by Stanley Morgan (12 receiving and 1 Punt Return TD) in the 1979 season
13 TDs were scored by Antowain Smith (12 rushing and 1 receiving) in their 2001 Championship Season
12 TDs were scored by James White (7 receiving and 5 rushing) during their 2018 Championship Season
12 TDs were scored through the air by Rob Gronkowski during their 2014 Championship Season
12 TDs were scored on the ground by Stevan Ridley during their 2012 season
12 TDs were scored by Robert Edwards (9 rushing and 3 receiving) during the 1998 season
12 TDs were scored by Mack Herron (7 rushing and 5 receiving) during the 1974 season

Everyone Who Has Scored at Least Seven TDs in the Playoffs

12 TDs by Rob Gronkowski (12 TD receptions)
8 TDs by James White (5 rushing TDs and 3 TD receptions)
8 TDs by LeGarrette Blount (8 rushing TDs)
7 TDs by David Givens (7 TD receptions)

Everyone Who Has Scored at Least 50 TDs While Playing for the Patriots

92 TDs by Rob Gronkowski (79 Regular Season and 12 Playoff TD Receptions + 1 Rushing TD)
71 TDs by Stanley Morgan (67 Regular Season and 3 Playoff TD receptions + 1 Punt Return TD)
51 TDs by Randy Moss (50 Regular Season receptions and 1 TD reception in the Playoffs)
51 TDs by Ben Coates (50 Regular Season receptions and 1 TD reception in the Playoffs)

Every Game That the Patriots Scored at Least 50 points

The Patriots blew out the Buffalo Bills 52-21 @ BU Field on 10-22-61
The Patriots beat the New York Jets 55-21 @ Schaefer Stadium on 10-29-78
The Patriots destroyed the New York Jets 56-3 @ Schaefer Stadium on 09-09-79
The Patriots roughed up the Washington Redskins 52-7 @ Gillette Stadium on 10-28-07
The Patriots blasted the Buffalo Bills 56-10 @ Ralph Wilson Stadium on 11-18-07
The Patriots shutout to the Tennessee Titans 59-0 @ Gillette Stadium on 10-18-09
The Patriots defeated the Buffalo Bills 52-28 @ Ralph Wilson Stadium on 09-30-12
The Patriots crushed the Indianapolis Colts 59-24 @ Gillette Stadium on 11-18-12
The Patriots smashed the Pittsburgh Steelers 55-31 @ Gillette Stadium on 11-03-13
The Patriots buried the Chicago Bears 51-23 @ Gillette Stadium on 10-26-14
The Patriots jolted the Jacksonville Jaguars 51-17 @ Gillette Stadium on 09-27-15

Only Patriots Player Who Has Returned a Punt for a TD in a Playoff Game

Troy Brown returned a punt 55 yards for a TD in their **Divisional** win over the Steelers on 01-27-02

Only Patriots Player Who Has Returned a Kickoff for a TD in the Playoff Game

Dion Lewis returned a kickoff 98 yards for a TD in their **Divisional** win over Houston on 01-14-17

Only Patriots Player Who Has Returned an Interception for a TD in a Super Bowl Game

Ty Law returned a pass by Kurt Warner 47 yards for a TD in their **Super Bowl** win on 02-03-02

10 Greatest Comebacks by the Patriots

Trailing 28-3 PATS beat Atlanta 34-28 in OT with James White's 2 yard TD run in Super Bowl on 02-05-17
Trailing 24-0 the Patriots beat Denver 34-31 in OT (Nate Ebner's fumble recovery in OT) on 11-24-13
Trailing 23-0 the Patriots beat the Seattle Seahawks 38-23 (Led by Tony Eason) on 09-16-84
Trailing 22-0 the Patriots defeated the Giants 23-22 on Ben Coates' 13 yard TD reception on 12-21-96
Trailing 21-0 the Patriots beat the Jets 31-27 on Keith Byars' 4 yard TD reception with 4:03 left, on 11-10-96
Trailing 28-7 the Patriots defeated the Colts 31-28 on Adam Vinatieri's 26 yard field goal on 09-19-99
Trailing 27-6 the Patriots beat the Bears 33-30 on David Patten's 20 yard TD reception on 11-10-02
Trailing 21-0 the Patriots crushed the Bills 49-21 (Led by Tom Brady) on 01-01-12
Trailing 20-0 the Patriots defeated the Vikings 26-20 in OT with Kevin Turner's TD reception on 11-13-94
Trailing 24-7 the Boston Patriots defeated the NY Titans 28-24 on Chuck Shonta's 54 yard TD on 09-17-60
Trailing 20-3 the Boston Patriots beat the San Diego Chargers 24-20 on 10-19-62
Trailing 20-3 the Patriots beat the Jets 30-20 (Led by Tony Eason) on 10-28-84
Trailing 17-0 the Patriots beat the Dolphins 27-24 (Helped by Tom Brady's 2 rushing TDs) on 12-24-11

BONUS TRIVIA

Players Who have Been Mentioned or Appeared in Football-Related Movies

Matt Bahr and Greg Hawthorne appeared in the Rocky Bleier Movie *Fighting Back*
Drew Bledsoe had a cameo appearance in *Jerry Maguire*
Doug Flutie was an actor in the movie *Second String*
Tim Fox broke the collarbone of Dennis Quaid while filming *Everybody's All American*
Bob Gladieux's name was mentioned twice in the restaurant scene of *Rudy*
Joe Kapp was an actor in *Semi Tough*, *The Longest Yard* and *Two Minute Warning*
Martin Imhoff and Harold Jackson were in scenes of the movie *North Dallas Forty*
Marty Schottenheimer and Pat Studstill appeared in *Paper Lion*

TWO POINT CONVERSIONS

Every Successful 2 Point Conversion by the Patriots

Jim Crawford caught a 2 point pass from Gino Cappelletti in their 35-0 win over the Chargers on 10-08-60

Gino Cappelletti ran for a 2 point conversion in their 27-14 loss to the Oakland Raiders on 10-16-60

Gino Cappelletti ran for a 2 point conversion in their 42-14 rout of the Dallas Texans on 11-18-60

Gino Cappelletti ran for a 2 point conversion in their 37-21 loss to the Houston Oilers on 12-18-60

Babe Parilli ran for a 2 point conversion in their 18-17 victory over the Dallas Texans on 10-29-61

Jim Crawford caught a 2 point pass from Babe Parilli in their 24-20 win over the Chargers on 10-19-62

Jim Colclough caught a 2 point pass from Babe Parilli in their 43-43 tie with the Raiders on 10-16-64

Gino Cappelletti caught a 2 point pass from Babe Parilli in their 36-28 win over the Bills on 11-15-64

Jim Colclough caught a 2 point pass from Babe Parilli in their 24-14 loss to the Bills on 12-20-64

Tony Romeo caught a 2 point pass from Babe Parilli in their 24-10 win over the Broncos on 09-18-66

Bob Cappadona caught a 2 point pass from Babe Parilli in their 38-28 loss to the Jets on 12-17-66

Kim Hammond ran for a 2 point conversion in their 28-18 loss to the San Diego Chargers on 12-07-69

Dave Meggett ran for a 2 point conversion in their 17-14 win over the Browns on 09-03-95

Curtis Martin caught a 2 point pass from Drew Bledsoe in their 35-25 win over the Ravens on 11-26-95

Dave Meggett caught a 2 point pass from Drew Bledsoe in their 41-27 loss to the Steelers on 12-16-95

Curtis Martin caught a 2 point pass from Drew Bledsoe in their 31-0 shutout of the Cardinals on 09-15-96

Sam Gash caught a 2 point pass from Drew Bledsoe in their 46-38 victory over the Ravens on 10-06-96

Ben Coates caught a 2 point pass from Drew Bledsoe in their 46-38 win over the Ravens on 10-06-96

Keith Byars caught a 2 point pass from Drew Bledsoe in their 34-8 loss to the Broncos on 11-17-96

Adam Vinatieri ran for a 2 point conversion in their 25-21 win over the Bills on 11-29-98

Kevin Faulk ran for a 2 point conversion in their 19-11 loss to the Browns on 11-12-00

Antowain Smith ran for a 2 point conversion in their 41-38 OT win vs the Chiefs on 09-22-02

Troy Brown caught a 2 point pass from Tom Brady in their 33-30 win over the Bears on 11-10-02

Christian Fauria caught a 2 point pass from Tom Brady in their 27-24 OT win vs the Dolphins on 12-29-02

Kevin Faulk ran for a 2 point conversion in their 32-29 **Super Bowl** win over the Panthers on 02-03-04

Corey Dillon ran for a 2 point conversion in their 24-3 win over the Baltimore Ravens on 11-28-04

Heath Evans ran for a 2 point conversion in their 23-16 victory over the Dolphins on 11-13-05

Reche Caldwell caught a 2 point pass from Tom Brady in their 17-14 loss to the Jets on 11-12-06

Troy Brown caught a 2 point pass from Tom Brady in their 28-21 win over the Lions on 12-03-06

Kevin Faulk ran for a 2 point conversion in their 24-21 **Divisional** win over San Diego on 01-14-07

Laurence Maroney ran for a 2 point conversion in their 38-35 win over the Giants on 12-29-07

Jabar Gaffney caught a 2 point pass from Matt Cassel in their 34-31 OT loss to the Jets on 11-13-08

Wes Welker caught a 2 point pass from Matt Cassel in their 24-21 win over the Seahawks on 12-07-08

Randy Moss caught a 2 point pass from Tom Brady in their 27-17 win over the Dolphins on 11-08-09

Sammy Morris ran for a 2 point conversion in their 28-21 **Divisional** loss to the Jets on 01-16-11

Danny Woodhead ran for a 2 point conversion in their 35-21 win over the Chargers on 09-18-11

Danny Woodhead ran for a 2 point conversion in their 49-21 win over the Dolphins on 01-01-12

Julian Edelman caught a 2 point pass from Tom Brady in their 27-26 win over the Browns on 12-08-13

Julian Edelman caught a 2 point pass from Tom Brady in their 34-20 victory over the Bills on 12-29-13

Stevan Ridley ran for a 2 point conversion in their 43-22 **Divisional** rout of the Indianapolis Colts on 1-11-14

Julian Edelman caught a 2 point pass from Tom Brady in their 35-14 win over the Dolphins on 01-01-17

James White ran for a 2 point conversion in their 34-28 OT **Super Bowl** win vs the Falcons on 02-05-17

Danny Amendola caught a 2 point pass from Tom Brady in their 34-28 OT **Super Bowl** Win on 02-05-17

James White ran for a 2 point conversion in their 17-10 victory over the Eagles on 11-17-19

Julian Edelman caught a 2 point pass from Tom Brady in their 24-17 win over Buffalo on 12-21 -19

Every *Unsuccessful Attempt* for a 2 Point Conversion

Gino Cappelletti's run, after his PAT was blocked, was stopped for no gain, in their 27-14 loss on 10-16-60

Butch Songin was sacked in their 27-15 loss to the Houston Oilers on 11-12-61

Jim Crawford's run was halted in their 24-24 Tie with the Chiefs on 11-17-63

Babe Parilli's pass to Art Graham was incomplete in their 25-24 win over the Chiefs on 11-06-64

Babe Parilli's pass was incomplete in their 24-14 loss to the Bills on 12-20-64

Jim Nance's run was stopped in their 44-16 loss to the Bills on 12-09-67

Babe Parilli's pass to Jim Colclough was incomplete in their 44-16 loss to the Bills on 12-09-67

Mike Taliaferro's pass to Carl Garrett, with 35 tics left, was incomplete in their 17-16 loss on 11-09-69

Tom Janik's pass to TE Eligible Charlie Long was incomplete in their 38-23 loss to Miami on 11-30-69

Drew Bledsoe's pass to Michael Timpson was incomplete in their 31-28 win over the Bengals on 09-18-94

Drew Bledsoe's pass was completed to Ben Coates but he was stopped in their 31-28 win on 09-18-94

Curtis Martin's run was halted in their 31-26 loss to the Chiefs on 10-15-95

Curtis Martin's run was halted in their 41-27 loss to the Steelers on 12-16-95

Curtis Martin's run was halted in their 27-22 loss to the Redskins on 10-13-96

Drew Bledsoe's pass to Keith Byars was incomplete in their 23-22 win over the Giants on 12-21-96

Adam Vinatieri's run after a fumbled snap was stopped in their 23-18 loss to the Vikings on 11-02-97

Drew Bledsoe's pass to Terry Glenn was incomplete in their 23-18 loss to the Vikings on 11-02-97

Drew Bledsoe's pass was completed to Mike Bartrum but he was stopped short in their 29-6 win on 09-13-98

Drew Bledsoe's pass was completed to M.Bartrum but he was stopped short in their 32-18 loss on 12-13-98

Drew Bledsoe's pass to Ben Coates was incomplete in their 19-7 win over the Browns on 10-03-99

Drew Bledsoe's pass was completed to Ben Coates but he was stopped short in their 20-15 loss on 12-12-99

Kevin Faulk's run was halted in their 21-16 loss to the Buccaneers on 09-03-00

Lee Johnson's run, after recovering the fumbled snap, was stopped in their 21-13 loss on 09-17-00

Ken Walter's pass to Grey Ruegamer was incomplete in their 34-17 win over the Saints on 11-25-01

Ken Walter took a direct snap but was stopped in their 41-38 OT win vs the Chiefs on 09-22-02

Tom Brady's pass to Mike Vrabel was incomplete in their 26-13 loss to Miami on 10-06-02

Tom Brady's pass to David Patten was incomplete in their 24-16 loss to the Broncos on 10-27-02

Kevin Faulk took a direct snap but was stopped in their 33-30 win over the Bears on 11-10-02

Tom Brady's pass to Troy Brown was incomplete in their 23-16 win over the Miami on 11-13-05

Tom Brady's pass to Christian Fauria was incomplete in their 26-16 loss to the Chiefs on 11-27-05

Matt Cassel's pass to Bam Childress was incomplete in their 28-26 loss to the Dolphins on 01-01-06

Kevin Faulk's run was halted in their 18-15 loss to the Indianapolis Colts on 11-02-08

Tom Brady's pass to Benjamin Watson was incomplete in their 25-24 win over the Bills on 09-14-09

Tom Brady's pass to Randy Moss was incomplete in their 25-24 win over the Bills on 09-14-09

Tom Brady's pass to Brandon Tate was incomplete in their 39-26 win over the Steelers on 11-14-10

Tom Brady's pass to Rob Gronkowski was incomplete in their 20-18 loss to the Cardinals on 09-16-12

Shane Vereen's run was stopped in their 27-26 comeback win over the Browns on 12-08-13

Shane Vereen's run was stopped in their 26-16 **AFC Championship** loss to the Broncos on 01-19-14

Tom Brady's pass was completed to Julian Edelman but he was stopped short in their 43-21 win on 11-02-14

Tom Brady's pass to Julian Edelman was intercepted in their 20-18 **AFC Championship** loss on 01-24-16

Tom Brady's pass was completed to James White but he was stopped short in their 22-17 win on 11-27-16

Tom Brady's pass was intercepted by Julian Stanford in their 25-6 win over Buffalo on 10-29-18

James White run was stopped in their 23-16 loss to the Chiefs on 12-08-19

(Julian Stanford fumbled his interception and if PATS had recovered fumble they would have scored 1 point)

CHAPTER 7

EVERYONE WHO HAS PLAYED
IN A REGULAR SEASON / PLAYOFF GAME

FOOTBALL-RELATED STATS OF 1,268 PLAYERS

ABDULLAH, Rabih (#27)
Born on April 27, 1975 in Martinsville, VA
6'1" and 235 pounds
Running Back   2004
13 carries for 13 yards + 1 TD and had 1 reception for 9 yards
Ran for a 1 yard touchdown in their 24-10 win over the Miami Dolphins on 10-10-04
Caught a 9 yard pass from Tom Brady in their 30-20 win over the Seattle Seahawks on 10-17-04
Longest run for 5 yards in their 23-7 win over the New York Jets on 12-26-04
9 Regular Season Games and 3 Playoff Games
Member of the 2004 World Championship Team
Lehigh Mountain Hawk

ABRAMS, Robert "Bobby" (#50)
Born on April 12, 1967 in Detroit, Michigan
6'3" and 242 pounds
Linebacker   1995
9 games/1 started (on 10-15-95)
Michigan Wolverine

ACKS, Ron (#51)
Born on October 3, 1944 in Herrin, IL
6'2" and 214 pounds
Linebacker   1972-73
1 interception for 11 yards, 1 sack and 5 fumble recoveries
Recovered fumbles by Dennis Shaw, Steve Davis, Don Nottingham, Carl Garrett and George Hoey
Had an 11 yard return of a pass by Joe Ferguson in their 31-13 loss to the Bills on 09-16-73
Sacked Bert Jones in their 24-16 win over the Baltimore Colts on 10-07-73
28 games/27 started
Illinois Fighting Illini

ADAMS, Robert "Bob" (#80)
Born on August 15, 1946 in Stockton, CA
6'2" and 225 pounds
TE/Tackle   1973-74
31 receptions for 441 yards and 2 carries for 7 yards
Longest reception was a 30 yard pass from Jim Plunkett in their 37-13 loss to the Bills on 12-09-73
Longest run for 4 yards in their 18-13 loss to the Baltimore Colts on 12-16-73
25 games/12 started
Pacific Tiger

ADAMS, George (#33)
Born on December 22, 1962 in Lexington, Kentucky
6'1" and 225 pounds
RB (KR)   1990-91
30 carries for 114 yards, 16 receptions for 146 yards + 1 TD and 1 kickoff return of 7 yards
Caught a 4 yard TD pass from Marc Wilson in their 17-10 loss to the Dolphins on 10-18-90
Longest reception was a 28 yard pass from Hugh Millen in their 14-0 loss to the Bills on 11-18-90
Returned Al Del Greco's kickoff 7 yards in their 34-14 loss to the Phoenix Cardinals on 11-25-90
Longest run for 13 yards in their 13-10 loss to the New York Giants on 12-30-90
18 games/8 started
Kentucky Wildcat

ADAMS JR., Julius (#85 and #69) *"Ju-Ju* **and** *The Jewel"*
Born on April 26, 1948 in Macon, GA
6'3" and 270 pounds
Defensive End (LB)   1971-87
Wore #69 for 3 games in 1987 (Oct 25th, Nov 1st + Nov 8th)
81.5 Regular Season sacks and 7 fumbles recoveries for 12 yards
Shared in a sack of Jim McMahon and had 1 ½ sacks of Al Woodhall
Sacked James Harris, Bill Nelson, Len Dawson, Bobby Douglass and Roman Gabriel
Sacked Lynn Dickey, Norm Snead, Marty Domres, Steve Ramsey and Mike Livingston
Sacked Bobby Avelini, Greg Landry, Jim Zorn, Joe Montana and Don Strock
Sacked Mike Phipps, David Woodley, Dan Manucci, Art Schlitcher and Joe Pisarcik
Sacked Joe Theisman and WR Mark Clayton
Had 2 sacks of Roger Staubach, Archie Manning, Vince Ferragamo, Mike Pagel and Dave Krieg
Had 2 sacked Earl Morrall and recorded 2 ½ sacks of Terry Bradshaw and Dan Fouts
Had 3 sacks of Pat Ryan and Ken O'Brien, 3 ½ sacks of Joe Namath and 4 sacks of Dennis Shaw
Had 5 sacks of Steve Bartkowski, Bert Jones and Joe Ferguson
Recorded 6 sacks of Bob Griese and Richard Todd
Recovered fumbles by Dennis Shaw, Bob Griese, John Keyworth, Lynn Dickey and Archie Manning
Recovered fumbles by Curt Warner and Joe Ferguson
NFL Defensive Player of the Week in their 34-13 rout of the Dolphins on 12-05-71
Sacked Steve Bartkowski 4 times in their 16-10 win over the Falcons on 12-04-77
Recovered his strip sack of Archie Manning in their 29-21 win over the Houston Oilers on 11-28-82
Sacked WR Mark Clayton in their 17-13 win over the Miami Dolphins on 11-03-85
Had a 12 yard return of a fumble by Joe Ferguson in their 23-6 win over the Detroit Lions on 12-08-85
AFC Pro Bowl Defensive End in 1980
206 Regular Season games/158 started 6 Playoff Games/6 started
3 sacks and 1 fumble recovery in the playoffs
Sacked Ken Stabler *3 times* in their 24-21 loss Divisional Playoff loss to the Oakland Raiders on 12-18-76
Recovered Joe Carter's fumble in their 31-14 AFC Championship Game win over Miami on 01-12-86
#27 pick in the 1971 NFL Draft
Texas Southern Tiger

ADAMS, Phillip (#26)
Born on July 20, 1988 in Rock Hill, SC
6'0" and 193 pounds
Defensive Back   2011
Intercepted a pass by Tyler Palko in their 34-3 rout of the Kansas City Chiefs on 11-21-11
6 games
South Carolina State Bulldog

ADAMS, Samuel "Sam" (#61) *"Pimpin' Sam"*
Nicknamed "*Pimpin' Sam*" because of his elaborate 3 piece suits
Born on September 20, 1948 in Jasper, TX
6'3" and 256 pounds
Guard/Tackle (TE)   1972-80
Recovered fumbles by Carl Garrett, Jim Plunkett, Sam Cunningham and Horace Ivory
Occasionally used as a Blocking Tight End
119 Regular Season Games/105 started and 2 Playoff Games
Pairie View A & M Panther

ADAMS, Titus (#62)
Born on January 28, 1983 in Omaha, NE
6'3" and 305 pounds
Defensive Lineman   2009
2 games (on Dec. 13th and Dec. 20th)
Nebraska Cornhusker

ADDISON, Thomas "Tom" (#53) *"Plugger"*
Born on April 12, 1936 in Lancaster, SC
6'2" and 230 pounds
Linebacker   1960-67
22 sacks, 16 interceptions for 103 yards + 1 TD, 1 blocked extra point and 4 fumble recoveries
Sacked Abner Hayes, Frank Tripucka, Tom Flores, Jack Kemp, George Shaw and Warren Rabb
Sacked John McCormick and 2 sacks of Tom Flores, John Hadl and George Blanda,
Recorded 2 ½ sacks of Len Dawson and 6 ½ sacks of Jacky Lee
Intercepted Tom Flores, George Herring, Lee Grosscup, Cotton Davidson and Tobin Rote
Intercepted Mickey Slaughter, Jacky Lee, Len Dawson, Dick Wood and Don Breaux
Had 2 interceptions of Jack Kemp, Dick Wood and George Blanda
Recovered fumbles by Bob Stransky, Curtis McClinton and Abner Hayes
Blocked an extra point attempt by Gene Mingo in their 31-24 loss to the Broncos on 10-23-60
Recovered a blocked punt in their 35-21 victory over the Oakland Raiders on 12-09-61
Had a 12 yard TD return of a pass by Lee Grosscup in their 43-14 win vs the NY Titans on 10-06-62
Had a career long 17 yard return of a pass by Tobin Rote in their 17-13 loss to the Chargers on 09-14-63
AFL All Star LB in 1960, 1961, 1962, 1963, 1964
First Team All Pro Linebacker in 1961
106 Regular Season Games/102 started and 2 Playoff Games/2 started
Fell on Jack Kemp's 4th down & goal fumble in their 26-8 Playoff win over Buffalo on 12-28-63
South Carolina Gamecock

AGNEW JR, Raymond "Ray" (#92)
Born on September 9, 1967 in Winston Salem, NC
6'3" and 285 pounds
Defensive Lineman   1990-94
8 sacks and 2 fumble recoveries
Sacked Boomer Esiason, Timm Rosenbach, Jeff George, Dan Marino, Steve DeBerg and Don Majkowski
Recorded 2 sacks of Dave Krieg and Jim Kelly
Recovered fumbles by Albert Bentley and Dave Krieg
66 Regular Season games/38 started and 1 Playoff Game (on 01-01-95)
#10 pick in the 1990 NFL Draft
North Carolina State Wolfpack

AIKEN, Daniel "Danny" (#48)
Born on August 28, 1988 in Roanoke, VA
6'4" and 250 pounds
Long Snapper   2011-14
Long Snapper for Kicker Stephen Gostkowski and Punter's Zoltan Mesko and Ryan Allen
63 Regular Season Games and 10 Playoff Games
Snapped the ball over Punter Ryan Allen in their 43-22 Divisional win over the Colts on 01-11-14
Member of the 2014 Championship Team
Virginia Cavalier

AIKEN, Kamar (#16)
Born on May 30, 1989 in Hollywood, FL
6'2" and 216 pounds
Wide Receiver   2012
Only game played was on 12-23-12
Central Florida Knight

AIKEN JR, Samuel "Sam" (#88)
6'2" and 204 pounds
Born on December 14, 1980 in Kenansville, NC
Wide Receiver   2008-09
28 receptions for 427 yards + 2 TDs
Caught a 54 yard TD pass from Tom Brady in their 35-7 rout of Tampa on 10-25-09
Hauled in a career long 81 yard TD pass from Tom Brady in their 22-21 loss to Miami on 12-06-09
28 Regular Season Games/9 started and 1 Playoff Game/1 started (on 01-10-10)
Caught a 5 yard pass from Tom Brady in their 33-14 Wild Card loss to the Baltimore Ravens on 01-10-10
North Carolina Tar Heel

AKBAR, Akmal "Hakin" (#29)
Born on August 11, 1980 in Riverside, CA
6'0" and 222 pounds
Defensive Back   2001
6 games
Member of the 2001 World Championship Team
#163 pick in the 2001 NFL Draft
Washington Husky

AKINS, Chris (#34)
Born on November 29, 1976 in Little Rock AK
5'11" and 200 pounds
Safety   2003
12 Regular Season Games and 3 Playoff Games
Member of the 2003 World Championship Team
Arkansas Pine Bluff Golden Lion

ALEXANDER, Eric (#49 and #52)
Born on August 1, 1982 in Tyler, TX
6'3" and 230 pounds
LB/Special Team   2004-09
Wore #49 from 2004-05 and #52 from 2006-09
Forced Chris Carr's fumbled kickoff return of the opening kickoff in their 27-21 win over the Ravens
          on 10-04-09
45 Regular Season Games and 7 Playoff Games
Sacked Peyton Manning in their 38-34 AFC Championship Game loss to the Colts on 01-21-07
Member of the 2004 World Championship Team
LSU Fighting Tiger

ALEXANDER, Rogers (#91)
Born on August 11, 1964 in Washington, DC
6'3" and 222 pounds
Linebacker (KR)   1987
Returned Goran Lingmerth's kickoff 4 yards in their 20-10 loss to the Cleveland Browns on 10-04-87
3 games/2 started
Penn State Nittany Lion

ALLARD, Don (#12)
Born on April 21, 1936 in Cambridge, MA
6'1" and 188 pounds
Quarterback   1962
4 games
Member of the 1964 ACFL Boston Sweepers and 1965 ACFL New Bedford Sweepers Championship Teams
Boston College Eagle

ALLEN, Dwayne (#83)
Born on February 24, 1990 in Fayetteville, NC
6'3" and 265 pounds
Tight End   2017-18
13 receptions for 113 yards + 1 TD and 1 fumble recovery
Caught an 11 yard TD pass from Tom Brady in their 41-16 rout of the Broncos on 11-12-17
Recovered Rex Burkhead's fumble in their 33-6 rout of the Raiders on 11-19-17
Longest reception was a 22 yard pass from Tom Brady in their 34-17 rout of Buffalo on 12-24-17
29 Regular Season Games/16 started and 6 Playoff Games/1 started (on 01-20-19)
Member of the 2018 World Championship Team
Clemson Tiger

ALLEN, Marvin (#39)
Born on November 23, 1965 in Wichita Falls, TX
5'10" and 215 pounds
RB/KR   1988-91
94 carries for 378 yards + 2 TDs, 7 receptions for 57 yards and 43 kickoff returns for 844 yards
Recovered fumbled punt returns by Erroll Tucker, Wendell Davis, Marvin Hargrove and Leo Lewis
Recovered fumbled kickoff returns by Leonard Harris and Jamie Morris
Downed a 49 yard punt by Jeff Feagles, on the Colts 2 yard line, in their 21-17 win over the Colts on 10-02-88
Downed a 38 yard punt by Jeff Feagles, on the Colts 4 yard line, in their 21-17 win over the Colts on 10-02-88
Had a 3 yard advancement of a fumbled KR by Jamie Morris in their 37-7 loss to the Chiefs on 12-02-90
Longest run was 29 yards in their 37-7 loss to the Kansas City Chiefs on 12-02-90
Longest was a 34 yard return of Gary Anderson's opening kickoff in their 24-3 loss to Pittsburgh on 12-09-90
Longest reception was a 19 yard pass from Tommy Hodson in their 42-7 loss to the Jets on 12-23-90
37 games/3 started
#294 pick in the 1988 NFL Draft
Tulane Green Wave

ALLEN, Ryan (#6)
Born on February 28, 1990 in Salem, OR
6'2" and 220 pounds
Punter   2013-18
409 punts for 18,526 yards
Had a career long punt of 67 yards in their 43-21 rout of the Broncos on 11-02-14
Had another punt of 67 yards in their 28-21 victory over the Steelers on 09-10-15
AFC Special Team Player of the Week in their 23-14 win over San Diego on 12-07-14
AFC Special Team Player of the Week in their 27-0 shutout of Houston on 09-22-16
Holder for Stephen Gostkowski
96 Regular Season Games and 16 Playoff Games
58 punts for 2,487 yards in the playoffs
Had a 68 yard free kick after a safety in their 43-22 Divisional win over the Colts on 01-11-14
Member of the 2014, 2016 and 2018 World Championship Teams
Louisiana Tech Bulldog

ALLEN JR., Terry (#22)
Born on February 21, 1968 in Commerce, GA
5'10" and 204 pounds
Running Back   1999
254 carries for 896 yards + 8 TDs and 14 receptions for 125 yards + 1 TD
Caught an 8 yard TD pass from Drew Bledsoe in their 31-28 win over the Colts on 09-19-99
Longest run for 39 yards in their 24-23 win over the Denver Broncos on 10-24-99
Longest reception was a 38 yard pass from Drew Bledsoe in their 27-3 win over Arizona on 10-31-99
Ran for a 3 yard game winning TD in their 13-6 win over the Dallas Cowboys on 12-05-99
16 games/13 started
Clemson Tiger

AMENDOLA, Daniel "Danny" (#80) *"Playoff"*
Born on November 2, 1985 in The Woodlands, TX
5'11" and 190 pounds
WR/PR/KR (QB)   2013-17
230 receptions for 2,383 yards + 12 TDs, 3 carries for 12 yards and 1 completion for 36 yards
85 punt returns for 773 yards, 34 kickoff returns for 799 yards and 1 recovery of an onside kick
Caught 2 TD passes from Jimmy Garoppolo and 1 Post Season TD pass from Julian Edelman
Caught 10 Regular Season TD passes and 5 Post Season TD passes from Tom Brady
Longest reception was a 57 yard pass from Tom Brady in their 55-31 rout of the Steelers on 11-03-13
Caught a Game Winning 1 yard TD pass from Tom Brady in their 27-26 win over the Browns on 12-08-13
Recovered Nick Folk's onside kick in their 27-25 win over the Jets on 10-16-14
Longest was an 81 yard return of a kickoff by Sam Martin in their 34-9 win over the Lions on 11-23-14
Longest run for 8 yards in their 27-10 win over the Redskins on 11-08-15
Longest was an 82 yard return of a punt by Brad Wing in their 27-26 win over the NY Giants on 11-15-15
Took the direct snap and tossed a 36 yard pass to Tom Brady in their 35-28 loss to the Eagles on 12-06-15
Led the NFL with the best average (12.0) yards per punt return in 2015
Returned a free kick by Drew Kaser 16 yards in their 21-13 win over the LA Chargers on 10-29-17
69 Regular Season Games/29 started and 13 Playoff Games/6 started
57 receptions for 709 yards + 6 TDs, 3 carries for 16 yards and 1 completion for 20 yards in the playoffs
9 kickoff returns for 213 yards and 9 punt returns for 106 yards in the playoffs
Caught a 15 yard TD pass from Tom Brady in their 35-31 Divisional win over the Ravens on 01-10-15
Caught a 51 yard flea flicker TD pass from Julian Edelman in their 35-31 Divisional win vs Balt on 01-10-15
Caught a 4 yard TD pass from Tom Brady in their 28-24 Super Bowl win over Seattle on 02-01-15
Caught a 6 yard TD pass from Tom Brady in their Epic 34-28 OT Super Bowl win over Atlanta on 02-05-17
Caught a 2 point pass from Tom Brady in their Epic 34-28 OT Super Bowl win vs the Falcons on 02-05-17
Caught a 9 yard TD pass from Tom Brady in their 24-20 Championship win over Jacksonville on 01-21-18
Caught a 4 yard TD pass from Tom Brady in their 24-20 Championship win vs the Jaguars on 01-21-18
Caught Tom Brady's lateral and tossed 20 yard pass to Dion Lewis in 24-20 Championship win on 01-21-18
Member of the 2014 and 2016 World Championship Teams
Texas Tech Red Raider

ANDERSEN, Jason (#67)
Born on September 3, 1975 in Hayward, CA
6'6" and 319 pounds
Center   1999-2000
16 games
#211 pick in the 1998 NFL Draft
BYU Cougar

ANDERSON, Bobby (#33)
Born on October 11, 1947 in Midland, MI
6'0" and 208 yards
Running Back   1975
Ran for a 1 yard gain in their 24-17 loss to the St. Louis Cardinals on 11-02-75
5 games
Appeared in Kevin Costner's "American Flyers" Movie in 1985
Colorado Buffalo

ANDERSON, Darren (#25)
Born on January 1, 1969 in Cincinnati, Ohio
5'10" and 185 pounds
DB   1992
Only game played was on 09-27-92
#93 pick in the 1992 NFL Draft
Toledo Rocket

ANDERSON, Mark (#95)
Born on May 26, 1983 in Tulsa, OK
6'4" and 255 pounds
Defensive End   2011
10 sacks and 1 fumble recovery
Sacked Chad Henne, Philip Rivers, Mark Sanchez, Ben Roethlisberger and Tyler Palko
Sacked Tim Tebow and Ryan Fitzpatrick as well
Recovered Tim Tebow's fumble in their 41-23 victory over Denver on 12-18-11
16 Regular Season Games/1 started (on 12-11-11) and 3 Playoff Games
2.5 sacks in the playoffs
Sacked Joe Flacco in their 23-20 AFC Championship win over the Ravens on 01-22-12
Sacked Eli Manning 1 ½ times in their 21-17 Super Bowl loss to the NY Giants on 02-05-12
Alabama Crimson Tide

ANDERSON, Ralph (#49) *"Sticks"*
Born on April 3, 1949 in Dallas, TX
6'2" and 180 pounds
Defensive Back   1973
2 interceptions, 2 fumble recoveries and blocked an extra point
Intercepted Roman Gabriel and Dan Pastorini and recovered fumbles by Mike Adamle and Bob Gresham
Blocked an extra point attempt by George Hunt in their 18-13 loss to the Baltimore Colts on 12-16-73
13 games/11 started
West Texas A & M University Buffalo

ANDREWS, David (#60)
Born on July 10, 1992 in Wesleyan, GA
6'3" and 300 pounds
Center (G)   2015-18
Recovered 1 fumble by Danny Amendola and 3 Regular Season fumbles by Tom Brady
Used at Right Guard in their 27-26 win over the New York Giants on 11-08-15
60 Regular Season Games/57 started and 11 Playoff Games/9 started
Used as a blocking fullback in their 20-18 Championship Game loss to the Broncos on 01-24-16
Recovered a fumble by Tom Brady in their 13-3 Super Bowl win over the Rams on 02-03-19
Member of the 2016 and 2018 World Championship Teams
Georgia Bulldog

ANDREWS, Willie (#23)
Born on November 2, 1983 in Longview, TX
5'9" and 182 pounds
KR (DB)   2006-07
4 kickoff returns for 149 yards + 1 TD
Longest was a 77 yard TD return of a kickoff by Jay Feely in their 49-28 win over Miami on 10-21-07
30 Regular Season Games and 6 Playoff Games
#229 pick in the 2006 NFL Draft
Baylor Bear

ANDRUZZI, Joe (#63)
Born on August 23, 1975 in Brooklyn, NY
6'3" and 312 pounds
Offensive Guard   2000-04
3 fumble recoveries for 2 yards and 1 reception for no gain
Recovered 2 fumbles by Tom Brady and advanced a fumble by Drew Bledsoe
Advanced Drew Bledsoe's fumble 2 yards in their 10-3 loss to the Dolphins on 09-24-00
Caught a Tom Brady pass for no gain in their 30-26 win over the Broncos on 11-30-03
72 Regular Season Games/72 started and 9 Playoff Games/9 started
Member of the 2001, 2003 and 2004 World Championship Teams
Ron Burton Community Service Award in 2003
Southern Connecticut State Owl

ANTRUM, Glenn (#10)
Born on February 3, 1966 in Derby, CT
5'11" and 175 pounds
Wide Receiver   1989
Only game played was on 11-19-89
UCONN Husky

ANTWINE, Houston (#65) *"Twine"*
Born on April 11, 1939 in Louise, MS
6'0" and 270 pounds
DT (G/DE)   1961-71
Offensive Guard in 1961 and Defensive End in 1970
38 sacks, 1 interception for 2 yards and 4 fumble recoveries
Sacked Cotton Davidson, Tobin Rote, Dick Wood, George Blanda, John Hadl, Don Breaux and Joe Namath
Sacked Jim LeClair, Don Trull, Steve Tensi, Greg Cook, Rick Norton, Fran Tarkenton and Johnny Unitas
Recorded 1 ½ sacks of Mickey Slaughter and 2 sacks of Tom Flores, Pete Beathard and Earl Morrall
Had 2 ½ sacks of Jack Kemp and Len Dawson and 3 sacks of Dan Darragh
Recorded 4 sacks of Daryle Lamonica and 4 ½ sacks of Bob Griese
Recovered fumbles by Paul Lowe, Darrell Lester, Bert Coan and Dennis Shaw
Returned a pass by Jacky Lee 2 yards in their 28-20 win over the Broncos on 12-12-65
Sacked Dan Darragh *3 times* in their 16-7 victory over the Broncos on 09-08-68
AFL Defensive Player of the Week in their 16-7 win over Denver on 09-08-68
AFL All Star Defensive Tackle from 1963-68
First Team All Pro Defensive Tackle in 1963
142 Regular Season Games/129 started and 2 Playoff Games/2 started
Inducted into the Patriots Hall of Fame on 08-05-15
Southern Illinois Saluki

ARMSTRONG, Bruce (#78) *"Army"*
Born on September 7, 1965 in Miami, FL
6'4" and 295 pounds
Tackle   1987-2000
Recovered fumbles by John Stephens, Hugh Millen, Sam Gash, Robert Edwards and Terry Allen
Recovered a fumble by Marc Wilson and 3 fumbles by Drew Bledsoe as well
Advanced Marc Wilson's fumble 4 yards in their 17-10 loss to the Dolphins on 10-18-90
AFC Pro Bowl Tackle in 1990, 1991, and from 1994-97
212 Regular Season Games/212 started and 7 Playoff Games/7 started
#23 pick in the 1987 NFL Draft
His Uniform # 78 was retired by the Patriots on 09-30-01
Inducted into the Patriots Hall of Fame on 09-30-01
Louisville Cardinal

ARRINGTON, Kyle (#27, #24, #25)
Born on August 12, 1986 in Accokeek, MD
5'10" and 196 pounds
Defensive Back   2009-14
Wore #27 from 2009-10, #24 from 2011-12 and #25 from 2013-14
9 interceptions for 133 yards + 1 TD, 3 sacks and 3 fumble recoveries for 9 yards + 1 TD
Returned 2 blocked field goal attempts 97 yards for 2 TDs and had a recovery of an onside kick
Intercepted Matt Flynn, Chad Henne, Tony Romo, Eli Manning and Drew Brees
Had 2 interceptions of Ryan Fitzpatrick and Tyler Palko
Sacked Ryan Tannehill, Joe Flacco and Matt Cassel
Recovered fumbles by Delone Carter, Fred Jackson and Brandon Tate
Had a 35 yard TD return of a blocked field goal in their 41-14 rout of the Dolphins on 10-04-10
Had a career long 36 yard TD return of a pass by Matt Flynn in their 31-27 win over Green Bay on 12-19-10
Had a 9 yard TD return of Brandon Tate's fumbled kickoff return in their 45-17 win vs the Bengals on 10-05-14
Recovered onside kick by Stephen Gostkowski in their 27-26 comeback win over the Browns on 12-08-13
Had a 62 yard TD return of a blocked field goal in their 41-13 rout of the Dolphins on 12-14-14
86 Regular Season Games/56 started and 12 Playoff Games/8 started
Recovered Tom Zbikowski's fumbled punt return in their 33-14 Wild Card loss to the Ravens on 01-10-10
Member of the 2014 Championship Team
Hofstra University Flying Dutchman

ARTHUR, Mike (#65)
Born on May 7, 1968 in Minneapolis, MN
6'3" and 280 pounds
Center   1993-94
Recovered fumbles by Scott Secules and Drew Bledsoe
25 Regular Season Games/22 started and 1 Playoff Game/1 started (on 01-01-95)
Texas A & M Aggie

ASHTON JR, Josh (#31)
Born on August 24, 1949 in Eagle Lake, TX
6'1" and 205 pounds
RB/KR   1972-74
247 carries for 950 yards + 3 TDs and 33 receptions for 320 yards + 1 TD
15 kickoff returns for 309 yards and 2 fumble recoveries
Recovered fumbles by Bob Windsor and Sam Cunningham
Longest was a 31 yard return of a kickoff by Boris Shlapak in their 24-17 loss to Baltimore on 11-06-72
Caught a 24 yard TD pass from Jim Plunkett in their 24-23 win over the Redskins on 10-01-72
Longest run for 35 yards in their 37-21 loss to the Dolphins on 12-03-72
Longest reception was a 51 yard pass from Jim Plunkett in their 31-13 loss to the Bills on 09-16-73
Recovered Sam Cunningham's fumble, for a 1st down, in their 42-3 rout of the Colts on 10-06-74
38 games/20 started
#209 pick in the 1971 NFL Draft
Tulsa Golden Hurricane

ASHWORTH, Tom (#68)
Born on October 10, 1977 in Denver, CO
6'6" and 305 pounds
Tackle (FB/TE)   2002-05
1 fumble recovery and 1 reception for a 1 yard TD
Recovered Tom Brady's fumble in their 40-21 loss to the Indianapolis Colts on 11-07-05
As a Fullback, he caught a 1 yard TD pass from Tom Brady in their 28-0 shutout of Tampa on 12-17-05
37 Regular Season Games/30 started and 5 Playoff Games/4 started
Member of the 2003 and 2004 World Championship Teams
Colorado Buffalo

ATCHASON, Jack (#85)
Born on November 16, 1936 in Springfield IL
6'4" and 215 pounds
Offensive End   1960
2 receptions for 22 yards
Longest reception was a 14 yard pass from Tom Greene in their 13-0 loss to Buffalo on 09-23-60
Caught an 8 yard pass from Butch Songin in their 13-0 loss to the Buffalo Bills on 09-23-60
Only game played was on 09-23-60
Western Illinois Leatherneck

ATESSIS, Bill (#73)
Born on July 16, 1949 in Houston, TX
6'3" and 240 pounds
Defensive Lineman   1971
5 games
Texas Longhorn

ATKINSON JR, Richard "Ricky" (#22)
Born on August 28, 196 in Middletown, CT
6'0" and 170 pounds
Defensive Back   1987
Only game played was on 10-18-87
Southern Connecticut State Owl

AVEZZANO, Joe (#50)
Born on November 17, 1943 in Yonkers, NY
6'2" and 235 pounds
Center   1966
3 games
6th Round Draft Pick in 1966
Was the Head Coach of the Milano Seamen in the Italian Football League
Florida State Seminole

AYERS, Akeem (#55)
Born on July 10, 1989 in Los Angeles, CA
6'3" and 255 pounds
Linebacker   2014
Sacked Jay Cutler, Peyton Manning, Matthew Stafford and Kyle Orton
Intercepted a pass by Philip Rivers in their 41-13 rout of the Dolphins
9 Regular Season Games/4 started and 3 Playoff Games
Member of the 2014 Championship Team
UCLA Bruin

AYI, Bamikole "Kole" (#99)
Born on September 27, 1978 in Ann Arbor, MI
6'1" and 231 pounds
Special Team   2001
Only game played was on 11-18-01
Member of the 2001 World Championship Team
UMASS Minuteman

BAAB, Mike (#68)
Born on September 5, 1959 in Fort Worth, TX
6'4" and 270 pounds
Center   1988-89
Recovered a fumble by Eric Sievers in their 27-26 loss to the New York Jets on 11-05-89
31 games/28 started
Texas Longhorn

BADEMOSI, Johnson (#29)
Born on July 23, 1990 in Washington, DC
6'0" and 219 pounds
Special Team/DB   2017
16 Regular Season Games/3 started and 3 Playoff Games
Stanford Cardinal

BAHR, Matt (#3)
Born on July 6, 1956 in Philadelphia, PA
5'10" and 175 pounds
Kicker (Punter)   1993-95
Kicked 55 field goals and 73 extra points
Only punt was 29 yards in their 27-14 win over the Bills on 10-23-95
Kicked a career long 55 yard field goal in their 34-17 win over the Dolphins on 11-12-95
AFC Special Team Player of the Week in their 34-17 win over Miami on 11-12-95
35 Regular Season Games and 1 Playoff Game
Kicked 2 FG's and 1 extra point in their 20-13 Wild Card Playoff loss to the Browns on 01-01-95
Pro Soccer Player for the Colorado Caribous and Tulsa Roughnecks in the NASL in 1978
Penn State Nittany Lion

BAILEY, Jacob *"Jake"* (#7)
6'2" and 205 pounds
Born on June 18, 1997 in Phoenix, AZ
Punter　　　　　　　　　2019--
81 punts for 3,638 yards
AFC Special Team Player of the Week in their 30-14 win over the Jets on 09-22-19
AFC Special Team Player of the Week in their 17-10 win over the Eagles on 11-17-19
Had his career longest punt of 65 yards in their 13-9 win over the Cowboys on 11-24-19
Had another 65 yard punt in their 34-13 win over the Bengals on 12-15-19
Holder for Stephen Gostkowski, Mike Nugent, Kai Forbath and Nick Folk in 2019
16 Regular Season Games and 1 Playoff Game
#163 Pick in the 2019 NFL Draft
Stanford Cardinal

BAILEY, William "Teddy" (#37)
Born on August 12, 1944 in Cincinnati, OH
6'1" and 255 pounds
Running Back　　　　　　1969
2 games (on Sept. 21st and Sept. 28th)
Cincinnati Bearcat

BAIN, Bill (#62)
Born on August 9, 1952 in Los Angeles, CA
6'4" and 279 pounds
Tackle　　　　　　　　　1986
3 Regular Season Games and 1 Playoff Game (on 01-04-87)
USC Trojan

BAKER, Chris (#86)
Born on November 18, 1979 in St. Albans, NY
6'3" and 258 pounds
Tight End　　　　　　　2009
14 receptions for 142 yards + 2 TDs
Caught 2 TD passes from Tom Brady
Longest reception was a 36 yard TD pass from Tom Brady in their 26-10 win over Atlanta on 09-27-09
16 Regular Season Games/7 started and 1 Playoff Game/1 started
Made a fair catch on Billy Cundiff's 30 yard kickoff in their 33-14 Wild Card loss to the Ravens on 01-10-10
Michigan State Spartan

BAKER, Melvin "Mel" (#83)
Born on August 12, 1950 in Beaumont, TX
6'0" and 189 pounds
Special Team　　　　　　1975
Recovered Jackie Wallace's fumbled punt return in their 21-10 win vs the Baltimore Colts on 10-19-75
Only game played was on 10-19-75
Texas Southern Tiger

BAKER, Rashad (#32)
Born on February 22, 1982 in Camden, NJ
5'10" and 198 pounds
Defensive Back   2006-07
13 Regular Season Games and 1 Playoff Game (on 01-21-07)
Tennessee Volunteer

BALDINGER, Rich (#74)
Born on December 31, 1959 in Camp Lejeune, NC
6'4" and 285 pounds
Guard/Tackle   1993
15 games/15 started
Wake Forest Demon Deacon

BALLOU, Mikell "Mike" (#51) *"Cat"*
Born on September 11, 1947 in Los Angeles, CA
6'3" and 238 pounds
Linebacker   1970
Nicknamed *"Cat"* because of the Lee Marvin Movie "Cat Ballou"
Led the Boston Patriots with 9 tackles in the *"Bob Gladieux Game"* on 09-20-70
14 games/4 started
#56 pick in the 1970 NFL Draft
UCLA Bruin

BANKS, Willie (#78)
Born on March 17, 1946 in Greenville, MS
6'2" and 250 pounds
Guard/Special Team   1973
Blocked a punt by Julian Fagan in their 9-7 loss to the Jets on 10-14-73
13 games/1 started (on 12-16-73)
Alcorn State Brave

BANTA-CAIN, Tully (#48 and #95)
Born on August 28, 1980 in Mountain View, CA
6'2" and 245 pounds
LB (KR)   2003-06 and 2009-10
Wore #48 from 2003-04 and #95 from 2005-06 and 2009-10
23.5 sacks, 1 interception for 4 yards, 1 fumble recovery and 4 kickoff returns for 60 yards
Shared in a sack of Gus Frerotte, Chad Pennington, Brett Favre, Chad Henne and Carson Palmer
Sacked Brad Johnson, Kyle Orton and Matt Flynn
Recorded 1 ½ sacks of Ben Roethlisberger, Brooks Bollinger and David Garrard
Had 2 sacks of David Carr, Ryan Fitzpatrick and 2 ½ sacks of Drew Bledsoe
Recorded 3 sacks of Trent Edwards and 4 sacks of Mark Sanchez
Had a 4 yard return of a pass by J.P. Losman in their 29-6 rout of the Buffalo Bills on 11-14-04
Longest was a 21 yard return of a kickoff by Lawrence Tynes in their 27-19 win over the Chiefs on 11-22-04
Recovered a short kickoff by Adam Vinatieri in their 23-7 win over the Jets on 12-26-04
Recovered a fumble by Maurice Hicks in their 21-7 win over the San Francisco 49ers on 01-02-05
85 Regular Season Games/21 started and 12 Playoff Games/3 started
Recovered a fumble by Philip Rivers in their 24-21 Divisional win over the San Diego Chargers on 01-14-07
Intercepted a pass by Joe Flacco in their 33-10 Wild Card loss to the Baltimore Ravens on 01-10-10
Member of the 2003 and 2004 World Championship Teams
#239 pick in the 2002 NFL Draft
California Golden Bear

BARKER, Chris (#64)
Born on August 3, 1990 in West Covina, CA
6'3" and 305 pounds
Guard   2013-15
6 games
Nevada Runnin Rebel

BARNARD, Brooks (#8)
Born on November 4, 1979 in Arnold, MD
6'2" and 188 pounds
Punter   2003
10 punts for 365 yards
Longest punt was 49 yards in their 12-0 shutout of the Miami Dolphins in the snow on 12-07-03
Only game played was on 12-07-03
Member of the 2003 World Championship Team
Maryland Terrapin

BARNER, Kenjon (#38)
Born on April 28, 1990 in Lynwood, CA
5'9" and 195 pounds
RB   2018
19 carries for 71 yards
Longest run was 11 yards in their 38-7 rout of the Dolphins on 09-30-18
5 games
Member of the 2018 World Championship Team
Oregon Duck

BARNES, Bruce (#3)
Born on June 21, 1951 in Coshocton, OH
5'11" and 215 pounds
Punter   1973-74
100 punts for 3,738 yards
Longest punt was 53 yards in their 13-10 win over the Chicago Bears on 10-21-73
23 games
#290 pick in the 1973 NFL Draft
UCLA Bruin

BARNES, Pete (#59)
Born on August 31, 1945 in Keatchie, LA
6'1" and 239 pounds
Linebacker   1976-77
13 sacks, 1 interception for 13 yards and 2 fumble recoveries for 11 yards
Sacked Richard Todd, Gary Marangi, Steve Ramsey, Bobby Douglass, Steve Myer and Joe Ferguson
Strip sacked Mike Livingston and had 2 sacks of Bob Griese and 4 sacks of Bert Jones
Intercepted a pass by Richard Todd and recovered fumbles by Tony Galbreath and Mike Livingston
Sacked Bert Jones *3 times*, all in the 4th Qtr, in their 21-14 win over the Colts on 11-14-76
Had an 11 yard return of his strip sack of Mike Livingston in their 21-17 win over the Chiefs on 09-18-77
Had a 13 yard return of a pass by Richard Todd in their 30-27 loss to the New York Jets on 10-02-77
25 Regular Season Games/18 started and 1 Playoff Game (on 12-18-76)
Southern University Jaguar

BARNES, Rodrigo (#55)
Born on February 10, 1950 in Waco, TX
6'1" and 215 pounds
Linebacker   1974-75
Recovered Cotton Speyrer's fumble in their 27-17 win over the Baltimore Colts on 11-24-74
6 games
Rice Owl

BARNETT, Harlon (#42)
Born on January 2, 1967 in Cincinnati, OH
5'11" and 200 pounds
Defensive Back   1993-94
4 interceptions for 91 yards and 2 fumble recoveries for 7 yards
Intercepted Rick Mirer, Don Majkowski and had 2 interceptions of Dan Marino
Had a career long 40 yard return of a pass by Rick Mirer in their 10-9 loss to the Seahawks on 10-24-93
Had a 2 yard return of a fumble by Cris Carter in their 26-20 Overtime win vs the Vikings on 11-13-94
Had a 5 yard return of a fumble by Don Majkowski that help seal their 12-10 win vs the Colts 11-27-94
30 Regular Season Games/28 started and 1 Playoff Game/1 started (on 01-01-95)
Michigan State Spartan

BARNETT, Troy (#98) *"Laptop"*
Born on May 24, 1971 in Jacksonville, NC
6'5" and 293 pounds
Defensive End   1994-96
3 sacks, 1 fumble recovery, 1 blocked extra point and 2 blocked field goal attempts
Sacked David Klinger, Jim Kelly and Jim Harbaugh
Blocked a 38 yard field goal attempt by Kevin Butler in their 13-3 win over the Bears on 12-24-94
Blocked a 54 yard field goal attempt by Pete Stoyanovich in their 20-3 loss to the Dolphins on 09-10-95
Recovered Dan Marino's fumble in their 34-17 win over the Dolphins on 11-12-95
Blocked an extra point attempt by Doug Christie in their 35-25 win over the Bills on 11-26-95
31 Regular Season Games/15 started and 1 Playoff Game
North Carolina Tar Heel

BARRETT, Joshua "Josh" (#30)
Born on November 22, 1984 in Reno, NV
6'2" and 226 pounds
Safety   2011
12 solo tackles and 3 assists
5 games/4 started
Arizona State Sun Devil

BARTRUM, Mike (#86)
Born on June 23, 1970 in Gallipolis, OH
6'4" and 245 pounds
TE/LS   1996-99
2 receptions for 2 yards + 2 TDs
Caught two 1 yard TD passes from Drew Bledsoe
Long Snapper for Punter Tom Tupa and Kicker Adam Vinatieri
57 Regular Season Games and 4 Playoff Games
Fell on Chris Hudson's fumbled PR in their 20-6 AFC Championship win over the Jaguars on 01-12-97
Marshall Thundering Herd

BATY, Greg (#48 and #85)
Born on August 28, 1964 in Hastings, MI
6'5" and 241 pounds
Tight End   1986-87
Wore #48 in 1986 and #85 in 1987
52 receptions for 469 yards + 4 TDs
Caught 1 TD pass from Steve Grogan and 3 TD passes from Tony Eason
Caught a 13 yard TD pass in the 4th Qtr from Tony Eason in their 22-19 win over Buffalo on 11-23-86
Longest reception was a 22 yard pass from Tony Eason in their 21-20 win over the Saints on 11-30-86
21 Regular Season Games/7 started and 1 Playoff Game/1 started on 01-04-87
#220 pick in the 1986 NFL Draft
Stanford Cardinal

BAUMANN, Bruce "Charlie" (#8)
Born on August 25, 1967 in Erie, PA
6'1" and 203 pounds
Kicker   1991-92
Kicked 18 field goals and 31 extra points
Kikced a career long 46 yard field goal in their 16-13 win over the Bills on 11-24-91
Kicked an 18 yard Overtime Game Winning Field Goal in their 37-34 win over the Colts on 11-15-92
Recovered Bernie Parmalee's fumbled kickoff return in their 16-13 OT loss to Miami on 12-27-92
23 games
West Virginia Mountaineer

BAVARO, David (#52)
Born on March 27, 1967 in Danvers, MA
6'0" and 234 pounds
Linebacker   1993-94
Recovered Johnny Bailey's fumble in their 23-21 win vs the Phoenix Cardinals on 10-10-93
Recovered Ronnie Harris' fumbled punt return in their 17-14 loss to the Steelers on 12-05-93
21 Regular Season Games/5 started and 1 Playoff Game
Syracuse Orangeman

BAXTER, Fred (#49 and #84)
Born on June 14, 1971 in Brundidge, AL
6'3" and 268 pounds
Tight End   2002-03
Wore #49 in 2002 and #84 in 2003
13 games
Member of the 2003 World Championship Team
Auburn Tiger

BEACH III, Walter (#26 and #41)
Born on January 31, 1935 in Pontiac, MI
6'0" and 190 pounds
RB/KR (PR/DB)   1960-61
Wore #26 in 1960 and #41 in 1961
6 carries for a net loss of 4 yards and 9 receptions for 132 yards + 1 TD
9 kickoff returns for 184 yards, 1 punt return for 21 yards and 1 interception for 37 yards
Returned a punt by Billy Atkins 21 yards in their 13-0 loss to the Buffalo Bills on 09-23-60
Longest was a 33 yard return of a kickoff by Ben Agajanian in their 35-0 shutout of the LA Chargers on 10-08-60
Longest run for 3 yards in their 45-16 loss to the Los Angeles Chargers on 10-28-60
Longest reception was a 59 yard TD pass from Butch Songin in their 45-16 loss to the LA Chargers on 10-28-60
Returned a pass by Frank Tripucka pass 37 yards in their 21-20 loss to the New York Titans on 09-09-61
Recovered Dick Christy's fumble in their 37-30 loss to the New York Titans on 10-01-61
Advanced Larry Garron's handoff on a kickoff return 20 yards in their 38-27 loss to the Chargers on 10-07-61
18 games/12 started
Central Michigan Chippewa

BEAUDOIN, Doug (#27)
Born on May 15, 1954 in Dickinson, ND
6'1" and 193 pounds
DB/KR (PR)   1976-79
4 interceptions for 55 yards, 10 kickoff returns for 207 yards, 3 punt returns for 18 yards and 2 fumble recoveries
Intercepted Bill Troup and Joe Ferguson and had 2 interceptions of Bob Griese
Recovered fumbles by Mickey Shuler and Walter Payton
Had a career long 30 yard return of a pass by Joe Ferguson in their 31-0 loss to the Bills on 11-25-79
Longest was a 44 yard return of a kickoff by Toni Linhart in their 21-14 win over the Colts on 11-14-76
Had an 11 yard return of a punt by Marv Bateman in their 20-10 victory over the Bills on 11-07-76
45 Regular Season games/20 started and 1 Playoff Game
Shared in a sack of Dan Pastorini in their 31-14 Divisional loss to the Houston Oilers on 12-31-78
Shared in 1/3 of another sack of Dan Pastorini in their 31-14 Divisional loss to the Oilers on 12-31-78
#243 pick in the 1976 NFL Draft
Minnesota Golden Gopher

BEAUHARNAIS, Steve (#58)
Born on May 2, 1990 in Saddlebrook, NJ
6'1" and 240 pounds
Special Team (LB)   2013
Was in on 10 Special Team plays and on 1 play as a Linebacker on 12-22-13
2 games (on Oct. 20th and Dec. 22nd)
Rutgers Scarlet Knight

BEER, Tom (#82) *"Tarzan"*
Born on December 21, 1944 in Detroit, MI
6'4" and 235 pounds
TE (KR)   1970-72
25 receptions for 381 yards and 3 TDs, 2 kickoff returns for 19 yards and 1 fumble return of 5 yards
Caught 3 TD passes from Jim Plunkett
Lateraled a kickoff from Jim O'Brien to Carl Garrett in their 27-3 loss to the Baltimore Colts on 10-25-70
Lateraled 2 kickoffs from Grant Guthrie to Carl Garrett in their 45-10 loss to the Buffalo Bills on 11-01-70
Longest reception was a 31 yard TD pass from Jim Plunkett in their 44-21 loss to the Cowboys on 10-24-71
Returned Ike Hill's fumbled punt return 5 yards in their 38-33 win over the Buffalo Bills on 11-14-71
Longest was a 15 yard return of a kickoff by Bobby Howfield in their 34-10 loss to the NY Jets on 10-29-72
42 games/12 started
Houston Cougar

BEISEL, Monty (#52)
Born on August 20, 1978 in Douglass, KS
6'3" and 254 pounds
Linebacker   2005
Sacked Matt Schaub in their 31-28 victory over the Atlanta Falcons on 10-09-05
15 Regular Season Games/6 started and 2 Playoff Games
Kansas State Wildcat

BELL, Bill (#8)
Born on December 9, 1947 in Fort Knox, KY
6'0" and 192 pounds
Kicker   1973
Kicked 1 field goal and 4 extra points
Kicked a 36 yard field goal in their 44-23 loss to the Miami Dolphins on 09-30-73
3 games
Kansas Jayhawk

BELLINO, Joe (#27)
Born on March 13, 1938 in Winchester, MA
5'9" and 185 pounds
RB/KR/PR   1965-67
30 carries for 64 yards and 11 receptions for 151 yards + 1 TD
43 kickoff returns for 905 yards and 19 punt returns for 148 yards
Longest run for 10 yards in their 24-10 loss to the Oakland Raiders on 10-08-65
Longest reception was a 25 yard TD pass from Babe Parilli in their 20-10 win over Buffalo on 10-08-66
Longest was a 43 yard return of a kickoff by Booth Lusteg in their 20-10 win over the Bills on 10-08-66
Caught a deflected pass, while on his back, in their 14-3 win over Buffalo in "The Game" on 12-04-66
Had another 10 yard run in their 28-14 loss to the San Diego Chargers on 09-09-67
Had a career long 18 yard return of a punt by Mike Eischeid in their 48-14 loss to the Raiders on 10-22-67
35 games/3 started
19th Round Draft Pick in 1961
Won the Heisman Trophy in 1960
Navy Midshipman

BENNETT, Martellus (#88) *"The Black Unicorn"*
Born on March 10, 1987 in San Diego, CA
6'6" and 275 pounds
Tight End   2016-17
61 receptions for 754 yards + 7 TDs and 2 carries for 10 yards
Caught a 20 yard TD pass from Tom Brady in their 31-24 win over the Dolphins on 09-18-16
Caught a 3 TD passes (7 yds, 5 yds + 37 yds) from Tom Brady in their 33-13 rout of the Browns on 10-09-16
Snared a 19 yard TD pass from Tom Brady in their 30-23 win over the Ravens on 12-12-16
Caught a 5 yard TD pass from Tom Brady in their 41-3 rout of the Jets on 12-24-16
Caught a 2 yard TD pass from Tom Brady in their 35-14 rout of the Dolphins on 01-01-17
Longest reception was a 58 yard pass from Jacoby Brissette in their 16-0 loss to Buffalo on 10-02-16
Longest run for 6 yards in their 27-0 shutout of Houston on 09-22-16
18 Regular Season games/12 started and 3 Playoff Games/3 started
11 receptions for 98 yards in the playoffs
Member of the 2016 World Championship Team
Texas A & M Aggie

BENNETT JR., Michael (#77)
Born on November 13, 1985 in Avondale, LA
6'4" and 275 pounds
Defensive Lineman   2019
2.5 sacks
Sacked Ryan Fitzpatrick and Luke Falk and shared in a sack of Colt McCoy
6 games/1 started (on 09-08-19)
Texas A & M Aggie

BENNETT, Phil (#52)
Born on February 14, 1935 in Pittsburgh, PA
6'3" and 225 pounds
Special Team   1960
2 games (on Sept. 9th and Sept. 17th)
Miami Hurricane

BENSON, Thomas (#53)
Born on September 6, 1961 in Ardmore, OK
6'2" and 238 pounds
Special Team   1988
12 games
Oklahoma Sooner

BENTLEY, Ja'Whaun (#51)
Born on August 24, 1996 in Glenarden, MD
6'2" and 255 pounds
Linebacker   2018-19
Intercepted a pass by Matthew Stafford in their 26-10 loss to the Lions on 09-23-18
19 Regular Season Games/4 started and 1 Playoff Game
Member of the 2018 World Championship Team
#143 pick in the 2018 NFL Draft
Purdue Boilermaker

BEQUETTE, Jake (#92)
Born on February 21, 1989 in Little Rock, AR
6'5" and 274 pounds
Defensive End   2012-13
8 games
#90 pick in the 2012 NFL Draft
Arkansas Razorback

BERGER, Ron (#88) *"The Whopper"*
Born on September 30, 1943 in Detroit, MI
6'8" and 290 pounds
DT/DE (KR)   1969-72
15.5 sacks, 3 fumble recoveries and 1 kickoff return of 20 yards
Sacked Jack Kemp, Rick Norton, Marty Domres, Earl Morrall, Dennis Shaw and Johnny Unitas
Had 2 sacks of Al Woodhall, 3 ½ sacks of James Harris and 4 sacks of Bob Griese
Recovered fumbles by Bob Davis, Wendell Hayes and John Riggins
Had a 20 yard return of a kickoff by Dennis Partee in their 13-10 loss to San Diego on 10-19-69
Sacked Bob Griese *3 times* in their 27-14 victory over the Miami Dolphins on 09-20-70
Sacked James Harris *3 times* in their 14-10 win over the Buffalo Bills on 11-29-70
NFL Defensive Player of the Week in their 27-14 win over the Dolphins on 09-20-70
41 games/23 started
Pacific Division All Star DE for the Orange County Ramblers in the Continental Football League in 1967
Wayne State Tartar

BETHEL, Justin (#29)
Born on June 17, 1990 in Sumter, SC
6'0" and 200 pounds
CB/Special Team   2019--
Recovered muffed punt returns by Cyrus Jones and Alex Erickson
9 Regular Season Games and 1 Playoff Game
Presbyterian College Blue Hose

BEVERLY, Randolph "Randy" (#27)
Born on April 3, 1944 in Wildwood, NJ
5'11" and 190 pounds
DB (KR)   1970-71
2 interceptions for 19 yards, 2 fumbles recoveries and 1 kickoff return for no gain
Intercepted John Brodie and Dan Pastorini and recovered fumbles by Odell Lawson and Jim Kiick
Had no return of a kickoff by Dennis Partee in their 16-14 loss to the San Diego Chargers on 11-15-70
Had a 19 yard return of a pass by John Brodie in their 27-10 loss to the 49ers on 10-31-71
21 games/4 started
Colorado State Ram

BIANCHINI, Frank (#30)
Born on May 27, 1961 in East Islip, NY
5'8" and 190 pounds
Special Team   1987
Only game played was on 10-04-87
Member of the 1987 Arena Football League Denver Dynamite Championship Team
Hofstra Flying Dutchman

BILLIPS, Terry (#23)
Born on February 9, 1975 in Wiesbaden, Germany
5'9" and 180 pounds
Special Team   1999
2 games/1 started (on 01-02-00)
North Carolina Tar Heel

BISCAHA, Joe (#34)
Born on June 1, 1937 in Clifton, NJ
6'1" and 190 pounds
Offensive End   1960
Only game played was on 09-09-60
Richmond Spider

BISHOP, Michael (#7)
Born on May 15, 1976 in Galveston, TX
6'2" and 215 pounds
Quarterback   2000
3 completions for 80 yards + 1 TD and 7 carries for a net loss of 1 yard
Longest run for 2 yards in their 20-19 loss to the New York Jets on 09-11-00
Longest completion was a 44 yard TD pass to Tony Simmons in their 24-16 win vs the Colts on 10-08-00
8 games
#227 pick in the 1999 NFL Draft
Drafted by the Cleveland Indians
Kansas State Wildcat

BISHOP, Richard (#64)
Born on March 23, 1950 in Cleveland, OH
6'1" and 275 pounds
NT/DE   1976-81
30.5 sacks, 6 fumble recoveries and 1 blocked field goal attempt
Shared in a sack of Ken Stabler and Dan Manucci
Sacked Mike Rae, Ron Jaworski, Ken Anderson, Scott Hunter, Greg Landry and Matt Robinson
Sacked Marc Wilson and David Woodley and had 1 ½ sacks of Dan Fouts
Had 2 sacks of Joe Ferguson and Jack Thompson and 3 sacks of Bob Griese
Recorded 5 sacks of Bert Jones and 8 sacks of Richard Todd
Recovered fumbles by Terry Bradshaw, Mike Hogan, John Riggins, Joe Washington and Richard Todd
Recovered Bobby Walden's fumbled punt attempt in their 30-27 win over the Steelers on 09-26-76
Sacked Bob Griese for a safety in their 33-24 win over Miami on 10-22-78
Blocked a 40 yard field goal attempt by Mark Moseley in their 24-22 loss to the Redskins on 10-25-81
85 Regular Season games/50 started and 2 Playoff Games
Participated in 3 sacks of Dan Pastorini in their 31-14 Divisional Playoff loss to Houston on 12-31-78
Louisville Cardinal

BJORNSON, Eric (#86)
Born on December 15, 1971 in San Francisco, CA
6'4" and 236 pounds
Tight End   2000
20 receptions for 152 yards + 2 TDs, 1 onside kick recovery and 1 fumble recovery
Caught 2 TD passes from Drew Bledsoe
Longest reception was a 19 yard pass from Drew Bledsoe on in their 20-19 loss to the Jets 09-11-00
Recovered an onside kick by Danny Kight in their 24-16 win over the Colts on 10-08-00
Recovered JR Redmond's fumble in their 30-23 loss to the Indianapolis Colts on 10-22-00
8 games/6 started
Washington Husky

BLACK, Melvin "Mel" (#94 and #51)
Born on February 2, 1962 in New Haven, CT
6'2" and 228 pounds
Special Team   1986-87
Wore #94 in 1986 and #51 in 1987
6 games/2 started
Eastern Illinois Panther

BLACKMON, Don (#55) *"Gator"*
Born on March 14, 1958 in Pompano Beach, FL
6'3" and 255 pounds
Linebacker   1981-86
31 sacks, 5 interceptions for 63 yards, recorded 2 safeties and had 6 fumble recoveries for 47 yards
Shared in a sack of David Humm, Pat Ryan, Dan Marino and Dave Archer
Sacked Richard Todd, Brian Sipe, Jim Zorn, Ken Stabler, Jeff Kemp, John Elway and Jim McMahon
Sacked Steve DeBerg, Mike Pagel, Matt Kofler, Jack Trudeau, Jim Everett and Jim Kelly
Had 1 ½ sacks of Cliff Stoudt and Dave Krieg and 2 sacks of Joe Ferguson and Boomer Esiason
Had 3 sacks of Lynn Dickey, Gary Hogenboom and Ken O'Brien
Intercepted Art Schlitcher, David Woodley, Vince Ferragamo, Dan Marino and Steve DeBerg
Recovered fumbles by Cleveland Franklin, Earl Campbell, Pat Beach, Tony Nathan, Rueben Mays and Marc Wilson
Had a career long 39 yard return of a pass by Vince Ferragamo in their 21-7 win over the LA Rams on 12-11-83
Sacked Lynn Dickey *for a safety* in their 26-20 win over the Green Bay Packers on 09-08-85
Blocked an extra point attempt by Al Del Greco in their 26-20 win over Green Bay on 09-08-85
Sacked Steve DeBerg *for a safety* in their 32-14 win over the Buccaneers on 10-27-85
Sacked Gary Hogenboom *3 times* in their 33-3 rout of the Indianapolis Colts on 09-07-86
Blocked a 53 yard field goal attempt by Mick Luckhurst in their 25-17 win over Atlanta on 11-02-86
89 Regular Season games/72 started and 6 Playoff Games/6 started
4 sacks in the playoffs
Sacked Pat Ryan in their 26-14 Wild Card win over the New York Jets at the Meadowlands on 12-28-85
Sacked Marc Wilson *twice* in their 27-20 Divisional win over the LA Raiders at the LA Coliseum on 01-05-86
Sacked John Elway in their 22-17 Divisional loss to the Denver Broncos at Mile High Stadium on 01-04-87
#102 pick in the 1981 NFL Draft
Tulsa Golden Hurricane

BLAHAK, Joe (#21)
Born on August 29, 1950 in Columbus, NE
5'9" and 187 pounds
Defensive Back   1976
2 Regular Season Games + 1 Playoff Game (on 12-18-76)
Nebraska Cornhusker

BLANCHARD, Dick (#49)
Born on January 17, 1949 in Waukesha, WI
6'3" and 225 pounds
Linebacker   1972
Had a 20 yard return of a pass by Archie Manning in their 17-10 win over the Saints on 12-10-72
14 games/1 started (on 09-17-72)
Tulsa Golden Hurricane

BLANKS, Sidney "Sid" (#22)
Born on April 29, 1940 in Del Rio, TX
6'1" and 200 pounds
RB/PR/KR   1969-70
20 carries for 74 yards, 7 receptions for 65 yards, 14 punt returns for 93 yards and 13 kickoff returns 283 yards
Longest run for 12 yards in their 24-0 shutout of the Oilers on 11-02-69
Fell on Carl Garrett's fumbled punt return in their 24-0 shutout of the Houston Oilers on 11-02-69
Longest was a 22 yard return of a punt by Larry Seiple in their 27-14 win vs Miami on 09-20-70
Had another run of 12 yards in their 14-6 loss to the Baltimore Colts on 10-04-70
Longest was a 29 yard return of a kickoff by Fred Cox in their 35-14 loss to the Vikings on 12-13-70
Longest reception was an 18 yard pass from Joe Kapp in their 45-7 loss to the Bengals on 12-20-70
28 games
Texas A & I Javelina

BLEDSOE, Drew (#11)
Born on February 14, 1972 in Ellensburg, WA
6'5" and 238 pounds
Quarterback   1993-2001
2,544 completions for 29,657 yards + 166 TDs and threw 6 Two Point conversion passes
Threw 1 TD pass to Derrick Cullors, Terry Allen, Marv Cook, Rod Rutledge, Greg McMurtry,
      Will Moore, Dave Meggett and Lamont Warren
Tossed 1 Post Season TD pass to David Patten on 01-27-02
Threw 2 TDs to Hason Graham, Mike Bartrum, Eric Bjornson, Jermaine Wiggins, Kevin Faulk,
      JR Redmond and Robert Edwards
Tossed 3 TDs to Lovett Purnell and Kevin Turner
Threw 4 TDs to Ray Crittenden and Tony Simmons
Threw 2 TDs to Mike Batrum, Eric Bjornson, Jermaine Wiggins, Kevin Faulk, JR Redmond and Robert Edwards
Completed 4 TD passes to Ray Crittenden and Tony Simmons and 3 TDs to Lovett Purnell and Kevin Turner
Threw 5 touchdown passes to Sam Gash, Curtis Martin and Michael Timpson
Completed 5 Regular Season TD passes and 1 Post Season TD pass to Leory Thompson
Threw 5 Regular Season TD passes and 2 Post Season TD passes to Keith Byars
Completed 12 Regular Season TD passes and 1 Post Season TD pass to Troy Brown
Threw 13 TD passes to Shawn Jefferson, 14 TDs to Vincent Brisby and 21 TD passes to Terry Glenn
Threw 45 Regular Season TD passes and 1 Post Season TD pass to Ben Coates
Tossed a 54 yard TD pass, on 4th and 1, to Ben Coates, in their 38-14 loss to the Bills on 09-05-93
Threw a 36 yard TD pass to Michael Timpson to defeat Miami 33-27 in Overtime on 01-02-94
Threw a 14 yard TD pass to Kevin Turner to defeat Minnesota 26-20 in OT at Foxboro Stadium on 11-13-94
Tossed a 2 point pass to Curtis Martin in their 35-25 win over the Ravens on 11-26-95
Tossed a 2 point pass to Dave Meggett in their 41-27 loss to the Steelers on 12-16-95
Tossed a 2 point pass to Curtis Martin in their 31-0 shutout of the Cardinals on 09-15-96
Tossed a 2 point pass to Sam Gash and Ben Coates in their 46-38 win over the Ravens on 10-06-96
Threw an 84 yard TD pass to Ben Coates in their 42-23 victory over the Dolphins on 11-03-96
Tossed a 2 point pass to Keith Byars in their 34-8 loss to the Broncos on 11-17-96
Threw a 13 yard TD pass, on 4th + 7, to Ben Coates, to defeat the Giants 23-22 at Giants Stadium on 12-21-96
Tossed a 1 yard touchdown pass to Ben Coates, with no time left, to defeat Buffalo 25-21 on 11-29-98
Tossed a career long 86 yard TD pass to Terry Glenn in their 23-9 win over the Steelers on 12-06-98
Fired a 1 yard TD, on 4th + 1, to Jermaine Wiggins in their 30-24 win over the Chiefs on 12-04-00
270 carries for 553 yards + 2 TDs
Longest run for 25 yards in their 13-10 loss to the Buffalo Bills on 12-26-99
Caught his own deflected pass for a 9 yard loss in their 41-27 loss to the Steelers on 12-16-95
AFC Offensive Player of the Week 6 Times and NFL Player of the Week 3 Times
AFC Offensive Player of the Month in December 1994
Led NFL with the most passing attempts, completions and yards passing in 1994
Led NFL with the most passing attempts and pass completions in 1996
AFC Pro Bowl Quarterback in 1994, 1996, 1997
124 Regular Season Games/123 started and 7 Playoff Games/6 started
129 completions for 1,335 yards + 6 TDs in the playoffs
Threw a 13 yard TD pass to Leroy Thompson in their 20-13 Wild Card loss to the Browns on 01-01-95
Tossed a 34 yard TD pass to Keith Byars in their 28-3 Divisional win over the Steelers on 01-05-97
Fired a 1 yard TD to Keith Byars + a 4 yard TD to Ben Coates in their 35-21 Super Bowl loss to GB on 01-26-97
Tossed a 24 yard TD pass to Troy Brown in their 17-3 Wild Card win over the Dolphins on 12-28-97
Threw an 11 yard TD pass to David Patten in their 24-17 Championship win over the Steelers on 01-27-02
Member of the 2001 World Championship Team
1st Overall Pick in the 1993 NFL Draft
Inducted into the Patriots Hall of Fame on 09-15-11
Washington State Cougar

BLEIER, John "Bob" (#10)
Born on June 1, 1964 in Rochester, NY
6'3" and 210 pounds
Quarterback   1987
14 completions for 181 yards + 1 TD and 5 carries for a net loss of 5 yards + 1 TD
Longest completion was a 35 yard pass to Wayne Coffey in their 20-10 loss to Cleveland on 10-04-87
Threw a 6 yard TD pass to Larry Linne in their 20-10 loss to the Browns on 10-04-87
Longest run was a 1 yard game winning TD in their 14-7 win over the Buffalo Bills on 10-11-87
Holder for Tony Franklin's 3 extra points in their 21-7 win over the Houston Oilers on 10-18-87
3 games/2 started
Richmond Spider

BLOUNT, LeGarrette (#29) *"Blount Force Trauma"*
Born on December 5, 1986 in Madison, FL
6'0" and 247 pounds
RB/KR   2013-16
677 carries for 2,917 yards + 34 TDs, 19 receptions for 137 yards + 1 TD and 17 kickoff returns for 494 yards
Longest run was a 47 yard TD in their 30-23 win over the Atlanta Falcons on 09-29-13
Longest reception was a 32 yard pass from Tom Brady in their 27-26 comeback win over the Browns on 12-08-13
Longest was an 83 yard return of a kickoff by Dan Carpenter in their 34-20 win over Buffalo on 12-29-13
Caught an 11 yard TD pass from Tom Brady in their 34-27 win over the Indianapolis Colts on 10-18-15
AFC Offensive Player of the Week on 12-29-13 and NFL Ground Player of the Week on 12-29-13
AFC Offensive Player of the Month in September 2016
Led the NFL with 18 rushing TDs in 2016
49 Regular Season Games/22 started and 8 Playoff Games/2 started
111 carries for 470 yards + 8 TDs, 1 reception for 8 yards and 2 kickoff returns for 37 yards in the playoffs
Ran for 4 TDs in their 43-22 Divisional Playoff win over the Colts on 01-11-14
Member of the 2014 and 2016 World Championship Teams
Oregon Duck

BODDEN, Leigh (#23)
Born on September 24, 1981 in Hyattsville, MD
6'1" and 195 pounds
Cornerback   2009-11
5 interceptions for 60 yards + 1 TD and 1 fumble recovery
Intercepted Joe Flacco and Peyton Manning and had 3 interceptions of Mark Sanchez
Had 3 interceptions of Mark Sanchez in their 31-14 rout of the Jets on 11-22-09
Had a 53 yard TD return of a pass by Mark Sanchez in their 31-14 win over the Jets on 11-22-09
AFC Defensive Player of the Week in their 31-14 victory over the NY Jets on 11-22-09
20 Regular Season Games/15 started and 1 Playoff Game/1 started (on 01-10-10)
Duquesne Duke

BOLDEN, Brandon (#38)
Born on January 26, 1990 in Baton Rouge, LA
5'11" and 220 pounds
RB/Special Team　　　　2012-17 and 2019
231 carries for 980 yards + 9 TDs, 56 receptions for 484 yards + 3 TDs, 23 kickoff returns for 515 yards
Caught 3 TD passes from Tom Brady
Longest run for 46 yards in their 23-3 victory over Tampa on 09-22-13
Blocked a punt by Mike Scifres in their 23-14 victory over San Diego on 12-07-14
Tackled Colt Anderson for a 1 yard loss, on a Fake Punt, in their 34-27 win over the Colts on 10-18-15
Longest reception was a 63 yard TD pass from Tom Brady in their 30-24 OT loss to Denver on 11-29-15
98 Regular Season Games/8 started and 16 Playoff Games/2 started
Ran for a 2 yard TD in their 35-14 Divisional Playoff rout of Tennessee on 01-13-18
Member of the 2014 and 2016 World Championship Teams
Mississippi Rebel

BOLTON, Ron (#27) *"Gamebreaker"*
Born on April 16 1950 in Petersburg, VA
6'2" and 180 pounds
Defensive Back　　　　1972-75
18 interceptions for 116 yards, 1 sack, 1 fumble recovery and 1 blocked field goal attempt
Intercepted Bobby Douglass, Jerry Tagge, Lynn Dickey, John Hadl, Joe Ferguson and Dan Pastorini
Intercepted Bob Griese and Norm Snead as well
Had 2 interceptions of Roman Gabriel, Fran Tarkenton, Ken Stabler, Joe Namath and Dan Fouts
Blocked a 32 yard field goal attempt by Bill Bell in their 21-20 win over Atlanta on 09-24-72
Recovered a fumble by John Riggins in their 9-7 loss to the New York Jets on 10-14-73
Had a career long 56 yard return of a pass by Roman Gabriel in their 24-23 loss to the Eagles on 11-04-73
Sacked Dan Pastorini in their 32-0 shutout of the Houston Oilers on 11-25-73
Intercepted a pass by Fran Tarkenton on the 1 yard line in their 17-14 win over the Vikings on 10-27-74
Pick off another pass by Fran Tarkenton on the 1 yard line in their 17-14 win over Minnesota on 10-27-74
After his 2nd interception of Fran Tarkenton, Ron broke his hand trying to punch him on 10-27-74
55 games/45 started
#124 pick in the 1972 NFL Draft
Norfolk State Spartan

BOSTIC II, Jonathan (#58)
Born on May 5, 1991 in Wellington, FL
6'1" and 245 pounds
Linebacker　　　　2015
11 games/1 started (on 12-13-15)
Florida Gator

BOUDREAUX, Jim (#78 and #64) *"The Falcon"*
Born on October 11, 1942 in Ville Platte, LA
6'4" and 260 pounds
OT/DE   1966-68
Wore #78 from 1966-67 and #64 in 1968
Recovered Les "Speedy" Duncan's fumbled punt return in their 28-14 loss to San Diego on 09-09-67
12 games
2nd Round Draft Pick in 1966
Louisiana Tech Bulldog

BOWMAN, Jim (#28)
Born on October 26, 1963 in Cadillac, MI
6'2" and 210 pounds
DB/Special Team   1985-89
3 interceptions for 3 yards, shared in a sack, 3 fumble recoveries for 2 yards and recovered an onside kick
Intercepted a pass by Boomer Esiason and 2 passes by Gary Hogenboom
Recovered fumbles by Eric Dickerson, Irving Fryar and Thomas Everett
Recovered an onside kick by Morton Andersen in their 21-20 win over the New Orleans Saints on 11-30-86
Had a 3 yard return of a pass by Gary Hogenboom in their 24-0 shutout of the Colts on 11-22-87
Had a 2 yard return of a fumble by Eric Dickerson in their 24-0 shutout of the Colts on 11-22-87
Shared in a sack of Randall Cunningham in their 34-31 Overtime loss to the Eagles on 11-29-87
Advanced a lateral from Ed Williams 8 yards in their 31-20 loss to Denver on 12-06-87
Picked off a pass by Boomer Esiason, on the last play, in their 27-21 win over the Bengals on 10-16-88
73 Regular Season Games/12 started and 5 Playoff Games
Recovered Fulton Walker's fumbled punt return in their 27-20 Divisional win over the Raiders on 01-05-86
Recovered Sam Seale's fumbled kickoff return for a TD in their 27-20 Playoff win over LA on 01-05-86
#52 pick in the 1985 NFL Draft
Central Michigan Chippewa

BOYCE, Josh (#82)
Born on May 6, 1991 in Copperas Coe, TX
5'11" and 206 pounds
WR/KR   2013-14
9 receptions for 121 yards and 9 kickoff returns for 214 yards
Longest was a 41 yard return of a kickoff by Randy Bullock in their 34-31 win over Houston on 12-01-13
Longest reception was a 30 yard pass from Tom Brady in their 24-20 loss to Miami on 12-15-13
10 games/3 started
Member of the 2014 World Championship Team
#102 pick in the 2013 NFL Draft
Texas Christian Horned Frog

BOYD, Greg (#29)
Born on December 30, 1950 in Scottsdale, AZ
6'2" and 201 pounds
Safety　　　　　　1973
2 games (on Dec. 9th and Dec. 16th)
Arizona Wildcat

BOYD, Greg (#65) *"Too Strong"*
Born on September 15, 1952 in Merced, CA
6'6" and 274 pounds
Defensive End　　　　1977-78
Sacked Mike Livingston and Ron Jaworski
23 games
#170 pick in the 1976 NFL Draft
San Diego State Aztec

BRACE III, Ron (#92 and #97)
Born on December 18, 986 in Springfield, MA
6'3" and 329 pounds
Defensive Lineman　　　2009-12
Wore #92 in 2009 and #97 from 2010-12
39 Regular Season Games/7 started and 1 Playoff Game (on 01-22-12)
#40 pick in the 2009 NFL Draft
Boston College Eagle

BRADSHAW JR., Morris (#88)
Born on October 19, 1952 in Highland, IL
6'1" and 195 pounds
Wide Receiver　　　　1982
6 receptions for 111 yards + 1 TD
Longest reception was a 48 yard pass from Steve Grogan in their 16-0 shutout of Seattle on 12-19-82
Caught an 11 yard TD pass from Steve Grogan in their 30-19 win over Buffalo on 01-02-83
8 games/5 started
Ohio State Buckeye

BRADY, Kyle (#88)
Born on January 14, 1972 in New Cumberland, PA
6'6" and 278 pounds
Tight End　　　　　2007
9 receptions for 70 yards + 2 TDs
Caught 2 TD passes from Tom Brady
Longest reception was a 20 yard pass from Tom Brady in their 38-7 win over Buffalo on 09-23-07
14 Regular Season games/9 started and 3 Playoff Games/2 started
Penn State Nittany Lion

BRADY, Thomas "Tom" (#12) "G.O.A.T"
Born on August 3, 1977 in San Mateo, CA
6'4" and 225 pounds
Quarterback   2000-19
6,377 completions for 74,571 yards + 541 TDs and 606 carries for 1,037 yards + 22 TDs
3 receptions for 65 yards and 2 punts for 68 yards and completed 10 Two point conversions
Threw 1 TD pass to 24 players: Dwayne Allen, Tom Ashworth, LeGarrette Blount, Antonio Brown,
        Larry Centers, Cam Cleeland, Andre' Davis, Heath Evans, Michael Floyd, Terry Glenn,
        Michael Hoomanawanui, Ryan Izzo, Charles Johnson, Matt LaCosse, Matt Lengel,
        Laurence Maroney,Matthew Mulligan, Chad Ochocinco, Patrick Pass, Elandon Roberts,
        Mohamed Sanu, David Thomas, Brian Tyms and Dedric Ward
Tossed 2 TD passes to 11 players: Sam Aiken, Chris Baker, Kyle Brady, Alge Crumpler, Corey Dillon,
        Tim Dwight, Marc Edwards, Donald Hayes, N'Keal Harry, Keyshawn Martin and Brandon Tate
Tossed 3 TD passes to Brandon Bolden, Doug Gabriel, Chad Jackson, Cordarrelle Patterson,
        Antowain Smith and Jermaine Wiggins
Completed 4 TDs to Rex Burkhead, Reche Caldwell, Scott Chandler, Aaron Dobson, Josh Gordon,
        Bethel Johnson, Brandon Lloyd, Malcolm Mitchell, Donte' Stallworth, Kenbrell Thompkins and
        Danny Woodhead
Tossed 5 TDs to Dion Lewis and 6 TD passes to Martellus Bennett, Jabar Gaffney and Tim Wright
Tossed 7 regular season TD passes to Brandin Cooks, Phiilip Dorsett, Brandon LaFell and Shane Vereen
Completed 8 TDs to Mike Vrabel and 10 TD passes to Danny Amendola and Kevin Faulk
Tossed 11 TD passes to Chris Hogan and 12 TD passes to David Givens
Completed 13 TDs to Christian Fauria and 15 TD passes to Troy Brown
Completed 16 TDs to David Patten and 17 TD passes to Daniel Graham and Benjamin Watson
Tossed 18 TDs to Aaron Hernandez and 24 TD passes to Deion Branch and James White
Threw 34 TDs to Wes Welker and 36 TD passes to Julian Edelman
Completed 39 TDs to Randy Moss and 78 regular season touchdown passes to Rob Gronkowski
Completed a Team Record 6 TD passes in one game on Oct. 21, 2007 and on Oct. 18, 2009
Caught a 23 yard pass from Kevin Faulk in their 20-13 win over the Dolphins on 12-22-01
Tossed a 20 yard Game Winning TD pass, with 21 seconds left, to David Patten on 11-10-02
Threw an 82 yard Overtime Game Winning TD pass to Troy Brown on 10-19-03
Tossed an 18 yard Game Winning TD pass, with 30 seconds left, to David Givens on 11-03-03
His 36 yard punt was downed by David Givens on 1 yard line in their 12-0 win vs Miami on 12-07-03
Longest run was 22 yards in their 38-13 rout of the Bengals on 10-01-06
Threw an 8 yard Game Winning TD pass, with 44 seconds left, to Jabar Gaffney on 12-03-07
Tossed a 56 yard Flea Flicker TD pass to Jabar Gaffney in their 34-13 rout of the Steelers on 12-09-07
Tossed a 16 yard Game Winning TD pass, with 50 ticks left, to Benjamin Watson on 09-14-09
Tossed a 40 yard Flea Flicker TD pass to Randy Moss in their 59-0 shutout of Tennessee on 10-18-09
Longest completion was a 99 yard TD pass to Wes Welker in their 38-24 win over Miami on 09-12-11
Threw an 8 yard Game Winning TD pass, with 22 seconds left, to Aaron Hernandez on 10-16-11
Tossed a 17 yard Game Winning TD pass, with 5 ticks left, to Kenbrell Thompkins on 10-13-13
Threw a 1 yard Game Winning TD pass, with 31 seconds left, to Danny Amendola on 12-08-13
Had a 32 yard pooch punt, on 3rd + 32, in their 34-20 win over the Buffalo Bills on 12-29-13
Caught a 36 yard pass from Danny Amendola in their 35-28 loss to the Eagles on 12-06-15
Tossed a 25 yard Game Winning TD pass, with 23 seconds left, to Brandin Cooks, on 09-24-17
Caught a 6 yard pass from Julian Edelman in their 34-10 loss to the Titans on 11-11-18
Led the NFL with the highest QB Rating in 2007 + 2010
Led the NFL with the most yards passing in 2005, 2007 and 2017
Led the NFL with the highest pass completion % (68.9) in 2007
Led the NFL with the lowest pass interception % in 2010, 2012, 2015 and 2016
Led the NFL with the most passing attempts in 2017

Led the NFL with the most TD passes in 2002, 2007, 2010 and 2015

Completed the longest pass in the NFL Regular Season in 2011

NFL Player of the Week 11 times

AFC Offensive Player of the Week 30 times

AFC Offensive Player of the Month 10 times

14 Time AFC Pro Bowl Quarterback (2001, 2004, 2005, 2007, 2009-17)

First Team All Pro Quarterback in 2007, 2010, 2017

League MVP in 2007, 2010, 2017

2009 Comeback Player of the Year

NFL Record of most regular season touchdowns thrown to a different receiver (77)

285 Regular Season Games/283 started and 41 Playoff Games/41 started

1,025 completions for 11,388 yards + 73 TDs and 100 carries for 136 yards + 6 TDs in the playoffs

Completed 1 Post Season TD pass to Troy Brown, Reche Caldwell, Alge Crumpler, James Develin,

Tossed a Post Season TD pass to Kevin Faulk, Daniel Graham, Bethel Johnson, Brandon Lloyd, Randy Moss

Threw 1 Post Season TD pass to David Patten, Nate Solder, Dion Lewis and Danny Woodhead

Threw 2 Post Season TDs to Phillip Dorsett, Aaron Hernandez, Brandon LaFell, Shane Vereen and Mike Vrabel

Completed 3 Post Season TD passes to Jabar Gaffney, Benjamin Watson and James White.

Threw 4 Post Season TD passes to Deion Branch, Chris Hogan and Wes Welker

Completed 5 Post Season TD passes to Danny Amendola and Julian Edelman

Threw 7 Post Season TD passes to David Givens and 12 Post Season TD passes to Rob Gronkowski

Ran for the last TD scored in a game played at Foxboro Stadium in their 16-13 OT win vs Oakland on 01-19-02

Longest completion was a 73 yard pass to Deion Branch in their 27-13 Divisional loss to Denver on 01-14-06

His 48 yard punt, on 3rd + 10, was downed on the 10 yard line in their 45-10 Divisional rout of Denver
        on 01-14-12

Lateraled it to Julian Edelman for a 51 yard double pass TD in their 35-31 Divisional win vs Balt on 01-10-15

Took lateral from Dion Lewis + tossed 34 yard TD to Chris Hogan in their 36-17 Championship win on 01-22-17

Completed a 2 point pass to Danny Amendola in their 34-28 OT Super Bowl win vs Atlanta on 02-05-17

Longest run was 15 yards in their Epic 34-28 OT Super Bowl win over Atlanta on 02-05-17

Lateraled it to Danny Amendola for a 20 yard pass play in 24-20 Championship win vs Jacksonville on 01-21-18

Super Bowl MVP 4 Times

Super Bowl Record of the most games played (9)

Super Bowl Record of the most career completions (235) and most career passing attempts (357)

Super Bowl Record of the most career yards passing (2,576) and most career passing TDs (18)

Super Bowl Record of the most attempts (48) without an interception in a game (on 02-03-08 and 02-04-18)

Super Bowl Record of the most attempts (62) and most completions (43) in a game (on 02-05-17)

Super Bowl Record of the most yards passing in a game (505 yards) (on 02-04-18)

Super Bowl Record of the most consecutive completions (16) in a game (on 02-05-12)

Member of the 2001, 2003, 2004, 2014, 2016 and 2018 Championship Teams

#199 pick in the 2000 NFL Draft

Michigan Wolverine

BRAMLETT, John (#57) *"Bull"*

Born on July 7, 1941 in Memphis, TN

6'1" and 220 pounds

Linebacker   1969-70

2 sacks, 2 interceptions for 42 yards, blocked an extra point and advanced a lateral 17 yards

Sacked Bob Griese and Johnny Unitas and intercepted John Hadl and Dennis Shaw

Blocked an extra point attempt by Karl Kremser in their 38-23 win over the Miami Dolphins on 11-30-69

Had a 26 yard return of a pass by John Hadl in their 28-18 loss to the San Diego Chargers on 12-07-69

Advanced Jim Cheyunski's lateral 17 yards, after Jim's fumble recovery, in their 27-23 loss to Houston on 12-14-69

24 games/23 started

Played minor league baseball for the St. Louis Cardinals

Memphis Tiger

BRANCH, Alan (#97)
Born on December 29, 1984 in Albuquerque, NM
6'6" and 350 pounds
Defensive Lineman   2014-17
2.5 sacks and blocked a field goal attempt
Sacked Tyrod Taylor twice and shared in a sack of Bryce Petty
Blocked Nick Folk's 54 yard field goal attempt in their 22-17 win over the Jets on 11-27-16
52 Regular Season Games/39 started and 8 Playoff Games/5 started
Sacked Peyton Manning in their 20-18 Championship loss to the Denver Broncos on 01-24-16
Shared in a sack of Matt Ryan in their epic 34-28 Super Bowl win in Overtime vs Atlanta on 02-05-17
Recovered the strip sack fumble of Matt Ryan in their 34-28 OT Super Bowl win over Atlanta on 02-05-17
Member of the 2014 and 2016 World Championship Teams
Michigan Wolverine

BRANCH, Anthony "Deion" (#83 and #84)
Born on July 18, 1979 in Albany, GA
5'9" and 193 pounds
WR/KR/PR   2002-05 and 2010-12
Wore #83 from 2002-05 and #84 from 2010-12
328 career receptions for 4,297 yards + 24 TDs, 3 carries for 11 yards and 1 fumble recovery
36 kickoff returns for 863 yards and 7 punt returns for 84 yards and 1 recovery of an onside kick
Caught 24 Regular Season and 4 Post Season TD passes from Tom Brady
Had a career long 40 yard return of a punt by Tom Rouen in their 24-16 loss to the Broncos on 10-27-02
Longest was a 63 yard return of a kickoff by Jason Hanson in their 20-12 win over the Lions on 11-28-02
Longest run for 11 yards in their 20-17 loss to the Redskins on 09-28-03
Lost 1 yard returning a fumble by Patrick Pass in their 23-12 win over Arizona on 09-19-04
Had a career long 79 yard TD reception in their 45-24 rout of the Detroit Lion on 11-25-10
Recovered Pat McAfee's onside kick in their 31-24 win over the Colts on 12-04-11
89 Regular Season Games/71 started and 14 Playoff Games/11 started
56 receptions for 852 yards + 4 TDs in the playoffs
Caught a 5 yard TD pass from Tom Brady in their 32-29 Super Bowl win over the Panthers on 02-01-04
Hauled in a 60 yard TD pass from Tom Brady in their 41-27 Championship win over the Steelers on 01-23-05
Caught a 13 yard TD pass from Tom Brady in their 28-21 Divisional Playoff Game loss to the Jets on 01-16-11
Hauled in a 61 yard TD pass from Tom Brady in their 45-10 Divisional Game rout of the Broncos on 01-14-12
Longest reception was a 73 yard pass from Tom Brady in their 27-13 Divisional loss to Denver on 01-14-06
3 carries for 41 yards in the playoffs
Member of the 2003 and 2004 World Championship Teams
Super Bowl XXXIX MVP
#65 pick in the 2002 NFL Draft
Louisville Cardinal

BRIGANCE, Orenthial James "O.J." (#59)
Born on September 29, 1969 in Houston, TX
6'0" and 236 pounds
Special Team   2002
Only game played was on 09-15-02
Member of the 1995 Baltimore Stallions Grey Cup Championship Team
Rice Owl

BRISBY, Vincent (#82) *"Ultimate" and "Briz"*
Born on January 25, 1971 in Houston, TX
6'3" and 190 pounds
Wide Receiver   1993-99
217 receptions for 3,142 yards + 14 TDs and 1 fumble recovery
Caught 14 TD passes from Drew Bledsoe
Recovered a fumble by Kevin Turner in their 17-13 loss to the Miami Dolphins on 11-21-93
Longest reception was a 72 yard pass from Scott Zolak in their 30-17 loss to the Falcons on 10-01-95
83 Regular Season Games/45 started and 6 Playoff Games/1 started (on 01-01-95)
11 receptions for 132 yards in the playoffs
#58 pick in the 1993 NFL Draft
Northeast Louisiana Indian

BRISCOE, Marlin (#88)
Born on September 10, 1945 in Oakland, CA
5'11" and 178 pounds
Wide Receiver   1976
10 receptions for 136 yards + 1 TD
Longest reception was a 21 yard pass from Steve Grogan in their 27-13 loss to Baltimore on 09-12-76
Caught a 16 yard TD pass from Steve Grogan in their 48-17 rout of the Raiders on 10-03-76
Was sacked by Lawrence Fillers while attempting an end around pass and caught a 13 yard pass on 10-18-76
14 Regular Season Games/5 started and 1 Playoff Game
Caught a 7 yard pass from Steve Grogan in their 24-21 Divisional Game loss to the Raiders on 12-18-76
University of Nebraska Omaha Maverick

BRISSETT, Jacoby (#7)
Born on December 11, 1993 in West Palm Beach, FL
6'4" and 235 pounds
Quarterback   2016
34 completions for 400 yards and 16 carries for 83 yards + 1 TD
Ran for a 23 yard TD in their 27-0 shutout of Houston on 09-22-16
Longest completion was a 58 yard pass to Martellus Bennett in their 16-0 loss to Buffalo on 10-02-16
3 games/2 started
Member of the 2016 World Championship Team
#91 pick in the 2016 NFL Draft
North Carolina State Wolfpack

BRITT, Kenny (#85)
Born on September 19, 1988 in Bayonne, NJ
6'3" and 230 pounds
Wide Receiver   2017
2 receptions for 23 yards
Longest reception was a 16 yard pass from Tom Brady in their 37-16 rout of Buffalo on 12-24-17
3 games
Rutgers Scarlet Knight

BRITT, Wesley (#65)
Born on November 21, 1981 in Cullman, AL
6'8" and 314 pounds
Tackle   2006-08
16 games/2 started
Alabama Crimson Tide

BROCK, Pete (#58) *"Deep Threat"*
Born on July 14, 1954 in Portland, OR
6'5" and 267 pounds
Center/LS/OL (TE)   1976-87
Nicknamed *"Deep Threat"* after catching a 6 yard TD pass
Recovered fumbles by Doug Beaudoin, Horace Ivory and Matt Cavanaugh and 2 fumbles by Steve Grogan
Long Snapper for Punters Rich Camarillo, Luke Prestridge, Mike Hubach and Ken Hartley
Long Snapper for Kickers John Smith, Fred Steinfort and Tony Franklin
Caught a 6 yard TD pass from Steve Grogan in their 38-24 victory over the Jets on 11-21-76
Was *"Mr. Versatility"* for playing Tackle, Wing Back, TE and Long Snapper in same series on 10-14-79
154 Regular Season games/88 started and 8 Playoff Games/6 started
Recovered Steve Grogan's fumble in their 28-13 First Round Playoff Game loss to Miami on 01-08-83
Recovered Tony Eason's fumble in their 22-17 Divisional Playoff Game loss to Denver on 01-04-87
#12 pick in the 1976 NFL Draft
Colorado Buffalo

BROOKS, Terrence (#25)
Born on March 2, 1992 in Dunnellon, FL
5'11" and 205 pounds
Special Team   2019--
15 Regular Season Games and 1 Playoff Game (on 01-04-20)
Florida State Seminole

BROWN, Antonio (#17)
Born on July 10, 1988 in Miami, FL
5'10" and 185 pounds
WR   2019
4 receptions for 56 yards + 1 TD and 1 carry for 5 yards
Caught a 20 yard TD pass from Tom Brady in their 43-0 shutout of the Dolphins on 09-15-19
1 game
Central Michigan Chippewa

BROWN, Bill (#54)
Born on April 25, 1936 in Mount Kisko, NY
6'1" and 230 pounds
Linebacker   1960
Had an 8 yard return of a pass by Al Dorow in their 28-24 win over the NY Titans on 09-17-60
Sacked Tom Flores in their 34-28 victory over the Oakland Raiders on 11-04-60
14 games/10 started
Syracuse Orangeman

BROWN, Chadwick "Chad" (#98)
Born on July 12, 1970 in Pasadena, CA
6'2" and 245 pounds
Linebacker   2005 and 2007
17 Regular Season Games/5 started and 2 Playoff Games
Colorado Buffalo

BROWN, Corwin (#30) *"Cornflakes"*
Born on April 25, 1970 in Chicago, IL
6'1" and 200 pounds
Defensive Back   1991-96
3 fumble recoveries for 42 yards + 1 TD and 1 recovery of an onside kick
Recovered fumbles by Pete Metzelaars, Rob Carpenter and Bryan Still
Recovered Matt Stover's onside kick in their 46-38 win over the Baltimore Ravens on 10-06-96
Had a 42 yard TD return of a fumble by Bryan Still in their 45-7 rout of the San Diego Chargers on 12-01-96
61 Regular Season Games/14 started and 4 Playoff Games
Caught a 21 yard pass from Punter Pat O'Neill in their 20-13 Wild Card loss to the Browns on 1-01-95
Recovered Matt Bahr's onside kick in their 20-13 Wild Card Playoff Game loss to Cleveland on 01-01-95
#110 pick in the 1993 NFL Draft
Michigan Wolverine

BROWN, Joseph "Barry" (#66 and #86)
Born on April 17, 1943 in Boston, MA
6'3" and 230 pounds
LB/TE   1969-70
Wore #66 in 1969 and #86 in 1970
21 receptions for 214 yards and 1 recovery on an onside kick
Longest reception was a 22 yard pass from Joe Kapp in their 45-10 loss to Buffalo on 11-01-70
Recovered an onside kick by Grant Guthrie in their 14-10 win over Buffalo on 11-29-70
21 games/12 started
Florida Gator

BROWN, Malcom (#90)
Born on February 2, 1994 in Brenham, TX
6'2" and 320 pounds
Defensive Lineman   2015-18
8.5 sacks, 3 fumble recoveries and made a tackle that resulted in a safety
Shared in a sack of Nathan Peterman, and sacked WR Antonio Brown, Eli Manning and Brock Osweiler
Sacked Trevor Siemian, Josh McCown and Tyrod Taylor and had 2 sacks of Charlie Whitehurst
Recovered fumbles by Kenjon Barber, Bryan Hoyer and Jason Croom
Sacked WR Antonio Brown on a HB option play in their 28-21 win over the Steelers on 09-10-15
Tackled RB Kenneth Dixon in the end zone for a safety in their win 30-23 over the Ravens on 12-12-16
60 Regular Season Games/51 started and 11 Playoff Games/10 started
Sacked Brock Osweiler in their 34-16 Divisional Playoff Game win over Houston on 01-14-17
Member of the 2016 World Championship Team
#32 pick in the 2015 NFL Draft
Texas Longhorn

BROWN, Montague "Monty" (#93)
Born on April 13, 1970 in Bridgeport, MI
6'0" and 238 pounds
Linebacker   1996
11 games
Ferris State Bulldog

BROWN, Preston (#87 and #81)
Born on March 2, 1958 in Nashville, TN
5'10" and 184 pounds
PR/KR/WR   1980 and 1982
Wore #87 for 5 games in 1980 and #81 for 9 games in 1982
10 punt returns for 42 yards, 9 kickoff returns for 156 yards and 4 receptions for 114 yards + 1 TD
Longest return was a 14 yard return of a punt by Johnny Evans in their 34-17 win over Cleveland on 09-07-80
Longest return was a 26 yard return of a kickoff by Fred Steinfort in their 23-14 win over Denver on 09-29-80
Hauled in a 38 yard TD pass from Matt Cavanaugh in their 10-7 loss to the Cleveland Browns on 11-21-82
Longest reception was a 41 yard pass from Steve Grogan in their 26-13 loss to the Chicago Bears on 12-05-82
14 Regular Season Games/4 started and 1 Playoff Game/1 started
Caught an 8 yard pass from Steve Grogan in their 28-13 First Round Playoff loss to Miami on 01-08-83
#160 pick in the 1980 NFL Draft
Vanderbilt Commodore

BROWN, Roger (#47)
Born on December 16, 1966 in Baltimore, MD
6'0" and 196 pounds
Defensive Back   1992
Recovered Marcus Dowdell's fumbled punt return in their 31-14 loss to the Saints on 11-08-92
16 games/2 started
Virginia Tech Hokie

BROWN, Sergio (#38 and #31)
Born on May 22, 1988 in Maywood, IL
6'2" and 210 pounds
Safety   2010-11
Wore #38 in 2010 and #31 in 2011
Recovered CJ Spiller's fumbled punt return in their 34-3 rout of the Buffalo Bills on 12-26-10
Had a 2 yard return of a pass by Philip Rivers in their 35-21 win over the San Diego Chargers on 09-18-11
26 Regular Season games/3 started and 4 Playoff Games
Notre Dame Fighting Irish

BROWN, Sidney (#21)
Born on January 27, 1956 in New Orleans, LA
6'0" and 186 pounds
Cornerback   1978
16 Regular Season Games and 1 Playoff Game (on 12-31-78)
#82 pick in the 1977 NFL Draft
Oklahoma Sooner

BROWN, Tarell (#25)
Born on January 6, 1985 in New York, NY
5'11" and 190 pounds
Cornerback   2015
3 games/2 started
Texas Longhorn

BROWN, Trent (#77)
Born on April 13, 1993 in Albany, GA
6'8" and 380 pounds
Tackle   2018
16 Regular Season Games/16 started and 3 Playoff Games/3 started
Member of the 2018 World Championship Team
Florida Gator

BROWN, Troy (#86 and #80) *"Mr. Patriot"*
Born on July 2, 1971 in Barnwell, SC
5'10" and 196 pounds
WR/PR/KR (DB)   1993-2007
Wore #86 in 1994 and #80 in 1993 and from 1995-2007
557 receptions for 6,366 yards + 31 TDs and 29 carries for 178 yards and
252 punt returns for 2,625 yards + 3 TDs, 87 kickoff returns for 1,862 yards and 1 onside kick recovery
3 interceptions for 22 yards and 3 special team fumble recoveries for 75 yards + 1 TD
Caught a TD pass from Dave Meggett, David Patten, Adam Vinatieri and Vinny Testaverde
Caught 12 Regular Season TD passes and 1 Post Season TD pass from Drew Bledsoe
Caught 15 Regular Season TD passes and 1 Post Season TD pass from Tom Brady
Recovered fumbled kickoff returns by Dave Meggett and Allen Rossum
Recovered a fumbled punt return by Randall Gay in their 42-15 win over Cleveland on 12-05-04
Intercepted Drew Bledsoe, Luke McCown and Jon Kitna
Advanced Dave Meggett's fumbled kickoff return 75 yards for a TD in their 31-28 win over the Jets on 12-10-95
Grabbed a 35 yard HB Option TD pass from Dave Meggett in their 27-24 win vs Miami on 11-23-97
Caught an 18 yard TD pass from Drew Bledsoe in the 4th Qtr to defeat the Colts 20-17 on 11-30-97
Recovered an onside kick by Mike Hollis in their 26-20 win over the Jaguars on 12-07-97
Longest was a 54 yard return of Matt Stover's opening kickoff in their 20-3 rout of the Ravens on 01-02-00
Returned a punt by Mark Royals 66 yards for a TD in their 21-16 loss to Tampa on 09-03-00
Longest run for 35 yards in their 21-6 loss to the Tampa Bay Buccaneers on 09-03-00
Hauled in a 60 yard TD pass from WR David Patten in their 38-17 win over the Colts on 10-21-01
Had a career long 85 yard TD return of a punt by Chris Gardocki in their 27-16 win vs the Browns on 12-09-01
Led the NFL with the best punt return average and had the most punts returned for a TD in 2001
Returned a punt by Todd Sauerbrun 68 yards for a TD in their 38-6 rout of the Panthers on 01-06-02
Caught a 2 point conversion pass from Tom Brady in their 33-30 win over the Bears on 11-10-02
Had a 6 yard return of a blocked FGA by Richard Seymour in their 19-13 OT win vs the Dolphins on 10-19-03
Caught a career long 82 yard TD pass from Tom Brady to beat Miami 19-13 in Overtime on 10-19-03
Caught a 4 yard TD pass from Adam Vinatieri in their 40-22 win vs the St. Louis Rams on 11-07-04
Had a career long 17 yard return of a pass by Drew Bledsoe in their 29-6 win over Buffalo on 11-14-04
Intercepted a pass by Luke McCown in their 42-15 rout of the Cleveland Browns on 12-05-04
Had a 5 yard return of a pass by Jon Kitna in their 35-28 win over the Bengals on 12-12-04
Caught a 2 point conversion pass from Tom Brady in their 28-21 win over the Lions on 12-03-06
Snared a 6 yard TD pass from Vinny Testaverde in their 40-23 win over Tennessee on 12-31-06
AFC Special Team Player of the Month in December 2001
AFC Pro Bowl Wide Receiver in 2001
192 Regular Season games/70 started and 20 Playoff Games/8 started
Wore #86 in the Wild Card Playoff Game on 01-01-95
58 receptions for 694 yards + 2 TDs and 2 carries for minus 19 yards in the playoffs
33 punt returns for 315 yards + 1 TD and 5 kickoff returns for 85 yards in the playoffs
Caught a 24 yard TD pass from Drew Bledsoe in their 17-3 Wild Card win over Miami on 12-28-97
Returned a punt by Josh Miller 55 yards for a TD in their 24-17 AFC Championship win vs Pitt on 01-27-02
Returned a blocked FGA 11 yards + lateraled to Antwan Harris in their 24-17 Playoff win on 01-27-02
Returned a free kick by Hunter Smith 16 yards in their 24-14 Championship win over the Colts on 01-18-04
Used as a Nickel Defensive Back in their 24-21 Super Bowl win over the Eagles on 02-06-05
Caught an 11 yard TD pass from Tom Brady in their 28-3 Wild Card win over Jacksonville on 01-07-06
Member of the 2001, 2003 and 2004 World Championship Teams
#198 pick in the 1993 NFL Draft
Awarded the Ron Burton Community Service Award in 2004
Inducted into the Patriots Hall of Fame on 09-15-12
Marshall Thundering Herd

BROWN, Vincent (#59) *"The Undertaker"*
Born on January 9, 1965 in Atlanta, GA
6'2" and 245 pounds
Linebacker   1988-95
16.5 sacks, 10 interceptions for 95 yards + 1 TD and 7 fumble recoveries for 30 yards and 1 TD
Shared in a sack of Dave Krieg and Browning Nagle and had 1 ½ sacks of Boomer Esiason
Sacked Jack Trudeau, Bobby Hebert, Bubby Brister, Tom Tupa, Rich Gannon and Jim Kelly
Sacked Steve DeBerg, Vinny Testaverde, Steve Bono and Glenn Foley
Had 2 sacks of Steve Beuerlein and Jeff George
Intercepted Bobby Hebert, Jack Trudeau, Rick Mirer, Jim Kelly, Brett Favre and Stan Humphries
Intercepted Steve Young, Dan Marino, Neil O'Donnell and Glenn Foley
Recovered fumbles by Kenny Johnson, Jack Trudeau, Brad Baxter and Thurman Thomas
Recovered fumbles by Rodney Culver, Boomer Esiason and Darick Holmes
Had a 25 yard TD return of a fumble by Thurman Thomas in their 16-7 loss to the Bills on 11-01-92
Had a career long 49 yard TD return of a pass by Bobby Hebert in their 31-14 loss to the Saints on 11-08-92
Tipped a pass by Jeff George that Chris Singleton returned 82 yards for a TD in their 37-34 OT win on 11-15-92
Had a diving interception of Glenn Foley's deflected pass in their 20-7 win over the Jets on 11-05-95
123 Regular Season games/103 started and 1 Playoff Game/1 started (on 01-01-95)
#43 pick in the 1988 NFL Draft
Mississippi Valley State Delta Devil

BROWN, Wilbert (#60)
Born on May 9, 1977 in Texarkana, TX
6'2" and 320 pounds
Offensive Lineman   2003
1 Regular Season Game (on 09-21-03) and 2 Playoff Games
Member of the 2003 World Championship Team
Houston Cougar

BROWNER, Brandon (#39)
Born on August 2, 1984 in Sylmar, CA
6'4" and 221 pounds
Cornerback   2014
1 interception return of 30 yards and 1 advancement of a lateral for 2 yards
Had a 30 yard return of a pass by Peyton Manning in their 43-21 win over Denver on 11-02-14
Advanced a lateral from Jamie Collins 2 yards in their 17-16 win over the Jets on 12-21-14
9 Regular Season Games/9 started and 3 Playoff Games/3 Started
Member of the 2014 World Championship Team
Member of the 2008 Calgary Stampeders Grey Cup Championship Team
Oregon State Beaver

BROWNING, Dave (#74)
Born on August 18, 1956 in Spokane, WA
6'5" and 245 pounds
Defensive End   1983
2 sacks
Sacked Dan Fouts and Brian Sipe
12 games
Washington Husky

BRUNEY, Fred (#33) *"Fearless"*
Born on December 30, 1931 in Martins Ferry, OH
5'10" and 184 pounds
DB/PR (KR)   1960-62
8 interceptions for 125 yards + 1 TD, 1 sack and 3 fumble recoveries
30 punt returns for 148 yards, 2 kickoff returns for 39 yards and attempted an onside kick
Intercepted Tom Flores, Al Dorow, Cotton Davidson, Jack Kemp, Hunter Enis and George Blanda
Intercepted George Shaw and Lee Grosscup as well
Recovered fumbles by Jack Rudolph, Johnny Robinson and Charley Hennigan
Longest was a 19 yard return of a punt by Rick Sapienza in their 28-24 win over the NY Titans on 09-17-60
Longest was a 20 yard return of a kickoff by Bill Shockley in their 28-24 win over the Titans on 09-17-60
Attempted an onside kick in their 28-24 comeback win over the NY Titans at the Polo Grounds on 09-17-60
Had a career long 33 yard TD return of a pass by George Shaw in their 41-16 win over Denver on 09-21-62
Sacked Frank Tripucka in their 41-16 win over the Denver Broncos on 09-21-62
Holder for Gino Cappelletti in 1960
Led the AFL with 23 punt returns in 1961
AFL All Star Defensive Back in 1961 and 1962
40 games/36 started
Ohio State Buckeye

BRUSCHI, Tedy (#54)
Born on June 9, 1973 in San Francisco, CA
6'1" and 247 pounds
Linebacker (KR)　　　　1996-2008
30.5 sacks, 7 fumble recoveries for 13 yards and 12 interceptions for 187 yards + 4 TDs
6 kickoff returns for 47 yards and returned a blocked punt 4 yards for a TD
Shared in a sack of Brett Favre and had 1 ½ sacks of Drew Bledsoe and 3 sacks of Vinny Testaverde
Sacked Stan Humphries, Glenn Foley, Jim Harbaugh, Todd Collins, Mark Brunell and Danny Wuerffel
Sacked Elvis Grbac, Tim Couch, Rob Johnson, Kordell Stewart, Brian Griese and Chris Chandler
Sacked Donovan McNabb, Marc Bolger, Kyle Boller, Luke McCown and Jon Kitna
Had 2 sacks of Rick Mirer, Chris Simms and Derek Anderson and 2 ½ sacks of Dante Culpepper
Intercepted Ky Detmer, Brian Griese, Kurt Warner, Rich Gannon, Joey Harrington and Donovan McNabb
Intercepted Jay Fiedler, Peyton Manning and Drew Bledsoe and had 3 interceptions of Chad Pennington
Recovered fumbles by Jim Harbaugh, Reggie Barlow, Eric Moulds, Edgerrin James and Drew Bledsoe
Recovered fumbles by Ronnie Brown and J.P. Losman as well
Returned 4 consecutive interceptions for a TD
Longest was an 11 yard return of Sebastian Janikowski's opening kickoff in 27-20 loss to Oakland on 11-17-02
Had a career long 48 yard TD return of a pass by Rich Gannon in their 27-20 loss to the Raiders on 11-17-02
Had a 27 yard TD return of a pass by Joey Harrington in their 20-12 win over the Lions on 11-28-02
Had an 18 yard TD return of a pass by Donovan McNabb in their 31-10 rout of the Eagles on 09-14-03
Had an 5 yard TD return of a pass by Jay Fiedler in their 12-0 shutout of the Dolphins on 12-07-03
Had a 13 yard return of a fumble by Drew Bledsoe in their 31-0 shutout of the Buffalo Bills on 12-27-03
Returned a blocked punt 4 yards for a TD in their 46-38 win over the Ravens on 10-06-96
AFC Defensive Player of the Week in their 31-10 rout of the Eagles on 09-14-03
AFC Defensive Player of the Week in their 12-0 shutout of the Dolphins on 12-07-03
AFC Defensive Player of the Week in their 31-17 victory over the Bills on 10-03-04
AFC Defensive Player of the Week in their 21-7 win over San Francisco on 01-02-05
AFC Defensive Player of the Week in their 21-16 win over Buffalo on 10-03-05
AFC Pro Bowl Linebacker in 2004
189 Regular Season games/139 started and 22 Playoff Games/17 started
4.5 sacks, 2 interceptions for 12 yards and 3 fumble recoveries for 1 yard in the playoffs
Sacked Brett Favre *twice* in their 35-21 Super Bowl loss to the Green Bay Packers on 01-26-97
Sacked Rich Gannon in their 16-13 Divisional OT win vs the Oakland Raiders on 01-19-02
Shared in a sack of Kordell Stewart in their 24-17 Championship win over the Steelers on 01-27-02
Sacked Donovan McNabb in their 24-21 Super Bowl win over the Eagles on 02-06-05
Returned a pass by Mark Brunell 12 yards in their 20-6 AFC Championship win over the Jaguars on 01-12-97
Intercepted a pass by Donovan McNabb in their 24-21 Super Bowl win over the Eagles on 02-06-05
Returned Kordell Stewart's fumble 1 yard in their 24-17 Playoff win over the Steelers on 01-27-02
Ripped the ball from Dominic Rhodes in their 20-3 Divisional rout of the Colts on 01-16-05
Recovered Reggie Wayne's fumble in their 20-3 Divisional Playoff rout of the Colts on 01-16-05
NFL Defensive Player of the Week in their 20-3 Divisional win over the Colts on 01-16-05
Returned Mike Vanderjagt's 2nd half kickoff 15 yards in their 20-3 Divisional win over the Colts on 01-16-05
Member of the 2001, 2003 and 2004 World Championship Teams
#86 pick in the 1996 NFL Draft
Inducted into the Patriots Hall of Fame on 07-29-13
Played Saxophone along with the Boston Pops Orchestra
Arizona Wildcat

BRYANT, Hubert "Hubie" (#45 and #84) *"Fashion Plate"*
Born on February 10, 1946 in Pittsburgh, PA
5'10" and 170 pounds
WR/PR/KR   1971-72
Wore #45 in 1971 and #84 for 2 games in 1972
14 receptions for 212 yards + 1 TD and 4 carries for 1 yard
10 punt returns for 24 yards and 10 kickoff returns for 252 yards
Longest was a 16 yard return of a punt by David Lee in their 23-3 loss to the Baltimore Colts on 10-03-71
Longest was a 45 yard return of a kickoff by Jim O'Brien in their 23-3 loss to the Baltimore Colts on 10-03-71
Snared a 10 yard TD pass from Jim Plunkett in their 28-20 win over the Oilers on 11-07-71
Longest reception was a 48 yard pass from Bob Gladieux in their 28-20 victory over Houston on 11-07-71
Longest run for 1 yard in their 27-20 loss to the Buffalo Bills on 11-28-71
13 games/2 started
Minnesota Golden Gopher

BUBEN, Mark (#63)
Born on March 23, 1957 in Geneva, NY
6'3" and 260 pounds
Defensive Lineman   1979-81
Fell on Pat Ryan's fumble, after he was strip sacked by Julius Adams, in their 56-3 rout of the Jets on 09-09-79
Returned a Bert Jones fumble 31 yards in their 29-28 loss to the Baltimore Colts on 09-06-81
Had a 49 yard interception return of a pass by Bill Kenney in their 33-17 win over the Chiefs on 10-04-81
32 games
Tufts Jumbo

BUCHANAN, Michael (#99)
Born on January 24, 1991 in Homewood, IL
6'6" and 255 pounds
Defensive Lineman   2013-14
Sacked Geno Smith and Matt Ryan
Recovered Julian Edelman's fumbled punt return in their 34-31 OT win against Denver on 11-24-13
18 Regular Season Games and 2 Playoff Games
Member of the 2014 World Championship Team
#226 Pick in the 2013 NFL Draft
Illinois Fighting Illini

BUCKLEY, Douglas "Terrell" (#27 and #22) *"T Buck"*
Born on June 6, 1971 in Pascagoula, MS
5'10" and 180 pounds
DB (WR)   2001-02
Wore #27 in 2001 and wore #27 and #22 in 2002
7 interceptions for 126 yards + 1 TD and 1 sack and was a Wide Receiver in one game
Intercepted Kurt Warner, Vinny Testaverde, Tim Couch, Drew Bledsoe and Steve McNair
Had 2 interceptions of Kordell Stewart and 1 sack of Rob Johnson
Sacked Rob Johnson in their 21-11 victory over the Buffalo Bills on 11-11-01
Was targeted once as a wide receiver in their 21-11 win over Buffalo on 11-11-01
Had a career long 52 yard return of a pass by Kurt Warner in their 24-17 loss to St. Louis on 11-18-01
Picked off a pass by Vinny Testaverde to seal the 17-16 win over the NY Jets on 12-02-01
31 Regular Season Games/3 started and 3 Playoff Games
Intercepted Kordell Stewart in their 24-17 Championship win over the Steelers on 01-27-02
Returned Ricky Proehl's fumble 15 yards in their 20-17 Super Bowl victory over the Rams on 02-03-02
Member of the 2001 World Championship Team
Florida State Seminole

BUGENHAGEN, Gary (#67)
Born on February 6, 1945 in Buffalo, NY
6'2" and 240 pounds
Guard   1970
10 games/7 started
Syracuse Orangeman

BUONICONTI, Nicholas "Nick" (#85*) "Skip"*
Born on December 15, 1940 in Springfield, MA
5'11" and 220 pounds
Linebacker (PR)   1962-68
23 sacks, 6 fumble recoveries for 7 yards + 1 TD and 24 interceptions for 223 yards
Blocked an extra point, blocked 2 field goal attempts and had an 8 yard punt return
Shared in a sack of Mickey Slaughter and had 3 ½ sacks of Jack Kemp
Sacked Warren Rabb, Don Trull, Joe Namath, Pete Beathard, Dan Darragh and Jim LeClair
Sacked Cotton Davidson, Len Dawson and Daryle Lamonica
Recorded 2 sacks of Tom Flores and Jacky Lee and 3 sacks of Dick Wood and George Blanda
Intercepted Cotton Davidson, George Blanda, Jack Kemp, Don Trull, Mickey Slaughter and Max Choboian
Had 2 interceptions of John Hadl, Pete Beathard and Jacky Lee
Had 3 interceptions of Len Dawson, Dick Wood, Tom Flores and Dan Darragh
Recovered fumbles by Jack Kemp, George Blanda, Bill Tobin, Wray Carlton, Jack Clancy and Mike Garrett
Had an 8 yard return of a punt by Curley Johnson in their 43-14 win over the NY Titans on 10-06-62
Had a 3 yard retun of a pass by Tom Flores with 2 minutes left in their 20-14 win over the Raiders on 09-22-63
Had a 7 yard TD return of a fumble by Bill Tobin in their 46-28 win over the Oilers on 12-08-63
Blocked a 36 yard FGA by George Blanda in their 31-10 loss to the Houston Oilers on 09-19-65
Blocked an extra point attempt by Fletcher Smith in their 43-24 loss to the Chiefs on 09-25-66
Had a career long 41 yard return of a pass by John Hadl in their 35-17 win over San Diego on 10-23-66
Tackled RB Roy Hopkins in the end zone for a safety in their 18-7 win over the Oilers on 11-05-67
Blocked a 40 yard FGA by John Wittenborn in their 16-0 loss to the Houston Oilers on 10-13-68
Had 3 interceptions for 22 yards of Dan Darragh in their 23-6 win over Buffalo on 10-20-68
AFL Defensive Player of the Week in their 18-7 win over Houston on 11-05-67
AFL Defensive Player of the Week in their 23-6 win over Buffalo on 10-20-68
AFL All Star Linebacker in 1963, 1964, 1965, 1966, 1967
First Team All Pro Linebacker in 1964, 1965, 1966, 1967
91 Regular Season Games/91 started and 2 Playoff Games/2 started
13th Round Draft Pick in 1962
Inducted into the Patriots Hall of Fame in 1992
Inducted into the Pro Football Hall of Fame on 08-04-01
Notre Dame Fighting Irish

BURGESS, Derrick (#53)
Born on August 12, 1978 in Lake City, SC
6'2" and 266 pounds
Linebacker   2009
5 sacks and 1 fumble recovery
Sacked Trent Edwards, Josh Freeman, Matt Moore, Ryan Fitzpatrick and Matt Schaub
Recovered a fumble by Mark Sanchez in their 31-14 win over the NY Jets on 11-22-09
16 Regular Season games/6 started and 1 Playoff Game (on 01-10-10)
Mississippi Rebel

BURKE, John (#85)

Born on September 7, 1971 in Elizabeth, NJ
6'3" and 248 pounds
Tight End (KR)   1994-96
25 receptions for 241 yards, 4 kickoff returns for 18 yards and 1 fumble recovery
Recovered OJ McDuffie's fumbled punt return in their 20-3 loss to Miami on 09-10-95
Longest reception was a 21 yard pass from Drew Bledsoe in their 27-14 win over the Bills on 10-23-95
Longest was a 7 yard return of a kickoff by Norm Johnson in their 41-27 loss to the Steelers on 12-16-95
43 Regular Season games/12 started and 4 Playoff Games/1 started (on 01-12-97)
#121 pick in the 1994 NFL Draft
Virginia Tech Hokie

BURKHEAD, Rex (#34)

Born on July 2, 1990 in Plano, TX
5'10" and 210 pounds
Running Back   2017-19
186 carries for 752 yards + 8 TDs and 71 receptions for 664 yards + 4 TDs
Had a 17 yard kickoff return and blocked a punt
Caught 4 TD passes from Tom Brady
Blocked a punt by Riley Dixon in their 41-16 rout of the Denver Broncos on 11-12-17
Returned Steven Hauschka's kickoff 17 yards in their 23-3 victory over the Bills on 12-03-17
Deflected Jonathan Jones' deflection of Ryan Allen's punt which was recovered on the 1 yard line on 12-16-18
Longest reception was a 32 yard pass from Tom Brady in their 43-0 shutout of the Dolphins on 09-15-19
Longest run was a 33 yard TD in their 34-13 rout of the Bengals on 12-15-19
31 Regular Season Games/8 started and 6 Playoff Games/1 started (on 01-13-19)
30 carries for 123 yards + 3 TDs and 11 receptions for 123 yards
Ran for a 6 yard TD in their 41-28 Divisional Playoff Win over the Los Angeles Chargers on 01-13-19
Ran for a 4 yard TD with 39 seconds left in their 37-31 OT AFC Championship win over the Chiefs on 01-20-19
Ran for the game winning 2 yard TD to defeat the Chiefs 37-31 in OT for the AFC Championship on 01-20-19
Lost 1 yard on a kickoff return lateral from Dion Lewis in their 41-33 Super Bowl loss on 02-04-18
Member of the 2018 World Championship Team
Nebraska Husker

BURKS, Steve (#82)

Born on August 6, 1953 in Little Rock, AR
6'5" and 211 pounds
WR/KR   1975-77
13 receptions for 264 yards, 1 carry for 2 yards and 4 kickoff returns for 65 yards
Longest reception was a 76 yard pass from Jim Plunkett in their 34-31 loss to Dallas on 11-16-75
Longest was a 25 yard return of a kickoff by Toni Fritsch in their 34-31 loss to the Cowboys on 11-16-75
Ran for a 2 yard gain in their 31-14 win over Tampa on 12-12-76
Recovered Tim Fox's onside kick recovery fumble in their 14-6 win over the Eagles on 11-27-77
34 Regular Season games/1 started (on 12-12-76) and 1 Playoff Game (on 12-18-76)
#91 pick in the 1975 NFL Draft
Arkansas State Indian

BURTON, Ron (#22)
Born on July 25, 1936 in Springfield, OH
5'10" and 190 pounds
HB/PR/KR   1960-65
429 carries for 1,536 yards + 9 TDs and 111 receptions for 1,205 yards + 8 TDs
56 punt returns for 389 yards, 46 kickoff returns for 1,119 yards + 1 TD and 2 fumble recoveries
Caught 2 TD passes from Tom Yewcic and 6 TD passes from Babe Parilli
Recovered fumbled punt returns by Fred Bruney and Dave Cloutier
Longest run for 77 yards in their 31-24 loss to the Denver Broncos on 10-23-60
Handed off to Larry Garron on a reverse kickoff return in their 31-31 tie with the Oilers on 10-13-61
Had a 91 yard TD return of a kickoff by Ben Agajanian in their 28-21 win vs the Dallas Texans on 11-03-61
Longest was a 62 yard return of a punt by Jim Norton in their 27-15 loss to the Oilers on 11-12-61
Returned Gene Mingo's missed FGA 91 yards for a TD in their 33-29 win over the Broncos on 11-11-62
Advanced Gino Cappelletti's lateral 7 yards in their 43-43 tie with the Oakland Raiders on 10-16-64
Returned Dick Guesman's missed FGA 18 yards in their 12-7 win vs Denver on 11-20-64
Had a career long 73 yard TD reception from Babe Parilli in their 13-13 tie with San Diego on 10-17-65
Returned Herb Travenio's missed FGA 19 yards in their 13-13 tie with San Diego on 10-17-65
69 Regular Season Games and 2 Playoff Games/2 started
1st Overall Draft Pick of the Boston Patriots
Northwestern Wildcat

BUTLER, Adam (#70)
Born on April 12, 1994 in Duncanville, TX
6'5" and 300 pounds
Defensive Lineman   2017-19
Shared in a sack of Luke Faulk and Josh Allen and strip sacked Sam Darnold
Sacked Matt Ryan, Jay Cutler, Ryan Tannehill, Kirk Cousins and Carson Wentz
Recorded 2 sacks of Ryan Fitzpatrick and Baker Mayfield
Strip sacked Sam Darnold and Kyle Van Noy returned it 46 yds for a TD in 38-3 rout of the Jets on 12-30-18
48 Regular Season Games/8 started and 7 Playoff Games
Sacked Marcus Mariota in their 35-14 Divisional Playoff win over the Titans on 01-13-08
Sacked Blake Bortles in their 24-20 AFC Championship win over the Jaguars on 01-21-08
Member of the 2018 World Championship Team
Vanderbilt Commodore

BUTLER, Darius (#28)
Born on March 18, 1986 in Tamarac, FL
5'10" and 180 pounds
CB/KR   2009-10
3 interceptions for 91 yards + 1 TD and 5 kickoff returns for 104 yards
Intercepted Kerry Collins, Josh Johnson and Matt Schaub
Had a 91 yard TD return of a pass by Matt Schaub in their 34-27 loss to the Texans on 01-03-10
Longest was a 26 yard return of a kickoff by Kris Brown in their 34-27 loss to Houston on 01-03-10
Recovered Julian Edelman's fumbled punt return in their 31-27 win over Green Bay on 12-19-10
29 Regular Season Games and 1 Playoff Game
#41 pick in the 2009 NFL Draft
UCONN Husky

BUTLER, Malcolm (#21) "Strap"
Born on March 2, 1990 in Vickburg, MS
5'11" and 190 pounds
Cornerback   2014-17
8 interceptions for 36 yards, 2 sacks and 2 fumble recoveries
Intercepted Tyrod Taylor, Zach Mettenberger, Landry Jones, Jared Goff and Bryce Petty
Intercepted Ryan Fitzpatrick Cam Newton and Brock Osweiler
Sacked Colin Kaepernick and Tyrod Taylor and recovered fumbles by Robby Anderson and Khiry Robinson
Had a career long 21 yard return of a Ryan Fitzpatrick pass in their 41-3 rout of the Jets on 12-24-16
AFC Pro Bowl Cornerback in 2015
59 Regular Season Games/48 started and 11 Playoff Games/7 started
Had a 3 yard return of a pass by Russell Wilson to seal their 28-24 Super Bowl win vs Seattle on 02-01-05
Member of the 2014 and 2016 World Championship Teams
West Alabama Tiger

BUTTS, Marion (#44)
Born on August 1, 1966 in Sylvester, GA
6'1" and 248 pounds
Running Back   1994
243 carries for 703 yards + 8 TDs and 9 receptions for 54 yards
Longest reception was a 15 yard pass from Drew Bledsoe in their 38-35 loss to Buffalo on 09-11-94
Longest run for 26 yards in their 24-13 win over the Jets on 12-04-94
16 games/15 started
Florida State Seminole

BYARS, Keith (#41)
Born on October 14, 1963 in Dayton, OH
6'1" and 245 pounds
Fullback (WR/TE)   1996-97
13 carries for 26 yards, 47 receptions for 438 yards + 5 TDs, caught a 2 point pass and recovered an onside kick
Caught 5 Regular Season TD passes and 2 Post Season TD passes from Drew Bledsoe
Recovered an onside kick by Steve Christie in their 28-25 win over the Buffalo Bills on 10-27-96
Caught a 2 yard TD from Drew Bledsoe in the 4th Qtr in their 31-27 win over the Jets on 11-10-96
Caught a 2 point conversion pass from Drew Bledsoe in their 34-8 loss to the Denver Broncos on 11-17-96
Longest run for 5 yards in their 27-24 OT win over the New York Jets on 09-14-97
Longest reception was a 51 yard pass from Drew Bledsoe in their 27-24 win over Miami on 11-23-97
26 Regular Season Games/14 started and 5 Playoff Games/4 started
Used as a Wide Receiver and Tight End in the Playoffs
14 receptions for 112 yards + 2 TDs and 3 carries for 9 yards in the playoffs
Caught a 34 yard TD pass from Drew Bledsoe in their 28-3 Divisional Playoff win vs the Steelers on 01-05-97
Caught a 1 yard TD pass from Drew Bledsoe in their 35-21 Super Bowl loss to the Packers on 01-26-97
Ohio State Buckeye

BYRD, Dennis (#78)
Born on August 31, 1946 in Lincolnton, NC
6'4" and 260 pounds
DE/DT   1968
Sacked Daryle Lamonica, Len Dawson, John Stofa and shared in a sack of Joe Namath
14 games/14 started
#6 pick in the 1968 NFL Draft
North Carolina State Wolfpack

CADE, Eddie (#41)
Born on August 4, 1973 in Casa Grande, AZ
6'1" and 206 pounds
Safety   1995
10 games
Arizona State Sun Devil

CADET, Travaris (#39)
Born on January 2, 1989 in Miami, FL
6'1" and 210 pounds
Running Back   2015
Caught a 2 yard pass from Tom Brady in their 40-32 win over the Bills on 09-20-15
Only game played was on 09-20-15
Appalachian State Mountaineer

CAGLE, John (#62)
Born on March 26, 1947 in Anderson, SC
6'3" and 260 pounds
Defensive End   1969
6 games/1 started (on 09-14-69)
#344 pick in the 1969 NFL Draft
Clemson Tiger

CALDWELL JR., Donald "Reche" (#87)
Born on March 28, 1979 in Tampa, FL
6'0" and 215 pounds
Wide Receiver   2006
61 receptions for 760 yards + 4 TDs, 1 carry for 5 yards and caught a pass for a 2 point conversion
Caught 4 Regular Season TD passes and 1 Post Season TD pass from Tom Brady
Ran for a 5 yard gain in their 28-6 rout of the Buffalo Bills on 10-22-06
Caught a 2 point conversion pass from Tom Brady in their 17-14 loss to the Jets on 11-12-06
Advanced Benjamin Watson's fumble 8 yards in their 17-13 win over the Chicago Bears on 11-26-06
Had a career long 62 yard TD reception from Tom Brady in their 40-23 win over Tennessee on 12-31-06
16 Regular Season Games/14 started and 3 Playoff Games/3 started
16 receptions for 176 yards + 1 TD and 1 fumble recovery in the playoffs
Caught a 4 yard TD pass from Tom Brady in their 24-21 Divisional win over the Chargers on 01-14-07
Recovered Marlon McCree's fumbled interception return in their 24-21 Divisional win vs San Diego on 01-14-07
Florida Gator

CALHOUN, Don (#44) *"Houn"*
Born on April 29, 1952 in Sumner, OK
6'0" and 206 pounds
RB/KR   1975-81
820 carries for 3,391 yards + 23 TDs, 82 receptions for 614 yards + 2 TDs and 12 kickoff returns for 238 yards
Caught 1 TD pass from Steve Grogan and Tom Owen
Hauled in a career long 62 yard TD from Steve Grogan in their 34-14 loss to the Bills on 12-14-75
Longest was a 33 yard return of a kickoff by George Jakowenko in their 20-10 win over Buffalo on 11-07-76
Longest run for 74 yards in their 16-6 win over the St. Louis Cardinals on 09-10-78
Grabbed a 6 yard TD pass from Tom Owen in their 24-17 win over the Lions on 10-07-79
93 Regular Season games/49 started and 1 Playoff Game (on 12-18-76)
Kansas State Wildcat

CALHOUN, Shilique (#90)
Born on March 20, 1992 in Middletown Township, NJ
6'4" and 260 pounds
Defensive End   2019--
15 Regular Season Games/1 started (on 09-08-19) and 1 Playoff Game
Michigan State Spartan

CALLOWAY, Chris (#82)
Born on March 29, 1968 in Chicago, IL
5'10" and 188 pounds
Wide Receiver   2000
5 receptions for 95 yards
Longest reception was a 28 yard pass from Drew Bledsoe in their 24-16 win over the Colts on 10-08-00
7 games/2 started
Michigan Wolverine

CAMARILLO, Richard "Rich" (#3)
Born on November 29, 1959 in Whittier, CA
5'11" and 202 pounds
Punter   1981-87
468 punts for 19,922 yards and 1 fumble advancement of 6 yards
Had the longest punt in the NFL in 1981, 1983 and 1985
Longest punt was 76 yards in their 31-7 loss to the New York Jets on 09-19-82
Advanced the football 6 yards, after his punt was blocked, in their 30-16 loss to the Colts on 10-25-87
AFC Pro Bowl Punter in 1983
85 Regular Season Games and 6 Playoff Games
Had a 56 yard free kick after a Bears safety in their 46-10 Super Bowl loss to Chicago on 01-12-86
Had an 11 yard onside free kick after a Broncos safety in their 22-17 Divisional loss to Denver on 01-04-87
Washington Husky

CANALE, John "Whit" (#67)
Born on December 27, 1941 in Sarasota, FL
6'3" and 245 pounds
Defensive Lineman   1968
Recovered Larry Carwell's fumbled kickoff return in their 45-17 loss to the Oilers on 12-15-68
13 games
Tennessee Volunteer

CANALE, Justin (#63)
Born on April 11, 1943 in Memphis, TN
6'2" and 250 pounds
Guard/K (KR)   1965-68
Recovered a short kickoff by Herb Travenio in their 13-13 tie with San Diego on 10-17-65
Recovered an onside kick by Herb Travenio in their 22-6 win over the San Diego Chargers on 10-31-65
Kicked an extra point in their 18-7 victory over the Houston Oilers on 11-05-67
His onside kick was recovered by Billy Johnson in their 29-24 loss to the Jets on 11-19-67
Caught Tom Sherman's deflected pass for no gain in their 27-17 loss to San Diego on 11-10-68
Kicked off in 54 games
56 games/14 started
6th Round Draft Pick in 1965
Mississippi State Bulldog

CANNON, Marcus (#61)
Born on May 6, 1988 in Odessa, TX
6'6" and 335 pounds
Offensive Lineman   2011-19
115 Regular Season Games/69 started and 19 Playoff Games/11 started
Member of the 2014, 2016 and 2018 World Championship Teams
#138 Pick in the 2011 NFL Draft
Texas Christian Horned Frog

CANTY, Chris (#26) *"Can He or Can't He?"*
Born on March 30, 1976 in Long Beach, CA
5'9" and 185 pounds
CB/PR/KR   1997-98
Sacked Trent Dilfer, Danny Wuerffel and had 2 sacks of Dan Marino
16 punt returns for 170 yards and 15 kickoff returns for 313 yards
Recovered Dave Meggett's fumbled punt return in their 31-6 win over the Colts on 09-07-97
Longest was a 63 yard return of John Hall's opening kickoff in their 27-24 OT win vs the Jets on 09-14-97
Advanced Derrick Cullors' fumbled kickoff return 9 yards in their 14-12 win over Miami on 12-22-97
Returned a Peyton Manning pass 12 yards in their 29-6 rout of the Colts on 09-13-98
Longest was a 36 yard return of a punt by Klaus Wilmsmeyer in their 12-9 OT loss to Miami on 10-25-98
32 Regular Season Games/10 started and 3 Playoff Games
Strip sacked Dan Marino in their 17-3 Wild Card win over the Miami Dolphins Game on 12-28-97
#29 pick in the 1997 NFL Draft
Kansas State Wildcat

CAPPADONA, Robert "Bob" (#33)
Born on December 13, 1942 in Watertown, MA
6'1" and 225 pounds
RB/KR   1966-67
50 carries for 188 yards + 1 TD, 6 receptions for 104 yards + 1 TD and 6 kickoff returns for 72 yards
Longest return was a 21 yard return of a kickoff by Verlon Biggs in their 24-24 tie with the Jets on 10-02-66
Longest run for 13 yards in their 35-17 win over San Diego on 10-23-66
Ran for a 1 yard touchdown in their 38-14 rout of the Houston Oilers on 12-11-66
Caught a 2 point conversion pass from Babe Parilli in their 38-28 loss to the Jets on 12-17-66
Longest reception was a 42 yard pass from Babe Parilli in their 44-16 loss to Buffalo on 12-09-67
Snared a 19 yard TD pass from Babe Parilli in their 41-32 loss to the Miami Dolphins on 12-17-67
27 games/3 started
3rd Round Draft Pick in 1965
Northeastern University Husky

CAPPELLETTI, Gino (#20) *"Duke"*
Born on March 26, 1934 in Keewatin, MN
6'0" and 190 pounds
WR/K (PR/DB/KR/RB) 1960-70
4 interceptions for 61 yards, 4 kickoff returns for 100 yards and 1 punt return of 3 yards
292 receptions for 4,589 yards + 42 TDs and 1 carry for 2 yards
Intercepted a pass by Bob Laraba and had 3 interceptions of Tom Flores
Kicked 176 field goals and 342 extra points
Caught 1 TD pass from Tom Yewcic and 2 TD passes from Tom Sherman
Caught 4 TD passes from Butch Songin and 35 touchdown passes from Babe Parilli
Had a 3 yard return of a punt by George Herring in their 13-10 loss to Denver on 09-09-60
Completed a 2 point pass to Jim Crawford in their 35-0 shutout of the LA Chargers on 10-08-60
Had 3 interceptions of Tom Flores in their 27-14 loss to the Oakland Raider on 10-16-60
Had a career long 37 yard return of a pass by Tom Flores in their 27-14 loss to the Raiders on 10-16-60
Ran for 2 points on Fred Bruney's fake PAT lateral in their 27-14 loss to Oakland on 10-16-60
Returned Bob Laraba's pass 20 yards + lateraled it to Clyde Washington in their 45-16 loss to LA on 10-28-60
Ran for 2 points after receiving a lateral from Fred Bruney on a fake PAT in their 42-14 rout of Dallas on 11-18-60
Ran for 2 points on Fred Bruney fake PAT lateral in their 37-21 loss to Houston on 12-18-60
Longest was a 37 yard return of a kickoff by Charlie Milstead in their 37-21 loss to the Oilers on 12-18-60
Threw a 27 yard TD pass to Larry Garron on a fake FGA in their 37-30 loss to the NY Titans on 10-01-61
His onside kick was recovered by Jim Lee Hunt in their 26-10 victory over the NY Jets on 09-27-64
Advanced Jim Colclough's lateral 14 yards in their 43-43 tie with the Raiders on 10-16-64
Had 3 touchdown receptions and caught a 2 point pass in their 36-28 victory over the Bills on 11-15-64
Caught a 2 point conversion pass from Babe Parilli in their 36-28 win over Buffalo on 11-15-64
Kicked a career long 53 yard field goal in their 27-23 victory over the New York Jets on 11-28-65
Set Patriots Team Record with 28 points scored in their 42-14 rout of the Houston Oilers on 12-18-65
Had a career long 63 yard TD reception from Babe Parilli in their 27-21 win vs Houston on 11-13-66
Ran for a 2 yard gain as a Running Back in their 41-10 loss to the Oakland Raiders on 10-06-68
His onside kick was recovered by Carl Garrett in their 38-23 loss to the Raiders on 09-28-69
Led the AFL and the NFL with the most points scored in a season 5 times
Only Professional Football Player to score at least 20 points in a game 8 times
AFL All Star Wide Receiver in 1961, 1963, 1964, 1966, 1968
AFL All Star Kicker in 1964, 1966, 1968
AFL MVP and Player of the Year in 1964
153 Regular Season Games and 2 Playoff Games
6 receptions for 181 yards and kicked 5 field goals and 3 extra points in the playoffs
His Uniform # 20 was retired by the Patriots
Inducted into the Patriots Hall of Fame in 1992
Minnesota Golden Gopher

CARDONA, Joe (#49)
Born on April 16, 1992 in El Cajon, CA
6'3" and 245 pounds
Long Snapper   2015-19
Long Snapper for Punter's Ryan Allen and Jake Bailey
Long Snapper for Kicker's Stephen Gostkowski, Mike Nugent, Nick Folk and Kai Forbath
80 Regular Season Games and 11 Playoff Games
Member of the 2016 and 2018 World Championship Teams
#166 pick in the 2015 NFL Draft
Ron Burton Community Service Award in 2018
Naval Midshipman

CAREY, Brian (#81)
Born on November 6, 1963 in Woburn, MA
6'0" and 200 pounds
Wide Receiver   1987
2 games (on Oct. 4th and Oct. 11th)
AIC Yellow Jacket

CARLSON, Jeff (#17)
Born on May 23, 1966 in Long Beach, CA
6'3" and 215 pounds
Quarterback   1992
18 completions for 232 yards + 1 TD and 11 carries for 32 yards
Longest completion was a 40 yard pass to Irving Fryar in their 27-20 loss to the Chiefs on 12-13-92
Tossed a 6 yard TD pass to Kevin Turner in their 27-20 loss to the Kansas City Chiefs on 12-13-92
Longest run for 7 yards in their 20-10 loss to the Bengals on 12-20-92
3 games/2 started
Weber State Wildcat

CARPENTER, Robert III "Bobby" (#59)
Born on August 1, 1983 in Lancaster, OH
6'3" and 255 pounds
LB/Special Team   2012
4 games
Ohio State Buckeye

CARPENTER, Robert "Rob" (#81)
Born on August 1, 1968 in Amityville, NY
6'2" and 190 pounds
Wide Receiver   1991
3 receptions for 45 yards
Longest reception was a 23 yard pass from Hugh Millen in their 23-17 OT win vs the Colts on 12-08-91
9 games/1 started (on 12-22-91)
Syracuse Orangeman

CARTER, Antonio "Tony" (#30)
Born on August 23, 1972 in Columbus, OH
6'0" and 230 pounds
RB (KR)   1998-2000
45 carries for 119 yards + 2 TDs, 47 receptions for 347 yards and 1 kickoff return for 16 yards
Longest reception was a 49 yard pass from Drew Bledsoe in their 26-23 win over Miami on 11-23-98
Recovered Terry Allen's fumble in their 27-3 victory over the Arizona Cardinals on 10-31-99
Had a 16 yard return of a kickoff by Todd Sauerbrun in their 30-24 win over the Chiefs on 12-04-00
43 Regular Season Games/27 started and 1 Playoff Game/1 started (on 01-03-99)
Minnesota Golden Gopher

CARTER, Chris (#42)
Born on September 27, 1974 in Tyler, TX
6'1" and 201 pounds
Safety   1997-99
2 sacks, 3 interceptions and 2 fumble recoveries
Sacked Steve Young and Damon Huard and recovered fumbles by Jonathan Linton and Ty Law
Had 1 interception of Ray Lucas and 2 interceptions of Peyton Manning
Intercepted Peyton Manning *twice*, including 1 with 12 seconds left, in their 31-28 win vs the Colts on 09-19-99
47 Regular Season Games/15 started and 3 Playoff Games
#89 pick in the 1997 NFL Draft
Texas Longhorn

CARTER, Kent (#51)
Born on May 25, 1950 in Los Angeles, CA
6'3" and 235 pounds
Special Team   1974
2 games (on Dec. 1st and Dec. 15th)
USC Trojan

CARTER, Rubin "Andre" (#93 and #96)
Born on May 12, 1979 in Denver, CO
6'4" and 265 pounds
Defensive End   2011 and 2013
Wore #93 in 2011 and #96 in 2013
12 sacks
Shared in a sack of Chad Henne and Tyler Palko and sacked Rex Grossman and Joe Flacco
Had 2 sacks of Tony Romo, 3 sacks of Ben Roesthlisberger and 4 sacks of Mark Sanchez
Sacked Mark Sanchez *4 times* in their 37-16 rout of the Jets on 11-13-11
AFC Defensive Player of the Week in their 37-16 win over the NY Jets on 11-13-11
AFC Pro Bowl Defensive End in 2011
23 Regular Season Games/14 started and 2 Playoff Games
California Golden Bear

CARTER JR., Tony (#29)
Born on May 24, 1986 in Tallahassee, FL
5'9" and 177 pounds
Cornerback   2010
2 games (on December 19, 2010 and January 2, 2011)
Florida State Seminole

CARTER, Wayne "Allen" (#21)
Born on December 12, 2952 in Pomona, CA
5'11" and 208 pounds
RB/KR   1975-76
22 carries for 95 yards, 2 receptions for 39 yards and 33 kickoff returns for 898 yards + 1 TD
Longest reception was a 26 yard pass from Steve Grogan in their 36-7 loss to the New York Jets on 10-05-75
Longest was a 99 yard TD return of Toni Linhart's opening kickoff in their 34-21 loss to the Colts on 12-21-75
Longest run for 19 yards in their 34-21 loss to the Baltimore Colts on 12-21-75
Led the NFL with the best Kickoff Return Average of 27.5 yards per return in 1975
15 games
#86 pick in the 1975 NFL Draft
USC Trojan

CARTHEN, Jason (#99)
Born on November 16, 1970 in Toledo, OH
6'3" and 255 pounds
Linebacker   1993-94
6 games
Ohio University Bobcat

CARWELL, Larry (#41) *"Cardinal"*
Born on August 5, 1944 in Vada, GA
6'1" and 188 pounds
DB/PR (KR)   1969-72
9 interceptions for 167 yards + 1 TD, 13 punt returns for 93 yards and 2 kickoff returns for 58 yards
Intercepted Daryle Lamonica, Jack Kemp, George Blanda and John Brodie
Intercepted Bob Griese, Joe Namath and Billy Kilmer
Intercepted Rick Norton twice in their 38-23 win over Miami on 11-30-69
Returned a short kickoff by Mike Eischeid 28 yards in their 38-23 loss to the Raiders on 09-28-69
Longest was a 30 yard return of a kickoff by Dave Williams in their 31-0 loss to St. Louis on 11-08-70
Longest was a 45 yard return of a punt by Steve O'Neal in their 17-3 loss to the New York Jets on 11-22-70
Had a career long 53 yard TD return of a pass by Bob Griese in their 34-13 rout of the Dolphins on 12-05-71
Blocked a 51 yard FGA by Horst Mulmann and returned it 45 yards for a TD in their 31-7 loss on 09-17-72
51 games/48 started
Iowa State Cyclone

CASH, Richard "Rick" (#63) *"Thumper"*
Born on July 1, 1945 in St. Louis, MO
6'5" and 248 pounds
DT/DE   1972-73
Defensive Right Tackle in 1972 and Defensive Right End in 1973
4 sacks, 3 fumble recoveries and blocked a field goal attempt
Sacked Dennis Shaw, Bob Griese, Bill Demory and Al Woodhall
Recovered fumbles by Wayne Patrick, Archie Manning and Floyd Rice
Blocked a 48 yard field goal attempt by Garo Yepremian in their 52-0 loss to the Dolphins on 11-12-72
28 games/27 started
NE Missouri Bulldog

CASILLAS, Jonathan (#52)
Born on June 3, 1987 in Jersey City, NJ
6'0" and 225 pounds
Linebacker   2014
8 Regular Season Games/3 started and 3 Playoff Games
Member of the 2014 Championship Team
Wisconsin Badger

CASSEL, Matthew "Matt" (#16)
Born on May 17, 1982 in Northbridge, CA
6'4" and 225 pounds
Quarterback (P)   2005-08
349 completions for 3,946 yards + 23 TDs and 85 carries for 298 yards + 3 TDs
Completed 1 TD pass to Tim Dwight and 2 touchdown passes to Jabar Gaffney
Threw 3 TD passes to Benjamin Watson, Kevin Faulk and Wes Welker and 11 TD passes to Randy Moss
Recovered a bad snap fumble, for a 9 yard loss, on FGA by Stephen Gostkowski on 09-09-07
Longest run for 19 yards in their 34-31 OT loss to the Jets on 11-13-08
Tossed a 2 point conversion pass to Jabar Gaffney in their 34-31 OT loss to the Jets on 11-13-08
Tossed a 2 point conversion pass to Wes Welker in their 24-21 win over Seattle on 12-07-08
Tossed a 78 yard TD pass to Randy Moss in their 47-7 rout of the Arizona Cardinals on 12-21-08
His 57 yard punt, on 3rd down, was downed by Sammy Morris on 2 yard line in 13-0 win vs Buffalo on 12-28-08
AFC Offensive Player of the Week in their 41-7 rout of Denver on 10-20-08
AFC Offensive Player of the Week in their 48-28 rout of the Dolphins on 11-23-08
Holder for Stephen Gostkowski
30 Regular Season Games/15 started and 4 Playoff Games
#230 pick in the 2005 NFL Draft
Drafted to play baseball by the Oakland Athletics
USC Trojan

CATANHO, Alcides (#54)
Born on January 20, 1972 in Elizabeth, NJ
6'4" and 230 pounds
Special Team   1995
Recovered Dexter Carter's fumbled kickoff return in their 20-7 win over the Jets on 11-05-95
12 games
Rutgers Scarlet Knight

CAVANAUGH, Matthew "Matt" (#12)
Born on October 27, 1956 in Youngstown, OH
6'2" and 212 pounds
Quarterback   1979-82
206 completions for 3,018 yards + 19 TDs and 39 carries for 190 yards + 3 TDs
Threw 1 TD pass to Lin Dawson and Tony Collins, Harold Jackson, Carlos Pennywell, Don Westbrook,
        Ken Toler, Preston Brown and Stanley Morgan
Completed 3 TD passes to Don Hasselbeck and 4 TD passes to Russ Francis and Andy Johnson
Longest run for 22 yards in their 24-2 win over the Buffalo Bills on 12-14-80
Caught a 9 yard flea flicker pass from Andy Johnson in their 27-21 OT loss to the Steelers on 09-27-81
Holder for John Smith's 33 yard field goal in the "Snow Plow" 3-0 win over Miami on 12-12-82
Heaved a career long 75 yard TD pass to Stanley Morgan in their 37-14 loss to the Steelers on 12-26-82
Holder for Rex Robinson and Dan Miller in 1982
52 Regular Season Games/15 started and 1 Playoff Game (on 01-08-83)
Holder for John Smith in their 28-13 First Round Playoff Game loss to Miami on 01-08-83
#50 pick in the 1978 NFL Draft
Pittsburgh Panther

CENTERS, Larry (#31)
Born on June 1, 1968 in Tatum, TX
6'0" and 225 pounds
Fullback   2003
21 carries for 82 yards and 19 receptions for 106 yards + 1 TD
Longest run for 13 yards in their 31-0 loss to the Buffalo Bills on 09-07-03
Recovered Tom Brady's fumble in their 23-16 victory over the New York Jets on 09-21-03
Caught a 7 yard TD pass from Tom Brady in their 20-17 loss to the Washington Redskins on 09-28-03
Longest reception was a 14 yard pass from Tom Brady in their 20-17 loss to the Redskins on 09-28-03
9 Regular Season Games/3 started and 3 Playoff Games/2 started
Member of the 2003 World Championship Team
Stephen F. Austin State Lumberjack

CHANDLER, Albert "Al" (#87 and #82)
Born on November 18, 1950 in Oklahoma, City, OK
6'2" and 233 pounds
Tight End   1976-79
Wore #87 from 1976-77 and #82 from 1978-79
13 receptions for 119 yards + 3 TDs and 2 fumble recoveried for 4 yards
Caught 3 Regular Season and 1 Post Season TD pass from Steve Grogan
Longest reception was a 29 yard pass from Steve Grogan in their 27-13 loss to the Baltimore Colts on 09-12-76
Had aa 4 yard return of Nat Moore's fumbled punt return in their 30-14 win over Miami on 09-19-76
Recovered John "Frenchy" Fuqua's fumbled punt return in their 30-27 win over Pittsburgh on 09-26-76
39 Regular Season Games/6 started and 1 Playoff Game (on 12-18-76)
Caught a 1 yard TD pass from Steve Grogan in their 24-21 Divisional Playoff loss to Oakland on 12-18-76
Oklahoma Sooner

CHANDLER, Edgar (#50)
Born on August 31, 1946 in Cedartown, GA
6'3" and 225 pounds
Linebacker   1973
½ sack and 2 fumble recoveries for 14 yards
Shared in a sack of Joe Ferguson in their 37-13 loss to Buffalo on 12-09-73
Recovered a fumble by Dennis Shaw in their 31-13 loss to the Bills on 09-16-73
Had a 14 yard return of Norm Bulaich's fumble in their 24-23 loss to the Eagles on 11-04-73
12 games/11 started
Member of the 1974 World Football League Birmingham Americans Championship Team
Georgia Bulldog

CHANDLER, William "Scott" (#88)
Born on July 23, 1985 in Bedford, TX
6'7" and 270 pounds
Tight End   2015
23 receptions for 259 yards + 4 TDs
Caught 4 TD passes from Tom Brady
Longest reception was a 30 yard pass from Tom Brady in their 35-28 loss to the Eagles on 12-06-15
15 Regular Season Games/4 started and 2 Playoff Games
Iowa Hawkeye

CHAPPLE, Dave (#10)
Born on March 30, 1947 in Arcadia, CA
6'0" and 184 pounds
Punter   1974
26 punts for 967 yards
Longest punt was 57 yards in their 34-27 loss to the Miami Dolphins on 12-15-74
5 games
California Gaucho

CHARLES, John (#25)
Born on May 9, 1944 in Newark, NJ
6'0" and 205 pounds
Defensive Back   1967-69
6 interceptions for 110 yards + 2 TDs, blocked an extra point and blocked 2 FGA's and recovered 1 fumble
Intercepted Bob Davis and Pete Beathard and had 2 interceptions of Jack Kemp and Joe Namath
Blocked an extra point attempt by Gary Kroner in their 26-21 loss to the Denver Broncos on 09-03-67
Had a career long 35 yard TD return of a pass by Joe Namath in their 30-23 loss to the NY Jets on 10-29-67
Blocked a 47 yard FGA by Mike Mercer in their 16-7 win over the Buffalo Bills on 09-08-68
Blocked a 25 yard FGA by John Wittenborn in their 16-0 loss to the Houston Oilers on 10-13-68
Recovered Gene Foster's fumble in their 13-10 loss to the San Diego Chargers on 10-19-69
Had a 25 yard TD return of a pass by Joe Namath in their 23-17 loss to the NY Jets on 10-26-69
39 games/34 started
#21 pick in the 1967 NFL Draft
Purdue Boilermaker

CHATHAM, Matt (#58)
Born on June 28, 1977 in Newton, IA
6'4" and 250 pounds
LB/Special Team   2000-05
Strip sacked Donovan McNabb, shared in a sack of Kerry Collins and sacked Gus Frerotte
Returned a fumble by Tiki Barber 38 yards for a TD and recovered a fumble by Travis Henry
66 Regular Season Games/4 started and 10 Playoff Games
Member of the 2001, 2003 and 2004 World Championship Teams
South Dakota Coyote

CHERRY, Je'Rod (#30)
Born on May 30, 1973 in Charlotte, NC
6'1" and 210 pounds
DB/Special Team   2001-04
1 fumble recovery and 1 sack
Recovered a blocked field goal in their 38-17 rout of the Indianapolis Colts on 10-21-01
Sacked Drew Bledsoe in their 31-0 shutout of the Buffalo Bills on 12-27-03
55 Regular Season Games and 6 Playoff Games
Member of the 2001, 2003 and 2004 World Championship Teams
California Golden Bear

CHEYUNSKI, Jim (#50) *"Chey"*
Born on December 29, 1945 in Bridgewater, MA
6'1" and 225 pounds
Linebacker   1968-72
5 sacks, 3 interceptions for 82 yards, 4 fumble recoveries and 1 recovery of an onside kick
Shared in a sack of James Harris and Al Woodhall
Sacked Len Dawson and Steve Tensi and had 2 sacks of Bob Griese
Intercepted John Stofa, Greg Cook and Dan Pastorini
Recovered fumbles by Jess Phillips, Ron Sayers, Larry Brown and Bob Davis
Had a 21 yard return of a pass by John Stofa in their 33-14 win over the Cincinnati Bengals on 12-01-68
Had a career long 37 yard return of a pass by Greg Cook in their 25-14 win over the Bengals on 11-16-69
Had a 24 yard return of a pass by Dan Pastorini in their 28-20 win over the Houston Oilers on 11-07-71
Recovered a fumble by Bob Davis and lateraled it to John Bramlett in their 27-23 loss to the Oilers on 12-14-69
Recovered George Blanda's onside kick in their 41-10 loss to the Oakland Raiders on 10-06-68
AFL Defensive Player of the Week in their 25-14 win over the Bengals on 11-16-69
NFL Defensive Player of the Week in their 21-20 win over the Falcons on 09-24-72
66 games/54 started
#305 pick in the 1968 NFL Draft
Syracuse Orangeman

CHILDRESS, Brandon "Bam" (#13)
Born on March 31, 1982 in Warrensville Heights, OH
5'10" and 185 pounds
WR/DB   2005-06
5 receptions for 39 yards
Longest reception was a 21 yard pass from Tom Brady in their 28-26 loss to Miami on 01-01-06
3 games
Ohio State Buckeye

CHILDRESS, Freddie (#61)
Born on September 17, 1966 in Little Rock, AR
6'4" and 331 pounds
Guard/Tackle (LS)   1991
Recovered a fumble in the end zone for a TD in their 26-23 OT win vs the Minnesota Vikings on 10-20-91
Was the long snapper on Charlie Baumann's 37 yard field goal in their 30-20 loss to Miami on 11-10-91
15 games
Arkansas Razorback

CHILTON, Gene (#63)
Born on March 27, 1964 in Houston, TX
6'3" and 281 pounds
Center/Tackle   1990-92
Recovered 2 fumbles by Hugh Millen
36 games/35 started
Texas Longhorn

CHRISTY, Richard "Dick" (#23)
Born on November 24, 1935 in Philadelphia, PA
5'10" and 191 pounds
HB/KR/PR   1960
78 carries for 363 yards + 4 TDs and 26 receptions for 268 yards + 2 TDs
24 kickoff returns for 617 yards and 8 punt returns for 73 yards and 1 lateral advancement of 5 yards
Completed 6 Half Back Option passes for 94 yards + 2 TDs
Longest run for 48 yards in their 13-0 loss to the Buffalo Bills on 09-23-60
Longest completion was a 39 yard HB Option pass to Walter Beach in their 13-0 loss to Buffalo on 09-23-60
Longest was a 29 yard return of a punt by Wayne Crow in their 27-14 loss to the Raiders on 10-16-60
Longest reception was a 53 yard pass from Butch Songin in their 34-28 win over the Raiders on 11-04-60
Longest was a 52 yard return of Bill Shockley's opening kickoff in their 38-21 win over the Titans on 11-11-60
Advanced Joe Johnson's pass reception lateral 5 yards in their 42-14 rout of the Dallas Texans on 11-18-60
Advanced Bob Dee's kickoff return lateral 19 yards in their 38-14 loss to the Buffalo Bills on 12-04-60
13 games
North Carolina State Wolfpack

CHUNG, Patrick (#25 and #23)
Born on August 19, 1987 in Kingston, Jamaica
5'11" and 215 pounds
Safety (KR/PR)   2009-12 and 2014-19
Wore #25 from 2009-12 and #23 since 2014
11 interceptions for 171 yards + 1 TD, 4 ½ sacks, 4 fumble recoveries and blocked a field goal attempt
9 kickoff returns for 161 yards, 3 punt returns for 11 yards, blocked a punt and recovered an onside kick
Intercepted Vince Young, Jason Campbell, Ryan Tannehill, Charlie Whitehusrt and Brock Osweiler
Intercepted Andrew Luck and had 2 interceptions of Ryan Fitzpatrick and 3 interceptions of Chad Henne
Shared in a sack of Andrew Luck, sacked John Johnson and Colin Kaepernick and had 2 sacks of Chad Henne
Recovered fumbles by Cyrus Jones, Seth Roberts, Kenyan Drake and Derek Anderson
Had a 26 yard return of a pass by Ryan Fitzpatrick, from the end zone, in their 38-30 win vs Buffalo on 09-26-10
Blocked a punt by Brandon Fields in their 41-14 rout of the Miami Dolphins on 10-04-10
Blocked a 53 yard field goal attempt by Dan Carpenter in their 41-14 rout of the Dolphins on 10-04-10
Had a career long 51 yard TD return of a pass by Chad Henne in their 41-14 rout of the Dolphins on 10-04-10
Had a 27 yard return, from the end zone, of a pass by Chad Henne in their 23-16 win over the Jaguars on 12-23-12
Intercepted another pass by Chad Henne on the last play in their 23-16 win over Jacksonville on 12-23-12
Longest was a 30 yard return of a kickoff by Caleb Sturgis in their 33-20 loss to Miami on 09-07-14
Longest was a 7 yard return of a punt by Sam Koch in their 30-23 win over the Ravens on 12-12-16
Recovered an onside kick by Justin Tucker in their 30-23 win over Baltimore on 12-12-16
Had a 4 yard return of a free kick by Lac Edwards in their 26-6 victory over the Jets on 12-31-17
141 Regular Season Games/112 started/ 22 Playoff Games/19 started
Ran for no gain on a fake punt play in their 28-21 Divisional Playoff Game loss to the Jets on 01-16-11
Lost 1 yard on a return of a punt by Matt Bosher in their 34-28 OT Super Bowl win vs Atlanta on 02-05-17
Member of the 2014, 2016 and 2018 World Championship Teams
#34 pick in the 2009 NFL Draft
Oregon Duck

CHUNG, Yon, "Eugene" (#69)
Born on June 14, 1969 in Prince George Co., MD
6'4" and 301 pounds
Offensive Lineman   1992-94
34 games/30 started
#13 pick in the 1992 NFL Draft
Virginia Tech Hokie

CINDRICH, Ralph (#55)
Born on October 29, 1949 in Washington, PA
6'1" and 228 pounds
Linebacker   1972
Had 16 tackles and 7 assists in their 37-21 loss to the Miami Dolphins on 12-03-72
12 games/3 started
Pittsburgh Panther

CLARK, Allan (#35)
Born on June 8, 1957 in Grand Rapids, MI
5'10" and 186 pounds
RB/KR   1979-80
28 carries for 140 yards + 3 TDs, 2 receptions for 35 yards and 40 kickoff returns for 837 yards
3 fumble recoveries for 15 yards and 1 TD
Recovered Chris Pane's muffed punt return and fumbled kickoff returns by Ben Garry and Kim Anderson
Longest was a 38 yard return of the 2nd half kickoff by Bob Thomas in their 27-7 rout of the Bears on 10-14-79
Longest run for 19 yards in their 50-21 rout of the Baltimore Colts on 11-18-79
Longest reception was a 20 yard pass from Steve Grogan in their 50-21 rout of the Colts on 11-18-79
Had a 15 yard TD return of Kim Anderson's fumbled kickoff return in their 47-21 rout of the Colts on 11-23-80
27 games
#271 pick in the 1979 NFL Draft
Northern Arizona Lumberjack

CLARK, Gail (#54)
Born on April 14, 1951 in Bellefontaine, OH
6'2" and 226 pounds
Linebacker   1974
8 games
Michigan State Spartan

CLARK, Philip (#22)
Born on April 28, 1945 in Burlington, KY
6'3" and 208 pounds
Defensive Back   1971
2 games (on Sept. 26th and Oct. 3rd)
Northwestern Wildcat

CLARK, Rico (#39)
Born on June 6, 1974 in Atlanta, GA
5'10" and 181 pounds
Special Team   1999
Only game played was on 01-02-00
Louisville Cardinal

CLARK, Stevan "Steve" (#65)
Born on October 29, 1959 in Chattanooga, TN
6'5" and 258 pounds
Defensive End   1981
7 games
#130 pick in the 1981 NFL Draft
Kansas State Wildcat

CLAY, Willie (#32) *"Big Play"*
Born on September 5, 1970 in Pittsburgh, PA
5'10" and 193 pounds
Free Safety   1996-98
13 interceptions for 178 yards + 1 TD and 4 fumble recoveries for 17 yards
Intercepted Jim Kelly, Boomer Esiason, Vinny Testaverde, Frank Reich and Jim Everett
Intercepted Bobby Hebert, Alex Van Pelt, Kordell Stewart, Dan Marino and Doug Flutie
Intrercepted and Steve Young and had 2 interceptions of John Elway
Recovered fumbles by Cliff Groce, Horace Copeland, Marshall Faulk and Peyton Manning
Had a 17 yard return of a fumble by Cliff Groce in their 27-9 win over the Indianapolis Colts on 10-20-96
Had a career long 53 yard TD return of a pass by Jim Everett in their 41-7 rout of San Diego on 08-31-97
Intercepted a pass by Steve Young, to help set up the GW FG, in their 24-21 win over the 49ers on 12-20-98
AFC Defensive Player of the Week in their 24-21 win over San Francisco on 12-20-98
48 Regular Season Games/48 started and 6 Playoff Games/6 started
2 interceptions for 14 yards in the playoffs
Had a 14 yard return of a pass by Mike Tomczak in their 28-3 Divisional win over the Steelers on 01-05-97
Intercepted Mark Brunell in the end zone in their 20-6 Championship win vs Jacksonville on 01-12-97
Georgia Tech Yellow Jacket

CLAYBORN, Adrian (#94)
Born on July 6, 1988 in St. Louis, MO
6'3" and 280 pounds
Defensive End   2018
2.5 sacks
Shared in a sack of Aaron Rodgers and sacked Mitchell Trubisky and Derek Anderson
14 Regular Season Games/1 started (on 09-23-18) and 3 Playoff Games
Member of the 2018 World Championship Team
Iowa Hawkeye

CLAYBORN, Raymond (#26) *"Mr. Reliable, Claybo, Bones"*
Born on January 2, 1955 in Fort Worth, TX
6'0" and 186 pounds
CB/KR　　　　　　　　1977-88
36 interceptions for 555 yards + 1 TD, 1 sack and 9 fumble recoveries for 71 yards + 1 TD
57 kickoff returns for 1,538 yards + 3 TDs and returned a blocked field goal 71 yards for a TD
Intercepted Ken Stabler, Richard Todd, Bill Troup, Dan Fouts, Joe Ferguson, Don Strock and Tommy Kramer
Intercepted Jim Zorn, Don Strock, Bert Jones, Steve DeBerg, David Humm, Paul McDonald and Danny White
Intercepted Gary Danielson, Ken O'Brien, Matt Kofler, Dan Marino, Bubby Brister and Joe Montana
Intercepted Rusty Hilger, Todd Rutledge and Chris Miller and had 3 interceptions of David Woodley
Had 2 interceptions of Pat Ryan, Vince Ferragamo, John Elway, Chris Chandler and Jim Kelly
Recovered fumbles by Wilbert Montgomery, Brian Sipe, Louie Giammona, Tony Nathan and Calvin Thomas
Recovered fumbles by Pete Metzelaars, Boomer Esiason and George Wonsley and sacked Steve Bartkowski
Returned a kickoff by Pat Leahy 100 yards for a TD in their 30-27 loss to the Jets on 10-02-77
Returned a kickoff by Carson Long 93 yards for a TD in their 24-14 loss to the Bills on 11-06-77
Forced Punter Mike Michel out of end zone *for a safety* in their 17-5 loss to the Dolphins on 11-13-77
Had a 78 yard return (after a penalty) of a kickoff by Fred Steinfort on 12-04-77
Sacked Steve Bartkowski in their 16-10 win over the Atlanta Falcons on 12-04-77
Had a career long 101 yard TD return of a kickoff by Toni Linhart in their 30-24 loss to the Colts on 12-18-77
Had a 44 yard return of a pass by Richard Todd in their 19-17 victory over the New York Jets on 11-19-78
Had a 27 yard return of a pass by Tommy Kramer in their 27-23 win over the Vikings on 12-16-79
Picked off a pass by Jim Zorn, to seal their 37-31 win over the Seattle Seahawks on 09-21-80
Took a David Woodley pass, that Joe Rose bobbled, 16 yards in their 34-0 shutout of Miami on 10-12-80
Has a career long 85 yard return of a pass by Paul McDonald, on the last play, in 17-16 win vs Clev on 10-07-84
Picked off a pass by Vince Ferragamo in their 17-14 victory over the Buffalo Bills on 09-22-85
Had a 27 yard TD return of a pass by Vince Ferragamo in their 14-3 win over Buffalo on 10-13-85
Picked off a pass by Ken O'Brien in their 20-13 victory over the New York Jets on 10-20-85
Had a 71 yard TD return of a blocked field goal in their 21-7 win over the Oilers on 10-18-87
Picked off a pass by Chris Chandler, with 23 seconds left, in their 21-17 win over the Colts on 10-02-88
Led NFL with the longest kickoff return ave, longest kickoff return and most kickoff returns for a TD in 1977
AFC Pro Bowl Cornerback in 1983, 1985, 1986
191 Regular Season Games/179 started and 7 Playoff Games/7 started
2 kickoff returns for 68 yards in their 31-14 Divisional Playoff Game loss to the Houston Oilers on 12-31-78
Picked off a pass by Dan Marino in their 31-14 Championship win over Miami at the Orange Bowl on 01-12-86
Recovered a fumble by Matt Suhey in their 46-10 Super Bowl loss to Da' Bears on 01-26-86
#16 pick in the 1977 NFL Draft
Inducted into the Patriots Hall of Fame on 07-29-17
Texas Longhorn

CLAYTON, Stan (#76)
Born on January 31, 1965 in Philadelphia, PA
6'3" and 265 pounds
Guard/Tackle　　　　　1990
11 games/3 started
Penn State Nittany Lion

CLAYTON, Thomas (#22)
Born on April 26, 1984 in Alexandria, VA
5'11" and 225 pounds
Running Back   2010
6 carries for 17 yards
Longest run for 5 yards in their 38-7 rout of the Miami Dolphins on 01-02-11
Only game played was on 01-02-11
Kansas State Wildcat

CLEELAND, Cameron "Cam" (#85)
Born on August 15, 1975 in Sedro-Woodley, WA
6'5" and 272 pounds
Tight End   2002
16 receptions for 112 yards + 1 TD
Caught a 1 yard TD pass from Tom Brady in their 44-7 rout of the New York Jets on 09-15-02
Longest catch was a 22 yard pass from Tom Brady in 27-20 loss to Oakland on 11-27-03
12 games
Washington Husky

CLEVELAND, Asante (#44)
Born on March 21, 1992 in Sacramento, CA
6'5" and 260 pounds
Tight End   2015
Caught a 1 yard pass from Tom Brady in their 30-24 OT loss to the Denver Broncos on 11-29-15
4 games
Miami Hurricane

CLOUD, Mike (#21 and #34)
Born on July 1, 1975 in Charleston, SC
5'10" and 205 pounds
RB (KR)   2003 and 2005
Wore #21 for 5 games in 2003 and #34 for 6 games in 2005
50 carries for 177 yards + 5 TDs, 1 reception for 8 yards and 3 kickoff returns for 53 yards
Longest run for 42 yards in their 38-30 win over Tennessee on 10-05-03
Caught an 8 yard pass from Tom Brady in their 23-20 OT win vs Houston on 11-23-03
Longest was a 19 yard return of a kickoff by Kris Brown in their 23-20 OT win vs Houston on 11-23-03
11 games/1 started (on 10-12-03)
Member of the 2003 World Championship Team
Boston College Eagle

CLOUTIER, Dave (#28)
Born on November 22, 1938 in Gardiner, ME
6'0" and 195 pounds
PR/DB (KR)   1964
20 punt returns for 136 yards
Longest was a 40 yard return of a punt by Curley Johnson in their 35-14 loss to the Jets on 10-31-64
Returned Keith Lincoln's kickoff 46 yards in their 26-17 loss to the San Diego Chargers on 10-09-64
12 games
Maine Black Bear

COATES, Ben (#87)
Born on August 16, 1969 in Greenwood, SC
6'5" and 245 pounds
Tight End (KR)   1991-99
490 receptions for 5,471 yards + 50 TDs, caught a 2 point pass and 3 carries for a net loss of 4 yards
2 kickoff returns for 26 yards and recovered 3 onside kicks and 2 fumbles
Caught 1 TD pass from Scott Zolak and Scott Secules and 3 TD passes from Hugh Millen
Caught 45 Regular Season TD passes and 1 Post Season TD pass from Drew Bledsoe
Recovered fumbles by Drew Bledsoe and Kevin Turner
Caught a 2 yard TD from Hugh Millen, on last play to force OT, in their 23-17 OT win vs the Colts on 12-08-91
Longest run for 2 yards in their 6-0 loss to the Indianapolis Colts on 12-06-92
Caught a 2 yard TD from Scott Secules in the 4th Qtr to defeat Phoenix 23-21 on 10-10-93
Caught a 2 point conversion pass from Drew Bledsoe in their 46-38 win over the Ravens on 10-06-96
Caught a career long 84 yard TD pass from Drew Bledsoe in their 42-23 win over Miami on 11-03-96
Caught a 13 yard TD from Drew Bledsoe, on 4th + 7, to defeat the Giants 23-22 at Giants Stadium on 12-21-96
Recovered an onside kick by Chris Gardocki in their 20-17 win over the Colts on 11-30-97
Longest was a 20 yard return of an onside kick by Mike Hollis in their 26-20 win over the Jaguars on 12-07-97
Cradled a 1 yard TD pass from Drew Bledsoe, with no time left, to defeat the Bills 25-21 on 11-29-98
Recovered an onside kick by Brad Daluiso in their 16-14 win over the New York Giants on 09-26-99
AFC Pro Bowl Tight End in 1994, 1995, 1996, 1997, 1998
First Team All Pro Tight End in 1994 and 1995
142 Regular Season Games/105 started and 7 Playoff Games/7 started
22 receptions for 204 yards + 1 TD in the playoffs
Caught a 4 yard TD pass from Drew Bledsoe in their 35-21 Super Bowl loss to the Packers on 01-26-97
#124 pick in the 1991 NFL Draft
Inducted into the Patriots Hall of Fame on 09-20-08
Livingstone College Fighting Blue Bear

COBBS, Cedric (#34)
Born on Janaury 9, 1981 in Little Rock, AR
6'1" and 225 pounds
Running Back   2004
22 carries for 50 yards
Longest run for 13 yards in their 21-7 win over the 49ers on 01-02-05
3 games
Member of the 2004 World Championship Team
#128 pick in the 2004 NFL Draft
Arkansas Razorback

COBBS, Robert "Duffy" (#43)
Born on January 17, 1964 in Bad Kreuznach, Germany
5'11" and 178 pounds
Special Team   1987
3 games
Penn State Nittany Lion

COFFEY, Wayne (#83)
Born on May 30, 1964 in Rantoul, IL
5'7" and 158 pounds
Wide Receiver   1987
3 receptions for 66 yards
Longest reception was a 35 yard pass from Bob Bleier in their 20-10 loss to Cleveland on 10-04-87
3 games
Member of the 1987 Arena Football League Denver Dynamite Championship Team
Southwest Texas State Bobcat

COHEN, Abraham "Abe" (#62)
Born on March 23, 1933 in Plymouth, PA
6'0" and 230 pounds
Guard   1960
Blocked a punt by George Herring in their 31-24 loss to Denver on 10-23-60
14 games
Tennessee Chattanooga Moccasin

COHEN, Landon (#66 and #98)
Born on August 3, 1986 in Spartanburg, SC
6'3" and 274 pounds
Defensive Lineman   2010-11
Wore #66 for 2 Regular Season Games and in 1 Playoff Game
Wore #98 in the game played on 09-25-11
3 Regular Season games/1 started (on 12-26-10) and 1 Playoff Game (on 01-16-11)
Ohio University Bobcat

COLCLOUGH, Jim (#81)
Born on March 31, 1936 in Medford, MA
6'0" and 185 pounds
Wide Receiver (KR)   1960-68
283 receptions for 5,001 yards + 39 TDs, 4 carries for 51 yards and caught 2 Two Point conversion passes
Caught 1 TD pass from Eddie Wilson and 5 TD passes from Tom Yewcic
Caught 14 TD passes from Ed "Butch" Songin and 19 TD passes from Vito "Babe" Parilli
Scored the 1st AFL TD on a 10 yard TD pass from Butch Songin in their 13-10 loss to Denver on 09-09-60
Advanced Billy Lott's fumble 10 yards in their 23-21 win over the Bills on 09-23-61
Longest run for 16 yards in their 18-17 win over the Dallas Texans on 10-29-61
Had another run from scrimmage of 16 yards in their 35-21 win over the Oaklans Raiders on 12-09-61
Caught a career long 78 yard TD pass from Tom Yewcic in their 24-17 win over the NY Titans on 11-30-62
Caught a 2 point pass from Babe Parilli in their 43-43 tie with the Oakland Raiders on 10-16-64
Caught a 37 yard pass and then tossed a lateral to Gino Cappelletti in their 43-43 tie with the Raiders on 10-16-64
Caught a 2 point pass from Babe Parilli in their 24-14 loss to the Buffalo Bills on 12-20-64
Returned George Blanda's onside kick 2 yards in their 27-21 win over Houston on 11-13-66
Led the AFL with the best yards per reception (21.7) in 1962
AFL All Star Wide Receiver in 1962
126 Regular Season Games and 2 Playoff Games
4 receptions for 35 yards in the playoffs
Boston College Eagle

COLE, Marquice (#23)
Born on November 13, 1983 in Hazel Crest, IL
5'11" and 184 pounds
Defensive Back   2012-13
2 interceptions and 1 fumble recovery
Intercepted Chad Henne and Ryan Tannehill and recovered a fumbled punt return by Trindon Holliday
27 Regular Season games/1 started (on 12-23-12) and 2 Playoff Games
Northwestern Wildcat

COLEMAN, Dennis (#53)
Born on December 19, 1948 in Aberdeen, MS
6'4" and 225 pounds
Linebacker   1971
Intercepted a pass by Earl Morrall in their 23-3 loss to the Baltimore Colts n 10-03-71
9 games
Mississippi Rebel

COLEMAN, Eric (#22)
Born on December 27, 1966 in Denver, CO
6'0" and 190 pounds
Defensive Back   1989-90
Had a 1 yard return of a pass by Warren Moon in their 23-13 win over Houston on 10-08-89
15 games
#43 pick in the 1989 NFL Draft
Wyoming Cowboy

COLEMAN, Frederick "Fred" (#84)
Born on January 31, 1975 in Tyler, TX
6'0" and 190 pounds
Wide Receiver   2001-02
2 receptions for 50 yards, 1 recovery of an onside kick and 1 fumble recovery
Longest reception was a 46 yard pass from Tom Brady in their 17-16 win over the Jets on 12-02-01
Recovered an onside kick by Olindo Mare in their 20-13 win over the Dolphins on 12-22-01
Recovered Ed Perry's fumbled kickoff return in their 20-13 win over Miami on 12-22-01
9 Regular Season Games and 3 Playoff Games
Member of the 2001 World Championship Team
Washington Husky

COLEMAN, Justin (#22)
Born on March 27, 1993 in Brunswick, GA
5'11" and 190 pounds
Defensive Back   2015-16
Recovered Eli Manning's fumble in their 27-26 win over the NY Giants on 11-15-15
20 Regular Season games/3 started and 5 Playoff Games
Member of the 2016 World Championship Team
Tennessee Volunteer

COLEMAN, Pat (#47)
Born on April 8, 1967 in Cleveland, MS
5'7" and 176 pounds
Kickoff Returnman   1990
2 kickoff returns for 18 yards
Longest was a 12 yard return of a kickoff by Al Del Greco in their 34-14 loss to Phoenix on 11-25-90
Only game played was on 11-25-90
Mississippi Rebel

COLLIE, Austin (#10)
Born on November 11, 1985 in Hamilton, Canada
6'1" and 200 pounds
Wide Receiver   2013
6 receptions for 63 yards
Caught a 4th down pass for a 1st down in their 30-27 comeback win over the Saints on 10-13-13
Longest reception was a 19 yard pass from Tom Brady in their 24-20 loss to Miami on 12-15-13
7 Regular Season games/1 started (on 10-27-13) and 2 Playoff Games
5 receptions for 72 yards in the playoffs
BYU Cougar

COLLINS, Jamie (#91)
Born on October 20, 1989 in McCall Creek, MS
6'3" and 250 pounds
Linebacker   2013-16 and 2019
17.5 sacks, 8 interceptions for 167 yards + 1 TD and 5 fumble recoveries for 17 yards + 1 TD
Blocked an extra point and a field goal attempt
Sacked Aaron Rodgers, Kyle Orton, Blake Bortles, Marcus Mariota, Carson Palmer, Josh Allen and Colt McCoy
Had 1 ½ sacks of Baker Mayfield and 2 sacks of Philip Rivers and Luke Falk
Recorded 2 ½ sacks of Tyrod Taylor and Ryan Fitzpatrick
Intercepted Kyle Orton, Geno Smith, Zach Mettenberger, Ryan Tannehill, Brock Osweiler and Josh Allen
Had 2 interceptions of Ryan Fitzpatrick
Recovered fumbles by Pierre Thomas, A.J. Green, Kyle Orton, Ryan Fitzpatrick and Trey Quinn
Had a career long 69 yard TD return of a pass by Ryan Fitzpatrick in their 43-0 sshuout of Miami on 09-15-09
Blocked a 41 yard FGA by Caleb Sturgis that was returned for a TD in their 41-13 win vs Miami on 12-14-14
Jumped over long snapper and blocked Adam Vinatieri's extra point attempt in 34-27 win vs the Colts on 10-18-15
Had a 14 yard TD return of a fumble by Ryan Fitzpatrick in their 26-20 OT loss to the Jets on 12-27-15
Led the NFL with 5 forced fumbles in 2015
AFC Pro Bowl Linebacker in 2015
66 Regular Season Games/56 started and 8 Playoff Games/7 started
3 sacks and 2 interceptions for 45 yards in the playoffs
Sacked Andrew Luck in their 43-22 Divisional Playoff win over the Colts on 01-14-14
Sacked Peyton Manning *twice* in their 20-18 AFC Championship Game loss to Denver on 01-24-16
Returned a pass by Andrew Luck 20 yards in their 43-22 Divisional Playoff win over the Colts on 01-14-14
Returned a pass by Andrew Luck 25 yards in their 45-7 Divisional Playoff win over the Colts on 01-18-15
Member of the 2014 and 2016 World Championship Teams
#52 pick in the 2013 NFL Draft
Southern Mississippi

COLLINS, Todd (#54 and #59) *"The Swamp Chicken"*
Born on May 27, 1970 in New Market, TN
6'2" and 248 pounds
Linebacker   1992-94 and 1996-98
Wore #54 from 1992-94 and #59 from 1996-98
2.5 sacks, 2 interceptions for 15 yards and 2 fumble recoveries for 2 yards
Shared in a sack of Brad Johnson and sacked Neil O'Donnell and Dan Marino
Intercepted Rick Mirer and Kent Graham and recovered a fumbles by Terance Mathis and Tommy Vardell
Recovered Terance Mathis' fumble of the opening kickoff in their 30-21 loss to the Jets on 10-04-92
Had an 8 yard return of a pass by Rick Mirer in their 17-14 loss to the Seahawks on 09-19-93
Had a 2 yard return of a fumble by Tommy Vardell in their 20-17 win over the Browns on 12-19-93
Returned a pass by Kent Graham 7 yards in their 31-0 shutout of the Arizona Cardinals on 09-15-96
76 Regular Season games/53 started and 5 Playoff Games/5 started
Returned a Dan Marino pass 40 yards for a TD in their 17-3 Wild Card win over Miami on 12-28-97
#64 pick in the 1994 NFL Draft
Carson-Newman Eagle

COLLINS, Anthony "Tony" (#33) *"The Blade"*
Born on May 27, 1959 in Sanford, FL
5'11 and 208 pounds
RB/KR (PR)   1981-87
1,191 carries for 4,647 yards + 32 TDs and 261 receptions for 2,356 yards + 12 TDs
65 kickoff returns for 1,335 yards and 3 punt returns for 15 yards
Caught 1 TD pass from Matt Cavanaugh and 1 Half Back Option TD pass from Mosi Tatupu
Caught 2 TD passes from Tom Ramsey and Tony Eason and 3 TD passes from Craig James and Steve Grogan
Longest was a 15 yard return of a punt by Greg Cater in their 19-10 loss to Buffalo on 12-13-81
Longest run for 54 yards in their 24-13 win over the Baltimore Colts on 09-12-82
Ran for a Patriots Team Record 212 yards in their 23-13 victory over the Jets on 09-18-83
Ran for a 3 yard game winning TD to beat the Saints 7-0 on 12-04-83
Ran for a 2 yard game winning TD to beat the Browns 17-16 on 10-07-84
Longest was a 46 yard return of a kickoff by Rich Karlis in their 26-19 loss to Denver on 11-04-84
Recovered Tony Eason's fumble in their 38-31 win over the Indianapolis Colts on 12-01-85
Caught a 10 yard HB Option TD from Craig James, on 4th down, in their 20-6 win over the Jets on 09-11-86
Had a career long 49 yard reception in their win vs Tampa on 10-27-85 and in their win vs Atlanta on 11-02-86
Snared a 15 yard HB Option TD from Mosi Tatupu, on 4th down, in their 26-23 win over LA Raiders on 11-01-87
AFC Pro Bowl Running Back in 1983
102 Regular Season Games/83 started and 6 Playoff Games/6 started
47 carries for 220 yards and 13 receptions for 119 yards + 1 TD in the playoffs
Caught a 4 yard TD pass from Tony Eason in their 31-14 AFC Championship win over Miami on 01-12-86
#47 pick in the 1981 NFL Draft
East Carolina Pirate

COLLONS, Ferric (#92)
Born on December 4, 1969 in Scott AFB, IL
6'7" and 290 pounds
Defensive End   1995-99
7.5 sacks, 1 fumble recovery for 5 yards and blocked a field goal attempt
Sacked Jim Kelly, Stoney Casey and had 1 ½ sacks of Troy Aikman
Recorded 2 sacks of Steve Young and Jim Harbaugh
Had a 5 yard return of a fumble by Rick Mirer in their 31-3 rout of the Bears on 09-21-97
Blocked a 47 yard field goal attempt by Morton Anderson in their 41-10 loss to Atlanta on 11-08-98
64 Regular Season Games/27 started and 4 Playoff Games/4 started
Sacked Brett Favre in their 35-21 Super Bowl loss to the Green Bay Packers on 01-26-97
California Golden Bear

COLON, Harry (#40)
Born on February 14, 1969 in Kansas City, MO
6'0" and 203 pounds
Defensive Back   1991
Recovered fumbles by Merrill Hoge and Mark Higgs
16 games/14 started
#196 pick in the 1991 NFL Draft
Missouri Tiger

COLTON, George (#63)
Born on July 28, 1963 in Lindenhurst, NY
6'4" and 279 pounds
Guard   1987
Recovered Michael LeBlanc's fumble in their 20-10 loss to the Browns on 10-04-87
3 games/3 started
#248 pick in the 1986 College Draft
Maryland Terrapin

COLVIN III, Rosevelt (#59)
Born on September 5, 1977 in Indianapolis, IN
6'3" and 250 pounds
Linebacker   2003-08
26.5 sacks, 1 interception of 4 yards and 5 fumble recoveries for 17 yards + 1 TD
Shared in a sack of Jake Delhomme and had 1 ½ sacks of Brooks Bollinger
Sacked Donovan McNabb, Trent Green, Kyle Boller, Matt Schaub, Kelly Holcomb and Trent Green
Sacked Chris Simms, Brett Favre, A.J. Feeley, David Carr and Vince Young
Had 2 sacks of J.P. Losman, Chad Pennington, Jon Kitna and Philip Rivers
Recorded 2 ½ sacks of Peyton Manning and 3 sacks of Drew Bledsoe
Recovered fumbles by Donovan McNabb, Kelly Holcomb, Vince Young, Jason Campbell and Peyton Manning
Had a 4 yard return of a pass by Philip Rivers in their 38-14 rout of the San Diego Chargers on 09-16-07
Returned Mike Vrabel's strip sack of Jason Campbell 11 yds for a TD in 52-7 rout of Washington on 10-28-07
Returned Peyton Manning's fumble 5 yards in their 24-20 win over the Indianapolis Colts on 11-04-07
65 Regular Season Games/42 started and 8 Playoff Games/6 started
2 sacks and 1 interception in the playoffs
Sacked Byron Leftwich in their 28-3 Wild Card win over the Jacksonville Jaguars on 01-07-06
Batted down a backward lateral by Chad Pennington in their 37-16 Wild Card win over the Jets on 01-07-07
Intercepted a pass by Philip Rivers, that he tipped to himself, in their 24-21 Divisional win vs SD on 01-14-07
Sacked Peyton Manning in their 38-34 Championship Game loss to the Indianapolis Colts on 01-21-07
Member of the 2003 and 2004 World Championship Teams
Purdue Boilermaker

COMPTON, Mike (#77)
Born on September 18, 1970 in Richlands, VA
6'6" and 310 pounds
Offensive Lineman   2001-03
34 Regular Season Games/34 started and 3 Playoff Games/3 started
Member of the 2001 and 2003 World Championship Teams
West Virginia Mountaineer

CONDON, Tom (#63)
Born on October 26, 1952 in Derby, CT
6'3" and 255 pounds
Offensive Guard   1985
Only game played was on 09-15-85
Boston College Eagle

CONN, Richard "Dick" (#22)
Born on January 9, 1951 in Louisville, KY
6'0" and 185 pounds
DB/KR/PR   1975-79
Returned a pass by Ken Stabler pass 24 yards on the last play in their 21-14 win over the Raiders on 09-24-78
3 kickoff returns for 55 yards
Had a career long 26 yard return of a kickoff by Dave Green in their 31-14 win over Tampa on 12-12-76
Had another return of 26 yards of a a kickoff by Garo Yepremian in their 23-3 loss to Miami on 12-18-78
Had a 2 yard return of a punt by George Roberts in their 33-24 win over the Dolphins on 10-22-78
Holder for Steve Zabel's extra point on 12-12-76 and for David Posey in 1978
46 Regular Season games/1 started (on 09-12-76) and 2 Playoff Games
Georgia Bulldog

CONNOLLY, Dan (#63)
Born on September 2, 1982 in St. Louis, MO
6'4" and 311 pounds
OL (KR/FB/TE)   2008-14
4 kickoff returns for 106 yards
Longest was a 71 yard return of a kickoff by Mason Crosby in their 31-27 win over Green Bay on 12-19-10
AFC Special Team Player of the Week in their 31-27 win over the Packers on 12-19-10
Used as a Fullback in 4 games and as a blocking TE in 2009
85 Regular Season games/71 started and 11 Playoff Games/11 started
Long Snapper on Tom Brady's 48 yard punt in their 45-10 Divisional rout of the Broncos on 01-14-12
Member of the 2014 World Championship Team
Southeast Missouri State Redhawk

COOK, Marv (#46 and #85)
Born on February 24, 1966 in Iowa City, IO
6'4" and 234 pounds
TE/LS (KR)   1989-93
Wore #46 from 1989-90 and #85 from 1991-93
210 receptions for 1,843 yards + 11 TDs and 1 kickoff return of 8 yards
Caught a TD pass from Jon Vaughn, Steve Grogan and Drew Bledsoe
Caught 2 TD passes from Marc Wilson and 3 TD passes from Tommy Hodson and Hugh Millen
Longest reception was a 49 yard pass from Hugh Millen in their 24-20 win over Houston on 09-22-91
Had an 8 yard return of a kickoff by Pete Stoyanovich in their 33-27 OT win vs the Miami Dolphins on 01-02-94
Recovered fumbles by Leonard Russell and Scott Zolak and a fumbled kickoff return by James Brooks
Long Snapper for Punters Shawn McCarthy and Mike Saxon
AFC Offensive Player of the Week in their 24-20 win over Houston on 09-22-91
AFC Pro Bowl Tight End in 1991, 1992
First Team All Pro Tight End in 1991
80 games/59 started
#63 pick in the 1989 NFL Draft
Iowa Hawkeye

COOKS, Brandin (#14)
Born on September 25, 1993 in Stockton, CA
5'10" and 183 pounds
Wide Receiver   2017
65 receptions for 1,082 yards + 7 TDs and 9 carries for 40 yards
Caught 7 TD passes from Tom Brady
Longest run for 13 yards in their 36-20 win over the New Orleans Saints on 09-17-17
Caught a 25 yard TD pass with 23 seconds left from Tom Brady in their 36-33 win over Houston on 09-24-17
Caught a 2 point pass from Tom Brady for the last points scored in their 36-33 win over Houston on 09-24-17
Longest reception was a 64 yard TD pass from Tom Brady in their 33-8 rout of the Raiders on 11-19-17
16 Regular Season Games/15 started and 3 Playoff Games/3 started
Oregon State Beaver

COOKS, Terrence (#58)
Born on October 25, 1966 in New Orleans, LA
6'0" and 230 pounds
Linebacker   1989
3 games
Nicholls State Colonel

CORBETT, Steve (#62)
Born on August 11, 1951 in Dover, NH
6'4" and 250 pounds
Guard   1975
14 games
#30 pick in the 1974 NFL Draft
Boston College Eagle

CORCORAN, James "King" (#15)
Born on July 6, 1943 in Jersey City, NJ
6'0" and 200 pounds
Quarterback   1968
3 completions for 33 yards and ran for a 1 yard loss
Longest completion was a 14 yard pass to Jim Whalen in their 34-10 loss to Miami on 11-24-68
Ran for a 1 yard loss on the last play in their 34-10 loss to the Miami Dolphins on 11-24-68
2 games (on Nov. 24th and Dec.15th)
Member of the American Football Association Semi-Pro Football Hall of Fame
Maryland Terrapin

CORSETTI, Enrico "Rico" (#93)
Born on January 13, 1963 in Newton, MA
6'1" and 225 pounds
Special Team Player   1987
2 games (on Oct. 4th and Oct. 11th)
Bates Bobcat

COSTICT, Ray (#55)
Born on March 19, 1955 in Moss Point, MS
6'0" and 217 pounds
Special Team/LB   1977-79
2 sacks, 4 fumble recoveries for 16 yards and 1 interception for 22 yards
Sacked Jack Thompson and Greg Landry
Recovered fumbles by Bo Matthews, Johnnie Dirden, Don McCauley and Roland Hooks
Had a 22 yard return of a pass by Richard Todd in their 56-3 rout of the New York Jets on 09-09-79
Returned Don McCauley's fumble 16 yards in their 31-26 loss to the Baltimore Colts on 10-28-79
46 Regular Season games/7 started and 1 Playoff Game (on 12-31-78)
#313 pick in the 1977 NFL Draft
Mississippi State Bulldog

COTTRELL, Dana (#45)
Born on January 11, 1974 in Boston, MA
6'3" and 234 pounds
Special Team/LB   1998
2 Regular Season Games and 1 Playoff Game (on 01-03-99)
Syracuse Orangeman

COWAN, Lawrence "Larry" (#44)
Born on July 11, 1960 in Mobile, AL
5'11" and 194 pounds
Special Team   1982
6 Regular Season Games and 1 Playoff Game (on 01-08-83)
Jackson State Tiger

COWART, Byron (#99)
Born on May 20, 1996 in Seffner, FL
6'3" and 300 pounds
Defensive Lineman   2019--
5 games
#159 pick in the 2019 NFL Draft
Maryland Terrapin

COX, Bryan (#51*) "Mr. Attitude"***
Born on February 17, 1968 in St. Louis, MO
6'4" and 250 pounds
Linebacker (RB)   2001
Nicknamed *"Mr. Attitude"* after his ferocious hit on Jerome Pathon in their 44-13 rout of the Colts on 09-30-01
Had a 9 yard return of a fumble by LaDanian Tomlinson in their 29-26 OT win vs San Diego on 10-14-01
Caught a 7 yard pass, as a RB, from Tom Brady in their 29-26 OT win vs San Diego on 10-14-01
11 Regular Season games/7 started and 3 Playoff Games
Stuffed Zack Crockett on 3rd down in their 16-13 OT Divisional Playoff win over the Raiders on 01-19-02
Member of the 2001 World Championship Team
Western Illinois Leatherneck

CRABLE, Shawn (#98)
Born on December 26, 1984 in Massillon, OH
6'5" and 241 pounds
Linebacker   2010
Shared in a sack of Ben Roethlisberger in their 39-26 victory over the Steelers on 11-14-10
6 games
#78 pick in the 2008 NFL Draft
Michigan Wolverine

CRABTREE, Eric (#10)
Born on November 3, 1944 in Monessen, PA
6'0" and 185 pounds
Wide Receiver   1971
9 receptions for 120 yards + 1 TD and 2 carries for 11 yards
Hauled in a career long 31 yard TD pass from Jim Plunkett in their 38-33 win vs Buffalo on 11-14-71
Longest run for 18 yards in their 38-33 victory over the Buffalo Bills on 11-14-71
6 games/4 started
Pittsburgh Panther

CRAWFORD, Elbert (#65)
Born on June 20, 1966 in Chicago, IL
6'3" and 280 pounds
Center/Guard   1990-91
30 games/16 started
Arkansas Razorback

CRAWFORD, Jim (#30) *"Cowboy"*
Born on August 26, 1935 in Greybull, NY
6'1" and 205 pounds
RB (KR)   1960-64
302 carries for 1,078 yards + 5 TDs and 52 receptions for 501 yards + 2 TDs
2 kickoff returns for 24 yards in 1962 and 2 completions for 27 yards
Recovered Eddie Bell's interception return fumble in their 28-24 win vs the NY Titans on 09-17-60
Caught a 2 point pass from Gino Cappelletti in their 35-0 shutout of the LA Chargers on 10-08-60
Longest run was a 39 yard TD in their 42-14 rout of the Dallas Texans on 11-18-60
Snared a 13 yard TD pass from Babe Parilli in their 41-16 victory over the Broncos on 09-21-62
Longest reception was a 44 yard pass from Tom Yewcic in their 41-16 win over Denver on 09-21-62
Caught a 2 point pass from Babe Parilli in their 24-20 win over the San Diego Chargers on 10-19-62
Ran 1 yard for the game winning TD to beat San Diego 24-20 on 10-19-62
Longest was an 18 yard return of a kickoff by Mack Yoho in their 21-10 win over Buffalo on 11-23-62
Advanced Bob Dee's kickoff return lateral 6 yards in their 21-10 victory over the Bills on 11-23-62
Recovered Tom Yewcic's fumble in their 21-10 victory over the Buffalo Bills on 11-23-62
Caught a 43 yard TD pass from Tom Yewcic in their 20-14 win over the Chargers on 12-09-62
Tossed a 15 yard half back option pass to Larry Garron in their 17-13 loss to San Diego on 09-14-63
Tossed a 12 yard half back option pass to Tony Romeo in their 24-24 with the Chiefs on 11-17-63
54 games/10 started
Wyoming Cowboy

CRAWFORD, Vernon (#99)
Born on June 25, 1974 in Texas City, TX
6'4" and 245 pounds
LB/Special Team   1997-99
Fell on Derrick Cullors' fumbled kickoff return in their 26-20 win over Jacksonville on 12-07-97
41 Regular Season games/1 started (on 11-15-98) and 1 Playoff Game (on 01-03-99)
#159 pick in the 1997 NFL Draft
Florida State Seminole

CRESWELL III, Smiley (#92)
Born on December 11, 1959 in Everett, WA
6'4" and 251 pounds
Defensive End   1985 Playoffs
2 Playoff Games
#118 pick in the 1983 NFL Draft
Michigan State Spartan

CRITTENDEN, Ray (#81)
Born on March 1, 1970 in Washington, DC
6'1" and 192 pounds
KR/WR/PR   1993-94
44 receptions for 672 yards + 4 TDs and 1 carry for a 3 yard loss
47 kickoff returns for 938 yards and 21 punt returns for 192 yards
Caught 4 TD passes from Drew Bledsoe
Longest reception was a 44 yard pass from Drew Bledsoe in their 45-7 loss to the NY Jets on 09-26-93
Ran for a 3 yard loss in their 45-7 loss to the New York Jets on 09-26-93
Longest was a 30 yard return of a punt by Greg Montgomery in their 28-014 loss to Houston on 10-17-93
Longest was a 44 yard return of a kickoff by John Kasay in their 10-9 loss to Seattle on 10-24-93
Recovered Corey Croom's fumble in their 38-35 loss to the Buffalo Bills on 09-11-94
32 Regular Season games/4 started and 1 Playoff Game (on 01-01-95)
Virginia Tech Hokie

CROOM, Corey (#26)
Born on May 22, 1971 in Sandusky, OH
5'11" and 208 pounds
RB/KR　　　　　1993-95
73 carries for 252 yards + 1 TD, 9 receptions for 100 yards and 10 kickoff returns for 172 yards
Longest reception was a 21 yard pass from Drew Bledsoe in their 17-14 loss to the Steelers on 12-05-93
Ran for a 5 yard TD and had his career longest run of 22 yards in their 38-0 shutout of the Colts on 12-26-93
Longest was a 24 yard return of a kickoff by Steve Christie in their 38-35 loss to Buffalo on 09-11-94
43 Regular Season Games/2 started and 1 Playoff Game/1 started (on 01-01-95)
Ball State Cardinal

CROSS, Robert "Bobby" (#77)
Born on July 4, 1931 in Ranger, TX
6'4" and 240 pounds
Offensive Tackle　　　　　1960
4 games
Kilgore Jr. College Ranger

CROSSEN, Keion (#35)
Born on April 17, 1996 in Garysburg, NC
5'10" and 180 pounds
DB　　　　　2018
11 Regular Season Games and 3 Playoff Games
Member of the 2018 World Championship Team
#243 pick in the 2018 NFL Draft
Western Carolina Catamount

CROSTON, Cole (#74)
Born on December 25, 1993 in Sergeant Bluff, IA
6'5" and 310 pounds
Offensive Lineman　　　　　2017-18
5 Regular Season Games and 1 Playoff Game (on 01-21-18)
Iowa Hawkeye

CROUTHAMEL, John "Jake" (#34)
Born on June 27, 1938 in Perkasie, PA
6'0" and 195 pounds
RB/KR　　　　　1960
4 carries for 16 yards and 2 kickoff returns for 27 yards
Had his longest run of 6 yards in their 31-24 loss to the Broncos on 10-23-60
Had his longest kickoff return of 15 yards in their 31-24 loss to Denver on 10-23-60
2 games (on Oct. 23rd and Oct. 28th)
Dartmouth Big Green

CROW, Albert "Al" (#72)
Born on August 20, 1932 in Norfolk, VA
6'7" and 260 pounds
DT　　　　　1960
3 games/2 started
William & Mary Tribe

CRUMP, George (#91)
Born on July 22, 1959 in Portsmouth, VA
6'4" and 260 pounds
Defensive End   1982
Forced Archie Manning's intentional grounding safety in their 29-21 win over the Oilers on 11-28-82
9 Regular Season Games and 1 Playoff Game (on 01-08-83)
#85 pick in the 1982 NFL Draft
East Carolina Pirate

CRUMP, Harry (#31) "*Harry the Thump*"
Born on June 18, 1940 in Framingham, MA
6'1" and 205 pounds
FB (KR)   1963
49 carries for 120 yards + 5 TDs, 6 receptions for 46 yards and 3 kickoff returns for 33 yards
Longest was a 14 yard return of a kickoff by Dick Guesman in their 31-24 loss to the Jets on 10-05-63
Longest run for 21 yards in their 28-21 loss to the Buffalo Bills on 10-26-63
Longest reception was a 12 yard pass from Babe Parilli in their 7-6 loss to San Diego on 11-10-63
14 Regular Season Games and 2 Playoff Games
Boston College Eagle

CRUMPLER, Algernon "Alge" (#82)
Born on December 23, 1977 in Wilmington, NC
6'2" and 262 pounds
Tight End   2010
6 receptions for 52 yards + 2 TDs and 5 kickoff returns for 18 yards
Caught 2 Regular Season TD passes from Tom Brady and 1 Post Season TD pass from Tom Brady
Longest was a 7 yard return of Jeff Reed's onside kick in their 39-26 win over Pittsburgh on 11-14-10
Longest reception was a 27 yard pass from Tom Brady in their 45-24 rout of the Lions on 11-25-10
16 Regular Season games/10 started and 1 Playoff Game (on 01-16-11)
Caught a 2 yard TD pass from Tom Brady in their 28-21 Divisional Playoff loss to the Jets on 01-16-11
North Carolina Tar Heel

CRYDER, Robert "Bob" (#75)
Born on September 7, 1956 in East St. Louis, IL
6'4" and 275 pounds
Offensive Lineman   1978-83
75 Regular Season Games/36 started and 1 Playoff Game (on 01-08-83)
#18 pick in the 1978 NFL Draft
Alabama Crimson Tide

CUDZIK, Walt (#56 and #54)
Born on February 21, 1932 in Chicago, IL
6'2" and 231 pounds
C/LS/LB (Kicker)   1960-63
Wore #56 in 1960 and #54 from 1961-63
Caught Butch Songin's deflected pass for an 11 yard gain in their 45-16 loss to the LA Chargers on 10-28-60
Attempted a 48 yard field goal in their 34-0 loss to the Dallas Texans on 12-11-60
Recovered an onside kick by Billy Atkins in their 23-21 win over the Buffalo Bills on 09-23-61
56 Regular Season Games/28 started and 2 Playoff Games/2 started
Purdue Boilermaker

CULLORS, Derrick (#29) *"Flying"*
Born on December 26, 1972 in Dallas, TX
6'0" and 195 pounds
RB/KR   1997-98
Nicknamed *"Flying Cullors"* after his 86 yard TD kickoff return
40 carries for 149 yards, 16 receptions for 154 yards + 1 TD and 60 kickoff returns for 1,471 yards + 1 TD
Longest was an 86 yard TD return of a kickoff by Steve Christie in their 31-10 win over Buffalo on 11-09-97
Longest run for 24 yards in their 27-7 loss to the Tampa Bay Buccaneers on 11-16-97
Longest reception was a 43 yard pass from Drew Bledsoe in their 30-27 win over the Saints on 10-04-98
Caught a 9 yard TD pass from Drew Bledsoe in their 25-21 win over the Buffalo Bills on 11-29-98
31 Regular Season Games/1 started (on 12-22-97) and 3 Playoff Games/2 started
Murray State Racer

CUNNINGHAM, Jay (#21) *"The Dart"*
Born on October 9, 1943 in Youngstown, OH
5'10" and 185 pounds
DB/KR/PR   1965-67
Nicknamed *"The Dart"* because of his blazing speed
3 interceptions for 70 yards + 1 TD, 64 kickoff returns 1,372 yards and 22 punt returns for 140 yards
Advanced Tom Hennessey's fumbled punt return 12 yards in their 31-10 loss to the Oilers on 09-19-65
Tackled Punt Returner Les "Speedy" Duncan in the end zone for a safety in their 22-6 win vs SD on 10-31-65
Had a career long 45 yard return of a kickoff by Jim Turner in their 30-20 loss to the Jets on 11-14-65
Returned a Len Dawson pass 6 yards in their 10-10 Tie with the Kansas City Chiefs on 11-21-65
Returned a George Blanda pass 10 yards in their 42-14 rout of the Houston Oilers on 12-18-65
Had a 17 yard return of Gary Kroner's missed field goal attempt in their 17-10 loss to Denver on 11-06-66
Had a 54 yard TD return of a pass by Rick Norton in their 41-10 rout of the Dolphins on 10-15-67
Had a career long 44 yard return of a punt by Mike Eischeid on their 48-14 loss to the Raiders on 10-22-67
Had a 10 yard return of Paul Maguire's free kick in their 44-16 loss to the Buffalo Bills on 12-09-67
40 games/2 started
14th Round Draft Pick in 1964
Bowling Green State Falcon

CUNNINGHAM, Jermaine (#96)
Born on August 24, 1988 in the Bronx, NY
6'2" and 248 pounds
Defensive End   2010-12
Sacked Joe Flacco, Jake Locker and Ryan Fitzpatrick and shared in a strip sack of Mark Sanchez
Recovered fumbles by Willis McGahee and Ryan Fitzpatrick
36 Regular Season games/14 started and 3 Playoff Games
#53 pick in the 2010 NFL Draft
Florida Gator

CUNNINGHAM, Korey (#74)
Born on May 17, 1995 in Montevalo, AL
6'6" and 305 pounds
Tackle   2019
Only game played was on 09-15-09
Cincinnati Bearcat

CUNNINGHAM JR, Sam (#39) "Sam Bam"
Born on August 15, 1950 in Santa Barbara, CA
6'3" and 226 pounds
Running Back   1973-79 and 1981-82
1,385 carries for 5,453 yards + 43 TDs and 210 receptions for 1,905 yards + 6 TDs
Caught 3 TD passes from Jim Plunkett and Steve Grogan
Caught a 34 yard TD pass from Jim Plunkett, on the 1st play, in their 30-14 loss to Miami on 10-28-73
Longest run was a 75 yard TD, on 1st play of the game, in their 30-28 loss to Buffalo on 10-20-74
Longest reception was a 41 yard pass from Steve Grogan in their 48-17 rout of the Raiders on 10-03-76
Dove for a game winning 1 yard TD in their 21-14 win over the Oakland Raiders on 09-24-78
Ran for a game winning 3 yard TD in their 10-3 victory over the Bengals on 10-15-78
Only Patriot to score a TD on the 1st offensive play via a TD reception and on a rushing play
AFC Pro Bowl Running Back in 1978
107 Regular Season Games/94 started and 2 Playoff Games/2 started
#11 pick in the 1973 NFL Draft
Inducted into the Patriots Hall of Fame on 08-12-10
USC Trojan

CURRIER, Bill (#28)
Born on January 5, 1955 in Glen Burnie, MD
6'0" and 196 pounds
DB/KR   1980
6 kickoff returns for 98 yards
Longest was a 26 yard return of a kickoff by Nick Mike Mayer in their 31-13 loss to Buffalo on 10-26-80
16 games
South Carolina Gamecock

CUSICK, Pete (#76)
Born on October 27, 1952 in San Bernardino, CA
6'1" and 255 pounds
Nose Tackle   1975
1 sack and 2 blocked field goal attempts
Sacked Joe Namath in their 30-28 loss to the NY Jets on 12-07-75
Blocked a 48 yard FGA and a 46 yard FGA by Pat Leahy in their 30-28 loss to the Jets on 12-07-75
13 games
#66 pick in the 1975 NFL Draft
Ohio State Buckeye

DALTON, Antico (#93)
Born on December 31, 1975 in Eden, NC
6'1" and 240 pounds
Special Team   2000
Recovered Curtis Jackson's fumbled kickoff return in their 13-10 OT win vs the Bills on 12-17-00
3 games
Hampton Pirate

DAMKROGER, Maurice "Maury" (#51)
Born on January 8, 1952 in Cambridge, NE
6'2" and 230 pounds
Linebacker   1974-75
13 games
#178 pick in the 1974 NFL Draft
Nebraska Cornhusker

DANENHAUER, William "Bill" (#77)
Born on June 3, 1934 in Clay Center, KS
6'5" and 245 pounds
Defensive End   1960
3 games
Emporia State Hornet

DAVEY, Rohan (#6)
Born on April 14, 1978 in Clarendon, Jamaica
6'2" and 245 pounds
Quarterback   2002-04
8 completions for 88 yards and 6 carries for a net loss of 5 yards
Longest completion was a 20 yard pass to Bethel Johnson in their 42-15 rout of the Browns on 12-05-04
Longest run for 3 yards in their 21-7 victory over the San Francisco 49ers on 01-02-05
7 games
Member of the 2003 and 2004 World Championship Teams
#117 pick in the 2002 NFL Draft
Member of the 2004 NFL Europe Berlin Thunder Championship Team (Europe League MVP)
LSU Fighting Tiger

DAVIS, Andre' (#18)
Born on June 12, 1979 in Niskayuna, NY
6'1" and 195 pounds
WR/KR   2005
9 receptions for 190 yards + 1 TD and 3 kickoff returns for 108 yards
Longest was a 60 yard TD pass from Tom Brady, which he dunked, in their 24-17 win vs the Saints on 11-20-05
Longest was a 65 yard return of a kickoff by Olindo Mare in their 28-26 loss to the Dolphins on 01-01-06
9 Regular Season Games/4 started and 2 Playoff Games
Virginia Tech Hokie

DAVIS, Don (#51)
Born on December 17, 1972 in Olathe, KS
6'1" and 235 pounds
DB/LB   2003-06
59 Regular Season Games/2 started and 8 Playoff Games
Member of the 2003 and 2004 World Championship Teams
Kansas Jayhawk

DAVIS, Elgin (#40)
Born on October 23, 1965 in Jacksonville, FL
5'10" and 192 pounds
RB/KR   1987-88
9 carries for 43 yards and 11 kickoff returns for 240 yards
Longest run was 27 yards in their 21-7 victory over the Houston Oilers on 10-18-87
Longest was a 43 yard return of John Teltschik's opening kickoff in their 34-31 OT loss Philly on 11-29-87
9 games
#330 pick in the 1987 NFL Draft
Central Florida Golden Knight

DAVIS, Gregory "Greg" (#5)
Born on October 29, 1965 in Rome, GA
6'0" and 202 pounds
Kicker   1989
Kicked 16 field goals and 13 extra points
Kicked a career long 52 yard field goal in their 16-15 loss to the Atlanta Falcons on 10-15-89
Booted a 51 yard game winning field goal in Overtime to beat the Colts 23-20 on 10-29-89
9 games
Citadel Bulldog

DAVIS, Ja'Gared (#53)
Born on September 11, 1990 in Crockett, TX
6'1" and 235 pounds
Linebacker   2013-14
4 Regular Season Games and 2 Playoff Games
Member of the 2014 World Championship Team
SMU Mustang

DAVIS, John "Jack" (#65)
Born on March 12, 1932 in Braddock, PA
6'0" and 225 pounds
Guard   1960
Had a 5 yard return of a blocked punt in their 31-24 loss to the Denver Broncos on 10-23-60
14 games/13 started
Maryland Terrapin

DAVIS, Kanorris (#36)
Born on January 21, 1990 in Perry, GA
5'10" and 207 pounds
Safety   2013
3 Regular Season Games and 2 Playoff Games
Troy Trojan

DAVIS, Keionta (#58)
Born on March 1, 1994 in Chattanooga, TN
6'3" and 280 pounds
Defensive Lineman   2018
6 games
Member of the 2018 World Championship Team
Tennessee Chattanooga Moccasin

DAVIS, Shockmain (#84)
Born on August 20, 1977 in Port Arthur, TX
6'0" and 205 pounds
WR/KR   2000
2 receptions for 12 yards and 2 kickoff returns for 45 yards
Longest was a 32 yard return of a kickoff by Mitch Berger in their 21-13 loss to the Vikings on 09-17-00
Longest reception was a 9 yard pass from Drew Bledsoe in their 34-9 loss to the Lions on 11-23-00
12 games
Angelo State Ram

DAWSON, Bill "Red" (#83)
Born on December 4, 1942 in Valdosta, GA
6'3" and 240 pounds
DE/OE/LB   1965
Played on both sides of the line of scrimmage
9 games
19ᵗʰ Round Draft Pick in 1964
Florida State Seminole

DAWSON, James "Lin" (#87)
Born on June 24, 1959 in Norfolk, VA
6'3" and 240 pounds
Tight End   1981-90
117 receptions for 1,233 yards + 8 TDs
Caught 1 TD pass from Matt Cavanaugh, 2 TDs from Steve Grogan and Doug Flutie and 3 TDs
        from Tony Eason
Longest reception was a 42 yard pass from Matt Cavanaugh in their 23-21 loss to the Baltimore Colts on 12-20-81
Recovered a fumble by Craig James in their 20-17 loss to the Dallas Cowboys on 11-22-84
105 Regular Season Games/75 started and 5 Playoff Games/5 started
Caught a 13 yard TD pass from Tony Eason in their 27-20 Divisional win over the LA Raiders on 01-05-86
#212 pick in the 1981 NFL Draft
Appeared in 2 episodes of the "Spenser for Hire" TV Show, which was occasionally filmed in the Boston Area
North Carolina State Wolfpack

DEADERICK, Brandon (#71)
Born on August 19, 1987 in Elizabethtown, KY
6'4" and 297 pounds
Defensive Lineman   2010-12
Sacked Joe Flacco, Philip Rivers, Rex Grossman, Matt Moore and Ryan Tannehill
34 Regular Season Games/14 started and 6 Playoff Games/5 started
Sacked Eli Manning in their 21-17 Super Bowl loss to the NY Giants on 02-05-12
Alabama Crimson Tide

DEE, Robert "Bob" (#89) *"Bubba"*
Born on May 18, 1933 in Quincy, MA
6'3" and 248 pounds
Defensive End (LB)   1960-67
32 ½ sacks, 13 fumble recoveries for 34 yards and 1 interception return of 14 yards
Blocked a field goal and blocked a punt
Shared in a sack of Al Dorow, Hunter Enis, Randy Duncan, and Rick Norton
Sacked George Blanda, M.C. Reynolds, Johnny Green, Tobin Rote, Eddie Wilson and Dick Wood
Sacked Tom Flores and Bob Griese and had 1 ½ sacks of Joe Namath
Had 2 sacks of Jack Kemp and 2 ½ sacks of Jacky Lee and John McCormick
Had 3 sacks of Frank Tripucka, John Hadl and Len Dawson and 5 sacks of Cotton Davidson
Recovered fumbles by Al Carmichael, Art Baker, Cotton Davidson, Wayne Crow and Jacky Lee
Recovered fumbles by Paul Lowe, Bill Tobin, Wray Carlton, Lee Grosscup and Max Chobian
Had a 14 yard return of a pass Babe Parilli in their 27-14 loss to the Oakland Raiders on 10-16-60
Protected a boy who went onto the field trying to recover Bob Laraba's fumble on the last play on 10-28-60
Fielded a kickoff and lateraled it to Dick Christy in their 38-14 loss to Buffalo on 12-04-60
Had a 30 yard return of a fumble by Warren Rabb in their 52-21 rout of the Buffalo Bills on 10-22-61
Blocked a 37 yard field goal attempt by Gene Mingo in their 41-16 rout of the Broncos on 09-21-62
Recovered a blocked field goal in their 41-16 rout of the Denver Broncos on 09-21-62
Recovered Lee Grosscup's lateral in their 43-14 rout of the New York Titans on 10-06-62
Fielded a kickoff and lateraled it to Jim Crawford in their 21-10 win over Buffalo on 11-23-62
Had a 14 yard return of a kickoff by Bill Shockley in their 24-17 win over the Titans on 11-30-62
Recovered his strip sack of Jacky Lee in their 45-3 rout of the Houston Oilers on 11-01-63
Recovered George Blair's onside kick in their 33-28 win over the San Diego Chargers on 09-20-64
Blocked a punt by Jim Fraser in their 39-10 rout of the Denver Broncos on 10-04-64
Returned Len Dawson's fumble 4 yards in their 27-27 Tie with the Chiefs on 11-20-66
Led the AFL with 5 fumble recoveries in 1961
AFL All Star DE in 1961, 1963, 1964, 1965
112 Regular Season games/112 started and 2 Playoff Games/2 started
Intercepted 2 passes by Daryle Lamonica in their 26-8 AFL Divisional Playoff win vs Buffalo on 12-28-63
His Uniform #89 was retired on "Dee Day" on 10-13-68
Inducted into the Patriots Hall of Fame on 08-18-93
Holy Cross Crusader

DELLENBACH, Jeff (#66)
Born on February 14, 1963 in Wausau, WI
6'6" and 290 pounds
Center   1995-96
17 games/5 started
Long Snapper in 2 games for Punter Tom Tupa and Kicker Adam Vinatieri
Wisconsin Badger

DELUCCA, Gerald "Jerry" (#74)
Born on July 17, 1936 in Peabody, MA
6'2" and 247 pounds
Tackle (KR)   1960-64
Had an 8 yard return of a kickoff by Ben Agajanian in their 45-16 loss to the LA Chargers on 10-28-60
31 games/25 started
Middle Tennessee State Blue Raider

DENNARD, Alfonzo (#37)
Born on September 9, 1989 in Rochelle, GA
5'10" and 204 pounds
Cornerback   2012-14
5 interceptions for 95 yards + 1 TD and had a 3 yard fumble return
Intercepted Mark Sanchez, Sam Bradford, Andrew Luck, Geno Smith and Ryan Tannehill
Had an 87 yard TD return of a pass by Andrew Luck in their 59-24 rout of the Colts on 11-18-12
Had a 3 yard advancement of a fumble by Jamie Collins in their 43-17 win over the Bengals on 10-05-14
29 Regular Season Games/20 started and 4 Playoff Games/4 started
Member of the 2014 World Championship Team
#224 pick in the 2012 NFL Draft
Nebraska Cornhusker

DENSON, Damon (#61)
Born on February 8, 1975 in Pittsburgh, PA
6'4" and 305 pounds
Guard   1997-99
Used as a Defensive Lineman on special teams
14 Regular Season Games and 1 Playoff Game (on 01-03-99)
#97 pick in the 1997 NFL Draft
Michigan Wolverine

DEOSSIE, Steve (#50 and #99)
Born on November 22, 1962 in Tacoma, WA
6'2" and 248 pounds
LS/LB (KR)   1994-95
Wore #50 for the first 3 games in 1994
Long Snapper for Punter Pat O'Neill and Kicker Matt Bahr
Had a 14 yard return of a kickoff by Fuad Reveiz in their 26-20 OT win over the Vikings on 11-13-94
32 Regular Season Games and 1 Playoff Game (on 01-01-95)
Boston College Eagle

DERBY, Adam James "A.J." (#86)
Born on September 20, 1991 in Iowa City, IA
6'5" and 240 pounds
Tight End   2016
4 games
Member of the 2016 World Championship Team
#202 pick in the 2015 NFL Draft
Arkansas Razorback

DERIGGI, Fred (#71)
Born on January 15, 1967 in Scranton, PA
6'2" and 265 pounds
Nose Tackle   1990
2 games (on Dec.23rd and Dec.30th)
Syracuse Orangeman

DEVELIN JR, James (#46) *"Tasmanian"*
Born on July 23, 1988 in Gilbertsville, PA
6'3" and 255 pounds
Fullback (KR)   2012-19
15 carries for 26 yards + 5 TDs, 31 receptions for 222 yards and 4 kickoff returns for 50 yards
Caught 5 Regular Season TD passes and 1 Post Season TD pass from Tom Brady
Longest reception was a 31 yard pass from Tom Brady in their 27-26 win over Cleveland on 12-08-13
Longest run for 5 yards in their 43-17 rout of the Cincinnati Bengals on 10-05-14
Recovered own fumble after his 3 yard pass reception from Tom Brady in their 43-21 rout of Denver on 11-02-14
Longest (tie) was a 15 yard return of a kickoff by Andrew Franks in their 35-14 win over Miami on 01-01-17
Longest (tie) was a 15 yard return of a kickoff by Jason Meyers in their 27-13 win vs the Jets on 11-25-18
AFC Pro Bowl Fullback in 2017
83 Regular Season Games/31 started and 14 Playoff Games/6 started
4 receptions for 20 yards + 1 TD, 1 carry for no gain amd 1 kickoff return of 5 yards in the playoffs
Caught a 1 yard TD pass from Tom Brady in their 45-7 AFC Championship rout of the Colts on 01-18-15
Returned Steven Hauschka's kickoff 5 yards, to end the half, in their 28-24 Super Bowl win vs Seattle on 02-01-15
Member of the 2014, 2016 and 2018 World Championship Teams
Brown Bear

DEVEY, Jordan (#65)
Born on January 11, 1988 in American Fork, UT
6'6" and 320 pounds
Offensive Lineman   2014
7 games
Member of the 2014 World Championship Team
Eagle Scout
Memphis Tiger

DEVREE, Tyson (#85)
Born on November 12, 1984 in Hudsonville, MI
6'6" and 245 pounds
Tight End   2008
2 games (on Dec. 7th and Dec.21st)
Colorado Buffalo

DILLON, Corey (#28) *"Clock Killin"*
Born on October 24, 1974 in Seattle, WA
6'1" and 225 pounds
Running Back   2004-06
753 carries for 3,180 yards + 37 TDs and 52 receptions for 431 yards + 2 TDs
Recovered Tom Brady's fumble in their 27-24 victory over the Indianapolis Colts on 09-09-04
Ran for a 2 point conversion in their 24-3 rout of the Baltimore Ravens on 11-28-04
Caught a 2 yard TD pass from Tom Brady in their 29-28 loss to the Dolphins on 12-20-04
Caught a 2 yard TD pass from Tom Brady in their 28-0 shutout of Tampa on 12-17-05
Longest run for 50 yards in their 17-14 loss to the New York Jets on 11-12-06
Longest reception was a 52 yard pass from Tom Brady in their 40-23 win over Tennessee on 12-31-06
AFC Offensive Player of the Month in December 2004
AFC Pro Bowl Running Back in 2004
43 Regular Season Games/37 started and 8 Playoff Games/6 started
120 carries for 508 yards + 4 TDs and 12 receptions for 74 yards in the playoffs
Member of the 2004 World Championship Team
Washington Husky

DIMITROFF, Tom (#15)
Born on June 6, 1935 in Strongsville, OH
5'11" and 200 pounds
Quarterback   1960
Threw 2 incomplete passes in their 42-14 win over the Dallas Texans on 11-18-60
3 games
Miami Redskin

DISCENZO, Tony (#76)
Born on February 3, 1936 in Cleveland, OH
6'5" and 240 pounds
Tackle/Kicker   1960
Kicked off for the Boston Patriots for their first 3 games in 1960
5 games
Michigan State Spartan

DOBSON, Aaron (#17)
Born on July 23, 1991 in Dunbar, WV
6'3" and 210 pounds
Wide Receiver   2013-15
53 receptions for 698 yards + 4 TDs
Caught 4 TD passes from Tom Brady
Longest reception was an 81 yard TD pass from Tom Brady in their 55-31 rout of the Steelers on 11-03-13
24 Regular Season Games and 1 Playoff Game
Member of the 2014 World Championship Team
#59 Pick of the 2013 NFL Draft
Marshall Thundering Herd

DOIG, Steve (#59)
Born on March 28, 1960 in Melrose, MA
6'2" and 240 pounds
LB/Special Team   1986-87
Recovered Larry Lee's fumbled kickoff return in their 34-27 win over Miami on 12-22-86
6 Regular Season Games and 1 Playoff Game (on 01-04-87)
New Hampshire Wildcat

DOMBROSKI, Paul (#47)
Born on August 8, 1956 in Sumter, SC
6'0" and 185 pounds
DB (KR)   1981-84
1 interception for 23 yards, 1 fumble recovery and 3 3 kickoff returns for 64 yards
Longest was a 24 yard return of a kickoff by Mike Wood in their 23-21 loss to Baltimore on 12-20-81
Recovered Dennis Gentry's fumbled punt return in their 26-13 loss to the Bears on 12-05-82
Returned a pass by Dave Krieg 23 yards in their 38-23 comeback win over Seattle on 09-16-84
Downed Luke Prestridge's 82 yard punt on the Jets 1 yard line in their 30-20 win over the Jets on 10-28-84
Downed Rich Camarillo's 57 yard punt on Colts 3 yard line, the next play was a safety, on 11-18-84
36 Regular Season Games and 1 Playoff Game (on 01-08-83)
Linfield Wildcat

DONNALLEY, Kevin (#23)
Born on January 17, 1958 in Warren, OH
5'11" and 177 pounds
Special Team   1981
Only game played was on 10-25-81
North Dakota State Bison

DORSETT II, Phillip (#13)
Born on January 5, 1993 in Ft. Lauderdale, FL
5'10" and 192 pounds
Wide Receiver　　　　　　2017-19
73 receptions for 881 yards + 8 TDs and 8 carries for 57 yards
Longest run for 17 yards in their 24-12 win over the Buffalo Bills on 12-23-18
Longest reception was a 58 yard TD pass from Tom Brady in their 33-3 rout of the Steelers on 09-08-19
45 Regular Season Games/8 started and 6 Playoff Games/1 started (on 01-04-20)
8 receptions for 126 yards + 2 TDs in the playoffs
Caught a 15 yard TD pass from Tom Brady in their 41-28 Divisional Playoff win vs the LA Chargers on 01-13-19
Caught a 29 yard TD pass from Tom Brady in their 37-31 Championship Game win over the Chiefs on 01-20-19
Member of the 2018 World Championship Team
Miami Hurricane

DORSEY, Nate (#66)
Born on December 6, 1950 in Tampa, FL
6'4" and 240 pounds
Defensive End　　　　　　1973
Tackled OJ Simpson for a 1 yard loss on the last play, limiting him to only 250 yards rushing, on 09-16-73
2 games (on Sept. 16th and Oct. 21st)
Mississippi Valley State Delta Devil

DOUGLAS, David (#67)
Born on March 20, 1963 in Spring City, TN
6'4" and 280 pounds
Offensive Lineman　　　　1989-90
16 games
Tennessee Volunteer

DOWLING, Brian (#14) *"B.D."*
Born on April 1, 1947 in Cleveland, OH
6'2" and 210 pounds
Quarterback　　　　　　1972-73
29 completions for 383 yards + 2 TDs and 7 carries for 35 yards + 3 TDs
Threw a TD pass to Running Back John Tarver and WR Bob Reynolds
Recovered Dennis Wirgowski's poor snap on Mike Walker's FGA in their 31-7 loss to the Bengals on 09-17-72
Longest completion was a 42 yard pass to Carl Garrett in their 33-3 loss to the Steelers on 10-22-72
Longest run for 11 yards in their 45-21 loss to the Denver Broncos on 12-17-72
Holder for Mike Walker, Charlie Gogolak, Bill Bell and Jeff White
25 games
Yale Bulldog

DOWLING, Ras-I (#21)
Born on May 9, 1988 in Chesapeake, VA
6'1" and 198 pounds
Cornerback   2011-12
9 games/2 started
#33 Pick in the 2011 NFL Draft
Virginia Cavalier

DRESSLER, Doug (#44)
Born on August 19, 1948 in Beaver Falls, PA
6'3" and 228 pounds
Running Back   1975
3 carries for 8 yards and 1 reception for a loss of 1 yard
Longest run for 6 yards in their 36-7 loss to the New York Jets on 10-05-75
Caught a pass from Steve Grogan for a 1 yard loss in their 36-7 loss to the NY Jets on 10-05-75
5 games
California State Wildcat

DUKES, Mike (#54) *"The Moon Man"*
Born on March 16, 1936 in Louisville, KY
6'3" and 235 pounds
Linebacker (KR)   1964-65
4 sacks, 2 interceptions for 16 yards, 4 fumble recoveries and 5 kickoff returns for 78 yards
Shared in a sack of Joe Namath, sacked Dick Wood 1 ½ times and had 2 sacks of Mickey Slaughter
Intercepted Dick Wood and John Hadl
Recovered fumbles by John Hadl, Hagood Clarke, Joe Namath and Cookie Gilchrist
Had a 6 yard return of a pass by Dick Wood in their 26-10 win over the New York Jets on 09-27-64
Longest was a 20 yard return of a kickoff by Herb Travenio in their 13-13 tie with San Diego on 10-17-65
Had a 10 yard return of a pass by John Hadl in their 22-6 win over the San Diego Chargers on 10-31-65
25 games
Clemson Tiger

DULAC, Bill (#68)
Born on January 15, 1951 in Detroit, MI
6'4" and 250 pounds
Guard   1974-75
Recovered a fumble by Leon McQuay and a fumbled punt return by Darryl Stingley
26 games/2 started
Eastern Michigan Huron

DUMLER, Doug (#58)
Born on December 15, 1950 in Hoisington, KS
6'3" and 243 pounds
Center   1973-75
42 games/3 started
#108 pick in the 1973 NFL Draft
Nebraska Cornhusker

DUPARD, Jon "Reggie" (#21)
Born on October 30, 1963 in New Orleans, LA
5'11" and 206 pounds
RB/KR   1986-89
186 carries for 571 yards + 6 TDs, 43 receptions for 303 yards and 7 kickoff returns for 111 yards
Longest was a 21 yard return of a kickoff by Morton Andersen in their 21-20 win over the Saints on 11-30-86
Had another 21 yard return of a kickoff by Roger Ruzik in their 23-17 OT loss to Dallas on 11-15-87
Longest run for 49 yards in their 31-20 loss to the Denver Broncos on 12-06-87
Recovered Doug Flutie's fumble in their 45-3 loss to the Green Bay Packers on 10-09-88
Ran for a 4 yard game winning TD to beat the New York Jets 27-24 on 09-10-89
Longest reception was a 45 yard pass from Tony Eason in their 24-10 loss to Miami on 09-17-89
Received a lateral from Doug Flutie, after his 7 yard run, in their 31-10 loss to Buffalo on 10-01-89
37 Regular Season Games/7 started and 1 Playoff Game (on 01-04-87)
5 carries for 18 yards in their 22-17 Divisional Playoff Game loss to Denver on 01-04-87
#26 pick in the 1986 NFL Draft
SMU Mustang

DURKO, Sandy (#22)
Born on August 29, 1948 in Los Angeles, CA
6'1" and 185 pounds
DB/PR   1973-74
3 interceptions for 26 yards and 4 punt returns for 22 yards
Had an 8 yard return of a blocked punt and recovered an onside kick
Intercepted Bill Demory, Dan Fouts and Marty Domres
Co-recovered a blocked punt (w/Art Moore) and returned it 8 yards in their 9-7 loss to the NY Jets on 10-14-73
Longest was a 15 yard return of a punt by Tom ONeil in their 24-23 loss to the Eagles on 11-04-73
Had a career long 16 yard return of a pass by Dan Fouts in their 30-14 win over the San Diego Chargers
          on 12-02-73
Recovered an onside kick by Garo Yepremian in their 34-24 win over Miami on 09-15-74
25 games/18 started
USC Trojan

DWIGHT JR., Tim (#86)
Born on July 13, 1975 in Iowa City, IA
5'8" and 180 pounds
WR/PR/KR   2005
19 receptions for 332 yards + 3 TDs and 4 carries for 11 yards
32 punt returns for 273 yards and 10 kickoff returns for 250 yards
Caught 2 TD passes from Tom Brady and 1 TD pass from Matt Cassel
Longest was a 29 yard return of a punt by Hunter Smith in their 40-21 loss to the Colts on 11-07-05
Longest reception was a 59 yard pass from Tom Brady in their 23-16 win over Miami on 11-13-05
Longest run for 12 yards in their 26-16 loss to the Kansas City Chiefs on 11-27-05
Longest was a 38 yard return of a kickoff by Olindo Mare in their 28-26 loss to Miami on 01-01-06
16 Regular Season Games/1 started (on 11-20-05) and 2 Playoff Games
7 punt returns for 68 yards in the playoffs
Iowa Hawkeye

DYKES, Hart Lee (#88)
Born on September 2, 1966 in Bay City, TX
6'4" and 218 pounds
Wide Receiver   1989-90
83 receptions for 1,344 yards + 7 TDs and recovered an onside kick by the Patriots
Caught 1 TD pass from Tony Eason, 2 TD passes from Marc Wilson and 4 TD passes from Steve Grogan
Recovered an onside kick by his Teammate Jason Staurovsky in their 28-24 loss to the Saints on 11-12-89
Longest reception was a 42 yard pass from Marc Wilson in their 22-16 win over the Colts on 12-03-89
26 games/16 started
#16 pick in the 1989 NFL Draft
Won the National Punt, Pass and Kick Competition as a young man
Oklahoma State Cowboy

EASLEY, Dominique (#74 and #99)
Born on April 28, 1992 in Staten Island, NY
6'2" and 263 pounds
Defensive Lineman   2014-15
Wore #74 in 2014 and #99 in 2015
3 sacks and 1 interception
Shared in a sack of Andrew Luck and Tyrod Taylor and sacked Jay Cutler and Brian Hoyer
Intercepted a pass by Matt Cassel in their 30-7 win over the Vikings on 09-14-14
22 games/3 started
Member of the 2014 World Championship Team
#29 pick in the 2014 NFL Draft
Florida Gator

EASON IV, Charles "Tony" (#11)
Born on October 8, 1959 in Blythe, CA
6'4" and 212 pounds
Quarterback   1983-89
876 completions for 10,732 yards + 60 TDs and 126 carries for 474 yards + 6 TDs
Tossed 1 TD pass to Craig James, Bo Robinson and Hart Lee Dykes
Completed 2 Regular Season TD passes to Willie Scott, Tony Collins and Clarence Weathers
Tossed 3 Regular Season TD passes to Greg Baty and Lin Dawson and 4 TD passes to Cedric Jones
Completed 5 TD passes to Stephen Starring and 8 Regular Season TD passes to Derrick Ramsey
Tossed 10 TD passes to Irving Fryar and 18 Regular Season TD passes to Stanley Morgan
Completed 1 Post Season TD pass to Lin Dawson, Tony Collins, Derrick Ramsey and Robert Weathers
Tossed 3 Post Season TD passes to Stanley Morgan
Threw a career long 90 yard TD pass to Craig James in their 20-7 loss to the Bears on 09-15-85
Tossed a 50 yard TD to Stanley Morgan in their 34-23 playoff clinching win vs the Bengals on 12-22-85
Completed a 25 yard "Hail Mary" TD to Irving Fryar in their 30-28 win over the LA Rams on 11-16-86
Threw a 13 yard Game Winning TD pass to Greg Baty in their 22-19 win over Buffalo on 11-23-86
Longest run for 26 yards in their 30-28 comeback win over the LA Rams on 11-16-86
AFC Offensive Player of the Week in their 38-23 comeback win vs Seattle on 09-16-84
AFC Offensive Player of the Week in their last second 30-28 win vs the Rams on 11-16-86
Advanced a fumble by John Stephens 2 yards in their 10-7 Overtime win vs the Buccaneers on 12-11-88
Holder for Tony Franklin and Fred Steinfort
72 Regular Season Games/49 started and 5 Playoff Games/5 started
42 completions for 561 yards + 7 TDs in the playoffs and 14 carries for 26 yards in the playoffs
Threw a 36 yard TD pass to Stanley Morgan in their 26-14 Wild Card win over the Jets on 12-28-85
Threw a 13 yard TD pass to Lin Dawson in their 27-20 Divisional win over the LA Raiders on 01-05-86
Tossed a 4 yard TD pass to Tony Collins in their 31-14 Championship win over the Miami on 01-12-86
Fired a 1 yard TD pass to Derrick Ramsey in their 31-14 Championship win over Miami on 01-12-86
Lofted a 2 yard TD pass to Robert Weathers in their 31-14 Championship win over Miami on 01-12-86
Threw a 19 yard TD pass to Stanley Morgan in their 22-17 Divisional loss to the Broncos on 01-04-87
Threw a 45 yard Flea Flicker TD pass to Stanley Morgan in their 22-17 Divisional loss to Denver on 01-04-87
#15 pick in the 1983 NFL Draft
Illinois Fighting Illini

EATON, Chad (#90)
Born on April 6, 1972 in Exeter, NH
6'5" and 303 pounds
DL (KR)   1996-2000
14 sacks, blocked 3 field goal attempts and had 4 fumble recoveries for 53 yards + 1 TD
Sacked Sean Salisbury, Jim Harbaugh, Vinny Testaverde, Dan Marino, Damon Huard and Brian Griese
Sacked Charlie Batch and had 2 sacks of Doug Flutie and Elvis Grbac and 3 sacks of Kordell Stewart
Recovered fumbles by Steve Bono, Damon Huard, Jonathan Linton and Tony Banks
Had a 13 yard return of a kickoff by Craig Hentrich in their 27-16 win over Tennessee on 09-20-98
Blocked a 38 yard field goal attempt by John Hall in their 24-14 loss to the Jets on 10-19-98
AFC Defensive Player of the Week in their 23-9 win over Pittsburgh on 12-06-98
AFC Special Team Player of the Week in their 13-10 OT victory vs Buffalo on 12-17-00
Had a career long 30 yard return of a fumble by Jonathan Linton in their 13-10 OT loss to Buffalo on 12-26-99
Had a 23 yard TD return of a fumble by Tony Banks in their 20-3 rout of the Ravens on 01-02-00
Blocked a 23 yard field goal attempt by Steve Christie in their 13-10 OT win over the Bills on 12-17-00
Blocked a 30 yard field goal attempt by Steve Christie in their 13-10 OT win over Buffalo on 12-17-00
65 Regular Season games/44 started and 6 Playoff Games/1 started (on 01-03-99)
Shared in a sack of Mike Tomczak in their 28-3 Divisional win over the Steelers on 01-05-97
Washington State Cougar

EBNER, Nate (#43) *"Leonidas"*
Born on December 14, 1988 in Dublin, OH
6'0" and 215 pounds
DB/ST (K)   2012-19
Nicknamed "Leonidas" (Greek Warrior King) because of his intense workout regiment
3 fumble recoveries, 1 carry for 14 yards, 1 onside kick, 1 free kick of 24 yards and blocked a punt
Fell on Tony Carter's muffed punt return in Overtime in their 34-31 OT win vs Denver on 11-24-13
Fell on John Denney's poor snap, which deflected off the facemask of Brandon Fields, on a FGA on 12-15-13
Had a 24 yard (drop) kickoff and an onside kick in their 35-28 loss to the Philadelphia Eagles on 12-06-15
Recovered a fumbled kickoff return by Cyrus Jones in their 31-24 loss to Seattle on 11-13-16
Ran for a 14 yard gain on a fake punt play in their 35-17 win over the Dolphins on 11-26-17
Blocked a punt by Dustin Colquitt in their 23-16 loss to the Chiefs on 12-08-19
111 Regular Season Games and 16 Playoff Games
Member of the 2014, 2016 and 2018 World Championship Teams
Member of the 2016 USA Olympic Rugby Team
Ohio State Buckeye

ECKEL, Kyle (#38)
Born on December 30, 1981 in Philadelphia, PA
5'11" and 237 pounds
RB/Special Team   2007
33 carries for 90 yards + 2 TDs
Longest run for 14 yards in their 56-10 demolition of the Buffalo Bills on 11-18-07
Caught a 6 yard pass from Tom Brady in their 56-10 rout of the Bills on 11-18-07
12 Regular Season Games and 1 Playoff Game (on 01-20-08)
Navy Midshipman

EDDS, Andrew "A.J." (#90)
Born on September 18, 1987 in Marion, IN
6'4" and 246 pounds
Special Team   2011
2 games (on Sept. 12th and Sept. 18th)
Iowa Hawkeye

EDELMAN, Julian (#11) *"Jules, Minitron* and *Squirrel"*
Born on May 22, 1986 in Redwood City, CA
5'10" and 198 pounds
WR/PR/KR/DB   2009-19
599 receptions for 6,507 yards + 36 TDs, 56 carries for 391 yards and 4 completions for 90 yards + 1 TD
177 punt returns for 1,986 yards + 4 TDs, 30 kickoff returns for 626 yards and caught three 2 point receptions
Caught 36 Regular Season TD passes and 5 Post Season TD passes from Tom Brady
Had a career long 94 yard TD return of a punt by Brandon Fields in their 38-7 rout of Miami on 01-02-11
Longest was a 37 yard return of a kickoff by Dan Carpenter in their 38-24 win over Miami on 09-12-11
Returned a punt by Dustin Colquit 72 yards for a TD in their 34-3 rout of the Chiefs on 11-21-11
Advanced his own fumbled punt return 8 yards in their 31-24 win over the Colts on 12-04-11
Returned a punt by Pat McAfee 68 yards for a TD in their 59-24 rout of the Colts on 11-18-12
Longest run for 47 yards in their 59-24 rout of the Indianapolis Colts on 11-18-12
Returned Joe McNight's fumbled kickoff return 22 yards for a TD in their 49-19 win over the Jets on 11-22-12
Advanced his own fumbled punt return 8 yards in their 34-31 OT win vs the Broncos on 11-24-13
Caught a 2 point pass from Tom Brady in their 27-26 comeback win over the Browns on 12-08-13
Caught a 2 point pass from Tom Brady in their 34-20 win over the Buffalo Bills on 12-29-13
Advanced his own fumbled punt return 2 yards in their 33-20 loss to the Dolphins on 09-07-14
Returned a punt by Britton Colquit 84 yards for a TD in their 43-21 rout of the Broncos on 11-02-14
Recovered Tom Brady's fumble, after being strip sacked, in their 30-6 win over the Cowboys on 10-11-15
Returned a free kick by Britton Colquitt 9 yards in their 33-13 win over Cleveland on 10-09-16
Returned a free kick by Kevin Huber 16 yards in their 35-17 win over Cincinnati on 10-16-16
Returned a free kick by Sam Koch 19 yards in their 30-23 win over Baltimore on 12-12-16
Caught a career long 77 yard TD pass from Tom Brady in their 35-14 rout of the Dolphins on 01-01-17
Caught a 2 point pass from Tom Brady in their 35-14 win over the Miami Dolphins on 01-01-17
Longest completion was a 37 yard pass to James White in their 31-17 win over GB on 11-04-18
Tossed a 6 yard pass to Tom Brady in their 34-10 loss to the Tennessee Titans on 11-11-18
Tossed a 15 yard TD pass to Phillip Dorsett in their 17-10 win over the Eagles on 11-17-19
Caught a 2 point pass from Tom Brady in their 24-17 win over the Buffalo Bills on 12-22-19
Played in 8 games as a defensive back in 2011
AFC Special Team Player of the Week in their 34-3 rout of Kansas City on 11-21-11
AFC Special Team Player of the Week in their 43-21 rout of Denver on 11-02-14
AFC Offensive Player of the Week in their 35-14 rout of Miami on 01-01-17
AFC Pro Bowl Wide Receiver in 2014
131 Regular Season Gaames/84 started and 19 Playoff Games/15 started
118 receptions for 1,442 yards + 5 TDs, 11 carries for 81 yards + 1 TD and threw a 51 yard TD pass in the playoffs
39 punt returns for 443 yards and 4 kickoff returns for 83 yards in the playoffs
Caught a 6 yard TD pass from Tom Brady in their 33-14 Wild Card loss to the Ravens on 01-10-10
Caught a 1 yard TD pass from Tom Brady in their 33-14 Wild Card loss to the Ravens on 01-10-10
Caught a 7 yard TD pass from Tom Brady in their 26-16 AFC Championship loss to Denver on 01-11-14
Recovered his own fumble in their 35-31 Divisional comeback win over the Ravens on 01-10-15
Caught a lateral from Tom Brady + threw a 51 yard TD pass to Danny Amendola in Divisional win on 01-10-15
Caught a 3 yard TD pass from Tom Brady in their 28-24 Super Bowl win over Seattle on 02-01-15
Caught a 10 yard TD pass from Tom Brady in their 36-17 AFC Championship Rout of the Steelers on 01-22-17
Made a huge double catch of a pass that deflected off Robert Alford in their Super Bowl win vs Atlanta on 02-05-17
Ran for a 5 yard TD in their 20-13 Wild Card Playoff Loss to the Tennessee Titans on 01-04-20
Member of the 2014, 2016 and 2018 World Championship Teams
Super Bowl LIII MVP
#232 pick in the 2009 NFL Draft
Kent State Golden Flash

EDMUNDS, George "Randy" (#51)
Born on June 24, 1946 in Washington, GA
6'2" and 220 pounds
Special Team   1971
Recovered Hubert Ginn's fumbled kickoff return in their 34-13 win over Miami on 12-05-71
14 games
Georgia Tech Yellow Jacket

EDWARDS, Marc (#44)
Born on November 17, 1974 in Cincinnati, OH
6'0" and 249 pounds
FB (KR)   2001-02
82 carries for 237 yards + 1 TD, 48 receptions for 362 yards + 2 TDs and 4 kickoff returns for 50 yards
Longest was a 23 yard return of a kickoff by Hunter Smith in their 44-13 win over the Colts on 09-30-01
Advanced Tom Brady's fumble 2 yards in their 29-26 OT win vs the San Diego Chargers on 10-14-01
Snared a 15 yard TD from Tom Brady in their 24-10 win over Atlanta on 11-04-01
Caught a 2 yard TD pass from Tom Brady in their 34-17 win over the Saints on 11-25-01
Ran for a 4 yard touchdown in their 17-16 victory over the Jets on 12-02-01
Longest reception was a 27 yard pass from Tom Brady in their 24-17 win over the Vikings on 11-24-02
Longest run for 17 yards in their 20-12 win over the Lions on 11-28-02
32 Regular Season games/23 started and 3 Playoff Games/3 started
3 carries for 8 yards and 9 receptions for 62 yards in the playoffs
Member of the 2001 World Championship Team
Notre Dame Fighting Irish

EDWARDS III, Robert (#47)
Born on October 2, 1974 in Tennille, GA
5'11" and 218 pounds
Running Back   1998
291 carries for 1,115 yards + 9 TDs and 35 receptions for 331 yards + 3 TDs
Caught 1 TD pass from Scott Zolak and 2 TD passes from Drew Bledsoe
Longest run for 53 yards in their 27-16 win over Tennessee on 09-20-98
Had another run of 53 yards in their 32-18 loss to the St. Louis Rams on 12-13-98
Longest reception was a 46 yard pass from Drew Bledsoe in their 26-23 win over Miami on 11-23-98
16 Regular Season Games/15 started and 1 Playoff Game/1 started (on 01-03-99)
17 carries for 28 yards + 1 TD and 3 receptions for 33 yards in the playoffs
Ran for a 1 yard TD in their 25-10 Wild Card Playoff Game loss to the Jaguars on 01-03-99
#18 pick in the 1998 NFL Draft
Georgia Bulldog

EDWARDS, Tim (#98)
Born on August 29, 1968 in Philadelphia, MS
6'1" and 270 pounds
Defensive Tackle   1992
Sacked Jim Kelly in their 16-7 loss to the Buffalo Bills on 11-01-92
14 games
#307 pick in the 1991 NFL Draft
Delta State Statesman

EGU, Okechukwu "Patrick" (#33)
Born on February 20, 1967 in Owerri, Nigeria
5'11" and 205 pounds
RB/KR   1989
3 carries for 20 yards + 1 TD and 2 kickoff returns for 26 yards
Longest run was a 15 yard TD, on his 1st carry in the NFL, in their 33-24 win over Buffalo on 11-19-89
Longest was a 22 yard return of a kickoff by Gary Anderson in their 28-10 loss to Pittsburgh on 12-17-89
7 games
Nevada Reno Wolf Pack

EISENHAUER, Larry (#72) *"Wildman"*
Born on February 22, 1940 in Hicksville, NY
6'5" and 250 pounds
Defensive End   1961-69
Nicknamed *"Wild Man"* because of his pre-game tactics
45 sacks, 1 interception, 12 fumble recoveries for 19 yards and 1 blocked field goal attempt
Shared in a sack of Johnny Green, Dick Wood and Cotton Davidson
Sacked Frank Tripucka, Butch Songin, Harold Stephens, Tobin Rote, Max Choboian, Pete Beathard
        and Bob Griese
Had 1 ½ sacks of Joe Namath and 2 sacks of Steve Tensi and Daryle Lamonica
Had 3 sacks of Tom Flores, Mickey Slaughter, Dick Wood and George Blanda
Had 3 ½ sacks of Len Dawson, 4 sacks of Jack Kemp, 5 ½ sacks of Jacky Lee and 6 sacks of Don Trull
Recovered fumbles by Warren Rabb, Len Dawson, Eddie Wilson, Daryle Lamonica, Charley Mitchell
        and Joe Auer
Recovered Gene Mingo's lateraled fumble in their 45-17 rout of the Denver Broncos on 09-16-61
Strip sacked John Hadl and returned the fumble 9 yards in their 20-14 win vs the Chargers on 12-09-62
Strip sacked Tom Flores and returned the fumble 7 yards in their 20-14 win vs the Raiders on 10-11-63
Intercepted a pass by Jack Kemp in their 17-7 win over the Buffalo Bills on 12-01-63
Strip sacked and recovered George Blanda's fumble in their 34-17 win over the Oilers on 11-29-64
Blocked a 35 yard field goal attempt by Herb Travenio in their 22-6 win over San Diego on 10-31-65
Recovered his own blocked field goal in their 22-6 win over the San Diego Chargers on 10-31-65
Had a 3 yard return of a fumble by Joe Auer in their 41-10 rout of the Dolphins on 10-15-67
AFL Defensive Player of the Week in their 23-0 shutout of the Bills on 09-24-67
AFL All Star Defensive End in 1962, 1963, 1964, 1966
First Team All Pro Defensive End in 1962, 1963, 1964
115 Regular Season Games/114 started and 2 Playoff Games/2 started
Recovered a fumble by Paul Lowe in their 51-10 AFL Championship Game loss to San Diego on 01-05-64
6th Round Draft Pick in 1961
Boston College Eagle

EITZMANN, Chris (#46)
Born on April 1, 1977 in Belleville, KS
6'5" and 255 pounds
Tight End   2000
5 games/1 started (on 11-12-00)
Harvard Crimson

ELLARD, Henry (#18)

Born on July 21, 1961 in Fresno, CA
5'11" and 180 pounds
Wide Receiver   1998
5 receptions for 86 yards
Longest reception was a 19 yard pass from Drew Bledsoe in their 21-16 win over the Colts on 11-01-98
5 games
Qualified for the 1992 USA Olympic Track Team in the Triple Jump
Fresno State Bulldog

ELLIS, Edward (#66)

Born on October 13, 1975 in New Haven, CT
6'5" and 325 pounds
Tackle   1997-99
9 games/1 started (on 09-19-99)
#125 pick in 1997 NFL Draft
Buffalo Bull

ELLIS, MeShaunda "Shaun" (#94)

Born on June 24, 1977 in Anderson, SC
6'5" and 285 pounds
Defensive End   2011
Sacked Matt Moore in their 27-24 win over the Dolphins on 12-24-11
14 Regular Season games/10 started and 3 Playoff Games
Sacked Tim Tebow in their 45-10 Divisional Playoff rout of the Denver Broncos on 01-14-12
Tennessee Volunteer

ELLISON, Jerry (#35)

Born on December 20, 1971 in Augusta, GA
5'10" and 204 pounds
RB (KR)   1999
2 carries for 10 yards, 4 receptions for 50 yards and 1 kickoff return for 13 yards
Longest run for 8 yards in their 27-3 rout of the Arizona Cardinals on 10-31-99
Longest reception was a 23 yard pass from Drew Bledsoe in their 24-9 loss to the Eagles on 12-19-99
Had a 13 yard return of a kickoff by David Akers in their 24-9 loss to Philadelphia on 12-19-99
12 games
Tennessee Chattanooga Moccasin

ELUEMUNOR, Jermaine (#65)

Born on December 13, 1994 in London, England
6'4" and 335 pounds
Guard   2019--
10 games
Texas A & M Aggie

EMANUEL, Bert (#87)

Born on October 26, 1970 in Kansas City, MO
5'10" and 180 pounds
Wide Receiver   2001
4 receptions for 25 yards
Longest reception was a 16 yard pass from Drew Bledsoe in their 23-17 loss to the Bengals on 09-09-01
2 games/1 started (on 09-09-01)
Member of the 2001 World Championship Team
Rice Owl

EVANS, Bryan "Heath" (#44)
Born on December 30, 1978 in West Palm Beach, FL
6'0" and 245 pounds
Fullback (KR)　　　　　　　2005-08
123 carries for 455 yards + 3 TDs, 24 receptions for 224 yards + 1 TD and 1 kickoff return for 13 yards
Ran for a 2 point conversion in their 23-16 win over the Dolphins on 11-13-05
Caught a 1 yard TD pass from Tom Brady in their 20-10 win over the Dolphins on 10-08-06
Longest run for 35 yards in their 31-7 win over the Vikings on 10-30-06
Longest reception was a 29 yard pass from Tom Brady in their 49-28 rout of the Dolphins on 10-21-07
Had a 13 yard return of a kickoff by Matt Stover in their 27-24 win over the Ravens on 12-03-07
54 Regular Season games/9 started and 7 Playoff Games
5 carries for 13 yards and 6 receptions for 49 yards in the playoffs
Auburn Tiger

FAIRCHILD, Paul (#66)
Born on September 14, 1961 in Carroll, IA
6'4" and 270 pounds
Guard　　　　　　　1984-90
83 Regular Season Games/38 started and 5 Playoff Games
#124 pick in the 1984 NFL Draft
Kansas Jayhawk

FALCON, Theodore "Terry" (#68)
Born on August 30, 1955 in Culbertson, MT
6'3" and 260 pounds
Special Team　　　　　　　1978-79
18 Regular Season Games and 1 Playoff Game (on 12-31-78)
#198 pick in the 1978 NFL Draft
Montana Grizzly

FARMER, Lonnie (#55)
Born on March 28, 1940 in Steubenville, OH
6'0" and 220 pounds
Linebacker　　　　　　　1964-66
3 sacks, 1 interception for 16 yards and 1 fumble recovery
Shared in a sack of Len Dawson and Buddy Humphrey and sacked Mickey Slaughter and Don Trull
Had a 16 yard return of a pass by Jack Kemp in their 24-7 loss to Buffalo on 09-11-65
Recovered Daryle Lamonica's fumble in their 14-3 win over Buffalo on 12-04-66
31 games
20th Round Draft Pick in 1964
Tennessee Chattanooga Moccasin

FARRELL, Sean (#62) *"Dirty"*
Born on May 25, 1960 in Southampton, NY
6'3" and 260 pounds
Left Guard　　　　　　　1987-89
Caught a Doug Flutie pass, deflected by Joe Nash, for a 4 yard gain, in their 13-7 win vs Seattle on 12-04-88
43 games/43 started
Penn State Nittany Lion

FAULK, Kevin (#33) *"Swiss Army Knife"*
Born on June 5, 1976 in Lafayette, LA
5'8" and 202 pounds
RB/KR/PR   1999-2011
864 carries for 3,607 yards + 16 TDs, 431 receptions for 3,701 yards + 15 TDs and 2 completions for 23 yards
181 kickoff returns for 4,098 yards + 2 TDs and 101 punt returns for 943 yards
Caught 2 TD passes from Drew Bledsoe and 3 TD passes from Matt Cassel
Caught 10 Regular Season TD passes and 1 Post Season TD pass from Tom Brady
Longest was a 95 yard return of a kickoff by John Hall in their 24-17 loss to the Jets on 11-15-99
Ran for a 2 point conversion in their 19-11 loss to the Cleveland Browns on 11-12-00
Hauled in a career long 52 yard TD pass from Drew Bledsoe in their 27-24 loss to Miami on 12-24-00
Completed a 23 yard pass to Tom Brady in their 20-13 win over the Dolphins on 12-22-01
Longest run was a 45 yard TD in their 38-7 rout of the Detroit Lions on 11-03-02
Returned a kickoff by Sebastian Janikowski 86 yards for a TD in their 27-20 loss to Oakland on 11-17-02
Returned a kickoff by John Hall 87 yards for a TD in their 30-17 loss to the Jets on 12-22-02
Returned Brian Moorman's free kick 23 yards in their 19-17 win over Buffalo on 09-10-06
Longest was a 43 yard return of a punt by Kyle Larson in their 38-13 win over the Bengals on 10-01-06
Completed a pass to Wes Welker for a 2 yard loss in their 18-15 loss to the Colts on 11-02-08
161 Regular Season Games/47 started and 19 Playoff Games/4 started
88 carries for 425 yards, ran for 2 Two point conversions and 51 receptions for 412 yards + 1 TD in the playoffs
2 kickoff returns for 30 yards and 1 punt return for no gain in the playoffs
Caught a 7 yard TD pass from Tom Brady in their 37-16 Wild Card win over the Jets on 01-07-07
Ran for 2 points in their 24-21 Divisional Playoff win over the San Diego Chargers on 01-14-07
Ran for 2 points in their 32-29 Super Bowl win over the Carolina Panthers on 02-01-04
Member of the 2001, 2003 and 2004 World Championship Teams
#46 pick in the 1999 NFL Draft
Inducted into the Patriots Hall of Fame on 08-01-16
Ron Burton Community Service Award in 2009
LSU Fighting Tiger

FAURIA, Christian (#88)
Born on September 22, 1971 in Northbridge, CA
6'4" and 250 pounds
Tight End (KR/DB)   2002-05
79 receptions for 790 yards + 13 TDs
Caught 13 TD passes and a two point pass from Tom Brady
Recovered 1 onside kick in the Regular Season and 3 onside kicks in the playoffs
Longest reception (tie) was a 33 yard pass from Tom Brady in their 27-20 loss to Oakland on 11-17-02
Longest reception (tie) was a 33 yard pass from Tom Brady in their 27-17 win over Buffalo on 12-08-02
Caught a 2 point conversion pass from Tom Brady in their 27-24 OT win vs the Dolphins on 12-29-02
Recovered an onside kick by Craig Hentrich in their 38-30 victory over Tennessee on 10-05-03
Recovered Corey Dillon's fumble in their 23-7 victory over the New York Jets on 12-26-04
Used as an extra defensive back on hail mary passing plays in 3 games during the 2004 season
64 Regular Season Games/45 started and 8 Playoff Games/3 started
6 receptions for 76 yards in the playoffs and 3 onside kick recoveries in the playoffs
Recovered Mike Vanderjagt's onside kick in their 24-14 Championip win over the Colts on 01-18-04
Recovered Jeff Reed's onside kick in their 41-27 Championship win over the Steelers on 01-23-05
Recovered David Akers' onside kick in their 24-21 Super Bowl win over the Eagles on 02-06-05
Member of the 2003 and 2004 World Championship Teams
Colorado Buffalo

FEACHER, Richard "Ricky" (#83)
Born on Feburary 11, 1954 in Crystal River, FL
5'10" and 174 pounds
WR/KR　　　　　　　1976
2 receptions for 38 yards and 10 kickoff returns for 240 yards
Longest reception was a 21 yard pass from Steve Grogan in their 27-13 loss to the Baltimore Colts on 09-12-76
Longest was a 46 yard return of Roy Gerela's opening kickoff in their 30-27 win over Pittsburgh on 09-26-76
3 games
#270 pick in the 1976 NFL Draft
Mississippi Valley State Delta Devil

FEAGLES, Jeff (#6)
Born on March 7, 1966 in Anaheim, CA
6'1" and 215 pounds
Punter　　　　　　　1988-89
154 punts for 5,874 yards
Recovered a poor snap in the end zone for a Vikings safety in 36-6 loss to Minn on 09-11-88
Longest punt was 74 yards in their 21-17 win over the Indianapolis Colts on 10-02-88
Recovered his own fumble and threw an incomplete pass in their 24-10 loss to Miami on 09-17-89
Had the longest punt in the NFL of 74 yards in 1988
32 games
Miami Hurricane

FEGGINS, Howard (#27)
Born on May 6, 1965 in South Hill, VA
5'10" and 190 pounds
Defensive Back　　　　1989
Returned a pass by Jack Trudeau 4 yards in their 22-16 victory over the Indianapolis Colts on 12-03-89
11 games
North Carolina Tar Heel

FELDHAUSEN, Paul (#66)
Born on June 14, 1946 in Provo, UT
6'6" and 260 pounds
Offensive Tackle　　　1968
2 games (on Dec. 8th and Dec.15th)
#238 pick in the 1968 NFL Draft
Northland College Lumberjack

FELLS, Daniel (#86)
Born on September 23, 1983 in Anaheim, CA
6'4" and 252 pounds
Tight End　　　　　　2012
4 receptions for 85 yards
Longest reception was a 35 yard pass from Tom Brady in their 24-23 loss to Seattle on 10-14-12
13 Regular Season Games/4 started and 1 Playoff Game (on 01-20-13)
UC Davis Aggie

FELT, Richard "Dick" (#24)
Born on March 3, 1933 in Provo, UT
6'1" and 185 pounds
Defensive Back   1962-66
12 interceptions for 199 yards, 2 fumble recoveries for 50 yards and blocked an extra point attempt
Intercepted Cotton Davidson, George Shaw, Charley Tolar, Mike Taliaferro, John McCormick and Pete Beathard
Had 3 interceptions of George Blanda and Dick Wood
Recovered fumbles by Tobin Rote and Johnny Olszewski
Had a 50 yard return of a fumble by Johnny Olszewski in their 41-16 rout of the Denver Broncos on 09-21-62
Had a career long 35 yard return of a pass by Dick Wood in their 38-14 win over the NY Jets on 09-08-63
Blocked an extra point attempt by Fletcher Smith in their 43-24 loss to the Chiefs on 09-25-66
AFL All Star Defensive Back in 1962
52 Regular Season Games/37 started and 2 Playoff Games
BYU Cougar

FERENTZ, James (#66)
Born on June 5, 1989 in Iowa City, IA
6'2" and 300 pounds
Center (FB)   2018-19
Used as a blocking Full Back in their 33-0 shutout of the Jets on 10-21-19
17 Regular Season Games/2 started and 1 Playoff Game
Member of the 2018 World Championship Team
Iowa Hawkeye

FERGUSON, Vasquero "Vagas" (#43)
Born on March 6, 1957 in Richmond, IN
6'1" and 204 pounds
Running Back   1980-82
290 carries for 1,163 yards + 5 TDs, 26 receptions for 212 yards and 1 fumble recovery
Longest run for 44 yards in their 34-0 shutout of the Miami Dolphins on 10-12-80
Recovered Harold Jackson's fumble in their 27-20 loss to the St. Louis Cardinals on 11-29-81
Longest reception was a 20 yard pass from Tom Owen in their 19-10 loss to the Bills on 12-13-81
31 games/21 started
#25 pick in the 1980 NFL Draft
Notre Dame Fighting Irish

FLEMING, Cameron (#71)
Born on September 3, 1992 in Fort Hood, TX
6'6" and 320 pounds
T/G (TE)   2014-17
Used as an eligible receiver and blocking tight end
47 Regular Season Games/20 started and 8 Playoff Games/2 started
Member of the 2014 and 2016 World Championship Teams
#140 pick in the 2014 NFL Draft
Stanford Cardinal

FLEMING, Darius (#58 and #53)
Born on July 19, 1989 in Chicago, IL
6'2" and 245 pounds
Linebacker   2014-15
Wore #58 in 2014 and #53 in 2015
11 Regular Season Games and 5 Playoff Games
Recovered a muffed punt return by Josh Cribbs in their 45-7 Championship rout of the Colts on 01-18-15
Member of the 2014 World Championship Team
Notre Dame Fighting Irish

FLETCHER, Bradley (#24)
Born on June 25, 1986 in Cleveland, OH
6'0" and 196 pounds
Cornerback   2015
Forced fumble by Percy Harvin in their 40-32 win over the Buffalo Bills on 09-20-15
2 games (on Sept. 10th and Sept. 20th)
Iowa Hawkeye

FLETCHER, Dane (#52)
Born on September 14, 1986 in Bozeman, MT
6'2" and 244 pounds
Linebacker   2010-13
4 sacks, 2 fumble recoveries for 1 yard, 1 interception and recovered an onside kick
Sacked Matt Flynn, Ryan Fitzpatrick, Ryan Tannehill and Ben Roethlisberger
Recovered C.J. Spiller's fumble and returned Quan Cosby's fumbled punt return 1 yard
Recovered an onside kick by Kris Brown in their 23-20 win over the Chargers on 10-24-10
Intercepted a pass by Ryan Fitzpatrick in their 34-3 rout of the Bills on 12-26-10
38 Regular Season Games/6 started and 6 Playoff Games
Montana State Bobcat

FLETCHER, Derrick (#64)
Born on September 9, 1975 in Houston, TX
6'6" and 348 pounds
Guard   2000
2 games/2 started (on Sept.3rd and Sept. 11th)
#154 pick in the 1999 NFL Draft
Baylor Bear

FLICK, Tom (#10)
Born on August 20, 1958 in Patuxent River, MD
6'2" and 190 pounds
Quarterback   1982
Holder for John Smith
3 games
Washington Husky

FLOWERS, Marquis (#59)
Born on February 16, 1992 in Independence, MO
6'2" and 245 pounds
Linebacker   2017
Recorded 1 sack of Bryce Petty and 2 ½ sacks of Tyrod Taylor
16 Regular Season Games/2 started and 3 Playoff Games
Sacked Marcus Mariota in their 35-14 Divisional Playoff Game win over Tennessee on 01-13-18
Arizona Wildcat

FLOWERS III, Robert "Trey" (#98) *"Technique and The Quiet Storm"*
Born on August 16, 1993 in Huntsville, AL
6'2" and 265 pounds
Defensive Lineman   2015-18
21 sacks and 2 fumble recoveries for a net loss of 3 yards
Shared in a sack of Andrew Luck, Ben Roethlisberger, Jamieson Winston, Derek Carr and Aaron Rodgers
Sacked Tyrod Taylor, EJ Manuel, Joe Flacco, Josh McCown, Kirk Cousins and Sam Darnold
Had 2 sacks of Russell Wilson, Trevor Siemian, Alex Smith, Matt Moore and Ryan Tannehill
Recorded 2 ½ sacks of Deshaun Watson
Recovered a fumble by Jay Ajayi in their 31-24 win over Miami on 09-18-16
Lost 3 yards returning Chris Long's strip sack of Ryan Fitzpatrick in their 22-17 win vs the Jets on 11-27-16
46 Regular Season Games/37 started and 9 Playoff Games/9 started
5.5 sacks in the playoffs
Sacked Matt Ryan *2.5 times* in their Epic 34-28 OT Super Bowl win over the Atlanta Falcons on 02-05-17
Sacked Marcus Mariota in their 35-14 Divisional rout of the Tennessee Titans on 01-13-18
Sacked Philip Rivers in their 41-28 Divisional win over the Los Angeles Chargers on 01-13-19
Sacked Patrick Mahomes in their 37-31 OT Championship win over the Kansas City Chiefs on 01-20-19
Member of the 2016 and 2018 World Championship Teams
#101 pick in the 2015 NFL Draft
Arkansas Razorback

FLOYD, Chris (#37)
Born on June 23, 1975 in Detroit, MI
6'2" and 231 pounds
Fullback   1998-2000
14 carries for 33 yards and 4 receptions for 43 yards
Longest run for 10 yards in their 24-21 win over the San Francisco 49ers on 12-20-98
Longest reception was a 21 yard pass from Drew Bledsoe in their 20-19 loss to the Jets on 09-11-00
40 Regular Season Games/2 started and 1 Playoff Game (on 01-03-99)
#81 pick in the 1998 NFL Draft
Michigan Wolverine

FLOYD, Michael (#14)
Born on November 27, 1989 in St. Paul, MN
6'3" and 220 pounds
Wide Receiver   2016
4 receptions for 42 yards + 1 TD
Longest reception was a 14 yard TD pass from Tom Brady in their 35-14 rout of the Dolphins on 01-01-17
2 Regular Season Games/1 started (on 01-01-17) and 1 Playoff Game/1 started (on 01-14-17)
Caught a 9 yard pass from Tom Brady in their 34-16 Divisional Playoff win over Houston on 01-14-17
Member of the 2016 World Championship Team
Notre Dame Fighting Irish

FLUTIE, Doug (#2)
Born on October 23, 1962 in Manchester, MD
5'10" and 180 pounds
Quarterback   1987-89 and 2005
148 completions for 1,871 yards + 11 TDs, 65 carries for 308 yards + 1 TD and kicked 1 extra point
Threw 1 TD pass to Larry Linne and 2 TD passes to Lin Dawson and Cedric Jones
Completed 3 TD passes to Irving Fryar and Stanley Morgan
Ran for a 13 yard game winning TD, to beat the Colts 21-17 at Sullivan Stadium on 10-02-88
AFC Offensive Player of the Week in their 21-17 win over Indianapolis on 10-02-88
AFC Special Team Player of the Week in their 28-26 loss to Miami on 01-01-06
Longest completion was an 80 yard TD to Irving Fryar, on the 1st play, in their 30-7 win vs Chicago on 10-30-88
Longest run for 22 yards in their 31-10 loss to the Buffalo Bills on 10-01-89
Lateraled to Reggie Dupard, on 4th + 1, for a 14 yard gain, in their 31-10 loss to the Buffalo Bills on 10-01-89
Drop kicked an extra point in their 28-26 loss to the Dolphins at Gillette Stadium on 01-01-06
22 games/13 started
Won Grey Cup Championships with the 1992 Calgary Stampeders and 1996-97 Toronto Argonauts
Boston College Eagle

FOLK, Nicholas "Nick" (#2)
Born on November 5, 1984 in Hollywood, CA
6'1" and 211 pounds
Kicker   2019--
14 field goals and 12 extra points
Longest field goal was 51 yards in their 24-17 win over Buffalo on 12-21-19
7 Regular Season Games and 1 Playoff Game (on 01-04-20)
Arizona Wildcat

FORBATH, Kai (#2)
Born on September 2, 1987 in Santa Monica, CA
5'11" and 197 pounds
Kicker   2019
Kicked 1 extra point and a 23 yard field goal in their 28-22 loss to Houston on 12-01-19
Only game played was on 12-01-19
UCLA Bruin

FOREMAN, Walter "Chuck" (#22)
Born on October 26, 1950 in Frederick, MD
6'2" and 210 pounds
Running Back   1980
23 carries for 63 yards + 1 TD and 14 receptions for 99 yards
Longest run for 7 yards in their 37-21 loss to the Atlanta Falcons on 09-14-80
Dove for a 1 yard TD, on 4th + 1, with 26 seconds left, in their 37-21 win over the Baltimore Colts on 10-19-80
Longest reception was an 18 yard pass from Steve Grogan in their 38-34 loss to the Houston Oilers on 11-10-80
16 games
Miami Hurricane

FORSTON, Marcus (#98)
Born on September 28, 1989 in Miami, FL
6'3" and 305 pounds
Defensive Lineman   2012-13
4 games
Miami Hurricane

FORTE, Donald "Ike" (#38)
Born on March 8, 1954 in Texarkana, AR
6'0" and 203 pounds
RB (PR)   1976-77
87 carries for 257 yards + 3 TDs, 11 receptions for 97 yards + 1 TD and 2 punt returns for 9 yards
Longest run for 26 yards in their 38-14 rout of the Denver Broncos on 11-28-76
Caught a 6 yard TD pass from Steve Grogan in their 27-6 rout of the New Orleans Saints on 12-05-76
Longest reception was a 22 yard pass from Steve Grogan in their 24-14 loss to the Buffalo Bills on 11-06-77
Longest was a 6 yard return of a punt by Marv Bateman in their 20-7 win over the Buffalo Bills on 11-20-77
23 games/1 started (on 10-31-76)
#35 pick in the 1976 NFL Draft
Arkansas Razorback

FOSTER, Darryll James "D.J." (#27)
Born on November 22, 1993 in Scottsdale, AZ
6'0" and 195 pounds
RB (KR)   2016
7 carries for 24 yards, 1 reception for 2 yards and 1 kickoff return for 30 yards
Longest run for 7 yards in their 31-24 win over the Dolphins on 09-18-16
Caught a 2 yard pass from Jimmy Garoppolo in their 31-24 win over Miami on 09-18-16
Had a 30 yard return of a kickoff by Mike Nugent in their 35-17 rout of the Bengals on 10-16-16
3 games
Member of the 2016 World Championship Team
Arizona State Sun Devil

FOSTER, William "Will" (#55)
Born on October 2, 1948 in Grady, AL
6'2" and 230 pounds
Linebacker   1973-74
2 fumble recoveries for 1 TD
Recovered a blocked punt in the end zone for a TD in their 9-7 loss to the Jets on 10-14-73
Recovered a fumbled kickoff return by Margene Adkins in their 33-13 loss to the Jets on 11-11-73
21 games/1 started on 10-28-73
Eastern Michigan Huron

FOX, Timothy "Tim" (#48) *"Foxie"*
Born on November 1, 1953 in Canton, OH
5'11" and 186 pounds
Safety   1976-81
17 interceptions for 215 yards, 4 sacks, 7 fumble recoveries and had a 7 yard return of a missed FGA
Recovered an onside kick, recorded a safety and blocked an extra point
Intercepted Joe Namath, Gary Marangi, Brian Sipe, Ron Jaworski, Steve Bartkowski and Scott Hunter
Intercepted David Whitehurst, Joe Ferguson, Vince Ferragamo, Bill Kenney, Ken Stabler and Bert Jones
Had 2 interceptions of Ken Anderson and 3 interceptions of Richard Todd
Recovered a fumble by Howard Satterwhite, Roland Hooks, Terry Miller and Jon Keyworth
Recovered 3 fumbles by Eddie Ray
Sacked Mike Livingston twice and recorded 1 sack of Bill Troup and Greg Landry
Had a career long 29 yard interception return of a pass by Gary Marangi in their 20-10 win vs Buffalo on 11-07-76
Strip sacked Mike Livingston and sacked Mike Livingston again in their 21-17 win over the Chiefs on 09-18-77
Returned a pass by Ron Jaworski 27 yards, from the 1 yard line, in their 14-6 win over the Eagles on 11-27-77
Recovered Ove Johansson's onside kick in their 14-6 win over the Eagles on 11-27-77
Returned a pass by Steve Bartkowski 5 yards to help seal their 16-10 win over Atlanta on 12-04-77
Picked off a pass by Ken Anderson, with 13 ticks left, in their 10-3 win over the Bengals on 10-15-78
Forced Punter Rusty Jackson out of the end zone for a safety in their 26-24 win over Buffalo on 12-10-78
Blocked an extra point attempt by Chester Marcol in their 27-14 loss to Green Bay on 10-01-79
Had a 7 yard return on Fred Steinfort's 73 yard missed FGA in their 23-14 win over Denver on 09-29-80
AFC Pro Bowl Safety in 1980
91 Regular Season Games/91 started and 2 Playoff Games/2 started
Picked off a pass by Dan Pastorini in their 31-14 Divisional loss to the Houston Oilers at Schaefer on 12-31-78
#21 pick in the 1976 NFL Draft
Broke Dennis Quaid's collarbone while filming the most dramatic shot of the Movie "Everybody's All American"
Ohio State Buckeye

FRAIN, Todd (#44 and #85)
Born on January 31, 1962 in Council Bluffs, IA
6'2" and 240 pounds
Tight End   1987
Wore # 44 on 10-04-87 and #85 on 10-11-87 and 10-18-87
2 receptions for 22 yards
Caught an 11 yard pass from Bob Bleier in their 20-10 loss to Cleveland on 10-04-87
Caught an 11 yard pass from Bob Bleier in their 14-7 win over Buffalo on 10-11-87
3 games/2 started
Nebraska Cornhusker

FRANCIS, Justin (#94)
Born on February 8, 1989 in Opa-Locka, FL
6'2" and 270 pounds
Defensive Lineman   2012
Sacked Ryan Tannehill *3 times* in their 28-0 shutout of the Dolphins on 12-30-12
10 Regular Season Games and 2 Playoff Games/1 started (on 01-20-13)
Rutgers Scarlet Knight

FRANCIS, Russ (#81 and #49) *"All World Tight End"*
Born on April 3, 1953 in Seattle, WA
6'6" and 240 pounds
Tight End   1975-80 and 1987-88
Nicknamed the *"All World Tight End"* by Howard Cosell
Wore #81 from 1975-80, #49 on 12-28-87 and #81 again in 1988
207 receptions for 3,157 yards + 28 TDs, 2 carries for 12 yards and 1 fumble recovery
Caught 1 TD pass from Neil Graff and Jim Plunkett and 4 TD passes from Matt Cavanaugh
Caught 22 Regular Season TDs and 1 Post Season TD from Steve Grogan
Caught 1 Post Season TD pass from Tom Owen
Longest run was for 8 yards in their 41-7 rout of the NY Jets on 10-18-76
Recovered James McAllister's fumble in their 16-6 win over the St. Louis Cardinals on 09-10-78
Longest reception was a 53 yard pass from Steve Grogan in their 21-14 win over Oakland on 09-24-78
Caught a 5 yard TD from Steve Grogan in the 4th Qtr in their 27-21 win over Chargers on 09-23-79
AFC Pro Bowl Tight End in 1976, 1977, 1978
92 Regular Season Games/83 started and 2 Playoff Games/2 started
12 receptions for 197 yards + 2 TDs in the playoffs
Caught a 26 yard TD pass from Steve Grogan in their 24-21 Divisional loss to the Raiders on 12-18-76
Caught a 24 yard TD pass from Tom Owen in their 31-14 Divisional loss to the Oilers on 12-31-78
#16 pick in the 1975 NFL Draft
Oregon Duck

FRANKLIN, Arnold (#87)
Born on December 16, 1963 in Cincinnati, OH
6'3" and 246 pounds
Tight End   1987
3 games
North Carolina Tar Heel

FRANKLIN, Anthony "Tony" (#1)
Born on November 18, 1956 in Big Spring, TX
5'8" and 182 pounds
Kicker   1984-87
Kicked with a bare foot
Kicked 93 field goals and 163 extra points and lost 5 yards on a lateral
Kicked a career long 50 yard field goal in their 32-14 win over Tampa Bay on 10-27-85
Kicked a career long 50 yard field goal in their 23-6 rout of the Detroit Lions on 12-08-85
Lost 5 yards after getting lateral from Tony Eason, on a mishandled 51 yard FGA, on 11-17-85
Led the NFL with 32 field goals and 140 points scored in 1986
AFC Pro Bowl Kicker in 1986
62 Regular Season Games and 5 Playoff Games
Kicked 9 field goals and 12 extra points in the playoffs
Texas A & M Aggie

FRASER, Jim (#51)
Born on May 29, 1936 in Philadelphia, PA
6'3" and 236 pounds
Punter and Linebacker   1966
55 punts for 2,044 yards, 1 ½ sacks and 1 interception for 3 yards
Longest punt was 68 yards in their 24-10 win over the Broncos on 09-18-66
Sacked Jack Kemp in their 14-3 victory over the Buffalo Bills on 12-04-66
Had a 3 yard return of a pass by Jack Kemp in their 14-3 win over Buffalo on 12-04-66
Shared in a sack of Buddy Humphrey in their 38-14 victory over the Houston Oilers on 12-11-66
14 games
Wisconsin Badger

FRAZIER, Charley (#81) *"Razor"*
Born on August 12, 1939 in Houston, TX
6'0" and 190 pounds
Wide Receiver   1969-70
28 receptions for 392 yards + 7 TDs
Caught 7 TD passes from Mike Taliaferro
Caught a 34 yard TD from Mike Taliaferro on the 1st play of their 35-21 win over Buffalo on 11-23-69
Had a career long 50 yard TD reception (from Mike Taliaferro) in their 38-23 win over Miami on 11-30-69
23 games/13 started
Texas Southern Tiger

FREEMAN, Arturo (#25)
Born on October 27, 1976 in Orangeburg, SC
6'1" and 200 pounds
Safety   2005
2 games/1 started (on 10-30-05)
South Carolina Gamecock

FREENY, Jonathan (#55 and #44)
Born on June 15, 1989 in Margate, FL
6'2" and 245 yards
Linebacker   2015-17
Wore #55 from 2015-16 and #44 for 1 game on 12-11-17
1 sack, 2 fumble recoveries for 12 yards and recovered a Patriots onside kick
Sacked Brock Osweiler in their 30-24 OT loss to the Denver Broncos on 11-29-15
Had a 7 yard return of a fumble by Jason Witten in their 30-6 win over the Dallas Cowboys on 10-11-15
Returned Leodis McKelvin's muffed punt return 5 yards in their 20-13 win over Buffalo on 11-23-15
Recovered an onside kick by Stephen Gostkowski in their 27-10 win over the Redskins on 11-08-15
19 Regular Season Games/11 started and 2 Playoff Games
Recovered Peyton Manning's fumble in their 20-18 AFC Championship Game loss to Denver on 01-24-16
Member of the 2016 World Championship Team
Rutgers Scarlet Knight

FRIESZ, John (#17)
Born on May 19, 1967 in Missoula, MT
6'4" and 214 pounds
Quarterback   1999-2000
11 completions for 66 yards
Knelt on the last 2 snaps in their 27-3 rout of the Arizona Cardinals on 10-31-99
Longest completion was a 17 yard pass to Troy Brown in their 16-13 OT loss to Buffalo on 11-05-00
2 games (on Oct. 31, 1999 and Nov. 5, 2000)
Idaho Vandal

FRISCH, David (#88)
Born on June 22, 1970 in Kirkwood, MO
6'7" and 260 pounds
TE (KR)   1995
Had an 8 yard return of a kickoff by Chris Gardocki in their 24-10 loss to the Colts on 11-19-95
2 games (On Nov. 5th and Nov. 19th)
Colorado State Ram

FRYAR, Irving (#80)
Born on September 28, 1962 in Mount Holly, NJ
6'0" and 200 pounds
WR/PR/KR   1984-92
363 receptions for 5,726 yards + 38 TDs and 35 carries for 188 yards + 1 TD
206 punt returns for 2,055 yards + 3 TDs and 26 kickoff returns for 495 yards
Caught 1 TD pass from Tom Ramsey and 2 TD passes from Marc Wilson and Tommy Hodson
Caught 3 TD passes from Doug Flutie, 6 TD passes from Hugh Millen and 10 TD passes from Tony Eason
Caught 14 Regular Season TD passes and 1 Post Season TD pass from Steve Grogan
Returned a free kick by Rohn Stark 18 yards in their 50-17 rout of the Colts on 11-18-84
Returned a free kick by Joe Prokop 24 yards in their 26-20 win over Green Bay on 09-08-85
Longest was an 85 yard TD return of a punt by John Kidd in their 17-14 win over Buffalo on 09-22-85
Returned a free kick by Frank Garcia 16 yards in their 32-14 win over Tampa on 10-27-85
Returned a punt by Rohn Stark 77 yards for a TD in their 34-15 win over the Colts on 11-10-85
Ran for an 8 yard touchdown in their 20-13 win over the Seahawks on 11-17-85
Caught a 13 yard TD pass in the 4th Qtr from Steve Grogan in their 20-13 win over Seattle on 11-17-85
Longest run for 31 yards in their 34-7 rout of the Dolphins on 10-05-86
Returned a punt by Rick Donnelly 59 yards for a TD in their 25-17 win over the Falcons on 11-02-86
Recovered Mosi Tatupu's fumble in their 30-21 win vs the Indianapolis Colts on 11-09-86
Caught a 25 yard TD pass on the last play from Tony Eason in their 30-28 win over the Rams on 11-16-86
Returned a free kick by John Kidd 16 yards in their 22-19 win over Buffalo on 11-23-86
Caught a career long 80 yard TD pass on the 1st play from Doug Flutie in their 30-7 rout of the Bears on 10-30-88
Longest was a 47 yard return of a kickoff by Mike Lansford in their 24-20 loss to the LA Rams on 12-24-89
Following Hugh Millen's 18 yard run, he advanced Hugh's lateral another 8 yards in their 30-21 loss on 10-04-92
Led the NFL with the most punt returns, best punt return average and longest punt return in 1985
AFC Offensive Player of the Week in their 16-13 win over Buffalo on 11-24-91
AFC Pro Bowl Return Specialist in 1985
129 Regular Season Games/105 started and 4 Playoff Games/3 started
6 receptions for 82 yards + 1 TD and 8 punt returns for 47 yards in the playoffs
Caught an 8 yard TD pass, on 4th down, from Steve Grogan, in 46-10 Super Bowl loss to Da' Bears on 01-26-86
Recovered a fumble by Stanley Morgan, after his 22 yard reception, in Divisional Playoff Game on 01-05-86
1st Overall Pick in the 1984 NFL Draft
Nebraska Cornhusker

FULLINGTON, Darrell (#29)
Born on April 17, 1964 in New Smyrna Beach, FL
6'1" and 197 pounds
Defensive Back   1991
5 games
Miami Hurricane

FUNCHESS, Tom (#73) *"Moose"*
Born on September 12, 1944 in Crystal Springs, MS
6'5" and 265 pounds
Tackle (DE)   1968-70
39 games/38 started
#32 pick in the 1968 NFL Draft
Jackson State Tiger

FUSSELL, Tom (#83)
Born on May 25, 1945 in Cleveland, OH
6'3" and 250 pounds
Defensive End   1967
12 games/4 started
#206 pick in the 1967 NFL Draft
LSU Fighting Tiger

GABRIEL, Doug (#85)
Born on August 27, 1980 in Miami, FL
6'2" and 215 pounds
Wide Receiver   2006
25 receptions for 344 yards + 3 TD passes from Tom Brady
Longest reception was a 45 yard pass from Tom Brady in their 31-7 rout of the Vikings on 10-30-06
12 games/5 started
Central Florida Golden Knight

GADBOIS, Dennis (#82 and #48)
Born on September 18, 1963 in Biddeford, ME
6'1" and 183 pounds
Wide Receiver   1987-88
Wore #82 for 3 games in 1987 and #48 for 2 games in 1988
3 receptions for 51 yards
Longest reception was a 20 yard pass from Doug Flutie in their 21-7 win over Houston on 10-18-87
5 games/1 started on 10-18-87
Boston University Terrier

GAFFNEY, Derrick "Jabar" (#10)
Born on December 1, 1980 in Jacksonville, FL
6'1" and 205 pounds
Wide Receiver   2006-08
85 receptions for 1,059 yards + 8 TDs
Caught 2 TD passes from Matt Cassel, 6 Regular Season and 3 Post Season TD passes from Tom Brady
Hauled in a career long 56 yard TD pass from Tom Brady in their 34-13 win over Pittsburgh on 12-09-07
Caught a 2 point pass from Matt Cassel in their 34-31 OT loss to the New York Jets on 11-13-08
43 Regular Season Games/20 started and 6 Playoff Games/4 started
25 receptions for 282 yards + 3 TDs in the playoffs
Caught a 6 yard TD pass from Tom Brady in their 24-21 Divisional win over San Diego on 01-14-07
Caught a 6 yard TD pass from Tom Brady in their 38-34 Championship game loss to the Colts on 01-21-07
Caught a 12 yard TD pass from Tom Brady in their 21-12 Divisional win over San Diego on 01-20-08
Florida Gator

GAITER JR., Tony (#17)
Born on July 15, 1974 in Miami, FL
5'8" and 169 pounds
Wide Receiver   1997
Only game played was on 11-30-97
Miami Hurricane

GALLAHER, Allen (#64)
Born on November 30, 1950 in San Fernando, CA
6'3" and 250 pounds
Tackle   1974
14 games
#82 pick in the 1973 NFL Draft
USC Trojan

GALLOWAY, Joseph "Joey" (#13)
Born on April 20, 1971 in Bellaire, OH
5'11" and 197 pounds
Wide Receiver   2009
7 receptions for 67 yards
Longest reception was a 19 yard pass from Tom Brady in their 16-9 loss to the Jets on 09-20-09
3 games
Ohio State Buckeye

GAMBLE, R.C. (#13)
Born on September 27, 1946 in Greenville, SC
6'3" and 220 pounds
HB (KR)   1968-69
94 carries for 346 yards + 1 TD, 18 receptions for 129 yards + 1 TD and 2 kickoff returns for 25 yards
Longest run was a 45 yard TD in their 16-7 win over Buffalo on 09-08-68
Caught a 1 yard TD pass from Tom Sherman in their 31-17 loss to the Kansas City Chiefs on 11-17-68
Longest reception was a 20 yard pass from Mike Taliaferro in their 35-7 loss to Denver on 09-14-69
Longest was a 23 yard return of a kickoff by Karl Kremser in their 17-16 loss to Miami on 11-09-69
27 games/13 started
#88 pick in the 1968 NFL Draft
South Carolina State Bulldog

GAMBOL, Chris (#74)
Born on September 14, 1964 in Pittsburgh, PA
6'6" and 303 pounds
Guard/Tackle   1990
16 games/15 started
Iowa Hawkeye

GANNON, Chris (#91)
Born on January 20, 1966 in Brandon, FL
6'6" and 265 pounds
DE/TE/LS   1990-93
Shared in a sack and had 1 fumble recovery
Long Snapper for Punters Brian Hansen, Shawn McCarthy and Mike Saxon and Kicker Scott Sisson
Snapped the ball over the head of Punter Brian Hansen for a safety in their 25-10 loss to the Redskins on 12-15-90
Shared in a sack of Jeff Hostetler in their 13-10 loss to the New York Giants on 12-30-90
Recovered a fumbled punt return by Al Edwards in their 22-17 loss to the Bills on 11-03-91
30 games/2 started
#73 pick in the 1989 NFL Draft
Southwest Louisiana Ragin' Cajun

GARCIA, Alfonso "Teddy" (#7)
Born on June 4, 1964 in Caddo Parish, LA
5'10" and 187 pounds
Kicker   1988
Kicked 6 field goals and 11 extra points
Kicked a career long 50 yard field goal in their 36-6 loss to the Vikings on 09-11-88
Made potential TD saving tackle on Bobby Joe Edwards' 43 yard kickoff return in 13-7 win vs Seattle on 12-04-88
16 games
#100 pick in the 1988 NFL Draft
Northeast Louisiana Indian

GARDIN, Ron (#37)
Born on September 25, 1944 in New Haven, CT
5'11" and 180 pounds
KR/PR   1971
14 kickoff returns for 321 yards and 4 punt returns for 14 yards
Longest was a 5 yard return of a punt by Steve O'Neal in their 20-0 shutout of the Jets on 10-10-71
Had another 5 yard return of a punt by Jim McCann in their 27-10 loss to San Francisco on 10-31-71
Longest was a 34 yard return of Mark Moseley's 2nd half kickoff in their 28-20 win over Houston on 11-07-71
8 games
Arizona Wildcat

GAROPPOLO, Jimmy (#10)
Born on November 2, 1991 in Arlington Heights, IL
6'2" and 225 pounds
Quarterback   2014-16
63 completions for 690 yards + 5 TDs, 25 carrries for 10 yards and 1 reception for 3 yards
Longest completion was a 37 yard TD pass to Chris Hogan in their 23-21 win over Arizona on 09-11-16
Caught his own deflected pass for a 3 yard gain in their 23-21 win over the Arizona Cardinals on 09-11-16
Longest run for 10 yards in their 23-21 win over the Arizona Cardinals on 09-11-16
17 games/2 started
Member of the 2014 and 2016 World Championship Teams
#62 pick in the 2014 NFL Draft
Eastern Illinois Panther

GARRETT, Carl (#30) *"The Roadrunner"*
Born on August 31, 1947 in Denton, TX
5'11" and 210 pounds
RB/KR/PR   1969-72
537 carries for 2,235 yards + 15 TDs and 107 receptions for 1,158 yards + 3 TDs
92 kickoff returns for 2,251 yards and 43 punt returns for 487 yards
Snared a 1 yard TD from Mike Taliaferro in their 38-23 loss to the Raiders on 09-28-69
Recovered an onside kick by Gino Cappelletti in their 38-23 loss to the Raiders on 09-28-69
Grabbed a 7 yard TD from Mike Taliaferro in their 13-10 loss to the Chargers on 10-19-69
Longest run was an 80 yard TD in their 17-16 loss to the Dolphins on 11-09-69
Longest was a 63 yard return of kickoff by Bruce Alford in their 35-21 win over Buffalo on 11-23-69
Longest was a 62 yard return of a punt by Steve O'Neal in their 31-21 loss to the Jets on 09-27-70
Recovered Jim Kearney's interception return fumble in their 23-10 loss to the Chiefs on 10-11-70
Returned Tom Beer's kickoff return lateral 21 yards in their 27-3 loss to the Baltimore Colts on 10-25-70
Returned a kickoff return lateral from Tom Beer 27 yards in their 45-10 loss to the Bills on 11-01-70
Returned another kickoff return lateral from Tom Beer 15 yards in their 45-10 loss to Buffalo on 11-01-70
Fell on the interception return fumble by John Pitts in their 45-10 loss to Buffalo on 11-01-70
Longest reception was an 80 yard TD pass from Jim Plunkett in their 38-33 win over Buffalo on 11-14-71
Ran for a 12 yard game winning TD in their 21-20 win over the Atlanta Falcons on 09-24-72
AFL All Star Running Back in 1969
AFL Rookie of the Year in 1969
51 games
#58 pick in the 1969 NFL Draft
New Mexico Highlands Cowboy

GARRETT, John "J.D." (#32) *"Red River"*
Born on November 28, 1941 in Natchitoches, LA
5'11" and 195 pounds
RB/KR (PR)   1964-67
116 carries for 434 yards + 3 TDs and 17 receptions for 169 yards + 2 TDs
3 punt returns for 47 yards and 48 kickoff returns for 1,054 yards
Longest was 42 yard return of a kickoff by Keith Lincoln in their 33-28 win over San Diego on 09-20-64
Longest run for 58 yards in their 39-10 rout of the Denver Broncos on 10-04-64
Longest reception was a 57 yard pass from Babe Parilli in their 39-10 rout of the Broncos on 10-04-64
Advanced Jim Hunt's kickoff return lateral 24 yards in their 43-43 tie with the Oakland Raiders on 10-16-64
Had a 12 yard return of a free kick by Jim Fraser in their 12-7 win over the Denver Broncos on 11-20-64
Longest was a 28 yard return of a punt by Jim Fraser in their 12-7 win over the Broncos on 11-20-64
Ran for a 1 yard game winning TD to beat the Kansas City Chiefs 31-24 on 12-06-64
Fell on a blocked punt in the end zone for a TD, in their 41-32 loss to Miami on 12-17-67
50 games
8th Round Draft Pick in 1964
Grambling State Tiger

GARRON, Larry (#46 and #40)
Born on May 23, 1937 in Marks, MS
6'0" and 195 pounds
RB/KR (DB/PR)   1960-68
Wore #46 in 1960 and #40 from 1961-68
759 carries for 2,981 yards + 14 TDs and 185 receptions for 2,502 yards + 26 TDs
89 kickoff returns for 2,299 yards + 2 TDs, 1 punt return for 23 yards and 1 completion of 39 yards
Caught 1 TD pass from Gino Cappelletti + 25 Regular Season and 2 Post Season TD passes from Babe Parilli
Recovered fumbles by Dick Christy, Bob Suci and Babe Parilli
Played in 3 games as a Defensive Back in 1960
Advanced John Simerson's kickoff return lateral 26 yards in their 45-17 win over Denver on 09-16-61
Caught a 27 yard fake field goal TD pass from Gino Cappelletti in their 37-30 loss to the NY Titans on 10-01-61
Advanced Ron Burton's kickoff return reverse handoff 11 yards in their 31-31 tie with Houston on 10-13-61
Returned a kickoff by George Blanda 89 yards for a TD in their 31-31 tie with Houston on 10-13-61
Longest run was a *Team Record* 85 yard TD in their 52-21 rout of the Bills on 10-22-61
Advanced Rommie Loudd's kickoff return lateral 36 yards in their 26-16 win over Oakland on 10-26-62
Tossed a 39 yard Half Back Option pass to Ron Burton in their 26-16 win over the Oakland Raiders on 10-26-62
Had a 95 yard TD return of a kickoff by Mack Yoho in their 28-28 tie with Buffalo on 11-03-62
Caught a career long 76 yard TD pass from Babe Parilli in their 45-3 rout of the Oilers on 11-01-63
Had a 23 yard return of a punt by Jerrel Wilson in their 35-3 loss to the Kansas City Chiefs on 12-14-63
AFL All Star Running Back in 1961, 1963, 1964, 1967
99 Regular Season Games/81 started and 2 Playoff Games/2 started
Ran for a 7 yard TD in their 51-10 AFL Championship Game loss to the San Diego Chargers on 01-05-64
Caught 2 TD passes from Babe Parilli in their 26-8 AFL Divisional Playoff win over Buffalo on 12-28-63
Western Illinois Leatherneck

GASH JR., Samuel "Sam" (#33)
Born on March 7, 1969 in Hendersonville, NC
6'0" and 242 pounds
Fullback (KR)   1992-97
105 carries for 291 yards + 2 TDs, 104 receptions for 826 yards + 6 TDs and 1 kickoff return of 9 yards
Caught 1 TD pass from Scott Zolak and 5 TD passes and one 2 point pass from Drew Bledsoe
Recovered a fumbled punt return by Ron Lewis in their 24-12 loss to the 49ers on 10-11-92
Longest run for 14 yards in their 38-14 loss to the Buffalo Bills on 09-05-93
Longest reception was a 30 yard pass from Drew Bledsoe in their 17-14 win over the Browns on 09-03-95
Had a 9 yard return of a kickoff by Pete Stoyanovich in their 23-3 loss to the Dolphins on 10-30-94
Caught a 2 point pass from Drew Bledsoe in their 46-38 win over the Baltimore Ravens on 10-06-96
88 Regular Season Games/36 started and 3 Playoff Games/2 started
#205 pick in the 1992 NFL Draft
Penn State Nittany Lion

GAY JR., Randall (#21) *"Blue"*
Born on May 5, 1982 in Baton Rouge, LA
5'11" and 186 pounds
Cornerback   2004-07
5 interceptions for 75 yards and 3 fumble recoveries for 56 yards + 2 TDs
Intercepted Jay Fiedler, Kyle Boller, Carson Palmer, Cleo Lemon and J.P. Losman
Recovered Jerald Sowell's fumble, on the Patriots 7 yard line, in their 13-7 win over the Jets on 10-24-04
Had a 41 yard TD return of a fumble by William Green in their 42-15 rout of the Browns on 12-05-04
Returned a punt by Derrick Frost for no gain in their 42-15 rout over the Cleveland Browns on 12-05-04
Had a 15 yard TD return of a fumble by Kellen Winslow in their 34-17 win over the Browns on 10-07-07
Had a career long 31 yard return of a pass by Cleo Lemon in their 49-28 win over the Dolphins on 10-21-07
39 Regular Season Games/14 started and 6 Playoff Games/4 started
Member of the 2004 World Championship Team
LSU Fighting Tiger

GEDDES, Robert "Bob" (#59)
Born on April 22, 1946 in Seattle, WA
6'2" and 240 pounds
Linebacker   1973-75
½ sack and 2 interceptions for 32 yards + 1 TD
Shared in a sack of Norm Snead and had a 3 yard return of a pass by Norm Snead in their 28-20 win on 09-22-74
Had a 29 yard TD return of a pass by Al Woodall in their 24-0 shutout of the NY Jets on 10-13-74
24 games/6 started
UCLA Bruin

GEORGE JR., Houston "Tony" (#41)
Born on August 10, 1975 in Cincinnati, OH
5'11" and 205 pounds
Safety   1999-2000
Had a 24 yard return of a fumble by Sylvester Morris in their 30-24 win over the Chiefs on 12-04-00
Recovered a fumble on a poor snap to Punter Lee Johnson in their 13-10 OT win vs Buffalo on 12-17-00
31 games/1 started (on 01-02-00)
#91 pick in the 1999 NFL Draft
Florida Gator

GERMANY JR., Willie (#29)
Born on May 9, 1948 in Columbus, GA
6'0" and 192 pounds
Safety   1976
10 Regular Season Games and 1 Playoff Game (on 12-18-76)
Morgan State Bear

GIBSON, Ernest (#43)
Born on October 3, 1961 in Jacksonville, FL
5'10" and 189 pounds
DB (PR)   1984-88
4 interceptions for 21 yards, recovered a fumble by Joe Ferguson and had 1 punt return for 3 yards
Intercepted Joe Pisarcik, Jack Trudeau and had 2 interceptions of Dan Marino
Had a 3 yard return of a punt by Chuck Ramsey in their 28-21 win over the Jets on 09-30-84
Had a career long 17 yard return of a pass by Dan Marino in their 24-10 win over Miami on 12-28-87
67 Regular Season Games/14 started and 5 Playoff Games
#151 pick in the 1984 NFL Draft
Furman Paladin

GILLEN, John (#54)
Born on November 5, 1958 in Arlington Heights, IL
6'3" and 227 pounds
Linebacker   1983
8 games
Illinois Fighting Illini

GILLISLEE JR., Mike (#35)
Born on November 1, 1990 in Deland, FL
5'11" and 210 pounds
Running Back   2017
104 carries for 383 yards + 5 TDs and 1 reception for 15 yards
Longest run was 16 yards in their 42-27 loss to the Kansas City Chiefs on 09-07-17
Caught a 15 yard pass from Tom Brady in their 37-16 win over the Bills on 12-24-17
9 games/2 started
Florida Gator

GILMORE, Stephon (#24)
Born on September 19, 1990 in Rock Hill, SC
6'1" and 202 pounds
Cornerback   2017--
10 interceptions for 185 yards + 2 TDs and 2 fumble recoveries
Intercepted Matt Moore, Josh McCown, Ryan Fitzpatrick, Daniel Jones, Sam Darnold
Intercepted Dak Prescott and had 2 interceptions of Deshaun Watson and Andy Dalton
Recovered fumbles by Aaron Jones and Travis Kelce
Had a 54 yard TD return of a pass by Ryan Fitzpatrick in their 43-0 shutout of the Dolphins on 09-15-19
Had a career long 64 yard return of a pass by Andy Dalton in their 34-13 win over the Bengals on 12-15-19
AFC Defensive Player of the Month in October 2019
AFC Pro Bowl Cornerback in 2018 and 2019
First Team All Pro Cornerback in 2018 and 2019
NFL Defensive Player of the Year in 2019
45 Regular Season Games/45 started and 7 Playoff Games/7 started
Intercepted a pass by Philip Rivers in their 41-28 Divisional win over the LA Chargers on 01-13-18
Intercepted a pass by Jared Goff in their 13-3 Super Bowl win over the LA Rams on 02-03-19
Member of the 2018 World Championship Team
South Carolina Gamecock

GIPSON, Paul (#46)
Born on March 21, 1946 in Jacksonville, TX
6'0" and 210 pounds
Running Back   1973
5 carries for a net loss of 1 yard and 1 fumble recovery for 20 yards
Longest run was 4 yards in their 10-7 loss to the Kansas City Chiefs on 09-23-73
Had a 20 yard return of Bruce Laird's fumbled punt return in their 24-16 win over the Colts on 10-07-73
5 games
Houston Cougar

GISLER, Mike (#67)
Born on August 26, 1969 in Runge, TX
6'4" and 295 yards
Center (KR)   1993-97
3 kickoff returns for 28 yards
Longest was an 11 yard return of a kickoff by Doug Brien in their 31-17 loss to the Saints on 12-03-95
73 Regular Season Games/7 started and 3 Playoff Games
Houston Cougar

GIVENS, David (#87)
Born on August 16, 1980 in Youngstown, OH
6'0" and 212 pounds
Wide Receiver (KR)   2002-05
158 receptions for 2,214 yards + 12 TDs, 2 carries for 13 yards and 2 kickoff returns for 31 yards
Caught 12 Regular Season TD passes and 7 Post Season TD passes from Tom Brady
Caught an 18 yard TD pass from Tom Brady with 30 ticks left to beat Denver 30-26 at Invesco Field on 11-03-03
Longest reception was a 57 yard pass from Tom Brady in their 12-0 shutout of Dallas on 11-16-03
Longest run was 9 yards in their 28-0 shutout of the Tampa Bay Buccaneers on 12-17-05
Longest was a 20 yard return of a kickoff by Olindo Mare in their 19-13 OT win over Miami on 10-19-03
53 Regular Season Games/27 started and 8 Playoff Games/6 started
35 receptions for 324 yards + 7 TDs in the playoffs
Caught a 7 yard TD pass from Tom Brady in their 24-14 Championship win over the Colts on 01-18-04
Caught a 5 yard TD pass from Tom Brady in their 32-29 Super Bowl victory over the Panthers on 02-01-04
Caught a 5 yard TD pass from Tom Brady in their 20-3 Divisional win over the Colts on 01-16-05
Snared a 9 yard TD pass from Tom Brady in their 41-27 Championship win over the Steelers on 01-23-05
Grabbed a 4 yard TD pass from Tom Brady in their 24-21 Super Bowl win over the Eagles on 02-06-05
Caught a 3 yard TD pass from Tom Brady in their 28-3 Wild Card rout of the Jaguars on 01-07-06
Caught a 4 yard TD pass from Tom Brady in their 27-13 Divisional loss to the Broncos on 01-14-06
Member of the 2003 and 2004 World Championship Teams
#253 pick in the 2002 NFL Draft
Notre Dame Fighting Irish

GLADIEUX, Bob (#24) *"Harpo"*
Born on January 2, 1947 in Louisville, OH
5'11" and 195 pounds
RB/KR/PR   1969-72
65 carries for 239 yards, 25 receptions for 252 yards and 1 pass completion of 48 yards
10 kickoff returns for 146 yards, 6 punt returns for minus 6 yards and 2 fumble recoveries
Recovered fumbles by Hubert Ginn and Ricky Harris
Longest was a 20 yard return of a kickoff by Jim Turner in their 23-14 loss to the New York Jets on 10-05-69
Threw a left handed HB option pass of 48 yards to Hubie Bryant in their 28-20 win over Houston on 11-07-71
Longest run was 31 yards in their 38-33 win over Buffalo on 11-14-71
Longest reception was a 31 yard pass from Jim Plunkett in their 24-23 win over the Redskins on 10-01-72
43 games/5 started
#188 pick in the 1969 NFL Draft
Notre Dame Fighting Irish

GLENN, Terrance "Terry" (#88)
Born on July 23, 1974 in Columbus, OH
5'11" and 195 pounds
Wide Receiver   1996-2001
329 receptions for 4,669 yards + 22 TDs and 11 carries for 80 yards
Caught 21 TD passes from Drew Bledsoe and 1 TD pass from Tom Brady
Grabbed a career long 86 yard TD from Drew Bledsoe in their 23-9 win over Pittsburgh on 12-06-98
Recovered Kevin Faulk's fumble on a reverse in their 16-14 loss to the Chiefs on 10-10-99
Longest run was 35 yards in their 30-24 win over the Kansas City Chiefs on 12-04-00
Caught Tom Brady's 1st NFL TD pass in their 29-26 OT win vs the San Diego Chargers on 10-14-01
AFC Offensive Player of the Week in their 19-7 win over Cleveland on 10-03-99
AFC Pro Bowl Wide Receiver in 1999
68 Regular Season Games/63 started and 5 Playoff Games/4 started
Member of the 2001 World Championship Team
#7 pick in the 1996 NFL Draft
Ohio State Buckeye

GLENN, Vencie (#25)
Born on October 26, 1964 in Grambling, LA
6'0" and 205 pounds
Defensive Back   1986
4 games
#54 pick in the 1986 NFL Draft
Indiana State Sycamore

GOAD, Tim (#72)
Born on February 26, 1966 in Claudville, VA
6'3" and 280 pounds
NT/LS (DT and DE)   1988-94
11.5 sacks and 4 fumble recoveries for 27 yards + 1 TD
Shared in a sack of Jeff Hostetler, Mike Tomczak and Jeff George
Sacked Don Majkowski, Jim Kelly, Bubby Brister, Jack Trudeau, David Klinger, and Brett Favre
Had 2 sacks of Boomer Esiason and Dan Marino
Recovered fumbles by Dave Meggett, Christian Okoye, and 2 fumbles by Boomer Esiason
Long Snapper for Punter Shawn McCarthy in their 38-17 loss to the Miami Dolphins on 10-18-92
Had a 19 yard TD return of a fumble by Christian Okoye, on 1st play, in their 27-20 loss to KS on 12-13-92
Long Snapper for Kickers Charlie Baumann and Jason Staurovsky
109 games/105 started
#87 pick in the 1988 NFL Draft
North Carolina Tar Heel

GOGOLAK, Charlie (#7)
Born on December 29, 1944 in Budapest, Hungary
5'10" and 165 pounds
Kicker   1970-72
Kicked 20 field goals and 42 extra points and had 2 of his onside kicks recovered by a teammate
His onside kick was recovered by teammate Clarence Scott in their 35-14 loss to the Vikings on 12-13-70
Kicked a career long 51 yard field goal in their 41-3 loss to the Miami Dolphins on 10-17-71
His onside kick was recovered by teammate Clarence Scott in their 24-17 loss to the Colts on 11-06-72
26 games
Princeton Tiger

GOLDEN, Timothy "Tim" (#59)
Born on November 15, 1959 in Pahokee, FL
6'1" and 220 pounds
Linebacker (KR)   1982-84
3 fumble recoveries and 1 kickoff return of 10 yards
Recovered fumbles by Ricky Smith and Jeff Groth and a fumbled kickoff return by Tony Collins
Had a 10 yard return of a kickoff by Ray Wershing in their 33-13 loss to the 49ers on 10-02-83
40 Regular Season Games/1 started (on 10-23-83) and 1 Playoff Game (on 01-08-83)
Florida Gator

GOLIC, Robert "Bob" (#51)
Born on October 26, 1957 in Cleveland, OH
6'2" and 264 pounds
DL/LB   1979-81
Recovered Cleveland Franklin's fumble in their 23-21 loss to the Baltimore Colts on 12-20-81
33 games/12 started
#52 pick in the 1979 NFL Draft
Notre Dame Fighting Irish

GONZALEZ, Noe (#38)
Born on February 5, 1951 in Alice, TX
6'1" and 210 pounds
Special Team　　　　　　1974
2 games (on Dec. 8th and Dec. 15th)
Southwest Texas State Bobcat

GORDON, Joshua "Josh" (#10)
Born on April 13, 1991 in Houston, TX
6'3" and 225 pounds
WR (DB)　　　　　　2018-19
60 receptions for 1,007 yards + 4 TDs and 1 carry for 1 yard
Caught 4 TD passes from Tom Brady
Longest reception was a 55 yard pass from Tom Brady in their 38-31 win over Chicago on 10-21-18
Used as a defensive back for 3 plays in their 38-31 win over the Chicago Bears on 10-21-18
Longest reception (tie) was a 55 yard TD pass from Tom Brady in their 31-17 win over the Packers on 11-04-18
Ran for a 1 yard gain in their 30-14 win over the Jets on 09-22-19
17 games/17 started
Member of the 2018 World Championship Team
Baylor Bear

GORDON, Timothy "Tim" (#41)
Born on May 7, 1965 in Ardmore, OK
6'0" and 188 pounds
Defensive Back　　　　1991-92
Recovered fumbles by Greg Lewis and Alton Montgomery
21 games/15 started
Tulsa Golden Hurricane

GORIN, Brandon (#76)
Born on July 17, 1978 in Muncie, IN
6'6" and 308 pounds
Tackle　　　　　　2003-05
32 Regular Season Games/18 started and 7 Playoff Games/5 started
Member of the 2003 and 2004 World Championship Teams
Purdue Boilermaker

GOSTKOWSKI, Stephen (#3) *"The Kicker"*
Born on January 28, 1984 in Baton Rouge, LA
6'1" and 215 pounds
Kicker　　　　　　　　　2006-19
Kicked 374 field goals and 653 extra points and 3 of his onside kicks were recovered by a teammate
Kicked a career long 62 yard field goal in their 33-8 win over Oakland in Mexico City on 11-19-17
Onside kick was recovered by teammate Kyle Arrington in their 27-26 win over Cleveland on 12-08-13
Onside kick was recovered by teammate Jonathan Freeney in their 27-10 win over Washington on 11-08-15
Onside kick was recovered by teammate Rashaan Melvin in their 35-28 loss to the Eagles on 12-06-15
Recovered Leodis McKelvin's fumbled kickoff return in their 25-24 win over Buffalo on 09-14-09
AFC Special Team Player of the Week 6 times and AFC Special Team Player of the Month 3 times
Led the NFL with the most extra points kicked in 2007, 2008 and 2012
Led the NFL with the most field goals kicked in 2008, 2013, 2014
Led the NFL in scoring the most points in a regular season 5 times
AFC Pro Bowl Kicker in 2008, 2013-15
First Team All Pro Kicker in 2008, 2015
204 Regular Season Games and 28 Playoff Games
Kicked 39 field goals and 88 extra points and had 5 punts for 209 yards in the playoffs
Member of the 2014, 2016 and 2018 World Championship Teams
#118 pick in the 2006 NFL Draft
Memphis Tiger

GRAFF, Neil (#15)
Born on January 12, 1950 in Sioux Falls, SD
6'3" and 205 pounds
Quarterback　　　　　　　1974-75
19 completions for 241 yards + 2 TDs and 2 carries for 2 yards
Longest run was 2 yards in their 7-0 loss to the Houston Oilers on 09-21-75
Longest completion was a 31 yard TD pass to Randy Vataha in their 22-14 loss to Miami on 09-28-75
Threw a 5 yard TD pass to Russ Francis in their 22-14 loss to the Dolphins on 09-28-75
Holder for John Smith
25 games/2 started
Wisconsin Badger

GRAHAM III, Arthur "Artie" (#84)
Born on July 31, 1941 in Somerville, MA
6'1" and 205 pounds
WR (PR/KR)　　　　　　　1963-68
199 receptions for 3,107 yards + 20 TDs, 2 punt returns for 11 yards and 1 kickoff return of 9 yards
Caught 1 TD pass from Tom Sherman, 3 TD passes from Tom Yewcic and 16 TD passes from Babe Parilli
Made a potential game saving tackle on Hoot Gibson's punt return in their 17-14 win vs Oakland on 09-13-64
Made a potential game saving tackle on Lance Alworth's punt return in their 33-28 win vs SD on 09-20-64
Caught a career long 80 yard TD from Babe Parilli in their 34-17 win vs Houston on 11-29-64
Longest was a 6 yard return of a punt by Larry Seiple in their 38-7 loss to Miami on 12-08-68
Had a 9 yard return of a kickoff by Doug Moreau in their 38-7 loss to the Dolphins on 12-08-68
75 Regular Season Games and 2 Playoff Games/2 started
1st Round Draft Pick in 1963
Boston College Eagle

GRAHAM, Daniel (#82)
Born on November 16, 1978 in Torrance, CA
6'3" and 257 pounds
Tight End   2002-06
120 receptions for 1,393 yards + 17 TDs
Caught 17 Regular Season TD passes and 1 Post Season TD pass from Tom Brady
Lost 10 yards returning a fumble by Tom Brady in their 27-17 win over Buffalo on 12-08-02
Caught a 4th down 4 yard TD pass, to tie the game, in their 23-20 OT win vs Houston on 11-23-03
AFC Offensive Player of the Week in their 9-3 win over Cleveland on 10-26-03
63 Regular Season Games/49 started and 11 Playoff Games/6 started
13 receptions for 143 yards + 1 TD in the playoffs
Caught a 1 yard TD pass from Tom Brady in their 37-16 Wild Card win over the Jets on 01-07-07
Member of the 2003 and 2004 World Championship Teams
#21 pick in the 2001 NFL Draft
Colorado Buffalo

GRAHAM, Hason (#81)
Born on March 21, 1971 in Decatur, GA
5'10" and 176 pounds
Wide Receiver   1995-96
15 receptions for 220 yards + 2 TDs
Caught a career long 37 yard TD pass from Drew Bledsoe in their 31-27 win over the Jets on 12-10-95
Hauled in a 31 yard TD pass from Drew Bledsoe in their 10-7 loss to the Colts on 12-23-95
19 Regular Season Games/1 started (on 12-23-95) and 1 Playoff Game
Had an 18 yard return of a kickoff by Chris Jacke in their 35-21 Super Bowl loss to Green Bay on 01-26-97
Georgia Bulldog

GRAHAM, Michael "Shayne" (#5)
Born on December 9, 1977 in Radford, VA
6'0" and 197 pounds
Kicker   2010
Kicked 12 field goals and 35 extra points
Longest field goal was 41 yards in their 45-3 rout of the New York Jets on 12-06-10
8 Regular Season Games and 1 Playoff Game
Kicked 2 field goals and 1 extra point in their 28-21 Divisional loss to the Jets on 01-16-11
Virginia Tech Hokie

GRAHAM, Milt (#70)
Born on July 28, 1934 in Chatham, MA
6'6" and 235 pounds
OT/DT   1961-63
Played on both sides of the line of scrimmage
Pounced on Tom Yewcic's fumble in their 31-24 loss to the New York Jets on 10-05-63
28 Regular Season Games/23 started and 2 Playoff Games/2 started
Member of the 1960 Canadian Football League Grey Cup Champion Ottawa Rough Riders Team
Colgate Red Raider

GRANT JR., Rupert (#34)
Born on November 5, 1973 in Washington, DC
6'1" and 233 pounds
RB (KR)   1995
Had a 7 yard return of a kickoff by Morten Andersen in their 30-17 loss to the Falcons on 10-01-95
Caught a 4 yard pass from Drew Bledsoe in their 37-3 loss to the Denver Broncos on 10-08-95
Recovered Drew Bledsoe's fumble in their 10-7 loss to the Indianapolis Colts on 12-23-95
7 games/1 started (on 10-08-95)
Howard Bison

GRAVES III, White (#44)
Born on March 20, 1942 in Jackson, MS
6'0" and 190 pounds
DB (PR)   1965-67
3 interceptions, 1 fumble recovery, 1 punt return for 5 yards and blocked a punt
Intercepted a pass by John McCormick and 2 passes by George Blanda
Recovered Joe Beauchamp's fumble of the opening kickoff in their 35-17 win over San Diego on 10-23-66
Had a 5 yard return of a punt by Bob Scarpitto in their 17-10 loss to the Denver Broncos on 11-06-66
Blocked a punt by Bob Scarpitto in their 17-10 loss to Denver on 11-06-66
40 games
17ᵗʰ Round Draft Pick in 1964
LSU Fighting Tiger

GRAY, Jonas (#35)
Born on June 27, 1990 in Pontiac, MI
5'9" and 223 pounds
Running Back   2014
89 carries for 412 yards + 5 TDs and 1 reception for 7 yards
Longest run was 20 yards in their 42-20 rout of the Colts on 11-16-14
Caught a 7 yard pass from Tom Brady in their 41-13 rout of the Dolphins on 12-14-14
Ran for a Patriots Team Record 4 TDs on 11-16-14
AFC Offensive Player of the Week in their 42-20 rout of Indianapolis on 11-16-14
8 Regular Season Games/3 started and 1 Playoff Game (on 01-18-15)
Member of the 2014 Championship Team
Notre Dame Fighting Irish

GRAY, Leon (#70) *"Big Dog"*
Born on November 15, 1951 in Olive Branch, MS
6'3" and 256 pounds
Tackle   1973-78
4 fumble recoveries
Recovered fumbles by Don Calhoun and Jess Phillips and 2 fumbles by Sam Cunningham
Pounced on Tom Owen's fumble in their 31-14 Playoff Game loss to the Houston Oilers on 12-31-78
AFC Pro Bowl Tackle in 1976, 1978
First Team All Pro Tackle in 1978
78 Regular Season Games/77 started and 2 Playoff Games/2 started
Inducted in the Patriots Hall of Fame on July 29, 2019
Jackson State Tiger

GREEN, David (#38)
Born on April 18, 1972 in Mount Kisco, NY
5'11" and 193 pounds
Running Back   1995
2 games
Boston College Eagle

GREEN, Jarvis (#97)
Born on January 12, 1979 in Thibodaux, LA
6'3" and 290 pounds
DE/NT (KR)   2002-09
28 sacks, 5 fumble recoveries for 1 TD and 1 kickoff return of 10 yards
Sacked Kordell Stewart, Dante Culpepper, Donovan McNabb, Matt Hasselbeck and Marc Bulger
Sacked Matt Moore, Joey Harrington, Cleo Lemon and A.J. Feeley
Shared in a sack of Steve McNair, Jay Fiedler, Matt Schaub and Ben Roethlisberger
Sacked Kerry Collins 1 ½ times, Trent Edwards and Carson Palmer 2 ½ times
Sacked Brooks Bollinger 3 times and Chad Pennington 4 ½ times
Strip sacked Carson Palmer, David Garrard, Vince Young and Peyton Manning
Recovered fumbles by Marc Bulger, Chad Pennington, J.P. Losman, Kyle Boller and Matt Leinhart
Had a 10 yard return of a kickoff by Olindo Mare in their 26-13 loss to the Miami Dolphins on 10-06-02
Shared in a sack of Jay Fiedler *for a safety* in their 12-0 shutout of Miami on 12-07-03
Fell on Kyle Boller's fumble in the end zone for a TD in their 24-3 rout of the Ravens on 11-28-04
Strip sacked Carson Palmer and then sacked him 2 more times in their 38-13 rout of Cincy on 10-01-06
Recovered his strip sack of Carson Palmer in their 38-13 win over the Bengals on 10-01-06
Strip sacked David Garrard to preserve their 24-21 victory over the Jaguars on 12-24-06
Strip sacked Vince Young in their 40-23 win over the Tennessee Titans on 12-31-06
Strip sacked Peyton Manning in their 24-20 win over the Colts on 11-04-07
AFC Defensive Player of the Week in their 38-13 rout of Cincinnati on 10-01-06
121 Regular Season Games/46 started and 15 Playoff Games/4 started
5 sacks in the playoffs
Had 2 ½ sacks of Peyton Manning in their 24-14 Championship win vs the Colts on 01-18-04
Sacked Ben Roethlisberger in their 41-27 Championship win over the Steelers on 01-23-05
Shared in a sack of Jake Plummer in their 27-13 Divisional loss to the Broncos on 01-14-06
Sacked Eli Manning in their 17-14 Super Bowl loss to the New York Giants on 02-03-08
Member of the 2003 and 2004 World Championship Teams
Ron Burton Community Service Award in 2006
#126 pick in the 2002 NFL Draft
LSU Fighting Tiger

GREEN, Jerome "Jerry" (#45)
Born on April 16, 1936 in Atlanta, GA
6'0" and 190 pounds
Offensive End   1960
3 receptions for 52 yards
Longest reception was a 31 yard pass from Tom Greene in their 28-24 win vs the NY Titans on 09-17-60
2 games (on Sept. 9th and Sept. 17th)
Georgia Tech Yellow Jacket

GREEN, Justin (#41)
Born on February 26, 1991 in Louisville, KY
5'11" and 195 pounds
Special Team   2013
2 games (on Nov. 24th and Dec. 29th)
Illinois Fighting Illini

GREEN, Victor (#27)
Born on December 8, 1969 in Americus, GA
5'11" and 210 pounds
Safety   2002
3 fumble recoveries and 1 interception for 90 yards + 1 TD
Recovered fumbles by Jerome Bettis, Ricky Williams and Dante Culpepper
Had a 90 yard TD return of a pass by Vinny Testaverde in their 44-7 rout of the Jets on 09-15-02
16 games/5 started
Akron Zip

GREENE, Tom (#14)
Born on January 1, 1938
6'1" and 190 pounds
QB/P/RB (KR)   1960
27 completions for 251 yards + 1 TD, 7 carries for 44 yards and 3 receptions for 43 yards
61 punts for 2,253 yards and 1 kickoff return of 3 yards
Threw a 15 yard TD pass to Oscar Lofton in their 28-24 win over the NY Titans on 09-17-60
Longest completion was a 31 yard pass to Jerry Green in their 28-24 win over the Titans on 09-17-60
Longest reception was a 31 yard pass from Butch Songin in their 28-24 win over the Titans on 09-17-60
Longest run was 21 yards in their 13-0 loss to the Buffalo Bills on 09-23-60
Longest punt was 66 yards in their 27-14 loss to the Oakland Raiders on 10-16-60
Had a 3 yard return of a kickoff by Ben Agajanian in their 45-16 loss to the LA Chargers on 10-28-60
10 games
Holy Cross Crusader

GREEN-ELLIS, BenJarvus (#42) "Law Firm of"
Born on July 2, 1985 in New Orleans, LA
5'11" and 215 pounds
RB (KR)   2008-11
510 carries for 2,064 yards + 29 TDs, 26 receptions for 292 yards and 1 kickoff return for no gain
Lateraled to Tom Brady, who then threw a 40 yard TD pass, in their 59-0 shutout of Tennessee on 10-18-09
Recovered a short kickoff by Rian Lindell in their 38-30 win over Buffalo on 09-26-10
Longest run was a 33 yard TD in their 31-27 win over the Green Bay Packers on 12-19-10
Longest reception was a 53 yard pass from Tom Brady in their 49-21 rout of the Bills on 01-01-12
53 Regular Season Games/20 started and 4 Playoff Games/2 started
Ran for a 7 yard TD in their 23-20 Championship win over the Baltimore Ravens on 01-22-12
Mississippi Rebel

GREGORY, Stephen "Steve" (#28)
Born on January 8, 1983 in New York, NY
5'11" and 185 pounds
Safety   2012-13
3 interceptions, 1 sack and 2 fumble recoveries for 30 yards + 1 TD
Intercepted Joe Flacco, Mark Sanchez and Ryan Tannehill
Recovered and returned fumbles by Mark Sanchez and Brandon Spikes
Had a career long 36 yard return of a pass by Joe Flacco in their 31-30 loss to the Ravens on 09-23-12
Returned Mark Sanchez's "butt fumble" 32 yards for a TD in their 49-19 rout of the NY Jets on 11-22-12
Lost 2 yards returning a fumble by Brandon Spikes in their 49-19 rout of the NY Jets on 11-22-12
Sacked Thad Lewis in their 34-20 win over the Buffalo Bills 12-29-13
26 Regular Season Games/23 started and 4 Playoff Games/4 started
Syracuse Orangeman

GRIER, Marrio (#35)
Born on December 5, 1971 in Charlotte, NC
5'10" and 229 pounds
Running Back   1996-97
60 carries for 180 yards + 2 TDs and 1 reception for 8 yards
Recovered Marvin Harrison's fumbled punt return in their 27-9 rout of the Colts on 10-20-96
Longest run was 26 yards in their 27-13 victory over the Colts on 11-24-96
Caught an 8 yard pass from Drew Bledsoe in their 23-22 comeback win over the NY Giants on 12-21-96
32 Regular Season Games and 5 Playoff Games
#195 pick in the 1996 NFL Draft
Tennessee Chattanooga Moccasin

GRIFFITH, Rich (#88)
Born on July 31, 1969 in Tucson, AZ
6'5" and 262 pounds
Special Team   1993
3 games
#138 pick in the 1993 NFL Draft
Arizona Wildcat

GRIGSBY, Nicholas (#50)
Born on July 2, 1992 in Trotwood, OH
6'2" and 230 pounds
Special Team   2017-18
Recovered Ryan Allen's punt on 1 yard line (tipped back by Jonathan Jones and Rex Burkhead) on 12-16-18
14 Regular Season Games and 3 Playoff Games
Member of the 2018 World Championship Team
Pittsburgh Panther

GRIMES, Reggie (#97)
Born on November 7, 1976 in Nashville, TN
6'4" and 300 pounds
Defensive Tackle   2000
8 games
Alabama Crimson Tide

GRISSOM, Geneo (#92 and #96)
Born on June 4, 1992 in Hutchinson, KS
6'4" and 265 pounds
LB/Special Team   2015-18
Wore #92 from 2015-17 and #96 for 5 games in December 2017 and 4 games in 2018
Sacked Ryan Tannehill in their 20-10 loss to the Miami Dolphins on 01-03-16
38 Regular Season Games and 6 Playoff Games
Sacked Marcus Mariota *twice* in their 35-14 Divisional win over Tennessee on 01-13-18
Member of the 2016 and 2018 World Championship Teams
#97 pick in the 2015 NFL Draft
Oklahoma Sooner

GROGAN, Steven "Steve" (#14) *"Grogs"*
Born on July 24, 1953 in San Antonio, TX
6'4" and 210 pounds
Quarterback   1975-90
1,879 completions for 26,886 yds + 182 TDs, 445 carries for 2,176 yds + 35 TDs and 3 receptions for 19 yards
Threw 1 TD pass to Pete Brock, Greg Baty, Marv Cook, Greg Hawthorne, Willie Scott and Don Calhoun
Tossed 1 TD pass to Ike Forte, Mark van Eeghen, Mosi Tatupu, Craig James, Marlin Briscoe and Ray Jarvis
Completed 1 TD pass to Ken Toler, Morris Bradshaw and Sammy Martin
Tossed 2 TD passes to Lin Dawson, Horace Ivory and Carlos Pennywell
Threw 3 TD passes for Al Chandler, Tony Collins, Sam Cunningham and Clarence Weathers
Completed 4 touchdown passes to Hart Lee Dykes
Tossed 6 TDs to Andy Johnson, Derrick Ramsey, Stephen Starring and Randy Vataha
Threw 8 TD passes to Cedric Jones and 9 TD passes to Darryl Stingley
Completed 12 TD Regular Season TD passes and 1 Post Season TD pass to Don Hasselbeck
Threw 14 Regular Season TD passes and 1 Post Season TD pass to Irving Fryar
Tossed 22 Regular Season TD passes and 1 Post Season TD pass to Russ Francis
Tossed 17 TD passes to Harold Jackson and 39 TD passes to Stanley Morgan
Holder for John Smith in 1975
Longest run was a 41 yard TD in their 41-7 Monday Night win over the Jets on 10-18-76
Advanced Don Calhoun's fumble 6 yards for a TD in their 41-7 rout of the Jets on 10-18-76
Ran 10 yards for the game winning TD in their 26-22 win over the Buffalo Bills on 10-24-76
Ran for a 3 yard game winning TD in their 21-14 win over the Baltimore Colts on 11-14-76
Threw a 6 yard TD pass to TE Pete Brock in their 38-24 victory over the Jets on 11-21-76
Ran for a 4 yard game winning TD in their 28-23 win over the San Diego Chargers on 10-01-78
Completed 5 TDs (3 to Harold Jackson and 2 to Stanley Morgan) in their 56-3 rout of the Jets on 09-09-79
Caught a 16 yard pass from Andy Johnson in their 29-28 loss to the Baltimore Colts on 09-06-81
Caught an 11 yard pass from Andy Johnson in their 27-17 loss to the Oakland Raiders on 11-01-81
Fired a career long 76 yard TD pass to Stanley Morgan in their 30-27 OT loss to Miami on 11-08-81
Threw a career long 76 yard TD pass to Stephen Starring in their 28-23 win vs Pittsburgh on 09-25-83
Caught his own deflected pass for an 8 yard loss in their 21-7 win over the Buffalo Bills on 11-06-83
Ran 3 yards on a fake bootleg for the game winning TD in their 20-13 win over the Jets on 10-20-85
Scored on a 1 yard run was the game winning TD in their 17-13 win over Miami on 11-03-85
149 Regular Season Games/135 started and 4 Playoff Games/3 started
48 completions for 571 yards + 3 TDs in the playoffs
Threw a 26 yard TD pass to Russ Francis in their 24-21 Divisional loss to the Raiders on 12-18-76
Threw a 22 yard TD to Don Hasselbeck in their 28-13 First Round Playoff loss Miami on 01-08-83
Tossed an 8 yard TD, on 4th down, to Irving Fryar, in their 46-10 Super Bowl loss to Da' Bears on 01-26-86
#116 pick in the 1975 NFL Draft
Inducted into the Patriots Hall of Fame in 1995
Kansas State Wildcat

GRONKOWSKI, Dan (#82)
Born on January 21, 1985 in Amherst, NY
6'6" and 255 pounds
Tight End   2011
5 games/1 started (on 10-16-11)
Maryland Terrapin

GRONKOWSKI, Robert "Rob" (#87) *"Gronk"*
Born on May 14, 1989 in Amherst, NY
6'6" and 265 pounds
Tight End (KR/DB)   2010-18
521 receptions for 7,861 yards + 79 TDs and 1 carry for a 2 yard TD
3 kickoff returns for 16 yards, 1 fumble recovery and 1 reception for a 2 point conversion
Caught 1 TD pass from Jimmy Garoppolo and 78 Regular Season TD passes from Tom Brady
Caught 3 TD passes from Tom Brady (19 yds, 9 yds & 25 yds) in their 39-26 win over Pittsburgh on 11-14-10
Longest was an 11 yard return of a kickoff by Dan Carpenter in their 38-24 win over Miami on 09-12-11
Advanced a lateral from Tom Brady 2 yards for a TD in their 31-24 win over the Colts on 12-04-11
Caught a 13 yard TD pass from Jimmy Garoppolo in their 41-14 loss to the Chiefs on 09-29-14
Caught 3 TD passes from Tom Brady (6 yds, 2 yds + 46 yds) in their 51-23 romp over the Bears on 10-26-14
Recovered a fumble by Dion Lewis, after his 19 yard reception, in their 28-21 win over Pittsburgh on 09-10-15
Caught a career long 76 yard TD pass from Tom Brady in their 27-26 win over the NY Giants on 11-15-15
Caught a 2 point pass from Tom Brady in their 27-24 win over the Steelers on 12-17-17
Used as a Safety on "Hail Mary" passes on 10-16-11, 10-30-11, 09-24-17 and on 12-09-18
Led the NFL with most the TD receptions in 2011 with 17
Set NFL record with the most TDs scored by a TE in a season with 18 in 2011
AFC Offensive Player of the Week in their 34-27 win over Washington on 12-11-11
AFC Offensive Player of the Week in their 27-24 win over Pittsburgh on 12-17-17
AFC All Pro Tight End in 2011, 2012, 2014, 2015, 2017
First Team All Pro Tight End in 2011, 2014, 2015, 2017
115 Regular Season Games/100 started and 16 Playoff Games/16 started
81 receptions for 1,163 yards + 12 TDs in the playoffs
Caught 3 TDs from Tom Brady (10 yds, 12 yds + 19 yds) in their 45-10 Divisional win vs Denver on 01-14-12
Caught a 5 yard TD pass from Tom Brady in their 35-31 Divisonal win over Baltimore on 01-10-15
Was a Safety on Joe Flacco's "Hail Mary" pass attempt in their 35-31 Divisional win vs the Ravens on 01-10-15
Caught a 5 yard TD pass from Tom Brady in their 45-7 Championship win over the Colts on 01-18-15
Caught a 22 yard TD pass from Tom Brady in their 28-24 Super Bowl win over Seattle on 02-01-15
Caught 2 TDs from Tom Brady (8 yds + 16 yds) in their 27-20 Divisional win over the Chiefs on 02-16-16
Caught a 4 yard TD pass from Tom Brady in their 20-18 Championship loss to Denver on 01-24-16
Caught a 4 yard TD pass from Tom Brady in their 35-14 Divisional win over Tennessee on 01-13-18
Caught 2 TDs from Tom Brady (5 yds + 4 yds) in their 41-33 Super Bowl loss to the Eagles on 02-04-18
Holds the NFL Record of Most Career Playoff TDs (12) by a Tight End
Member of the 2014, 2016 and 2018 World Championship Teams
Ron Burton Community Service Award in 2016
#42 pick in the 2010 NFL Draft
Arizona Wildcat

GUTIERREZ, Matt (#7)
Born on June 9, 1984 in Concord, CA
6'4" and 235 pounds
Quarterback   2007-08
Completed a 15 yard pass to Donte' Stallworth in their 49-28 rout of the Dolphins on 10-21-07
Knelt 5 times for minus 13 yards
5 games
Idaho State Bengals

GUY, Lawrence (#93)
Born on March 17, 1990 in Las Vegas, NV
6'4" and 315 pounds
Defensive Lineman   2017-19
5 sacks, 1 interception for 5 yards, 2 fumble recoveries and 1 blocked field goal attempt
Sacked Ben Roethlisberger, Sam Darnold, Lamar Jackson, Josh Allen and Ryan Fitzpatrick
Recovered fumbles by Carson Wentz and Mark Ingram
Blocked Nick Novak's 51 yard field goal attempt in their 21-13 win over the LA Chargers on 10-29-17
Had a 5 yard return of a pass by Baker Mayfield in their 27-13 win over the Browns on 10-27-19
48 Regular Season Games/46 started and 7 Playoff Games/7 started
1.5 sacks in the playoffs
Sacked Blake Bortles in their 24-20 Championship win over the Jaguars on 01-21-18
Shared in a sack of Patrick Mahomes in their 37-31 Championship win over the Chiefs on 01-20-19
Member of the 2018 World Championship Team
Arizona State Sun Devil

GUYTON JR., Gary (#59)
Born on November 14, 1985 in Hinesville, GA
6'2" and 245 pounds
Linebacker   2008-11
4.5 sacks, 3 interceptions for 89 yards + 1 TD and 3 fumble recoveries for 42 yards + 1 TD
Shared in a sack of David Garrard and strip sacked Ryan Fitzpatrick
Sacked Trent Edwards, Ben Roethliseberger and Shaun Hill
Intercepted Carson Palmer, Jay Cutler and Ben Roethlisberger
Recovered fumbles by Patrick Ramsey, Jerricho Cotchery and Johnny Knox
Returned Patrick Ramsey's fumble 7 yards in their 41-7 rout of the Denver Broncos on 10-20-08
Had a career long 59 yard TD return of a pass by Carson Palmer in their 38-24 win vs the Bengals on 09-12-10
Returned Johnny Knox's fumble 35 yards for a TD in their 36-7 rout of the Bears on 12-12-10
Strip sacked Ryan Fitzpatrick in their 34-3 rout of the Buffalo Bills on 12-26-10
60 Regular Season Games/32 started and 2 Playoff Games/2 started
Georgia Tech Yellow Jacket

GUYTON, Myron (#29)
Born on August 26, 1967 in Metcalf, GA
6'1" and 205 pounds
Safety   1994-95
5 interceptions for 86 yards, 4 fumble recoveries for 31 yards and 1 recovery of an onside kick
Intercepted Scott Mitchell, Dan Marino and Jim Harbaugh and had 2 interceptions of Jim Kelly
Recovered fumbles by Terry Kirby, Tyrone Montgomery, Andrew Reed and Lamont Warren
Recovered an onside kick by Doug Pelfrey in their 31-28 win over the Cincinnati Bengals on 09-18-94
Had a 3 yard return of a Scott Mitchell pass, tipped by Chris Slade, to seal 23-17 win vs Detroit on 09-25-94
Had a career long 26 yard return of a fumble by Andrew Reed in their 41-17 rout of the Bills on 12-18-94
Had a carrer long 45 yard return of a pass by Dan Marino in their 34-17 win over Miami on 11-12-95
Intercepted Jim Harbaugh and lateraled it to Ricky Reynolds in their 24-10 loss to the Colts on 11-19-95
30 Regular Season Games/30 started and 1 Playoff Game/1 started (on 01-01-95)
Eastern Kentucky Colonel

GUZIK III, John (#97)
Born on September 25, 1962 in Cleveland, OH
6'4" and 270 pounds
Defensive Lineman   1987
3 games/2 started
Ohio University Bobcat

HAGEN, Halvor (#62)
Born on February 4, 1947 in Oslo, Norway
6'5" and 245 pounds
Guard/DE (KR)   1971-72
Had a 7 yard return of a kickoff by Bruce Gossett in their 27-10 loss to the 49ers on 10-31-71
Sacked Earl Morrall in their 52-0 loss to the Miami Dolphins on 11-12-72
26 games/15 started
Weber State Wildcat

HAGGERTY, Mike (#75)
Born on October 14, 1945 in Royal Oak, MI
6'4" and 245 pounds
Tackle   1971
13 games
Miami Hurricane

HALEY, Darryl (#68)
Born on February 16, 1961 in Gardena, CA
6'4" and 269 pounds
Tackle   1982-86
57 Regular Season Games/24 started and 1 Playoff Game/1 started (on 01-04-87)
#55 pick in the 1982 NFL Draft
Utah Ute

HALL, Ron (#23) *"Haystacks"*
Born on April 30, 1937 in Goreville, IL
6'0" and 190 pounds
Safety   1961-67
29 interceptions for 476 yards + 1 TD
Intercepted Jacky Lee, George Shaw, Frank Tripucka, Mickey Slaughter, Joe Namath and Max Choboian
Intercepted Dick Wood, John McCormick, Cotton Davidson and Daryle Lamonica
2 interceptions of Warren Rabb, Tom Flores, Tobin Rote, Dick Wood, Len Dawson and George Blanda
Had 3 interceptions of John Hadl and 4 interceptions of Jack Kemp
Recovered fumbles by Don Norton, Clem Daniels and Curtis McClinton
Shared in a sack of Cotton Davidson, sacked Mickey Slaughter and Jack Kemp and had 2 sacks of Tom Flores
Attempted to return a punt by Wayne Crow for no gain in their 28-28 win over Buffalo on 11-03-62
Blocked Tommy Brooker's potential GW 28 yard FGA, with 26 ticks left, in 10-10 tie with KS on 11-21-65
Had a career long 87 yard return of a pass by John McCormick in their 24-10 win vs Denver on 09-18-66
AFL All Star Defensive Back in 1963 and First Team All Pro Safety in 1964
88 Regular Season Games/81 started and 2 Playoff Games/2 started
Missouri Valley Viking

HAMILTON, Bobby (#91)
Born on July 1, 1971 in Denver, CO
6'5" and 280 pounds
Defensive End   2000-03
10.5 sacks, 2 fumble recoveries, 1 interception and 1 kickoff return for no gain
Sacked Shane Matthews, Chris Chandler, Jay Fiedler and Brett Favre
Shared in a sack of Rob Johnson and had 3 sacks of Vinny Testaverde and Peyton Manning
Recovered fumbles by Vinny Testaverde and Peyton Manning
Recovered Paul Edinger's squibbed kickoff in their 24-17 loss to the Chicago Bears on 12-10-00
Intercepted a pass by Joey Harrington in their 20-12 victory over the Detroit Lions on 11-28-02
64 Regular Season Games/62 started and 6 Playoff Games/6 started
Sacked Kurt Warner in their 20-17 Super Bowl win over the St. Louis Rams on 02-03-02
Member of the 2001 and 2003 World Championship Teams
Southern Mississippi Golden Eagle

HAMILTON, Ray (#71) *"Sugar Bear"*
Born on January 20, 1951 in Omaha, NE
6'1" and 244 pounds
NT/DE   1973-81
Nicknamed *"Sugar Bear"* since high school
54 sacks, 14 fumble recoveries for 23 yards + 1 TD and blocked 2 field goal attempts
Shared in a sack of Dennis Shaw, John Hadl, Jim Zorn and David Humm
Sacked Len Dawson, Wayne Clark, Dan Fouts, Joe Namath, Norm Snead, Earl Morrall, Gary Marangi
        and Jim Hart
Sacked Sam Adkins, James Harris, Bill Munson, Ron Jaworski, Steve Bartkowski, Mike Phipps and Don Strock
Sacked Brian Sipe, Clint Longley, Vince Ferragamo and Dan Manucci as well
Recored 2 sacks of Roger Staubach, Ken Stabler, Joe Ferguson and Bill Troup
Had 3 sacks of Steve Ramsey and David Woodley and 4 sacks of Richard Todd
Recorded 5 sacks of Bob Griese and 5 ½ sacks of Bert Jones
Recovered fumbles by Bobby Douglass, Perry Williams, John Hadl and Ken Stabler
Recovered fumbles by Roland Hooks, Steve Myers, Haskel Stanback, Jim Otis and Brian Sipe
Recovered 2 fumbles by Joe Ferguson and 3 fumbles by Jim Hart
Had a 23 yard TD return of a fumble by Jim Hart in their 24-17 loss to the St. Louis Cardinals on 11-02-75
Blocked a 44 yard FGA by Jim Bakken in their 24-17 loss to the St. Louis Cardinals on 11-02-75
Blocked a 19 yard FGA by Ove Johansson in their 14-6 win over the Philadelphia Eagles on 11-27-77
Deflected Steve Mick-Mayer's kickoff out of bounds in their 20-17 loss to the Buffalo Bills on 11-22-81
132 Regular Season Games/117 started and 2 Playoff Games/2 started
#342 pick in the 1973 NFL Draft
Oklahoma Sooner

HAMILTON, Woodrow (#74)
Born on December 20, 1992 in Raleigh, MS
6'3" and 315 pounds
Defensive Lineman   2016
2 games/1 started (on 10-19-16)
Member of the 2016 World Championship Team
Mississippi Rebel

HAMMOND, Kim (#15)
Born on October 12, 1944 in Miami, FL
6'1" and 190 pounds
Quarterback   1969
2 completions for 31 yards and ran for a 2 point conversion
Longest was an 18 yard pass to Ron Sellers in their 28-18 loss to San Diego on 12-07-69
Ran for a 2 point conversion in their 28-18 loss to the San Diego Chargers on 12-07-69
3 games
Florida State Seminole

HANKERSON, Leonard (#15)
Born on January 30, 1989 in Ft. Lauderdale, FL
6'1" and 205 pounds
Wide Receiver   2015
Only game played was on 12-20-15
Miami Hurricane

HANNAH, John (#73) *"Hog"*
Born on April 4, 1951 in Canton, GA
6'2" and 265 pounds
Left Guard   1973-85
Nicknamed *"Hog"* because of his fierce tenacity in the pit
10 fumble recoveries for 1 TD and 1 kickoff return for no gain
Recovered fumbles by Chris Farasopoulous, Sam Cunningham, Vegas Ferguson and Tony Collins
Recovered fumbles by Tom Owen and Steve Grogan and fell on 3 fumbles by Stanley Morgan
Recovered a fumbled punt return by Chris Farasopoulos in their 33-13 loss to the Jets on 11-11-73
Recovered a bad snap in the end zone for a TD in their 34-27 loss to the Dolphins on 12-15-74
Recovered a short kickoff by John Leypoldt in their 37-13 loss to the Buffalo Bills on 12-09-73
AFC Pro Bowl Guard in 1976, 1978-1985
First Team All Pro Guard in 1976, 1978, 1979, 1980, 1981, 1983, 1985
183 Regular Season Games/183 started and 7 Playoff Games/7 started
#4 pick in the 1973 NFL Draft
Inducted into the Pro Football Hall of Fame on 07-27-91
His Uniform # 73 was retired by the Patriots on 09-30-90
Inducted into the Patriots Hall of Fame in 1991
Alabama Crimson Tide

HANNEMAN, Craig (#74)
Born on July 1, 1949 in Salem, OR
6'3" and 240 pounds
Defensive Lineman   1974-75
4.5 sacks and 1 fumble recovery
Shared in a sack of Dan Fouts, sacked Bob Griese and Joe Namath and had 2 sacks of Bert Jones
Recovered Lynn Swann's fumble in their 21-17 loss to the Pittsburgh Steelers on 12-08-74
20 games/3 started
Oregon State Beaver

HANSEN, Brian (#10)
Born on October 26, 1960 in Hawarden, IA
6'4" and 215 pounds
Punter   1990
90 punts for 3,752 yards and 1 fumble recovery
Longest punt was 69 yards in their 37-13 loss to the New York Jets on 09-30-90
Recovered a fumbled punt return by Anthony Edwards in their 48-20 loss to the Eagles on 11-04-90
16 games
Sioux Falls Cougar

HANSEN, Bruce (#24 and #35)
Born on September 18, 1961 in American Fork, UT
6'1" and 225 pounds
FB (KR)   1987
Wore #24 for 3 games and #35 for 3 games
16 carries for 44 yards, 1 reception for 22 yards, 1 kickoff return for 14 yards and 1 fumble recovery
Longest run was 7 yards in their 14-7 win over the Buffalo Bills on 10-11-87
Recovered Michael LeBlanc's fumble in their 14-7 victory over the Buffalo Bills on 10-11-87
Caught a 22 yard pass from Doug Flutie in their 21-7 win over the Houston Oilers on 10-18-87
Had a 14 yard return of a kickoff by Lee Johnson in their 21-7 win over the Houston Oilers on 10-18-87
6 games/2 started
BYU Cougar

HANSON, Chris (#6)
Born on October 25, 1976 in Senoia, GA
6'2" and 223 pounds
Punter   2007-09
149 punts for 6,185 yards
Longest punt was 70 yards in their 17-10 win over the Chiefs on 09-07-08
Had a 41 yard punt, on 3rd down, in very windy conditions, in their 13-0 shutout of Buffalo on 12-28-08
AFC Special Team Player of the Week in their 13-0 shutout of the Bills on 12-28-08
48 Regular Season Games and 4 Playoff Games
Marshall Thundering Herd

HARBOR, Clayton "Clay" (#81)
Born July 2, 1987 in Dwight, IL
6'3" and 240 pounds
Tight End   2016
3 games
Member of the 2016 World Championship Team
Missouri State Bear

HARE, Edward "Eddie" (#8)
Born on May 30, 1957 in Ulysses, KS
6'4" and 209 pounds
Punter   1979
83 punts for 3,038 yards and 1 completion for 4 yards
Longest punt was 58 yards in their 16-13 Overtime loss to the Steelers on 09-03-79
Recovered poor snap and tossed a 4 yard pass to Mosi Tatupu in their 28-13 win vs Miami on 10-21-79
16 games
#106 pick in the 1979 NFL Draft
Tulsa Golden Hurricane

HARLOW, Pat (#77)
Born on March 16, 1969 in Norco, CA
6'6" and 295 pounds
Tackle   1991-95
74 Regular Season Games/64 started and 1 Playoff Game/1 started (on 01-01-95)
#11 pick in the 1991 NFL Draft
USC Trojan

HARMON, Duron (#30 and #21) *"The Closer"*
Born on January 24, 1991 in Dover, DE
6'1" and 205 pounds
Defensive Back　　　　　　2013-19
Wore #30 from 2013-17 and wore #21 from 2018-19
17 interceptions for 193 yards and 3 fumble recoveries for 3 yards
Intercepted Tyrod Taylor, Deshaun Watson, Derek Carr, Matt Moore and Patrick Mahomes
Intercepted Kirk Cousins, Daniel Jones and Sam Darnold
Had 4 interceptions of Ryan Tannehill and 5 interceptions of Ben Roethlisberger
Recovered fumbles by Dane Sanzenbacher, Charles James and DJ Clark
Had a career long 60 yard return of a pass by Ryan Tannehill in their 41-13 rout of the Dolphins on 12-14-14
Intercepted Ryan Tannehill's 4th down pass in the end zone to preserve their 31-24 win over Miami on 09-18-16
Had a 4 yard return of a fumble by DJ Clark in their 31-20 loss to the Jaguars on 09-16-18
111 Regular Season Games/29 started and 17 Playoff Games/6 started
3 interceptions for 39 yards in the playoffs
Intercepted Joe Flacco in the end zone in their 35-31 Divisional win over the Ravens on 01-10-15
Had a 31 yard return of a pass by Brock Osweiler in their 34-16 Divisional win over Houston on 01-14-17
Had an 8 yard return of a pass by Nick Foles in their 41-33 Super Bowl loss to the Eagles on 02-04-18
Member of the 2014, 2016 and 2018 World Championship Teams
#91 pick in the 2012 NFL Draft
Rutgers Scarlet Knight

HARPER, Chris (#14)
Born on December 7, 1993 in Northbridge, CA
5'11" and 176 pounds
PR/WR　　　　　　　　2015
3 punt returns for 17 yards and 1 reception for 6 yards
Longest was a 10 yard return of a punt by Britton Colquitt in their 30-24 OT loss to Denver on 11-29-15
Caught a 6 yard pass from Tom Brady in their 20-10 loss to the Miami Dolphins on 01-03-16
5 games
California Golden Bear

HARRIS, Damien (#37)
Born on February 11, 1997 in Richmond, KY
5'11" and 213 pounds
Running Back　　　　　2019--
4 carries for 12 yards
Longest run was 13 yards in their 33-0 shutout of the New York Jets on 10-21-19
2 games
#87 pick in the 2019 NFL Draft
Alabama Crimson Tide

HARRIS, David (#45)
Born on January 21, 1984 in Grand Rapids, MI
6'2" and 250 pounds
Linebacker　　　　　　2017
Sacked Tyrod Taylor and shared in a sack of Nathan Peterman in their 23-3 rout of Buffalo on 12-03-17
10 games/6 started
Michigan Wolverine

HARRIS, Marshall (#78)
Born on December 6, 1955 in San Antonio, TX
6'6" and 261 pounds
Defensive Lineman   1983
Sacked Cliff Stoudt in their 28-23 victory over the Pittsburgh Steelers on 09-25-83
6 games/2 started
Texas Christian Horned Frog

HARRIS, Melvin "Antwan" (#23)
Born on May 29, 1977 in Raleigh, NC
5'9" and 194 pounds
Defensive Back   2000-03
Returned a pass by Peyton Manning 11 yards, late in the 4th Qtr, in their 24-16 win vs the Colts on 10-08-00
Recovered Troy Brown's fumbled punt return in their 16-13 win over the Bengals on 11-19-00
Sacked Jay Fiedler in their 27-24 loss to the Miami Dolphins on 12-24-00
52 Regular Season Games/2 started and 3 Playoff Games
Advanced Troy Brown's lateral 49 yards for a TD in their 24-17 Championship win over the Steelers on 01-27-02
Forced a fumble by Ricky Proehl in their 20-17 Super Bowl win over the St. Louis Rams on 02-03-02
Member of the 2001 and 2003 World Championship Teams
187th pick in the 2000 NFL Draft
Virginia Cavalier

HARRIS, Raymont (#28)
Born on December 23, 1970 in Lorain, OH
6'0" and 226 pounds
Running Back   2000
3 carries for 14 yards and 2 receptions for 1 yard
Longest run was 7 yards in their 24-17 loss to the Chicago Bears on 12-10-00
Longest reception was a 2 yard pass from Drew Bledsoe in their 24-17 loss to the Bears on 12-10-00
Only game played was on 12-10-00
Ohio State Buckeye

HARRIS, Rickie (#25)
Born on May 15, 1943 in St. Louis, MO
5'11" and 182 pounds
DB/PR   1971-72
3 interceptions for 45 yards, 9 punt returns for 24 yards, 2 sacks and 4 fumble recoveries for 2 yards
Sacked Terry Bradshaw and Joe Namath
Recovered fumbles by Vic Washington, Jim Braxton, OJ Simpson and returned Wayne Patrick's fumble 2 yards
Longest was a 9 yard return of a punt by David Lee in their 21-17 win over the Baltimore Colts on 12-19-71
Had a career long 32 yard return of a pass by Joe Namath in their 41-13 loss to the NY Jets on 10-15-72
Had a 13 yard return of a pass by Archie Manning to help seal their 17-10 win vs the Saints on 12-10-72
28 games/21 started
Arizona Wildcat

HARRIS, Ronald "Ronnie" (#84)
Born on June 4, 1970 in Granada Hills, CA
5'11" and 179 pounds
WR/PR   1993-94
26 punt returns for 227 yards, 6 kickoff returns for 90 yards and had 1 reception for 11 yards
Returned (Team Record) 10 punts in their 17-14 loss to the Steelers on 12-05-93
Longest was a 21 yard return of a punt by Brian Hansen in their 20-17 win over the Browns on 12-19-93
Longest was a 19 yard return of a kickoff by Matt Stover in their 20-17 win over Cleveland on 12-19-93
Caught an 11 yard pass from Drew Bledsoe in their 24-17 loss to the Jets on 10-16-94
6 games
Oregon Duck

HARRISON, James (#92) *"Deebo"*
Born on May 4, 1978 in Akron, OH
6'0" and 242 pounds
LB/DE   2017
Sacked Bryce Petty *twice,* on the last 2 plays, in their 26-6 victory over the New York Jets on 12-31-17
1 Regular Season Game and 3 Playoff Games
Kent State Golden Flash

HARRISON, Rodney (#37) *"The Hitman"*
Born on December 15, 1972 in Markham, IL
6'1" and 220 pounds
Safety   2003-08
8 interceptions for 16 yards, 9 sacks and 2 fumble recoveries for 16 yards
Intercepted Chad Pennington, Trent Green, Luke McCown, Brad Johnson, Peyton Manning and
          J.T. O'Sullivan
Recorded 2 interceptions of Kerry Collins as well
Sacked Tony Banks, Drew Bledsoe, J.P. Losman, Tony Romo and Cleo Lemon
Recorded 1 strip sack and one regular sack of Jay Fiedler and Josh McCown
Had a 16 yard return of a fumble by Chris Chambers and recovered a 4th Qtr fumble by David Garrard
Returned a Kerry Collins pass 2 yards, tipped by Richard Seymour, in their 17-6 win vs the Giants on 10-12-03
Lost 2 yards returning another pass by Kerry Collins in their 17-6 win over the NY Giants on 10-12-03
Had a 12 yard return of a pass by Trent Green, from the end zone, in their 27-19 win vs the Chiefs on 11-22-04
AFC Defensive Player of the Week in their 23-12 win over Arizona on 09-19-04
First Team All Pro Safety in 2003
63 Regular Season Games/62 started and 9 Playoff Games/9 started
7 interceptions for 118 yards + 1 TD and 1 strip sack in the playoffs
Had a 7 yard return of a pass by Steve McNair in their 17-14 Divisional win over the Titans on 01-10-04
Intercepted Peyton Manning in the end zone in their 24-14 Championship win over the Colts on 01-18-04
Strip sacked Jake Delhomme in their 32-29 Super Bowl win over the Panthers on 02-01-04
Had a 9 yard end zone return of a pass by Peyton Manning in their 20-3 Divisional win vs the Colts on 01-16-05
Had an 87 yard TD return of a pass by Ben Roethlisberger in their 41-27 Championship win vs Pitt on 01-23-05
Sacked Donovan McNabb in their 24-21 Super Bowl win over the Philadelphia Eagles on 02-06-05
Lost 1 yard returning a pass by Donovan McNabb in their 24-21 Super Bowl win over the Eagles on 02-06-05
Returned a Donovan McNabb pass 6 yards, tipped by LJ Smith, in their 24-21 SB win vs Philly on 02-06-05
Had a 10 yard return of a pass by David Garrard in their 31-20 Divisional win over the Jaguars on 01-12-08
Member of the 2003 and 2004 World Championship Teams
Inducted in the Patriots Hall of Fame on July 29, 2019
Western Illinois Leatherneck

HARRY, N'Keal (#15)
Born on December 17, 1997 in Toronto, Ontario
6'4" and 225 pounds
Wide Receiver   2019--
12 receptions for 105 yards + 2 TDs and 5 carries for 49 yards
Caught 2 TD passes from Tom Brady
Longest run was 18 yards in their 24-17 win over Buffalo on 12-21-19
Longest reception was an 18 yard pass from Tom Brady in their 27-24 loss to Miami on 12-29-19
7 Regular Season Games/5 started and 1 Playoff Game
#32 pick in the 2019 NFL Draft
Arizona State Sun Devil

HARTLEY, Ken (#7)
Born on April 28, 1957 in Hamilton, Bermuda
6'2" and 200 pounds
Punter   1981
9 punts for 266 yards
Longest punt was 41 yards in their 28-24 loss to the NY Jets on 10-11-81
2 games (on Oct. 11th and Oct. 18th)
Catawba Indian

HARVEY JR., Richard (#58)
Born on September 11, 1966 in Pascagoula, MS
6'1" and 235 pounds
Linebacker   1990-91
17 games/9 started
Tulane Green Wave

HASSELBECK, Don (#80) *"Hass"*
Born on April 1, 1955 in Cincinnati, OH
6'7" and 245 pounds
Tight End (KR)   1977-83
99 receptions for 1,444 yards + 15 TDs and 1 kickoff return of 7 yards
Caught 3 TDs from Matt Cavanaugh
Caught 12 Regular Season passes and 1 Post Season TD pass from Steve Grogan
Snared a 4 yard 4th Qtr TD pass from Steve Grogan in their 24-20 win over San Diego on 10-16-77
Caught 16 yard TD pass from S. Grogan with 3 minutes left in their 37-31 win vs Seattle on 09-21-80
Had a 7 yard return of a kickoff by Rafael Septien in their 35-21 loss to the Dallas Cowboys on 09-21-81
Longest reception was a 51 yard pass from Steve Grogan in their 28-24 loss to the Jets on 10-11-81
86 Regular Season Games/30 started and 2 Playoff Games
7 receptions for 87 yards + 1 TD in the playoffs
Caught a 22 yard TD pass from Steve Grogan in their 28-13 First Round Playoff loss to Miami on 01-08-83
#52 pick in the 1977 NFL Draft
Colorado Buffalo

HAUCK, Timothy "Tim" (#40)
Born on December 20, 1966 in Butte, MT
5'10" and 187 pounds
Defensive Back   1990
10 games
Montana Grizzly

HAUSER, Art (#67)
Born on June 19, 1929 in Rubican, WI
6'0" and 237 pounds
G/T/DL   1960
Played on both sides of the line of scrimmage
Shared in a sack of Hunter Enis in their 42-14 victory over the Dallas Texans on 11-18-60
8 games/7 started
Xavier Musketeer

HAWKINS JR., Artrell (#25)
Born on November 24, 1976 in Johnstown, PA
5'10" and 190 pounds
Defensive Back   2005-06
Sacked Chris Simms in their 28-0 shutout of the Tampa Bay Buccaneers on 12-17-05
Recovered a fumbled kickoff return by Terrence Wilkins in their 27-20 loss to the Colts on 11-05-06
Intercepted a pass by Chad Pennington in their 17-14 loss to the NY Jets on 11-12-06
19 Regular Season Games/16 started and 5 Playoff Games/5 started
Cincinnati Bearcat

HAWKINS, Mickal "Mike" (#59)
Born on November 29, 1955 in Bay City, TX
6'2" and 235 pounds
Linebacker   1978-81
11 sacks, 5 interceptions for 56 yards and 1 TD, 2 fumble recoveries and 1 recovery of a free kick
Sacked Terry Bradshaw, Greg Landry, WR Terry LeCount, Joe Montana, Joe Ferguson and Marc Wilson
Sacked Richard Todd *5 times* (4 times in their 56-3 rout of the New York Jets on 09-09-79)
Sacked WR Terry LeCount in their 27-23 win over the Vikings on 12-16-79
Intercepted Don Strock, Bob Griese, Richard Todd, Ken Stabler and Bill Kenney
Recovered fumbles by Danny White and Ottis Anderson
Recovered the free kick by George Roberts in their 33-24 win over the Dolphins on 10-22-78
Had a career long 35 yard TD return of a pass by Don Strock in their 28-13 win over Miami on 10-21-79
Intercepted a pass by Richard Todd, tipped by Mel Lunsford, in their 34-21 win vs the NY Jets on 11-02-80
59 Regular Season Games/45 started and 1 Playoff Game (on 12-31-78)
#188 pick in the 1978 NFL Draft
Texas A & I Javelina

HAWKINS, Steven (#80)
Born on March 16, 1971 in Detroit, MI
6'5" and 210 pounds
Wide Receiver   1994
2 receptions for 22 yards
Recovered (teammate) Matt Bahr's short kickoff in their 21-17 loss to the LA Raiders on 10-09-94
Longest reception was a 14 yard pass from Drew Bledsoe in their 13-6 loss to the Browns on 11-06-94
7 games
#166 pick in the 1994 NFL Draft
Western Michigan Bronco

HAWTHORNE, Greg (#27)
Born on September 5, 1956 in Fort Worth, TX
6'2" and 228 pounds
WR/TE (RB/KR)   1984-86
34 receptions for 361 yards + 1 TD and 4 kickoff returns for 40 yards
Longest was a 14 yard return of a kickoff by Rafael Septien in their 20-17 loss to Dallas on 11-22-84
Longest reception was a 28 yard TD pass from Steve Grogan in their 17-13 win over Miami on 11-03-85
Caught a 28 yard flea flicker TD pass, on 4th + 1, in their 17-13 win over the Dolphins on 11-03-85
Ran for a 5 yard gain and recovered Reggie Dupard's fumble in their 34-27 win over Miami on 12-22-86
43 Regular Season Games/11 started and 5 Playoff Games
Recovered Lorenzo Hampton's fumbled kickoff return in their 31-14 Championship win vs Miami on 01-12-86
Baylor Bear

HAYES, Chris (#29)
Born on May 7, 1972 in San Bernardino, CA
6'0" and 206 pounds
Safety   2002
4 games
Washington State Cougar

HAYES JR., Donald (#81)
Born on July 13, 1975 in Century, FL
6'4" and 220 pounds
Wide Receiver   2002
12 receptions for 133 yards + 2 TDs
Caught 2 TD passes from Tom Brady
Longest reception was a 40 yard TD pass from Tom Brady in their 30-14 win over the Steelers on 09-09-02
12 games/1 started (on 09-22-02)
Wisconsin Badger

HAYNES, Mike (#40)
Born on July 1, 1953 in Denison, TX
6'2" and 192 pounds
CB/PR　　　　　　　　　1976-82
28 interceptions for 388 yds + 1 TD, 111 punt returns for 1,159 yds + 2 TDs and a 65 yd lateral TD return
Intercepted Gary Marangi, Steve Ramsey, Ken Stabler, Pat Ryan, Bill Troup, Jeff Komlo and Mike Pagel
Intercepted a pass by Kansas City Chiefs WR Henry Marshall
Had 2 interceptions of Joe Namath, Richard Todd, Steve Myer, Steve Bartkowski and Joe Ferguson
Had 2 interceptions of Bob Griese, Matt Robinson and Jim Zorn and 4 interceptions of Bert Jones
Recovered fumbles by Franco Harris, Gary Marangi, Sidney Thornton, Larry Csonka and Don Hardeman
Recovered a fumble by Reggie McKenzie and returned a fumble by Curtis Brown 6 yards
Had a career long 89 yard TD return of a punt by Marv Bateman in their 20-10 win over Buffalo on 11-07-76
Intercepted a Joe Namath *twice* and Richard Todd once, in their 38-24 win over the Jets on 11-21-76
Returned a punt by Billy Van Heusen 62 yards for a TD in their 38-14 win over the Denver Broncos on 11-28-76
Had a 50 yard return of a pass by Pat Ryan, to the 1 yard line, in their 55-21 rout of the NY Jets on 10-29-78
Had a 65 yard TD return of a lateral from John Zamberlin, after a blocked FGA, in their 21-11 win on 10-05-80
Had a 3 yard return of a pass by WR Henry Marshall in their 33-17 win over the Chiefs on 10-04-81
AFC Pro Bowl Cornerback in 1976-80, 1982
AFC Rookie of the Year in 1976
90 Regular Season Games/86 started and 3 Playoff Games/3 started
#5 pick in the 1976 NFL Draft
Inducted into the Pro Football Hall of Fame on 07-26-97
His Uniform # 40 was retired by the Patriots
Inducted into the Patriots Hall of Fame in 1994
Arizona State Sun Devil

HAYNESWORTH III, Albert (#92)
Born on June 17, 1981 in Hartsville, SC
6'6" and 320 pounds
Defensive Lineman　　　　2011
6 games
Tennessee Volunteer

HENDERSON, Jerome (#36 and #26)
Born on August 8, 1969 in Portsmouth, VA
5'10" and 193 pounds
DB/PR　　　　　　　　　1991-93 and 1996
Wore #36 from 1991-93 and #26 in 1996
7 interceptions for 52 yards and 27 punt returns for 201 yards
Intercepted Warren Moon, Dan Marino, Jeff George, Sean Salisbury and Glenn Foley and had 2 int's of Jim Kelly
Longest was a 39 yard return of a punt by Reggie Roby in their 20-10 loss to the Dolphins on 10-06-91
Had a career long 34 yard return of a pass by Dan Marino in their 38-17 loss to Miami on 10-18-92
Had 9 yard return of a Jeff George pass that set up OT Game Winning FG in 37-34 win vs Indy on 11-15-92
40 Regular Season Games/10 started and 3 Playoff Games
#41 pick in the 1991 NFL Draft
Clemson Tiger

HENDLEY, David (#28)
Born on June 29, 1964
6'0" and 188 pounds
Defensive Back   1987
2 games (on Oct. 4th and Oct. 11th)
Southern Connecticut State Fighting Owl

HENKE, Karl (#80)
Born on March 8, 1945 in Ventura, CA
6'4" and 245 pounds
Defensive End   1969
Sacked Steve Tensi in their 35-7 loss to the Denver Broncos on 09-14-69
10 games/7 started
Tulsa Golden Hurricane

HENNESSEY, Tom (#30) *"Brookline Blur"*
Born on February 15, 1942 in Boston, MA
6'0" and 180 pounds
DB/PR   1965-66
8 interceptions for 113 yards and 12 punt returns for 60 yards
Intercepted George Blanda, John Hadl, Cotton Davidson, Dick Wood and Jack Kemp
Intercepted Kansas City Chiefs WR Otis Taylor and had 2 interceptions of Joe Namath
Had a career long 33 yard return of a Joe Namath pass, from 2 yard line, in their 24-24 Tie with the Jets
        on 10-02-66
Longest was an 11 yard return of a punt by Mike Eischeid in their 24-21 win over the Raiders on 10-30-66
Intercepted the only career pass attempt of WR Otis Taylor in their 27-27 Tie with the Chiefs on 11-20-66
Intercepted a pass by Jack Kemp in the end zone in their 14-3 win over the Bills at Fenway Park on 12-04-66
28 games
Holy Cross Crusader

HENSON, Luther (#70)
Born on March 25, 1959 in Sandusky, OH
6'0" and 275 pounds
Nose Tackle   1982-84
Sacked Mike Pagel once and Joe Ferguson *twice*
21 Regular Season Games/2 started and 1 Playoff Game (on 01-08-83)
Ohio State Buckeye

HERLINE, Alan (#6)
Born on September 16, 1964 in Monroe, LA
6'0" and 168 pounds
Punter   1987
25 punts for 861 yards
Longest punt was 50 yards in their 14-7 win over Buffalo on 10-11-87
3 games
Vanderbilt Commodore

HERNANDEZ, Aaron (#85 and #81)
Born on November 6, 1989 in Bristol, CT
6'2" and 250 pounds
Tight End (RB)   2010-12
Wore #85 in 2010 and #81 from 2011-12
175 receptions for 1,956 yards + 18 TDs and 9 carries for 97 yards
Caught 18 Regular Season and 2 Post Season TD passes from Tom Brady
Longest reception was a 46 yard pass from Tom Brady in their 28-14 loss to the Jets on 09-19-10
Had another 46 yard reception of a pass from Tom Brady in their 42-23 win over Denver on 12-18-11
Longest run was 19 yards in their 49-21 rout of the Buffalo Bills on 01-01-12
38 Regular Season Games/29 started and 6 Playoff Games/5 started
35 receptions for 360 yards + 2 TDs in the playoffs
Caught a 17 yard TD pass from Tom Brady in their 45-10 Divisional rout of Denver on 01-14-12
Caught a 12 yard TD pass from Tom Brady in their 21-17 Super Bowl loss to the NY Giants on 02-05-12
Florida Gator

HEROCK, KEN (#36)
Born on July 16, 1941 in Munhall, PA
6'2" and 230 pounds
Linebacker   1969
6 games
West Virginia Mountaineer

HERRON, Mack (#42) *"Mini"*
Born on July 24, 1948 in Biloxi, MS
5'5" and 170 pounds
RB/PR/KR   1973-75
353 carries for 1,298 yards + 9 TDs and 61 receptions for 789 yards + 6 TDs
74 punt returns for 888 yards and 71 kickoff returns for 1,796 yards + 1 TD (including 11 yard return
        of free kick)
Caught 6 TD passes from Jim Plunkett
Advanced Lennie St. Jean's kickoff return lateral 30 yards in their 24-23 loss to the Eagles on 11-04-73
Returned a free kick by Skip Butler 11 yards in their 32-0 shutout of the Houston Oilers on 11-25-73
Longest was a 92 yard TD return of a kickoff by Denis Partee in their 30-14 win over the Chargers on 12-02-73
Advanced his own fumble 6 yards in their 18-13 loss to the Baltimore Colts on 12-16-73
Longest was a 66 yard return of a punt by David Lee in their 42-3 rout of the Baltimore Colts on 10-06-74
Longest reception was a 48 yard pass from Jim Plunkett in their 21-17 loss to the Steelers on 12-08-74
Longest run was 53 yards in their 27-10 loss to the Cincinnati Bengals on 10-12-75
Led the NFL with the most kickoff return yards in 1973 and the NFL with 2,444 All Purpose Yards in 1974
35 games/20 started
Kansas State Wildcat

HICKS, Akiem (#72)
Born on November 16, 1989 in Elk Grove, CA
6'5" and 332 pounds
Defensive Lineman   2015
Sacked Brian Hoyer, T.J. Yates and Marcus Mariota
Recovered a fumble by Marcus Mariota in the end zone for a TD in their 33-16 win over the Titans on 12-20-15
13 Regular Season Games and 2 Playoff Games
Regina Ram

HIGHTOWER, Qualin "Dont'a" (#54) *"Zeus, Tim Duncan and The Stripper"*
Born on March 12, 1990 in Lewisburg, TN
6'3" and 260 pounds
Linebacker   2012-19
25.5 sacks, 5 fumbles recoveries for 32 yards + 2 TDs and had a 6 yard return of a blocked field goal
Blocked a punt, 1 interception for 27 yards and recorded 2 safeties
Shared in a sack of Jay Cutler, Tyrod Taylor and Luke Falk
Sacked Ryan Fitzpatrick, Chad Henne, Aaron Rodgers, Ben Roethlisberger and Brandon Weeden
Sacked Colin Kaepernick, Cam Newton, Josh McCown, Carson Wentz and DeShaun Watson
Had 1 ½ sacks of Andy Dalton, Josh Allen and Colt McCoy
Had 2 sacks of Matt Cassel, Geno Smith, Mark Sanchez and 3 ½ sacks of Ryan Tannehill
Recovered fumbles by Jake Locker, Ryan Tannehill, Ryan Fitzpatrick, DeShaun Watson and Nick Chubb
Returned Jake Locker's fumble 6 yards for a TD in their 34-13 win over Tennessee on 09-09-12
Forced Cody Kessler's lateral/fumble for a safety in their 33-13 win over the Browns on 10-09-16
Sacked Andy Dalton *for a safety* in their 35-17 win over the Bengals on 10-16-16
Had a 6 yard return of a blocked field goal in their 22-17 win over the Jets on 11-27-16
Recovered Deshaun Watson's fumble on the 1st play of the game in their 27-20 win on 09-09-18
Blocked a punt by Pat O'Donnell, that Kyle Van Noy returned for a TD, in their 38-31 win on 10-21-18
Returned a pass by Patrick Mahomes 27 yards, to the 4 yard line, in their 43-40 win on 10-14-18
Had a 26 yard TD return of a fumble by Nick Chubb in their 27-13 win over the Browns on 10-27-19
AFC Defensive Player of the Week in their 35-17 win over the Bengals on 10-16-16
AFC Special Team Player of the Week in their 38-31 win over the Bears on 10-21-18
AFC Pro Bowl Linebacker in 2016
102 Regular Season Games/99 started and 16 Playoff Games/16 started
Had a 3 yard return of a pass by Andrew Luck in their 43-22 Divisional Playoff win vs the Colts on 01-11-14
Stopped Marshawn Lynch on the play prior to Malcolm Butler's Epic Super Bowl interception on 02-01-15
Recovered a fumble by Knile Davis in their 27-20 Divisional Playoff win vs the Chiefs on 01-16-16
Strip sacked Matt Ryan in their 34-28 Epic Super Bowl Overtime win vs the Falcons on 02-05-17
Sacked Jared Goff *twice* in their 13-3 Super Bowl win vs the LA Rams on 02-03-19
Member of the 2014, 2016 and 2018 World Championship Teams
#25 pick in the 2012 NFL Draft
Alabama Crimson Tide

HILL, Jeremy (#33)
Born on October 20, 1992 in Baton Rouge, LA
6'1" and 230 pounds
Running Back   2018
4 carries for 25 yards and had 1 reception for 6 yards
Longest run was 11 yards in their 27-20 victory over the Houston Texans on 09-09-18
Caught a 6 yard pass from Tom Brady in their 27-20 win over the Houston Texans on 09-09-18
Partially blocked a punt by Daniel Trevor in their 27-20 win over the Texans on 09-09-18
Only game played was on 09-09-18
Member of the 2018 World Championship Team
LSU Fighting Tiger

HILL, Marquise (#91)
Born on August 7, 1982 in New Orleans, LA
6'6" and 297 pounds
Defensive End   2004-06
13 Regular Season Games and 1 Playoff Game (on 01-14-06)
Member of the 2004 World Championship Team
#63 pick in the 2004 NFL Draft
LSU Fighting Tiger

HILLIARD, Lex (#30)
Born on July 30, 1984 in Kalispell, MT
5'11" and 233 pounds
Running Back   2012
Ran for a 2 yard gain in their 20-18 loss to the Arizona Cardinals on 09-16-12
2 games (on Sept. 9th and Sept. 16th)
Montana Grizzly

HINTON, Eddie (#82)
Born on June 26, 1947 in Lawton, OK
6'0" and 200 pounds
WR/KR   1974
2 receptions for 36 yards, 1 carry for 1 yard and 3 kickoff returns for 83 yards
Longest was a 53 yard return of a kickoff by John Leypoldt in their 29-28 loss to the Bills on 11-03-74
Recovered Sam Cunningham's fumble in their 21-14 loss to the Browns on 11-10-74
Ran for a 1 yard gain in their 21-16 loss to the New York Jets on 11-17-74
Longest reception was a 20 yard pass from Jim Plunkett in their 34-27 loss to the Dolphins on 12-15-74
9 games/1 started (on 12-08-74)
Oklahoma Sooner

HITCHCOCK, Jimmy (#31 and #37)
Born on November 9, 1970 in Concord, NC
5'10" and 190 pounds
Cornerback   1995-97 and 2002
Wore #31 from 1995-97 and #37 in 2002
4 interceptions for 118 yards + 1 TD
Intercepted Mark Brunell and Alex Van Pelt and had 2 interceptions of Dan Marino
Had a career long 100 yard TD return of a pass by Dan Marino in their 27-24 win over Miami on 11-23-97
37 games/20 started
#88 pick in the 1995 NFL Draft
North Carolina Tar Heel

HOBBS III, Ellis (#27) *"Mr. 108"*
Born on May 16, 1983 in Niagara Falls, NY
5'9" and 188 pounds
CB/KR   2005-08
Nicknamed *"Mr. 108"* after his 108 yard kickoff return for a TD
9 interceptions for 87 yards, 2 ½ sacks, 3 fumble recoveries for 47 yards + 1 TD
105 kickoff returns for 2,913 yards + 3 TDs
Intercepted Gus Frerotte, J.P. Losman, David Carr, Eli Manning, Damon Huard and Trent Edwards
Intercepted Matt Leinhart and had 2 interceptions of Brooks Bollinger
Strip sacked J.P. Losman, sacked Damon Huard and shared in a sack of Ben Roethlisberger
Had a 7 yard return of a fumble by Randy McMichael and a 5 yard return of a fumble by Lee Evans
Had a career long 70 yard return of a pass by Brooks Bollinger in their 31-7 rout of the Vikings on 10-30-06
Returned a kickoff by Kris Brown 93 yards for a TD in their 40-7 rout of Houston on 12-17-06
Longest was a 108 yard TD return of the 2nd half kickoff by Mike Nugent in their 38-14 rout of the Jets
          on 09-09-07
Had a career long 35 yard TD return of a fumble by Dwayne Wright in their 56-10 rout of Buffalo on 11-18-07
Returned a kickoff by Sebastian Janikowski 95 yards for a TD in their 49-26 rout of Oakland on 12-14-08
AFC Special Team Player of the Week in their 38-14 rout of the Jets on 09-09-07
AFC Special Team Player of the Week in their 49-26 rout of the Raiders on 12-14-08
63 Regular Season games/49 started and 8 Playoff Games/7 Started
Lost 3 yards returning an interception of Philip Rivers in their 21-12 Championship win vs SD on 01-20-08
Had a 23 yard return of a pass by Eli Manning in their 17-14 Super Bowl loss to the Giants on 02-03-08
#84 pick in the 2005 NFL Draft
Iowa State Hawkeye

HOBBY JR., Marion (#60)
Born on November 7, 1966 in Birmingham, AL
6'4" and 277 pounds
DE (KR)   1990-92
5 sacks and 3 kickoff returns for 11 yards
Sacked Jim Kelly, Timm Rosenbach, Troy Taylor, Dan Marino and John Elway
Had an 11 yard return of a kickoff by Dean Biasucci in their 37-34 OT win vs the Colts on 11-15-92
42 games/8 started
Tennessee Volunteer

HOCHSTEIN, Russ (#71)
Born on October 7, 1977 in Hartington, NE
6'4" and 305 pounds
G/C (FB/TE)　　　　　2002-08
Occasionally used as a Full Back and as a Tight End
Recovered a fumble by Tom Brady on the last play in their 17-14 loss to the NY Jets on 11-12-06
92 Regular Season Games/20 started and 14 Playoff Games/5 started
Member of the 2003 and 2004 World Championship Teams
Nebraska Cornhusker

HODGE, Milford (#97)
Born on March 11, 1961 in Los Angeles, CA
6'3" and 278 pounds
DE/NT (KR)　　　　　1986-89
3 sacks, 2 kickoff returns for 19 yards and 1 fumble return of 2 yards
Sacked Dave Wilson and had 2 sacks of Ken O'Brien
Returned Ken O'Brien's fumble 2 yards in their 28-3 rout of the New York Jets on 09-04-88
Had an 11 yard return of a kickoff by Mike Lansford in their 24-20 loss to the LA Rams on 12-24-89
49 Regular Season Games/8 started and 1 Playoff Game (on 01-04-87)
#224 pick in the 1985 NFL Draft
Washington State Cougar

HODSON, Thomas "Tommy" (#13)
Born on January 28, 1967 in Mathews, LA
6'3" and 195 pounds
Quarterback　　　　　1990-92
171 completions for 1,809 yards + 7 TDs and 21 carries for 90 yards
Threw 1 TD pass to John Stephens and Michael Timpson, 2 TDs to Irving Fryar and 3 TDs to Marv Cook
Longest completion was a 56 yard pass to Irving Fryar in their 25-10 loss to the Redskins on 12-15-90
Longest run was 23 yards in their 42-7 loss to the New York Jets on 12-23-90
Caught his own deflected pass for a 6 yard loss in their 38-17 loss to the Dolphins on 10-18-92
Recovered a blocked field goal in their 38-17 loss to Miami on 10-18-92
32 games/12 started
#59 pick in the 1990 NFL Draft
LSU Fighting Tiger

HOEY, George (#23)
Born on November 14, 1946 in Gaffney, SC
5'10" and 174 pounds
DB/KR　　　　　1972-73
9 kickoff returns for 210 yards
Longest was a 30 yard return of a kickoff by Roy Gerela in their 33-3 loss to the Steelers on 10-22-72
Returned a pass by Marty Domres 25 yards in their 31-0 loss to the Baltimore Colts on 11-26-72
25 games
Michigan Wolverine

HOGAN, Chris (#15)
Born on October 24, 1988 in Ramapo, NJ
6'1" and 210 pounds
Wide Receiver   2016-18
107 receptions for 1,651 yards + 12 TDs and 6 carries for 26 yards
Caught 1 TD pass from Jimmy Garoppolo
Caught 11 Regular Season TDs and 4 Post Season TDs from Tom Brady
Caught a 37 yard TD from Jimmy Garoppolo in their 23-21 win over the Arizona Cardinals on 09-11-16
Longest reception was a 79 yard TD pass from Tom Brady in their 30-23 win over the Ravens on 12-12-16
Longest run was 13 yards in their 42-27 loss to the Kansas City Chiefs on 09-07-17
40 Regular Season Games/28 started and 9 Playoff Games/7 started
34 receptions for 542 yards + 4 TDs in the playoffs
Snared a 16 yard TD pass from Tom Brady in their 36-17 Championship win over the Steelers on 01-22-17
Caught a 34 yard flea flicker TD from Tom Brady in their 36-17 Championship win vs Pittsburgh on 01-22-17
Snared a 4 yard TD from Tom Brady in their 35-14 Divisional win over Tennessee on 01-13-18
Caught a 26 yard TD pass from Tom Brady in their 41-33 Super Bowl loss to the Eagles on 02-04-18
Ran for a 4 yard gain in their 41-33 Super Bowl loss to the Eagles on 02-04-18
Member of the 2016 and 2018 World Championship Teams
Monmouth Hawk

HOLLISTER, Jacob (#47)
Born on November 18, 1993 in Bend, OR
6'4" and 245 pounds
Tight End   2017-18
8 receptions for 94 yards and had 1 carry for 5 yards
Recovered Isaiah McKenzie's muffed punt return in their 41-16 win over Denver on 11-12-17
Ran for a 5 yard gain in their 37-16 rout of the Buffalo Bills on 12-24-17
Longest reception was a 23 yard pass from Tom Brady in their 31-20 loss to Jacksonville on 09-16-18
23 Regular Season Games and 1 Playoff Game
Caught a pass from Tom Brady for no gain in their 35-14 Divisional win over Tennessee on 01-13-18
Member of the 2018 World Championship Team
Wyoming Cowboy

HOLLOWAY, Brian (#76)
Born on July 25, 1959 in Omaha, NE
6'7" and 284 pounds
Tackle   1981-86
Recovered a fumble by Steve Grogan and Craig James and 2 fumbles by Tony Eason
Caught Steve Grogan's deflected pass for a 5 yard gain in their 34-7 win over Miami on 10-05-86
AFC Pro Bowl Tackle in 1983, 1984, 1985
88 Regular Season Games/77 started and 6 Playoff Games/6 started
#19 pick in the 1981 NFL Draft
Stanford Cardinal

HOLMBERG, Robert "Rob" (#50 and #47)
Born on May 6, 1971 in McKeesport, PA
6'3" and 230 pounds
Linebacker　　　　　　　2000-01
Wore #50 in 2000 and #47 in 2 games in 2001 (on Oct 7th and 14th)
18 games/5 started
Member of the 2001 World Championship Team
Penn State Nittany Lion

HOLMES, Darryl (#41)
Born on September 6, 1964 in Birmingham, AL
6'2" and 190 pounds
Defensive Back　　　　　1987-89
1 interception return of 4 yards, 2 fumble recoveries and blocked a field goal attempt
Recovered fumbles by Carl Byrum and Wendell Davis
Returned a pass by Brent Pease 4 yards in their 21-7 victory over the Oilers on 10-18-87
Blocked a 23 yard field goal attempt by Mike Cofer in their 37-20 loss to the 49ers on 10-22-89
44 games/3 started
Fort Valley State Wildcat

HOLMES, Ernie (#63)
Born on July 11, 1948 in Jamestown, TX
6'3" and 260 pounds
Defensive Lineman　　　1978
Recovered a fumble by Gary Davis in their 23-3 loss to the Miami Dolphins on 12-18-78
3 Regular Season Games and 1 Playoff Game (on 12-31-78)
Texas Southern Tiger

HOLSEY, Leonard "Bernard" (#60)
Born on December 10, 1973 in Rome, GA
6'2" and 286 pounds
Defensive Lineman　　　2002
Sacked Chad Pennington in their 44-7 rout of the New York Jets on 09-15-02
8 games
Duke Blue Devil

HOOMANAWANUI, Michael (#47) *"Hoo-Man"*
Born on July 4, 1988 in Bloomington, IL
6'4" and 265 pounds
Tight End　　　　　　　2012-15
20 receptions for 289 yards + 1 TD
Longest reception was a 41 yard pass from Tom Brady in their 41-34 loss to the 49ers on 12-16-02
Caught a 13 yard TD pass from Tom Brady in their 24-20 loss to Miami on 12-15-13
45 Regular Season Games/28 started and 7 Playoff Games/5 started
9 receptions for 92 yards in the playoffs
Member of the 2014 World Championship Team
Illinois Fighting Illini

HOWARD, Bob (#24)
Born on November 19, 1944 in Tallulah, LA
6'2" and 174 pounds
Defensive Back   1975-77
10 interceptions for 90 yards + 1 TD and 1 fumble recovery
Intercepted Norm Snead, Dan Fouts, Gary Marangi, Joe Namath, Steve Ramsey and Ron Jaworski
Had 2 interceptions of Joe Ferguson and Steve Myer
Recovered Don Hardeman's fumble in their 7-0 loss to the Houston Oilers on 09-21-75
Had a 44 yard TD return of a pass by Dan Fouts in their 33-19 win over the San Diego Chargers on 11-09-75
41 Regular Season Games/40 started and 1 Playoff Game/1 started (on 12-18-76)
San Diego State Aztec

HOWARD, David (#99)
Born on December 8, 1961 in Enterprise, AL
6'2" and 232 pounds
Linebacker   1991-92
2 sacks, 1 interception return of 1 yard and 1 fumble recovery
Sacked Rich Gannon and Kelly Stouffer
Had a 1 yard return of a pass by Scott Mitchell in their 38-17 loss to the Dolphins on 10-18-92
Recovered Christian Okoye's fumble in their 27-20 loss to the Chiefs on 12-13-92
32 games/15 started
Long Beach State 49er

HOYER, Brian (#8 and #2)
Born on October 13, 1985 in North Olmstead, OH
6'2" and 216 pounds
Quarterback   2009-11 and 2017-18
Wore #8 from 2009-11 and #2 from 2017-18
32 completions for 335 yards + 1 TD and 28 carries for 11 yards + 1 TD
Ran for a 1 yard TD in their 59-0 shutout of Tennessee in the snow at Gillette Stadium on 10-18-09
Longest run was 20 yards in their 35-7 win over Tampa at Wembley Stadium on 10-25-09
Longest completion was a 42 yard TD pass to Brandon Tate in their 38-7 rout of the Dolphins on 01-02-11
23 Regular Season Games and 1 Playoff Game
Member of the 2018 World Championship Team
Michigan State Spartan

HUARD, Damon (#19)
Born on July 9, 1943 in Yakima, WA
6'3" and 215 pounds
Quarterback   2002-03
2 carries for 3 yards
Longest run was a 4 yard QB sneak, for a 1st down, in their 33-30 win over Denver on 11-10-02
Holder for Adam Vinatieri
4 games
Member of the 2001 and 2003 World Championship Teams
Washington Husky

HUARTE, John (#7)
Born on May 20, 1943 in Anaheim, CA
6'0" and 185 pounds
Quarterback　　　　　1966-67
8 completions for 88 yards and 9 carries for 45 yards
Longest run was 13 yards in their 20-14 win over the Dolphins on 11-27-66
Longest completion was a 17 yard pass to Tony Romeo in their 38-14 win over Houston on 12-11-66
18 games
Notre Dame Fighting Irish

HUBACH, Mike (#6)
Born on January 26, 1958 in Cleveland, OH
5'10" and 185 pounds
Punter/Kicker　　　　　1980-81
82 punts for 3,118 yards
Longest punt was 69 yards in their 34-0 shutout of the Miami Dolphins on 10-12-80
His onside kick was recovered by Mosi Tatupu in their 38-34 loss to the Houston Oilers on 11-10-80
Recovered a high snap in the end zone for a safety in their 24-2 win over Buffalo on 12-14-80
Kicked off in every game he played for the Patriots
21 games
#293 pick in the 1980 NFL Draft
Kansas Jayhawk

HUDSON, Bill (#61)
Born on July 9, 1935 in Lamar, SC
6'4" and 270 pounds
Defensive Tackle　　　　　1963
4 games/4 started
Clemson Tiger

HUMBER II, Ramon (#50)
Born on August 10, 1987 in Brooklyn Park, MN
5'11" and 232 pounds
Special Team　　　　　2018
Returned a blocked punt 6 yards in their 34-33 loss to the Miami Dolphins on 12-09-18
6 Regular Season Games and 3 Playoff Games
Member of the 2018 World Championship Team
North Dakota State Bison

HUNT, Jim Lee (#79) "Earthquake"
Born on October 5, 1938 in Atlanta, TX
5'11" and 255 pounds
DT/DE (KR)   1960-71
Nicknamed *"Earthquake"* after returning a pass 78 yards for a TD on 11-01-63
34.5 sacks, 16 fumble recoveries for 67 yards + 1 TD, 1 kickoff return of 8 yards and 1 onside kick recovery
Shared in a sack of Jacky Lee and in 2 sacks of Len Dawson, Joe Namath, Don Trull and James Harris
Sacked Frank Tripucka, George Herring, Max Chobian, Daryle Lamonica, Steve Tensi and Rick Norton
Sacked Joe Namath, Jim LeClair and James Harris as well
Had 2 sacks of Tom Flores, John Hadl, Len Dawson, Don Trull, Pete Beathard, Bob Griese and Earl Morrall
Had 3 ½ sacks of Len Dawson and John McCormick and recorded 5 sacks of Jack Kemp
Recovered fumbles by Al Dorow, Tom Flores, Mickey Slaughter, Ode Burrell, Daryle Lamonica and Steve Tensi
Recovered fumbles by Bobby Burnett, Bob Cappadona, Marlin Briscoe, Robert Holmes and Larry Csonka
Had an 11 yard return of a fumble by Cotton Davidson in their 42-14 win vs the Dallas Texans on 11-18-60
Returned Charlie Milstead's kickoff 8 yards in their 24-10 loss to the Houston Oilers on 11-25-60
Had a 78 yard TD return of a pass by Jacky Lee in their 45-3 rout of the Houston Oilers on 11-01-63
Recovered Gino Cappelletti's onside kick in their 26-10 win over the Jets at BC Alumni Stadium on 09-27-64
Lateraled a kickoff return to JD Garrett, who advanced it 24 yards, in their 43-43 tie with Oakland on 10-16-64
Returned Darrell Lester's fumble 5 yards for a TD in their 17-10 loss to the Broncos on 11-06-66
Sacked Jack Kemp for a safety in their 44-16 loss to the Buffalo Bills on 12-09-67
Had a career long 51 yard return of a fumble by Don Trull in their 45-17 loss to the Oilers on 12-15-68
Recovered a fumbled snap in their 38-23 win over the Miami Dolphins on 11-30-69
AFL All Star Defensive Tackle in 1961, 1966, 1967, 1969
146 Regular Season Games/135 started and 2 Playoff Games/2 started
His Uniform # 79 was retired by the Patriots
Inducted into the Patriots Hall of Fame on 08-18-93
Prairie View A & M Panther

HUNT, Richard "Kevin" (#62)
Born on November 29, 1948 in Framingham, MA
6'5" and 260 pounds
Tackle   1973
Only game played was on 11-11-73
Doanne Tiger

HUNT, Sam (#50) *"Big Backer"*
Born on August 6, 1951 in Loongview, TX
6'1" and 248 pounds
Linebacker (KR)   1974-79
5 sacks, 7 interceptions for 68 yards + 1 TD, 5 fumble recoveries for 13 yards and 1 kickoff return of 21 yards
Shared in a sack of Joe Namath and Ken Stabler
Sacked Earl Morrall, Dan Fouts and and recorded 2 sacks of Joe Ferguson
Intercepted Joe Namath, Steve Ramsey and Steve Spurrier
2 interceptions of Bob Griese and Joe Ferguson
Recovered fumbles by Roger Staubach, Gary Hayman, Lydell Mitchell, Clark Gaines and Curtis Brown
Had a 21 yard return of a kickoff by Pat Leahy in their 21-16 loss to the NY Jets on 11-17-74
Recovered a blocked punt in their 24-16 victory over the San Francisco 49ers on 10-26-75
Had a 6 yard return of a fumble by Roger Staubach in their 34-31 loss to the Cowboys on 11-16-75
Had a 7 yard return of a fumble by Gary Hayman in their 34-14 loss to the Buffalo Bills on 12-14-75
Had a career long 68 yard TD return of a pass by Steve Spurrier in their 31-14 win over Tampa on 12-12-76
Recovered a blocked field goal in their 14-6 win over the Eagles on 11-27-77
84 Regular Season Games/82 started and 2 Playoff Games
#374 pick in the 1974 NFL Draft
Stephen F. Austin State Lumberjack

HUNTER, Ivy Joe (#45)
Born on November 16, 1966 in Gainesville, FL
6'0" and 237 pounds
Running Back   1991
18 carries for 53 yards, 11 receptions for 97 yards and 1 fumble recovery
Longest run was 9 yards in their 20-10 loss to the Dolphins on 10-06-91
Recovered Hugh Millen's fumble in their 26-23 Overtime win vs the Vikings on 10-20-91
Recovered a fumbled punt return by Al Edwards in their 22-17 loss to Buffalo on 11-03-91
Longest reception was a 25 yard pass from Hugh Millen in their 30-20 loss to the Dolphins on 11-10-91
13 games/11 started
Kentucky Wildcat

HURST, Maurice (#37)
Born on September 17, 1967 in New Orleans, LA
5'10" and 185 pounds
DB (PR)   1989-95
27 interceptions for 263 yards + 1 TD, 3 sacks and 1 punt return of 6 yards
Intercepted Warren Moon, Jim Everett, Todd Philcox, Ken O'Brien, Tom Tupa and Browning Nagle
Intercepted Rodney Peete, Steve Beuerlein, Stan Gelbaugh and Vinny Testaverde
Intercepted Scott Mitchell, Jeff Hosterler, Mark Rypien, Frank Reich and John Elway
Had 2 interceptions of Jack Trudeau, Dan Marino, Jeff George, Stan Humphries and 4 int's of Jim Kelly
Sacked Stan Gelbaugh, Jeff Hostetler and Don Majkowski
Had a 6 yard return of a punt by Tommy Barnhardt in their 28-24 loss to the Saints on 11-12-89
Had a 16 yard TD return of a pass by Jim Kelly in their 33-24 victoty over Buffalo on 11-19-89
Intercepted a pass by Jeff George in the 4ᵗʰ Qtr to help seal their 16-14 win over the Colts on 09-16-90
Had a career long 36 yard return of a pass by Ken O'Brien in their 37-13 loss to the Jets on 09-30-90
Blocked a punt by Dan Stryzinski in their 24-3 loss to the Pittsburgh Steelers on 12-09-90
Had a 9 yard return of a pass by Vinny Testaverde to help seal their 20-17 win vs the Browns on 12-19-93
105 Regular Season Games/102 started and 1 Playoff Game (on 01-01-95)
#96 pick in the 1989 NFL Draft
Southern Jaguar

HUTSON, Brian (#36)
Born on February 20, 1965 in Jackson, MS
6'1" and 198 pounds
Defensive Back   1990
2 games (on Oct. 7th and Oct. 18th)
Mississippi State Bulldog

HYLAND, Bob (#60)
Born on July 21, 1945 in White Plains, NY
6'5" and 255 pounds
Center   1977
3 games
Boston College Eagle

IHEDIGBO, James (#44)
Born on December 3, 1983 in Northampton, MA
6'1" and 202 pounds
Safety   2011
16 Regular Season Games/12 started and 3 Playoff Games/3 started
Sacked Joe Flacco in their 23-20 Championship win over the Ravens on 01-22-12
UMASS Minuteman

ILG III, Raymond "Ray" (#45)
Born on November 25, 1945 in Wellesley, MA
6'1" and 220 pounds
Linebacker (KR)   1967-68
Sacked Rick Norton in their 41-10 rout of the Miami Dolphins on 10-15-67
Had a 10 yard return of a kickoff by Verlon Biggs in their 29-24 loss to the Jets on 11-19-67
28 games/7 started
#336 pick in the 1967 NFL Draft
Colgate Red Raider

IMHOF, Martin (#64)
Born on October 9, 1949 in Seattle, WA
6'6" and 255 pounds
Defensive End   1975
Recovered Carl Garrett's fumble in their 30-28 loss to the New York Jets on 12-07-75
5 games/3 started
San Diego State Aztec

INGRAM, Brian (#51)
Born on October 31, 1959 in Memphis, TN
6'4" and 236 pounds
Linebacker   1982-86
39 Regular Season Games and 5 Playoff Games
#111 pick in the 1982 NFL Draft
Tennessee Volunteer

INGRAM, Jake (#47)
Born on October 23, 1985 in Albuquerque, NM
6'3" and 232 pounds
Long Snapper   2009-10
Long Snapper for Chris Hanson, Zoltan Mesko, Stephen Gostkowski and Wes Welker
Long Snapper for Wes Welker's extra point in their 34-14 loss to the Cleveland Browns on 11-07-10
24 Regular Season Games and 1 Playoff Game (on 01-10-10)
Hawaii Rainbow

IOSEFA, Marvin "Joey" (#47)
Born on June 19, 1991 in American Samoa
6'0" and 245 pounds
Full Back   2015
15 carries for 51 yards
Longest run was 15 yards in their 33-16 victory over Tennessee on 12-20-15
2 games (on Dec. 20th and Dec. 27th)
Hawaii Rainbow

IRWIN, Heath (#63)
Born on June 27, 1973 in Boulder, CO
6'4" and 300 pounds
Guard/Center   1996-99
44 Regular Season Games/17 started and 3 Playoff Games
#101 pick in the 1996 NFL Draft
Colorado Buffalo

ISAIA, Sale (#72)
Born on June 13, 1972 in Honolulu, HI
6'5" and 320 pounds
Guard   2000
Recovered JR Redmond's fumble in their 24-17 loss to the Chicago Bears on 12-10-00
16 games
UCLA Bruin

ISRAEL, Steve (#21)
Born on March 16, 1969 in Camden, NJ
5'11" and 194 pounds
Cornerback   1997-99
4 interceptions, 4 sacks and 2 fumble recoveries
Intercepted Dan Marino, Kordell Stewart, Steve Bono and Rick Mirer
Sacked Mark Brunell, Chris Chandler, Steve Young and Tom Tupa
Recovered fumbles by Rob Konard and Jonathan Linton
Recovered a blocked field goal in their 41-10 loss to the Atlanta Falcons on 11-08-98
29 Regular Season Games/20 started and 3 Playoff Games/1 started (on 01-03-98)
Picked off a pass by Kordell Stewart in their 7-6 Divisional playoff loss to the Steelers on 01-03-98
Pittsburgh Panther

IVORY, Horace (#23)
Born on August 8, 1954 in Fort Worth, TX
6'0" and 197 pounds
RB/KR　　　　　　　　　1977-81
329 carries for 1,336 yards + 14 TDs and 49 receptions for 433 yards + 2 TDs
45 kickoff returns for 1,191 yards + 1 TD and recovered fumbles by Stanley Morgan and Steve Grogan
Ran for a 5 yard game winning TD in their 14-10 win over the Buffalo Bills on 11-05-78
Snared a 6 yard TD from Steve Grogan in their 26-6 win over the Bills on 11-04-79
Longest reception was a 24 yard pass from Tom Owen in their 45-10 loss to Denver on 11-11-79
Longest run was 52 yards in their 50-21 rout of the Baltimore Colts on 11-18-79
Caught a 5 yard TD pass from Steve Grogan in their 27-23 victory over the Vikings on 12-16-79
Handed off to Don Westbrook, who threw a 24 yard pass to Don Hasselbeck, in their win over Minn on 12-16-79
Longest was a 98 yard TD return of a kickoff by Steve Mick-Mayer in their 37-21 win over the Colts on 10-19-80
Led the NFL with the longest kickoff return average and most kickoffs and kickoff return yards in 1980
46 Regular Season Games/12 started and 1 Playoff Game
#44 pick in the 1977 NFL Draft
Oklahoma Sooner

IWUOMA, Chidi (#29)
Born on February 19, 1978 in Los Angeles, CA
5'8" and 184 pounds
Special Team　　　　　　　2006
3 games
California Golden Bear

IZZO, Larry (#53) *"H to the Izzo"*
Born on September 26, 1974 in Fort Belvoir, VA
5'10" and 228 pounds
Special Team/LB　　　　　2001-08
Had 1 fumble recovery, 1 onside kick recovery, 1 interception, 1 rushing attempt and 1 kickoff return
Recovered Kurt Warner's fumble in their 24-17 loss to the St. Louis Rams on 11-18-01
Recovered Seth Marler's onside kick in their 27-13 win over the Jaguars on 12-14-03
Intercepted Travis Brown in the end zone with 13 seconds left in their 31-0 shutout of Buffalo on 12-27-03
Ran for no gain on a direct snap fake punt rushing attempt in their 35-28 win over the Bengals on 12-12-04
Fell on Lawrence Tyne's squibbed kickoff in their 26-16 loss to the Kansas City Chiefs on 11-27-05
AFC Special Team Player of the Week in their 41-38 OT win vs the Chiefs on 09-22-02
AFC Pro Bowl Special Team in 2002, 2004
127 Regular Season Games and 17 Playoff Games
Recovered 2 fumbled punt returns by Troy Brown in their 16-13 Divisional OT win vs the Raiders on 01-19-02
Member of the 2001, 2003 and 2004 World Championship Teams
Rice Owl

IZZO, Ryan (#85)
Born on December 21, 1995 in Highland Lakes, NJ
6'5" and 255 pounds
Tight End　　　　　　　　2019--
6 receptions for 114 yards and 1 TD
Longest reception was a 41 yard pass from Tom Brady on 09-22-19
Caught a 10 yard TD pass from Tom Brady on 10-06-19
6 games/4 started
#250 pick in the 2019 NFL Draft
Florida State Seminole

JACKSON, Chad (#17)
Born on March 6, 1985 in Birmingham, AL
6'1" and 205 pounds
WR/KR/PR   2006-07
13 receptions for 152 yards + 3 TDs, 4 carries for 22 yards, 6 KRs for 106 yards and 5 PRs for 83 yards
Caught 3 TD passes from Tom Brady
Longest reception was a 35 yard TD pass from Tom Brady in their 28-6 win over the Bills on 10-22-06
Longest run was 14 yards in their 28-6 victory over the Buffalo Bills on 10-22-06
Longest was a 39 yard return of a punt by Craig Hentrich in their 40-23 win over the Titans on 12-31-06
Longest was a 39 yard return of a kickoff by Jeff Reed in their 34-13 win over the Steelers on 12-09-07
14 Regular Season Games/1 started (on 10-08-06) and 3 Playoff Games
#36 pick in the 2006 NFL Draft
Florida Gator

JACKSON, Curtis (#82)
Born on September 22, 1971 in Fort Worth, TX
5'10" and 190 pounds
WR/KR   2000-01
7 receptions for 60 yards and 15 kickoff returns for 353 yards
Longest was a 47 yard return of Todd Sauerbrun's opening kickoff in their 30-24 win over KS on 12-04-00
Longest reception was a 13 yard pass from Drew Bledsoe in their 24-17 loss to Chicago on 12-10-00
7 games
Member of the 2001 World Championship Team
Texas Longhorn

JACKSON JR., Eddie (#29)
Born on December 19, 1980 in Americus, GA
6'0" and 190 pounds
Cornerback   2007
3 games
Arkansas Razorback

JACKSON, Harold (#29) *"Two-Nine"*
Born on January 6, 1946 in Hattiesburg, MS
5'10" and 175 pounds
Wide Receiver   1978-81
156 receptions for 3,162 yards + 18 TDs, 11 carries for 42 yards and 2 completions for 35 yards
Caught 17 Regular Season TD passes from Steve Grogan and 1 TD pass from Matt Cavanaugh
Caught 1 Post Season TD pass from RB Andy Johnson
Longest reception was a 59 yard pass from Steve Grogan in their 20-14 win over the Bengals on 09-16-79
Longest run was 16 yards in their 23-14 win over the Denver Broncos on 09-29-80
Longest completion was a 23 yard pass to Russ Francis in their 34-21 victory over the Jets on 11-02-80
Completed a 12 yard pass to Russ Francis in their 16-13 OT loss to the Dolphins on 12-08-80
64 Regular Season Games/59 started and 1 Playoff Game/1 started
Caught a 24 yard HB Option TD pass from Andy Johnson in their 31-14 Divisional loss to Houston on 12-31-78
Jackson State Tiger

JACKSON, Honor (#29)
Born on November 21, 1948 in New Orleans, LA
6'1" and 195 pounds
Defensive Back   1972-73
5 interceptions for 133 yards and recovered a fumble by OJ Simpson
Intercepted Marty Domres, Earl Morrall, Jim Del Daizo, Archie Manning and Bobby Douglass
Longest interception was a 55 yard return of a pass by Archie Manning in their 17-10 win vs NO on 12-10-72
20 games/12 started
Pacific Tiger

JACKSON, Jerald Christopher "J.C." (#27)
Born on November 17, 1995 in Immokalee, FL
6'1" and 198 pounds
DB   2018-19
8 interceptions for 48 yards
Intercepted Ryan Tannehill, Mitchell Trubisky and Patrick Mahomes
Had 2 interceptions of Andy Dalton and 3 interceptions of Josh Allen
Had a career long 19 yard return of a pass by Josh Allen in their 16-10 win over Buffalo on 09-29-19
29 Regular Season Games/11 started and 4 Playoff Games/2 started
Member of the 2018 World Championship Team
Maryland Terrapin

JACKSON, Steven (#39)
Born on July 22, 1983 in Las Vegas, NV
6'3" and 229 pounds
Running Back   2015
21 carries for 50 yards + 1 TD and 1 reception for 20 yards
Longest run was 7 yards in their 26-20 OT loss to the New York Jets on 12-27-15
Ran for a 2 yard TD in their 20-10 loss to the Miami Dolphins on 01-03-16
Caught a 20 yard pass from Tom Brady in their 20-10 loss to the Dolphins on 01-03-16
2 Regular Season Games and 2 Playoff Games
Ran for a 1 yard TD in their 20-18 Championship loss to the Denver Broncos on 01-24-16
Oregon State Beaver

JACKSON, Martrevius "Tre" (#63)
Born on December 14, 1992 in Jesup, GA
6'4" and 323 pounds
Guard   2015
13 games/9 started
#111 pick in the 2015 NFL Draft
Florida State Seminole

JACOBS, Harry (#83)
Born on February 4, 1937 in Canton, IL
6'1" and 226 pounds
LB/DE   1960-62
5.5 sacks, 4 interceptions for 26 yards, 1 fumble recovery, 1 blocked FGA and 1 recovery of an onside kick
Shared in a sack of M.C. Reynolds, sacked Jack Kemp and Tom Flores and sacked Frank Tripucka 3 times
Intercepted a pass by Jack Kemp, Hunter Enis, Jacky Lee and George Blanda
Sacked Frank Tripucka *3 times* in their 31-24 loss to the Denver Broncos on 10-23-60
Blocked a 35 yard field goal attempt by Ben Agajanian in their 45-16 loss to the LA Chargers on 10-28-60
Recovered a fumble by Richie Lucas in their 23-21 win over the Bills on 09-23-61
Recovered an onside kick by Jim Fraser in their 33-29 win over the Denver Broncos on 11-11-62
37 games/18 started
Bradley Brave

JACOBS, Herschel "Ray" (#87)
Born on November 21, 1938 in Corsicana, TX
6'3" and 285 pounds
Defensive End   1969
Recovered fumbles by Matt Snell and Emerson Boozer in their 23-17 loss to the New York Jets on 10-26-69
8 games/5 started
Howard Payne Yellow Jacket

JAGIELSKI, Harry (#73) "Moose"
Born on December 25, 1931 in Pittsburgh, PA
6'0" and 257 pounds
Defensive Tackle   1960-61
Recovered fumbles by Tony Teresa and Bill Mathis
19 games/18 started
Indiana Fighting Hoosier

JAMES, Jesse "Craig" (#32)
Born on January 2, 1961 in Jacksonville, TX
6'0" and 215 pounds
Running Back   1984-88
585 carries for 2,469 yards + 11 TDs, 81 receptions for 819 yards + 2 TDs
3 completions for 26 yards + 3 TDs and recovered an onside kick
Recovered fumbles by Steve Grogan and Leroy Irvin
Longest run was 73 yards in their 33-10 loss to the St. Louis Cardinals on 12-02-84
Hauled in a 90 yard TD pass from Tony Eason in their 20-7 loss to the Chicago Bears on 09-15-85
Longest completion was an 11 yard HB Option TD pass to Tony Collins in their 32-14 win vs Tampa on 10-27-85
Recovered an onside kick by Raul Allegre in their 38-31 win over the Indianapolis Colts on 12-01-85
Recovered Leroy Irvin's interception return fumble in their 30-28 win over the LA Rams on 11-16-86
Advanced Willie Scott's lateral 20 yards on the last play in their 16-14 loss to the Buffalo Bills on 09-18-88
AFC Pro Bowl Running Back in 1985
52 Regular Season Games/33 started and 5 Playoff Games/5 started
Ran for a 2 yard TD in their 27-20 Divisional win over the Los Angeles Raiders on 01-05-86
Completed an 8 yard pass to Tony Collins in their 27-20 Divisional win over the LA Raiders on 01-05-86
#187 pick in the 1983 NFL Draft
SMU Mustang

JAMES, Roland (#38)
Born on February, 18, 1958 in Xenia, OH
6'2" and 191 pounds
DB/PR   1980-90
29 interceptions for 383 yards, 42 punt returns for 400 yards + 1 TD, 5 sacks and 8 fumble recoveries
Intercepted Greg Landry, Joe Montana, Marc Wilson, Archie Manning, Jim Zorn and Brian Sipe
Intercepted Vince Ferragamo, Dave Krieg, Ken O'Brien, Danny White and Tommy Kramer
Intercepted Cody Carlson, Vinny Testaverde and Jim Kelly
Had 2 interceptions of David Woodley, Richard Todd, Pat Ryan and Mike Pagel
Had 3 interceptions of Joe Ferguson (all in the 3rd Qtr on 10-23-83) and 4 interceptions of Dan Marino
Recovered fumbles by Jerry Butler, Arthur Cox, Mike Barber, Eric Dickerson and Byron Franklin
Recovered fumbles by Sammy Winders, Rick Sanford and Bubby Brister (after Bubby bumped into a referee)
Sacked Richard Todd, Jim McMahon, David Woodley, Dave Krieg and Steve Dils
Returned a punt by Chuck Ramsey 75 yards for a TD in their 34-21 win over the Jets on 11-02-80
Intercepted a pass by David Woodley, on last play, in their 3-0 shutout of Miami on 12-12-82
Had a career long 46 yard return of a pass by Joe Ferguson in their 31-0 shutout of the Bills on 10-23-83
Recovered Rick Sanford's fumbled punt return in their 21-7 win over the LA Rams on 12-11-83
Tackled RB Frank Middleton for a safety in their 38-10 rout of the Buffalo Bills on 11-18-84
Had a 26 yard return of a blocked field goal in their 16-10 win over the Indianapolis Colts on 12-16-84
Sealed the win with his interception of Dave Krieg in their 20-13 win over Seattle on 11-17-85
145 Regular Season Games/122 started and 5 Playoff Games/5 started
Recovered Freeman McNeil's fumble in their 26-14 Playoff Game win vs the Jets on 12-28-85
#14 pick in the 1980 NFL Draft
Tennessee Volunteer

JANIK, Tom (#21)
Born on September 6, 1940 in Poth, TX
6'3" and 190 pounds
Punter/DB   1969-71
243 punts for 9,516 yards, 1 interception for 8 yards and recovered an onside kick
His 49 yard punt went to 1 yard line, and on the next play the Patriots recorded a safety, on 11-16-69
Had an 8 yard return of pass by Greg Cook in their 25-14 win over the Bengals on 11-16-69
Longest punt was 58 yards in their 44-21 loss to the Dallas Cowboys on 10-24-71
Recovered an onside kick by John Leypoldt in their 38-33 win over the Buffalo Bills on 11-14-71
Holder for Gino Cappelletti and Charlie Gogolak
42 games/3 started (as a Defensive Back)
Texas A & M Longsville Tribe

JAROSTCHUK, Ilia (#50)
Born on August 1, 1964 in Utica, NY
6'3" and 231 pounds
Linebacker   1990
12 games/1 started (on 12-30-90)
New Hampshire Wildcat

JARVIS, Leon "Ray" (#87)
Born on February 2, 1949 in Chesapeake, VA
6'0" and 200 pounds
Wide Receiver　　　　　1979
2 receptions for 30 yards + 1 TD
Caught a 15 yard pass from Steve Grogan in their 27-14 loss to the Green Bay Packers on 10-01-79
Caught a 15 yard TD pass from Steve Grogan in their 28-13 win over the Miami Dolphins on 10-21-79
7 games
Norfolk State Spartan

JEAN-FRANCOIS, Ricky (#94)
Born on November 23, 1986 in Miami, FL
6'2" and 309 pounds
Defensive Lineman　　　2017
6 Regular Season Games/1 started (on 12-24-17) and 3 Playoff Games/1 started (on 01-21-18)
Sacked Marcus Mariota in their 35-14 Divisional win over the Tennessee Titans on 01-13-18
LSU Tiger

JEFFERSON, Vanchi La"Shawn" (#84)
Born on February 22, 1969 in Jacksonville, FL
5'11" and 185 pounds
Wide Receiver　　　　　1996-99
178 receptions for 3,081 yards + 14 TDs, 2 carries for 21 yards and 2 fumble recoveries
Caught 13 TD passes from Drew Bledsoe and 1 TD pass from Scott Zolak
Recovered fumbles by Robert Edwards and Rod Rutledge
Longest reception was a 76 yard pass from Drew Bledsoe in their 23-28 loss to the Vikings on 11-02-97
Snared a 25 yard TD from Drew Bledsoe with 34 seconds left in their 26-23 win vs Miami on 11-23-98
Hauled in a 51 yard TD from Scott Zolak in their 24-21 victory over the 49ers on 12-20-98
Longest run was 15 yards in their 24-21 win over the San Francisco 49ers on 12-20-98
63 Regular Season Games/61 started and 6 Playoff Games/5 started
Central Florida Golden Knight

JELLS, Dietrich (#18 and #83)
Born on April 11, 1972 in New York, NY
5'10" and 186 pounds
Wide Receiver　　　　　1996-97
Wore #18 in the game played on 09-08-96
2 receptions for 14 yards
Longest reception was a 9 yard pass from Drew Bledsoe in their 27-7 loss to Tampa on 11-16-97
18 games/1 started (on 09-08-96)
Pittsburgh Panther

JENKINS, Eddie "Ed" (#30)
Born on August 31, 1950 in Jacksonville, FL
6'2" and 210 pounds
Special Team　　　　　1974
Recovered Hubie Ginn's fumbled kickoff return in their 34-27 loss to Miami on 12-15-74
3 games
Holy Cross Crusader

JETER, Gary (#99)
Born on January 24, 1955 in Weirton, WV
6'4" and 259 pounds
Defensive Lineman   1989
Sacked Dave Krieg, Steve Young, Jack Trudeau, Ken O'Brien, Bobby Hebert, Jim Kelly and Steve Beuerlein
14 games
USC Trojan

JOHNSON, Anderson "Andy" (#32)
Born on October 18, 1952 in Athens, GA
6'0" and 204 pounds
RB/KR (WR/PR)   1974-76 and 1978-81
491 carries for 2,017 yards + 13 TDs and 161 receptions for 1,807 yards + 9 TDs
7 completions for 194 yards + 4 TDs in the Regular Season and 1 TD pass in the Post Season
28 kickoff returns for 544 yards, 6 punt returns for 60 yards and 3 fumble recoveries
Caught 6 TD passes from Steve Grogan and 3 TD passes from Matt Cavanaugh
Recovered a fumble by Bruce Laird and 2 fumbles by Steve Grogan
Longest was a 41 yard return of a kickoff by Pat Leahy in their 21-16 loss to the Jets on 11-17-74
Longest was a 15 yard return of a punt by Greg Gantt in their 30-28 loss to the Jets on 12-07-75
Longest run was a 69 yard TD in their 31-14 win over the Tampa Bay Buccaneers on 12-12-76
Longest reception was a 53 yard pass from Steve Grogan in their 31-14 win over Tampa on 12-12-76
Recovered Chris Bahr's onside kick in their 20-14 win over the Bengals on 09-16-79
Recovered Don Cockroft's onside kick in their 34-17 win over the Browns on 09-07-80
Tossed an 8 yard TD pass to Mosi Tatupu in their 29-28 loss to the Baltimore Colts on 09-06-81
Completed a 66 yard TD pass to Stanley Morgan in their 33-17 win over the Chiefs on 10-04-81
Threw a 28 yard TD pass to Stanley Morgan in their 38-10 rout of the Houston Oilers on 10-18-81
Completed a 56 yard TD pass to Stanley Morgan in their 20-17 loss to the Bills on 11-22-81
Was the Starting Wide Receiver for 3 games in 1974
94 Regular Season Games/43 started and 3 Playoff Games
Ran for a 1 yard TD in their 24-21 Divisional loss to the Oakland Raiders on 12-18-76
Completed a 24 yard HB Option TD pass to Harold Jackson in their 31-14 Divisional loss to Houston
          on 12-31-78
#113 pick in the 1974 NFL Draft
Georgia Bulldog

JOHNSON, Anthony (#65)
Born on January 24, 1993 in Baton Rouge, LA
6'3" and 275 pounds
Defensive Lineman   2016
4 games/1 started (on 10-23-16)
Member of the 2016 World Championship Team
LSU Fighting Tiger

JOHNSON, Bethel (#81)
Born on February 11, 1979 in Dallas, TX
5'11" and 200 pounds
WR/KR (PR)　　　　　2003-05
30 receptions for 450 yards + 4 TDs and 3 carries for a net loss of 4 yards
102 kickoff returns for 2,557 yards + 2 TDs, 6 punt returns for 21 yards and 3 fumble recoveries
Caught 4 Regular Season TD passes from Tom Brady and 1 Post Season TD pass from Tom Brady
Recovered fumbles by Brian Westbrook, Eric Brown and Patrick Pass
Recovered Eric Brown's interception return fumble in their 23-20 OT win vs the Houston Texans on 11-23-03
Had a 92 yard TD return of a kickoff by Mike Vanderjagt in their 38-34 victory over the Colts on 11-30-03
Made a fair catch on Matt Turk's free kick in their 12-0 shutout of the Miami Dolphins on 12-07-03
Had a career long 93 yard TD return of Phil Dawson's opening kickoff in their 42-15 win vs Cleveland
　　　　on 12-05-04
Longest run was 11 yards in their 21-7 victory over the 49ers on 01-02-05
Caught a career long 55 yard TD pass from Tom Brady in their 31-28 win over Atlanta on 10-09-05
Longest was an 11 yard return of a punt by Brian Moorman in their 21-16 win over Buffalo on 10-30-05
AFC Special Team Player of Week on 11-30-03
39 Regular Season Games/7 started and 6 Playoff Games
4 receptions for 70 yards + 1 TD in the playoffs
Caught a 41 yard TD pass from Tom Brady in their 17-14 Divisional win over Tennessee on 01-10-04
Member of the 2003 and 2004 World Championship Teams
#45 pick in the 2003 NFL Draft
Texas A & M Aggie

JOHNSON, Billy (#47)
Born on February 19, 194 in Stanton, NE
5'10" and 180 pounds
DB/KR/PR　　　　　1966-68
2 interceptions for 33 yards, 1 fumble return of 3 yards and recovered 2 onside kicks
24 kickoff returns for 453 yards, a 13 yard return of a free kick and 23 punt returns for 195 yards
Advanced Joe Bellino's fumbled punt return 3 yards in their 24-21 win vs the Raiders on 10-30-66
Recovered an onside kick by Gary Kroner in their 17-10 loss to Denver on 11-06-66
Longest was a 52 yard return of a punt by Jim Norton in their 18-7 victory over Houston on 11-05-67
Had a career long 19 yard return of a pass by Len Dawson in their 29-24 loss to the Jets on 11-19-67
Recovered an onside kick by Patriots Kicker Justin Canale in their 29-24 loss to the Jets on 11-19-67
Longest was a 36 yard return of Bruce Alford's opening kickoff in their 23-6 win over Buffalo on 10-20-68
Had a 14 yard return of a pass by John Hadl in their 27-17 loss to San Diego on 11-10-68
Had a 13 yard return of Wayne Walker's missed 54 yard FGA in their 45-17 loss to Houston on 12-15-68
32 games
Nebraska Cornhusker

JOHNSON, Charles (#81)
Born on January 3, 1972 in San Bernardino, CA
6'0" and 200 pounds
Wide Receiver　　　　　2001
14 receptions for 111 yards + 1 TD
Longest reception was a 24 yard TD pass from Tom Brady in their 34-17 win over the Saints on 11-25-01
14 Regular Season Games/2 started and 3 Playoff Games
Member of the 2001 World Championship Team
Colorado Buffalo

JOHNSON, Damian (#68)
Born on December 18, 1962 in Great Bend, KS
6'5" and 290 pounds
Guard   1990
16 games/16 started
Kansas State Wildcat

JOHNSON, Damaris (#15)
Born on November 22, 1989 in Norco, LA
5'8" and 175 pounds
WR/PR   2015
2 punt returns for 3 yards and 1 carry for 6 yards
Ran for a 6 yard gain and had a 3 yard return of a punt by Donnie Jones in their 35-28 loss to Philly on 12-06-15
Only game played was on 12-06-15
Tulsa Golden Hurricane

JOHNSON, Daryl (#23)
Born on August 11, 1946 in Richmond, VA
5'11" and 190 pounds
DB (KR/PR)   1968-70
5 interceptions for 85 yards, 3 kickoff returns for 63 yards and 3 punt returns for 11 yards
Recovered 2 fumbles for 41 yards + 1 TD, had 1 sack of Bob Griese and tackled Jess Phillips for a safety
Intercepted Dan Darragh, Joe Namath, Greg Cook, Bob Griese and Al Woodhall
Recovered fumbles by Alvin Reed and Hoyle Granger
Longest was a 26 yard return of a kickoff by Bobby Howfield in their 20-17 win over Denver on 09-29-68
Had a career long 32 yard TD return of a fumble by Hoyle Granger in their 24-0 win vs Houston on 11-02-69
Tackled Jess Phillips for a safety in their 25-14 victory over the Bengals on 11-16-69
Sacked Bob Griese in their 27-14 victory over the Miami Dolphins on 09-20-70
Had a career long 42 yard return of a pass by Al Woodall in their 17-3 loss to the New York Jets on 11-22-70
Longest was a 6 yard return of a punt by Paul Maguire in their 45-10 loss to Buffalo on 11-01-70
42 games
#197 pick in the 1968 NFL Draft
Morgan State Bear

JOHNSON, Ellis (#38)
Born on July 9, 1943 in Baton Rouge, LA
6'0" and 195 pounds
RB/E/KR/DB   1965-66
19 carries for 29 yards, 4 receptions for 29 yards and 4 kickoff returns for 74 yards
Longest reception was a 23 yard pass from Babe Parilli in their 24-7 loss to Buffalo on 09-11-65
Longest run was 9 yards in their 24-10 loss to the Oakland Raiders on 10-08-65
Longest was a 23 yard return of a kickoff by Dick Van Raaphorst in their 24-0 loss to San Diego on 09-10-66
28 games
4ᵗʰ Round Draft Pick in 1965
Southeast Louisiana Lion

JOHNSON, Garrett (#60)
Born on December 31, 1975 in Belleville, IL
6'3" and 295 pounds
Nose Tackle   2000
Recovered Doug Flutie's fumble, on the Bills 1 yard line, in their 13-10 OT win vs Buffalo on 12-17-00
8 games/2 started
Illinois Fighting Illini

JOHNSON, Joe (#24)
Born on November 3, 1929 in New Haven, CT
6'0" and 185 pounds
Tight End   1960-61
20 receptions for 268 yards + 4 TDs
Caught 4 TD passes from Butch Songin
Caught a Butch Songin pass and then lateraled it to Dick Christy in their 42-14 win over Dallas on 11-18-60
Caught a career long 51 yard TD pass from Butch Songin in their 24-10 loss to Houston on 11-25-60
13 games/11 started
Boston College Eagle

JOHNSON, Leland "Lee" (#10)
Born on November 27, 1961 in Dallas, TX
6'2" and 200 pounds
Punter   1999-2001
203 punts for 8,578 yards, 1 carry for 13 yards, 1 fumble recovery and 1 completion for 18 yards
Ran for a 13 yard gain in their 17-7 loss to the Buffalo Bills on 11-28-99
Recovered the fumbled snap on a missed extra point attempt in their 21-13 loss to the Vikings on 09-17-00
Completed 18 yard pass to Eric Bjornson, for a 1st down, in their 24-16 win over the Colts on 10-08-00
Longest punt was 76 yards in their 23-17 loss to the Bengals on 09-09-01
Holder for Adam Vinatieri
37 games
Member of the 2001 World Championship Team
BYU Cougar

JOHNSON, Leonard (#34)
Born on March 30, 1990 in Clearwater, FL
5'10" and 194 pounds
Defensive Back   2015
4 games/3 started
Iowa State Cyclone

JOHNSON JR., Mario (#98)
Born on January 30, 1970 in St. Louis, MO
6'3" and 292 pounds
Nose Tackle   1993
6 games
Missouri Tiger

JOHNSON JR., Olrick (#51)
Born on August 20, 1977 in Miami, FL
6'0" and 244 pounds
Linebacker   2000
12 games
Florida A & M Rattler

JOHNSON, Preston (#48)
Born on February 18, 1945 in Roxbury, MA
6'2" and 230 pounds
Running Back   1968
2 carries for 6 yards
Longest run was 6 yards in their 31-17 loss to the Chiefs on 11-17-68
3 games
Florida A & M Rattler

JOHNSON, Rufus (#59)
Born on August 28, 1990 in Mesquite, TX
6'5" and 280 pounds
Linebacker   2015
Only game played was on 09-20-15
Tarleton State Texan

JOHNSON, Steve (#85)
Born on June 22, 1965 in Huntsville, AL
6'6" and 245 pounds
Tight End   1988
Caught a 5 yard pass from Steve Grogan in their 31-6 loss to the Houston Oilers on 09-25-88
14 games/3 started
#154 pick in the 1988 NFL Draft
Virginia Tech Hokie

JOHNSON, Ted (#52)
Born on December 4, 1972 in Alameda, CA
6'4" and 253 pounds
Linebacker   1995-2004
11.5 sacks, 1 interrcpetion, 7 fumble recoveries and 1 broken helmet of an opponent
Shared in a sack of Vinny Testaverde and Jay Fiedler
Sacked Mark Brunell, Dan Marino and Kyle Boller and had 1 ½ sacks of Drew Bledsoe
Recorded 2 sacks of Neil O'Donnell, Danny Wuerffel and Tony Banks
Recovered fumbles by Boomer Esiason, Johnny Mitchell, Karim Abdul-Jabbar and Bert Emanuel
Recovered fumbles by Elvis Grbac, Marlon Barnes and Edgerrin James
Intercepted a pass by Stan Humphries, tipped by Ferric Collins, in their 45-7 rout of the Chargers on 12-01-96
Hit Miami Dolphins Lineman Jamie Nails so hard it broke his helmet in their 19-13 OT win on 10-19-03
AFC Defensive Player of the Week in their 20-3 rout of the Ravens on 01-02-00
125 Regular Season Games/107 started and 14 Playoff Games/7 started
2.5 sacks in the playoffs
Sacked Kordell Stewart in their 28-3 Divisional rout of the Pittsburgh Steelers on 01-05-97
Sacked Dan Marino in their 17-3 Wild Card victory over the Miami Dolphins on 12-28-97
Shared in a sack of Kordell Stewart in their 24-17 AFC Championship win over the Steelers on 01-27-02
Member of the 2001, 2003 and 2004 World Championship Teams
#57 pick in the 1995 NFL Draft
Colorado Buffalo

JONES II, Aaron (#97)
Born on December 18, 1966 in Orlando, FL
6'5" and 261 pounds
Defensive Lineman   1993-95
8.5 sacks and 3 fumble recoveries for 28 yards
Shared in a sack of Jeff George and sacked Boomer Esiason, Frank Reich and Glenn Foley
Recorded 2 sacks of Warren Moon and 3 sacks of David Klinger
Recovered a fumble by Steve Walsh and 2 fumbles by Don Majkowski
Sacked David Klinger *twice* in their 7-2 win over the Bengals on 12-12-93
Had a 21 yard return of a fumble by Don Majkowski in their 12-10 win over the Colts on 11-27-94
Had a 7 yard return of a fumble by Don Majkowski in their 28-13 win over the Colts on 12-11-94
Recovered Steve Walsh's fumble in their 13-3 win over the Chicago Bears on 12-24-94
37 Regular Season Games /1 started (on 09-05-93) and 1 Playoff Game
Eastern Kentucky Colonel

JONES, Cedric (#83)
Born on June 1, 1960 in Norfolk, VA
6'1" and 184 pounds
WR/KR   1982-90
191 receptions for 2,703 yards + 16 TDs and 2 carries for a net loss of 4 yards
14 kickoff returns for 207 yards, 1 recovery of an onside kick and 3 fumble recoveries for 15 yards + 2 TDs
Caught 2 TD passes from Doug Flutie and Marc Wilson, 4 TDs from Tony Eason and 8 TDs from Steve Grogan
Recovered fumbles by Mosi Tatupu, Joe Carter and Hart Lee Dykes
Longest was a 23 yard return of Raul Allegre's 2nd half kickoff in their 29-23 OT loss to the Colts on 09-04-83
Fell on Mosi Tatupu's fumble in the endzone for a TD, in their 27-17 loss to the Philadelphia Eagles on 12-09-84
Tackled Kickoff Returnman Phil Freeman on Tampa's 2 yard line which helped set up safety on 10-27-85
Returned Joe Carter's fumbled kickoff return 15 yards for a TD, in their 30-27 loss to the Dolphins on 12-16-85
Recovered an onside kick by Pat Leahy in their 14-13 win over the Jets on 11-13-88
Caught an 11 yard pass from Tony Eason and lateraled it to Stanley Morgan in their OT win vs Tampa
          on 12-11-88
Longest reception was a 65 yard TD pass from Marc Wilson in their 27-26 loss to the Jets on 11-05-89
Ran for a 3 yard gain in their 24-21 loss to the Los Angeles Raiders on 11-26-89
Recovered a fumble by Hart Lee Dykes in their 22-16 win over the Colts on 12-03-89
120 Regular Season Games/38 started and 6 Playoff Games
#56 pick in the 1982 NFL Draft
Duke Blue Devil

JONES, Chandler (#95)
Born on February 27, 1990 in Rochester, NY
6'5" and 265 pounds
Defensive End   2012-15
36 sacks, 2 fumble recoveries for 58 yards
2 TDs, 1 interception and 1 blocked FGA that he returned for a TD
Shared in a sack of Andy Dalton and Alex Smith, and had 1 sack of Sam Bradford and Josh Freeman
Sacked Drew Brees, Cam Newton, Peyton Manning, Kirk Cousins and Zach Mettenberger
Strip sacked Jake Locker, Kevin Kolb, Kyle Orton, Ryan Tannehill, Eli Manning and Marcus Mariota
Recorded 2 sacks of Russell Wilson Ben Roethlisberger, Ryan Fitzpatrick and Matt Cassel
Had 2 ½ sacks of Andrew Luck, 4 ½ sacks of Ryan Tannehill and 5 sacks of Geno Smith
Recovered a fumbled snap by Gino Gradkowski for a TD in their 41-7 rout of the Ravens on 12-22-13
Blocked Blair Walsh's 48 yard FGA and returned it 58 yards for a TD in their 30-7 win vs Minn on 09-14-14
Intercepted a pass by Brock Osweiler in their 30-24 OT loss to the Denver Broncos on 11-29-15
AFC Defensive Player of the Week in their 30-7 rout of the Vikings on 09-14-14
AFC Defensive Player of the Month in November 2013
AFC Pro Bowl Defensive End in 2015
55 Regular Season Games/52 started and 9 Playoff Games/8 started
Sacked Russell Wilson in their 28-24 Super Bowl win over the Seattle Seahawks on 02-01-15
Sacked Alex Smith in their 27-20 Divisional win over the Kansas City Chiefs on 01-16-16
Member of the 2014 World Championship Team
#21 pick in the 2012 NFL Draft
Syracuse Orangeman

JONES, Christopher "Chris" (#94)
Born on July 12, 1990 in Brownsburg, IN
6'1" and 293 pounds
Defensive Lineman   2013-15
9 sacks and 1 blocked field goal
Shared in a sack of Alex Smith and Philip Rivers and sacked Thaddeus Lewis and Aaron Rodgers
Recorded 1 ½ sacks of Ryan Tannehill, 2 sacks of Geno Smith and 2 ½ sacks of Andy Dalton
Blocked Nick Folk's potential game winning 58 yard FGA in their 27-25 win over the Jets on 10-16-14
AFC Special Team Player of the Week in their 27-25 win over the Jets on 10-16-14
28 Regular Season Games/23 started and 4 Playoff Games
Sacked Andrew Luck in their 42-22 Divisional win over the Colts on 01-11-14
Recovered Danny Amendola's fumbled kickoff return in their 35-31 Divisional win vs Balt on 01-10-15
Member of the 2014 World Championship Team
Bowling Green Falcon

JONES, Cyrus (#24 and #41)
Born on November 29, 1993 in Baltimore, MD
5'10" and 195 pounds
PR/KR/CB   2016 and 2018
Wore #24 in 2016 and #41 in 2018
16 punt returns for 94 yards and 8 kickoff returns for 180 yards
Longest was a 43 yard return of a kickoff by Steven Hauschka in their 31-24 loss to Seattle on 11-13-16
Longest was a 24 yard return of a punt by Matt Haack in their 38-7 rout of the Dolphins on 09-30-18
12 games/1 started (on 12-12-16)
Member of the 2016 and 2018 World Championship Teams
#60 pick in the 2016 NFL Draft
Alabama Crimson Tide

JONES, Don (#29)
Born on May 14, 1990 in Tuscumbia, AL
5'11" and 195 pounds
Safety   2014
9 games
Member of the 2014 World Championship Team
Arkansas State Red Wolf

JONES, Ezell (#74) *"Easy"*
Born on July 11, 1947 in Collierville, TN
6'4" and 255 pounds
Tackle/Special Team   1969-70
2 fumble recoveries, recorded a safety and blocked a punt
Recovered Clarence Scott's fumble of the opening kickoff in their 24-0 shutout of the Oilers on 11-02-69
Tackled Punt Returner Mercury Morris for a safety in their 38-23 win over the Dolphins on 11-30-69
Blocked a punt by Larry Seiple in their 38-23 victory over the Miami Dolphins on 11-30-69
Recovered Ken Houston's fumbled kickoff return in their 27-23 loss to the Oilers on 12-14-69
18 games
Minnesota Golden Gopher

JONES, Jonathan (#31)
Born on September 20, 1993 in Carrolton, GA
5'10" and 190 pounds
Defensive Back   2016-19
4 interceptions for 40 yards, 2.5 sacks and 2 fumble recoveries
Intercepted Philip Rivers, Andrew Luck, Mitchell Trubisky and Kirk Cousins
Shared in a sack of Ryan Tannehill and sacked Matt Moore and Ben Roethlisberger
Recovered fumbles by Jordan Norwood and Danny Amendola
Had a 28 yard return of a pass by Andrew Luck, tipped by Zach Pascal, in their 38-24 win vs the Colts
          on 10-04-18
Deflected back Ryan Allen's punt, which was downed on 1 yard line, in their 17-10 loss to the Steelers
          on 12-16-18
63 Regular Season Games/19 started and 8 Playoff Games/2 started
Sacked Jared Goff in their 13-3 Super Bowl win over the Los Angeles Rams on 02-03-19
Member of the 2016 and 2018 World Championship Teams
Auburn Tiger

JONES, Kenyatta (#74)
Born on January 18, 1979 in Gainesville, FL
6'3" and 307 pounds
Tackle   2001-02
18 games/11 started
Member of the 2001 World Championship Team
#96 pick in the 2001 NFL Draft
South Florida Bull

JONES, Mike (#96)

Born on August 25, 1969 in Columbia, SC
6'4" and 290 pounds
Defensive Lineman   1994-97
15 sacks, 3 fumble recoveries for 31 yards, 1 safety and blocked a field goal attempt
Shared in a sack of Brett Favre and had 1 ½ sacks of Boomer Esiason and Don Majkowski
Sacked David Klinger, Mark Rypien, Frank Reich, Steve Bono, Glenn Foley, Dave Brown and Dan Marino
Recorded 2 sacks of Jim Harbaugh and 2 ½ sacks of Stan Humphries
Recovered a fumbled snap by Jeff Dellenbach in their 39-35 loss to Miami on 09-04-94
Had a 31 yard return of a fumble by Kent Graham in their 31-0 shutout of the Arizona Cardinals on 09-15-96
Forced Jim Kelly to ground the ball for a safety in their 28-25 win over the Buffalo Bills on 10-27-96
Blocked John Hall's potential game winning 29 yard FGA in their 27-24 OT win vs the Jets on 09-14-97
Recovered Neil O'Donnell's fumble in their 27-24 Overtime win vs the Jets on 09-14-97
61 Regular Season Games/38 started and 6 Playoff Games/1 started (on 01-01-95)
Shared in a sack of Mike Tomczak in their 28-3 Divisional win over the Steelers on 01-05-97
North Carolina State Wolfpack

JONES, Nathan "Nate" (#23)

Born on June 15, 1982 in Newark, NY
5'10" and 185 pounds
Defensive Back   2011
5 Regular Season Games/1 started (on 12-04-11) and 1 Playoff Game (on 01-22-12)
Rutgers Scarlet Knight

JONES, Tebucky (#34)

Born on October 6, 1974 in New Britain, CT
6'2 and 218 pounds
DB (KR)   1998-2002
4 interceptions for 16 yards, 2 ½ sacks and 3 fumbles recoveries for 24 yards + 1 TD
5 kickoff returns for 113 yards and blocked an extra point attempt
Intercepted a pass by Brian Griese, Peyton Manning, Tim Couch and Drew Bledsoe
Fell on fumbles by Derrick Cullors and Priest Holmes and had a 24 yard TD return of fumble by
     Vinny Testaverde
Shared in a sack of Trent Green, sacked Michael Vick and strip sacked Vinny Testaverde
Longest was a 28 yard return of a kickoff by John Hall in their 24-17 loss to the Jets on 11-15-99
Had a career long 20 yard return of a pass by Peyton Manning in their 24-16 win over the Colts on 10-08-00
Blocked a 25 yard field goal attempt by Mike Vanderjagt in their 38-17 win over the Colts on 10-21-01
Strip sacked Vinny Testaverde and returned it 24 yards for a TD in their 44-7 rout of the Jets on 09-15-02
Blocked an extra point attempt by Olindo Mare in their 26-13 loss to the Miami Dolphins on 10-06-02
72 Regular Season Games/36 started and 4 Playoff Games/3 started
Had a 19 yard return of a pass by Kordell Stewart in their 24-17 Championship win vs Pitt on 01-27-02
Member of the 2001 World Championship Team
#22 pick in the 1998 NFL Draft
Syracuse Orangeman

JONES, Todd (#63)
Born on July 3, 1967 in Hope, AR
6'3" and 295 pounds
Tackle (LS)   1993
4 games
Long Snapper for Scott Sisson's 2 extra points in their 17-14 loss to the Steelers on 12-05-93
Henderson State Reddy

JORDAN, Lamont (#32)
Born on November 11, 1978 in Suitland, MD
5'10" and 242 pounds
Running Back   2008
80 carries for 363 yards + 4 TDs
Longest run was a 49 yard TD in their 49-26 win over the Oakland Raiders on 12-14-08
8 games
Maryland Terrapin

JORDAN, Shelby (#63 and #74) *"The Gentle Giant"*
Born on January 23, 1952 in St. Louis, MO
6'7" and 260 pounds
Tackle   1975, 1977-82
Wore #63 in 1975 and #74 from 1977-82
Recovered fumbles by Leon McQuay, Steve Grogan and Jim Plunkett
Advanced Jim Plunkett's fumble 12 yards in their 34-31 loss to the Cowboys on 11-16-75
Made a game saving tackle on Bob Horn's interception return in their 27-21 win over San Diego on 09-23-79
95 Regular Season Games/87 started and 2 Playoff Games/2 started
Washington University Bear

JORDAN, Timothy "Tim" (#93)
Born on April 26, 1964 in Madison, WI
6'3" and 226 pounds
Linebacker   1987-89
3 sacks, 3 fumble recoveries and 1 interception return of 31 yards
Sacked Ken O'Brien, Chris Chandler and Don Majkowski
Fell on a fumble by Mike Rozier, a fumbled PR by Irving Fryar and a fumbled KR by Don Beebe
Had a 31 yard return of a pass by Boomer Esiason in their 27-21 win over Bengals on 10-16-88
30 games/10 started
#107 pick in the 1987 NFL Draft
Wisconsin Badger

KACZUR, Nicholas "Nick" (#77)
Born on July 29, 1979 in Brantford, Canada
6'4" and 315 pounds
Tackle   2005-10
Recovered a fumble by Sammy Morris in their 20-17 OT loss to the Broncos on 10-11-09
68 Regular Season Games/62 started and 8 Playoff Games/7 started
#100 Pick in the 2005 NFL Draft
Toledo Rocket

KADZIEL, Ron (#52)
Born on February 27, 1949 in Pomona, CA
6'4" and 230 pounds
Linebacker   1972
Recovered a fumble by Mercury Morris in their 37-21 loss to the Dolphins on 12-03-72
14 games/1 started (on 09-17-72)
Stanford Cardinal

KAMALU, Ufomba (#97)
Born on November 2, 1992 in Fayetteville, GA
6'6" and 295 pounds
DE   2018
2 games
Member of the 2018 World Championship Team
Miami Hurricane

KAPP, Joe (#11)
Born on March 19, 1938 in Santa Fe, NM
6'2" and 215 pounds
Quarterback   1970
98 completions for 1,104 yards + 3 TDs and 20 carries for 71 yards
Threw 1 TD pass to Ron Sellers and 2 TD passes to Bake Turner
Longest run was 14 yards in their 16-0 loss to the New York Giants on 10-18-70
Longest completion was a 48 yard pass to Ron Sellers in their 27-3 loss to Baltimore on 10-25-70
11 games
Member of the 1965 British Columbia Lions Grey Cup Championship Team
California Golden Bear

KARRAS, Ted (#75)
Born on March 15, 1993 in Chicago, IL
6'4" and 305 pounds
G/C   2016-19
60 Regular Season Games/20 started and 10 Playoff Games/1 started (on 1-04-20)
Member of the 2016 and 2018 World Championship Teams
#221 pick in the 2016 NFL Draft
Illinois Fighting Illini

KASPER, Kevin (#10)
Born on December 23, 1977 in Hinsdale, IN
6'1" and 200 pounds
KR (WR)   2004
3 kickoffs for 61 yards
Longest was a 21 yard return of Wes Welker's opening kickoff in their 24-10 win over Miami on 10-10-04
Had another 21 yard return of a kickoff by Toby Gowin in their 23-7 win over the Jets on 12-26-04
Occasionally used as a wide receiver
8 games
Member of the 2004 World Championship Team
Iowa Hawkeye

KATULA, Matt (#48)
Born on August 22, 1982 in Brookfield, WI
6'6" and 265 pounds
Long Snapper   2010
Long Snapper for Punter Zoltan Mesko and Kicker Shayne Graham
8 Regular Season Games and 1 Playoff Game (on 01-16-11)
Wisconsin Badger

KATZENMOYER, Andy (#59)
Born on December 2, 1977 in Westerville, OH
6'3" and 255 pounds
Linebacker   1999-2000
3.5 sacks and 1 interception return for a 57 yard TD
Shared in a sack of Elvis Grbac, sacked Doug Flutie and recorded 2 sacks of Damon Huard
Returned a pass by Dan Marino 57 yards for a TD in their 31-30 loss to Dolphins on 10-17-99
24 games/14 started
#28 pick in the 1999 NFL Draft
Ohio State Buckeye

KECMAN JR., Daniel "Dan" (#45)
Born on June 10, 1948 in Pittsburgh, PA
6'2" and 230 pounds
Special Team   1970
Only game played was on 09-27-70
Maryland Terrapin

KEETON, Durwood (#29)
Born on August 14, 1952 in Bonham, TX
5'11" and 178 pounds
Special Team   1975
Recovered Andy Johnson's fumbled kickoff return in their 22-14 loss to Miami on 09-28-75
12 games
Oklahoma Sooner

KELLEY, Ethan (#99)
Born on February 12, 1980 in Amarillo, TX
6'2" and 320 pounds
Defensive Tackle   2004
Only game played was in their 21-7 victory over the 49ers on 01-02-05
Member of the 2004 World Championship Team
#243 pick in the 2003 NFL Draft
Baylor Bear

KELLY, Ben (#31)
Born on September 15, 1978 in Cleveland, OH
5'9" and 185 pounds
KR/Special Team   2001-02
7 kickoff returns for 123 yards in 2001 and 1 fumble recovery
Recovered his own fumble of the opening kickoff in their 34-17 win over the Saints on 11-25-01
Longest was a 28 yard return of a kickoff by Toby Gowin in their 34-17 win over New Orleans on 11-25-01
9 games
Member of the 2001 World Championship Team
Colorado Buffalo

KELLY, Tommy (#93)
Born on December 27, 1980 in Jackson, MS
6'6" and 310 pounds
Defensive Lineman   2013
2.5 sacks and 1 fumble recovery
Shared in a sack of Josh Freeman and sacked Geno Smith and Andy Dalton
Recovered a fumble by CJ Spiller in their 23-21 win over the Buffalo Bills on 09-08-13
5 games/5 started
Mississippi State Bulldog

KERRIGAN, Mike (#19)
Born on April 27, 1960 in Chicago, IL
6'3" and 205 pounds
Quarterback   1983-84
7 completions for 85 yards and had 1 carry for 14 yards
Longest completion was a 19 yard pass to Stanley Morgan in their 24-6 loss to Seattle on 12-18-83
Ran for a 14 yard gain in their 24-6 loss to the Seahawks on 12-18-83
2 games (on Dec. 19, 1983 and Nov. 18, 1984)
Northwestern Wildcat

KEY, David (#26)
Born on March 27, 1968 in Columbus, OH
5'10" and 190 pounds
Special Team   1991
Recovered A.B. Brown's fumbled kickoff return in their 6-3 win over the Jets on 12-15-91
3 games
#140 pick in the 1991 NFL Draft
Michigan Wolverine

KHAYAT, Ed (#73)
Born on September 14, 1935 in Moss Point, MS
6'3" and 240 pounds
Defensive Lineman   1966
14 games
Tulane Green Wave

KIGHT, Kelvin (#19)
Born on July 2, 1982 in Atlanta, GA
6'0" and 213 pounds
Wide Receiver   2006
1 reception of 9 yards and 1 carry for 8 yards
Caught a 9 yard pass from Tom Brady in their 24-21 win over the Jaguars on 12-24-06
Ran for an 8 yard gain in their 40-23 win over Tennessee on 12-31-06
4 games/1 started (on 12-24-06)
Florida Gator

KIMBER, Bill (#86)
Born on January 31, 1936 in Winter Park, FL
6'2" and 192 pounds
End   1961
4 games
Was a teammate of Burt Reynolds at Florida State
Florida State Seminole

KINCHEN, Brian (#46)
Born on August 6, 1965 in Baton Rouge, LA
6'2" and 240 pounds
Long Snapper   2003
2 Regular Season Games and 3 Playoff Games
Long Snapper for Adam Vinatieri's game winning 41 yard field goal in their 32-29 Super Bowl win on 02-01-04
Member of the 2003 World Championship Team
LSU Fighting Tiger

KINER, Steve (#57)
Born on June 12, 1947 in Sandstone, MN
6'1" and 220 pounds
Linebacker   1971 and 1973
7.5 sacks, 4 interceptions for 14 yards, 2 fumble recoveries for 13 yards and blocked a field goal
Shared in a sack of Bill Nelson and sacked Dan Pastorini for a safety
Sacked Bob Griese and Dennis Shaw and had 2 sacks of Daryle Lamonica and John Brodie
Intercepted John Brodie, Dan Pastorini, Joe Namath and Johnny Unitas
Recovered fumbles by Emerson Boozer and Len Dawson
Recovered the loose ball after Charlie Gogolak's 46 yard FGA was blocked on 10-03-71
Had a career long 14 yard return of a pass by Dan Pastorini in their 28-20 win over the Oilers on 11-07-71
Intercepted a pass by Johnny Unitas, that was tipped by Dave Rowe, in their 21-17 win vs the Colts on 12-19-71
Had an 11 yard return of a fumble by Len Dawson in their 10-7 loss to the Chiefs on 09-23-73
Blocked a 39 yard field goal attempt by Jan Stenerud in their 10-7 loss to the Chiefs on 09-23-73
NFL Defensive Player of the Week in their 28-20 win over Houston on 11-07-71
28 games/28 started
Tennessee Volunteer

KING, Brandon (#36)
Born on June 8, 1993 in Alabaster, AL
6'2" and 220 pounds
Special Team   2015-18
Tackled Punt Returner Travis Benjamin for a safety in their 21-13 win over the Chargers on 10-29-17
57 Regular Season Games and 11 Playoff Games
Member of the 2016 and 2018 World Championship Teams
Auburn Tiger

KING, Claude (#41)
Born on December 3, 1938 in Vicksburg, MS
5'11" and 185 pounds
RB/KR   1962
21 carries for 144 yards + 1 TD, 5 receptions for 42 yards and 9 kickoff returns for 177 yards
Longest run was a 71 yard TD in their 41-16 win over the Denver Broncos on 09-21-62
Longest reception was a 33 yard pass from Tom Yewcic in their 41-16 win over the Broncos on 09-21-62
Longest was a 28 yard return of a kickoff by Cotton Davidson in their 26-16 win over the Raiders on 10-26-62
14 games
Houston Cougar

KING, George "Steve" (#52) *"Reno"*
Born on June 10, 1951 in McAlester, OK
6'4" and 232 pounds
Linebacker   1973-81
8 sacks, 1 interception for 9 yards and 1 recovery of a blocked punt
Sacked Hall of Fame QB's Bob Griese, Joe Namath and Fran Tarkenton and shared in a sack of Terry Bradshaw
Sacked Greg Landry, Richard Todd and had 2 sacks of Joe Ferguson
Had a 9 yard return of a pass by Joe Namath, deflected by Ron Bolton, in their 24-0 rout of the Jets on 10-13-74
Recovered a blocked punt, on the 49ers 6 yard line, in their 24-16 win over San Francisco on 10-26-75
124 Regular Season Games/41 started and 2 Playoff Games
Tulsa Golden Hurricane

KITCHEN, Ishmaa'ily (#70)
Born on June 24, 1988 in Youngstown, OH
6'1" and 334 pounds
Defensive Lineman   2015
Only game played was on 01-03-16
Kent State Golden Flash

KLECKO, Dan (#90)
Born on January 12, 1981 in Colts Neck, NJ
5'11" and 275 pounds
DT (RB/KR)   2003-05
2 carries for 5 yards, 3 receptions for 18 yards and 3 kickoff returns for 20 yards
2 sacks, 1 fumble return of 4 yards and a blocked field goal attempt
Shared in a sack of Kelly Holcomb and Jake Plummer and sacked Patrick Ramsey
Blocked a 48 yard field goal attempt by John Hall in their 20-17 loss to the Redskins on 09-28-03
Longest was a 10 yard return of a kickoff by Craig Hentrich in their 38-30 win over Tennessee on 10-05-03
Longest run was 5 yards in their 17-6 win over the NY Giants on 10-12-03
Had a 4 yard return of a fumble by Peyton Manning in their 38-34 win over the Colts on 11-30-03
Had another 10 yard return of a kickoff by Doug Brien in their 21-16 win over the Jets on 12-20-03
Made a fair catch of a short kickoff by Dolphins Kicker Wes Welker in their 24-10 win over Miami on 10-10-04
Longest reception was an 11 yard pass from Tom Brady in their 30-20 win over Seattle on 10-17-04
29 Regular Season Games/3 started and 1 Playoff Game (on 01-10-04)
Member of the 2003 and 2004 World Championship Teams
#117 pick in the 2003 NFL Draft
Temple Owl

KLEIN, Richard "Dick" (#62) *"Sleepy"*
Born on February 11, 1934 in Pana, IL
6'4" and 254 pounds
DT/OT   1961-62
Defensive Tackle in 1961 and Offensive Tackle in 1962
5.5 sacks, 1 fumble recovery and blocked 2 punts
Shared in a sack of MC Reynolds, Jack Kemp and Johnny Green
Sacked Frank Tripucka, Hunter Enis, George Shaw and Cotton Davidson
Blocked a punt by Billy Atkins in their 52-21 rout of the Buffalo Bills on 10-22-61
Blocked a punt by Jerry Burch in their 35-21 victory over the Oakland Raiders on 12-09-61
Recovered a fumble by Clem Daniels in their 20-0 loss to the Oakland Raiders on 12-16-62
AFL All Star Offensive Tackle in 1962
24 games
Iowa Hawkeye

KLEMM, Adrian (#70)
Born on May 21, 1977 in Inglewood, CA
6'3" and 312 pounds
Tackle/Guard (TE)   2000 and 2002-04
26 games/10 started
Member of the 2003 and 2004 World Championship Teams
#46 pick in the 2000 NFL Draft
Hawaii Rainbow

KLINE, Josh (#67)
Born on December 29, 1989 in Hoffman Estates, IL
6'3" and 300 pounds
Offensive Lineman   2013-15
Recovered an onside kick by Pat McAfee in their 34-27 win over the Colts on 10-18-15
33 Regular Season Games/18 started and 4 Playoff Games/3 started
Member of the 2014 World Championship Team
Kent State Golden Flash

KNIEF, Gayle (#84)
Born on December 28, 1946 in Denison, IA
6'3" and 205 pounds
Wide Receiver   1970
3 receptions for 39 yards + 1 TD
Longest reception was a 22 yard TD pass from Mike Taliaferro in their 37-20 loss to Miami on 12-06-70
3 games
Morningside Chief

KOONTZ, Ed (#54)
Born on June 11, 1946 in Hanover, PA
6'2" and 230 pounds
Linebacker   1968
6 games
#440 pick in the 1968 NFL Draft
Catawba Indian

KOPP, Jeff (#91)
Born on July 8, 1971 in Danville, CA
6'3" and 244 pounds
Linebacker   1999
6 games
USC Trojan

KOPPEN, Dan (#67)
Born on September 12, 1979 in Dubuque, IA
6'2" and 296 pounds
Center   2003-11
Recovered 6 fumbles by Tom Brady
Long Snapper on Tom Brady's 36 yard punt in their 12-0 shutout of the Dolphins on 12-07-03
AFC Pro Bowl Center in 2007
121 Regular Season Games/120 started and 14 Playoff Games/14 started
Member of the 2003 and 2004 World Championship Teams
#164 pick in the 2003 NFL Draft
Boston College Eagle

KOUTOUVIDES, Niko (#90)
Born on March 25, 1981 in New Britain, CT
6'2" and 238 pounds
Special Team/LB   2011-12
Recovered Joe McKnight's fumbled punt return in their 37-16 win over the Jets on 11-13-11
22 Regular Season Games/1 started (on 12-04-11) and 5 Playoff Games
Purdue Boilermaker

KRAKAU, Mervin "Merv" (#53)
Born on May 16, 1951 in Jefferson, IA
6'2" and 242 pounds
Linebacker   1978
Only game played was in their 26-24 playoff clinching win over the Bills on 12-10-78
Iowa State Cyclone

KRATCH, Robert "Bob" (#61)
Born on January 6, 1966 in New York, NY
6'3" and 288 pounds
Guard   1994-96
40 Regular Season Games/36 started and 4 Playoff Games
Iowa Hawkeye

KUBERSKI JR., Robert "Bob" (#93)
Born on April 5, 1971 in Chester, PA
6'4" and 298 pounds
Defensive Tackle   1999
5 games
Navy Midshipman

KUEHN, Art (#78)
Born on February 12, 1953 in Victoria, Canada
6'3" and 257 pounds
Center   1983
2 games (on Dec. 11th and Dec. 18th)
UCLA Bruin

KURPEIKIS, Justin (#47)
Born on July 17, 1977 in Alison Park, PA
6'3" and 245 pounds
Special Team   2004
5 games
Member of the 2004 World Championship Team
Member of the 2007 Hamburg Sea Devils NFL Europe World Bowl Championship Team
Penn State Nittany Lion

LACOSSE, Matthew "Matt" (83)
Born on September 21, 1992 in Naperville, IL
6'6" and 255 pounds
Tight End   2019
13 receptions for 131 yards and 1 TD
Longest reception was a 24 yard pass from Tom Brady in their 28-22 loss to Houston on 12-01-19
Caught an 8 yard TD pass from Tom Brady in their 24-17 win over the Bills on 12-21-19
11 Regular Season Games/8 started and 1 Playoff Game (on 01-04-20)
Illinois Fightin' Illini

LADD, Anthony (#18)
Born on December 23, 1973 in Homestead, FL
6'1" and 188 pounds
Special Team   1998
4 games
Cincinnati Bearcat

LAFELL, Brandon (#19)
Born on November 4, 1986 in Houston, TX
6'3" and 210 pounds
Wide Receiver (KR)   2014-15
111 receptions for 1,468 yards + 7 TDs, 4 carries for 22 yards and 1 kickoff return for no gain
Caught 7 Regular Season TD passes and 2 Post Season TD passes from Tom Brady
Longest reception was a 56 yard TD pass from Tom Brady in their 37-22 win over Buffalo on 10-12-14
Recovered a squibbed kickoff by Caleb Sturgis in their 41-13 win over the Dolphins on 12-14-14
Had a career long run of 9 yards in their loss to Buffalo on 12-28-14 and in their OT loss to the Jets on 12-27-15
27 Regular Season Games/20 started and 5 Playoff Games/4 started
16 receptions for 125 yards + 2 TDs in the playoffs
Caught a 23 yard TD for the last points scored in their 35-31 Divisional win over the Ravens on 01-10-15
Caught an 11 yard TD for the 1st points scored in their 28-24 Super Bowl win over Seattle on 02-01-15
Member of the 2014 World Championship Team
LSU Fighting Tiger

LAMBERT, Dion (#28)
Born on February 12, 1969 in Lakeview Terrace, CA
6'0" and 190 pounds
Defensive Back   1992-93
1 sack, 1 fumble recovery and 1 interception
Sacked Browning Nagle and recovered Rob Carpenter's fumble in their 24-3 win over the Jets on 11-22-92
Intercepted a pass by Vinny Testaverde in their 20-17 win over the Browns on 12-19-93
30 games/4 started
#90 pick in the 1992 NFL Draft
UCLA Bruin

LANE, Max (#68)
Born on February 22, 1971 in Norbone, MO
6'6" and 315 pounds
Guard/Tackle (TE)   1994-2000
Recovered fumbles by Keith Byars and Troy Brown and 3 fumbles by Drew Bledsoe
Advanced Troy Brown's pass reception fumble 30 yards in their 31-26 loss to the Chiefs on 10-15-95
Occasionally used as a Blocking Tight End
100 Regular Season Games/70 started and 7 Playoff Games/6 started
#168 pick in the 1994 NFL Draft
Navy Midshipman

LANGHAM, Collie "Antonio" (#38)
Born on July 31, 1972 in Town Creek, AL
6'0" and 181 pounds
Defensive Back   2000
Had a 24 yard return of a pass by Vinny Testaverde in their 20-19 loss to the Jets on 09-11-00
15 games/7 started
Alabama Crimson Tide

LANGI, Havea "Harvey" (#48)
Born on September 24, 1992 South Jordan, UT
6'2" and 250 pounds
Special Team   2017
Only game played was in their 42-27 loss to the Chiefs on 09-07-17
BYU Cougar

LARSON, Bill (#34)

Born on July 26, 1938 in Rockford, IL

5'10" and 190 pounds

Full Back   1960

Only game played was in their 13-10 loss to the Denver Broncos on 09-09-60

Illinois Wesleyan Titan

LASSITER, Ike (#87)

Born on November 15, 1940 in Wilson, NC

6'5" and 270 pounds

Defensive End   1970-71

7 sacks and 1 fumble recovery

Sacked Pro Football Hall of Famer's Bob Griese, Johnny Unitas and Roger Staubach

Had 2 sacks of Earl Morrall and Greg Landry

Recovered Earl Morrall's fumble in their 14-6 loss to the Baltimore Colts on 10-04-70

19 games/17 started

St. Augustine's Mighty Falcon

LAW, Tajuan "Ty" (#24)

Born on February 10, 1974 in Aliquippa, PA

5'11" and 200 pounds

Cornerback   1995-2004

36 interceptions for 583 yards + 6 TDs, 4 sacks and 4 fumble recoveries for 17 yards

Intercepted Jim Kelly, Jim Everett, Boomer Esiason, Glenn Foley, Rick Mirer, Bobby Hebert and Dan Marino

Intercepted Danny Wuerfferl, Kordell Stewart, Steve Young, Damon Huard, Dave Brown and Chris Weinke

Intercepted Trent Green, Brian Griese, Kelly Holcomb, Chad Pennington and Matt Hasselbeck

Had 2 interceptions of Troy Aikman, Alex Van Pelt, Steve McNair, Chris Chandler and Drew Bledsoe

Had 2 interceptions of Jay Fiedler and Quincy Carter and 4 Regular Season interceptions of Peyton Manning

Shared in a sack of Brad Johnson and Damon Huard and sacked Jim Harbaugh, Rob Johnson
        and Kordell Stewart

Recovered fumbles by Richard Anderson, Jerry Rice, Marcus Pollard and Rod Smith

Had a 38 yard TD return of a pass by Glenn Foley in their 34-10 win over the New York Jets on 12-08-96

Had a 59 yard TD return of a pass by Peyton Manning in their 29-6 rout of the Colts on 09-13-98

Had a 17 yard return of a fumble by Jerry Rice in their 24-21 comeback win over the 49ers on 12-20-98

Had a 24 yard TD return of a pass by Damon Huard in their 31-30 loss to Miami on 10-17-99

Had a 23 yard TD return of a pass by Peyton Manning in their 44-13 rout of the Indianapolis Colts on 09-30-01

Had a 46 yard TD return of a pass by Chris Weinke in their 38-6 rout of the Panthers on 01-06-02

Had a career long 65 yard TD return of a pass by Steve McNair in their 38-30 win over the Titans on 10-05-03

Led the NFL with 9 interceptions in 1998

AFC Pro Bowl Cornerback in 1998, 2001

First Team All Pro Cornerback in 1998, 2003

141 Regular Season Games/133 started and 12 Playoff Games/12 started

4 interceptions for 73 yards + 1 TD in the playoffs

Had a 47 yard TD return of a pass by Kurt Warner in their 20-17 Super Bowl win over the Rams on 02-03-02

Returned a Peyton Manning pass 6 yards in their 24-14 Championship win over the Colts on 01-18-04

Intercepted another pass by Peyton Manning in their 24-14 Championship victory over the Colts on 01-18-04

Returned a 3rd Peyton Manning pass 20 yards, on 4th down, in their 24-14 Championship win vs Indy on 01-18-04

Member of the 2001, 2003 and 2004 World Championship Teams

#23 pick in the 1995 NFL Draft

Inducted in the Patriots Hall of Fame on 08-01-14

Inducted in the Pro Football Hall of Fame on 08-03-19

Michigan Wolverine

LAWSON, Jamie (#29)
Born on October 2, 1965 in New Orleans, LA
5'10" and 240 pounds
Special Team   1990
Only game played was on 12-30-90
Nicholls State Colonel

LAWSON, Odell (#32)
Born on December 20, 1948 in Ponca City, OK
6'2" and 218 pounds
RB/KR   1970-71
64 carries for 107 yards, 11 receptions for 113 yards and 27 kickoff returns for 593 yards
Longest run was 15 yards in their 14-6 loss to the Baltimore Colts on 10-04-70
Recovered Mike Taliaferro's fumble in their 14-6 loss to the Baltimore Colts on 10-04-70
Advanced Marty Schottenheimer's kickoff return lateral 17 yards in their 16-0 loss to the NY Giants on 10-18-70
Longest was a 52 yard return of Dennis Partee's opening kickoff in their 16-14 loss to San Diego on 11-15-70
Longest reception was a 19 yard pass from Joe Kapp in their 14-10 win over Buffalo on 11-29-70
16 games/3 started
#160 pick in the 1970 NFL Draft
Langston Lion

LEBLANC, Michael (#40 and #27)
Born on May 5, 1962 in Missouri City, TX
5'11" and 199 pounds
RB (KR)   1987
Wore #40 on 10-04-87 and #27 for 3 games in 1987
49 carries for 170 yards + 1 TD, 2 receptions for 3 yards and 2 kickoff returns for 31 yards
Longest was a 24 yard return of a kickoff by Goran Lingmerth in their 20-10 loss to Cleveland on 10-04-87
Longest run was 42 yards in their 14-7 win over the Buffalo Bills on 10-11-87
Ran for a 3 yard TD in their 21-7 victory over the Houston Oilers on 10-18-87
Longest reception was a 3 yard pass from Doug Flutie in their 21-7 win over Houston on 10-18-87
4 games/2 started
Stephen F. Austin State Lumberjack

LEE, Bob (#60)
Born on July 4, 1935 in East Prairie, MO
6'1" and 245 pounds
Guard   1960
8 games
Missouri Tiger

LEE, Eric (#55)
Born on August 6, 1994 in Panama City, FL
6'3" and 255 pounds
Linebacker   2017
3.5 sacks, 1 interception return of 8 yards and recorded a safety
Shared in a sack of Nathan Peterman and sacked Matt Moore, Tyrod Taylor and Bryce Petty
Had an 8 yard return of a pass by Tyrod Taylor in their 23-3 win over Buffalo on 12-03-17
Sacked Bryce Petty for a safety in their 26-6 win over the Jets on 12-31-17
6 Regular Season Games/5 started and 3 Playoff Games/1 started (on 01-13-18)
South Florida Bull

LEE, John (#66)

Born on February 17, 1953 in Fort Monmouth, NJ
6'2" and 255 pounds
Defensive Tackle   1981
Sacked Joe Ferguson once and Neil Lomax *twice*
4 games/4 started
Nebraska Cornhusker

LEE, Keith (#22)

Born on December 22, 1957 in San Antonio, TX
5'11" and 192 pounds
DB/KR   1981-84
10 kickoff returns for 117 yards, 1 interception and 1 fumble recovery
Picked off a pass by Ken Stabler in their 38-10 rout of the Houston Oilers on 10-18-81
Longest was a 19 yard return of a kickoff by Rolf Benirschke in their 37-21 win over the Chargers on 10-16-83
Recovered Preston Brown's fumbled kickoff return in their 26-3 loss to the Jets on 11-27-83
54 Regular Season Games/8 started and 1 Playoff Game/1 started (on 01-08-03)
Recovered Andra Franklin's fumble in their 28-13 First Round Playoff loss to the Dolphins on 01-08-83
Colorado State Ram

LEE, Kevin (#86)

Born on January 1, 1971 in Mobile, AL
6'1" and 194 pounds
WR (KR)   1995
8 receptions for 107 yards, 1 carry for 4 yards and 1 kickoff return of 14 yards
Longest reception was a 33 yard pass from Drew Bledsoe in their 37-3 loss to Denver on 10-08-95
Ran for a 4 yard gain in their 27-14 victory over the Buffalo Bills on 10-23-95
Had a 14 yard return of a kickoff by Steve Christie in their 27-14 win over Buffalo on 10-23-95
7 games/2 started
#35 pick in the 1994 NFL Draft
Alabama Crimson Tide

LEGETTE, Burnie (#35)

Born on December 5, 1970 in Colorado Springs, CO
6'1" and 243 pounds
Special Team   1993-94
10 games
Michigan Wolverine

LENGEL, Matthew "Matt" (#82)

Born on December 27, 1990 in Mechanicsburg, PA
6'7" and 265 pounds
TE/Special Team   2016
2 receptions for 22 yards + 1 TD
Caught an 18 yard TD pass from Tom Brady in their 41-3 rout of the NY Jets on 12-24-16
6 Regular Season Games and 3 Playoff Games
Member of the 2016 World Championship Team
Eastern Kentucky Colonel

LENKAITIS, Bill (#67) *"Dr. Lenk"*
Born on June 30, 1946 in Cleveland, OH
6'4" and 255 pounds
Center/Guard   1971-81
3 fumble recoveries
Recovered fumbles by Andy Johnson, Steve Grogan and Sam Cunningham
151 Regular Season Games/119 started and 2 Playoff Games/2 started
Was the Patriots Team Dentist
Penn State Nittany Lion

LEO, Bobby (#24)
Born on January 19, 1945 in Everett, MA
5'10" and 180 pounds
WR/PR/KR   1967-68
1 reception for a 25 yard TD, 1 carry for 7 yards, 7 punt returns for 66 yards and 11 kickoff returns for 232 yards
Ran for a 7 yard gain in their 44-16 loss to the Buffalo Bills at Fenway Park on 12-09-67
Longest was a 43 yard return of a punt by Paul Maguire in their 44-16 loss to Buffalo on 12-09-67
Caught a 25 yard TD pass from Babe Parilli in their 44-16 loss to the Buffalo Bills on 12-09-67
Longest was a 31 yard return of a kickoff by Booth Lusteg in their 41-32 loss to the Dolphins on 12-17-67
3 games
#180 pick in the 1967 NFL Draft
Harvard Crimson

LEO, Charles 'Charley" (#63)
Born on August 29, 1934 in Niagara Falls, NY
6'0" and 240 pounds
Guard   1960-62
Recovered a punt that deflected off Bob McNamara in their 13-10 loss to the Broncos on 09-09-60
Recovered Billy Lott's fumble in their 45-17 rout of the Denver Broncos on 09-16-61
34 games/27 started
AFL All Star Guard in 1960, 1961
First Team All Pro Guard in 1961
Indiana Fighting Hoosier

LEONARD, Louis (#66)
Born on July 16, 1984 in Los Angeles, CA
6'5" and 325 pounds
Defensive Lineman   2010
Only game played was on 12-19-10
Fresno State Bulldog

LEVOIR, Mark (#64)
Born on July 29, 1982 in Minneapolis, MN
6'7" and 310 pounds
Tackle   2008-10
Recovered fumbles by Matt Cassel and Tom Brady
32 games/2 started
Notre Dame Fighting Irish

LEWIS, Bill (#75)
Born on July 12, 1963 in Sioux City, IA
6'6" and 285 pounds
Center   1993
7 games/5 started
Nebraska Cornhusker

LEWIS, Dion (#33)
Born on September 27, 1990 in Brooklyn, NY
5'8" and 195 pounds
RB/KR   2015-17
293 carries for 1,413 yards + 8 TDs and 85 receptions for 696 yards + 5 TDs
25 kickoff returns for 605 yards + 1 TD
Caught 5 Regular Season TD passes and 1 Post Season TD pass from Tom Brady
Longest reception was a 40 yard pass from Tom Brady in their 40-32 win over Buffalo on 09-20-15
Had a 103 yard TD return of a kickoff by Brandon McMann in their 41-16 win over Denver on 11-12-17
Longest run was 44 yards in their 23-3 win over the Buffalo Bills on 12-03-17
AFC Special Team Player of the Week in their 41-16 rout of the Broncos on 11-12-17
AFC Offensive Player of the Week in their 37-16 rout of the Bills on 12-24-17
30 Regular Season Games/19 started and 6 Playoff Games/5 started
58 carries for 214 yards + 1 TD and 21 receptions for 144 yards + 1 TD in the playoffs
11 kickoff returns for 268 yards + 1 TD in the playoffs
Ran for a 1 yard TD in their 34-16 Divisional win over the Houston Texans on 01-14-17
Caught a 13 yard TD pass from Tom Brady in their 34-16 Divisional win over Houston on 01-14-17
Had a 98 yard TD Return of a kickoff by Nick Novak in their 34-16 Divisional win vs the Texans on 01-14-17
1st NFL Player to score a rushing, receiving and on a return touchdown in the same playoff game on 01-14-17
Lateraled to Tom Brady, who completed a 34 yard TD pass, in their 36-17 Championship win on 01-22-17
Lateraled a kickoff return to Rex Burkhead in their 41-33 Super Bowl loss to the Eagles on 02-04-18
Member of the 2016 World Championship Team
Pittsburgh Panther

LEWIS, Vernon (#43)
Born on October 27, 1970 in Houston, TX
5'10" and 192 pounds
Defensive Back   1993-96
1.5 sacks, 2 fumble recoveries for 3 yards
Shared in a sack of Kerry Collins and sacked Steve Young
Had a 3 yard return of a blocked field goal in their 13-3 victory over the Chicago Bears on 12-24-94
Recovered a fumble by Kerry Collins in their 20-17 Overtime loss to the Panthers on 10-29-95
44 Regular Season Games/2 started and 1 Playoff Game (on 01-01-95)
Pittsburgh Panther

LIGHT, Matthew "Matt" (#72)
Born on June 23, 1978 in Greenville, OH
6'4" and 305 pounds
Tackle   2001-11
Recovered fumbles by David Givens and Tom Brady
AFC Pro Bowl Tackle in 2006, 2007 and 2010
First Team All Pro Tackle in 2007
155 Regular Season Games/153 started and 20 Playoff Games/20 started
Recovered a fumble by Tom Brady in their 37-16 Divisional Playoff win over the Jets on 01-14-07
Member of the 2001, 2003 and 2004 World Championship Teams
#48 pick in the 2001 NFL Draft
Ron Burton Community Service Award in 2005
Inducted in the Patriots Hall of Fame on 09-29-18
Purdue Boilermaker

LINDQUIST, Paul (#67)
Born on April 30, 1939 in Brockton, MA
6'3" and 265 pounds
Defensive Tackle   1961
Recovered Al Carmichael's fumble in their 45-17 rout of the Denver Broncos on 09-16-61
2 games (on Sept. 9th and Sept. 16th)
New Hampshire Wildcat

LINNE, Larry (#80)
Born on July 20, 1962 in Baltimore, MD
6'1" and 185 pounds
WR/PR   1987
11 receptions for 158 yards + 2 TDs and 5 punt returns for 22 yards
Caught a TD pass from Bob Bleier and Doug Flutie
Longest was a 16 yard return of a punt by Dale Walters in their 20-10 loss to the Browns on 10-04-87
Longest reception was a 30 yard pass from Doug Flutie in their 21-7 win over the Oilers on 10-18-87
3 games/3 started
Texas El Paso Miner

LIPPETT, Ronnie (#42)
Born on December 10, 1960 in Melbourne, FL
5'11" and 180 pounds
DB　　　　　　　　　1983-88 and 1990-91
24 interceptions for 420 yards + 2 TDs, 9 fumble recoveries for 6 yards, 1 sack and 1 blocked extra point
Intercepted a pass by Art Schlitcher, Boomer Esiason, Gary Hogenboom, Frank Reich and Jim McMahon
Intercepted a pass by Jeff George, Bubby Brister, 1 Regular Season and 2 Post Season passes by Marc Wilson
Had 2 interceptions of Jack Trudeau and Ken O'Brien and 3 interceptions of Joe Ferguson and Jim Kelly
Intercepted Dan Marino *6 times*
Recovered fumbles by Tony Nathan, Paul McDonald, Jo Jo Townsell, Steve Jordan and Johnny Hector
Recovered a fumbled punt return by Irving Fryar, a fumble by Marc Logan and 2 fumbles by Sammie Smith
Blocked an extra point attempt by Pat Leahy in their 23-13 win over the New York Jets on 09-18-83
Took a pass by Art Schlitcher 13 yards, with 38 ticks left, in their 16-10 win vs the Colts on 12-16-84
Picked off a pass by Jim Kelly, with 1:10 left, in their 22-19 win over Buffalo on 11-23-86
Returned a pass by Dan Marino 20 yards for the Game Winning TD in their 28-21 win vs Miami on 09-13-87
Sacked Jack Trudeau in their 30-16 loss to the Indianapolis Colts on 10-25-87
Returned a pass by Gary Hogenboom 45 yards for a TD in their 24-0 shutout of the Colts on 11-22-87
Longest interception return was 73 yards of a pass by Dan Marino in their 27-24 loss to the Miami on 09-09-90
Recovered an onside kick by Dean Biasucci in their 16-14 win over the Indianapolis Colts on 09-16-90
Had a career long 6 yard return of a fumble by Marc Logan in their 17-10 loss to Miami on 10-18-90
AFC Defensive Player of the Week in their 38-10 rout of the Bills on 11-11-84
AFC Defensive Player of the Week in their 34-7 rout of the Dolphins on 10-05-86
122 Regular Season Games/111 started and 4 Playoff Games/4 started
Intercepted 2 passes by Marc Wilson in their 27-20 Divisional win over the LA Raiders on 01-05-86
#214 pick in the 1983 NFL Draft
Miami Hurricane

LIVINGSTON, Walt (#24)
Born on September 12, 1934 in Ravenna, OH
6'0" and 185 pounds
RB (KR)　　　　　　　　1960
10 carries for 16 yards + 1 TD, 1 reception for no gain and 1 kickoff return for 3 yards
Longest run was 5 yards in their 13-10 loss to the Denver Broncos on 09-09-60
Had a 3 yard return of a kickoff by Gene Mingo in their 13-10 loss to Denver on 09-09-60
Ran for a 2 yard touchdown in their 28-24 win over the NY Titans on 09-17-60
Caught a pass from Tom Greene for no gain in their 28-24 win over New York on 09-17-60
3 games
Heidelberg College Student Prince

LLOYD, Brandon (#85)
Born on July 5, 1981 in Kansas City, MO
6'0" and 200 pounds
Wide Receiver　　　　　2012
74 receptions for 911 yards + 4 TDs and 1 fumble recovery for a TD
Caught 4 Regular Season TD passes and 1 Post Season TD pass from Tom Brady
Recovered Danny Woodhead's end zone fumble for a TD in their 42-14 win over Houston on 12-10-12
Longest reception was a 53 yard pass from Tom Brady in their 41-34 loss to the 49ers on 12-16-12
16 Regular Season Games/15 started and 2 Playoff Games/2 started
12 receptions for 102 yards + 1 TD in the playoffs
Caught a 5 yard TD pass from Tom Brady in their 41-28 Divisional win over the Houston Texans on 01-13-13
Illinois Fighting Illini

LOCKETT, Bret (#38)
Born on October 7, 1986 in San Dimas, CA
6'1" and 210 pounds
Special Team   2009
10 games
UCLA Bruin

LOCKHART, Eugene (#51)
Born on March 8, 1961 in Crockett, TX
6'2" and 234 pounds
Linebacker   1991-92
Recovered Scott Mitchell's fumble in their 38-17 loss to the Miami Dolphins on 10-18-92
32 games/21 started
Houston Cougar

LOCKWOOD, Scott (#40)
Born on March 23, 1968 in Los Angeles, CA
5'10" and 196 pounds
RB/KR   1992-93
35 carries for 162 yards, 11 kickoff returns for 233 yards and 1 fumble recovery
Longest was a 36 yard return of a kickoff by Nick Lowery in their 27-20 loss to Kansas City on 12-13-92
Recovered Dale Carter's fumbled punt return in their 27-20 loss to the Chiefs on 12-13-92
Longest run was 23 yards in their 16-13 OT loss to the Miami Dolphins on 12-27-92
6 games
#204 pick in the 1992 NFL Draft
USC Trojan

LOFTON, Oscar (#86)
Born on April 2, 1938 in McCall Creek, MS
6'6" and 218 pounds
Tight End   1960
19 receptions for 360 yards + 4 TDs
Caught 1 TD pass from Tom Greene and 3 TD passes from Butch Songin
Caught a career long 39 yard TD pass from Butch Songin in their 37-21 loss to the Oilers on 12-18-60
14 games/6 started
Southeast Louisiana Lion

LOFTON, Steve (#38)
Born on November 26, 1968 in Jacksonville, TX
5'9" and 180 pounds
Cornerback   1997-98
10 games
Texas A & M Aggie

LONG, Charles "Charley" (#76) *"Choo-Choo"*
Born on April 6, 1938 in DeKalb, AL
6'4" and 260 pounds
T/G/DE (TE/KR)　　　　1961-69
Occasionally used as a Tight End and as a Defensive End
2 fumble recoveries for 2 yards, shared in a QB sack and had 6 kickoff returns for 44 yards
Recovered a fumble by Carl Garrett and had a 2 yard advancement of a fumble by Ron Burton
Shared in a sack of Joe Namath in their 27-23 victory over the New York Jets on 11-28-65
Longest was an 11 yard return of Curley Johnson's short kickoff to end the 1ˢᵗ half on 10-01-61
Had another 11 yard return of a kickoff by Bobby Howfield in their 35-14 loss to Denver on 11-03-68
AFL All Star Tackle in 1962 and 1ˢᵗ Team All AFL (UPI) Tackle in 1962
AFL All Star Guard in 1963
124 Regular Season Games/77 started and 2 Playoff Games
8ᵗʰ Round Draft Pick in 1961
Tenn-Chattanooga Moccasin

LONG, Chris (#95)
Born on March 28, 1985 in Santa Monica, CA
6'3" and 270 pounds
Defensive End　　　　2016
4 sacks and 1 fumble recovery
Sacked Carson Palmer, Jared Goff, Bryce Petty and strip sacked Ryan Fitzpatrick
Recovered a fumble by Ryan Tannehill in their 31-24 win over Miami on 09-18-16
Strip sacked Ryan Fitzpatrick to help seal their 22 -17 victory over the New York Jets on 11-27-16
16 Regular Season Games/7 started and 3 Playoff Games
Member of the 2016 World Championship Team
Virginia Cavalier

LONG, Mike (#87)
Born on October 29, 1938 in Marlboro, MA
6'0" and 188 pounds
Tight End　　　　1960
2 receptions for 10 yards
Caught a 5 yard pass from Butch Songin in their 13-10 loss to the Broncos on 09-09-60
Caught a 5 yard pass from Tom Greene in their 28-24 win over the NY Titans on 09-17-60
2 games
Brandeis Judge

LOTT, Billy (#32)
Born on November 8, 1934 in Sumrall, MS
6'0" and 203 pounds
RB (PR)　　　　1961-63
143 carries for 573 yards + 7 TDs, 36 receptions for 395 yards + 7 TDs and 1 punt return of 8 yards
Caught 2 TD passes from Butch Songin and 5 TD passes from Babe Parilli
Had an 8 yard return of a punt by Curley Johnson in their 37-30 loss to the NY Titans on 10-01-61
Longest run was 38 yards in their 38-27 loss to the San Diego Chargers on 10-07-61
Caught a career long 55 yard TD pass from Babe Parilli in their 20-14 win over the Raiders on 09-22-63
35 Regular Season Games/8 started and 2 Playoff Games
Fell on Elbert Dubenion's fumbled kickoff return in their 26-8 AFL Divisional win over Buffalo on 12-28-63
Mississippi Rebel

LOUDD, Rommie (#60)
Born on June 8, 1933 in Madisonville, TX
6'2" and 227 pounds
LB (KR)   1961-62
8 sacks, 1 interception for 12 yards, 4 fumble recoveries for 10 yards and 2 kickoff returns for 15 yards
Sacked Warren Rabb, Cotton Davidson and had 1 ½ sacks of Randy Duncan and Jack Kemp
Recorded 3 sacks of Tom Flores
Recovered fumbles by Al Dorow, Larry Garron, Ron Burton and Luther Hayes
Had a 12 yard return of a pass by Nick Papac in their 35-21 win over the Oakland Raiders on 12-09-61
Had a 7 yard return of a fumble by Luther Hayes in their 41-0 shutout of San Diego on 12-17-61
Had a 15 yard return of a kickoff by Cotton Davidson in their 26-16 win over Oakland on 10-26-62
Received another kickoff and lateraled it to Larry Garron in their win 26-16 vs Oakland on 10-26-62
27 games/13 started
UCLA Bruin

LOUKAS, Angelo (#66)
Born on February 25, 1947 in Corinth, Greece
6'3" and 250 pounds
Guard   1970
2 games (on Dec. 13th and Dec. 20th)
Northwestern Wildcat

LOVE, Kyle (#74)
Born on November 18, 1986 in South Korea
6'1" and 310 pounds
Defensive Lineman   2010-12
5.5 sacks and 1 fumble recovery
Shared in a sack of Kevin Kolb and sacked Ben Roethlisberger, Vince Young and Mark Sanchez
Had 2 sacks of Ryan Fitzpatrick
Recovered a fumble by Philip Rivers in their 35-21 win over the San Diego Chargers on 09-18-11
41 Regular Season Games/25 started and 6 Playoff Games/4 started
Mississippi State Bulldog

LOWE, Omare (#23)
Born on April 20, 1978 in Seattle, WA
6'1" and 195 pounds
Special Team   2004
3 games
Member of the 2004 World Championship Team
Washington Husky

LOWERY, Dominic "Nick" (#7)
Born on May 27, 1956 in Munich, Germany
6'4" and 215 pounds
Kicker   1978
Kicked 7 extra points
2 games (on Sept. 24th and Oct. 1st)
Dartmouth Big Green

LOWRY, Orlando (#91)
Born on August 14, 1961 in Cleveland, OH
6'4" and 237 pounds
Special Team　　　　　1989
2 games (on Dec. 17th and Dec. 24th)
Ohio State Buckeye

LUCAS, Raymond "Ray" (#15)
Born on August 6, 1972 in Harrison, NJ
6'3" and 214 pounds
Special Team　　　　　1996
2 Regular Season Games and 2 Playoff Games
Rutgers Scarlet Knight

LUNSFORD, Melvin "Mel" (#72)
Born on June 13, 1950 in Cincinnati, OH
6'3" and 256 pounds
Defensive Lineman　　　1973-80
20.5 sacks, 4 fumble recoveries and 1 blocked field goal attempt
Shared in a sack of Norm Snead and John Hadl and had 1 ½ sacks of Bob Griese and Terry Bradshaw
Sacked Jerry Tagge, Joe Namath, Marty Domres, Gary Marangi, Bill Troup, Dan Fouts and Roger Staubach
Sacked Richard Todd and had 2 sacks of Bert Jones and Bobby Avellini and 3 sacks of Joe Ferguson
Recovered fumbles by John Hadl, Gary Marangi, Franco Harris and Don Strock
Blocked Don Cockroft's 39 yard field goal attempt in their 30-27 OT loss to the Browns on 09-26-77
92 Regular Season Games/74 started and 2 Playoff Games
Recovered a fumble by Clarence Davis in their 24-21 Divisional Playoff Game loss to Oakland on 12-18-76
Sacked Ken Stabler in their 24-21 Divisional Playoff loss to the Raiders on 12-18-76
Central State Maurader

LYLE, Rick (#96)
Born on February 26, 1971 in Monroe, LA
6'5" and 285 pounds
Defensive Lineman　　　2002-03
21 games
Member of the 2003 World Championship Team
Missouri Tiger

MAITLAND, John "Jack" (#40)
Born on February 8, 1948 in Pittsburgh, PA
6'2" and 211 pounds
RB (KR)　　　　　　1971-72
26 carries for 58 yards + 1 TD and 5 receptions for 39 yards
5 kickoff returns for 88 yards and 4 fumble recoveries for 3 yards
Recovered a fumbled snap to punter Jim McCann and fumbles by Tim Beamer, Josh Ashton and Jim Plunkett
Ran for a 2 yard touchdown in their 28-20 win over the Houston Oilers on 11-07-71
Longest was a 21 yard return of a kickoff by Garo Yepremian in their 34-13 win over the Dolphins on 12-05-71
Advanced Jim Plunkett's 4th down fumble, 3 yards for a 1st down, in their 13-6 loss to the Jets on 12-12-71
Longest reception was a 9 yard pass from Brian Dowling in their 52-0 loss to the Dolphins on 11-12-72
27 games
Williams Ephman

MALLARD, Wesly (#96)
Born on November 21, 1978 in Hinesville, GA
6'1" and 230 pounds
Special Team　　　　　2005
3 games
Oregon Duck

MALLETT, Ryan (#15)
Born on June 5, 1988 in Batesville, AR
6'6" and 240 pounds
Quarterback　　　　　2012
1 completion of 17 yards and 8 carries for a net loss of 9 yards
Completed a 17 yard pass to Shane Vereen in their 45-7 rout of St. Louis on 10-28-12
Knelt 8 times for minus 9 yards
4 games
#74 pick in the 2011 Draft
Arkansas Razorback

MALLORY, Irvin (#43)
Born on February 10, 1949 in Glen Allen, VA
6'1" and 196 pounds
Kickoff Returnman　　　1971
Returned Wayne Walker's kickoff 19 yards in their 34-7 loss to the Detroit Lions on 09-26-71
2 games (on Sept. 19th and Sept. 26th)
Virginia Union Panther

MANERI, Steve (#86)
Born on March 20, 1988 in Saddlebrook, NJ
6'6" and 275 pounds
Tight End　　　　　　2014
Only game played on 12-28-14
Member of the 2014 World Championship Team
Temple Owl

MANGIERO, Dino (#96)
Born on December 19, 1958 in New York, NY
6'2" and 265 pounds
Nose Tackle　　　　　1987
Sacked Willie Totten on the last play of their 14-7 win over the Buffalo Bills on 10-11-87
2 games
Rutgers Scarlet Knight

MANGUM, John (#74) *"Jumbo"*
Born on September 30, 1942 in Magee, MS
6'1" and 270 pounds
DT (KR)　　　　　　1966-67
1 kickoff return of 8 yards and 1 fumble recovery
Returned Booth Lusteg's opening kickoff 8 yards in their 14-3 win over the Bills on 12-04-66
Recovered a fumble by Rick Norton in their 41-10 rout of the Dolphins on 10-15-67
28 games/5 started
5th Round Draft Pick in 1966
Southern Mississippi Golden Eagle

MANKINS, Logan (#70)
Born on March 10, 1982 in Catheys Valley, CA
6'4" and 308 pounds
Guard   2005-13
1 fumble recovery and 1 reception for a 9 yard loss
Pounced on a fumble by Patrick Pass in their 26-16 loss to the Chiefs on 11-27-05
Caught a Tom Brady pass for a 9 yard loss in their 34-13 victory over the Bengals on 10-01-07
AFC Pro Bowl Guard in 2007, 2009-13
First Team All Pro Guard in 2010
130 Regular Season Games/130 started and 17 Playoff Games/17 started
2 fumble recoveries for a TD in the playoffs
Fell on Tom Brady's fumble for a TD in their 38-34 AFC Championship loss to the Colts on 1-21-07
Recovered a fumble by Danny Woodhead in their 28-21 Divisional loss to the Jets on 01-16-11
#32 pick in the 2005 NFL Draft
Fresno State Bulldog

MARION, Fred (#31)
Born on January 2, 1959 in Gainesville, FL
6'2" and 192 pounds
Safety (PR)   1982-91
29 interceptions for 457 yards + 1 TD, 1 sack, 2 punt returns for 12 yards and 13 fumble recoveries for 17 yards
Intercepted Richard Todd, Jim McMahon, Bernie Kosar, Steve DeBerg, Bubby Brister and Todd Rutledge
Intercepted Boomer Esiason, Pat Ryan, Bobby Hebert, Jim Everett, Jeff George and Mark Rypien as well
Had 2 interceptions of Joe Ferguson and Mike Pagel and 3 interceptions of Dave Krieg
Had 4 interceptions of Dan Marino and 6 interceptions of Jim Kelly
Recovered fumbles by Jim Smith, Ronnie Lippett, Lynn Dickey, Walter Payton and George Wonsley
Recovered fumbles by Ickey Woods, Ronnie Harmon, Andre Rison, Ferrell Edmunds, Tim Worley
        and Brad Baxter
Recovered 2 fumbles by Troy Stradford as well
Sacked Pat Ryan in their 28-21 victory over the NY Jets on 09-30-84
Recovered Ronnie Lippett's interception return fumble in their 16-10 win over the Colts on 12-16-84
Had a career long 9 yard return of a fumble by George Wonsley in their 34-15 win over the Colts on 11-10-85
Longest was an 83 yard return of a pass by Dave Krieg in their 20-13 victory vs Seattle on 11-17-85
Longest was a 12 yard return of a punt by Harry Newsome in their 34-0 shutout of the Steelers on 10-19-86
Had an 8 yard return of a fumble by Ickey Woods in their 27-21 victory over the Bengals on 10-16-88
Picked off a flea flicker pass by Mark Rypien in their 25-10 loss to the Redskins on 12-15-90
AFC Defensive Player of the Week in their 34-15 victory over the Colts on 11-10-85
AFC Defensive Player of the Week in their 27-21 victory over the Bengals on 10-16-88
AFC Pro Bowl Safety in 1985
144 Regular Season Games/114 started and 6 Playoff Games/5 started
3 interceptions for 69 yards in the playoffs
Returned a Ken O'Brien pass 26 yards in their 26-14 Wild Card win over the Jets at the Meadowlands
        on 12-28-85
Returned a Marc Wilson pass 22 yards in their 27-20 Divisional win vs the Raiders at the LA Coliseum
        on 01-05-86
Recovered Marcus Allen's fumble in their 27-20 win over the LA Raiders at the LA Coliseum on 01-05-86
Returned a Dan Marino pass 21 yards in their 31-14 Championship win vs Miami at the Orange Bowl
        on 01-12-86
#112 pick in the 1982 NFL Draft
Miami Hurricane

MARONEY, Laurence (#39) *"Kool Aid"*
Born on February 5, 1985 in St. Louis, MO
5'11" and 220 pounds
RB/KR   2006-09
582 carries for 2,430 yards + 21 TDs, 40 receptions for 409 yards + 1 TD and 1 run for a 2 point conversion
41 kickoff returns for 1,062 yards
NFL Ground Player of the Week in their 38-13 rout of Cincinnati on 10-01-06
AFC Special Team Player of the Week in their 31-7 rout of Minnesota on 10-30-06
Longest was a 77 yard return of a kickoff by Ryan Longwell in their 31-7 win over the Vikings on 10-30-06
Caught a 19 yard TD pass from Tom Brady in their 35-0 shutout of the Green Bay Packers on 11-19-06
Longest reception was a 43 yard pass from Tom Brady in their 27-24 win over Baltimore on 12-03-07
Longest run was a 59 yard TD in their 28-7 win over the Miami Dolphins on 12-23-07
Ran for a 2 point conversion in their 38-35 win over the New York Giants on 12-29-07
45 Regular Season Games/14 started and 7 Playoff Games/2 started
93 carries for 369 yards + 3 TDs and 6 receptions for 67 yards in the playoffs
12 kickoff returns for 257 yards in the playoffs
#21 pick in the 2006 NFL Draft
Minnesota Golden Gopher

MARSH, Aaron (#29)
Born on July 27, 1945 in Dayton, OH
6'1" and 190 pounds
WR/KR   1968-69
27 receptions for 439 yards + 4 TDs and 4 carries for 8 yards
10 kickoff returns for 210 yards, 1 fumble recovery and had a 9 yard return of a free kick
Caught 1 TD pass from Mike Taliaferro and 3 TD passes from Tom Sherman
Caught a career long 70 yard TD pass from Mike Taliaferro in their 47-31 loss to the Jets on 09-22-68
Recovered a fumble by Gene Thomas in their 20-17 victory over the Denver Broncos on 09-29-68
Longest run was 11 yards in their 35-14 loss to the Denver Broncos on 11-03-68
Longest was a 41 yard return of a kickoff by Bruce Alford in their 35-21 win over Buffalo on 11-23-69
Returned Larry Seiple's free kick 9 yards in their 38-23 win over Miami on 11-30-69
28 games/16 started
#60 pick in the 1968 NFL Draft
Eastern Kentucky Colonel

MARSH, Cassius (#55)
Born on July 7, 1992 in Mission Hills, CA
6'4" and 245 pounds
LB   2017
1 strip sack and 1 blocked field goal
Strip sacked Deshaun Watson in their 36-33 win over the Houston Texans on 09-24-17
Blocked Matt Bryant's 37 yard field goal attempt in their 23-7 win over Atlanta on 10-22-17
9 games/1 started (on 09-24-17)
UCLA Bruin

MARSHALL, Albert "Al" (#88)
Born on January 7, 1951 in Monroe, LA
6'2" and 190 pounds
Wide Receiver   1974
Caught a 17 yard TD pass (deflected by Nemiah Wilson) from Jim Plunkett in their 41-26 loss on 12-01-74
4 games
Boise State Bronco

MARTIN JR., Curtis (#28)
Born on May 1, 1973 in Pittsburgh, PA
6'2" and 250 pounds
Running Back   1995-97
958 carries for 3,799 yards + 32 TDs and 117 receptions for 890 yards + 5 TDs
Caught 5 TD passes from Drew Bledsoe and two 2 point passes from Drew Bledsoe
Ran for a 1 yard game winning TD in their 17-14 victory over the Cleveland Browns on 09-03-95
Caught a 2 point conversion pass from Drew Bledsoe in their 35-25 win over Buffalo on 11-26-95
Recovered Drew Bledsoe's fumble in their 31-17 loss to the New Orleans Saints on 12-03-95
Ran for a 1 yard game winning TD in their 31-28 victory over the New York Jets on 12-10-95
Caught a 2 point conversion pass from Drew Bledsoe in their 31-0 shutout of Arizona on 09-15-96
Longest reception was a 41 yard pass from Drew Bledsoe in their 42-23 win over Miami on 11-03-96
Longest regular season run was a 70 yard TD in their 31-3 rout of the Chicago Bears on 09-21-97
AFC Offensive Player of the Week in their 20-7 victory over the Jets on 11-05-95
AFC Offensive Player of the Week in their 35-25 win over the Bills on 11-26-95
AFC Pro Bowl Running Back in 1995, 1996
NFL Offensive Rookie of the Year in 1995
45 Regular Season Games/43 started and 3 Playoff Games/3 started
49 carries for 267 yards + 5 TDs and 8 receptions for 55 yards in the playoffs
#74 pick in the 1995 NFL Draft
Inducted in the Pro Football Hall of Fame 08-04-12
Pittsburgh Panther

MARTIN, Derrick (#26)
Born on May 16, 1985 in Denver, CO
5'10" and 198 pounds
Safety   2012
Sacked Ryan Tannehill in their 28-0 shutout of the Miami Dolphins on 12-30-12
5 games
Wyoming Cowboy

MARTIN, Don (#38)
Born on September 17, 1949 in Carrollton, MO
5'11" and 187 pounds
Special Team   1973
Had a 35 yard return of a blocked field goal in their 32-0 shutout of the Houston Oilers on 11-25-73
14 games/2 started
Yale Bulldog

MARTIN, Eric (#53)
Born on July 21, 1991 in Los Angeles, CA
6'2" and 250 pounds
Linebacker   2015
Wore #53 for 3 games and #52 in the game played on 12-13-15
4 games
Nebraska Cornhusker

MARTIN, Keshawn (#82)
Born on March 15, 1990 in Inkster, MI
5'10" and 190 pounds
WR/KR/PR   2015
24 receptions for 269 yards + 2 TDs, 10 kickoff returns for 257 yards and 8 punt returns for 92 yards
Caught 2 TD passes from Tom Brady
Longest was a 39 yard pass from Tom Brady in their 34-27 win over the Colts on 10-18-15
Longest was a 75 yard return of a kickoff by Ryan Succop in their 33-16 win over Tennessee on 12-20-15
Ran for a 6 yard gain in their 26-20 OT loss to the New York Jets on 12-27-15
Longest was a 21 yard return of a punt by Matt Darr in their 20-10 loss to the Dolphins on 01-03-16
9 Regular Season Games/8 started and 2 Playoff Games
Michigan State Spartan

MARTIN, Samson "Sammy" (#82)
Born on August 21, 1965 in Gretna, LA
5'11" and 175 pounds
WR/KR/PR   1988-91
21 receptions for 345 yards + 1 TD and 2 carries for 20 yards
88 kickoff returns for 2,012 yards + 1 TD and 20 punt returns for 165 yards
Returned Dean Biasucci's opening kickoff 95 yards for a TD in their 24-21 loss to the Colts on 11-27-88
Longest was a 28 yard return of a punt by Greg Montgomery in their 23-13 win over the Oilers on 10-08-89
Longest reception was a 37 yard pass from Steve Grogan in their 27-26 loss to the Jets on 11-05-89
Longest run was 13 yards in their 28-24 loss to the New Orleans Saints on 11-12-89
Caught a 19 yard TD pass from Steve Grogan in their 27-10 loss to the Buffalo Bills on 10-28-90
40 games
#97 pick in the 1988 NFL Draft
LSU Fighting Tiger

MARTIN, Steven (#90)
Born on May 31, 1974 in St. Paul, MN
6'4" and 320 pounds
Defensive Tackle   2002
14 games/5 started
Missouri Tiger

MASON, Dave (#28)
Born on December 16, 1973 in Menomonie, MI
6'0" and 199 pounds
Defensive Back   1973
Recovered Lydell Mitchell's fumble in their 18-13 loss to the Baltimore Colts on 12-16-73
8 games/1 started (on 12-16-73)
Nebraska Cornhusker

MASON, Shaquille "Shaq" (#69)
Born on August 28, 1993 in Columbia, TN
6'1" and 310 pounds
Guard (FB)   2015-19
Used as a blocking Fullback in their 27-10 win over the Washington Redskins on 11-08-15
Recovered a fumble by Tom Brady in their 36-33 win over the Houston Texans on 09-24-17
75 Regular Season Games/70 started and 12 Playoff Games/12 started
Member of the 2016 and 2018 World Championship Teams
#131 Pick in the 2015 Draft
Georgia Tech Yellow Jacket

MASS, Wayne (#75)
Born on March 11, 1946 in Portales, NM
6'4" and 240 pounds
Tackle   1972
6 games
Clemson Tiger

MASSEY, Jim (#47)
Born on April 24, 1948 in McMinnville, OR
5'11" and 198 pounds
Special Team   1974-75
Recovered Marshall Johnson's fumbled kickoff return in their 34-21 loss to the Colts on 12-21-75
15 games/1 started (on 11-23-75)
Linfield Wildcat

MATICH, Trevor (#64)
Born on October 9, 1961 in Sacramento, CA
6'4" and 277 pounds
Center/Guard   1985-88
26 Regular Season Games/11 started and 1 Playoff Game (on 01-04-87)
#28 pick in the 1985 NFL Draft
BYU Cougar

MATTHEWS, Bill (#53)
Born on March 12, 1956 in Santa Monica, CA
6'2" and 235 pounds
LB (KR)   1979-81
1 interception for 5 yards, 1 fumble recovery and 1 kickoff return of 5 yards
Returned a pass by Joe Ferguson 5 yards in their 31-13 loss to the Buffalo Bills on 10-26-80
Recovered George Wonsley's fumble in their 24-22 loss to the Washington Redskins on 10-25-81
Returned Nick Mike-Mayer's squibbed kickoff 5 yards in their 19-10 loss to the Bills on 12-13-81
48 games/10 started
#129 pick in the 1978 NFL Draft
South Dakota State Jack Rabbit

MATTHEWS JR., John "Henry" (#35)
Born on March 17, 1949 in Akron, OH
6'3" and 203 pounds
Kickoff Returnman   1972
3 kickoff returns for 74 yards
Longest was a 29 yard return of a kickoff by Garo Yepremian in their 37-21 loss to Miami on 12-03-72
3 games
Michigan State Spartan

MATTHEWS, Michael (#80)
Born on October 9, 1983 in Altadena, CA
6'4" and 270 pounds
Tight End   2009
4 games
Georgia Tech Yellow Jacket

MAY, Art (#71) *"Pops"*
Born on November 16, 1948 on Bessemer, AL
6'3" and 255 pounds
Defensive End   1971
3.5 sacks (shared in a sack of Bill Nelson, sacked James Harris, Dennis Shaw and Johnny Unitas)
11 games/5 started
Tuskegee Golden Tiger

MAYER, Shawn (#39 and #23)
Born on March 4, 1979 in Hillsborough, NJ
6'0" and 202 pounds
Safety   2003-04
Wore #39 for 9 games in 2003 and #23 for 3 games in 2004
12 Regular Season Games and 3 Playoff Games
Member of the 2003 and 2004 World Championship Teams
Member of the 2007 Hamburg Seal Devils NFL Europe World Bowl Championship Team
Penn State Nittany Lion

MAYO, Jerod (#51) *"Old Soul"*
Born on February 23, 1986 in Hampton, VA
6'2" and 230 pounds
Linebacker   2008-15
11 sacks, 3 interceptions for 4 yards and 7 fumble recoveries for 2 yards
Shared in a sack of Andy Dalton and sacked Matt Moore, Mark Sanchez, Josh Freeman and Sam Bradford
Sacked Ryan Fitzpatrick and had 1 ½ sacks of Chad Henne and 2 sacks of Peyton Manning and Ryan Tannehill
Intercepted Dan Orlovsky, Rex Grossman and Ryan Fitzpatrick
Recovered fumbles by Andre Hall, Kion Wilson, Jay Cutler, Ryan Fitzpatrick and Zach Miller
Recovered fumbles by Mike Wallace and Giovani Bernard as well
Had a 2 yard return of a pass by Rex Grossman, from 5 yard line, with 29 ticks left, to seal 34-27 win on 12-11-11
Had a 2 yard return of a fumble by Giovani Bernard in their 13-6 loss to the Bengals on 10-06-13
AFC Pro Bowl Linebacker in 2010, 2012
First Team All Pro Linebacker in 2010
103 Regular Season Games/93 started and 8 Playoff Games/7 started
Ron Burton Community Service Award in 2011
Member of the 2014 World Championship Team
#10 pick in the 2008 NFL Draft
Tennessee Volunteer

MAYS, Corey (#46)
Born on November 27, 1983 in Chicago, IL
6'1" and 245 pounds
Linebacker　　　　　　　　2006-07
9 Regular Season Games and 3 Playoff Games
Notre Dame Fighting Irish

McALLISTER, James (#37)
Born on September 5, 1951 in Little Rock, AR
6'1" and 205 pounds
RB/KR　　　　　　　　1978
19 carries for 77 yards + 2 TDs, 1 reception of 12 yards and 10 kickoff returns for 186 yards
Longest run was 16 yards in their 55-21 rout of the New York Jets on 10-29-78
Longest was a 32 yard return of a kickoff by Pat Leahy in their 55-21 rout of the Jets on 10-29-78
Caught a 12 yard pass from Tom Owen in their 23-3 loss to the Miami Dolphins on 12-18-78
16 Regular Season Games and 1 Playoff Game
UCLA Bruin

McCABE, Jerome "Jerry" (#52)
Born on January 25, 1965 in Detroit, MI
6'1" and 225 pounds
Linebacker　　　　　　　　1987
Sacked Brent Pease in their 21-7 victory over the Houston Oilers on 10-18-87
3 games/3 started
Holy Cross Crusader

McCALL, Bob (#24)
Born on April 26, 1950 in Sarasota, FL
6'0" and 205 pounds
RB/KR　　　　　　　　1973
10 carries for 15 yards, 3 receptions for 18 yards and 2 kickoff returns for 17 yards
Longest reception was a 14 yard pass from Jim Plunkett in their 33-13 loss to the Jets on 11-11-73
Longest run was 14 yards in their 33-24 win over the Green Bay Packers on 11-18-73
Longest was a 17 yard return of a kickoff by John Leypoldt in their 37-13 loss to the Bills on 12-09-73
8 games/1 started (on 11-18-73)
Arizona Wildcat

McCARRON, Riley (#17) *"Riles"*
Born on June 16, 1993 in East Dubuque, IA
5'9" and 198 pounds
WR/PR　　　　　　　　2018
Had a fair catch of a 37 yard punt by Trevor Daniel in their 27-20 win over the Texans on 09-09-18
Only game played was on 09-09-18
Member of the 2018 World Championship Team
Iowa Hawkeye

McCARTHY, Shawn (#11)
Born on February 22, 1968 in Fremont, OH
6'6" and 227 pounds
Punter   1991-92
169 punts for 6,877 yards, 1 completion of 11 yards and 1 fumble recovery
Longest punt was 93 yards in their 22-17 loss to the Buffalo Bills on 11-03-91
Completed an 11 yard pass to Ben Coates, on 4th + 13, in their 16-13 win over the Bills on 11-24-91
Recovered a high snap in the end zone for a Bills safety in their 16-7 loss to Buffalo on 11-01-92
29 games
Purdue Boilermaker

McCLAIN, Terrell (#93)
Born on July 20, 1988 in Pensacola, FL
6'2" and 302 pounds
Defensive Lineman   2012
Only game played was on 09-30-12
South Florida Bull

McCLELLAN, Albert (#59)
Born on June 4, 1986 in Lakeland, FL
6'2" and 235 pounds
LB/Special Team   2018
Blocked a punt, partially deflected another punt and recovered a fumble
Blocked a punt by Matt Haack and partially deflected a 2 yard punt in their 34-33 loss to Miami on 12-09-18
Recovered a fumble by De'Angelo Henderson in their 38-3 rout of the Jets on 12-30-18
7 Regular Season Games and 3 Playoff Games
Recovered Desmond King's fumbled punt return in their 41-28 Divisional win over the Chargers on 01-13-19
Member of the 2018 World Championship Team
Marshall Thundering Herd

McCLELLIN, Shea (#58)
Born on August 1, 1989 in Caldwell, ID
6'3" and 250 pounds
Linebacker (G)   2016
2 fumble recoveries for 69 yards, 1 sack and blocked an extra point attempt and a field goal attempt
Recovered Matthew Slater's kickoff return fumble in their 41-25 win over Buffalo on 10-30-16
Blocked an extra point attempt by Steven Hauschka in their 31-24 loss to Seattle on 11-13-16
Sacked Jared Goff in their 26-10 win over the Los Angeles Rams on 12-04-16
Blocked Justin Tucker's 34 yard field goal attempt in their 30-23 victory over Baltimore on 12-12-16
Played Left Guard for 1 play in their 16-3 win over the Denver Broncos on 12-18-16
Had a 69 yard return of a fumble by Damien Williams in their 35-14 rout of Miami on 01-01-17
14 Regular Season Games/4 started and 3 Playoff Games/1 started (on 02-05-17)
Member of the 2016 World Championship Team
Boise State Brono

McCOMB, Don (#85)
Born on March 24, 1934 in Cherry Hill, NJ
6'4" and 240 pounds
Defensive End   1960
Only game played on 09-09-60
Villanova Wildcat

McCOURTY, Devin (#32)
Born on August 13, 1987 in Nyack, NY
5'10" and 195 pounds
DB/KR   2010-19
26 interceptions for 431 yards + 1 TD, 3 sacks and 6 fumble recoveries for 61 yards
42 kickoff returns for 861 yards + 1 TD
Intercepted Philip Rivers, Brett Favre, Peyton Manning, Mark Sanchez, Chad Henne and Colin Kaepernick
Intercepted Matt Moore, Matt Schaub, Matt Cassel, Andrew Luck, Blake Bortles and Joe Flacco
Intercepted Josh McCown, Derek Anderson, Luke Falk, Josh Allen and Sam Darnold
Had 2 interceptions of Shaun Hill and Ben Roethlisberger and 5 interceptions of Ryan Fitzpatrick
Recovered fumbles by Stephen Hill, Jordan Norwood, Kareem Hunt and Jordan Wilkins
Recovered fumbles Elijah McGuire and Nick Chubb
Longest was a 104 yard TD return of a kickoff by Nick Folk in their 29-26 OT win vs the Jets on 10-21-12
Had a career long 44 yard return of a fumble by Stephen Hill in their 13-10 win over the Jets on 09-12-13
Returned a pass by Matt Cassel 60 yards, to the 1 yard line, in their 30-7 win over the Vikings on 09-14-14
Forced a fumble by Damien Williams that Shea McClellin returned 69 yards on 01-01-17
Had a career long 84 yard TD return of a pass by Derek Anderson in their 25-6 win over Buffalo on 10-29-18
AFC Special Team Player of the Week in their 29-26 OT win vs the Jets on 10-21-12
AFC Defensive Player of the Month in September 2019
AFC Pro Bowl Cornerback in 2010
AFC Pro Bowl Safety in 2014, 2016
155 Regular Season Games/155 started and 23 Playoff Games/23 started
Intercepted a pass by Joe Flacco in their 35-31 Divisional win over the Ravens on 01-10-15
Returned a pass by Brock Osweiler 4 yards in their 34-16 Divisional win over the Texans on 01-14-17
Ron Burton Community Service Award in 2014
Member of the 2014, 2016 and 2018 World Championship Teams
#27 pick in the 2010 NFL Draft
Rutgers Scarlet Knight

McCOURTY, Jason (#30)
Born on August 13, 1987 in Nyack, NY
5'11" and 195 pounds
DB   2018-19
2 interceptions for 16 yards
Intercepted a pass by Josh Allen in their 24-12 win over the Bills on 12-23-18
Had a 16 yard return of a pass by Colt McCoy in their 33-7 rout of the Redskins on 10-06-19
28 Regular Season Games/22 started and 3 Playoff Games/3 started
Member of the 2018 World Championship Team
Rutgers Scarlet Knight

McCRARY, Fred (#44)
Born on September 19, 1972 in Naples, FL
6'0" and 247 pounds
Running Back   2003
3 carries for 3 yards and 2 receptions for 12 yards
Longest run was 4 yards in their 19-13 OT win over the Miami Dolphins on 10-19-03
Longest reception was a 12 yard pass from Tom Brady in their 30-26 win over Denver on 11-03-03
6 games/3 started
Member of the 2003 World Championship Team
Mississippi State Bulldog

McCRAY, Prentice (#34) *"Pinhead"*
Born on March 1, 1951 in Los Angeles, CA
6'1" and 188 pounds
Cornerback   1974-80
15 interceptions for 352 yards + 2 TDs, 1 sack and 6 fumble recoveries for 2 yards
Intercepted John Hadl, Terry Bradshaw, Earl Morrall, Bob Griese, Ken Stabler Gary Marangi and Brian Sipe
Intercepted James Harris, Steve Bartkowski, David Whitehurst and Don Strock as well
Fell on a fumble by Mike Rozier, a fumbled PR by Irving Fryar and a fumbled KR by Don Beebe
Only Patriot Player to return 2 interceptions for a TD in the same game
Recovered fumbles by Roosevelt Leaks, Louie Giammona, Roland Hooks, Nesby Glasgow and Reggie Smith
Had a 33 yard return of a pass by John Hadl, with 1:39 left, in their 20-14 win over the LA Rams on 09-29-74
Returned Raymond Chester's fumble 2 yards in their 42-3 rout of the Baltimore Colts on 10-06-74
Had a 63 yd TD return + a 55 yd TD return of passes by Joe Namath in their 38-24 win over the Jets on 11-21-76
Sacked Jack Thompson in their 20-14 victory over the Cincinnati Bengals on 09-16-79
81 Regular Season Games/65 started and 1 Playoff Game (on 12-18-76)
Arizona State Sun Devil

McCURRY, David (#40)
Born on February 23, 1951 in Grinnel, IA
6'1" and 187 pounds
Defensive Back   1974
2 games (on Dec. 1st and Dec. 15th)
Iowa State Cyclone

McDERMOTT, Sean (#49)
Born on December 5, 1976 in Lufkin, TX
6'4" and 250 pounds
Long Snapper   2003
Only game played was on 12-14-03
Member of the 2003 World Championship Team
Kansas Jayhawk

McDONALD, Dewey (#31)
Born on June 10, 1990 in Ranson, WV
6'0" and 229 pounds
Safety   2015
Only game played was on 11-08-15
California University Vulcan

McDONALD, Nick (#65)
Born on June 27, 1987 in Salinas, CA
6'4" and 316 pounds
Offensive Lineman   2011-12
16 Regular Season Games/3 started and 2 Playoff Games
Grand Valley State Laker

McDOUGALD, Doug (#70)
Born on February 6, 1957 in Fayetteville, NC
6'5" and 271 pounds
Defensive End   1980
Shared in a sack of David Humm in their 24-2 victory over the Buffalo Bills on 12-14-80
8 games
#124 pick in the 1980 NFL Draft
Virginia Tech Hokie

McGEE, George (#75)
Born on October 7, 1935 in Baton Rouge, LA
6'2" and 255 pounds
Tackle   1960
14 games/14 started
Southern Jaguar

McGEE, Tony (#78) *"Mac the Sack"*
Born on January 18, 1949 in Battle Creek, MI
6'4" and 250 pounds
Defensive End   1974-81
Nicknamed *"Mac the Sack"* because of his skill in sacking the QB
72.5 sacks and 3 fumble recoveries for 8 yards
Sacked Mike Livingston, Marty Domres, Brian Sipe, Roger Staubach, Mike Rae, Bobby Scott and Pat Ryan
Sacked Steve Myer, Scott Hunter, James Harris, Stever Spurrier, David Humm, Greg Landry and
          Jack Thompson
Had 1 ½ sacks of Brian Sipe, Terry Bradshaw and Dan Manucci
Recorded 2 sacks of Ken Anderson, Ken Stabler, Ron Jaworski, Joe Theisman and Matt Robinson
Had 3 sacks of Richard Todd and Steve Ramsey and 4 sacks of Bill Troup and Dan Fouts
Recorded 6 sacks of Bert Jones, 8 sacks of Bob Griese and 8 ½ sacks of Joe Ferguson
Recovered fumbles by Tim Wilson, Bill Munson and David Woodley
Sacked Steve Ramsey *3 times* in their 38-14 rout of the Denver Broncos on 11-28-76
Had an 8 yard return of a fumble by Bill Munson in their 24-20 win vs the San Diego Chargers on 10-16-77
Sacked Bill Troup *4 times* in their 35-14 rout of the Baltimore Colts on 11-26-78
Sacked Joe Ferguson 3 ½ times in their 26-6 victory over the Buffalo Bills on 11-04-79
Recovered his strip sack fumble of David Woodley in their 30-27 OT loss to the Dolphins on 11-08-81
119 Regular Season Games/37 started and 2 Playoff Games
Bishop Cardinal

McGINEST JR, William "Willie" (#55) *"The Regulator"*
Born on December 11, 1971 in Long Beach, CA
6'5" and 270 pounds
DE/LB   1994-2005
78 sacks, 4 interceptions for 90 yards + 2 TDs and 15 fumble recoveries for 19 yards + 2 TDs
Shared in a sack of Sean Salisbury, Steve McNair, Dave Brown and Matt Hasselbeck
Shared in a sack of Jake Plummer and Brooks Bollinger
Sacked David Klinger, Steve Walsh, John Elway, Neil O'Donnell, Gus Frerotte, Paul Justin and Frank Reich
Sacked Alex Van Pelt, Danny Wuerffel, Tom Tupa, Tim Couch, Stoney Case, Shaun King and Rob Johnson
Sacked Doug Flutie, Chris Weinke, Richard Hundley, Kordell Stewart, Patrick Ramsey and Marc Bulger
Sacked JP Losman, Trent Green, Luke McCown, A.J. Feeley, Ken Dorsey and Aaron Brooks
Had 1 ½ sacks of Drew Bledsoe and 2 sacks of Don Majkowski, Boomer Esiason and Chris Simms
Had 2 sacks of Ben Roethlisberger, Chris Chandler and Josh McCown, Troy Aikman and Donovan McNabb
Had 2 ½ sacks of Chad Pennington, Peyton Manning, Damon Huard and Jay Fiedler
Had 3 sacks of Vinny Testaverde and 4 sacks of Dan Marino and Jim Harbaugh
Recorded 5 sacks of Brian Griese and 5 ½ sacks of Jim Kelly
Recovered fumbles by David Klinger, Leroy Hoard, Lamont Warren, Stan Humphries and Brett Favre
Recovered fumbles by Neil O'Donnell, Mark Brunell, Tom Tupa, Patrick Johnson and Brian Griese
Recovered fumbles by Doug Flutie, Travis Henry, Duce Staley, Rudi Johnson and Chris Simms
Sacked Peyton Manning, forcing a long FG that was missed, in their 27-24 win vs the Colts on 09-09-04
Had a 46 yard TD return of a pass by a pass by Jim Kelly in their 28-25 win over the Bills on 10-27-96
Fell on Stan Humphries' 22 yard fumble, in the end zone for a TD, in their 45-7 rout of the SD on 12-01-96
Fell on a fumble by QB Tom Tupa, in the end zone, for a TD, in their 30-28 win over the Jets on 09-12-99
Strip sacked and recovered Brian Griese's fumble in their 28-19 win over the Broncos on 10-01-00
Had a 2 yard return of a pass by Joey Harrington in their 20-12 victory over the Lions on 11-28-02
Advanced Anthony Pleasant's lateral 20 yards in their 31-10 rout of the Philadelphia Eagles on 09-14-03
Had a 15 yard TD return of a pass by Chad Pennington, tipped to himself, in their 21-16 win on 12-20-03
Had a 27 yard return of a pass by Matt Hasselbeck in their 30-20 win over Seattle on 10-17-04
Fell on Rudi Johnson's fumble, on the PATS 12 yard line, in their 35-28 win over the Bengals on 12-12-04
Had a career long 19 yard return of a fumble by Chris Simms in their 28-0 shutout of Tampa on 12-17-05
AFC Defensive Player of the Week in their 28-25 win over Buffalo on 10-27-96
AFC Defensive Player of the Week in their 45-7 rout of San Diego on 12-01-96
AFC Defensive Player of the Week in their 30-28 victory over the Jets on 09-12-99
AFC Defensive Player of the Week in their 21-16 win over the Jets on 12-20-03
AFC Defensive Player of the Month in October 1996
AFC Pro Bowl Defensive End in 1996
AFC Pro Bowl Linebacker in 2003
171 Regular Season Games. 146 started and 18 Playoff Games/15 started
16 sacks in the playoffs (NFL Record)
Sacked Vinny Testaverde, Brett Favre, Dan Marino, Kurt Warner and Frank Wycheck in the playoffs
Sacked Peyton Manning and Jake Delhomme once and Byron Leftwich 3 times in the playoffs
Had 1 ½ sacks of David Garrard, 2 sacks of Steve McNair and 2 ½ sacks of Kordell Stewart in the playoffs
Member of the 2001, 2003 and 2004 World Championship Teams
#4 pick in the 1994 NFL Draft
Inducted into the Patriots Hall of Fame on 08-05-15
USC Trojan

McGOVERN, Robert "Rob" (#58)
Born on October 1, 1966 in Teaneck, NJ
6'2" and 225 pounds
Linebacker   1992
4 games
Holy Cross Crusader

McGOWAN, Brandon (#30)
Born on September 16, 1983 in Jersey City, NJ
5'11" and 200 pounds
Safety   2009
2 fumble recoveries
Recovered Chris Carr's fumble of the opening kickoff in their 27-21 win over the Ravens on 10-04-09
Recovered Knowshon Moreno's fumble in their 20-17 Overtime loss to the Denver Broncos on 10-11-09
16 Regular Season Games/11 started and 1 Playoff Game (on 01-10-10)
Maine Bear

McGREW, Lawrence "Larry" (#50)
Born on July 23, 1957 in Berkeley, CA
6'5" and 233 pounds
Linebacker   1980-89
16.5 sacks, 6 interceptions for 49 yards, 5 fumble recoveries, blocked a punt and recorded a safety
Shared in a sack of David Humm, Mike Pagel and Danny White
Sacked Richard Todd, Joe Montana, Vince Ferragamo, Jim Kelly, Rusty Hilger and Tommy Kramer
Sacked Boomer Esiason, Ken O'Brien, Dave Krieg and Warren Moon
Recorded 1 ½ sacks of Chris Miller and 2 sacks of David Woodley
Intercepted Joe Ferguson, Lynn Dickey, John Elway, Ken O'Brien
Had 2 interceptions of Dan Marino
Recovered fumbles by Lindsay Scott, Ken O'Brien, James Brooks, Mickey Shuler and Ron Heller
Had a career long 27 yard return of a pass by Dan Marino in their 34-7 rout of Miami on 10-05-86
Blocked a punt by Hunter Newsome in their 34-0 shutout of the Steelers on 10-19-86
Strip sacked Jim Kelly, which resulted in a safety, in their 22-19 win over Buffalo on 11-23-86
122 Regular Season Games/98 started and 6 Playoff Games/6 started
Recovered Walter Payton's fumble on the 2nd play, in their 46-10 Super Bowl loss to Da' Bears on 01-26-86
#45 pick in the 1980 NFL Draft
USC Trojan

McGRUDER, Michael (#27) *"Scooter"*
Born on May 6, 1964 in Cleveland, OH
5'11" and 185 pounds
Cornerback   1996-97
1.5 sacks
Shared in a sack of Sean Salisbury and sacked Jim Harbaugh
17 Regular Season Games and 3 Playoff Games
Kent State Golden Flash

McHALE, Joe (#55)
Born on September 26, 1963 in Passaic, NJ
6'2" and 227 pounds
Linebacker   1987
3 games
Delaware Fighting Blue Hen

McKAY, Bob (#66) *"Booger"*
Born on December 27, 1947 in Seminole, TX
6'5" and 260 pounds
Guard/Tackle (KR)   1976-78
2 kickoff returns for 39 yards and 1 fumble recovery
Returned Toni Linhart's squibbed kickoff 23 yards in their 27-13 loss to the Baltimore Colts on 09-12-76
Pounced on Steve Grogan's fumble in their 14-10 victory over the Dolphins on 12-11-77
39 Regular Season Games and 1 Playoff Game (on 12-18-76)
Texas Longhorn

McKINNON, Don (#51)
Born on August 28, 1941 in Arlington, MA
6'3" and 230 pounds
Linebacker   1963-64
17 Regular Season Games and 2 Playoff Games
10th Round Draft Pick in 1963
Dartmouth Big Green

McMAHON, Arthur "Art" (#28) *"Irish Art"*
Born on February 24, 1946 in Newark, NJ
6'0" and 190 pounds
Defensive Back   1968-72
2 fumble recoveries and 3 interceptions for 99 yards
Recovered fumbles by Lee White and Ed Podolak
Intercepted Len Dawson, Don Trull and John Huarte
Had a career long 72 yard return of a pass John Huarte in their 23-10 loss to the Chiefs on 10-11-70
43 games/7 started
#385 pick in the 1968 NFL Draft
North Carolina State Wolfpack

McMICHAEL, Stephen "Steve" (#66)
Born on October 17, 1957 in Houston, TX
6'2" and 270 pounds
Defensive Tackle   1980
6 games
#73 pick in the 1980 NFL Draft
Texas Longhorn

McMURTRY, Greg (#86)
Born on October 15, 1967 in Jackson, MS
6'2" and 207 pounds
Wide Receiver   1990-93
120 receptions for 1,519 yards + 4 TDs and 2 carries for 3 yards
Snared a 34 yard TD from Hugh Millen on the last play to defeat the Houston Oilers 24-20 on 09-22-91
Grabbed an 18 yard TD from Hugh Millen in their 26-23 OT win vs the Vikings on 10-20-91
Caught a career long 65 yard TD pass from Scott Zolak in their 37-34 OT win vs the Colts on 11-15-92
Longest run was 2 yards in their 16-13 OT loss to the Miami Dolphins on 12-27-92
Cradled a 2 yard TD pass from Drew Bledsoe in their 38-14 loss to the Buffalo Bills on 09-05-93
58 games/41 started
#80 pick in the 1990 NFL Draft
Michigan Wolverine

McNEIL, Emanuel (#92)
Born on June 9, 1967 in Richmond, VA
6'3" and 285 pounds
Nose Tackle   1989
Only game played was on 12-24-89
#267 pick in the 1989 NFL Draft
Tennessee Martin Skyhawk

McQUAY, Leon (#31)
Born on March 19, 1950 in Tampa, FL
5'9" and 200 pounds
RB/KR   1975
33 carries for 47 yards, 4 receptions for 27 yards, 15 kickoff returns for 252 yards and 1 fumble recovery
Longest run was 9 yards in their 7-0 loss to the Houston Oilers on 09-21-75
Longest was a 34 yard return of a kickoff by Skip Butler in their 7-0 loss to the Houston Oilers on 09-21-75
Recovered Manfred Moore's fumbled punt return in their 24-16 win over the 49ers on 10-26-75
Longest reception was a 16 yard pass from Steve Grogan in their 20-7 loss to the Dolphins on 12-01-75
13 games
Tampa Spartan

McSWAIN, Anthony "Chuck" (#32)
Born on February 21, 1961 in Polk County, NC
6'0" and 193 pounds
RB/KR   1987
9 carries for 23 yards, 2 kickoff returns for 32 yards and 1 fumble recovery
Returned Goran Lingmerth's opening kickoff 24 yards in their 20-10 loss to Cleveland on 10-04-87
Longest run was 9 yards in their 20-10 loss to the Cleveland Browns on 10-04-87
Recovered Mike Katolin's bad snap in their 20-10 loss to the Browns on 10-04-87
3 games
Clemson Tiger

McSWAIN, Rodney "Rod" (#23)
Born on January 28, 1962 in High Shoals Township, NC
6'1" and 198 pounds
DB (KR)   1984-90
6 interceptions for 89 yards, 2 sacks, 2 fumble recoveries and 1 kickoff return for no gain
Blocked punt and returned it 31 yards for a touchdown
Intercepted John Elway, Boomer Esiason, Chris Chandler, Ken O'Brien
Had 2 interceptions of Dan Marino
Sacked Timm Rosenbach and Steve DeBerg
Recovered fumbles by Stump Mitchell and Tim Worley
Blocked a punt by Dale Hatcher and returned it 31 yards for a TD in their 30-28 win over the Rams on 11-16-86
Had a 3 yard return of pass by Dan Marino, with 38 seconds left, in their 34-27 win over Miami on 12-22-86
Had a career long 42 yard return of a pass by Chris Chandler in their 24-21 loss to the Colts on 11-27-88
Returned a kickoff by Pat Leahy for no gain in their 37-13 loss to the NY Jets on 09-30-90
90 Regular Season Games/17 started and 5 Playoff Games
Returned a pass by John Elway 2 yards in their 22-17 Divisional Playoff loss to Denver on 01-04-87
Clemson Tiger

MEGGETT, Dave (#22) *"Little Big Man"*
Born on April 30, 1966 in Charleston, SC
5'7" and 190 pounds
RB/PR/KR   1995-97
120 carries for 432 yards + 4 TDs, 104 receptions for 829 yards + 1 TD and threw a 35 yard TD pass
142 punt returns for 1,438 yards + 1 TD, 105 kickoff returns for 2,561 yards and 1 fumble recovery
Ran for a 2 point conversion and had a reception for a 2 point conversion
Ran for a 2 point conversion in their 17-14 victory over the Cleveland Browns on 09-03-95
Longest run was 25 yards in their 31-26 loss to the Kansas City Chiefs on 10-15-95
Longest was a 62 yard return of a kickoff by Doug Brien in their 31-17 loss to the Saints on 12-03-95
Caught a 2 point conversion pass from Drew Bledsoe in their 41-27 loss to the Steelers on 12-16-95
Recovered Chris Hudson's fumbled punt return in their 28-25 OT win vs Jacksonville on 09-22-96
Returned Chris Mohr's free kick 16 yards in their 28-25 win over the Bills on 10-27-96
Longest was a 60 yard TD return of a punt by Mike Horan in their 23-22 comeback win over the Giants
          on 12-21-96
Returned John Hall's free kick 21 yards in their 24-19 loss to the Jets on 10-19-97
Threw a 35 yard half back option TD pass to Troy Brown in their 27-24 win over Miami on 11-23-97
Longest reception was a 49 yard TD pass from Drew Bledsoe in their 24-21 OT loss to Pittsburgh on 12-13-97
Ran for a 5 yard game winning TD in their 14-12 win over the Miami Dolphins on 12-22-97
AFC Special Team Player of the Week in their 23-22 comeback win vs the Giants on 12-21-96
AFC Special Team Player of the Month in December 1996
AFC Pro Bowl Return Specialist in 1996
48 Regular Season Games/3 started and 5 Playoff Games
Recovered Drew Bledsoe's fumble in their 20-6 Championship win over the Jaguars on 01-12-97
Towson State Tiger

MEGNA, Marc (#99)
Born on July 30, 1976 in Fall River, MA
6'2" and 245 pounds
Special Team   2000
4 games
Richmond Spider

MEIXLER, Ed (#52)
Born on October 11, 1943 in Saratoga Springs, NY
6'3" and 245 pounds
Linebacker   1965
4 games
18ᵗʰ Round Draft Pick in 1965
Boston University Terrier

MELANDER, Jon (#64)
Born on December 27, 1966 in Fridley, MN
6'7" and 280 pounds
Guard/Tackle   1991
Recovered a blocked field goal in their 9-6 loss to the Denver Broncos on 10-27-91
11 games/3 started
#113 pick in the 1990 NFL Draft
Minnesota Golden Gopher

MELIFONWU, Henry-William "Obi" (#22)
Born on April 3, 1994 in London, England
6'4" and 224 pounds
DB   2018
2 Regular Season Games and 1 Playoff Game (on 01-20-19)
Member of the 2018 World Championship Team
UCONN Husky

MELVIN, Rashaan (#24)
Born on October 2, 1989 in Waukegan, IL
6'2" and 196 pounds
Special Team   2015
Recovered an onside kick by Stephen Gostkowski in their 35-28 loss to the Eagles on 12-06-15
8 games
Northern Illinois Husky

MERIWEATHER, Brandon (#31)
Born on January 14, 1984 in Apopka, FL
5'11" and 195 pounds
Defensive Back   2007-10
12 interceptions for 213 yards + 1 TD, 2 sacks and 1 fumble recovery
Intercepted Brett Favre, J.T. O'Sullivan, Chad Pennington, Mark Sanchez and Chad Henne
Intercepted David Garrard, Ryan Fitzpatrick and Peyton Manning
Had 2 interceptions of Josh Johnson and Jay Cutler
Sacked Russell Wilson and Carson Palmer
Had a 39 yard TD return of a pass by Josh Johnson in their 35-7 win over Tampa in London on 10-25-09
Had a career long 56 yard return of a pass by David Garrard in their 35-7 rout of the Jaguars on 12-27-09
Recovered a fumble by Peyton Hillis in their 34-14 loss to the Browns on 11-07-10
AFC Defensive Player of the Week in their 35-7 rout of the Buccaneers on 10-25-09
AFC Pro Bowl Safety in 2009, 2010
64 Regular Season Games/40 started and 5 Playoff Games/3 started
#24 pick in the 2007 NFL Draft
Miami Hurricane

MESKO, Zoltan (#14)
Born on March 16, 1986 in Timisoara, Romania
6'4" and 234 pounds
Punter   2010-12
175 punts for 7,738 yards
Holder for Shayne Graham, Stephen Gostkowski and Wes Welker
Longest punt was 65 yards in their 23-20 OT win vs the Ravens on 10-17-10
Holder for Wes Welker's extra point in their 34-14 loss to the Browns on 11-07-10
Had another 65 yard punt in their 27-24 win over the Dolphins on 12-24-11
48 Regular Season Games and 6 Playoff Games
Had a 62 yard free kick after a Giants safety in their 21-17 Super Bowl loss on 02-05-12
Ron Burton Community Service Award in 2012
#150 pick in the 2010 NFL Draft
Michigan Wolverine

MICHEL, Sony (#26)
Born on February 17, 1995 in Orlando, FL
5'11" and 215 pounds
RB   2018-19
456 carries for 1,843 yards and 13 TDs, 19 receptions for 144 yards and 4 kickoff returns for 77 yards
Longest run was a 34 yard TD in their 38-24 victory over the Colts on 10-04-18
Longest was a 26 yard return of a kickoff by Rigoberto Sanchez in their 38-24 win over the Colts on 10-04-18
Longest reception was a 19 yard pass from Tom Brady in their 35-14 rout of the NY Giants on 10-10-19
29 Regular Season Games/22 started and 4 Playoff Games/3 started
85 carries for 397 yards and 6 TDs and 3 receptions for 18 yards in the playoffs
Ran for 3 TDs in their 41-28 Divisional Playoff win over the LA Chargers on 01-13-19
Ran for 2 TDs in their 37-31 OT AFC Championship win vs the Chiefs on 01-20-19
Ran for a 2 yard TD in their 13-3 Super Bowl win over the LA Rams on 02-03-19
Member of the 2018 World Championship Team
#31 pick in the 2018 NFL Draft
Georgia Bulldog

MICKENS, William "Ray" (#38)
Born on January 4, 1973 in Frankfurt, Germany
5'8" and 180 pounds
Defensive Back   2006
4 Regular Season Games and 3 Playoff Games
Texas A & M Aggie

MILDREN JR., Larry "Jack" (#45)
Born on October 16, 1949 in Kingsville, TX
6'1" and 200 pounds
Defensive Back   1974
3 interceptions for 51 yards and 2 fumbles recoveries for 5 yards
Intercepted Joe Namath, Fran Tarkenton and Marty Domres
Recovered fumbles by OJ Simpson and Greg Pruitt
Had a 10 yard return of a pass by Fran Tarkenton in their 17-14 win over the Vikings on 10-27-74
Had a 5 yard return of a fumble by OJ Simpson in their 29-28 loss to the Bills on 11-03-74
Had a career long 41 yard return of a pass by Marty Domres in their 27-17 win over the Colts on 11-24-74
14 games
Oklahoma Sooner

MILLEN, Hugh (#7) *"Thrillen"*
Born on November 22, 1963 in Des Moines, IA
6'5" and 216 pounds
Quarterback   1991-92
370 completions for 4,276 yards + 17 TDs and 48 carries for 200 yards + 1 TD
Threw 1 TD pass to Kevin Turner and 2 TD passes to Greg McMurty and Michael Timpson
Completed 3 TD passes to Marv Cook and Ben Coates and 6 TD passes to Irving Fryar
Ran for a 2 yard game winning touchdown in their 16-13 victory over the Buffalo Bills on 11-24-91
Threw a 45 yard TD pass to Michael Timpson to defeat the Indianapolis Colts 23-17 in OT on 12-08-91
Nicknamed *"Thrillen' Hugh Millen"* after throwing an Overtime Game Winning TD pass on 12-08-91
Longest completion was a 60 yard TD pass to Michael Timpson in their 29-7 loss to the Bengals on 12-22-91
Longest run was 26 yards in their 14-0 loss to the Los Angeles Rams on 09-13-92
Had another run of 26 yards in their 30-21 loss to the Jets on 10-04-92
20 games/20 started
Washington Husky

MILLER, Alan (#32)
Born on June 19, 1937 in Mount Kisco, NY
6'0" and 219 pounds
Running Back   1960
101 carries for 416 yards + 1 TD and 29 receptions for 284 yards + 2 TDs
Ran for a 1 yard TD in their 35-0 shutout of the Los Angeles Chargers on 10-08-60
Hauled in a 47 yard TD pass from Butch Songin in their 31-24 loss to the Broncos on 10-23-60
Longest run was 33 yards in their 31-24 loss to the Denver Broncos on 10-23-60
Had a career long 48 yard TD reception of a pass from Butch Songin in their 38-21 win vs the Titans
        on 11-11-60
14 games/8 started
Boston College Eagle

MILLER, Danny (#6)
Born on December 30, 1960 in West Palm Beach, FL
5'10" and 172 pounds
Kicker   1982
Kicked 2 field goals and 4 extra points
Longest field goal was 25 yards in their 29-21 win over the Houston Oilers on 11-28-82
2 games (on Nov. 28th and Dec. 5th)
Miami Hurricane

MILLER, Joshua "Josh" (#8)
Born on July 14, 1970 in Queens, NY
6'4" and 225 pounds
Punter   2004-06
175 punts for 7,629 yards
Longest punt was 69 yards in their 35-28 win over the Bengals on 12-12-04
Holder for Adam Vinatieri
42 Regular Season Games and 5 Playoff Games
Member of the 2004 World Championship Team
Member of the 1995 Baltimore Stallions Grey Cup Championship Team
Arizona Wildcat

MILLOY, Lawyer (#36)
Born on November, 14, 1973 in St. Louis, MO
6'0" and 211 pounds
Safety　　　　　　　　　1996-2002
19 interceptions for 123 yards + 1 TD, 7 sacks and 7 fumble recoveries
Intercepted John Elway, Stan Humphries, Kordell Stewart, Dan Marino, Steve McNair and Doug Flutie
Intercepted Ray Lucas, Stoney Case, Dante Culpepper, Scott Mitchell and Aaron Brooks
Had 2 interceptions of Alex Van Pelt, Elvis Grbac, Peyton Manning and Vinny Testaverde
Shared in a sack of Rob Johnson, and had 1 ½ sacks of Tim Couch
Sacked Glenn Foley, Vinny Testaverde, Stoney Case, Doug Flutie and Michael Vick as well
Recovered fumbles by Sean Dawkins, Stan Humphries, Warrick Dunn and Jerome Bettis
Recovered fumbles by Tony Gonzalez, Peyton Manning and Dennis Northcutt
Intercepted a 4th down pass by Dan Marino, that helped seal their 14-12 win over Miami on 12-22-97
Had a career long 30 yard TD return of pass by Steve McNair in their 27-16 win over Tennessee on 09-20-98
AFC Defensive Player of the Week in their 21-16 win over the Colts on 11-01-98
AFC Defensive Player of the Week in their 16-13 win over the Bengals on 11-19-00
AFC Pro Bowl Safety in 1998, 1999, 2001, 2002
First Team All Pro Safety in 1999
112 Regular Season Games/106 started and 9 Playoff Games/9 started
Picked off a pass by Mike Tomczak in their 28-3 Divisional rout of the Pittsburgh Steelers on 01-05-97
Had an 11 yard return of a pass by Kordell Stewart in their 24-17 Championship win on 01-27-02
Member of the 2001 World Championship Team
#36 pick in the 1996 NFL Draft
Washington Husky

MINGO, Barkevious (#51) *"Keke"*
Born on October 4, 1990 in Belle Glade, FL
6'5" and 235 pounds
Linebacker　　　　　　2016
16 Regular Season Games and 3 Playoff Games
Member of the 2016 World Championship Team
LSU Fighting Tiger

MIRICH, Rex (#76)
Born on March 11, 1941 in Florence, AZ
6'4" and 250 pounds
Defensive Tackle　　　　1970
7 games/2 started
Arizona State Sun Devil

MITCHELL, Brandon (#98)
Born on June 19, 1945 in Abbeville, LA
6'3" and 290 pounds
Defensive End   1997-2001
6 sacks, 1 fumble recovery and blocked 2 field goal attempts (one in the playoffs)
Sacked John Elway, Dan Marino, Tim Couch, Damon Huard, Dave Brown and Kurt Warner
Recovered a fumble by Edgerrin James in their 31-28 win over the Colts on 09-19-99
Blocked Mike Vanderjagt's 46 yard field goal attempt in their 38-17 win over the Colts on 10-21-01
62 Regular Season Games/37 started and 5 Playoff Games/3 started
Blocked Kris Brown's 34 yard field goal attempt in their 24-17 Championship win over Pittsburgh on 01-27-02
Member of the 2001 World Championship Team
#59 pick in the 1997 NFL Draft
Texas A & M Aggie

MITCHELL, Leroy (#41)
Born on September 22, 1944 in Wharton, TX
6'1" and 190 pounds
Defensive Back   1967-68
10 interception for 50 yards, 1 fumble recovery and recovered a blocked field goal
Intercepted Tom Flores, Len Dawson, Jack Kemp, Jim LeClair, Steve Tensi and Marlin Briscoe
Had 2 interceptions of Dan Darragh and Joe Namath
Recovered Willie Frazier's fumble in their 31-31 Tie with the San Diego Chargers on 10-08-67
Recovered a blocked field goal in their 16-0 loss to the Houston Oilers on 10-13-68
Had a career long 20 yard return of a pass by Joe Namath in their 48-14 loss to the NY Jets on 10-27-68
AFL All Star Defensive Back in 1968
28 games/28 started
#283 pick in the 1967 NFL Draft
Texas Southern Tiger

MITCHELL, Malcolm (#19)
Born on July 20, 1992 in Valdosta, GA
6'1" and 200 pounds
Wide Receiver   2016
32 receptions for 401 yards + 4 TDs
Caught 4 TD passes from Tom Brady
Caught a career long 56 yard TD pass from Tom Brady in their 30-17 win over the 49ers on 11-20-16
14 Regular Season Games/6 started and 2 Playoff Games/2 started
7 receptions for 75 yards in the playoffs
Member of the 2016 World Championship Team
#112 Pick in the 2016 NFL Draft
Georgia Bulldog

MITCHELL III, Mel (#24)
Born on February 10, 1979 in Rockledge, FL
6'1" and 220 pounds
Defensive Back   2007
10 games
Western Kentucky Hilltopper

MOLDEN, Antwaum (#27)
Bornon January, 23, 1985 in Cleveland, OH
6'1" and 198 pounds
Cornerback   2011
2 interceptions for 40 yards and 1 fumble recovery
Recovered a fumbled punt return by Wes Welker in their 30-21 victory over the Jets on 10-09-11
Had a 27 yard return of a pass by Vince Young in their 38-20 win over the Eagles on 11-27-11
Had a 13 yard return of a pass by Ryan Fitzpatrick in their 49-21 rout of the Bills on 01-01-12
16 Regular Season Games/2 started and 3 Playoff Games
Eastern Kentucky Colonel

MONTLER, Mike (#64)
Born on January 10, 1944 in Columbus, OH
6'5" and 254 pounds
Tackle/Guard   1969-72
Recovered fumbles by Jim Plunkett and Bob Gladieux
53 games/50 started
#32 pick in the 1969 NFL Draft
Colorado Buffalo

MOORE, Art (#75)
Born on April 4, 1951 in Daingerfield, TX
6'5" and 253 pounds
NT/DT   1973-77
8 sacks, 1 fumble recovery and 3 blocked field goals
Shared in a sack of Bert Jones and had 1 ½ sacks of Brian Sipe
Sacked Bob Griese, Bobby Douglass, Bill Demory, Dan Fouts, Marty Domres and John Hadl
Recovered Bob Griese's fumble in their 44-23 loss to the Miami Dolphins on 09-30-73
Co-recovered a blocked punt (w/Sandy Durko) and returned it 8 yards in their 9-7 loss to the Jets on 10-14-73
Blocked a 43 yard field goal attempt by Skip Butler in their 32-0 shutout of the Oilers on 11-25-73
Blocked a 47 yard field goal attempt by Dennis Partee in their 30-14 win over the Chargers on 12-02-73
Blocked a 41 yard field goal attempt by David Ray in their 20-14 win over the LA Rams on 09-29-74
29 games
Tulsa Golden Hurricane

MOORE, Brandon (#70)
Born on June 21, 1970 in Ardmore, PA
6'6" and 290 pounds
Tackle   1993-95
26 games
Duke Blue Devil

MOORE, Eric (#98 and #92)
Born on February 28, 1981 in Pahokee, FL
6'4" and 268 pounds
Defensive Lineman   2010-11
Wore #98 for 4 games in 2010 and #92 for 2 games in 2011
Sacked Jay Cutler and Matt Flynn and recovered a fumble by Ryan Fitzpatrick
6 Regular Season Games/3 started and 1 Playoff Game/1 started (on 01-16-11)
Florida State Seminole

MOORE, Glenn "Rashad" (#95)
Born on March 16, 1979 in Huntsville, AL
6'3" and 324 pounds
Defensive Lineman   2007
Only Regular Season Game was on 12-23-07
2 Playoff Games
Tennessee Volunteer

MOORE, Greg (#54)
Born on March 28, 1965 in Cartersville, GA
6'1" and 240 pounds
Linebacker   1987
Recovered Willie Totten's fumble in their 14-7 win over the Buffalo Bills on 10-11-87
3 games/3 started
Tennessee Chattanooga Moccasin

MOORE, LeRoy (#61)
Born on September 16, 1935 in Pontiac, MI
6'2" and 240 pounds
Defensive End   1961-62
2 fumble recoveries for 1 TD
Recovered a deflected punt in the end zone for a TD in their 20-17 win over the Raiders on 11-17-61
Recovered James Stinnette's fumble in their 28-24 victory over the Denver Broncos on 12-03-61
19 games
Fort Valley State Wildcat

MOORE, Marty (#58 and #90) *"Mr. Irrelevant"*
Born on March 19, 1971 in Phoenix, AZ
6'1" and 244 pounds
Linebacker   1994-99 and 2001
Wore #58 from 1994-99 and #90 in 2001
2 interceptions for 7 yards and 1 fumble recovery
Intercepted Rick Mirer and Alex Van Pelt
Had a 7 yard return of a pass by Alex Van Pelt in their 33-6 rout of the Buffalo Bills on 10-12-97
Recovered Steve Bono's fumble in their 32-18 loss to the St. Louis Rams on 12-13-98
96 Regular Season Games/10 started and 7 Playoff Games/2 started
Member of the 2001 World Championship Team
#222 and last pick in the 1994 NFL Draft
Kentucky Wildcat

MOORE, Sterling (#29)
Born on February 3, 1990 in Antioch, CA
5'9" and 200 pounds
Defensive Back   2011-12
2 interceptions for 26 yards + 1 TD and 1 fumble return of 14 yards
Had a 5 yard return of a pass by Ryan Fitzpatrick in their 49-21 rout of the Bills on 01-01-12
Had a 21 yard TD return of a pass by Ryan Fitzpatrick in their 49-21 rout of Buffalo on 01-01-12
Had a 14 yard return of a fumble by Demarius Thomas in their 31-21 win over Denver on 10-07-12
14 Regular Season Games/3 started and 3 Playoff Games
SMU Mustang

MOORE, Stephen "Steve" (#67) *"Big House"*
Born on October 1, 1960 in Memphis, TN
6'4" and 293 pounds
Tackle (FB)   1983-87
Used a blocking full back on 11-03-85 and on 11-10-85
52 Regular Season Games/31 started and 4 Playoff Games/4 started
#80 pick in the 1983 NFL Draft
Tennessee State Tiger

MOORE III, Will (#83)
Born on February 21, 1970 in Dallas, TX
6'1" and 184 pounds
Wide Receiver   1995-96
46 receptions for 539 yards + 1 TD
Longest reception was a 33 yard pass from Drew Bledsoe in their 20-3 loss to Miami on 09-10-95
Caught a 6 yard TD pass from Drew Bledsoe in their 31-26 loss to the Chiefs on 10-15-95
16 games/14 started
Texas Southern Tiger

MOORE, Zach (#90)
Born on September 5, 1990 in Chicago, IL
6'6" and 275 pounds
Defensive Lineman   2014
1 fumble recovery and shared in a sack
Recovered a fumble by C.J. Spiller in their 37-22 win over the Bills on 10-12-14
Shared in a strip sack of Jay Cutler in their 51-23 rout of the Bears on 10-26-14
8 games/1 started (on 11-16-14)
Member of the 2014 World Championship Team
#198 pick in the 2014 NFL Draft
Concordia-St. Paul Golden Bear

MORELAND, Earthwind (#29)
Born on June 13, 1977 in Atlanta, GA
5'11" and 185 pounds
Cornerback   2004
1 fumble recovery
Recovered a fumble by Maurice Hicks in their 21-7 victory over the 49ers on 01-02-05
9 games/2 started
Member of the 2004 World Championship Team
Georgia Southern Eagle

MOREY, SEAN (#85)
Born on February 26, 1976 in Marshfield, MA
5'11" and 193 pounds
Special Team   1999
2 games (on December 26, 1999 and January 2, 2000)
#241 pick in the 1999 NFL Draft
Brown Bear

MORGAN, Stanley (#86) *"The Steamer"*
Born on February 17, 1955 in Easley, SC
5'11" and 181 pounds
WR/PR (KR)   1977-89
534 receptions for 10,352 yards + 67 TDs, 21 carries for 127 yards and 2 fumble returns for 23 yards
92 punt returns for 960 yards + 1 TD, 2 kickoff returns for 29 yards and 1 lateral return of 7 yards
Caught 2 TD passes from Matt Cavanaugh and 3 TD passes from Andy Johnson and Doug Flutie
Caught 18 Regular Season and 3 Post Season TD Passes from Tony Eason
Caught 39 touchdown passes from Steve Grogan
Snared a 75 yard TD pass from Steve Grogan in their 35-14 rout of the Colts on 11-26-78
Longest was a 17 yard return of a free kick by Rusty Jackson in their 26-24 win over Buffalo on 12-10-78
Longest run was 17 yards in their 56-3 rout of the New York Jets on 09-09-79
Had an 80 yard TD return of a punt by Bucky Dilts in their 50-21 rout of the Baltimore Colts on 11-18-79
Had a 3 yard advancement of a fumble by Don Calhoun in their 37-31 win over Seattle on 09-21-80
Hauled in a 66 yard HB Option TD pass from Andy Johnson in their 33-17 win over the Chiefs on 10-04-81
Caught a 28 yard HB Option TD pass from Andy Johnson in their 38-10 rout of the Oilers on 10-18-81
Had a career long 76 yard TD reception from Steve Grogan in their 30-27 OT loss to Miami on 11-08-81
Snared a 56 yard HB Option TD from Andy Johnson in their 20-17 loss to Buffalo on 11-22-81
Had a 20 yard advancement of a fumble by Tony Collins in their 30-0 loss to the Browns on 11-20-83
Had another 76 yard TD reception from Tony Eason in their 44-24 loss to Miami on 10-21-84
Caught an AFC Title Game Winning 30 yard TD pass to beat Miami 34-27 at the Orange Bowl on 12-22-86
Advanced a lateral from Cedric Jones 7 yards, on last play of 4th Qtr, in their 10-7 OT win vs Tampa on 12-11-88
Caught a 55 yard flea flicker TD pass from Steve Grogan in their 37-20 loss to the 49ers on 10-22-89
AFC Pro Bowl Wide Receiver in 1979, 1980, 1986, 1987
180 Regular Season Games/174 started and 7 Playoff Games/7 started
18 receptions for 302 yards + 3 TDs in the playoffs
Caught a 36 yard TD pass from Tony Eason in their 26-14 Wild Card win over the Jets on 12-28-85
Caught a 19 yard TD pass from Tony Eason in their 22-17 Divisional loss to the Broncos on 01-04-87
Caught a 45 yard flea flicker TD pass from Tony Eason in their 22-17 Divisional loss to Denver on 01-04-87
#25 pick in the 1977 NFL Draft
Inducted into the Patriots Hall of Fame on 08-27-07
Tennessee Volunteer

MORRIS, Aric (#29)
Born on July 22, 1977 in Winston-Salem, NC
5'10" and 210 pounds
Defensive Back   2003
Had a 33 yard return of a pass by Donovan McNabb in their 31-10 rout of the Eagles on 09-14-03
4 games
Member of the 2003 World Championship Team
Michigan State Spartan

MORRIS, James "Jamie" (#24)
Born on June 6, 1965 in Southern Pines, NC
5'7" and 188 pounds
KR/RB   1990
2 carries for 4 yards and 11 kickoff returns for 202 yards
Longest run was 3 yards in their 34-14 loss to the Phoenix Cardinals on 11-25-90
Longest was a 22 yard return of a kickoff by Gary Anderson in their 24-3 loss to Pittsburgh on 12-09-90
5 games
Michigan Wolverine

MORRIS, Jon (#56)
Born on April 5, 1942 in Washington, DC
6'4" and 254 pounds
Center   1964-74
3 fumble recoveries
Recovered fumbles by Ron Burton, Larry Garron and Jim Nance
AFL All Star Center from 1964-69
AFC Pro Bowl Center in 1970
First Team All Pro Center in 1966
130 games/126 started
4ᵗʰ Round Draft Pick in 1964
Inducted into the Patriots Hall of Fame on 09-15-11
Holy Cross Crusader

MORRIS, Mike (#64)
Born on February 22, 1961 in Centerville, IA
6'5" and 276 pounds
Center   1989
11 games
NE Missouri Bulldog

MORRIS III, Sammy (#34)
Born on March 23, 1977 in Oxford, England
6'0" and 220 pounds
Running Back (KR)   2007-10
334 carries for 1,486 yards + 12 TDs, 49 receptions for 353 yards and 7 kickoff returns for 103 yards
Ran for a 1 yard game winning TD to beat the Seattle Seahawks 24-21 on 12-07-08
Longest was a 24 yard return of a kickoff by Sebastian Janikowski in their 49-26 rout of the Raiders on 12-14-08
Longest reception for 42 yards in their 47-7 rout of the Arizona Cardinals on 12-21-08
Downed Matt Cassel's pooched punt on the Bills 2 yard line in their 13-0 shutout of Buffalo on 12-28-08
Longest run was 55 yards in their 35-7 rout of the Jaguars on 12-27-09
47 Regular Season Games/14 started and 2 Playoff Games
Ran for a 2 point conversion in their 28-21 Divisional loss to the New York Jets on 01-16-11
Texas Tech Red Raider

MORRISS, Guy (#75)
Born on May 13, 1951 in Colorado City, TX
6'4" and 255 pounds
Center/Guard   1984-87
Long Snapper for Rich Camarillo, Alan Herline, Tony Franklin and Eric Schubert
53 Regular Season Games/22 started and 5 Playoff Games
Texas Christian Horned Frog

MOSIER, John (#88)
Born on March 1, 1948 in Wichita Falls, TX
6'3" and 220 pounds
Tight End   1973
2 games (on Oct. 28ᵗʰ and Nov. 4ᵗʰ)
Kansas Jay Hawk

MOSS, Randy (#81) *"The Freak"*
Born on February 13, 1977 in Rand, WV
6'4" and 210 pounds
Wide Receiver (DB)   2007-10
259 receptions for 3,904 yards + 50 TDs, 2 lateral advancements of 9 yards and 1 interception
Caught 11 TD passes from Matt Cassel and 39 Regular Season TDs + 1 Post Season TD pass from Tom Brady
Advanced Wes Welker's pass reception lateral 11 more yards in their 38-7 rout of the Bills on 09-23-07
Recovered Kevin Faulk's fumble in their 56-10 rout of the Bills on 11-18-07
Caught a Patriots Team Record 4 TD passes on 11-18-07 (All of them in the 1st half)
Lost 2 yards recovering Tom Brady's fumbled lateral on their 56 yard Flea Flicker TD pass on 12-09-07
Longest reception was a 76 yard TD pass from Matt Cassel in their 47-7 rout of Arizona on 12-21-08
Intercepted a "Hail Mary Pass" by Kyle Orton, to end the half, in their 20-17 OT loss to Denver on 10-11-09
AFC Offensive Player of the Week in their 24-20 win over the Colts on 11-04-07
AFC Offensive Player of the Week in their 56-10 rout of the Bills on 11-18-07
AFC Offensive Player of the Month in November 2007
Led the NFL with 23 touchdown receptions in 2007
AFC Pro Bowl Wide Receiver in 2007
First Team All Pro Wide Receiver in 2007
52 Regular Season Games/51 started and 4 Playoff Games/4 started
12 receptions for 142 yards + 1 TD and 1 carry for 14 yards in the playoffs
Caught a 6 yard TD pass from Tom Brady in their 17-14 Super Bowl loss to the NY Giants on 02-03-08
Ran for a 14 yard gain in their 21-12 Championship win over the San Diego Chargers on 01-20-08
Inducted in the Pro Football Hall of Fame on 08-14-18
Marshall Thundering Herd

MOSS JR., Roland (#86)
Born on September 20, 1946 in St. Matthews, SC
6'3" and 215 pounds
Tight End   1971
9 receptions for 124 yards + 1 TD and blocked a punt and returned it 10 yards for a TD
Longest reception was a 20 yard TD pass from Jim Plunkett in their 20-6 win over the Raiders on 09-19-71
Blocked a punt by Spike Jones and returned it 10 yards for a TD in their 38-33 win over the Bills on 11-14-71
14 games/6 started
Toledo Rocket

MOSS, Zefross (#77)
Born on August 17, 1966 in Tuscaloosa, AL
6'6" and 325 pounds
Tackle   1997-99
42 Regular Season Games/42 started and 3 Playoff Games/3 started
Alabama State Hornet

MOWATT, Ezekiel "Zeke" (#81)
Born on March 5, 1961 in Wauchula, FL
6'3" and 238 pounds
Tight End   1990
6 receptions for 67 yards
Longest reception was a 16 yard pass from Tommy Hodson in their 24-3 loss to Pittsburgh on 12-09-90
10 games
Florida State Seminole

MRUCZKOWSKI, Gene (#64)
Born on June 6, 1980 in Cleveland, OH
6'2" and 305 pounds
Guard/Center   2004-06
18 Regular Season Games and 4 Playoff Games
Member of the 2004 World Championship Team
Purdue Boilermaker

MULLIGAN, Matthew (#88)
Born on January 18m, 1985 in West Enfield, ME
6'4" and 258 pounds
Tight End   2013
2 receptions for 16 yards + 1 TD and 1 fumble recovery
Caught a 1 yard TD pass from Tom Brady on in their 30-23 win over the Atlanta Falcons on 09-29-13
Longest reception was a 15 yard pass from Tom Brady in their 27-26 comeback win over the Browns on 12-08-13
Recovered LeGarrette Blount's fumble in their 34-20 win over the Buffalo Bills on 12-29-13
15 Regular Season Games/4 started and 2 Playoff Games/1 started (on 01-11-14)
Maine Black Bear

MURPHY JR., William "Bill" (#31)
Born on March 26, 1946 in Montclair, NJ
6'1" and 185 pounds
Wide Receiver   1968
18 receptions for 268 yards
Longest reception was a 26 yard pass from Tom Sherman in their 31-17 loss to the Chiefs on 11-17-68
6 games/5 started
Cornell Big Red

MURRELL, Marques (#93)
Born on March 20, 1985 in Fayetteville, NC
6'2" and 234 pounds
Special Team   2010
Only game played was on 09-12-10
Appalachian State Mountaineer

MYERS, Jakobi (#16)
Born on November 9, 1996 in Lithonia, GA
6'2" and 200 pounds
WR   2019--
26 receptions for 359 yards
Longest reception was a 35 yard pass from Tom Brady in their 23-16 loss to the Chiefs on 12-08-19
15 games
North Carolina State Wolfpack

MYERS JR., Leonard (#25)
Born on December 18, 1978 in Ft. Lauderdale, FL
5'10" and 196 pounds
Special Team   2001-02
Had a 35 yard return of a blocked field goal in their 38-17 rout of the Colts on 10-21-01
15 games/1 started (on 12-22-02)
Member of the 2001 World Championship Team
#200 pick in the 2001 NFL Draft
Miami Hurricane

NANCE, James "Jim" (#35) *"Big Bo"*
Born on December 30, 1942 in Indiana, PA
6'1" and 235 pounds
Fullback (KR)   1965-71
1,323 carries for 5,323 yards + 45 TDs, 129 receptions for 844 yards + 1 TD and 3 kickoff returns for 40 yards
Returned Rick Redman's free kick 16 yards in their 22-6 win over the San Diego Chargers on 10-31-65
Longest was a 19 yard return of a kickoff by Jim Turner in their 30-20 loss to the Jets on 11-14-65
Longest reception was a 45 yard pass from Babe Parilli in their 24-0 loss to the San Diego Chargers on 09-10-66
Longest run was a 65 yard TD in their 14-3 win over the Bills in "The Game" at Fenway Park on 12-04-66
Caught a 10 yard TD pass from Babe Parilli in their 26-21 loss to the Denver Broncos on 09-03-67
AFL Offensive Player of the Week in their 23-0 shutout of the Bills on 09-24-67
Led the AFL with the most rushing attempts, yards rushing and rushing TDs in 1966
Led the AFL with the most rushing attempts, yards rushing and rushing TDs in 1967
AFL All Star Fullback in 1966, 1967
First Team All Pro Running Back in 1966, 1967
AFL MVP and Player of the Year in 1966
AFL Comeback Player of the Year in 1969
94 games/87 started
19th Round Draft Pick in 1965
Inducted into the Patriots Hall of Fame on 08-20-09
Syracuse Orangeman

NAPOSKI, Eric (#91)
Born on December 20, 1966 in New York, NY
6'2" and 230 pounds
Linebacker   1988-89
4 games
UCONN Husky

NEAL, Stephen (#61) *"The Real Deal"*
Born on October 9, 1976 in San Diego, CA
6'4" and 305 pounds
Guard   2001-10
1 kickoff return of 27 yards
Had a 27 yard return of Jeff Reed's 4th Qtr kickoff in their 33-10 loss to the Steelers on 11-30-08
86 Regular Season Games/81 started and 12 Playoff Games/12 started
Member of the 2001, 2003 and 2004 World Championship Teams
California State-Bakersfield Roadrunner

NEBLETT, Andre (#71)
Born on June 7, 1988 in Rahway, NJ
6'0" and 297 pounds
Defensive Lineman   2013
Only game played was on 10-20-13
Temple Owl

NEIGHBORS, William "Billy" (#73) *"Spanky"*
Born on February 4, 1940 in Tuscaloosa, AL
6'0" and 250 pounds
Guard   1962-65
2 fumble recoveries
Recovered fumbles by Tom Yewcic and Babe Parilli
AFL All Star Guard in 1963 and First Team All Pro Guard in 1964
56 Regular Season Games/44 started and 2 Playoff Games/2 started
6th Round Draft Pick in 1962
Alabama Crimson Tide

NELSON, Edmund (#65)
Born on April 30, 1960 in Live Oak, FL
6'3" and 272 pounds
DE/NT   1988
12 games/1 started (on 10-30-88)
Auburn Tiger

NELSON, Steve (#57) *"Nellie"*
Born on April 26, 1951 in Farmington, MN
6'2" and 230 pounds
Linebacker   1974-87
17 interceptions for 226 yards, 19.5 sacks and 16 fumble recoveries
Blocked a field goal and blocked 2 extra point attempts
Intercepted Gary Marangi, Vince Ferragamo, Cliff Stoudt, Bob Griese, Joe Theisman and Dan Pastorini
Intercepted Joe Ferguson, Don Stock and Pat Ryan as well
Had 2 interceptions of Jim Hart, Dan Fouts, Bert Jones and Jack Trudeau
Sacked Joe Ferguson, Greg Landry, Matt Robinson Craig Morton, Paul McDonald and Matt Kofler
Sacked Art Schlichter, Marc Wilson, Vince Ferragamo and Jim Kelly and had 1 ½ sacks of Brian Sipe
Had 2 sacks of Bob Griese, Ron Jaworski and Dave Krieg and 3 sacks of Bert Jones
Recovered fumbles by Brian Sipe, Terry Bradshaw, Rocky Bleier, Gary Marangi and Benny Malone
Recovered fumbles by Wilbert Montgomery, Ron Jaworski and Keith Krepfle in their 24-14 win on 10-08-78
Recovered fumbles by Joe Washington, Robin Earl, Jim Zorn, George Rodgers and Bernie Kosar
Recovered fumbles by Ulysses Norris, Dan Marino and fell on a bad pitch by Jim Kelly to Ronnie Harmon
Had a 34 yard return of a pass by Gary Marangi, tipped by Steve Zabel, in their 20-10 win vs Buffalo on 11-07-76
Had a career long 37 yard return of a pass by Jim Hart in their 16-6 win vs the St. Louis Cardinals on 09-10-78
Returned a Dan Fouts pass 18 yards, from the 2 yard line, in their 27-21 victory over San Diego on 09-23-79
Blocked a 49 yard field goal attempt by Pat Leahy in their 21-11 win over the Jets on 10-05-80
Returned a Vince Ferragamo pass 33 yards in their 17-14 loss to the LA Rams on 11-16-80
Had a 6 interception return and then it lateraled to Clayton Weishuhn in their 28-23 win vs Pitt on 09-25-83
Blocked an extra point attempt by Uwe Von Schamann in their 44-24 loss to the Dolphins on 10-21-84
Blocked an extra point attempt by Neil O'Donoghue in their 33-10 loss to the St. Louis Cardinals on 12-02-84
AFC Pro Bowl Linebacker in 1980, 1984, 1985
174 Regular Season Games/171 started and 7 Playoff Games/7 started
Recovered Garin Veris' interception return fumble in their 26-14 Wild Card win vs the Jets on 12-28-85
#34 pick in the 1974 NFL Draft
His Uniform # 57 was retired by the Patriots on 07-11-88
Inducted into the Patriots Hall of Fame on 08-18-93
North Dakota State Bison

NEUMANN, Tom (#36)
Born on March 4, 1940 in Menomonie, WI
5'11" and 205 pounds
Running Back   1963
44 carries for 148 yards and 10 receptions for 48 yards + 1 TD
Caught a 15 yard TD pass from Babe Parilli in their 20-14 win over the Raiders on 10-11-63
Longest run was 17 yards in their 45-3 rout of the Houston Oilers on 11-01-63
Longest reception was a 16 yard pass from Babe Parilli in their 24-24 tie with the Chiefs on 11-17-63
10 Regular Season Games and 2 Playoff Games
17ᵗʰ Round Draft Pick in 1963
Northern Michigan Wildcat

NEVILLE JR., Tom (#77)
Born on August 12, 1943 in Montgomery, AL
6'4" and 260 pounds
Tackle/DT   1965-77
Played both Defensive Tackle and Offensive Tackle in 1965
4 fumble recoveries and 1 carry for a loss of 8 yards and 7 tackles as a defensive lineman
Recovered fumbles by Gino Cappelletti, Dick Anderson, Jack Tatum and John Tarver
Had 7 tackles as a defensive tackle in their 24-10 loss to the Oakland Raiders on 10-08-65
Recovered Dick Anderson's blocked FGA return fumble in their 37-20 loss to Miami on 12-06-70
Lost 8 yards after QB Jim Plunkett handled him the ball in their 23-3 loss to the Colts on 10-03-71
AFL All Star Offensive Tackle in 1966, 1968
160 Regular Season Games/114 started and 1 Playoff Game (on 12-18-76)
7ᵗʰ Round Draft Pick in 1965
Mississippi State Bulldog

NEWHOUSE, Marshall (#72)
Born on September 29, 1988 in Dallas, TX
6'4" and 330 pounds
Tackle   2019
15 Regular Season Games/9 started and 1 Playoff Game (on 01-04-20)
Texas Christian Horned Frog

NICHOLS, Bobby (#87)
Born on January 30, 1942 in Boston, MA
6'2" and 220 pounds
Tight End   1967-68
1 reception for 19 yards and blocked a punt
Caught a 19 yard pass from Babe Parilli in their 48-14 loss to the Oakland Raiders on 10-22-67
Blocked a punt by Larry Seiple in their 41-32 loss to the Miami Dolphins on 12-17-67
15 games/1 started (on 10-06-68)
#440 pick in the 1967 NFL Draft
Boston University Terrier

NINKOVICH, Robert "Rob" (#50) *"Nink"*
Born on February 1, 1984 in New Lenox, IL
6'2" and 260 pounds
Linebacker   2009-16
46 sacks, 5 interceptions for 42 yards + 1 TD and 14 fumble recoveries for 84 yards + 1 TD
Shared in a sack of Mark Sanchez, Kevin Kolb, Josh Freeman and Andy Dalton
Shared in a sack of Tyrod Taylor and shared in a strip sack of Mark Sanchez
Sacked Chad Henne, Matt Flynn, Tyler Palko, Vince Young, Dan Orlovsky, Tim Tebow and Sam Bradford
Sacked Matt Schaub, Matt Cassel, Matthew Stafford, Ben Roethlisberger and Jason Campbell
Sacked Thaddeus Lewis, Eli and Peyton Manning, Brock Osweiler, Brian Hoyer, Russell Wilson and Jared Goff
Strip sacked Matt Moore, Ryan Fitzpatrick, Andrew Luck, Ben Roethlisberger, Tyrod Taylor and
      Colin Kaepernick
Had another sack of Colin Kaepernick, Andew Luck and Ryan Fitzpatrick
Recorded 2 sacks of Cam Newton, Tyler Thigpen, Philip Rivers and Joe Flacco
Recorded 3 sacks of Ryan Tannehill and 4 sacks of Kyle Orton
Intercepted Peyton Manning and had 2 interceptions of Chad Henne and Mark Sanchez
Recovered fumbles by Cedric Benson, Philip Rivers, Ricky Williams, Mike Tolbert and Aaron Ross
Recovered fumbles by Lance Ball, Russell Wilson, Mark Sanchez, Andrew Luck and Chaz Schilens
Recovered fumbles by Marquise Goodwin, Ryan Tannehill, Jay Cutler and Matt Jones
Had a career long 63 yard return of a fumble by Philip Rivers in their 23-20 win over San Diego on 10-24-10
Returned Rian Lindell's short kickoff 10 yards, to end the 1st half, in their 34-31 loss to Buffalo on 09-25-11
Had a career long 18 yard return of a pass by Mark Sanchez in their 37-16 rout of the Jets on 11-13-11
Had a 12 yard TD return of another pass by Mark Sanchez in their 37-16 rout of the Jets on 11-13-11
Recovered a fumble by Mark Sanchez to help seal their 29-26 OT win vs the Jets on 10-21-12
Recovered his strip sack of Andrew Luck in their 59-24 rout of the Colts on 11-18-12
Returned Jay Cutler's fumble 15 yards for a TD in their 51-23 rout of the Redskins on 10-26-14
Long Snapper for Stephen Gostkowski and Ryan Allen in their 26-21 loss to Green Bay on 11-30-14
123 Regular Season Games/101 started and 17 Playoff Games/16 started
6 sacks in the playoffs
Strip sacked Tim Tebow in their 45-10 Divisional win over the Broncos on 01-14-12
Shared in a sack of Tim Tebow in their 45-10 Divisional rout of the Broncos on 01-14-12
Shared in a sack of Eli Manning in their 21-17 Super Bowl loss to the Giants on 02-05-12
Sacked Joe Flacco *twice* in their 28-13 Championship Game loss to the Ravens on 01-20-13
Sacked Russell Wilson in their 28-24 Super Bowl win over Seattle on 02-01-15
Sacked Brock Osweiler in their 34-16 Divisional win over Houston on 01-14-17
Returned a pass by Matt Schaub 6 yards in their 41-28 Divisional Playoff win over Houston on 01-13-13
Recovered a fumble by Eli Rogers in their 36-17 AFC Championship win over the Steelers on 01-22-17
Member of the 2014 and 2016 World Championship Teams
Purdue Boilermaker

NUGENT, David (#92) *"The Big Nuge"*
Born on October 27, 1977 in Cincinnati, OH
6'4" and 300 pounds
Defensive End   2000-01
15 games/1 started (on 12-09-01)
Member of the 2001 World Championship Team
Purdue Boilermaker

NUGENT, Michael "Mike" (#2)
Born on March 2, 1982 in Centerville, OH
5'10" and 190 pounds
Kicker   2019
Kicked 5 field goals and 15 extra points
Longest field goal was 37 yards in their 33-7 rout of the Redskins on 10-06-19
4 games
Ohio State Buckeye

O'CALLAGHAN, Ryan (#68)
Born on July 19, 1983 in Susanville, GA
6'7" and 330 pounds
Offensive Lineman   2006-08
Recovered Tom Brady's fumble in their 28-6 win over the Bills on 10-22-06
26 Regular Season Games/7 started and 3 Playoff Games
#136 pick in the 2006 NFL Draft
California Golden Bear

O'CONNELL, Kevin (#5)
Born on May 25, 1985 in Knoxville, TN
6'5" and 225 pounds
Quarterback   2008
4 completions for 23 yards
Longest completion was a 12 yard pass to Jabar Gaffney in their 38-13 loss to Miami on 09-21-08
2 games (on Sept. 21st and Dec. 21st)
#94 pick in the 2008 NFL Draft
San Diego State Aztec

O'HANLEY, Ross (#25) *"Rocky"*
Born on February 16, 1939 in Everett, MA
6'0" and 183 pounds
Defensive Back   1960-65
15 interceptions for 288 yards + 1 TD, 6 fumble recoveries for 24 yards and 3 returns of missed field goals
Intercepted Tommy O'Connell, Frank Tripucka, Cotton Davidson, Dick Wood and Jacky Lee
Intercepted Mickey Slaughter and Joe Namath and had 2 interception of Tom Flores
Had 6 interceptions of George Blanda
Recovered fumbles by Curtis McClinton, Al Carmichael, Bo Roberson and Willard Dewveall
Recovered 2 fumbles by Lionel Taylor
Had a 14 yard return of a missed FGA by Larry Barnes in their 27-14 loss to the Raiders on 10-16-60
Lateraled a bad snap on a field goal attempt to Gino Cappelletti in their 27-14 loss to Oakland on 10-16-60
Holder for Gino Cappelletti's extra point and field goal attempts in their 27-14 loss to the Raiders on 10-16-60
Had a 2 yard return of a missed FGA by Gene Mingo in their 45-17 rout of the Broncos on 09-16-61
Had a career long 10 yard return of a fumble by Al Carmichael in their 45-17 win over Denver on 09-16-61
Had a 6 yard return of a missed FGA by Dick Guesman in their 38-14 victory over the Jets on 09-08-63
Had a career long 61 yard return of a pass by Tom Flores in their 20-14 win over the Raiders on 10-11-63
Deflected a potential game winning TD pass by Tom Flores in their 17-14 win over the Raiders on 09-13-64
Had a 43 yard return of a pass by Mickey Slaughter to help seal their 12-7 win vs Denver on 11-20-64
Had a 47 yard TD return of a pass by George Blanda in their 34-17 win over the Oilers on 11-29-64
AFL All Star Defensive Back in 1960
77 Regular Season Games/74 started and 2 Playoff Games/2 started
Had a 13 yard return of a pass by Daryle Lamonica in their 26-8 Divisional win over the Bills on 12-28-63
Picked off a Jack Kemp pass in the end zone in their 26-8 Divisional win vs the Bills on 12-28-63
Boston College Eagle

O'NEAL III, Deltha (#21)
Born on January 30, 1977 in Palo Alto, CA
5'11" and 194 pounds
CB (PR)   2008
3 interceptions for 49 yards and 2 punt returns for 2 yards
Intercepted a pass thrown by J.T. O'Sullivan, Marc Bulger and Trent Edwards
Had a 2 yard return of a punt by Dustin Colquitt in their 17-10 victory over Kansas City on 09-07-08
Had a 47 yard return of a pass by Marc Bulger in their 23-16 victory over St. Louis on 10-26-08
16 games/10 started
California Golden Bear

O'NEILL, Pat (#5) *"Thunderfoot"*
Born on February 9, 1971 at Scott Air Force Base, IL
6'1" and 200 pounds
P (Place Kicker)   1994-95
110 punts for 4,355 yards and kicked off in every game he played for the Patriots
Longest punt was 67 yards in their 41-17 victory over the Buffalo Bills on 12-18-94
AFC Special Team Player of the Week in their 41-17 win over Buffalo on 12-18-94
24 Regular Season Games and 1 Playoff Game
Tossed a 21 yard pass to Corwin Brown in their 20-13 Wild Card loss to Cleveland on 01-01-95
#135 pick in the 1994 NFL Draft
Syracuse Orangeman

OAKES, Don (#71) *"Tree"*
Born on July 22, 1938 in Roanoke, VA
6'4" and 255 pounds
Tackle   1963-68
Recovered Dick Guesman's squibbed kickoff in their 12-7 win over Denver on 11-20-64
AFL All Star Tackle in 1967
82 Regular Season Games/68 started and 2 Playoff Games/2 started
Virgina Tech Hokie

OCHOCINCO, Chad (#85)
Born on January 9, 1978, as Chad Johnson, in Miami, FL
6'1" and 188 pounds
Wide Receiver   2011
15 receptions for 276 yards + 1 TD
Longest reception was a 53 yard pass from Tom Brady in their 37-16 win over the Jets on 11-13-11
Caught a 33 yard TD pass from Tom Brady in their 34-27 win over the Redskins on 12-11-11
15 Regular Season Games/3 started and 2 Playoff Games
Caught a 21 yard pass from Tom Brady in their 21-17 Super Bowl loss to the Giants on 02-05-12
Oregon State Beaver

OHRNBERGER, Rich (#60)
Born on February 14, 1986 in East Meadow, NY
6'2" and 291 pounds
Offensive Lineman   2009-10
5 games
#123 pick in the 2009 NFL Draft
Penn State Nittany Lion

OJINNAKA, Quinn (#69)
Born on April 23, 1984 in Seabrook, MD
6'5" and 295 pounds
Offensive Lineman   2010
8 Regular Season Games and 1 Playoff Game (on 01-16-11)
Syracuse Orangeman

OLSZEWSKI, Kaleb "Gunner" (#80)
Born on November 26, 1996 in Alvin, TX
6'0" and 190 pounds
WR/PR   2019--
2 receptions for 34 yards and 20 punt returns for 179 yards
Longest reception was a 29 yard pass from Tom Brady in their 35-14 win over the Giants on 10-10-19
Had a career long 22 yard return of a punt by Lac Edwards in their 33-0 shutout of the Jets on 10-21-19
8 games
Bemidji State Beaver

OSLEY, Willie (#37)
Born on April 10, 1957 in Detroit, MI
6'0" and 195 pounds
Defensive Back   1974
Blocked an extra point attempt by John Leypoldt in their 30-28 loss to the Bills on 10-20-74
10 games/4 started
Illinois Fighting Illini

OUTLAW, John (#44)
Born on January 8, 1945 in Clarksdale, MS
5'10" and 180 pounds
Defensive Back   1969-72
3 interceptions for 108 yards + 1 TD and 1 fumble recovery
Intercepted Earl Morrall, George Mira and Johnny Unitas
Drove from Curry College to Harvard Stadium, in full uniform, before their 27-14 win over Miami on 09-20-70
Had a 19 yard return of a pass by Earl Morrall in their 23-3 loss to the Baltimore Colts on 10-03-71
Had a 29 yard return of a pass by George Mira in their 34-13 lsos to the Dolphins on 12-05-71
Recovered a fumble by John Riggins in their 13-6 loss to the New York Jets on 12-12-71
Had a career long 60 yard TD return of a pass by Johnny Unitas in their 21-17 win vs the Colts on 12-19-71
33 games
#249 pick in the 1968 NFL Draft
Jackson State Tiger

OVERTON, Don (#29)
Born on September 24, 1967 in Columbus, OH
6'0" and 221 pounds
RB/KR   1990
5 carries for 8 yards, 2 receptions for 19 yards and 10 kickoff returns for 188 yards
Longest reception was a 15 yard pass from Tommy Hodson in their 41-7 loss to the Bengals on 09-23-90
Longest run was 6 yards in their 33-20 loss to Seattle on 10-07-90
Longest was 23 yard return of a kickoff by Norm Johnson in their 33-20 loss to the Seahawks on 10-07-90
7 games
Fairmont State Falcon

OWEN, Willis "Tom" (#17)
Born on September 1, 1952 in Shreveport, LA
6'1" and 195 pounds
Quarterback   1976-81
58 completions for 655 yards + 3 TDs
Threw 1 TD pass to Don Calhoun, 2 TD passes to Don Westbrook and 1 Post Season TD pass to Russ Francis
Longest completion was a 32 yard pass to Harold Jackson in their 24-17 win over the Detroit Lions on 10-07-79
12 Regular Season Games/1 started (on 12-20-81) and 1 Playoff Game
Threw a 24 yard TD pass to Russ Francis in their 31-14 Divisional Playoff Game loss to Houston on 12-31-78
Wichita State Shocker

OWENS, Dennis (#98)
Born on February 24, 1960 in Clinton, NC
6'1" and 257 pounds
Nose Tackle   1982-86
11 sacks and 3 fumble recoveries for 4 yards
Shared in a sack of Paul McDonald and had 1 ½ sacks of Ken O'Brien
Sacked Joe Montana, Dan Fouts, Steve Bartkowski, Dan Marino, Dave Krieg and Joe Theismann
Sacked Pat Ryan, Joe Pisarcik and Art Schlichter
Recovered fumbles by Richard Todd, Danny White and Curtis Dickey
Had a 4 yard return of a fumble by Curtis Dickey in their 29-23 OT loss to the Colts on 09-04-83
71 Regular Season Games/44 started and 5 Playoff Games
Sacked David Woodley *twice* in their 28-13 First Round Playoff loss to Miami on 01-08-83
Sacked Jim McMahon and William Perry in their 46-10 Super Bowl loss to Da' Bears on 01-26-86
North Carolina State Wolfpack

PAGE, Jarrad (#44)
Born on October 19, 1984 in Oakland, CA
6'0" and 225 pounds
Safety   2010
Intercepted Tyler Thigpen and Ryan Fitzpatrick
10 Regular Season Games/1 started (on 12-26-10) and 1 Playoff Game (on 01-16-11)
UCLA Bruin

PARILLI, Vito "Babe" (#15)
Born on May 7, 1930 in Rochester, PA
6'1" and 196 pounds
Quarterback (P)   1961-67
1,140 completions for 16,747 yards + 133 TDs, 6 Two Point Passes and 228 carries for 949 yards + 15 TDs
Punted 5 times for 180 yards, ran for a 2 point conversion and had 6 Two Point conversion completions
Threw 1 TD pass to Jim Crawford, Tom Neumann, Joe Bellino, Jim Nance, Bob Cappadona and Bobby Leo
Tossed 2 TD passes for JD Garrett, 5 TDs to Billy Lott and 6 TDs to Ron Burton
Threw 8 TD passes to Jim Whalen, 10 TD passes to Tony Romeo and 16 TD passes to Art Graham
Completed 18 TDs to Jim Colclough, 25 Regular Season TDs to Larry Garron and 34 TDs to Gino Cappelletti
Recovered fumbles by JD Garrett, Joe Bellino, Dainard Paulson and 2 fumbles by Larry Garron
Holder for Gino Cappelletti
Ran for a 2-point conversion as the holder on a fake extra point attempt in their 18-17 win over Dallas on 10-29-61
Advanced Larry Garron's fumble 1 yard for a TD in their 28-21 win vs the Dallas Texans on 11-03-61
Ran for the game winning 7 yard TD to beat the Denver Broncos 28-24 on 12-03-61
Longest run was a 32 yard TD in their 34-21 win over the Houston Oilers on 09-16-62
Tossed a 2 point pass to Jim Crawford in their 24-20 win over San Diego on 10-19-62
Tossed a 2 point pass to Jim Colclough in their 43-43 tie with the Raiders on 10-16-64
Tossed a 2 point pass to Gino Cappelletti in their 36-28 win over the Bills on 11-15-64
Threw a career long 80 yard TD pass to Art Graham in their 34-17 win over the Houston Oilers on 11-29-64
Longest punt was 45 yards in their 24-14 loss to the Buffalo Bills on 12-20-64
Tossed a 2 point pass to Jim Colclough in their 24-14 loss to the Buffalo Bills on 12-20-64
Tossed a 2 point pass to Tony Romeo in their 24-10 win over the Broncos on 09-18-66
Recovered Dainard Paulson's interception return fumble in their 30-20 loss to the Jets on 11-14-65
Tossed a 2 point pass to Bob Cappadona in their 38-28 loss to the Jets on 12-17-66
AFL All Star Quarterback in 1963, 1964, 1966
First Team All Pro Quarterback in 1964
AFL Player of the Week in their 35-17 win over the Chargers on 10-23-66
AFL Player of the Week in their 41-10 rout of the Dolphins on 10-15-67
AFL Comeback Player of the Year in 1966
AFL All Star Game MVP on 01-21-67
94 Regular Season Games/83 started and 2 Playoff Games/2 started
28 completions for 489 yards + 2 TDs in the playoffs
Tossed 2 TD passes to Larry Garron in their 26-8 Divisional win vs Buffalo on 12-28-63
Inducted into the Patriots Hall of Fame on 08-18-93
Kentucky Wildcat

PARKER JR., Riddick (#97)
Born on November 20, 1972 in Emporia, VA
6'3" and 295 pounds
Defensive Tackle   2001
Sacked Mark Rypien in their 44-13 rout of the Indianapolis Colts on 09-30-01
Recovered Chris Weinke's fumble in their 38-6 rout of the Carolina Panthers on 01-06-02
13 Regular Season Games and 2 Playoff Games
Member of the 2001 World Championship Team
North Carolina Tar Heel

PASS, Patrick (#35)
Born on December 31, 1977 in Scottsdale, GA
5'10" and 217 pounds
RB/KR   2000-06
128 carries for 526 yards + 3 TDs, 66 receptions for 570 yards + 1 TD and 36 kickoff returns for 745 yards
Recovered fumbles by Drew Bledsoe and Tom Brady and Steve Smith's kickoff return fumble
Caught a 23 yard TD pass from Tom Brady in their 20-13 win over the Dolphins on 12-22-01
Longest was a 36 yard return of a kickoff by John Hall in their 20-17 loss to the Redskins on 09-28-03
Longest reception was a 39 yard pass from Tom Brady in their 28-20 loss to the Broncos on 10-16-05
Longest run was 31 yards in their 24-17 victory over the Saints on 11-20-05
78 Regular Season Games/11 started and 10 Playoff Games
15 kickoff returns for 336 yards in the playoffs
Member of the 2001, 2003 and 2004 World Championship Teams
#239 pick in the 2000 NFL Draft
Georgia Bulldog

PATRICK, Charles "Mike" (#2)
Born on September 6, 1952 in Austin, TX
6'0" and 209 pounds
Punter   1975-78
222 punts for 8,481 yards
Longest punt was 64 yards in their 30-24 loss to the Baltimore Colts on 12-18-77
Holder for John Smith
43 Regular Season Games and 1 Playoff Game (on 12-18-76)
Mississippi State Bulldog

PATTEN, David (#86) *"Chief"*
Born on August 19, 1974 in Columbia, SC
5'10" and 190 pounds
WR (KR)   2001-04
165 receptions for 2,513 yards + 16 TDs, 9 carries for 82 yards + 1 TD and 3 kickoff returns for 60 yards
Caught 16 Regular Season TDs from Tom Brady and 1 Post Season TD from Drew Bledsoe and Tom Brady
Hauled in a career long 91 yard TD pass from Tom Brady in their 38-17 win vs Indy on 10-21-01
Longest run was a 29 yard TD in their 38-17 rout of the Indianapolis Colts on 10-21-01
Completed a 60 yard TD pass to Troy Brown in their 38-17 rout of the Colts on 10-21-01
AFC Offensive Player of the Week in their 38-17 rout of the Colts on 10-21-01
Longest was a 24 yard return of a kickoff by Toby Gowin in their 34-17 win over the Saints on 11-25-01
Caught a 20 yard TD pass from Tom Brady, with 21 seconds left, in their 33-30 win over the Bears on 11-10-02
54 Regular Season Games/44 started and 6 Playoff Games/3 started
15 receptions for 174 yards + 2 TDs and 1 carry for 22 yards in the playoffs
Caught an 11 yard TD pass from Drew Bledsoe in their 24-17 Championship win over the Steelers on 01-27-02
Caught an 8 yard TD pass from Tom Brady in their 20-17 Super Bowl win over the St. Louis Rams on 02-03-02
Ran for a 22 yard gain in their 20-17 Super Bowl win over the St. Louis Rams on 02-03-02
Member of the 2001, 2003 and 2004 World Championship Teams
Western Carolina Catamount

PATTERSON, Cordarrelle (#84)

Born on March 17, 1991 in Rock Hill, SC

6'2" and 220 pounds

WR/KR/RB　　　　　　　2018

21 receptions for 247 yards and 3 TDs and 42 carries for 228 yards and 1 TD

23 kickoff returns for 663 yards and 1 TD

Caught 3 TD passes from Tom Brady

Longest reception was a 55 yard TD pass from Tom Brady in their 38-7 rout of Miami on 09-30-18

Longest was a 95 yard TD return of a kickoff by Cody Parkey in their 38-31 win over the Bears on 10-21-18

Ran for a 5 yard TD in their 31-17 win over the Green Bay Packers on 11-04-18

Had a career long run of 27 yards in their 24-12 win over the Buffalo Bills on 12-23-18

15 Regular Season Games/5 started and 3 Playoff Games

Member of the 2018 World Championship Team

Tennessee Volunteer

PATTON, Jerry (#72)

Born on March 27, 1946 in Saginaw, MI

6'3" and 261 pounds

Defensive Tackle　　　　　1975

Blocked an extra point attempt by John Leypoldt in their 34-14 loss to Buffalo on 12-14-75

3 games

Nebraska Cornhusker

PAULK, Jeff (#46)

Born on April 26, 1976 in Phoenix, AZ

6'0" and 240 pounds

Fullback　　　　　　　2000

Only game played was on 12-24-00

Arizona State Sun Devil

PAXTON III, Leonidas "Lonie" (#66) *"The Snow Angel"*

Born on March 13, 1978 in Orange, CA

6'2" and 270 pounds

Long Snapper　　　　　2000-08

Downed Adam Vinatieri's 33 yard punt on the 1 yard line in their 27-16 win over the Browns on 12-09-01

Deliberately snapped the ball out of the end zone for a safety in their 30-26 win over Denver on 11-03-03

Recovered Shaun McDonald's fumbled punt return in their 40-22 win over the St. Louis Rams on 11-07-04

141 Regular Season Games and 14 Playoff Games

Long Snapper for Adam Vinatieri's 45 yd game tying FG in their 16-13 OT Divisional win vs Oakland
　　　on 01-19-02

Snapper for Adam Vinatieri's 23 yard OT GW FG in their 16-13 Divisional win over the Raiders on 01-19-02

Long Snapper for Adam Vinatieri's 48 yard Super Bowl GW FG in their 20-17 win over St. Louis on 02-03-02

Member of the 2001, 2003 and 2004 World Championship Teams

Sacramento State Hornet

PENNYWELL, Carlos (#88) *"Chilly"*
Born on March 18, 1956 in Crowley, LA
6'2" and 180 pounds
Wide Receiver   1978-81
12 receptions for 143 yards + 3 TDs, 1 carry for 3 yards and recovered an onside kick
Caught 1 TD pass from Matt Cavanaugh and 2 TD passes from Steve Grogan
Longest reception was a 28 yard pass from Steve Grogan in their 34-27 loss to Baltimore on 09-18-78
Recovered an onside kick by Don Cockroft in their 34-17 win over the Cleveland Browns on 09-07-80
Ran for a 3 yard gain in their 13-3 loss to the Philadelphia Eagles on 09-13-81
38 games/2 started
#77 pick in the 1977 NFL Draft
Grambling State Tiger

PEOPLES, George (#35)
Born on August 25, 1960 in Tampa, FL
6'0" and 211 pounds
Special Team   1983
Recovered Ricky Smith's fumbled kickoff return in their 12-7 loss to the Colts on 10-09-83
16 games
Auburn Tiger

PERKINS, Willis
Born on February 14, 1934 in Columbus, TX
6'0" and 260 pounds
Guard   1961
Only game played was on 09-23-61
Texas Southern Tiger

PERRYMAN, Robert (#34)
Born on October 16, 1964 in Raleigh, NC
6'1" and 233 pounds
RB (KR)   1987-90
369 carries for 1,294 yards + 9 TDs and 64 receptions for 430 yards
3 kickoff returns for 43 yards and 2 fumble recoveries
Recovered fumbles by Steve Grogan and John Stephens
Longest was a 16 yard return of a kickoff by Chris Bahr in their 26-23 win over the LA Raiders on 11-01-87
Longest run was 48 yards in their 24-0 shutout of the Indianapolis Colts on 11-22-87
Longest reception was an 18 yard pass from Doug Flutie in their 14-13 win over the NY Jets on 11-13-88
49 games/38 started
#79 pick in the 1987 NFL Draft
Michigan Wolverine

PETERSON, Joe (#45)
Born on August 15, 1964 in San Francisco, CA
5'10" and 185 pounds
Defensive Back   1987
1 interception and 1 fumble recovery
Picked off a pass by Willie Totten in their 14-7 victory over the Buffalo Bills on 10-11-87
Recovered a fumble by Oliver Williams in their 21-7 victory over the Houston Oilers on 10-18-87
3 games/3 started
Nevada Reno Wolf Pack

PETRUS, Jonathan "Mitch" (#67)
Born on May 11, 1987 in Carlisle, AR
6'3" and 311 pounds
Offensive Line　　　　　2012
2 games (on Nov. 18th and Nov. 22nd)
Arkansas Razorback

PHELPS, Leroy (#46)
Born in 1935 in San Bernardino, CA
5'11" and 176 pounds
Defensive Back　　　　　1960
2 games (on Oct. 23rd and Oct. 28th)
Oregon Duck

PHIFER, Roman (#95)
Born on March 5, 1968 in Plattsburgh, NY
6'2" and 248 pounds
Linebacker　　　　　　2001-04
4 sacks, 2 interceptions for 40 yards and 4 fumble recoveries
Shared in a sack of Steve McNair and A.J. Feely and sacked Rob Johnson, Tim Couch and Drew Bledsoe
Intercepted Peyton Manning and Marc Bulger
Recovered fumbles by Jon Kitna, Lamar Smith, Kordell Stewart and J.P. Losman
Had 14 yard return of a pass by Peyton Manning, tipped by T. Buckley, in 44-13 rout of the Colts on 09-30-01
Had a 26 yard return of a pass by Marc Bulger in their 40-22 rout of the Rams on 11-07-04
59 Regular Season Games/46 started and 9 Playoff Games/7 started
Shared in a sack of Peyton Manning in their 24-14 AFC Championship win over the Colts on 01-18-04
Member of the 2001, 2003 and 2004 World Championship Teams
UCLA Bruin

PHILLIPS JR, Jess (#35) *"Banacek"*
Born on February 28, 1947 in Beaumont, TX
6'1" and 210 pounds
RB/KR　　　　　　　1976-77
29 carries for 191 yards + 2 TDs, 1 reception of 18 yards, 1 fumble recovery and 20 kickoff returns for 490 yards
Caught an 18 yard pass from Steve Grogan in their 48-17 rout of the Oakland Raiders on 10-03-76
Longest run was 46 yards in their 41-7 rout of the New York Jets on 10-18-76
Longest was a 71 yard return of a kickoff by George Jakowenko in their 26-22 win over Buffalo on 10-24-76
Ran for an 11 yard Game Winning TD to beat the Chiefs 21-17 on 09-18-77
Recovered Eddie Payton's fumbled punt return in their 30-27 OT loss to the Browns on 09-26-77
27 Regular Season Games and 1 Playoff Game
Ran for a 3 yard TD in their 24-21 Divisional Playoff Game loss to the Oakland Raiders on 12-18-76
Michigan State Spartan

PHILPOTT, Ed (#52) *"Big Red"*
Born on September 14, 1945 in Wichita, KS
6'3" and 240 pounds
Linebacker   1967-71
9 interceptions for 91 yards, 7 sacks, 11 fumble recoveries for 35 yards + 1 TD and blocked an extra
    point attempt
Intercepted Babe Parilli, Jim LeClair, Daryle Lamonica, Rick Norton and Mike Livingston
Had 2 interceptions of Len Dawson and Jack Kemp
Had a career long 23 yard return of a pass by Mike Livingston in their 23-10 loss to the Chiefs on 10-11-70
Shared in a sack of Rick Norton and Al Woodall and sacked Bob Griese, Daryle Lamonica and George Mira
Recorded 3 sacks of Jim LeClair
Recovered fumbles by Clem Daniels, Mark Smolinski, Brad Hubbert, Earl Morrall and Daryle Lamonica
Recovered a fumble by Dave Osborn and returned fumbles by Daryle Lamonica, Matt Snell and Robert Holmes
Blocked an extra point attempt by Jim Turner in their 29-24 loss to the NY Jets on 11-19-67
Returned a backward lateral by Babe Parilli 10 yards for a TD in their 47-31 loss to the Jets on 09-22-68
Sacked Jim LeClair *3 times* in their 20-17 victory over the Denver Broncos on 09-29-68
Had a career long 17 yard return of a fumble by Matt Snell in their 31-21 loss to the Jets on 09-27-70
68 games/57 started
#101 pick in the 1967 NFL Draft
Miami Redskin

PICKERING, Clayton "Clay" (#48)
Born on June 2, 1961 in Jacksonville, FL
6'5" and 215 pounds
Wide Receiver   1987
Caught a 10 yard pass from Doug Flutie in their 21-7 win over the Houston Oilers on 10-18-87
Only game played was on 10-18-87
Maine Black Bear

PITTS, Mike (#93)
Born on September 26, 1960 in Pell City, AL
6'5" and 277 pounds
Defensive Lineman   1993-94
4 sacks and 2 fumble recoveries
Sacked Jeff George, Neil O'Donnell, Scott Mitchell and David Klinger
Recovered fumbles by Jim Kelly and David Klinger
32 Regular Season Games/31 started and 1 Playoff Game/1 started
Sacked Vinny Testaverde and recovered Eric Metcalf's fumble in their 20-13 Wild Card loss on 01-01-95
Blocked Matt Stover's 50 yard FGA in their 20-13 Wild Card Playoff loss to the Browns on 01-01-95
Alabama Crimson Tide

PLEASANT, Anthony (#98)
Born on January 27, 1968 in Century, FL
6'5" and 280 pounds
Defensive End   2001-03
10 sacks, 2 interceptions and 1 fumble return of 6 yards that he lateraled to Willie McGinest
Sahred in a sack of Trent Green and sacked Peyton Manning and Alex Van Pelt
Sacked Steve McNair 1 ½ times and had 2 sacks of Vinny Testaverde, Chris Chandler and Jay Fiedler
Intercepted a pass thrown by Aaron Brooks and Tim Couch
Returned Donovan McNabb's fumble 6 yds + lateraled to Willie McGinest in their 31-10 win vs Philly
          on 09-14-03
37 Regular Season Games/27 started and 3 Playoff Games/3 started
Sacked Kordell Stewart in their 24-17 AFC Championship win over the Steelers at Heinz Field on 01-27-02
Member of the 2001 and 2003 World Championship Teams
Tennessee State Tiger

PLUNKETT, Arthur "Art" (#70)
Born on September 13, 1987 in Chicago, IL
6'7" and 269 pounds
Tackle   1985-87
22 Regular Season Games/1 started (on 09-13-87) and 4 Playoff Games
Nevada Runnin' Rebel

PLUNKETT JR., James "Jim" (#16) *"Plunk"*
Born on December 5, 1947 in San Jose, CA
6'3" and 220 pounds
Quarterback   1971-75
729 completions for 9,932 yards + 62 TDs, 159 carries for 817 yards + 9 TDs and 2 fumble recoveries
Threw 1 TD pass to Tight End's Russ Francis, John Tanner and Roland Moss
Threw 1 TD pass to Running Back's Carl Garrett and Josh Ashton
Tossed 1 TD pass to WR's Eric Crabtree, Steve Schubert, Hubie Bryant, Tom Reynolds and Al Marshall
Completed 3 TD passes to Tom Beer, Sam Cunningham and Ron Sellers
Threw 5 TD passes for Darryl Stingley and 6 TDs to Bob Windsor and Mack Herron
Tossed 10 TD passes to Reggie Rucker and 16 TD passes to Randy Vataha
Recovered fumbles by Bob Gladieux and John Tarver
Threw a career long 88 yard TD pass to Randy Vataha in the 4th Qtr of their 21-17 win vs the Colts on 12-19-71
Ran 5 yards for the Game Winning TD in their 13-10 win over the Chicago Bears on 10-21-73
Lofted a 34 yard TD pass to Sam Cunningham, on their 1st play, in their 30-14 loss to Miami on 10-28-73
Fired a 10 yard TD pass to Bob Windsor on the final play in their 17-14 win over the Vikings on 10-27-74
Longest run was 37 yards in their 41-26 loss to the Oakland Raiders on 12-01-74
NFL Offensive Player of the Week in their 21-17 win over Baltimore on 12-19-71
NFL Offensive Player of the Week in their 33-24 win over Green Bay on 11-18-73
AFC Rookie of the Year in 1971
61 games/61 started
1st Overall Pick in the 1971 NFL Draft
Stanford Cardinal

POLITE, Lousaka (#36)
Born on September 14, 1981 in North Braddock, PA
6'0" and 245 pounds
Fullback   2011
1 Regular Season Game (on 01-01-12) and 3 Playoff Games
Pittsburgh Panther

POOL, David (#27)
Born on December 20, 1966 in Cincinnati, OH
5'9" and 188 pounds
Defensive Back   1991-92
2 interceptions for 54 yards + 1 TD and 1 fumble recovery
Recovered Steve Jordan's fumble in their 26-23 OT win vs the Vikings on 10-20-91
Had a 41 yard TD return of a pass by Jeff George in their 37-34 OT win vs the Colts on 11-15-92
Had a 13 yard return of a pass by Browning Nagle in their 24-3 rout of the Jets on 11-22-92
31 games/17 started
Carson-Newman Eagle

POOLE, Tyrone (#38)
Born on February 3, 1972 in La Grange, GA
5'8" and 188 pounds
CB/PR   2003-05
7 interceptions for 102 yards and 13 punt returns for 81 yards
Intercepted Kerry Collins, Jay Fiedler, Quincy Carter, Peyton Manning and Drew Bledsoe
Had 2 interceptions of Byron Leftwich
Intercepted Jay Fiedler in OT, which set up the game winning TD, in their 19-13 OT win vs Miami on 10-19-03
Longest was an 18 yard return of a punt by Chad Stanley in their 23-20 OT win vs Houston on 11-23-03
Had a career long 44 yard return of a pass by Byron Leftwich in their 27-13 win over the Jaguars on 12-14-03
22 Regular Season Games/21 started and 3 Playoff Games/3 started
Recovered Marvin Harrison's fumble in their 24-14 AFC Championship win over the Colts on 01-18-04
Member of the 2003 and 2004 World Championship Teams
Fort Valley State Wildcat

POPE, Kenith "Ken" (#41)
Born on December 28, 1951 in Galveston, TX
5'11" and 200 pounds
Defensive Back   1974
4 games
Oklahoma Sooner

PORELL, Tom (#65)
Born on September 23, 1964 in Cambridge, MA
6'3" and 275 pounds
Nose Tackle   1987
Started in his only game played on 10-04-87
Boston College Eagle

PORTER, Willie (#27)
Born on March 25, 1946 in Victoria, TX
5'11" and 190 pounds
KR/PR   1968
36 kickoff returns for 812 yards and 22 punt returns for 135 yards
2 fumble recoveries for 2 yards and had a 17 yard return of a free kick
Recovered fumbles by Richard Trapp, Floyd Little, Butch Atkinson, Max Anderson and Billy Johnson
Returned 8 kickoffs (Patriots Team Record) in their 47-31 loss to the NY Jets on 09-22-68
Fell on Floyd Little's fumbled punt return, on the 1 foot line, in their 20-17 win vs Denver on 09-29-68
Advanced Billy Johnson's fumbled punt return 2 yards in their 31-17 loss to the Chiefs on 11-17-68
Longest was a 61 yard return of a kickoff by Ray Jacobs in their 34-10 loss to Miami on 11-24-68
Longest was a 24 yard return of a punt by Larry Seiple in their 34-10 loss to Miami on 11-24-68
Had a 17 yard return of a free kick by Rex Keeling in their 33-14 win over the Bengals on 12-01-68
13 games
Texas Southern Tiger

POSEY, David (#9)
Born on April 1, 1956 in Painesville, OH
5'11" and 167 pounds
Kicker   1978
Kicked 11 field goals and 29 extra points
Had a career long 47 yard field goal in their 19-17 victory over the New York Jets on 11-19-78
Kicked a 21 yard field goal to defeat Buffalo 26-24, and win the AFC Divisional Title, on 12-10-78
11 Regular Season Games and 1 Playoff Game
Kicked 2 extra points in their 31-14 Divisional Playoff Game loss to the Houston Oilers on 12-31-78
Florida Gator

POTEAT II, Henry "Hank" (#31 and #32)
Born on August 30, 1977 in Philadelphia, PA
5'10" and 195 pounds
Defensive Back   2004-06
Wore #31 in 3 Playoff Games in 2004 and #32 from 2005-06
Sacked Brooks Bollinger in their 31-21 win over the New York Jets on 12-26-05
12 Regular Season Games/2 started and 5 Playoff Games
Member of the 2004 World Championship Team
Pittsburgh Panther

PRESIDENT, Andre (#88)
Born on June 16, 1971 in Temple, TX
6'3" and 255 pounds
Tight End   1995
Only game played was on 09-03-95
Angelo State Ram

PRESTRIDGE, Luke (#17)
Born on September 17, 1956 in Houston, TX
6'4" and 235 pounds
Punter   1984
44 punts for 1,884 yards
Longest punt was 89 yards in their 44-24 loss to Miami on 10-21-84
9 games
Baylor Bear

PRICE, Kenny (#54)
Born on April 7, 1950 in Houston, TX
6'2" and 225 pounds
Linebacker   1971
Only game played was on 12-19-71
Iowa Hawkeye

PRICE, Taylor (#17)
Born on October 8, 1987 in Hilliard, OH
6'0" and 204 pounds
Wide Receiver   2010-11
3 receptions for 41 yards
Longest reception was an 18 yard pass from Brian Hoyer in their 38-7 rout of the Dolphins on 01-02-11
4 games
#90 pick in the 2010 NFL Draft
Ohio University Bobcat

PROFIT, Eugene "Gene" (#22)
Born on November 11, 1964 in Baton Rouge, LA
5'10" and 168 pounds
Special Team/DB   1986-88
2 blocked punts
Blocked a punt by Brian Hansen in their 21-20 win over the Saints on 11-30-86
Blocked a punt by John Teltschik in their 34-31 Overtime loss to the Eagles on 11-29-87
12 Regular Season Games and 1 Playoff Game (on 01-04-87)
Yale Bulldog

PRUETT, Perry (#39)
Born on March 7, 1949 in Dallas, TX
6'0" and 185 pounds
Defensive Back   1971
11 games/1 started (on 09-26-71)
North Texas Mean Green Eagle

PRYOR, Myron (#91)
Born on June 13, 1986 in Louisville, KY
6'1" and 310 pounds
Defensive Lineman   2009-11
Shared in a sack of Carson Palmer and Chad Henne
24 Regular Season Games/2 started and 1 Playoff Game (on 01-10-10)
Kentucky Wildcat

PUETZ, Garry (#77)
Born on March 14, 1952 in Elmhurst, IL
6'3" and 263 pounds
Offensive Lineman   1979-81
36 games/5 started
Valparaiso Crusader

PURNELL, Lovett (#48 and #85)
Born on April 7, 1972 in Seaford, DE
6'3" and 245 pounds
Tight End   1996-98
Wore #48 on 09-01-96 and on 12-21-96 and #85 from 1997-98
17 receptions for 149 yards + 5 TDs and 1 fumble recovery
Caught 2 TD passes from Scott Zolak and 3 TD passes from Drew Bledsoe
Recovered Curtis Martin's fumble in their 31-10 victory over the Buffalo Bills on 11-09-97
Longest reception was a 22 yard pass from Drew Bledsoe in their 29-6 win over the Colts on 09-13-98
34 Regular Season Games/7 started and 3 Playoff Games
#216 pick in the 1996 NFL Draft
West Virginia Mountaineer

PURVIS, James "Vic" (#31)
Born on November 17, 1943 in Brandon, MS
5'11" and 190 pounds
KR/PR/DB   1966-67
8 kickoff returns for 185 yards and 5 punt returns for 43 yards
Longest was a 34 yard return of Fletcher Smith's opening kickoff in their 43-24 loss to KS on 09-25-66
Longest was an 18 yard return of a punt by Jerrel Wilson in their 43-24 loss to the Chiefs on 09-25-66
16 games
Southern Mississippi Golden Eagle

PYNE III, George (#75)
Born on July 12, 1941 in Milford, MA
6'4" and 285 pounds
Defensive Tackle   1965
2 sacks, blocked a field goal attempt and had 1 kickoff return for no gain
Sacked Jack Kemp and George Blanda
Blocked a 30 yard field goal attempt by Pete Gogolak in their 24-7 loss to the Buffalo Bills on 09-11-65
Recovered Jim Fraser's squibbed kickoff in their 27-17 loss to the Kansas City Chiefs on 10-03-65
14 games
16th Round Draft Pick in 1965
Olivet Comet

RADEMACHER, William "Bill" (#33)
Born on May 13, 1942 in Menomonie, MI
6'1" and 190 pounds
Wide Receiver   1969-70
21 receptions for 268 yards + 3 TDs and 1 fumble recovery
Caught 3 TD passes from Mike Taliaferro
Caught a career long 22 yard TD pass from Mike Taliaferro in their 23-17 loss to the Jets on 10-26-69
Recovered Jim Nance's fumble in their 16-0 loss to the New York Giants on 10-18-70
27 games/5 started
Northern Michigan Wildcat

RAKOCZY, Gregg (#71)
Born on May 18, 1965 in Camden, NJ
6'6" and 290 pounds
Guard (LS/KR)   1991-92
1 kickoff return of 9 yards
Long Snapper for Shawn McCarthy and Charlie Baumann
Returned Fuad Reveiz's kickoff 9 yards in their 23-20 OT win against the Vikings on 10-20-91
Long Snapper for Charlie Baumann in their 16-7 loss to the Buffalo Bills on 11-01-92
21 games/4 started
Miami Hurricane

RAMSEY, Derrick (#88)
Born on December 23, 1956 in Hastings, FL
6'4" and 230 pounds
Tight End   1983-85
118 receptions for 1,412 yards + 14 TDs
Caught 6 TD passes from Steve Grogan and 8 Regular Season and 1 Post Season TD pass from Tony Eason
Longest reception was a 39 yard pass from Steve Grogan in their 12-7 loss to the Colts on 10-09-83
46 Regular Season Games/23 started and 4 Playoff Games
Caught a 1 yard TD pass from Tony Eason in their 31-14 Championship Game win over Miami on 01-12-86
Kentucky Wildcat

RAMSEY, Thomas "Tom" (#12)
Born on July 9, 1961 in Encino, CA
6'1" and 189 pounds
Quarterback   1986-88
84 completions for 1,005 yards + 6 TDs and 17 carries for 77 yards + 1 TD
Threw 1 TD pass to Irving Fryar and Willie Scott and 2 TD passes to Stanley Morgan and Tony Collins
Longest completion was a 40 yard pass to Irving Fryar in their 34-31 OT loss to the Eagles on 11-29-87
Ran for a 1 yard touchdown in their 34-31 Overtime loss to the Eagles on 11-29-87
Longest run was 19 yards in their 31-20 loss to the Denver Broncos on 12-06-87
21 games/4 started
#267 pick in the 1983 NFL Draft
UCLA Bruin

RATKOWSKI, Raymond "Ray" (#23)
Born on November 10, 1939 in New York, NY
6'0" and 195 pounds
Kickoff Returnman   1961
Returned Bert Rechichar's opening kickoff 17 yards in their 21-20 loss to the NY Titans on 09-09-61
Only game played was on 09-09-61
17th Round Draft Pick in 1961
Notre Dame Fighting Irish

RAY JR., Edward "Eddie" (#36)
Born on April 5, 1947 in Vicksburg, MS
6'2" and 240 pounds
RB/TE   1970
5 carries for 13 yards
Longest run was 4 yards in their 23-10 loss to the Kansas City Chiefs on 10-11-70
5 games/1 started (on 10-11-70)
#83 pick in the 1970 NFL Draft
LSU Fighting Tiger

RAY, Terry (#23)
Born on October 12, 1969 in Shape, Belgium
6'1" and 205 pounds
Safety   1993-96
Intercepted a pass thrown by David Klinger, Don Majkowski, Jeff George and Dan Marino
Recovered fumbles by Bert Emanuel and Thurman Thomas
Had a 43 yard return of a pass by Dan Marino in their 24-10 loss to the Miami Dolphins on 09-01-96
Sacked Vinny Testaverde in their 46-38 victory over the Baltimore Ravens on 10-06-96
63 Regular Season Games/24 started and 4 Playoff Games
Oklahoma Sooner

REDD, Vince (#49)
Born on September 1, 1985 in Elizabethton, TN
6'6" and 260 pounds
Linebacker   2008
5 games
Liberty Flame

REDDING, Reggie (#70)
Born on September 22, 1968 in Cincinnati, OH
6'3" and 298 pounds
Guard/Tackle   1992
Recovered Jon Vaughn's fumble in their 34-0 loss to the Atlanta Falcons on 11-29-92
14 games
California State Titan

REDMOND, Joseph "J.R." (#21)
Born on September 28, 1977 in Los Angeles, CA
5'11" and 215 pounds
RB (KR)   2000-02
164 carries for 527 yards + 1 TD, 35 receptions for 263 yards + 2 TDs and 4 kickoff returns for 94 yards
Caught a 12 yard TD from Drew Bledsoe in their 28-19 victory over the Broncos on 10-01-00
Longest reception was a 20 yard pass from Drew Bledsoe in their 24-16 win over the Colts on 10-08-00
Hauled in a 19 yard TD pass from Drew Bledsoe in their 30-23 loss to the Colts on 10-22-00
Ran for a 1 yard touchdown in their 16-13 OT loss to the Buffalo Bills on 11-05-00
Longest run was 20 yards in their 19-11 loss to the Cleveland Browns on 11-12-00
Longest was a 30 yard return of a kickoff by Neil Rackers in their 23-17 loss to the Bengals on 09-09-01
33 Regular Season Games/5 started and 3 Playoff Games
7 carries for 6 yards and 9 receptions for 69 yards in the playoffs
Member of the 2001 World Championship Team
#76 pick in the 1999 NFL Draft
Arizona State Sun Devil

REED, Henry "Ben" (#71)
Born on May 7, 1963 in Baton Rouge, LA
6'5" and 265 pounds
Defensive End   1987
3 games/3 started
Mississippi Rebel

REEDY, Bernard (#17)
Born on December 31, 1991 in St. Petersburg, FL
5'9" and 175 pounds
Punt Returner   2017
4 punt returns for 32 yards
Longest was a 13 yard return of a punt by Matt Haack in their 27-20 loss to Miami on 12-11-17
2 games (on 12-03-17 and 12-11-17)
Toledo Rocket

REHBERG, Scott (#60)
Born on November 17, 1973 in Kalamazoo, MI
6'8" and 325 pounds
Tackle   1997-98
8 games
#230 pick in the 1997 NFL Draft
Central Michigan Chippewa

REHDER II, Thomas "Tom" (#76)
Born on January 27, 1965 in Sacramento, CA
6'7" and 280 pounds
Tackle (KR)   1988-89
Had a 14 yard return of a kickoff by Dean Biasucci in their 22-16 win over the Colts on 12-03-89
32 games
#69 pick in the 1988 NFL Draft
Notre Dame Fighting Irish

REID, Dexter (#42)
Born on March 18, 1981 in Norfolk, VA
5'11" and 203 pounds
Safety   2004
Recovered Jay Fiedler's fumble in their 24-10 win over the Dolphins on 10-10-04
13 Regular Season Games/2 started and 3 Playoff Games
Member of the 2004 World Championship Team
#113 pick in the 2004 NFL Draft
North Carolina Tar Heel

REILLY, Kevin (#55)
Born on April 10, 1951 in Wilmington, DE
6'2" and 220 pounds
Linebacker   1975
Had a 54 yard return of a pass by Joe Ferguson in their 34-14 loss to the Buffalo Bills on 12-14-75
4 games/1 started (on 12-15-75)
Villanova Wildcat

REILLY, Trevor (#51)
Born on January 17, 1988 in Valley Center, CA
6'5" and 240 pounds
Linebacker   2017
6 games/1 started (on 11-12-17)
Utah Ute

REMBERT, John "Johnny" (#52) *"Rambo"*
Born on January 19, 1961 in Hollandale, MS
6'3" and 234 pounds
Linebacker (KR)   1983-92
7 interceptions for 70 yards, 11 fumble recoveries for 40 yards + 2 TDs and 3 kickoff returns for 27 yards
Intercepted Jim Kelly, Randall Cunningham + Cody Carlson and 2 int's of Boomer Esiason and Dan Marino
Sacked Joe Montana, Steve Bartkowski, Bubby Brister, Jack Trudeau, Danny White and Ken O'Brien
Shared in sack of Chris Miller, 1 sack of Jeff George, 2 sacks of John Elway and Steve Young and 5 sacks
          of Jim Kelly
Recovered fumbles by James Brooks, Clarence Weathers, Oliver Williams, Mark Nichols and John Tice
Recovered fumbles by Gary Hogenboom, Lorenzo Hampton, Roger Vick, Al Toon and Vinny Testaverde
Fell on a fumble by Clarence Weathers for a TD in their 24-20 loss to the Browns on 10-06-85
Fell on Gary Hogeboom's fumble in the end zone, for a TD, in their 33-3 rout of the Colts on 09-07-86
Longest was a 14 yard return of a squibbed kickoff by Rich Karlis in their 27-20 loss to Denver on 09-28-86
Had a career long 37 yard return of a pass by Jim Kelly in their 23-3 win over Buffalo on 10-26-86
Had a career long 27 yard return of a fumble by Jim Kelly in their 33-24 win over the Buffalo Bills on 11-19-89
AFC Defensive Player of the Week in their 21-10 win over Miami on 11-06-88
AFC Pro Bowl Linebacker in 1988, 1989
126 Regular Season Games/72 started and 5 Playoff Games/5 started
Returned Johnny Hector's fumbled KR 15 yards for a TD in their 26-14 Wild Card win vs the Jets on 12-28-85
Intercepted a pass by John Elway in their 22-17 loss to the Denver Broncos on 01-04-87
#101 pick in the 1983 NFL Draft
Clemson Tiger

REVIS, Darrelle (#24) *"Revis Island"*
Born on July 14, 1985 in Aliquippa, PA
5'11" and 198 pounds
Cornerback   2014
2 inteceptions and 1 fumble recovery
Intercepted Matt Cassel and Jay Cutler and recovered a fumble by Lamar Miller
AFC Pro Bowl Cornerback in 2014
First Team All Pro Cornerback in 2014
16 Regular Season Games/16 started and 3 Playoff Games/3 started
Had a 30 yard return of a pass by Andrew Luck in their 45-7 Championship rout of the Colts on 01-18-15
Sacked Russell Wilson in their 28-24 Super Bowl win over the Seahawks on 02-01-15
Member of the 2014 World Championship Team
Pittsburgh Panther

REYNOLDS, Robert "Bob" (#74)
Born on January 22, 1939 in Nashville, TN
6'5" and 265 pounds
Tackle   1972-73
Recovered John Tarver's fumble in their 24-16 victory over the Baltimore Colts on 10-07-73
19 games/15 started
Bowling Green State Falcon

REYNOLDS, Edward "Ed" (#95)
Born on September 23, 1961 in Stuttgart, Germany
6'5" and 238 pounds
Linebacker   1983-91
4 sacks and 4 fumble recoveries
Sacked Dave Wilson and Jim Kelly and had 2 sacks of Jeff Rutledge
Recovered fumbles by Ricky Smith, Jeff Kemp, Rick Woods and Thurman Thomas
119 Regular Season Games/46 started and 5 Playoff Games
Virginia Cavalier

REYNOLDS, Derrick "Ricky" (#21)
Born January 19, 1965 in Sacramento, CA
5'11" and 190 pounds
Defensive Back   1994-96
6 interceptions for 24 yards + 1 TD, 4 ½ sacks and 4 fumble recoveries for 25 yards + 1 TD
Intercepted Vinny Testaverde, Dan Marino, Kerry Collins and Jim Kelly and had 2 int's of Boomer Esiason
Sacked Boomer Esiason, Stan Humphries, Jeff George and had 1 ½ sacks of Kerry Collins
Recovered fumbles by Carwell Gardner, Andre Reed, Larry Whigham and Bernie Parmalee
Had an 11 yard TD return of a pass by Boomer Esiason in their 24-13 win over the Jets on 12-04-94
Returned Carwell Gardner's fumble 25 yards for a TD in their 41-17 rout of Buffalo on 12-18-94
Recovered Larry Whigham's interception return fumble in their 41-17 rout of the Bills on 12-18-94
Had a 4 yard return of a pass by Kerry Collins in their 20-17 loss to the Carolina Panthers on 10-29-95
Advanced Myron Guyton's lateral 2 yards in their 24-10 loss to the Colts on 11-19-95
Had a 7 yard return of a pass by Jim Kelly in their 17-10 loss to the Buffalo Bills on 09-08-96
42 Regular Season Games/35 started and 1 Playoff Game/1 started (on 01-01-95)
Washington State Cougar

REYNOLDS JR., Raoul "Tom" (#21)
Born on April 11, 1949 in Pasadena, CA
6'3" and 200 pounds
Wide Receiver   1972
8 receptions for 152 yards + 2 TDs
Had a career long 36 yard TD reception of a pass from Jim Plunkett in their 37-21 loss to Miami on 12-03-72
Caught a 28 yard TD pass from Brian Dowling in their 45-21 loss to Denver on 12-17-72
Holder for Charlie Gogolak
12 games
#49 pick in the 1972 NFL Draft
San Diego State Aztec

RHEAMS, Leonta (#75)
Born on August 1, 1976 in Tyler, TX
6'2" and 303 pounds
Defensive Tackle   1998
6 games
#115 pick in the 1998 NFL Draft
Houston Cougar

RICE, Rodney (#43)
Born on June 18, 1966 in Albany, GA
5'8" and 180 pounds
DB/KR   1989
11 kickoff returns for 242 yards and 1 fumble recovery
Longest was a 46 yard return of a kickoff by Pat Leahy in their 27-24 win over the Jets on 09-10-89
Recovered a fumble by Ken Davis in their 31-10 loss to the Buffalo Bills on 10-01-89
10 games
#210 pick in the 1989 NFL Draft
BYU Cougar

RICHARDS, David (#62)
Born on April 11, 1966 in Staten Island, NY
6'5" and 315 pounds
Offensive Lineman   1996
5 games
UCLA Bruin

RICHARDS, Jordan (#37)
Born on January 21, 1993 in Sacramento, CA
5'11" and 210 pounds
Special Team/DB   2015-17
Recovered Tyler Ervin's fumbled kickoff return in their 27-0 shutout of Houston on 09-22-16
41 Regular Season Games/7 started and 5 Playoff Games
Member of the 2016 World Championship Team
Ron Burton Community Service Award in 2017
#64 pick in the 2015 NFL Draft
Stanford Cardinal

RICHARDSON, Al (#79)
Born on February 1, 1935 in New Orleans, LA
6'3" and 250 pounds
Defensive End   1960
3 games/2 started
Grambling State Tiger

RICHARDSON, Jesse (#75) *"Big Jess"*
Born on August 18, 1930 in Philadelphia, PA
6'2" and 261 pounds
Defensive Tackle   1962-64
Jesse was the last professional football player to play without a facemask
6.5 sacks
Sacked Dick Wood, Jack Kemp, Johnny Green, Tom Flores, Daryle Lamonica and had 1 ½ sacks of Jacky Lee
42 Regular Season Games/36 started and 2 Playoff Games
Alabama Crimson Tide

RICHARDSON, Mike (#35)
Born on February 18, 1984 in Sumter, SC
5'11" and 190 pounds
Defensive Back   2008
10 games
Notre Dame Fighting Irish

RICHARDSON, Tom (#49) *"The Glove"*
Born on October 15, 1944 in Greenville, MS
6'2" and 195 pounds
Wide Receiver   1969-70
1 reception of 5 yards and 1 fumble recovery
Caught a 5 yard pass from Mike Taliaferro in their 31-0 loss to the Kansas City Chiefs on 09-21-69
Recovered RC Gamble's fumble in their 24-0 shutout of the Houston Oilers on 11-02-69
15 games
Jackson State Tiger

RIDLEY, Stevan (#22)
Born on January 27, 1989 in Natchez, MS
5'11" and 220 pounds
Running Back   2011-14
649 carries for 2,817 yards + 22 TDs, 23 receptions for 146 yards and 7 kickoff returns for 152 yards
Longest was a 32 yard return of a kickoff by Nick Folk in their 30-21 win over the Jets on 10-09-11
Longest reception was a 24 yard pass from Tom Brady in their 30-23 win over the Falcons on 09-29-13
Longest run was 43 yards in their 43-17 victory over the Bengals on 10-05-14
52 Regular Season Games/25 started and 5 Playoff Games/1 started (on 01-20-13)
56 carries for 242 yards + 3 TDs in the playoffs
Ran for an 8 yard TD in their 41-28 Divisional Playoff win over the Houston Texans on 01-13-13
Ran for a 3 yard TD and a 1 yard TD in their 43-22 Divisional Playoff win over the Colts on 01-11-14
Ran for a 2 point conversion in their 43-22 Divisional Playoff win over the Colts on 01-11-14
2 receptions for 17 yards in the playoffs
Member of the 2014 World Championship Team
#73 pick in the 2011 NFL Draft
LSU Fighting Tiger

RIVERA, Mike (#59)
Born on January 10, 1986 in Shawnee, KS
6'3" and 255 pounds
Special Team/LB   2012
10 games
Kansas Jayhawk

RIVERS, Derek (#95)
Born on May 9, 1991 in Augusta, ME
6'5" and 250 pounds
Defensive End   2018-19
Sacked Sam Darnold in their 38-3 rout of the NY Jets on 12-30-18
6 Regular Season Games and 1 Playoff Game (on 01-13-18)
Member of the 2018 World Championship Team
Youngstown State University Penguin

RIVERS, Marcellus (#82)
Born on October 26, 1978 in Oklahoma City, OK
6'4" and 250 pounds
Tight End   2007
3 games
Oklahoma State Cowboy

ROBBINS, Randy (#48)
Born on September 14, 192 in Casa Grande, AZ
6'2" and 189 pounds
Defensive Back   1992
2 interceptions for 27 yards and 1 fumble recovery
Intercepted Jim Kelly and Bobby Hebert and recovered a fumble by Andre Reed
Recovered Andre Reed's fumble in their 41-7 loss to the Buffalo Bills on 09-27-92
Had a career long 20 yard return of a pass by Jim Kelly in their 16-7 loss to the Bills on 11-01-92
15 games/15 started
Arizona Wildcat

ROBERTS, Elandon (#52)
Born on April 22, 1994 in Port Arthur, TX
6'0" and 238 pounds
Linebacker/FB   2016-19
Used as a fullback in 8 games during the 2019 season
3 sacks, 1 fumble recovery and 1 reception for a 38 yard TD
Recovered Jonathan Stewart's fumble in their 33-30 loss to the Panthers on 10-01-17
Sacked Matt Moore *twice* in their 35-17 win over the Miami Dolphins on 11-26-17
Sacked Marcus Mariota in their 34-10 loss to the Tennessee Titans on 11-11-18
Caught a 38 yard TD pass from Tom Brady in their 27-24 loss to Miami on 12-29-19
60 Regular Season Games/33 started and 10 Playoff Games/7 started
Member of the 2016 and 2018 World Championship Teams
#214 pick in the 2016 NFL Draft
Houston Cougar

ROBERTS, Timothy "Tim" (#94)
Born on April 14, 1969 in Atlanta, GA
6'6" and 318 pounds
Defensive Tackle   1995
Sacked Jim Harbaugh in their 10-7 loss to the Indianapolis Colts on 12-23-95
13 games/12 started
Southern Mississippi Golden Eagle

ROBERTS, William (#76)
Born on August 5, 1962 in Miami, FL
6'5" and 291 pounds
Guard   1995-96
32 Regular Season Games/27 started and 3 Playoff Games/3 started
Ohio State Buckeye

ROBINSON, Melvin "Bo" (#41)
Born on May 27, 1956 in Lamesa, TX
6'2" and 228 pounds
RB/TE (KR)   1984
4 receptions for 32 yards + 1 TD, 3 kickoff returns for 38 yards and 1 fumble recovery
Caught a 4 yard TD pass from Tony Eason in their 28-21 win over the Jets on 09-30-84
Recovered Mosi Tatupu's fumble in their 20-14 victory over the Bengals on 10-14-84
Longest reception was a 17 yard pass from Tony Eason in their 44-24 loss to Miami on 10-21-84
Longest was 14 yard return of a kickoff by Uwe von Schamann in their 44-24 loss to Miami on 10-21-84
16 games/1 started (on 11-04-84)
West Texas State Buffalo

ROBINSON, Greg (#61 and #68)
Born on December 25, 1962 in Sacramento, CA
6'5" and 280 pounds
Tackle   1987
Wore #61 on 10-04-87 and #68 in the other 2 games
Fell on a fumble by Tony Collins, on the 1st play, in their 20-10 loss to the Browns on 10-04-87
3 games/3 started
#137 Pick in the 1987 NFL Draft
Sacramento State Hornet

ROBINSON JR., David "Junior" (#27)
Born on February 3, 1968 in High Point, NC
5'9" and 181 pounds
Kickoff Returnman   1990
11 kickoff returns for 211 yards
Longest was a 27 yard return of a kickoff by Scott Norwood in their 14-0 loss to Buffalo on 11-18-90
16 games
#110 pick in the 1990 NFL Draft
East Carolina Pirate

ROBINSON, Noble "Rex" (#7)
Born on March 17, 1959 in Marietta, GA
5'11" and 205 pounds
Kicker   1982
Kicked 1 field goal and 5 extra points
Kicked a 24 yard field goal in their 24-13 win over the Baltimore Colts on 09-12-82
3 games
Georgia Bulldog

ROBINSON-RANDALL, Greg (#77 and #64) *"Baby Face"*
Born on June 23, 1978 in Galveston, TX
6'5" and 322 pounds
Tackle   2000-02
Wore #77 in 2000 and #64 from 2001-02
Recovered Tom Brady's fumble in their 34-17 victory over the Saints on 11-25-01
35 Regular Season Games/23 started and 3 Playoff Games
Member of the 2001 World Championship Team
Michigan State Spartan

ROBOTTI, Frank (#51)
Born on April 6, 1939 in Stamford, CT
6'0" and 220 pounds
Linebacker   1961
1 sack and 2 interceptions for 18 yards
Sacked Tom Flores and intercepted Jacky Lee and Cotton Davidson
Had a career long 11 yard return of a pass by Jacky Lee in their 31-31 tie with the Houston Oilers on 10-13-61
Sacked Tom Flores in their 20-17 win over the Oakland Raiders on 11-17-61
12 games/7 started
Boston College Eagle

ROGERS, Doug (#65)
Born on June 23, 1960 in Chico, CA
6'5" and 266 pounds
Defensive End   1983-84
Shared in a sack of Joe Ferguson and sacked Dave Krieg and Pat Ryan
22 games
Stanford Cardinal

ROMANISZYN, Jim (#53)
Born on September 17, 1951 in Titusville, PA
6'2" and 224 pounds
LB/Special Team   1976
Recovered Jazz Jackson's fumbled punt return in their 41-7 rout of the NY Jets on 10-18-76
11 games/2 started
Edinboro Fighting Scot

ROMEO, Anthony "Tony" (#86) *"Reverend"*
Born on March 7, 1938 in St. Petersburg, FL
6'3" and 230 pounds
Tight End   1962-67
110 receptions for 1,724 yards + 10 TDs and caught a pass for 2 point conversion
Caught 10 TD passes from Babe Parilli
Longest reception was a 62 yard pass from Babe Parilli in their 41-16 win over the Broncos on 09-21-62
Had a 5 yard return of a kickoff by Keith Lincoln in their 33-28 win over the Chargers on 09-20-64
Caught a 2 yard 4th down game winning TD pass from Babe Parilli in their 27-23 win vs the Jets on 11-28-65
Caught a 2 point conversion pass from Babe Parilli in their 24-10 win over the Broncos on 09-18-66
75 Regular Season Games/52 started and 2 Playoff Games/2 started
Recovered a fumble by Babe Parilli in their 51-10 AFL Championship loss to the Chargers on 01-05-64
Had a 9 yard return of a kickoff by George Blair in their 51-10 AFL Championship loss to SD on 01-05-64
Florida State Seminole

ROMINE, Alton "Al" (#46)
Born on March 10, 1932 in Florence, AL
6'2" and 191 pounds
Defensive Back   1961
Only game played was on 09-09-61
Member of the 1955 and 1956 Ontario Rugby Football Union Kitchener-Waterloo Dutchmen
          Championship Teams
North Alabama Lion

ROWE, Dave (#76)
Born on June 20, 1945 in Neptune, NJ
6'7" and 280 pounds
DT/NT   1971-73
7 sacks and 1 fumble recovery
Sacked Terry Hanratty, Earl Morrall, Archie Manning, Len Dawson and Dan Pastorini
Shared in a sack of Al Woodhall and had 1 ½ sacks of Dennis Shaw
Recovered Jim Del Gaizo's fumble in their 52-0 loss to the Miami Dolphins on 11-12-72
42 games/33 started
Penn State Nittany Lion

ROWE JR., Nelson "Eric" (#25)
Born on October 3, 1992 in Cleveland, OH
6'1" and 205 pounds
Defensive Back   2016-18
Intercepted a pass by Ryan Fitzpatrick in their 41-3 rout of the NY Jets on 12-24-16
21 Regular Season Games/12 started and 6 Playoff Games/2 started
Member of the 2016 and 2018 World Championship Teams
Utah Ute

RUCCI, Todd (#71)
Born on July 14, 1970 in Upper Darby, PA
6'5" and 296 pounds
Guard   1993-2000
Downed a punt by Pat O'Neill, on the Jets 1 yard line, in their 24-13 win over the Jets on 12-04-94
85 Regular Season Games/75 started and 7 Playoff Games/7 started
#51 pick in the 1993 NFL Draft
Penn State Nittany Lion

RUCKER, Reginald "Reggie" (#33)
Born on September 21, 1947 in Washington, DC
6'2" and 195 pounds
WR/KR   1971-74
126 receptions for 1,884 yards + 10 TDs, 15 kickoff returns for 375 yards and 5 carries for 4 yards
Caught 10 TD passes from Jim Plunkett
Longest run was 5 yards in their 52-0 loss to the Miami Dolphins on 11-12-72
Longest was a 43 yard return of a kickoff by Garo Yepremian in their 44-23 loss to Miami on 09-30-73
Had a career long 69 yard TD reception in their 42-3 rout of the Colts on 10-06-74
43 games/38 started
Boston University Terrier

RUDOLPH, John "Jack" (#80)
Born on March 21, 1938 in St. Louis, MO
6'3" and 225 pounds
Linebacker   1960-65
16 sacks, 2 intereptions for 13 yards, 10 fumble recoveries, blocked a punt and 1 kickoff return for 4 yards
Shared in a sack of Eddie Wilson, Len Dawson and Jack Kemp
Sacked Al Dorow, Frank Tripucka, Cotton Davidson, John Hadl, Dick Wood, Tom Flores and Don Breaux
Sacked John McCormick and had 2 sacks of Dick Jamieson and had 4 ½ sacks of Jacky Lee (2 for a safety)
Intercepted Hunter Ennis and George Blanda
Recovered fumbles by Leon Burton, Don Norton, Howie Ferguson, Lionel Taylor, Dick Christy and Bob Suci
Recovered fumbles by Clem Daniels, Charley Frazier, Dainard Paulson and Abner Haynes
Had a career long 13 yard return of a pass by Hunter Ennis in their 34-0 loss to the Dallas Texans on 12-11-60
Blocked a punt by Curley Johnson in their 31-24 loss to the New York Jets on 10-05-63
Sacked Jacky Lee for a safety in their 46-28 victory over the Houston Oilers on 12-08-63
Sacked Jacky Lee for a safety in their 12-7 victory over the Denver Broncos on 11-20-64
Returned Gary Kroner's opening kickoff 4 yards in their 27-10 loss to the Broncos on 09-24-65
64 Regular Season Games/50 started and 2 Playoff Games/2 started
Sacked Tobin Rote in their 51-10 AFL Championship Game loss to the San Diego Chargers on 01-05-64
2nd Round Draft Pick in 1960
Georgia Tech Yellow Jacket

RUEGAMER, Christopher "Grey" (#67)
Born on June 11, 1976 in Las Vegas, NV
6'4" and 299 pounds
Center　　　　　　　　　2000-02
33 Regular Season Games/3 started and 3 Playoff Games
Member of the 2001 World Championship Team
Arizona State Sun Devil

RUSS, Bernard (#51)
Born on November 4, 1973 in Utica, NY
6'1" and 238 pounds
Special Team　　　　　　1997-99
9 games
West Virginia Mountaineer

RUSSELL, Leonard (#32)
Born on November 17, 1969 in Long Beach, CA
6'2" and 240 pounds
Running Back　　　　　　1991-93
689 carries for 2,437 yards + 13 TDs and 55 receptions for 350 yards
Longest run was 24 yards in their 20-0 loss to the Cleveland Browns on 09-08-91
Longest reception was a 38 yard pass from Drew Bledsoe in their 19-16 OT loss to the Lions on 09-12-93
Advanced Kevin Turner's lateral 69 yards in their 23-21 win over the Phoenix Cardinals on 10-10-93
Ran for a 4 yard Game Winning TD in their 20-17 win over the Browns on 12-19-93
Advanced Vincent Brisby's fumble 22 yards, in overtime, in their 33-27 OT win vs Miami on 01-02-94
43 games/40 started
NFL Offensive Rookie of the Year in 1991
#14 pick in the 1991 NFL Draft
Arizona State Sun Devil

RUTH, Mike (#65)
Born on June 25, 1964 in Norristown, PA
6'2" and 266 pounds
Nose Tackle　　　　　　1986-87
1 sack and 1 fumble recovery
Sacked Ken O'Brien in their 20-6 victory over the New York Jets on 09-11-86
Recovered Irving Fryar's fumbled punt return in their 31-24 loss to the Jets on 10-12-86
8 Regular Season Games and 1 Playoff Game (on 01-04-87)
#42 pick in the 1986 NFL Draft
Boston College Eagle

RUTLEDGE, Rodrick "Rod" (#83)
Born on August 12, 1975 in Birmingham, AL
6'5" and 262 pounds
Tight End　　　　　　1998-2001
27 receptions for 204 yards + 1 TD and 1 fumble recovery
Longest reception was a 16 yard pass from Drew Bledsoe in their 30-23 loss to the Colts on 10-22-00
Snared a 2 yard TD pass from Drew Bledsoe in their 19-11 loss to the Cleveland Browns on 11-12-00
Caught the 1st regular season pass completion of Tom Brady in their 34-9 loss to the Lions on 11-23-00
Recovered Kevin Faulk's fumble in their 13-10 Overtime win vs the Buffalo Bills on 12-17-00
63 Regular Season Games/31 started and 4 Playoff Games/3 started
Member of the 2001 World Championship Team
#54 pick in the 1998 NFL Draft
Alabama Crimson Tide

RYAN, Logan (#26)
Born on February 9, 1991 in Berlin, NJ
5'11" and 195 pounds
Defensive Back　　　　　2013-16
13 interceptions for 167 yards + 1 TD and 2 ½ sacks
Intercepted Geno Smith, Peyton Manning, Case Keenum, Matt Cassel and Matthew Stafford
Intercepted Tyrod Taylor, Brandon Weeden, Ryan Tannehill, Kirk Cousins and Trevor Siemian
Intercepted Matt Moore and had 2 interceptions of Joe Flacco
Sacked Jared Goff and had 1 ½ sacks of Ryan Tannehill
Had a career long 79 yard TD return of a pass by Geno Smith in their 30-27 loss to the Jets on 10-20-13
Strip sacked Ryan Tannehill in their 27-17 win over the Miami Dolphins on 10-27-13
64 Regular Season Games/40 started and 10 Playoff Games/5 started
Sacked Brock Osweiler in their 34-16 Divisional Playoff win over the Houston Texans on 01-14-17
Had a 23 yard return of a pass by Brock Osweiler in their 34-16 Divisional win over the Texans on 01-14-17
Member of the 2014 and 2016 World Championship Teams
Rutgers Scarlet Knight

SABB, Dwayne (#95)
Born on October 9, 1969 in Union City, NJ
6'4" and 248 pounds
Linebacker　　　　　　1992-96
6.5 sacks, 3 interceptions for 6 yards and recovered 2 squibbed kickoffs
Shared in a sack of Dan Marino, sacked Neil O'Donnell and Boomer Esiason
Recorded 2 sacks of Jim Kelly and David Klinger
Intercepted a pass by Dan Marino, Jeff Hostetler and Jim Harbaugh
Recovered Steve Christie's squibbed kickoff in their 13-10 OT loss to the Buffalo Bills on 11-07-93
Recovered Dean Biasucci's squibbed kickoff in their 38-0 shutout of the Colts on 12-26-93
Had a career long 5 yard return of a pass by Dan Marino in their 39-35 loss to Miami on 09-04-94
74 Regular Season Games/24 started and 4 Playoff Games
#116 pick in the 1992 NFL Draft
New Hampshire Wildcat

SACCO, Frank (#95)
Born on April 8, 1964 in Yonkers, NY
6'4" and 240 pounds
Linebacker　　　　　　1987
2 games (on Oct. 11th and Oct. 18th)
Fordham Ram

SAGAPOLUTELE, Pio (#75)
Born on November 28, 1969 in American Samoa
6'6" and 297 pounds
Defensive Lineman   1996
Sacked Jim Harbaugh, Stan Humphries and Glenn Foley
15 Regular Season Games/10 started and 3 Playoff Games
San Diego State Aztec

SALAS, GREG (#17)
Born on August 25, 1988 in Chino, CA
6'1" and 206 pounds
Wide Receiver   2012
Only game played was on 11-18-12
Hawaii Rainbow

SAM, Philip Kenwood "P.K." (#14)
Born on December 26, 1983 in Denver, CO
6'3" and 210 pounds
Wide Receiver   2004
2 games (on 10-03-04 and 10-10-04)
Member of the 2004 World Championship Team
#164 pick in the 2004 NFL Draft
Florida State Seminole

SAMUEL, Asante (#22)
Born on January 6, 1981 in Ft. Lauderdale, FL
5'10" and 185 pounds
Cornerback   2003-07
22 interceptions for 313 yards + 3 TDs
Intercepted Vinny Testaverde, Danny Kanell, Kelly Holcomb, Brooks Bollinger and Jon Kitna
Intercepted David Carr, Trent Edwards, Derek Anderson and Jason Campbell
Had 2 interceptions of J.P. Losman, Joey Harrington, Carson Palmer, Vince Young and A.J. Feeley
Recorded 3 interceptions of Rex Grossman (all of them were in their 17-13 win over the Bears on 11-26-06)
Had a 55 yard TD return of a pass by Vinny Testaverde in their 23-16 win over the NY Jets on 09-21-03
Had a 34 yard TD return of a pass by Carson Palmer in their 35-28 victory over the Bengals on 12-12-04
Had a 40 yard TD return of a pass by A.J. Feeley in their 31-28 win over the Eagles on 11-25-07
AFC Defensive Player of the Week in their 17-13 win over Chicago on 11-26-06
AFC Defensive Player of the Week in their 31-28 win over Philadelphia on 11-25-07
AFC Pro Bowl Cornerback in 2007 and First Team All Pro Cornerback in 2007
75 Regular Season Games/53 started and 14 Playoff Games/11 started
5 interceptions for 158 yards + 3 TDs in the playoffs
Had a 73 yard TD return of a pass by Byron Leftwich in their 28-3 Wild Card rout of the Jaguars on 01-07-06
Intercepted Jake Plummer in their 27-13 Divisional loss to the Denver Broncos on 01-14-06
Had a 36 yard TD return of a Chad Pennington pass in 37-16 Wild Card win vs the Jets on 01-07-07
Had a 39 yard TD return of a pass by Peyton Manning in their 38-34 Championship loss to the Colts
          on 01-21-07
Returned a pass by Philip Rivers 10 yards in their 21-12 Championship win over the Chargers on 01-20-08
Member of the 2003 and 2004 World Championship Teams
#120 Pick in the 2003 NFL Draft
Central Florida Golden Knight

SANDERS, James (#36)
Born on November 11, 1983 in Porterville, CA
5'10" and 207 pounds
Safety   2005-10
8 interceptions for 172 yards + 2 TDs, 1 sack and 4 funble recoveries
Intercepted J.P. Losman, David Carr, A.J. Feeley, Kyle Boller, Jay Cutler and Ben Roethlisberger
Intercepted Peyton Manning and Mark Sanchez and had 1 sack of Vince Young
Recovered fumbles by David Barrett, William Gay, Michael Turner and Richard Goodman
Had a 39 yard TD return of a pass by J.P. Losman, tipped by Tedy Bruschi, in their 35-7 rout of Buffalo
        on 12-11-05
Recovered Mike Nugent's kickoff that deflected off the leg of David Barrett in 31-21 win vs the Jets on 12-26-05
Had a 21 yard return of a pass by David Carr, tipped by Tedy Bruschi, in their 40-7 rout of the Texans on 12-17-06
Sacked Vince Young in their 40-23 win over the Tennessee Titans on 12-31-06
Forced Dwayne Wright to fumble and Ellis Hobbs returned it for a TD in their 56-10 rout of Buffalo on 11-18-07
Had a 1 yard return of a pass by A.J. Feeley, with 18 seconds left, in their 31-28 win over the Eagles on 11-25-07
Had a career long 42 yard return of a pass by Kyle Boller in their 27-24 win over the Ravens on 12-03-07
Had a 32 yard TD return of a pass by Ben Roethlisberger in their 39-26 win over the Steelers on 11-14-10
Intercepted Peyton Manning, on the 6 yard line, with 37 seconds left, in their 31-28 win vs Indy on 11-21-10
AFC Defensive Player of the Week in their 39-26 win over the Steelers on 11-14-10
84 Regular Season Games/50 started and 10 Playoff Games/7 started
Sacked Philip Rivers in their 24-21 Divisional Playoff win over the San Diego Chargers on 01-14-07
Recovered Ellis Hobbs' interception return fumble in their 21-12 Championship win vs San Diego on 01-20-08
#113 pick in the 2005 NFL Draft
Fresno State Bulldog

SANDERS, John (#25) *"Colonel"*
Born on January 11, 1950 in Chicago, IL
6'1" and 175 pounds
DB/Special Team   1974-76
6 interceptions for 75 yards + 1 TD and 5 fumble recoveries for 3 yards
Blocked 2 punts and blocked 2 extra point attempts
Intercepted Bert Jones, All Woodhall, Marty Domres, Bob Griese and had 2 interceptions of Earl Morrall
Recovered fumbles by Marv Hubbard, Don McCauley, Norm Bulaich, and 2 fumbles by OJ Simpson
Had a 23 yard TD return of a pass by Earl Morrall in their 34-27 loss to Miami on 12-15-74
Blocked a punt by Larry Seiple in their 22-14 loss to the Miami Dolphins on 09-28-75
Blocked an extra point attempt by Pat Leahy in their 36-7 loss to the New York Jets on 10-05-75
Blocked a punt by Tom Wittum in their 24-16 win over the San Francisco 49ers on 10-26-75
Blocked an extra point attempt by Steve Mike-Mayer in their 24-16 win over the 49ers on 10-26-75
Had a 3 yard reurn of a fumble by OJ Simpson in their 34-14 loss to the Buffalo Bills on 12-14-75
30 games/24 started
South Dakota Coyote

SANDERS, Lewis (#29)
Born on June 22, 1978 in Staten Island, NY
6'1" and 210 pounds
Defensive Back   2008
10 games/4 started
Maryland Terrapin

SANDHAM, Todd (#72)
Born on December 3, 1963 in Summit, NJ
6'3" and 255 pounds
Guard　　　　　　　1987
2 games (on Oct. 4ᵗʰ and Oct. 11ᵗʰ)
Northeastern Husky

SANDS, Terdell (#74)
Born on October 31, 1979 in Chattanooga, TN
6'7" and 335 pounds
Defensive Lineman　　　2009
Only game played was on 10-04-09
Member of the 2002 Berlin Thunder NFL Europe World Bowl Championship Team
Tennessee Chattanooga Moccasin

SANFORD, Richard "Rick" (#25) *"Bat"*
Born on January 9, 1957 in Rock Hill, SC
6'1" and 192 pounds
DB (KR/PR)　　　　　1979-84
Nicknamed *"Bat"* because he was always flying around everywhere
16 interceptions for 198 yards + 1 TD, 1 sack and 10 fumble recoveries for 60 yards + 2 TDs
14 kickoff returns for 261 yards and 2 punt returns for 1 yard
Had a 27 yard advancement of a lateral and returned a blocked punt 8 yards for a TD
Intercepted Matt Robinson, Richard Todd, David Woodley, Jim McMahon, Jim Zorn and Mike Pagel
Intercepted Dan Fouts, Dan Marino, Dave Krieg and Art Schlichter
Had 2 interceptions of Cliff Stoudt and 4 interceptions of Joe Ferguson
Recovered fumbles by Leonard Thompson, Keith Moody, Nesby Glasgow and Horace Ivory
Recovered fumbles by Wilbert Montgomery, Derrick Ramsey, Ottis Anderson and John Stallworth
Recovered a fumble by James Brooks, returned a blocked punt and advanced a lateral from Rod Shoate
Longest was a 1 yard return of a punt by Chuck Ramsey in their 56-3 rout of the NY Jets on 09-09-79
Had a 10 yard return of Leonard Thompson's fumbled kickoff return in their 24-17 win vs Detroit on 10-07-79
Advanced Rod Shoate's lateral 27 yards in their 26-6 win over the Buffalo Bills on 11-04-79
Blocked a punt by Bucky Dilts and returned it 8 yards for a TD in their 50-17 rout of Baltimore on 11-18-79
Sacked Bert Jones in their 47-21 rout of the Baltimore Colts on 11-23-80
Had a 22 yard TD return of Nesby Glasgow's kickoff return fumble in their 47-21 rout of the Colts on 11-23-80
Longest was a 27 yard return of a kickoff by Pat Leahy in their 17-6 loss to the Jetson 11-15-81
Had a career long 99 yard TD return of a pass by Jim McMahon in their 26-13 loss to the Bears on 12-05-82
Had a 26 yard return of a fumble by James Brooks in their 37-21 win over the San Diego Chargers on 10-16-83
Had the longest interception return in the NFL in 1982
89 Regular Season Games/60 started and 1 Playoff Game/1 started (on 01-08-83)
Had a 21 yard return of Andra Franklin's 1ˢᵗ fumble in their 28-13 Playoff loss to Miami on 01-08-83
Recovered Andra Franklin 2ⁿᵈ fumble in their 28-13 Playoff loss to the Dolphins on 01-08-83
#25 pick in the 1979 NFL Draft
South Carolina Gamecock

SANU, Mohamed (#14)
Born on August 22, 1989 in New Brunswick, NJ
6'2" and 215 pounds
Wide Receiver   2019
26 receptions for 207 yards and 1 TD and 1 carry for 8 yards
Longest reception was a 22 yard pass from Tom Brady on 12-29-19
8 Regular Season Games/6 started and 1 Playoff Game/1 started (on 01-04-20)
Rutgers Golden Knight

SARDISCO, Anthony "Tony" (#64)
Born on December 5, 1932 in Shreveport, LA
6'2" and 226 pounds
DE/Guard   1960-62
Defensive End in 1960 and Offensive Guard from 1961-62
2.5 sacks and 3 fumble recoveries
Shared in a sack of Al Dorow and sacked Tommy O'Connell and Jack Kemp
Recovered fumbles by Howard Clark, Johnny Green and Johnny Robinson
40 games/33 started
Tulane Green Wave

SATCHER, Douglas "Doug" (#58)
Born on May 28, 1945 in Sandersville, MS
6'0" and 220 pounds
Linebacker   1966-68
1 sack, 1 interception for 1 yard, 1 safety, and 5 fumble recoveries for 2 yards
Recovered fumbles by Joe Namath, Floyd Little, John Hadl and Billy Cannon
Recovered a blocked punt in their 17-10 loss to the Denver Broncos on 11-06-66
Sacked Steve Tensi in their 26-21 loss to the Denver Broncos on 09-03-67
Had a 2 yard return of a fumble by Billy Cannon in their 35-7 loss to the Raiders on 09-17-67
Had a 1 yard return of a pass by John Hadl in their 27-17 loss to the San Diego Chargers on 11-10-68
Tackled Paul Robinson in the end zone *for a safety* in their 33-14 win over the Bengals on 12-01-68
42 games/23 started
9th Round Draft Pick in 1966
Southern Mississippi Golden Eagle

SAUERBRUN, Todd (#18)
Born on January 4, 1973 in Setauket, NY
5'10" and 215 pounds
Punter   2006
10 punts for 408 yards
Longest punt was 58 yards in their 40-23 win over Tennessee on 12-31-06
2 Regular Season Games and 3 Playoff Games
14 punts for 640 yards in the playoffs
West Virginia Mountaineer

SAWYER, Jon (#31)
Born on April 6, 1964
5'9" and 175 pounds
Defensive Back   1987
2 games (on Oct. 4th and Oct. 11th)
Cincinnati Bearcat

SAXON, Michael "Mike" (#7)
Born on July 10, 1962 in Whittier, CA
6'3" and 205 pounds
Punter   1993
73 punts for 3,096 yards and 1 carry for 2 yards
Holder for Scott Sisson in their 13-10 OT loss to the Buffalo Bills on 11-07-93
Longest punt was 59 yards in their 17-13 loss to the Miami Dolphins on 11-21-93
Ran for a 2 yard gain in their 38-0 shutout of the Indianapolis Colts on 12-26-93
AFC Special Team Player of the Week in their 23-21 win over Phoenix on 10-10-93
16 games
San Diego State Aztec

SAYLER, James "Jace" (#94)
Born on February 27, 1979 in Rockford, IL
6'5" and 295 pounds
Defensive End   2001
2 games/1 started (on 09-09-01)
Member of the 2001 World Championship Team
Michigan State Spartan

SCARPITTO, Robert "Bob" (#46)
Born on January 7, 1939 in Rahway, NY
5'11" and 192 pounds
Punter (WR)   1968
34 punts for 1,382 yards and 2 receptions for 49 yards + 1 TD
Longest punt was 87 yards in their 20-17 win over the Denver Broncos on 09-29-68
Longest reception was a 33 yard TD pass from Tom Sherman in their 48-14 loss to the Jets on 10-27-68
14 games
Notre Dame Fighting Irish

SCHAUM, Greg (#76)
Born on January 1, 1954 in Baltimore, MD
6'4" and 246 pounds
Defensive End   1978
14 Regular Season Games and 1 Playoff Game (on 12-31-78)
Michigan State Spartan

SCHMIDT, Robert "Bob" (#74)
Born on July 9, 1936 in Rochester, NY
6'4" and 248 pounds
Tackle   1964
14 games/7 started
Minnesota Golden Gopher

SCHOLTZ, Bruce (#51)
Born on September 26, 1958 in La Grange, TX
6'6" and 240 pounds
Linebacker   1989
8 games/2 started
Texas Longhorn

SCHOTTENHEIMER, Martin "Marty" (#54)
Born on September 23, 1943 in Canonsburg, PA
6'3" and 225 pounds
LB (KR)　　　　　　　　1969-70
2 kickoff returns for 21 yards, 1 lateral of a kickoff return and 1 interception return of 3 yards
Had a 3 yard return of a pass by Jack Kemp in their 23-16 loss to the Buffalo Bills on 10-11-69
Longest was a 13 yard return of a kickoff by Karl Kremser in their 17-16 loss to Miami on 11-09-69
Fielded Pete Gogolak's kickoff and lateraled it to Odell Lawson in their 16-0 loss to the Giants on 10-18-70
23 games/5 started
Pittsburgh Panther

SCHUBERT, Eric (#1)
Born on May 28, 1962 in Abington, PA
5'8" and 185 pounds
Kicker　　　　　　　　1987
Kicked an extra point and a 23 yard field goal in their 20-10 loss to the Cleveland Browns on 10-04-87
Only game played was on 10-04-87
Pittsburgh Panther

SCHUBERT, Steve (#87)
Born on March 15, 1951 in Brooklyn, NY
5'10" and 185 pounds
WR/KR/PR　　　　　　　　1974
1 reception for a 21 yard TD, 5 kickoff returns for 112 yards and 3 punt returns for 15 yards
Had a 13 yard return of Charley Leigh's fumbled kickoff return in their 34-24 win over Miami on 09-15-74
Longest was a 32 yard return of a kickoff by Pete Gogolak in their 28-20 win over the NY Giants on 09-22-74
Longest was an 11 yard return of a punt by Spike Jones in their 30-28 loss to the Bills on 10-20-74
Only reception was a 21 yard TD pass from Jim Plunkett in their 17-14 comeback win vs the Vikings on 10-27-74
8 games/3 started
University of Massachusetts Minuteman

SCHWEDES, Gerhardt (#44)
Born on April 23, 1938 in Freiburg, Germany
6'1" and 205 pounds
Running Back　　　　　　　　1960-61
10 carries for 14 yards, 1 reception for 21 yards and recovered an onside kick
Caught a 21 yard pass from Butch Songin in their 27-15 loss to the Houston Oilers on 11-12-61
Recovered Gene Mingo's onside kick in their 28-24 win over the Denver Broncos on 12-03-61
Longest run was 5 yards in their 41-0 shutout of the San Diego Chargers on 12-17-61
7 games
1st Round Territorial Draft Pick in 1960
Syracuse Orangeman

SCHWENKE JR, Brian (#63)
Born on March 22, 1991 in Waukegan, IL
6'3" and 318 pounds
Offensive Lineman   2018
3 games
Member of the 2018 World Championship Team
California Golden Bear

SCOTT, Chad (#30)
Born on September 6, 1974 in Capitol Height, MD
6'1" and 205 pounds
Cornerback   2005-06
2 interceptions for 32 yards (Intercepted Brad Johnson and Peyton Manning)
Had a 32 yard return of a pass by Peyton Manning in their 27-20 loss to the Colts on 11-05-06
17 Regular Season Games/9 started and 3 Playoff Games
Maryland Terrapin

SCOTT, Clarence (#26)
Born on May 5, 1944 in Norristown, PA
6'1" and 186 pounds
DB (KR)   1969-72
1 interception for 18 yards, 6 kickoff returns for 43 yards and 3 fumble recoveries for 5 yards
Blocked a punt, had a 12 yard return of a free kick and recovered 2 onside kicks by the Patriots
Intercepted Al Woodhall and recovered fumbles by Jerry LeVias, John Guillory and Gene Washington
Longest was a 14 yard return of Roy Gerela's opening kickoff in their 24-0 win over Houston on 11-02-69
Blocked a punt by Horst Muhlmann in their 25-14 win over the Bengals on 11-16-69
Returned Dale Livingston's free kick 12 yards in their 25-14 win over the Bengals on 11-16-69
Had an 18 yard return of a pass by Al Woodall in their 17-3 loss to the New York Jets on 11-22-70
Recovered an onside kick by Patriots Kicker Charlie Gogolak in their 35-14 loss to the Vikings on 12-13-70
Recovered an onside kick by Patriots Kicker Charlie Gogolak in their 24-17 loss to the Colts on 11-06-72
43 games/24 started
Morgan State Bear

SCOTT, Guss (#29)
Born on May 21, 1981 in Jacksonville, FL
5'10" and 205 pounds
Safety   2005-06
6 games/2 started
#95 pick in the 2004 NFL Draft
Florida Gator

SCOTT, Trevor (#99)
Born on August 30, 1984 in Potsdam, NY
6'5" and 256 pounds
Defensive End   2012
Recorded 3 sacks of Ryan Tannehill
14 Regular Season Games/2 started and 2 Playoff Games
Buffalo Bull

SCOTT, Walter (#94)
Born on May 18, 1973 in Augusta, GA
6'3" and 285 pounds
Defensive End　　　　　1996
Only game played was on 10-20-96
East Carolina Pirate

SCOTT JR., Willie (#88)
Born on February 13, 1959 in Newberry, SC
6'4" and 245 pounds
Tight End　　　　　1986-88
14 receptions for 84 yards + 4 TDs and blocked a punt and returned it 3 yards for a TD
Caught 1 TD pass from Steve Grogan and Tom Ramsey and 2 TD passes from Tony Eason
Longest reception was a 15 yard pass from Doug Flutie in their 21-7 win over the Houston Oilers on 10-18-87
Blocked a punt by Rohn Stark and returned it 3 yards for a TD in their 24-0 win over the Colts on 11-22-87
Caught an 8 yard pass from Steve Grogan and lateraled it to Craig James in their 16-14 loss to Buffalo
　　　　on 09-18-88
26 Regular Season Games/2 started and 1 Playoff Game (on 01-04-87)
South Carolina Gamecock

SEALBY, Randall, "Randy" (#59 and #53)
Born on May 16, 1960 in Ann Arbor, MI
6'2" and 230 pounds
Linebacker　　　　　1987
Wore #59 on 10-04-87 and 10-11-87 and #53 on 10-18-87
Recovered Larry Mason's fumble in their 20-10 loss to the Cleveland Browns on 10-04-87
2 games/1 started (on 10-04-87)
Missouri Tiger

SEAU JR., Tiaina "Junior" (#55)
Born on January 19, 1969 in San Diego, CA
6'3" and 250 pounds
Linebacker (FB)　　　　　2006-09
4.5 sacks, 3 interceptions for 28 yards and 1 fumble recovery
Sacked Peyton Manning, had 1 ½ sacks of Cleo Lemon and 2 sacks of Chad Pennington
Intercepted a pass by Tony Romo and had 2 interceptions of Derek Anderson
Recovered a fumble by Ahmard Hall and was used as s blocking full back for 1 game
Used as a blocking full back on Heath Evans 1 yard TD run in their 38-14 win over the Jets on 09-09-07
Had a 23 yard return of a pass by Derek Anderson in their 34-17 victory over Cleveland on 10-07-07
Sacked Chad Pennington *twice* in their 20-10 win over the Jets on 12-16-07
Recovered Ahmard Hall's fumble in their 59-0 shutout of the Tennessee Titans on 10-18-09
38 Regular Season Games/16 started and 4 Playoff Games/2 started
Sacked Philip Rivers in their 21-12 AFC Championship win over the San Diego Chargers on 01-20-08
Inducted into the Pro Football Hall of Fame on 08-08-15
USC Trojan

SECULES, Thomas "Scott" (#10)
Born on November 8, 1964 in Newport News, VA
6'3" and 220 pounds
Quarterback   1993
75 completions for 918 yards + 2 TDs and 8 carries for 33 yards
Longest pass was an 82 yard pass to Kevin Turner/Leonard Russell in their 23-21 win over Phoenix on 10-10-93
Fired a game winning 2 yard TD pass to Ben Coates in their 23-21 win over the Cardinals on 10-10-93
Tossed a 7 yard TD pass to Kevin Turner in their 28-14 loss to the Houston Oilers on 10-17-93
Longest run was 13 yards in their 13-10 OT loss to the Buffalo Bills on 11-07-93
Holder for Scott Sisson
12 games/4 started
Virginia Cavalier

SELLERS, Ron (#34)
Born on February 5, 1947 in Jacksonville, FL
6'4" and 205 pounds
Wide Receiver   1969-71
79 receptions for 1,477 yards + 13 TDs
Caught 1 TD pass from Joe Kapp, 3 TDs from Jim Plunkett and 9 TD passes from Mike Taliaferro
Longest reception was a 77 yard pass from Mike Taliaferro in their 27-23 loss to Houston on 12-14-69
AFL Offensive Player of the Week in their 24-0 shutout of Houston on 11-02-69
AFL All Star Wide Receiver in 1969
35 games/30 started
#6 pick in the 1969 NFL Draft
Florida State Seminole

SERWANGA, Kato (#31)
Born on July 23, 1976 in Kampala, Uganda
6'0" and 205 pounds
Defensive Back   1999-2000
3 interceptions for 2 yards, 3 sacks and 3 fumble recoveries
Intercepted Dave Brown, Ky Detmer and Tony Banks and sacked Doug Flutie, Brian Griese and Charlie Batch
Recovered fumbles by David Dunn, Karl Williams and Charlie Batch
Had a 2 yard return of a pass by Dave Brown in their 27-3 win over the Arizona Cardinals on 10-31-99
Strip sacked Charlie Batch and recovered his fumble in their 34-9 loss to the Detroit Lions on 11-23-00
31 games/3 started
California Golden Bear

SEYMOUR, Richard (#93) *"Big Sey"*
Born on October 6, 1979 in Gadsden, SC
6'6" and 310 pounds
NT/DT/DE (FB)   2001-08
39 sacks, 1 interception for 6 yards, 6 fumble recoveries for 68 yards + 1 TD and blocked 5 field goal attempts
Shared in a sack of Dante Culpepper, Kelly Holcomb and Kurt Warner
Sacked Chris Chandler, Tim Couch, Kordell Stewart, Trent Green, Rich Gannon, Steve McNair
          and Kerry Collins
Sacked Quincy Carter, Tony Banks, Byron Leftwich, Kyle Boller, A.J. Feeley and Rex Grossman
Sacked Cleo Lemon and Trent Edwards and had 1 ½ sacks of Vinny Testaverde and Brooks Bollinger
Had 2 sacks of Jay Cutler, Brett Favre, Jay Fiedler, J.P.Losman and Marc Bulger
Had 2 ½ sacks of Ben Roethlisberger and 3 ½ sacks of Chad Pennington and Drew Bledsoe
Recovered fumbles by Richard Huntley, Randy Moss, Brooks Bollinger, Rex Grossman and Seneca Wallace
Had a 68 yard TD return of a fumble by Drew Bledsoe
Blocked a 43 yard field goal attempt by John Carney in their 34-17 win over the Saints on 11-25-01
Used as a blocking full back on Antowain Smith's 2 yard TD run in their 20-13 win over Miami on 12-02-01
Blocked a 49 yard FGA by Sebastian Janikowski in their 27-20 loss to the Oakland Raiders on 11-17-02
Blocked a 43 yard field goal attempt by Gary Anderson in their 24-17 win over the Vikings on 11-24-02
Returned a Drew Bledsoe pass, tipped by Anthony Pleasant, 6 yards, in their 27-17 win over the Bills
          on 12-08-02
Blocked a 35 yard FGA by Olindo Mare, which forced overtime, in their 19-13 OT win vs Miami on 10-19-03
Returned Drew Bledsoe's fumble 68 yards for a TD in their 31-17 win over the Bills on 10-03-04
Blocked a 45 yard field goal attempt by Robbie Gould in their 17-13 win over the Bears on 11-26-06
Intercepted a pass by David Carr, that he tipped to himself, in their 40-7 rout of the Texans on 12-07-06
AFC Special Team Player of the Week in their 19-13 OT win vs Miami on 10-19-03
AFC Special Team Player of the Week in their 17-14 Divisional win vs Tenn on 01-10-04
AFC Pro Bowl Defensive Lineman from 2002-06
First Team All Pro Defensive Lineman in 2003, 2004, 2005
111 Regular Season Games/105 started and 15 Playoff Games/13 started
4.5 sacks and 2 fumble recoveries in the playoffs
Sacked Kurt Warner in their 20-17 Super Bowl win over the St. Louis Rams on 02-03-02
Blocked a 31 yard FGA by Gary Anderson in their 17-14 Divisional Playoff Game win over Tennessee
          on 01-10-04
Used as a blocking full back in their 32-29 Super Bowl win over the Panthers on 02-01-04
Recovered Jake Delhomme's fumble in their 32-29 Super Bowl win over Carolina on 02-01-04
Sacked Donovan McNabb in their 24-21 Super Bowl win over the Eagles on 02-06-05
Shared in a sack of David Garrard in their 28-3 Wild Card rout of the Jaguars on 01-07-06
Recovered Alvin Pearman's fumble in their 28-3 Wild Card rout of the Jaguars on 01-07-06
Sacked Chad Pennington on 4th down, in their 37-16 Wild Card rout of the NY Jets on 01-07-07
Shared in 2 sacks of Jake Plummer in their 27-13 Divisional Playoff loss to the Denver Broncos on 01-14-07
Member of the 2001, 2003 and 2004 World Championship Teams
#6 pick in the 2001 NFL Draft
Georgia Bulldog

SHAW, Harold (#44)
Born on September 3, 1974 in Magee, MS
6'0" and 228 pounds
Running Back   1998-2000
18 carries for 35 yards and 4 receptions for 42 yards
Longest reception was a 29 yard pass from Drew Bledsoe in their 13-10 OT loss to Buffalo on 12-26-99
Longest run was 12 yards in their 20-3 win over the Baltimore Ravens on 01-02-00
35 Regular Season Games and 1 Playoff Game (on 01-03-99)
#176 pick in the 1998 NFL Draft
Southern Mississippi Golden Eagle

SHAW, Sedrick (#23)
Born on November 16, 1973 in Austin, TX
6'0" and 214 pounds
RB (KR)   1997-98
48 carries for 236 yards, 6 receptions for 30 yards and 1 kickoff return of 16 yards
Had a 16 yard return of a kickoff by Craig Hentrich in their 27-16 win over Tennessee on 09-20-98
Longest reception was an 11 yard pass from Drew Bledsoe in their 41-10 loss to Atlanta on 11-08-98
Longest run was 71 yards in their 31-10 loss to the Jets on 12-27-98
14 Regular Season Games/1 started (on 09-07-08) and 3 Playoff Games
11 carries for 26 yards in the playoffs
Caught a 13 yard pass from Drew Bledsoe in their 7-6 Divisional loss to the Steelers on 01-03-98
Returned a kickoff by Mike Hollis 14 yards in their 25-10 Wild Card loss to the Jaguars on 01-03-99
#61 pick in the 1997 NFL Draft
Iowa Hawkeye

SHAW, Terrance (#22)
Born on November 11, 1973 in Marshall, TX
6'0" and 200 pounds
Defensive Back   2001
13 Regular Season Games/3 started and 3 Playoff Games
Member of the 2001 World Championship Team
Stephen F. Austin State Lumberjack

SHEARD, Jabaal (#93)
Born on May 10, 1989 in Hollywood Hills, FL
6'3" and 265 pounds
Defensive Lineman   2015-16
13 sacks
Shared in a sack of Andy Dalton and Bryce Petty
Sacked Ben Roethlisberger, Blake Bortles, Zach Mettenberger, Ryan Fitzpatrick, Tyrod Taylor
      and Trevor Siemian
Had 2 sacks of Brandon Weeden, Brian Hoyer and Brock Osweiler
Strip sacked Ryan Fitzpatrick and Jamie Collins returned it 14 yds for a TD in their 26-20 loss to the Jets
      on 12-27-15
28 Regular Season Games/9 started and 5 Playoff Games
Shared in a sack of Matt Ryan in their Epic 34-28 Overtime Super Bowl win over the Falcons on 02-05-17
Member of the 2016 World Championship Team
Pittsburgh Panther

SHEGOG, Ronald "Ron" (#42)
Born on March 2, 1963 in Batesville, MS
5'11" and 190 pounds
Defensive Back   1987
Had a 7 yard return of a pass by Brent Pease in their 21-7 victory over the Oilers on 10-18-87
3 games/3 started
Austin Peay State Governor

SHELTON, Danny (#71)
Born on August 20, 1993 in Auburn, WA
6'2" and 345 pounds
DL   2018-19
3 sacks
Sacked Josh Rosen and Colt McCoy and strip sacked Carson Wentz
29 Regular Season Games/ 15 started and 3 Playoff Games/2 started
Member of the 2018 World Championship Team
Washington Husky

SHERMAN, Thomas "Tom" (#14)
Born on December 5, 1945 in Bellevue, PA
6'0" and 190 pounds
Quarterback   1968-69
90 completions for 1,199 yards + 12 TDs and 25 carries for 80 yards
Threw 1 TD pass to Bob Scarpitto, Art Graham and RC Gamble and 2 TD passes to Gino Cappelletti
Threw 3 TD passes to Jim Whalen and 4 TD passes Aaron Marsh
Completed a career long 87 yard TD pass to Jim Whalen in their 48-14 loss to the Jets on 10-27-68
Longest run was 17 yards in their 34-10 loss to the Miami Dolphins on 11-24-68
Holder for Gino Cappelletti
18 games/7 started
Penn State Nittany Lion

SHIANCOE, Visanthe (#80)
Born on June 18, 1980 in Birmingham, England
6'4" and 250 pounds
Tight End   2012
4 games
Morgan State Bear

SHINER, Richard "Dick" (#11)
Born on July 18, 1942 in Lebanon, PA
6'0" and 201 pounds
Quarterback   1973-74
5 completions for 68 yards
Longest completion was a 23 yard pass to Randy Vataha in their 32-0 shutout of the Oilers on 11-25-73
4 games
Maryland Terrapin

SHOATE, Roderick "Rod" (#56) *"Wolfgang"*
Born on April 26, 1953 in Spiro, OK
6'1" and 214 pounds
Linebacker   1975-81
5 interceptions for 50 yards + 1 TD, 22.5 sacks and 7 fumble recoveries for 7 yards
Intercepted Joe Ferguson, Richard Todd, Bert Jones, David Humm and Ken Stabler
Shared in a sack of Brian Sipe and Dan Fouts and had 2 sacks of Ron Jaworski and Ken Stabler
Sacked Bob Griese, Bert Jones, Bill Troup, Dan Fouts, Dan Pastorini and Terry Bradshaw
Sacked David Whitehurst, Steve Bartkowski, Greg Landry, Dan Manucci and Neil Lomax
Had 3 sacks of Richard Todd and 3 ½ sacks of Joe Ferguson
Recovered fumbles by Stanley Morgan, Earl Campbell, Tony Dorsett, Joe Washington
Recovered fumbles by Joe Cribbs, Kenny King and Andra Franklin
Recovered a blocked field goal in their 30-27 loss to the Cleveland Browns on 09-26-77
Picked off a pass by Joe Ferguson and lateraled it to Rick Sanford in their 26-6 win over Buffalo on 11-04-79
Had a career long 42 yard TD return of a pass by Bert Jones in their 47-21 win over Baltimore on 11-23-80
Had a 7 yard return of a fumble by Kenny King in their 27-17 loss to the Raiders on 11-01-81
79 Regular Season Games/64 started and 1 Playoff Game/1 started
#41 pick in the 1975 NFL Draft
Oklahoma Sooner

SHONTA, Charles "Chuck" (#40 and #34) *"Kemo"*
Born on August 29, 1937 in Detroit, MI
6'0" and 200 pounds
Defensive Back   1960-67
Wore #40 in 1960 and #34 from 1961-67
15 interceptions for 261 yards, 6 fumble recoveries for 52 yards + 1 TD and 1 reception of 9 yards
Recovered fumbles by Bill Groman, Gerry McDougall, Bill Mathis, Frank Jackson and Wray Carlton
Intercepted Frank Tripucka, Babe Parilli, Warren Rabb, Jack Spikes and Jack Kemp
Had 2 interceptions of Len Dawson, Mickey Slaughter, Tom Flores, Cotton Davidson and Joe Namath
Had a career long 52 yard return of a pass by Frank Tripucka in their 13-10 loss to Denver on 09-09-60
Had a career long 52 yard TD return of a bad snap to the Titans Punter on last play in their 28-24 win
          on 09-17-60
Caught a 9 yard pass, as a wide receiver, from QB Tom Yewcic, in their 41-0 shutout of San Diego on 12-17-61
Had a 9 yard return of a pass by Cotton Davidson, to help seal their 24-21 win over the Raiders on 10-30-66
AFL Defensive Player of the Week in their 34-28 win over Oakland on 11-04-60
AFL All Star Defensive Back in 1966
105 Regular Season Games/33 started and 2 Playoff Games
Eastern Michigan Huron

SHORTS, John "Peter" (#90)
Born on July 12, 1966 in Janesville, WI
6'8" and 278 pounds
Defensive Tackle   1989
Only game played was on 12-24-89
Illinois State Redbird

SIEVERS, Eric (#85)
Born on November 9, 1957 in Urbana, IL
6'4" and 236 pounds
Tight End   1989-90
62 receptions for 692 yards
Longest reception was a 46 yard pass from Steve Grogan in their 23-20 OT win over the Colts on 10-29-89
24 games/6 started
Maryland Terrapin

SILIGA, Tupaimoefitpo "Sealver" (#71 and #96)
Born on April 26, 1990 in West Jordan, UT
6'2" and 345 pounds
Defensive Lineman   2013-15
Wore #71 for 5 games in 2013 and #96 from 2014-15
5.5 sacks
Shared in a sack of Philip Rivers and sacked Joe Flacco, Thaddeus Lewis and Geno Smith
Recorded 2 sacks of Ryan Tannehill
25 Regular Season Games/13 started and 7 Playoff Games/5 started
Member of the 2014 World Championship Team
Utah Ute

SILVESTRO, Alex (#69)
Born on November 15, 1988 in Gibbstown, NJ
6'3" and 267 pounds
Defensive End   2011
Only game played was on 12-24-11
Rutgers Scarlet Knight

SIMERSON, John (#75)
Born on April 20, 1935 in Honolulu, HI
6'3" and 257 pounds
Tackle (KR)   1961
Received a kickoff by Jack Hill and lateraled it to Larry Garron in their 45-17 win over Denver on 09-16-61
10 games
Purdue Boilermaker

SIMMONS, Henry "Kendall" (#71)
Born on March 11, 1979 in Ripley, MS
6'3" and 315 pounds
Guard   2009
Only game played was on 10-18-09
Auburn Tiger

SIMMONS, Tony (#81)
Born on December 8, 1974 in Chicago, IL
6'1" and 210 pounds
WR/KR   1998-2000
56 receptions for 981 yards + 6 TDs and 10 kickoff returns for 214 yards
Caughtr 1 TD pass from Scott Zolak and Michael Bishop and 4 TD passes from Drew Bledsoe
Had a career long 63 yard TD reception of a pass by Drew Bledsoe in their 21-16 win vs the Colts on 11-01-98
Longest was 39 yard return of a kickoff by Danny Kight in their 24-16 win over the Colts on 10-08-00
38 Regular Season Games/9 started and 1 Playoff Game
3 receptions for 42 yards in their 25-10 Wild Card Playoff loss to Jacksonville on 01-03-99
#52 pick in the 1998 NFL Draft
Head Coach of the 2016 Champion Moscow Patriots Team in the Russian American Football League
Wisconsin Badger

SIMON, John (#51)
Born on October 14, 1990 in Youngstown, OH
6'2" and 260 pounds
Linebacker   2018-19
6 sacks and 1 interception for 6 yards
Sacked Ryan Fitzpatrick, and Sam Darnold and had 2 sacks of Ryan Tannehill and Josh Allen
Had a 6 yard return of pass by Daniel Jones in their 35-14 rout of the Giants on 10-10-19
27 Regular Season Games/14 started and 4 Playoff Games/2 started
Shared in a sack of Patrick Mahomes in their 37-31 OT Championship win vs the Chiefs on 01-20-19
Member of the 2018 World Championship Team
Ohio State Buckeye

SIMS, Kenneth (#77) *"Game Day"*
Born on October 31, 1959 in Kosse, TX
6'5" and 272 pounds
Defensive End   1982-89
17 sacks, 5 fumble recoveries for 6 yards and blocked 2 field goals
Shared in a sack of Dave Krieg, Steve DeBerg, Dave Archer and Rusty Hilger
Sacked Jim Zorn, Pat Ryan, Paul McDonald, Joe Ferguson, Marc Wilson, Vince Ferragamo
Sacked Dan Marino, Warren Moon and Steve Beuerlein
Had 2 ½ sacks of Archie Manning and 3 ½ sacks of Ken O'Brien
Recovered fumbles by Ron Davenport, Johnny Hector, Ernest Jackson and 2 fumbles by Ken O'Brien
Blocked a 40 yard field goal attempt by Al DelGreco in their 26-20 win over Green Bay on 09-08-85
Had a 6 yard return of a fumble by Ernest Jackson in their 34-0 shutout of the Steelers on 10-19-86
Blocked a 45 yard field goal attempt by Mike Cofer in their 37-20 loss to San Francisco on 10-22-89
74 Regular Season Games/64 started and 1 Playoff Game/1 started (on 01-08-83)
1st Overall Pick in the 1982 NFL Draft
Texas Longhorn

SINGER, Karl (#68)
Born on October 12, 1943 in Warren, OH
6'3" and 250 pounds
Tackle (KR)   1966-68
2 fumble recoveries and 3 kickoff returns for 56 yards
Recovered a fumbled kickoff return by Dave Grayson and fell on a fumble by Babe Parilli
Longest was a 27 yard return of a kickoff by Fletcher Smith in their 43-24 loss to the Chiefs on 09-25-66
39 games/7 started
1st Round Draft Pick in 1966
Purdue Boilermaker

SINGLETON, Chris (#55)
Born on February 20, 1967 in Omaha, NE
6'2" and 246 pounds
Linebacker   1990-93
4 sacks, 1 interception for 82 yards + 1 TD and 1 fumble return for 21 yards
Sacked Boomer Esiason, Todd Philcox, Dave Krieg and Jeff George
Had a 21 yard return of a fumble by Anthony Thompson in their 24-10 loss to the Phoenix Cardinals on 09-29-91
Had an 82 yard TD return of a pass by Jeff George in their 37-34 OT win vs the Colts on 11-15-92
41 games/26 started
#8 pick in the 1990 NFL Draft
Arizona Wildcat

SISSON, Scott (#9)
Born on July 21, 1971 in Marietta, GA
6'0" and 197 pounds
Kicker   1993
Kicked 14 field goals and 15 extra points and had an onside kick recovered by his teammate
His onside kick was recovered by his teammate Darryl Wren in their 28-14 loss to Houston on 10-17-93
Kicked a career long 40 yard field goal on 10-31-93 and on 11-21-93
13 games
#113 pick in the 1993 NFL Draft
Georgia Tech Yellow Jacket

SKENE, Douglas "Doug" (#74)
Born on June 17, 1970 in Fairview, TX
6'6" and 295 pounds
Guard   1994
6 games/6 started
Michigan Wolverine

SKINNER, Deontae (#55)
Born on December 18, 1990 in Macon, MS
6'2" and 250 pounds
Linebacker   2014
Sacked Kyle Orton in their 37-22 win over the Buffalo Bills on 10-12-14
7 games/1 started (on 10-05-14)
Member of the 2014 World Championship Team
Mississippi State Bulldog

SLADE, Chris (#53)
Born on January 30, 1971 in Newport News, VA
6'5" and 245 pounds
Linebacker   1993-2000
51 sacks, 3 interceptions for 3 yards + 1 TD and 3 fumble recoveries for 38 yards + 1 TD
Shared in a sack of Brett Favre, Stan Humphries, Dave Brown, Jay Fiedler and Doug Pederson
Sacked Steve DeBerg, David Klinger, Dan Marino, Don Majkowski, Bubby Brister and Boomer Esiason
Sacked Kent Graham, Mark Brunell, John Elway, Glenn Foley, Troy Aikman and Jim Harbaugh
Sacked Peyton Manning, Danny Wuerffel, Elvis Grbac, Steve Young, Doug Flutie and Dante Culpepper
Recorded 2 sacks of Rick Mirer, Brett Favre, Dan Marino, Brian Griese and Billy Joe Hobert
Had 2 sacks of Damon Huard, Mark Brunell, Vinny Testaverde and Scott Mitchell
Had 3 sacks of Rodney Peete, Stan Humphries and Neil O'Donnell and 3 ½ sacks of Jim Kelly
Intercepted Jim Kelly, Todd Collins and Rick Mirer
Recovered fumbles by Rodney Peete, Darick Holmes and Jim Kelly
Had an 11 yard return of a fumble by Darick Holmes in their 27-14 win over Buffalo on 10-23-95
Had a career long 27 yard TD return of a fumble by Jim Kelly in their 35-25 win over Buffalo on 11-26-95
Had a career long 2 yard return of a pass by Jim Kelly in their 17-10 loss to Buffalo on 09-08-96
Strip sacked Stan Humphries, and Willie McGinest fell on it for a TD, in their 45-7 rout of San Diego
        on 12-01-96
Had a 1 yard TD return of a pass by Todd Collins, tipped to himself, in their 31-10 win vs Buffalo on 11-09-97
Intercepted a pass by Rick Mirer, deflected by Ty Law, in their 30-28 victory over the Jets on 09-12-99
AFC Defensive Player of the Week in their 17-14 win over Cleveland on 09-03-95
AFC Defensive Player of the Month in September 1997
AFC Pro Bowl Linebacker in 1997
127 Regular Season Games/108 started and 7 Playoff Games/7 started
3.5 sacks and 1 fumble recovery in the playoffs
Shared in a sack of Mike Tomczak in their 28-3 Divisional win over Pittsburgh on 01-05-97
Shared another sack of Mike Tomczak in their 28-3 Divisional win over the Steelers on 01-05-97
Sacked Mark Brunell in their 20-6 AFC Championship win over the Jaguars on 01-12-97
Sacked Dan Marino in their 17-3 Wild Card win over the Miami Dolphins on 12-28-97
Shared in a sack of Kordell Stewart in their 7-6 Divisional loss to the Steelers on 01-03-98
Returned a Dan Marino pass 22 yards in their 17-3 Wild Card victory over Miami on 12-28-97
Recovered Dan Marino's fumble in their 17-3 Wild Card win over the Dolphins on 12-28-97
#31 pick in the 1993 NFL Draft
Virginia Cavalier

SLATER, Matthew (#18)
Born on September 9, 1985 in Los Angeles, CA
6'0" and 205 pounds
Gunner/KR (WR/S)   2008--
35 kickoff returns for 637 yards, 2 carries for 11 yards and 1 reception of 46 yards
1 fumble recovery, 1 blocked punt and played 3 games as a Safety (in 2011)
Longest run was 6 yards in their 17-10 win over Buffalo on 12-20-09
Longest was 35 yards on a kickoff by Kris Brown in their 34-27 loss to Houston on 01-03-10
Caught a 46 yard pass from Tom Brady in their 38-24 win over the Dolphins on 09-12-11
Tapped back Jake Bailey's punt, that was downed on the 1 yard line, in their 301-4 win over the Jets on 09-22-19
Recovered a muffed punt return by Braxton Berrios in their 33-0 shutout of the Jets on 10-21-19
Blocked a punt by Chris Jones, that was recovered by Nate Ebner, in their 13-9 win over Dallas on 11-24-19
AFC Pro Bowl Special Team Player from 2011-17, 2019
First Team All Pro Special Team Player in 2016, 2019
AFC Special Team Player of the Week in their 13-9 win over Dallas on 11-24-19
173 Regular Season Games/3 started and 24 Playoff Games/1 started (as a WR on 01-11-14)
3 kickoff returns for 65 yards in the playoffs
Ron Burton Community Service Award in 2013
Member of the 2014, 2016 and 2018 World Championship Teams
#153 pick in the 2008 NFL Draft
UCLA Bruin

SMALL, Torrance (#84)
Born on September 4, 1970 in Tampa, FL
6'3" and 209 pounds
Wide Receiver   2001
4 receptions for 29 yards
Longest reception was an 11 yard pass from Tom Brady in their 44-13 rout of the Colts on 09-30-01
3 games
Member of the 2001 World Championship Team
Alcorn State Brave

SMERLAS, Fred (#66 and #76)
Born on April 8, 1957 in Waltham, MA
6'3" and 277 pounds
Nose Tackle   1991-92
Wore #66 for the first 3 games in 1991
32 games/1 started (on 09-01-91)
Boston College Eagle

SMITH, Antowain (#32) *"Big Twan"*
Born on March 14, 1972 in Millbrook AL
6'2" and 232 pounds
Running Back   2001-03
721 carries for 2,781 yards + 21 TDs and 64 receptions for 527 yards + 3 TDs
Rand for a 2 point conversion and recovered 3 fumbles by Tom Brady
Caught 3 TD passes from Tom Brady
Recovered Tom Brady's fumble in their 29-26 OT win vs the San Diego Chargers on 10-14-01
Hauled in a career long 41 yard TD pass from Tom Brady in their 34-17 win over the Saints on 11-25-01
Longest run was 44 yards in their 20-13 victory over the Dolphins on 12-22-01
Ran for a 2 point conversion in their 41-38 Overtime win vs the Chiefs on 09-22-02
Recovered 2 fumbles by Tom Brady in their 24-17 victory over the Vikings on 11-24-02
45 Regular Season Games/36 started and 6 Playoff Games/6 started
117 carries for 456 yards + 2 TDs and 3 receptions for 13 yards in the playoffs
Ran for a 1 yard TD in their 17-14 Divisional win over Tennessee in brutal cold weather on 01-10-04
Ran for a 2 yard TD in their 32-29 Super Bowl win over the Carolina Panthers on 02-01-04
Member of the 2001 and 2003 World Championship Teams
Houston Cougar

SMITH, Donnell (#65)
Born on May 25, 1949 in Lakeland, FL
6'4" and 245 pounds
Defensive End   1973-74
4 sacks, 1 kickoff return for no gain, 1 blocked extra point attempt and 1 fumble recovery
Recored 1 sack of Bob Griese once and 3 sacks of Bert Jones
Sacked Bert Jones *3 times* in their 42-3 rout of the Baltimore Colts on 10-06-74
Fell on George Jakowenko's squibbed kickoff in their 41-26 loss to the Raiders on 12-01-74
Blocked an extra point attempt by Roy Gerela in their 21-17 loss to the Steelers on 12-08-74
Recovered John Tanner's fumbled kickoff return in their 34-27 loss to Miami on 12-15-74
21 games
Southern Jaguar

SMITH JR., Harold "Hal" (#70)
Born on October 3, 1935 in Santa Monica, CA
6'5" and 250 pounds
DT (KR)   1960
3 fumble recoveries and 1 kickoff return for 13 yards
Recovered fumbles by Gene Mingo, Frank Tripucka and Jack Larscheid
Had a 13 yard return of a kickoff by Bill Shockley in their 38-21 win over the NY Titans on 11-11-60
10 games/4 started
UCLA Bruin

SMITH, John (#1)
Born on December 30, 1949 in Leafield, England
6'0" and 186 pounds
Kicker   1974-83
Kicked 128 field goals and 308 extra points and had an onside kick recovered by a teammate
Kicked a 39 yard extra point (after numerous penalties) in their 17-14 win over the Vikings on 10-27-74
His onside kick was recovered by his teammate Don Westbrook in their 34-27 loss to the Colts on 09-18-78
Had a career long 50 yard field goal in their 33-17 win over the Chiefs on 10-04-81
Kicked a 33 yard field goal in their 3-0 "Snow Plow" win over the Dolphins at Schaefer on 12-12-82
Led the NFL with 115 points scored in 1979 and Led the NFL with 129 points scored in 1980
AFC Pro Bowl Kicker in 1980
116 Regular Season Games and 2 Playoff Games
Kicked 2 field goals and 6 extra points in the playoffs
Southampton (England)

SMITH, Jonathan (#81)
Born on November 28, 1981 in Argyle, GA
5'10" and 194 pounds
Wide Receiver   2006
2 games (on Sept. 24th and Oct. 1st)
Georgia Tech Yellow Jacket

SMITH, Le Kevin (#90)
Born on July 21, 1982 in Macon, GA
6'3" and 308 pounds
Defensive Lineman   2006-08
31 Regular Season Games and 2 Playoff Games
#206 pick in the 2006 NFL Draft
Nebraska Cornhusker

SMITH III, Otis (#45) *"My Man"*
Born on October 22, 1965 in New Orleans, LA
5'11" and 198 pounds
Defensive Back   1996 and 2000-02
10 interceptions for 278 yards + 2 TDs, 3 sacks and 4 fumble recoveries for 12 yards
Intercepted Stan Humphries, Dave Brown, Elvis Grbac, Peyton Manning and Chris Chandler
Intercepted Rob Johnson, Trent Green and Jim Miller and had 2 interceptions of Chris Weinke
Sacked Dave Brown, Aaron Brooks and Chris Weinke
Recovered fumbles by Brandon Bennett, Anthony Pleasant, Jed Weaver and Peerless Price
Had a 12 yard return of a fumble by Brandon Bennett in their 16-13 win over the Bengals on 11-19-00
Had a career long 78 yard TD return of a pass by Peyton Manning in their 44-13 rout of the Colts on 09-30-01
Had a 76 yard TD return of a pass by Chris Weinke in their 38-6 rout of the Panthers on 01-06-02
56 Regular Season Games/48 started and 6 Playoff Games/6 started
1 fumble return for a 47 yard TD, 1 sack and 1 interception return of 30 yards in the playoffs
Had a 47 yard TD return of a fumble by James Stewart in their 20-6 Championship vs the Jaguars on 01-12-97
Sacked Brett Favre in their 35-21 Super Bowl loss to the Green Bay Packers on 01-26-97
Had a 30 yard return of a pass by Kurt Warner in their 20-17 Super Bowl win over the Rams on 02-03-02
Member of the 2001 World Championship Team
Missouri Tiger

SMITH, Ricky (#27)
Born on July 20, 1960 in Quincy, FL
6'0" and 182 pounds
KR/PR   1982-84
67 kickoff returns for 1,505 yards + 1 TD and 54 punt returns for 537 yards
Had a 98 yard TD return of a kickoff by Pat Leahy in their 31-7 loss to the Jets on 09-19-82
Returned Cliff Parsley's free kick 19 yards in their 29-21 win over Houston on 11-28-82
Longest was 55 yard return of a punt by Rohn Stark in their 29-23 OT loss to the Colts on 09-04-83
Led the NFL with the longest kickoff return in 1982
26 Regular Season Games and 1 Playoff Game (on 01-08-83)
#141 pick in the 1982 NFL Draft
Alabama State Hornet

SMITH, Rodney "Rod" (#22)
Born on March 12, 1970 in St. Paul, MN
5'11" and 187 pounds
Defensive Back   1992-94
3 interceptions for 10 yards and shared in a sack of Dan Marino
Intercepted Steve Young, Brett Favre and Jeff Hostetler
Shared in a sack of Dan Marino in their 39-35 loss to the Miami Dolphins on 09-04-94
Had a career long 10 yard return of a pass by Brett Favre in their 17-16 win over the Packers on 10-02-94
48 Regular Season Games and 1 Playoff Game (on 01-01-95)
#35 pick in the 1992 NFL Draft
Notre Dame Fighting Irish

SMITH, Sean (#97)
Born on May 29, 1967 in Cincinnati, OH
6'7" and 280 pounds
Defensive Tackle   1990-91
Recorded 1 ½ sacks of Jeff Hostetler in their 13-10 loss to the New York Giants on 12-30-90
17 games/1 started (on 09-08-91)
#280 pick in the 1990 NFL Draft
Georgia Tech Yellow Jacket

SNYDER, Albert "Al" (#38) *Spike*
Born on June 20, 1941 in Baltimore, MD
6'1" and 196 pounds
Wide Receiver   1964
Caught a 12 yard pass from Babe Parilli in their 35-14 loss to the NY Jets on 10-31-64
2 games (on Oct. 31st and Nov. 6th)
23rd Round Draft Pick in 1963
Holy Cross Crusader

SOLDER, Nathaniel "Nate" (#77)
Born on April 12, 1988 in Denver, CO
6'8" and 325 pounds
Offensive Tackle   2011-17
98 Regular Season Games/95 started and 16 Playoff Games/16 started
Caught a 16 yard TD pass from Tom Brady in their 45-7 AFC Championship rout of the Colts on 01-18-15
Ron Burton Community Service Award in 2015
Member of the 2014 and 2016 World Championship Teams
#17 pick in the 2011 NFL Draft
Colorado Buffalo

SOLTIS, Robert "Bob" (#42)
Born on April 1, 1936 in Minneapolis, MN
6'2" and 205 pounds
Defensive Back   1960-61
2 interceptions for 33 yards
Had a 33 yard return of a pass by Babe Parilli in their 27-14 loss to the Oakland Raiders on 10-16-60
Picked off a pass by Jack Kemp in their 45-16 loss to the Los Angeles Chargers on 10-28-60
17 games
Minnesota Golden Gopher

SONGIN, Edward "Butch" (#11)
Born on May 11, 1924 in Walpole, MA
6'2" and 190 pounds
Quarterback   1960-61
285 completions for 3,905 yards + 36 TDs and 19 carries for 79 yards + 2 TDs
Threw 1 TD pass to Billy Wells and Walter Beach and 2 TDs to Alan Miller, Dick Christy and Billy Lott
Tossed 3 TD passes to Tight End's Oscar Lofton and Tom Stephens
Threw 4 TD passes to Gino Cappelletti and Joe Johnson and 14 TDs to Jim Colclough
Threw the 1st TD pass in the AFL with his 10 yard TD pass to Jim Colclough in their 13-10 loss on 09-09-60
Longest completion was a 78 yard pass to Billy Wells in their 35-0 shutout of the LA Chargers on 10-08-60
Longest run was 20 yards in their 37-21 loss to the Houston Oilers on 12-18-60
AFL Offensive Player of the Week in their 35-0 shutout of the LA Chargers on 10-08-60
28 games/18 started
Boston College Eagle

SOPOAGA, Isa'ako "Isaac" (#90)
Born on September 4, 1981 in Pago Pago, American Samoa
6'2" and 330 pounds
Defensive Tackle   2013
Sacked Case Keenum in their 34-31 win over the Houston Texans on 12-01-13
6 games/2 started
Hawaii Rainbow

SPACH, Stephen (#82)
Born on July 18, 1982 in Fresno, CA
6'4" and 260 pounds
Tight End   2007-08
5 Regular Season Games and 1 Playoff Game (on 01-20-08)
Fresno State Bulldog

SPANN, Antwain (#31)
Born on February 22, 1983 in Oceanside, CA
6'0" and 190 pounds
Defensive Back   2006-08
19 Regular Season Games and 3 Playoff Games
Louisiana-Lafayette Ragin' Cajun

SPEARS, Ronald "Ron" (#78)
Born on November 23, 1959 in Los Angeles, CA
6'6" and 255 pounds
Defensive End   1982-83
8 Regular Season Games/1 started (on 09-04-83) and 1 Playoff Game (on 01-08-83)
San Diego State Aztec

SPIKES, Brandon (#55)
Born on September 3, 1987 in Shelby, NC
6'3" and 250 pounds
Linebacker   2010-13
2 interceptions for 8 yards, 1 sack and 1 fumble recovery
Sacked Mark Sanchez in their 29-26 OT win over the NY Jets on 10-21-12
Recovered the football after a blocked punt in their 41-14 rout of the Dolphins on 10-04-10
Recovered Montee Ball's fumble in their 34-31 OT win over the Broncos on 11-24-13
Had a 5 yard return of a pass by Mark Sanchez in their 45-3 rout of the NY Jets on 12-06-10
Had a 3 yard return of a pass by Andy Dalton in their 13-6 loss to the Bengals on 10-06-13
51 Regular Season Games/39 started and 6 Playoff Games/5 started
Recovered Tim Tebow's fumble and sacked Tim Tebow in their 45-10 Divisional win vs Denver on 01-14-12
Had a 19 yard return of a pass by Joe Flacco in their 23-20 Championship win over the Ravens on 01-22-12
#62 pick in the 2010 NFL Draft
Florida Gator

SPIRES, Greg (#94)
Born on August 12, 1974 in Marianna, FL
6'1" and 265 pounds
Defensive End   1998-2000
9.5 sacks and 1 fumble recovery
Shared in a sack of Damon Huard and Doug Pederson and had 1 ½ sacks of Dante Culpepper
Sacked Elvis Grbac, Doug Flutie, Steve Young, Brian Griese and Scott Mitchell and 2 sacks of Peyton Manning
Recovered a fumble by Robert Smith in their 21-13 loss to the Minnesota Vikings on 09-17-00
42 Regular Season Games/3 started and 1 Playoff Game (on 01-03-99)
Sacked Mark Brunell *twice* in their 25-10 Wild Card Playoff loss to the Jaguars on 01-03-99
#83 pick in the 1998 NFL Draft
Florida State Seminole

SPRINGS, Shawn (#29)
Born on March 11, 1975 in Williamsburg, VA
6'0" and 204 pounds
Defensive Back   2009
Had an 8 yard return of a pass by David Garrard in their 35-7 rout of the Jaguars on 12-27-09
12 Regular Season Games/8 started and 1 Playoff Game/ 1 started (on 01-10-10)
Ohio State Buckeye

ST. JEAN, Lennie (#60) *"Boston Strong Boy"*
Born on October 27, 1941 in Newberry, MI
5'11 and 250 pounds
DE/Guard (LB/T)   1964-73
5.5 sacks, 4 fumble recoveries and 1 lateral on a kickoff return
Shared in a sack of Joe Namath, sacked Mickey Slaughter, Jacky Lee and Don Trull
Recorded 2 sacks of Dick Wood
Recovered fumbles by Don Trull and Jim Plunkett and 2 fumbles by Mike Taliaferro
Received Tom Dempsey's kickoff and lateraled it to Mack Herron in their 24-23 loss to the Eagles on 11-04-73
AFL All Star Guard on 1966
140 games/86 started
9th Round Draft Pick in 1964
Northern Michigan Wildcat

STALLWORTH, Donté (#18 and #19)
Born on November 10, 1980 in Sacramento, CA
6'0" and 197 pounds
Wide Receiver   2007 and 2012
Wore #18 in 2007 and Wore #19 for 1 game (on 12-10-12)
47 receptions for 760 yards + 4 TDs and 1 carry for 12 yards
Caught 4 TD passes from Tom Brady
Ran for a 12 yard gain in their 34-17 win over the Cleveland Browns on 10-07-07
Longest reception was a 69 yard TD pass from Tom Brady in their 48-27 win over Dallas on 10-14-07
17 Regular Season Games/9 started and 3 Playoff Games
Tennessee Volunteer

STANBACK, Isaiah (#15)
Born on August 16, 1984 in Seattle, WA
6'3" and 216 pounds
WR (KR)   2009
3 receptions for 22 yards and 1 kickoff return of 22 yards
Longest reception was a 9 yard pass from Tom Brady in their 35-34 loss to the Colts on 11-15-09
Had a 22 yard return of a kickoff by Kris Brown in their 34-27 loss to the Houston Texans on 01-03-10
6 games/2 started
Washington Husky

STANLEY, Sylvester (#63) *"Buster"*
Born on May 14, 1970 in Youngstown, OH
6'2" and 286 pounds
Nose Tackle   1994
7 games
Michigan Wolverine

STANLEY, Walter (#81)
Born on November 5, 1962 in Chicago, IL
5'9" and 180 pounds
WR/KR/PR   1992
3 receptions for 63 yards, 29 kickoff returns for 529 yards and 28 punt returns for 227 yards
Longest was a 40 yard return of a kickoff by Pete Stoyanovich in their 38-17 loss to Miami on 10-18-92
Longest reception was a 36 yard pass from Hugh Millen in their 19-17 loss to Cleveland on 10-25-92
Longest was a 50 yard return of a punt by Brian Hansen in their 19-17 loss to the Browns on 10-25-92
13 games
Colorado Buffalo

STARKS, Duane (#23)
Born on May 23, 1974 in Miami, FL
5'10" and 172 pounds
Cornerback   2005
7 games/6 started
Miami Hurricane

STARRING, Stephen (#81)
Born on July 30, 1961 in Baton Rouge, LA
5'10" and 172 pounds
WR/KR/PR (QB) 1983-87
112 receptions for 1,865 yards + 11 TDs, 107 kickoff returns for 2,259 yards and 19 punt returns 108 yards
Caught 5 TD passes from Tony Eason and 6 TD passes from Steve Grogan
Recovered 2 fumbles for 8 yards and ran one play as the Patriots QB
Caught a career long 76 yard TD pass from Steve Grogan to defeat the Steelers 28-23 on 09-25-83
Advanced Tony Collins' fumble 8 yards in their 38-23 win over the Seahawks on 09-16-84
Caught a 42 yard Flea Flicker TD from Tony Eason in their 17-16 win over the Browns on 10-07-84
Longest was a 53 yard return of a kickoff by Scott Norwood in their 17-14 win over Buffalo on 09-22-85
Tossed a QB run/option pitch to Tony Collins for a 14 yard gain in their 38-31 win over the Colts on 12-01-85
Recovered Cliff Austin's fumble in their 25-17 victory over the Atlanta Falcons on 11-02-86
Longest was a 17 yard return of a punt by Rohn Stark in their 30-16 loss to the Colts on 10-25-87
5 carries for a net loss of 3 yards and his longest run was 10 yards in their 24-10 win over Miami on 12-28-87
72 Regular Season Games/23 started and 5 Playoff Games/2 started
2 receptions for 39 yards and 15 kickoff returns for 315 yards in the playoffs
#74 pick in the 1983 NFL Draft
McNeese State Cowboy

STAUROVSKY, Jason (#4)
Born on March 23, 1963 in Tulsa, OK
5'9" and 167 pounds
Kicker 1988-91
Kicked 50 field goals and 57 extra points and had an onside kick recovered by his teammate
Kicked the Patriots 1st Overtime GW FG (of 27 yards) in their 10-7 win over Tampa on 12-11-88
His onside kick was recovered by his teammate Hart Lee Dykes in their 28-24 loss to the Saints on 11-12-89
Had a career long 53 yard field goal in their 33-20 loss to the Seahawks on 10-07-90
Booted a 42 yard game winning field goal in Overtime in their 26-23 win over the Vikings on 10-20-91
40 games
Tulsa Golden Hurricane

STEINFORT, Frederick "Fred" (#5) *"Suitcase"*
Born on November 3, 1952 in Wetter, Germany
5'11" and 180 pounds
Kicker 1983
Nicknamed *"Suitcase"* because he was always packing his suitcase to play for another team
Kicked 6 field goals and 16 extra points
Longest field goal was 35 yards in their 37-21 victory over San Diego on 10-16-83
9 games
Boston College Eagle

STENGER, Brian (#59)
Born on January 16, 1947 in Euclid, OH
6'4" and 241 pounds
Linebacker 1973
2 fumble recoveries
Recovered Ike Hill's fumbled punt return in their 13-10 victory over the Chicago Bears on 10-21-73
Recovered Kermit Alexander's fumble in their 24-23 loss to the Eagles on 11-04-73
10 games/2 started
Notre Dame Fighting Irish

STEPHENS, Calvin (#68)
Born on October 25, 1967 in Kings Mountain, NC
6'2" and 285 pounds
Guard   1992
13 games/1 started (on 12-27-92)
#56 pick in the 1991 NFL Draft
South Carolina Gamecock

STEPHENS, John (#44)
Born on February 23, 1966 in Shreveport, LA
6'1" and 220 pounds
Running Back   1988-92
891 carries for 3,249 yards + 17 TDs, 100 receptions for 781 yards + 1 TD
2 fumble recoveries for 4 yards + 1 TD and recovered a fumbled lateral by Eric Sievers
Advanced Doug Flutie's fumble 4 yards in their 45-3 loss to the Packers on 10-09-88
Fell on Robert Perryman's fumble in the endzone for a TD in their 27-21 win over Cincinnati on 10-16-88
Longest run was 52 yards in their 21-10 loss to the Denver Broncos on 12-17-88
Ran for a 10 yard game winning TD in their 22-16 victory over the Colts on 12-03-89
Recovered a fumbled lateral by Eric Sievers on the last play in their 17-10 loss to Miami on 10-18-90
Caught an 18 yard TD pass from Tommy Hodson in their 34-14 loss to Phoenix on 11-25-90
Longest reception was a 43 yard pass from Tommy Hodson in their 25-10 loss to Washington on 12-15-90
AFC Pro Bowl Running Back in 1988
NFL Offensive Rookie of the Year in 1988
76 games/59 started
#17 pick in the 1988 NFL Draft
Northwestern Louisiana State Demon

STEPHENS, Tom (#45)
Born on August 29, 1935 in Galveston TX
6'2" and 215 pounds
TE/DB/PR (KR)   1960-64
41 receptions for 506 yards + 5 TDs, 19 punt returns for 151 yards and 5 kickoff returns for 57 yards
3 fumble recoveries for 16 yards + 1 TD, 1 interception for 22 yards and 1 recovery of an onside kick
Caught 2 Half Back Option TD passes from Dick Christy and 3 TD passes from Butch Songin
Recovered fumbles by Jim Colcough and Paul Lowe
Longest reception was a 53 yard pass from Butch Songin in their 38-14 loss to the Buffalo Bills on 12-04-60
Had a 10 yard TD return of Paul Lowe's fumbled punt return in their 38-27 loss to San Diego on 10-07-61
Recovered Jim Colclough's fumble in their 20-17 victory over the Oakland Raiders on 11-17-61
Longest was a 31 yard return of a kickoff by Ben Agajanian in their 20-0 loss to the Raiders on 12-16-62
Had a 22 yard return of a pass by Dick Wood in their 38-14 win over the NY Jets on 09-08-63
Longest was a 26 yard return of a punt by Jim Norton in their 45-3 rout of the Houston Oilers on 11-01-63
Recovered George Blair's onside kick in their 33-28 win over the San Diego Chargers on 09-20-64
49 games/14 started
Syracuse Orangeman

STEVENS, Matt (#26)
Born on June 14, 1973 in Chapel Hill, NC
6'0" and 205 pounds
Defensive Back   2000-01
2 fumble recoveries for 9 yards
Had a 9 yard return of a fumble by Brian Griese in their 31-20 loss to Denver on 10-28-01
Recovered Tedy Bruschi's interception return fumble in their 31-20 loss to Denver on 10-28-01
16 Regular Season Games/4 started and 3 Playoff Games
Member of the 2001 World Championship Team
Appalachian State Mountaineer

STIDHAM, Jarret (#4)
Born on August 8, 1996 in Corbin, KY
6'3" and 215 pounds
QB   2019--
2 completions for 14 yards and knelt twice for minus 2 yards
Longest pass completion for 11 yards to Phillip Dorsett in their 30-14 win over the Jets on 09-22-19
3 games
#133 Pick in the 2019 NFL Draft
Auburn Tiger

STINGLEY, Darryl (#84) *"The Stinger"*
Born on September 18, 1951 in Chicago, IL
6'0" and 194 pounds
WR/PR (KR)   1973-77
110 receptions for 1,883 yards + 14 TDs and 28 carries for 244 yards + 2 TDs
19 punt returns for 136 yards and 8 kickoff returns for 187 yards and 1 fumble advancement of 14 yards
Caught 5 TD passes from Jim Plunkett and 9 TD passes from Steve Grogan
Longest was a 29 yard return of a kickoff by Chester Marcoll in their 33-24 win over Green Bay on 11-18-73
Ran for a 23 yard TD in their 42-3 rout of the Baltimore Colts on 10-06-74
Advanced Sam Cunningham's fumble 14 yards in their 22-14 loss to Miami on 09-28-75
Handed off to Andy Johnson on a reverse punt return in their 24-17 loss to St. Louis on 11-02-75
Longest was a 29 yard return of a punt by Mitch Hoopes in their 34-31 loss to Dallas on 11-16-75
Longest run was a 34 yard TD, on his 26th birthday, in their 21-17 win over the Chiefs on 09-18-77
Longest reception was a 68 yard pass from Steve Grogan in their 17-3 win over the Baltimore Colts on 10-23-77
60 Regular Season Games/53 started and 1 Playoff Game/1 started
#19 pick in the 1973 NFL Draft
Purdue Boilermaker

STOKES, Eric (#78)
Born on January 13, 1962 in Derby, CT
6'4" and 255 pounds
Guard   1987
Started and played in one game on 10-04-87
Northeastern University Husky

STOKES, Jerel "JJ" (#85)
Born on October 6, 1972 in San Diego, CA
6'4" and 218 pounds
Wide Receiver   2003
2 receptions for 38 yards
Longest reception was a 31 yard pass from Tom Brady in their 23-20 OT win vs Houston on 11-23-03
2 games (on Nov. 23rd and Nov. 30th)
Member of the 2003 World Championship Team
UCLA Bruin

STONE, Michael (#24)
Born on February 13, 1978 in Southfield, MI
6'0" and 201 pounds
Safety/Special Team   2005
Recovered a short kickoff by Michael Koenen in their 31-28 win over the Falcons on 10-09-05
13 Regular Season Games/3 started and 2 Playoff Games
Memphis Tiger

STORK, Bryan (#66)
Born on November 15, 1990 in Vero Beach, FL
6'4" and 315 pounds
Offensive Lineman   2014-15
Recovered a fumble by Tom Brady in their 27-26 win over the New York Giants on 11-15-15
21 Regular Season Games/17 started and 4 Playoff Games/4 started
Member of the 2014 World Championship Team
#105 pick in the 2014 NFL Draft
Florida State Seminole

STRIEGEL, Bill (#72)
Born on May 28, 1936 in Easton, KS
6'2" and 235 pounds
Offensive Lineman   1960
5 games
Pacific Tiger

STUCKEY, Shawn (#93)
Born on October 22, 1975 in Daleville, AL
6'0" and 230 pounds
Linebacker   1998
Recovered Lonnie Johnson's fumble in their 13-10 loss to the Buffalo Bills on 11-15-98
6 Regular Season Games/1 Playoff Game (on 01-03-99)
Troy State Trojan

STUDSTILL, Pat (#2)
Born on June 4, 1938 in Shreveport, LA
6'0" and 180 pounds
Punter   1972
75 punts for 2,859 yards and 1 carry for 11 yards
Longest punt was 57 yards in their 21-20 win over the Atlanta Falcons on 09-24-72
Advanced a bad snap 11 yards, on 4th & 3, in their 27-24 loss to the Buffalo Bills on 11-19-72
14 games
Houston Cougar

STURT, Fred (#63)
Born on January 6, 1951 in Toledo, OH
6'4" and 255 pounds
Guard   1976-78
29 Regular Season Games and 1 Playoff Game (on 12-18-76)
Bowling Green State Falcon

SUCI, Bob (#21)
Born on April 7, 1939 in Flint, MI
5'10" and 185 pounds
DB/PR/KR   1963
7 interceptions for 277 yards + 2 TDs and 2 fumble recovies for 5 yards
25 punt returns for 233 yards and 17 kickoff returns for 360 yards (including 2 lateraled kickoff returns)
Intercepted Johnny Green, Don Breaux and Tobin Rote
Had 2 interceptions of Jacky Lee and George Blanda
Longest was a 35 yard return of a kickoff by Dick Guesman in their 38-14 rout of the Jets on 09-08-63
Recovered Dave Watson's fumbled kickoff return in their 14-10 loss to Denver on 09-29-63
Longest was a 22 yard return of a punt by Jim Fraser in their 40-21 win over Denver on 10-18-63
Had a 5 yard return of a blocked field goal in their 28-21 loss to Buffalo on 10-26-63
Had a career long 98 yard TD return of a pass by George Blanda in their 45-3 rout of the Oilers on 11-01-63
Had a 52 yard TD return of a pass by Jacky Lee in their 46-28 win over the Oilers on 12-08-63
Advanced a lateral from Bob Yates 21 yards, on a free kick return, in their 46-28 win over Houston on 12-08-63
Advanced Bob Yates kickoff return lateral 22 yards in their 35-3 loss to the Kansas City Chiefs on 12-14-63
14 Regular Season Games/14 started and 2 Playoff Games/2 started
Michigan State Spartan

SUDFELD, Zachary "Zach" (#44)
Born on April 18, 1989 in Santa Cruz, CA
6'7" and 253 pounds
Tight End   2013
3 games
Nevada Runnin' Rebel

SULLIVAN, Chris (#74) *"Sully"*
Born on March 14, 1973 in North Attleboro, MA
6'4" and 279 pounds
DL (KR)   1996-99
3 sacks, 3 kickoff returns for 15 yards and 1 fumble recovery
Sacked Danny Wuerffel, Vinny Testaverde and Peyton Manning
Recovered Dave Meggett's fumbled punt return in their 27-9 win over the Colts on 10-20-96
Longest was a 9 yard return of a kickoff by Steve Christie in their 25-21 win over Buffalo on 11-29-98
63 Regular Season Games/20 started and 6 Playoff Games/2 started
#119 pick in the 1996 NFL Draft
Boston College Eagle

SVITEK, Will (#74)
Born on January 8, 1982 in Prague, Czech Republic
6'6" and 305 pounds
Tackle   2013
13 Regular Season Games/2 started and 2 Playoff Games
Stanford Cardinal

SWANSON, Terry (#36)
Born on January 8, 1944 in Cambridge, MA
6'0" and 210 pounds
Punter   1967-68
127 punts for 5,081 yards
Longest punt was 62 yards in their 23-0 shutout of the Buffalo Bills on 09-24-67
24 games
UMASS Minuteman

SWEET, Joe (#81)
Born on July 5, 1948 in Lakeland, FL
6'2" and 196 pounds
Wide Receiver   1974
4 games
Tennessee State Tiger

SYKES, Alfreddie "Al" (#13) *"The Wisp"*
Born on December 20, 1947 in Tallahassee, FL
6'2" and 170 pounds
Wide Receiver   1971
1 fumble recovery and 1 reception of 15 yards
Recovered Bob Gladieux's fumbled punt return in their 20-0 shutout of the Jets on 10-10-71
Caught a 15 yard pass from Jim Plunkett in their 44-21 loss to the Cowboys on 10-24-71
4 games/1 started (on 09-19-71)
#339 pick in the 1971 NFL Draft
Florida A & M Rattler

TALIAFERRO, Myron "Mike" (#17)
Born on July 26, 1941 in Houston, TX
6'2" and 202 pounds
Quarterback   1968-71
305 completions for 3,920 yards + 27 TDs and 23 carries for 46 yards
Threw 1 TD pass to Aaron Marsh and Gayle Knief and 2 TD passes to Carl Garrett
Tosssed 3 TD passes to Bill Rademacher and 4 TD passes to Jim Whalen
Completed 7 TD passes to Charley Frazier and 9 TD passes to Ron Sellers
Tossed a career long 70 yard TD pass to Aaron Marsh in their 47-31 loss to the Jets on 09-22-68
Longest run was 21 yards in their 23-6 win over the Buffalo Bills on 10-20-68
Holder for Gino Cappelletti
AFL All Star Quarterback in 1969
32 games/25 started
Illinois Fighting Illini

TALIB, Aqib (#31)
Born on February 13, 1986 in Cleveland, OH
6'1" and 205 pounds
Cornerback   2012-13
5 interceptions for 71 yards + 1 TD and 2 fumble recoveries for 5 yards
Intercepted Andrew Luck, Josh Freeman, Matt Ryan and had 2 interceptions of Geno Smith
Had a career long 59 yard TD return of a pass by Andrew Luck in their 59-24 rout of the Colts on 11-18-12
Had a 5 yard return of a fumble by Delanie Walker in their 41-34 loss to the 49ers on 12-16-12
Recovered Julian Edelman's fumbled punt return lateral in their 30-27 win over the Saints on 10-13-13
AFC Pro Bowl Cornerback in 2013
19 Regular Season Games/18 started and 4 Playoff Games/4 started
Kansas Jayhawk

TANNER, John (#53) *"Craze"*
Born on March 8, 1945 in Orlando, FL
6'4" and 241 pounds
LB/TE/DE (KR)   1973-74
Shared in a sack, had 2 receptions for 23 yards + 1 TD and 2 kickoff returns for 17 yards
Shared in a sack of Bert Jones in their 24-16 win over the Baltimore Colts on 10-07-73
Longest reception was a 21 yard pass from Jim Plunkett in their 29-28 loss to Buffalo on 11-03-74
Caught a 2 yard TD pass from Jim Plunkett in their 27-17 win over Baltimore on 11-24-74
Had a 17 yard return of a kickoff by Garo Yepremian in their 34-17 loss to the Miami on 12-15-74
Recovered Garo Yepremian's squibbed kickoff in their 34-17 loss to the Dolphins on 12-15-74
27 games/2 started
Tennessee Tech Golden Eagle

TARDITS, Richard (#53)
Born on July 30, 1965 in Biarritz, France
6'2" and 228 pounds
LB/Special Team   1990-92
Recovered Harry Newsome's punt that deflected off Tony Zackery in their 26-23 OT win vs Minn on 10-20-91
27 games/1 started (on 09-16-90)
Georgia Bulldog

TARPINIAN, Jeff (#53)
Born on October 16, 1987 in Omaha, NE
6'3" and 238 pounds
Linebacker   2011-12
10 games/1 started (on 11-13-11)
Iowa Hawkeye

TARVER, John (#36)
Born on January 1, 1949 in Bakersfield, CA
6'3" and 227 pounds
RB (KR)   1972-74
155 carries for 554 yards + 7 TDs, 29 receptions for 200 yards + 1 TD and 1 kickoff return of 17 yards
Longest reception was a 22 yard pass from Jim Plunkett in their 31-0 loss to the Baltimore Colts on 11-26-72
Caught an 8 yard TD pass from Brian Dowling 37-21 loss to the Miami Dolphins on 12-03-72
Had a 17 yard return of a kickoff by John Leypoldt in their 31-13 loss to the Buffalo Bills on 09-16-73
Longest run was 28 yards in their 9-7 loss to the New York Jets on 10-14-73
31 games/15 started
#186 pick in the 1972 NFL Draft
Colorado Buffalo

TATE, Brandon (#19)
Born on October 5, 1987 in Burlington, NC
6'1" and 195 pounds
WR/KR (PR)   2009-10
24 receptions for 432 yards + 3 TDs and 6 carries for 73 yards
45 kickoff returns for 1,161 yards + 2 TDs and 1 punt return of 4 yards
Caught 3 TD passes from Tom Brady
Had a 4 yard return of a punt by Kevin Huber in their 38-24 win over the Bengals on 09-12-10
Returned Mike Nugent's 2nd half kickoff 97 yards for a TD in their 38-24 win over the Bengals on 09-12-10
Returned Dan Carpenter's 2nd half kickoff 103 yards for a TD in their 41-14 rout of the Dolphins on 10-04-10
Longest run was 22 yards in their 23-20 OT win vs the Ravens on 10-17-10
Had a career long 65 yard TD reception of a pass by Tom Brady in their 28-18 win vs the Vikings on 10-31-10
18 Regular Season Games/11 started and 1 Playoff Game/1 started
5 kickoff returns for 108 yards in their 28-21 Divisional Playoff Game loss to the Jets on 01-16-11
North Carolina Tar Heel

TATUPU, Mosiula "Mosi" (#30)
Born on April 26, 1955 in Pago Pago, American Samoa
6'0" and 227 pounds
RB/ST (KR)   1978-90
His Fan Club was known as "Mosi's Mooses"
612 carries for 2,415 yards + 18 TDs and 96 receptions for 843 yards + 2 TDs
2 completions for 30 yards + 1 TD and 7 kickoff returns for 56 yards
Recovered 3 fumbles, returned a blocked punt 17 yards for a TD and recovered 3 onside kicks
Longest was a 17 yard return of the opening kickoff by George Roberts in their 23-3 loss to Miami on 12-18-78
Recovered an onside kick by Patriots Kicker Mike Hubach in their 38-34 loss to Houston on 11-10-80
Caught an 8 yard HB Option TD pass from Andy Johnson in their 29-28 loss to the Colts on 09-06-81
Longest reception was a 41 yard pass from Matt Cavanaugh in their 33-17 win over the Chiefs on 10-04-81
Recovered Kurt Sohn's fumbled punt return in their 28-24 loss to the New York Jets on 10-11-81
Recovered a fumble by George Wonsley in their 24-22 loss to the Redskins on 10-25-81
Recovered Bob Glazebrook's fumbled onside kick return in 24-13 loss to Atlanta on 10-30-83
Snared a 12 yard TD pass from Steve Grogan in their 24-13 loss to the Falcons on 10-30-83
Longest run was 55 yards in their 17-6 win over the Dolphins on 11-13-83
Recovered an onside kick by Al DelGreco in their 26-20 win over the Green Bay Packers on 09-08-85
Returned a blocked punt 17 yards for a TD in their 21-20 win over the Saints on 11-30-86
Threw a 15 yard TD pass, on 4th down, to Tony Collins in their 26-23 win over the LA Raiders on 11-01-87
Completed a 15 yard pass to John Stephens in their 24-21 loss to the Los Angeles Raiders on 11-26-89
AFC Pro Bowl Special Team Player in 1986
194 Regular Season Games/22 started and 7 Playoff Games
11 carries for 30 yards + 1 TD in the playoffs
Ran for a 1 yard TD in their 31-14 AFC Championship Game win over Miami on 01-12-86
Caught a 6 yard pass from Tony Eason in their 31-14 AFC Championship Game win over Miami on 01-12-86
Lateraled it back on a 45 yard Flea Flicker TD pass in their 22-17 Divisional loss on 01-04-87
#215 pick in the 1978 NFL Draft
USC Trojan

TAYLOR, Frederick "Fred" (#21)
Born on January 27, 1976 in Pahokee, FL
6'1" and 228 pounds
Running Back   2009-10
106 carries for 424 yards + 4 TDs and 4 receptions for 23 yards
Longest reception was a 13 yard pass from Tom Brady in their 27-21 win over Baltimore on 10-04-09
Longest run was 24 yards in their 38-24 victory over the Bengals on 09-12-10
13 Regular Season Games/1 started (on 09-14-09) and 1 Playoff Game
2 carries for 1 yard in their 33-14 Wild Card loss to the Baltimore Ravens on 01-10-10
Florida Gator

TAYLOR, Gene (#82)
Born on November 12, 1962 in Oakland, CA
6'2" and 189 pounds
Wide Receiver   1991
Only game played was on 11-17-91
#163 pick in the 1987 NFL Draft
Fresno State Bulldog

TAYLOR, Gregory "Greg" (#45)
Born on October 23, 1958 in Richmond, VA
5'8" and 175 pounds
Kickoff Returnman   1982
2 kickoff returns for 46 yards
Longest was a 27 yard return of a kickoff by Mike Wood in their 24-13 win over Baltimore on 09-12-82
Only game played was on 09-12-82
#308 pick in the 1982 NFL Draft
Virginia Cavalier

TAYLOR, Kitrick (#49)
Born on July 22, 1964 in Los Angeles, CA
5'11" and 194 pounds
Kickoff Returnman   1989
3 kickoff returns for 52 yards
Longest was a 22 yard return of a kickoff by Scott Norwood in their 33-29 win over Buffalo on 11-19-89
4 games
Washington State Cougar

TESTAVERDE, Vincent "Vinny" (#14)
Born on November 13, 1963 in New York, NY
6'5" and 235 pounds
Quarterback   2006
2 completions for 29 yards + 1 TD and knelt 8 times for minus 8 yards
Longest completion was a 23 yard pass to Chad Jackson in their 40-23 win over Tennessee on 12-31-06
Tossed a 6 yard TD pass to Troy Brown in their 40-23 victory over Tennessee on 12-31-06
(Set NFL Record for the oldest combined ages of the QB and Receiver on a TD pass on 12-31-06)
3 games
Miami Hurricane

THOMAS, Adalius (#96)
Born on August 18, 1977 in Equality, AL
6'2" and 270 pounds
Linebacker   2007-09
14.5 sacks and 1 interception return of 65 yards for a TD
Shared in a sack of Carson Palmer and had 1 ½ sacks of Chad Pennington
Sacked Ben Roethlisberger, Eli Manning, Brodie Coyle, Brett Favre, J.T. O'Sullivan and Trent Edwards
Sacked Chad Henne and Drew Brees and had 2 sacks of Marc Bulger and 2 ½ sacks of J.P. Losman
Had a 65 yard TD return of a pass by Philip Rivers in their 38-14 rout of the Chargers on 09-16-07
Strip sacked Chad Pennington in their 20-10 victory of the NY Jets on 12-16-07
39 Regular Season Games/35 started and 4 Playoff Games/4 started
Had 2 sacks of Eli Manning in their 17-14 Super Bowl loss to the Giants on 02-03-08
Southern Mississippi Golden Eagle

THOMAS JR., Benjamin "Ben" (#99)
Born on July 2, 1961 in Ashburn, GA
6'4" and 280 pounds
Defensive Lineman　　　　1985-86
Sacked John Elway in their 27-20 loss to the Denver Broncos on 09-28-86
19 Regular Season Games/1 started (on 09-07-86) and 4 Playoff Games
Sacked Steve Fuller in their 46-10 Super Bowl loss to Da' Bears on 01-26-86
#56 pick in the 1985 NFL Draft
Auburn Tiger

THOMAS, Blair (#32)
Born on October 7, 1967 in Philadelphia, PA
5'10" and 198 pounds
Running Back　　　　1994
19 carries for 67 yards + 1 TD, 2 receptions for 15 yards and 3 kickoff returns for 40 yards
Longest run was 13 yards in their 24-17 loss to the NY Jets on 10-16-94
Ran for a 4 yard touchdown in their 24-17 loss to the NY Jets on 10-16-94
Longest reception was a 9 yard pass from Drew Bledsoe in their 24-17 loss to the Jets on 10-16-94
Longest was a 16 yard return of Nick Lowery's 2nd half kickoff in their 24-17 loss to the Jets on 10-16-94
4 games
Penn State Nittany Lion

THOMAS, Donald (#64)
Born on September 25, 1985 in West Haven, CT
6'3" and 295 pounds
Guard　　　　2011-12
26 Regular Season Games/8 started and 2 Playoff Games
UCONN Husky

THOMAS, Donnie (#51)
Born on March 12, 1953 in Michigan City, IN
6'2" and 245 pounds
Linebacker　　　　1976
3 Regular Season Games/1 started (on 12-12-76) and 1 Playoff Game (on 12-18-76)
#298 pick in the 1976 NFL Draft
Indiana Fighting Hoosier

THOMAS, Eugene "Gene" (#22)
Born on September 1, 1942 in Barberton, OH
6'1" and 210 pounds
RB (KR)　　　　1968
88 carries for 215 yards + 2 TDs and 10 receptions for 85 yards
Had a 22 yard return of a kickoff by Jim Turner in their 47-31 loss to the Jets on 09-22-68
Longest reception was a 32 yard pass from Mike Taliaferro in their 20-17 win over Denver on 09-29-68
Longest run was 25 yards in their 23-6 win over the Buffalo Bills on 10-20-68
9 games/5 started
Florida A & M Rattler

THOMAS JR., Henry (#95)
Born on January 12, 1965 in Houston, TX
6'2" and 277 pounds
DT (TE/FB)   1997-2000
21 sacks, 2 interceptions for 40 yards + 1 TD and 3 fumble recoveries
Shared in a sack of Dante Culpepper and Rob Johnson and had 1 ½ sacks of Steve McNair
Had 2 sacks of Rick Mirer, Jim Harbaugh and Steve Bono and 2 ½ sacks of Vinny Testaverde
Sacked Stan Humphries, John Elway, Todd Collins, Dan Marino and Steve Young
Sacked Dave Brown and Doug Flutie and had 3 sacks of Tony Banks
Recovered fumbles by Stan Humphries, Donnell Bennett and Edgerrin James
Intercepted Danny Wuerffel and Jay Fiedler and forced Neil O'Donnell to ground the ball for a safety
Recovered his strip sack of Stan Humphries in their 41-7 rout of the San Diego Chargers on 08-31-97
Forced Neil O'Donnell to ground the ball for a safety in their 24-19 loss to the Jets on 10-19-97
Had a career long 24 yard TD return of a pass by Danny Wuerffel in their 30-27 win over the Saints on 10-04-98
Had a 16 yard return of a pass by Jay Fiedler in their 10-3 loss to the Miami Dolphins on 09-24-00
Used as a Tight End and as a Fullback in their 13-10 OT win vs the Buffalo Bills on 12-17-00
64 Regular Season Games/52 started and 3 Playoff Games/3 started
LSU Fighting Tiger

THOMAS, John "David" (#86)
Born on July 5, 1983 in Plainview, TX
6'3" and 248 pounds
Tight End   2006-08
21 receptions for 261 yards + 1 TD
Dove and caught a 22 yard TD pass from Tom Brady in their 24-21 win over Jacksonville on 12-24-06
Longest reception was a 36 yard pass from Tom Brady in their 24-21 win over the Jaguars on 12-24-06
32 Regular Season Games/13 started and 3 Playoff Games/1 started (on 01-14-07)
Recovered Eric Parker's fumbled punt return in their 24-21 Divisional Playoff win over San Diego on 01-14-07
#86 pick in the 2006 NFL Draft
Texas Longhorn

THOMAS, Santonio (#92)
Born on July 2, 1981 in South Bay, FL
6'4" and 305 pounds
Defensive Lineman   2007
4 games
Miami Hurricane

THOMPKINS, Kenbrell (#85)
Born on July 29, 1988 in Liberty City, FL
6'0" and 196 pounds
Wide Receiver   2013-14
38 receptions for 519 yards + 4 TDs
Caught 4 TD passes from Tom Brady
Longest reception was a 49 yard pass from Tom Brady in their 30-23 victory over the Falcons on 09-29-13
Caught a 17 yard Game Winning TD pass from Tom Brady to beat the Saints 30-27 at Gillette on 10-13-13
14 Regular Season Games/9 started and 1 Playoff Game (on 01-11-14)
Cincinnati Bearcat

THOMPSON, Reyna (#21)
Born on August 28, 1963 in Dallas, TX
6'0" and 194 pounds
Defensive Back   1993
Had a 4 yard return of a pass by Jim Kelly in their 38-14 loss to the Buffalo Bills on 09-05-93
15 games
Baylor Bear

THOMPSON, Ulys "Leroy" (#36)
Born on February 3, 1968 in Knoxville, TN
5'11" and 216 pounds
RB/KR   1994
102 carries for 312 yards + 2 TDs, 65 receptions for 465 yards + 5 TDs and 18 kickoff returns for 376 yards
Caught 5 Regular Season and 1 Post Season TD pass from Drew Bledsoe
Recovered Drew Bledsoe's fumble in their 39-35 loss to the Miami Dolphins on 09-04-94
Longest reception was a 27 yard TD pass from Drew Bledsoe in their 23-17 win over San Diego on 11-20-94
Had a career long run of 13 yards on 10-02-94, on 11-13-94 and on 12-04-94
Longest was a 30 yard return of a kickoff by Nick Lowery in their 24-13 win over the Jets on 12-04-94
16 Regular Season Games and 1 Playoff Game
Caught a 13 yard TD pass from Drew Bledsoe in their 2013 Wild Card loss to Cleveland on 01-01-95
Penn State Nittany Lion

THUNEY, Joe (#62)
Born on November 19, 1992 in Centerville, OH
6'5" and 308 pounds
Offensive Guard   2016-19
64 Regular Season Games/64 started and 10 Playoff Games/10 started
Recovered a fumble by Dion Lewis in their 34-16 Divisional win over the Texans on 01-14-17
Member of the 2016 and 2018 World Championship Teams
#78 pick in the 2016 NFL Draft
North Carolina State Wolfpack

TIMPSON, Michael (#45 and #83)
Born on June 6, 1967 in Baxley, GA
5'10" and 178 pounds
WR/KR (PR)   1989-94
Wore #45 from 1989-90 and #83 from 1991-94
172 receptions for 2,472 yards + 8 TDs and 3 carries for 10 yards
10 kickoff returns for 168 yards and 8 punt returns for 47 yards
Caught 1 TD pass from Tommy Hodson, 2 TDs from Hugh Millen and 5 TD passes from Drew Bledsoe
Cradled a 45 yard TD from Hugh Millen to beat the Colts 23-17 in OT at Foxboro Stadium on 12-08-91
Caught a career long 60 yard TD pass from Hugh Millen in their 29-7 loss to the Bengals on 12-22-91
Longest was a 14 yard return of a punt by Don Bracken in their 14-0 loss to the LA Rams on 09-13-92
Had a career long 28 yard return of a kickoff by Lee Johnson in their 20-10 loss to the Bengals on 12-20-92
Caught a 36 yard TD pass from Drew Bledsoe to beat the Miami Dolphins 33-27 in OT at Foxboro on 01-02-94
Had another 28 yard return of a kickoff by Steve Christie in their 38-35 loss to Buffalo on 09-11-94
Longest run was 10 yards in their 13-3 victory over the Chicago Bears on 12-24-94
70 Regular Season Games/25 started and 1 Playoff Game/1 started (on 01-01-95)
#100 pick in the 1989 NFL Draft
Penn State Nittany Lion

TIPPETT, Andre (#56) *"Tip"*
Born on December 27, 1959 in Birmingham, AL
6'3" and 240 pounds
Linebacker (DE)   1982-93
100 sacks, 17 fumble recoveries for 75 yards + 2 TDs, 1 interception for 10 yards and 1 blocked FGA
Shared in a sack of Steve DeBerg and Jeff Hosterler and had 1 ½ sacks of Scott Mitchell
Sacked Richard Todd, Cliff Stoudt, Joe Montana, Brian Sipe, Vince Ferragamo, Jeff Kemp and Paul McDonald
Sacked Neil Lomax, Jack Trudeau, Jeff Rutledge, Chris Chandler, Steve Young and Mike Tomczak
Sacked Browning Nagle and Boomer Esiason and had 2 sacks of Pat Ryan, Joe Pisarcik and Bubby Brister
Had 2 sacks of Tommy Kramer, Randall Cunningham, Rick Mirer and Steve Beuerlein
Had 2 ½ sacks of Mike Pagel and Bernie Kosar
Recorded 3 sacks of Lynn Dickey, Matt Kofler, Brent Pease and John Elway
Had 4 sacks of Art Schlichter and Gary Hogenboom
Recorded 4 ½ sacks of Joe Ferguson, Dan Marino, Jeff George and Danny White
Had 8 sacks of Dave Krieg and 8 ½ sacks of Ken O'Brien and Jim Kelly
Recovered fumbles by Theotis Brown, Eric Dickerson, Trey Dunkin, Greg Bell and Bubby Brister
Recovered fumbles by Mickey Shuler, Roger Vick, Jeff Dellenbach, Walter Reeves and Tony Martin
Recovered fumbles by James Lofton, Stan Gelbaugh, Jim Kelly, Thurman Thomas and Roosevelt Potts
Recovered 2 fumbles by Earnest Byner
Stole the ball from Eric Dickerson in their 21-7 win over the Los Angeles Rams on 12-11-83
Returned Trey Junkin's bad snap to Ray Guy 25 yards for a TD in their 35-20 loss to the Raiders on 09-29-85
Advanced Johnny Rembert's lateral 32 yards in their 23-3 rout of the Buffalo Bills on 10-26-86
Returned Roger Vick's fumble 29 yards for a TD in their 43-24 loss to the Jets on 09-21-87
Blocked a 48 yard field goal attempt by Tony Zendejas in their 21-7 win over Houston on 10-18-87
Had a 10 yard return of a pass by Jeff George in their 16-7 victory over the Colts on 09-01-91
Had a 14 yard return of a fumble by Roosevelt Potts in their 38-0 shutout of the Colts on 12-26-93
AFC Defensive Player of the Week in their 20-13 win over the Jets on 10-20-85
AFC Defensive Player of the Week in their 21-7 win over the Oilers on 10-18-87
AFC Pro Bowl Linebacker in 1984, 1985, 1986, 1987, 1988
First Team All Pro Linebacker in 1985, 1987
AFC Defensive Player of the Year in 1985
151 Regular Season Games/139 started and 6 Playoff Games/5 started
Tipped a Pat Ryan pass that was intercepted by Garin Veris in their 26-14 Wild Card win over the Jets on 12-28-85
Sacked Ken O'Brien in their 26-14 Wild Card victory over the NY Jets at the Meadowlands on 12-28-85
#41 pick in the 1982 NFL Draft
Inducted into the Patriots Hall of Fame on 11-15-99
Inducted into the Pro Football Hall of Fame on 08-02-08
Iowa Hawkeye

TIPTON, David "Dave" (#60)
Born on December 10, 1953 in Superior, WI
6'1" and 255 pounds
Nose Tackle   1975-76
2 sacks and 1 fumble recovery for 5 yards
Sacked Joe Namath and Steve Spurrier
Had a 5 yard return of a fumble by Gary Marangi in their 20-10 win over the Bills on 11-07-76
12 Regular Season Games and 1 Playoff Game (on 12-18-76)
Member of the 1983 United State Football League Michigan Panthers Championship Team
Western Illinois Leatherneck

TOLER, Kenneth "Ken" (#82)
Born on April 9, 1959 in Greenville, MS
6'2" and 195 pounds
WR/KR   1981-82
7 receptions for 133 yards + 2 TDs, 1 carry for 4 yards and 9 kickoff returns for 148 yards
Longest was a 32 yard return of a kickoff by Uwe von Schamann in their 30-27 OT loss to Miami on 11-08-81
Recovered a fumble by Tony Collins in their 19-10 loss to the Buffalo Bills on 12-13-81
Caught a 30 yard TD from Matt Cavanaugh in their 24-13 win over the Colts on 09-12-82
Ran for a 4 yard gain in their 10-7 loss to the Cleveland Browns on 11-21-82
Grabbed a 33 yard TD pass from Steve Grogan in their 30-19 win over the Bills on 01-02-83
25 Regular Season Games and 1 Playoff Game
#185 pick in the 1981 NFL Draft
Mississippi Rebel

TOMLINSON, Eric (#82)
Born on April 22, 1992 in Oklahoma City, OK
6'6" and 263 pounds
Tight End   2019
1 reception for 1 yard from Tom Brady on 10-21-19
2 games/2 started
Texas El Paso Miner

TONER, Edward (#75)
Born on September 11, 1944 in Reading, MA
6'2" and 250 pounds
DT/DE   1967-69
Sacked Dewey Warren in their 33-14 win over the Cincinnati Bengals on 12-01-68
26 games
3rd Round Draft Pick in 1966
University of Massachusetts Minuteman

TOWNS, Robert "Bobby" (#34) *"Paper"*
Born on March 17, 1938 in Elberton, GA
6'1' and 180 pounds
Defensive Back   1961
2 games (on Oct. 1st and Oct. 7th)
Georgia Bulldog

TRAYLOR, Byron "Keith" (#98)
Born on September 3, 1969 in Little Rock, AR
6'2" and 337 pounds
NT/DT   2004
16 Regular Season Games/10 started and 3 Playoff Games/2 started
Member of the 2004 World Championship Team
Central State Maurader

TRULL, Donald "Don" (#10)
Born on October 20, 1941 in Oklahoma City, OK
6'1" and 195 pounds
Quarterback   1967
27 completions for 442 yards + 1 TD and 19 carries for 35 yards + 3 TDs
Tossed a 40 yard touchdown pass to Jim Whalen in their 29-24 loss to the Jets on 11-19-67
Longest run was 10 yards in their 29-24 loss to the New York Jets on 11-19-67
Longest completion was a 52 yard pass to Jim Colclough in their 41-32 loss to Miami on 12-17-67
7 games/3 started
Baylor Bear

TUCKER, Erroll (#21)
Born on July 6, 1964 in Pittsburgh, PA
5'8" and 169 pounds
KR/PR   1989
13 kickoff returns for 270 yards and 13 punt returns for 102 yards
Longest was a 25 yard return of a punt by John Kidd in their 33-24 win over Buffalo on 11-19-89
Longest was 37 yard return of a kickoff by Jeff Jaeger in their 24-21 loss to the LA Raiders on 11-26-89
5 games
Utah Ute

TUCKER, Ross (#69)
Born on March 2, 1979 in Wyomissing, PA
6'4" and 316 pounds
Offensive Lineman   2005
Only Regular Season Game was on 01-01-06 and only Playoff Game was on 01-14-06
Princeton Tiger

TUITELE, Maugaula (#96 and #47 and #59)
Born on May 26, 1978 in Torrance, CA
6'2" and 255 pounds
Special Team   2000-02
Wore #96 on 11-23-00, Wore #47 on 12-02-01 and wore #59 for 3 games in 2002
5 games
Member of the 2001 World Championship Team
Colorado State Ram

TUPA JR., Thomas "Tom" (#19)
Born on February 6, 1966 in Cleveland, OH
6'4" and 225 pounds
Punter (QB)   1996-98
215 punts for 9,602 yards
Longest punt was 73 yards in their 34-13 loss to the Broncos on 10-06-97
AFC Special Team Player of the Week in their 28-25 win over Buffalo on 10-27-96
Took the last 2 snaps as the QB in their 40-10 rout of the Chiefs on 10-11-98
Holder for Adam Vinatieri
48 Regular Season Games and 6 Playoff Games
43 punts for 1,833 yards in the playoffs
Ohio State Buckeye

TURNER, Robert (#40) *"Bake"*
Born on July 22, 1940 in Alpine, TX
6'1" and 179 pounds
Wide Receiver　　　　　1970
28 receptions for 428 yards + 2 TDs
Caught 2 TD passes from Joe Kapp
Longest reception was a 43 yard pass from Joe Kapp in their 14-10 win over the Bills on 11-29-70
14 games/13 started
Texas Tech Red Raider

TURNER, William "Bill" (#74)
Born on March 56, 1960 in Norwood, MA
6'4" and 245 pounds
Guard　　　　　1987
2 games (on Oct. 4th and Oct. 11th)
Boston College Eagle

TURNER, Paul "Kevin" (#34)
Born on June 12, 1969 in Prattville, AL
6'1" and 231 pounds
RB (KR)　　　　　1992-94
96 carries for 382 yards + 1 TD and 98 receptions for 856 yards + 6 TDs
1 kickoff return of 11 yards and 5 fumble recoveries for 6 yards
Caught 1 TD pass from Hugh Millen, Jeff Carlson and Scott Secules and 3 TD passes from Drew Bledsoe
Recovered fumbles by Ron Lewis, Walter Stanley, Drew Bledsoe, Scott Secules and Ronald Humphrey
Had an 11 yard return of a kickoff by Louie Aguiar in their 30-21 loss to the Jets on 10-04-92
Caught a 13 yard pass and then lateraled it to Leonard Russell, for an 82 yard play, on 10-10-93
Advanced a fumble by Scott Secules 6 yards in their 28-14 loss to the Houston Oilers on 10-17-93
Longest run was 49 yards in their 20-17 win over the Cleveland Browns on 12-19-93
Ran for a 1 yard touchdown in their 39-35 loss to the Miami Dolphins on 09-04-94
Caught a 14 yard OT GW TD pass from Drew Bledsoe to beat Minnesota 26-20 in OT on 11-13-94
Longest reception was a 32 yard pass from Drew Bledsoe in their 23-17 win over the Lions on 09-25-94
48 Regular Season Games/19 started and 1 Playoff Game (on 01-01-95)
#71 pick in the 1992 NFL Draft
Alabama Crimson Tide

TURNER, Thomas III "T.J." (#99)
Born on October 1, 1978 in Dayton, OH
6'3" and 255 pounds
Special Team　　　　　2001
2 games (on Sept. 9th and Sept. 30th)
Member of the 2001 World Championship Team
#239 pick in the 2001 NFL Draft
Michigan State Spartan

TWOMBLY, Darren (#64)
Born on May 14, 1965 in Manchester, MA
6'4" and 270 pounds
Center   1987
Started in the only game he played on 10-04-87
Boston College Eagle

TYMS, Brian (#84)
Born on February 21, 1989 in Kent, WA
6'3" and 210 pounds
Wide Receiver   2014
5 receptions for 82 yards + 1 TD
Longest reception was a 43 yard TD pass from Tom Brady in their 37-22 win over Buffalo on 10-12-14
11 Regular Season Games/2 started and 1 Playoff Game (on 01-11-14)
Member of the 2014 World Championship Team
Florida A & M Rattler

UNDERWOOD, Tiquan (#10)
Born on February 17, 1987 in New Brunswick, NJ
6'1" and 175 pounds
Wide Receiver   2011
3 receptions for 30 yards
Longest reception was a 13 yard pass from Tom Brady in their 41-23 win over Denver on 12-18-11
6 games
Rutgers Scarlet Knight

VALENTINE, Vincent (#99)
Born on February 23, 1994 in Madison, IL
6'3" and 331 pounds
Defensive Lineman   2016
Sacked Carson Palmer in their 23-21 win over the Arizona Cardinals on 09-11-16
13 Regular Season Games/2 started and 3 Playoff Games
Member of the 2016 World Championship Team
#96 pick in the 2016 NFL Draft
Nebraska Cornhusker

VAN EEGHEN, Mark (#34)
Born on April 19, 1952 in Cambridge, MA
6'2" and 223 pounds
Running Back   1982-83
177 carries for 744 yards + 2 TDs, 12 receptions for 116 yards + 1 TD and 1 fumble recovery
Longest run was 17 yards in their 3-0 (Snow Plow) win over the Dolphins on 12-12-82
Caught a 5 yard TD pass from Steve Grogan in their 16-0 shutout of Seattle on 12-19-82
Longest reception was a 23 yard pass from Steve Grogan in their 21-7 win over the Bills on 11-06-83
Recovered Tony Eason's fumble in their 7-0 shutout of the New Orleans Saints on 12-04-83
24 Regular Season Games and 1 Playoff Game/1 started
Colgate Red Raider

VAN NOY, Kyle (#53)
Born on March 26, 1991 in Reno, NV
6'3" and 250 pounds
Linebacker   2016-19
16.5 sacks, 2 interceptions and 5 fumble recoveries for 97 yards and 3 TDs
Shared in a sack of Jameison Winston, Derek Carr, Tyrod Taylor, Ryan Tannehill and Luke Falk
Sacked Colin Kaepernick, Cam Newton, Matt Moore, Ben Roethlisberger and Daniel Jones
Sacked Baker Mayfield, Carson Wentz and DeShaun Watson
Recorded 2 sacks of Josh McCown, Derek Anderson and Josh Allen
Intercepted Jared Goff and Blake Bortles
Recovered fumbles by Ryan Tannehill, John Hilliman and 2 fumbles by San Darnold
Returned a blocked punt 29 yards for a TD in their 38-31 win over the Bears on 10-21-18
Returned Adam Butler's strip sack of Sam Darnold 46 yards for a TD in their 38-3 rout of the Jets on 12-30-18
Had a 22 yard TD return of a fumble by Jon Hilliman in their 35-14 rout of the Giants on 10-10-19
51 Regular Season Games/45 started and 10 Playoff Games/7 started
Shared in a sack of Matt Ryan in their Epic 34-28 Super Bowl OT win vs the Atlanta Falcons on 02-05-17
Sacked Blake Bortles in their 24-20 Championsip win over the Jaguars on 01-21-18
Sacked Pat Mahomes *twice* in their 37-31 AFC Championship OT win vs the Chiefs on 01-20-19
Sacked Jared Goff in their 13-3 Super Bowl win over the Los Angeles Rams on 02-03-19
Sacked Ryan Tannehill in their 20-13 Wild Card Playoff loss to the Titans on 01-04-20
AFC Defensive Player of the Week in their 16-10 win over Buffalo on 09-29-19
Member of the 2016 and 2018 World Championship Teams
Ron Burton Community Service Award in 2019
BYU Cougar

VATAHA, Randel "Randy" (#18) *"Rabbit"*
Born on December 4, 1948 in Santa Maria, CA
5'10" and 176 pounds
WR (DB)   1971-76
178 receptions for 3,055 yards + 23 TDs, 6 carries for 10 yards and 1 fumble advancement for a 46 yard TD
Caught 1 TD pass from Neil Graff, 6 TD passes from Steve Grogan and 16 TD passes from Jim Plunkett
Caught a career long 88 yard TD from Jim Plunkett in the 4th Qtr in 21-17 win over the Colts on 12-19-71
Advanced Mack Herron's fumble 46 yards for a TD in their 24-16 win over the Colts on 10-07-73
Longest run was 24 yards in their 27-17 win over the Baltimore Colts on 11-24-74
Was used a Defensive Back in the final series of their 30-27 win over the Pittsburgh Steelers on 09-26-76
80 Regular Season Games/63 started and 1 Playoff Game/1 started (on 12-18-76)
Stanford Cardinal

VAUGHN, Jon (#24)
Born on March 12, 1970 in Florissant, MO
5'9" and 203 pounds
RB/KR   1991-92
144 carries for 597 yards + 3 TDs, 22 receptions for 173 yards and 1 completion for a 13 yard TD
54 kickoff returns for 1,281 yards + 2 TDs
Longest reception was a 32 yard pass from Tommy Hodson in their 20-0 loss to Cleveland on 09-08-91
Threw a 13 yard HB Option (left handed) TD pass to Marv Cook in their 24-20 win vs Houston on 09-22-91
Had a 99 yard TD return of a kickoff by Greg Davis in their 24-10 loss to Phoenix on 09-29-91
Longest run was 36 yards in their 19-17 loss to the Cleveland Browns on 10-25-92
Had a 100 yard TD return of a kickoff by Lee Johnson in their 20-10 loss to the Bengals on 12-20-92
32 games
#112 pick in the 1991 NFL Draft
Michigan Wolverine

VELLANO, Joe (#72)
Born on October 30, 1988 in Clifton Park, NY
6'2" and 285 pounds
Defensive Lineman   2013-14
3 sacks and 1 fumble recovery
Sacked Matt Ryan, Ryan Tannehill and Alex Smith and recovered a fumble by Ben Roethlisberger
21 Regular Season Games/9 started and 3 Playoff Games
Sacked Andrew Luck in their 43-22 Divisional win over the Colts on 01-11-14
Member of the 2014 World Championship Team
Maryland Terrapin

VENTRONE, Raymond "Ray" (#41) *"Bubba"*
Born on October 21, 1982 in Pittsburgh, PA
5'10" and 200 pounds
Special Team   2007-08
17 Regular Season Games and 2 Playoff Games
Villanova Wildcat

VENTRONE, Ross (#35)
Born on September 27, 1986 in Pittsburgh, PA
5'8" and 190 pounds
Special Team   2011
8 games
Villanova Wildcat

VEREEN, Shane (#34)
Born on May 2, 1989 in Valencia, CA
5'10" and 205 pounds
RB (KR/RT)   2011-14
217 carries for 907 yards + 5 TDs, 107 receptions for 1,023 yards + 7 TDs and 3 kickoff returns for 66 yards
Caught 7 Regular Season and 2 Post Season TD passes from Tom Brady
Caught a career long 83 yard TD pass from Tom Brady in their 49-19 rout of the Jets on 11-22-12
Longest run was 21 yards in their 23-21 victory over the Buffalo Bills on 09-08-13
Longest was a 24 yard return of a kickoff by Dan Carpenter in their 34-20 win over the Buffalo Bills on 12-29-13
42 Regular Season Games/8 started and 7 Playoff Games/3 started (Used at Right Tackle on 01-10-15)
22 carries for 114 yards + 1 TD and 32 receptions for 324 yards + 2 TDs in the playoffs
Ran for a 1 yard TD in their 41-28 Divisional win over the Houston Texans on 01-13-13
Caught an 8 yard TD pass and a 33 yard TD pass in their 41-28 Divisional win over Houston on 01-13-13
Member of the 2014 World Championship Team
#56 pick in the 2011 NFL Draft
California Golden Bear

VERIS, Garin (#60 and #90) *"Ox"*
Born on February 27, 1963 in Chillicothe, OH
6'4" and 255 pounds
Defensive Lineman   1985-88 and 1990-91
Wore #60 from 1985-88 and #90 from 1990-91
39 sacks, 7 fumble recoveries and blocked an extra point attempt
Sacked Lynn Dickey, Steve DeBerg, Matt Kofler, Boomer Esiason and Gary Hogenboom
Sacked Steve Dils, Rusty Hilger, Randall Cunningham and Chris Chandler
Had 2 sacks of Dave Wilson, Mike Pagel, Bubby Brister, Jack Trudeau, Dan Marino and Jeff George
Had 2 ½ sacks of Dave Archer, 4 ½ sacks of Jim Kelly, 5 sacks of Dave Krieg and 6 sacks of Ken O'Brien
Recovered fumbles by Tony Paige, Dan Marino, Gary Hogenboom, Sammy Winder and Vance Mueller
Recovered fumbles by George Adams and Jim Kelly as well
Recovered Tony Paige's fumble on a 3rd & goal, in their 20-13 win over the Jets on 10-20-85
Sacked Ken O'Brien, on 4th down, with 52 seconds left, in their 20-13 win over the NY Jets on 10-20-85
Sacked Jim Kelly, with 58 ticks left, in their 13-7 win over Buffalo on 12-20-87
Blocked an extra point attempt by Scott Norwood in their 22-17 loss to the Buffalo Bills on 11-03-91
AFC Defensive Player of the Month in December 1986
78 Regular Season Games/46 started and 5 Playoff Games/5 started
4 sacks, 1 interception for 18 yards and 1 fumble recovery in the playoffs
Sacked Ken O'Brien once and Pat Ryan *twice* in their 26-14 Wild Card win over the Jets on 12-28-85
Had an 18 yard return of a pass by Pat Ryan in their 26-14 Wild Card win over the Jets on 12-28-85
Sacked Dan Marino in their 31-14 AFC Championship win over Miami at the Orange Bowl on 01-12-86
Recovered Tony Nathan's fumble in their 31-14 AFC Championship Game win over Miami on 01-12-86
#48 pick in the 1985 NFL Draft
Stanford Cardinal

VIAENE, David (#70)
Born on July 14, 1965 in Appleton, WI
6'5" and 300 pounds
Tackle   1989-90
20 games/8 started
Minnesota Golden Gopher

VILLA, Danny (#73 and #75)
Born on September 21, 1964 in Nogales, AZ
6'5" and 304 pounds
T/C/LS   1987-91 and 1997
Wore #73 from 1987-89 and #75 from 1990-91 and in 1997
3 fumble recoveries
Recovered fumbles by Tommy Hodson, Marv Cook and Pat Coleman's fumbled punt return
Long Snapper for Bryan Wagner, Shawn McCarthy, Charlie Baumann and Jason Staurovsky
75 Regular Season Games/62 started and 2 Playoff Games
#113 pick in the 1987 NFL Draft
Arizona State Sun Devil

VINATIERI, Adam (#4) *"Automatic"*
Born on December 28, 1972 in Yankton, SD
6'0" and 212 pounds
Kicker (P)   1996-2005
Kicked 263 field goals and 367 extra points and had 2 punts for 60 yards
Ran for a 2 point conversion and tosses a 4 yard TD pass
Tackled Hershell Walker on his 70 yard kickoff return in their 12-6 loss to Dallas on 12-15-96
Ran for a 2 point conversion in their 25-21 win over the Buffalo Bills on 11-29-98
Longest punt was 33 yards in their 27-16 win over Cleveland on 12-09-01
Kicked a career long 57 yard field goal in their 33-30 win over the Bears on 11-10-02
Caught the shotgun snap and tossed a 4 yard TD pass to Troy Brown in their 40-22 win vs the Rams
         on 11-07-04
Kicked 9 Overtime Game Winning Field Goals
AFC Special Team Player of the Week (8 times)
AFC Special Team Player of the Month (3 times)
Led the NFL with 31 field goals kicked and 141 points scored in 2004
AFC Pro Bowl Kicker in 2002, 2004
First Team All Pro Kicker in 2002, 2004
160 Regular Season Games and 17 Playoff Games
Kicked 26 field goals and 39 extra points in the playoffs
Kicked an incredible 45 yard Game Tying Field Goal in the snow in the "Tuck Rule" Game on 01-19-02
Booted a 23 yard GW FG to beat the Raiders 16-13 in Overtime in their Divisional Playoff win on 01-19-02
Kicked a 48 yard Super Bowl Game Winning field goal to beat the Rams 20-17 on the last play on 02-03-02
Kicked a 41 yard Super Bowl Game Winning field goal to beat the Panthers 32-29 on the last play on 02-01-04
Booted a 24 yard punt in their 28-3 Wild Card rout of the Jaguars on 01-07-06
Member of the 2001, 2003 and 2004 World Championship Teams
South Dakota State Jack Rabbit

VIRKUS, Scott (#70)
Born on September 7, 1959 in Rochester, MN
6'5" and 260 pounds
Defensive End   1984
5 games
Purdue Boilermaker

VOLLMER, Sebastian (#76) *"Seabass"*
Born on July 10, 1984 in Dusseldorf, Germany
6'8" and 315 pounds
Tackle   2009-15
Recovered Tom Brady's fumble in their 30-27 OT loss to the New York Jets on 10-20-13
88 Regular Season Games/80 started and 10 Playoff Games/10 started
Member of the 2014 World Championship Team
#58 Pick in the 2009 NFL Draft
Houston Cougar

VRABEL, Mike (#50) *"Vrabs"*
Born on August 14, 1975 in Akron, OH
6'4" and 261 pounds
LB/DE (TE/KR)   2001-08
48 sacks, 11 interceptions for 73 yards + 1 TD, 5 fumble recoveries and 8 receptions for 11 yards + 8 TDs
3 kickoff returns for 25 yards and recovered 2 onside kicks
Shared in a sack of Steve McNair, A.J. Feeley and Matt Schaub
Sacked Trent Green, Jim Miller, Donovan McNabb, Josh and Luke McCown, Matt Hasselbeck
        and Kerry Collins
Sacked Chris Simms, Brooks Bollinger, Vince Young, Kellen Clemens, Philip Rivers and JaMarcus Russell
Had 1 ½ sacks of Michael Vick, Tim Couch and Aaron Rodgers
Recorded 2 sacks of Drew Bledsoe, J.P. Losman and Damon Huard
Had 3 sacks of Jay Fiedler, Kelly Holcomb and Jason Campbell
Recorded 4 sacks of Peyton Manning and Cleo Lemon and 6 sacks of Chad Pennington
Intercepted Jay Fiedler, Vinny Testaverde, Kordell Stewart, Tony Banks, Drew Bledsoe and Peyton Manning
Intercepted Jake Delhomme, Brad Johnson, Ben Roethlisberger and had 2 interceptions of Jon Kitna
Recovered fumbles by Fred McCrary, Michael Bennett, Jay Fiedler, Kevin Jones and Trent Edwards
Recovered an onside kick by Jake Arians in their 21-11 win over the Bills on 11-11-01
Cradled a 1 yard TD pass from Tom Brady in their 21-14 loss to the Chargers on 09-29-02
Longest was a 14 yard return of Toby Gowin's 2nd half kickoff in their 12-0 shutout of Dallas on 11-16-03
Recovered Jay Fiedler's fumble on Miami's 10 yard line, in their 12-0 shutout of Miami on 12-07-03
Grabbed a 2 yard TD pass from Tom Brady in their 40-22 win over the St. Louis Rams on 11-07-04
Caught a 1 yard TD pass from Tom Brady in their 21-7 victory over the 49ers on 01-02-05
Had a 24 yard TD return of a pass by Jake Delhomme in their 27-17 loss to the Carolina Panthers on 09-18-05
Snared a 1 yard TD pass from Tom Brady in their 24-17 win over the Saints on 11-20-05
Caught a 1 yard TD and a 2 yard TD pass from Tom Brady in their 31-21 win over the Jets on 12-26-05
Caught a 1 yard TD pass from Tom Brady in their 34-13 rout of the Bengals on 10-01-07
Strip sacked Jason Campbell *3 times* in their 52-7 rout of the Redskins on 10-28-07
Snared a 1 yard TD pass from Tom Brady in their 52-7 rout of the Redskins on 10-28-07
Sacked Cleo Lemon *3 times* in their 28-7 victory over the Miami Dolphins on 12-23-07
Recovered an onside kick by Lawrence Tynes in their 38-35 victory over the NY Giants on 12-29-07
Sacked Damon Huard *twice* in their 17-10 win over the Kansas City Chiefs on 09-07-08
AFC Defensive Player of the Week in their 52-7 rout of the Redskins on 10-28-07
AFC Defensive Player of the Month in December 2003
AFC Pro Bowl Linebacker in 2007
First Team All Pro Linebacker in 2007
125 games/110 started and 17 Playoff Games/17 Started
Returned Jerome Bettis' fumble 1 yard in their 41-27 Championship win vs the Steelers at Heinz Field
        on 01-23-05
7 sacks and 2 receptions for 3 yards + 2 TDs in the playoffs
Sacked Steve McNair in their 17-14 Divisional win over the Tennessee Titans on 01-10-04
Sacked Jake Delhomme *twice* in their 32-29 Super Bowl win over the Panthers on 02-01-04
Caught a 1 yard TD pass from Tom Brady in their 33-29 Super Bowl win over the Panthers on 02-01-04
Sacked Peyton Manning in their 20-3 Divisional rout of the Indianapolis Colts on 01-16-05
Caught a 2 yard TD pass from Tom Brady in their 24-21 Super Bowl win over the Eagles on 02-06-05
Sacked Donovan McNabb in their 24-21 Super Bowl win over the Eagles on 02-06-05
Strip sacked Philip Rivers on 4th down, in their 24-21 Divisional win vs the Chargers on 01-14-07
Sacked Peyton Manning in their 38-34 Championship Game loss to the Colts on 01-21-07
Member of the 2001, 2003 and 2004 World Championship Teams
Ohio State Buckeye

WADDLE, LaAdrian (#68)
Born on July 21, 1991 in College Station, TX
6'6" and 315 pounds
Offensive Lineman   2015-18
31 Regular Season Games/7 started and 5 Playoff Games/1 started (on 01-13-18)
Member of the 2016 and 2018 World Championship Teams
Texas Tech Red Raider

WAGNER, Bryan (#8 and #9)
Born on March 28, 1962 in Escondido, CA
6'2" and 200 pounds
Punter (K)   1991 and 1995
Wore #8 in 1991 and #9 in 1995
51 punts for 2,105 yards
Longest punt was 57 yards in their 10-7 loss to the Indianapolis Colts on 12-23-95
Kicked off in 8 games in 1995
11 games
Cal State Northridge Matador

WALKER, Bruce (#91)
Born on July 18, 1972 in Compton, CA
6'4" and 310 pounds
Nose Tackle   1995
11 games/5 started
UCLA Bruin

WALKER, Casey (#98)
Born on December 6, 1989 in Garland, TX
6'1" and 345 pounds
Defensive Lineman   2014
Sacked Geno Smith in their 27-25 win over the Jets on 10-16-14
5 games/1 started (on 10-12-14)
Member of the 2014 World Championship Team
Oklahoma Sooner

WALKER, Michael "Mike" (#12) *"Superfoot"*
Born on October 18, 1949 in Lancaster, England
6'0" and 190 pounds
Kicker   1972
Kicked 2 field goals and 15 extra points
Kicked a career long 36 yard field goal in their 27-24 loss to Buffalo on 11-19-72
Kicked another 36 yard field goal in their 17-10 win over the Saints on 12-10-72
8 games
Won the "Superfoot" Kicking Contest in England

WALTER JR., Kenneth "Ken" (#13 and #15)
Born on August 15, 1972 in Cleveland, OH
6'1" and 207 pounds
Punter   2001-03 and 2006
Wore #13 from 2001-03 and #15 in 2006
211 punts for 8,143 yards and 1 carry for no gain
Longest punt was 58 yards in their 21-11 win over the Buffalo Bills on 11-11-01
AFC Special Team Player of Week on 12-22-01
Took a direct snap on a fake PAT and ran for no gain in their 41-38 OT win vs the Chiefs on 09-22-02
Holder for Adam Vinatieri
46 Regular Season Games and 6 Playoff Games
Member of the 2001 and 2003 World Championship Teams
Kent State Golden Flash

WARD, David (#94)
Born on March 10, 1964 in Helena, AR
6'2" and 230 pounds
Linebacker   1989
16 games
Southern Arkansas Mulerider

WARD, Dedric (#17)
Born on September 29, 1974 in Cedar Rapids, IA
5'9" and 187 pounds
Wide Receiver   2003
7 receptions for 106 yards + 1 TD
Longest reception was a 31 yard TD pass from Tom Brady in their 38-34 win over the Colts on 11-30-03
4 Regular Season Games and 3 Playoff Games
Member of the 2003 World Championship Team
Northern Iowa Panther

WARREN, Gerard (#92 and #98)
Born on July 25, 1978 in Lake City, FL
6'4" and 325 pounds
Defensive Lineman   2010-11
Wore #92 in 2010 and #98 in 2011
4.5 sacks
Shared in a sack of Ben Roethlisberger, sacked Jay Cutler and Tim Tebow and had 2 sacks of Mark Sanchez
28 Regular Season Games/10 started and 4 Playoff Games/1 started (on 01-16-11)
Florida Gator

WARREN, Lamont (#27)
Born on January 4, 1973 in Indianapolis, IN
5'11" and 202 pounds
RB (KR)   1999
35 carries for 120 yards, 29 receptions for 262 yards + 1 TD and 2 kickoff returns for 25 yards
Longest run was 18 yards in their 31-30 loss to the Miami Dolphins on 10-17-99
Longest was a 16 yard return of a kickoff by Pete Stoyanovich in their 16-14 loss to the Chiefs on 10-10-99
Longest reception was a 21 yard pass from Drew Bledsoe in their 31-30 loss to Miami on 10-17-99
Caught a 3 yard TD pass from Drew Bledsoe in their 27-3 rout of the Arizona Cardinals on 10-31-99
16 games
Colorado Buffalo

WARREN, Ty'ron "Ty" (#94) "*Boss Hog*"
Born on February 6, 1981 in Bryan, TX
6'5" and 300 pounds
DE/NT   2003-10
20.5 sacks, 1 safety and 6 fumble recoveries for 13 yards
Shared in a sack of Matt Hasselbeck, Chad Pennington and Gus Frerotte
Sacked Jay Fiedler, Carson Palmer, Joey Harrington, Vince Young, Tony Romo and Mark Sanchez
Had 1 ½ sacks of J.P. Losman, Aaron Rodger, Cleo Lemon and Trent Edwards
Had 2 sacks of Marc Bulger and Jon Kitna and 3 sacks of Trent Green
Recovered fumbles by Carson Palmer, Cleo Lemon and 2 fumbles by Jason Campbell
Had a 5 yard return of a fumble by Larry Johnson in their 26-16 loss to the Chiefs on 11-27-05
Sacked J.P. Losman for a safety for the final points scored in their 19-17 win over Buffalo on 09-10-06
Strip sacked and recovered Carson Palmer's fumble in their 38-13 win over the Bengals on 10-01-06
Recovered Mike Vrabel's strip sack of Cleo Lemon in their 49-28 rout of the Dolphins on 10-21-07
Recovered Mike Vrabel's strip sack of Jason Campbell in their 52-7 rout of the Redskins on 10-28-07
Recovered Mike Vrabel's 2nd strip sack of Jason Campbell in their 52-7 win over the Redskins on 10-28-07
Had a career long 8 yard return of a fumble by Jacob Hester in their 30-10 loss to the Chargers on 10-12-08
AFC Defensive Player of the Month in December 2006
106 Regular Season Games/92 started and 16 Playoff Games/11 started
Sacked David Garrard in their 31-20 Divisional win over the Jaguars on 01-12-08
Member of the 2003 and 2004 World Championship Teams
Ron Burton Community Service Award in 2007
#13 Pick in the 2003 NFL Draft
Texas A & M Aggie

WASHINGTON, Clyde (#31)
Born on March 21, 1938 in Carlisle, PA
6'1" and 197 pounds
DB/Punter (RB)   1960-61
7 interceptions for 58 yards, 17 punts for 539 yards, 3 carries for 13 yards and 3 fumble recoveries
Intercepted Frank Tripucka, Hunter Ennis, Richie Lucas, George Blanda and had 3 int's of Jack Kemp
Recovered Bob Dee's interception return fumble in their 27-14 loss to Oakland on 10-16-60
Recovered Jim Lee Hunt's kickoff return fumble in their 38-21 win over the NY Titans on 11-11-60
Advanced Gino Cappelletti's lateral 1 yard in their 45-16 loss to the LA Chargers on 10-28-60
Longest run was 7 yards in their 45-16 loss to the LA Chargers on 10-28-60
Longest punt was 48 yards in their 24-10 loss to the Houston Oilers on 11-25-60
Had a career long 33 yard return of a pass by Jack Kemp in their 41-0 shutout of the San Diego on 12-17-61
27 games/25 started
Purdue Boilermaker

WASHINGTON, John (#76)
Born on February 20, 1963 in Houston, TX
6'4" and 280 pounds
Defensive End   1993
16 games
Oklahoma State Cowboy

WASHINGTON, James "Kelley" (#15)
Born on August 21, 1979 in Stephens City, VA
6'3" and 218 pounds
Special Team/WR　　　　2007-08
Blocked a punt and had 1 reception for 3 yards
Blocked a punt by Ben Graham in their 20-10 win over the New York Jets on 12-16-07
Caught a 3 yard pass from Matt Cassel in their 17-10 win over the Chiefs on 09-07-08
24 Regular Season Games and 3 Playoff Games
Tennessee Volunteer

WASHINGTON SR., Leon (#33)
Born on August 29, 1982 in Jacksonville, FL
5'8" and 192 pounds
RB/KR　　　　2013
1 carry for 1 yard and 1 kickoff return of 19 yards
Only carry was for 1 yard in their 13-10 victory over the NY Jets on 09-12-13
Returned Mike Nugent's opening kickoff 19 yards in their 13-6 loss to the Bengals on 10-06-13
2 games (on Sept. 12th and Oct. 6th)
Florida State Seminole

WASHINGTON, Mark (#46)
Born on December 28, 1947 in Chicago, IL
5'10" and 188 pounds
DB (KR)　　　　1979
Had an 18 yard return of a kickoff by Dave Jacobs in their 27-26 loss to the Jets on 12-09-79
12 games
Morgan State Bear

WASHINGTON, Mickey (#21)
Born on July 8, 1968 in Galveston, TX
5'9" and 195 pounds
Defensive Back　　　　1990-91
Intercepted Jeff George and Warren Moon
25 games/4 started
Texas A & M Aggie

WASHINGTON JR., Theodore "Ted" (#92)
Born on April 13, 1968 in Tampa, FL
6'5" and 365 pounds
Nose Tackle　　　　2003
Sacked Donovan McNabb and Tony Banks
10 Regular Season Games/10 started and 3 Playoff Games/3 started
Member of the 2003 World Championship Team
Louisville Cardinal

WATERS, Brian (#54)
Born on February 18, 1977 in Waxahachie, TX
6'3" and 220 pounds
Guard　　　　2011
AFC Pro Bowl Guard in 2011
16 Regular Season Games/16 started and 3 Playoff Games/3 started
North Texas Mean Green

WATSON, Benjamin (#84)
Born on December 18, 1980 in Norfolk, VA
6'3" and 251 pounds
Tight End   2004-09 and 2019
184 receptions for 2,275 yards + 20 TDs, 1 carry for 11 yards and 1 onside kick recovery
Caught 3 TD passes from Matt Cassel
Caught 17 Regular Season TD passes and 3 Post Season TD passes from Tom Brady
Caught a game winning 17 yard TD pass from Tom Brady in their 23-16 win over Miami on 11-13-05
Returned an onside kick by Mike Nugent 1 yard in their 31-21 win over the New York Jets on 12-26-05
Longest reception was a 40 yard pass from Tom Brady in their 31-7 win over Minnesota on 10-30-06
Ran for an 11 yard gain in their 34-17 victory over the Cleveland Browns on 10-07-07
81 Regular Season Games/55 started and 10 Playoff Games/7 started
22 receptions for 233 yards + 3 TDs in the playoffs
Caught a 63 yard TD pass from Tom Brady in their 28-3 Wild Card win over the Jaguars on 01-07-06
Caught a 3 yard TD and a 6 yard TD pass from Tom Brady in their 31-20 Divisional win vs the Jaguars
        on 01-12-08
Member of the 2004 World Championship Team
#32 pick in the 2004 NFL Draft
Georgia Bulldog

WATSON, Carl "Dave" (#67 and #62)
Born on January 5, 1941 in Barbour County, AL
6'1" and 245 pounds
Guard (KR)   1963-64
Wore # 67 in 1963 and #62 in 1964
2 fumble recoveries, 1 kickoff return of 9 yards and 1 recovery of an onside kick
Recovered a fumble by Tom Yewcic and Jerry Robinson's fumbled punt return
Had a 9 yard return of a kickoff by Jim Fraser in their 14-10 loss to the Denver Broncos on 09-29-63
Recovered an onside kick by Mike Mercer in their 17-14 win over the Oakland Raiders on 09-13-64
28 Regular Season Games and 2 Playoff Games
11ᵗʰ Round Draft Pick in 1963
Georgia Tech Yellow Jacket

WATSON, Dekoda (#53 and #52)
Born on March 3, 1988 in Aiken, SC
6'2" and 245 pounds
Special Team   2015
Wore #53 for 2 games and #52 for 3 games
3 Regular Season Games and 2 Playoff Games
Florida State Seminole

WEATHERS, Clarence (#82)
Born on January 10, 1962 in Green Pond, SC
5'9" and 170 pounds
WR (KR/PR)   1983-84
27 receptions for 494 yards + 5 TDs and 1 carry for 28 yards
3 kickoff returns for 58 yards and 5 punt returns for 8 yards
Caught 3 TD passes from Steve Grogan and 2 TD passes from Tony Eason
Longest was a 33 yard return of a kickoff by Ray Wershing in their 33-13 loss to the 49ers on 10-02-83
Ran for a 28 yard gain in their 12-7 loss to the Baltimore Colts on 10-09-83
Caught a career long 58 yard TD pass from Steve Grogan in their 21-7 win over Buffalo on 11-06-83
Longest was a 7 yard return of a punt by Chris Norman in their 26-19 loss to Denver on 11-04-84
25 games
Delaware State Hornet

WEATHERS, Robert (#24)
Born on September 13, 1960 in Westfield, NY
6'2" and 220 pounds
RB (KR)   1982-86
159 carries for 733 yards + 4 TDs, 29 receptions for 268 yards and 4 kickoff returns for 86 yards
Longest reception was a 22 yard pass from Matt Cavanaugh in their 31-7 loss to the Jets on 09-19-82
Longest run was 77 yards in their 29-23 OT loss to the Baltimore Colts on 09-04-83
Longest was a 29 yard return of a kickoff by Ray Wershing in their 33-13 loss to the 49ers on 10-02-83
44 Regular Season Games/6 started and 4 Playoff Games
26 carries for 108 yards and 2 receptions for 5 yards + 1 TD in the playoffs
Caught a 2 yard TD pass from Tony Eason in their 31-14 AFC Championship win over Miami on 01-12-86
#40 pick in the 1982 NFL Draft
Arizona State Sun Devil

WEAVER, Timothy "Jed" (#85) *"Dream"*
Born on August 11, 1976 in Bend, OR
6'4" and 258 pounds
Tight End   2004
8 receptions for 93 yards
Longest reception was a 25 yard pass from Tom Brady in their 21-7 win over the 49ers on 01-02-05
10 games/1 started (on 11-14-04)
Member of the 2004 World Championship Team
Oregon Duck

WEBB, Donald "Don" (#42) *"Spider"*
Born on May 22, 1939 in Jefferson City, MO
5'10" and 182 pounds
DB/Special Team (WR) 1961-71
21 interceptions for 366 yards + 2 TDs and 10 fumble recoveries for 88 yards + 2 TDs
Blocked a punt and returned it 20 yards for a TD, recovered an onside kick and had 1 reception of 11 yards
Intercepted M.C. Reynolds, George Herring, Frank Tripucka, Mickey Slaughter and Tobin Rote
Intercepted Dick Wood, Buddy Humphrey, Rick Norton and Jim Hart
Had 2 interceptions of George Blanda, John Hadl, Len Dawson, Jack Kemp, Tom Flores and Pete Beathard
Recovered fumbles by Johnny Robinson, Lance Alworth, Jack Kemp, Abner Hayes and Bill Mathis
Recovered fumbles by OJ Simpson, Clint Jones, Jim Kiick and recovered a blocked punt and a blocked FGA
Advanced Larry Garron's kickoff return handoff 15 yards in their 37-30 loss to the NY Titans on 10-01-61
Had a 27 yard TD return of a pass by M.C. Reynolds in their 52-21 rout of the Bills on 10-22-61
Had a career long 49 yard TD return of a fumble by Johnny Robinson in their 18-17 win vs Dallas on 10-29-61
Had a career long 59 yard return of a pass by Frank Tripucka in their 28-24 victory over Denver on 12-03-61
Had a 31 yard TD return of a pass by Jack Kemp in their 41-0 shutout of San Diego on 12-17-61
Blocked a punt by Paul Maguire and returned it 20 yards for a TD in their 41-0 win over San Diego on 12-17-61
Caught an 11 yard pass, as a WR, from QB Tom Yewcic in their 43-14 rout of the NY Titans on 10-06-62
Recovered a blocked field goal in their 43-43 Tie with the Oakland Raiders at Fenway Park on 10-16-64
Picked off a Len Dawson pass to help secure their 31-24 win over Kansas City on 12-06-64
Recovered an onside kick by Jim O'Brien in their 21-17 win over the Baltimore Colts on 12-19-71
AFL All Star Defensive Back in 1969
134 games/99 started
24th Round Draft Pick in 1961
Iowa State Cyclone

WEBSTER, George (#90) *"Big Bird"*
Born on November 25, 1945 in Anderson, SC
6'4" and 220 pounds
Linebacker   1974-76
5 sacks, 2 fumble recoveries and 1 interception
Sacked Fran Tarkenton, Joe Ferguson, Marty Domres, Earl Morrall and Bob Griese
Recovered fumbles by Jim Bertelsen and Steve Ramsey
Picked off a pass by Bob Griese in their 22-14 loss to the Miami Dolphins on 09-28-75
37 Regular Season Games/25 started and 1 Playoff Game (on 12-18-76)
Recovered a squibbed kickoff by Ray Guy in their 24-21 Divisional Playoff loss to the Raiders on 12-18-76
Michigan State Spartan

WEBSTER, Jason (#23)
Born on September 8, 1977 in Houston, TX
5'9" and 187 pounds
Defensive Back   2008
3 games
Texas A & M Aggie

WEISACOSKY, Ed (#66)
Born on May 4, 1944 in Pottsville, PA
6'1" and 230 pounds
Linebacker   1971-72
3 sacks and 1 fumble recovery for 3 yards
Sacked Bob Berry and recorded 2 sacks of James Harris
Returned Steve Harkey's lateral 3 yards in their 34-10 loss to the New York Jets on 10-29-72
28 games/23 started
Miami Hurricane

WEISHUHN, Clayton (#53) *"The Happy Warrior of the NFL"*
Born on October 7, 1959 in San Angelo, TX
6'2" and 220 pounds
Linebacker   1982-86
Nicknamed *"The Happy Warrior of the NFL"* by Will McDonough
3 sacks, 4 fumble recoveries and 1 advancement of a lateral for a 27 yard TD
Shared in a sack of Jim McMahon, sacked David Woodley and had 1 ½ sacks of Joe Ferguson
Recovered fumbles by Freeman McNeil and Dan Fouts and 2 fumbles by Jack Kemp
Advanced Steve Nelson's lateral 27 yards for a TD in their 28-23 win over the Steelers on 09-25-83
30 Regular Season Games/26 started and 1 Playoff Game/1 started (on 01-08-03)
Forced a fumble that Rick Sanford returned 21 yards in their 28-13 First Round Playoff loss to Miami
        on 01-08-83
#60 pick in the 1982 NFL Draft
Angelo State Ram

WELCH, Claxton (#43)
Born on July 3, 1947 in Portland, OR
5'11" and 203 pounds
Running Back   1973
6 receptions for 22 yards, 1 fumble recovery and a recovery of a Patriots onside kick
Longest reception was an 8 yard pass from Jim Plunkett in their 33-13 loss to the Jets on 11-11-73
Recovered Rocky Turner's fumbled kickoff return in their 33-13 loss to the NY Jets on 11-11-73
Recovered an onside kick by Patriots Kicker Jeff White in their 33-13 loss to the Jets on 11-11-73
2 games/1 started (on 11-11-73)
Oregon Duck

WELCH, Dwayne "Thomas" (#66)
Born on June 19, 1987 in Deltona, FL
6'6" and 308 pounds
Offensive Lineman   2011
3 games/1 started (on 10-01-11)
Vanderbilt Commodore

WELKER, Wesley "Wes" (#83)
Born on May 1, 1981 in Oklahoma City, OK
5'9" and 185 pounds
WR/PR (K)   2007-12
672 receptions for 7,459 yards + 37 TDs, 18 carries for 146 yards and 1 reception on a 2 point pass
114 punt returns for 1,185 yards and 13 kickoff returns for 280 yards and kicked 1 extra point and 1 kickoff
Caught 3 TD passes from Matt Cassel and 34 Regular Season and 4 Post Season TD passes from Tom Brady
Longest run was 27 yards in their 34-13 rout of the Cincinnati Bengals on 10-01-07
Longest was a 33 yard return of a kickoff by Phil Dawson in their 34-17 win over Cleveland on 10-07-07
Caught a 2 point conversion pass from Matt Cassel in their 24-21 victory over Seattle on 12-07-08
Longest was 69 yard return of a punt by Pat McAfee in their 35-34 loss to the Colts on 11-15-09
Kicked an extra point and had a 45 yard kickoff in their 34-14 loss to the Cleveland Browns on 11-07-10
Recovered a lateral from Tom Brady in their 31-28 victory over the Colts on 11-21-10
Longest reception was a 99 yard TD pass from Tom Brady in their 38-24 win over Miami on 09-12-11
AFC Pro Bowl Wide Receiver from 2008-2012
First Team All Pro Wide Receiver in 2009, 2011
93 Regular Season Games/78 started and 9 Playoff Games/8 started
69 receptions for 686 yards + 4 TDs in the playoffs
Caught a 6 yard TD pass from Tom Brady in their 31-20 Divisional win over the Jaguars on 01-12-08
Caught a 6 yard TD pass from Tom Brady in their 21-12 Championship win over San Diego on 01-20-08
Caught a 7 yard TD pass from Tom Brady in their 45-10 Divisional playoff rout of Denver on 01-14-12
Caught a 1 yard TD pass from Tom Brady in their 28-13 Championship game loss to Baltimore on 01-20-13
Texas Tech Red Raider

WELLS, William "Billy" (#41)
Born on December 7, 1931 in Menomonie, MI
5'9" and 180 pounds
RB/PR/KR   1960
14 carries for 59 yards and 14 receptions for 206 yards + 1 TD
12 punt returns for 66 yards and 11 kickoff returns for 275 yards
Longest reception was a 78 yard pass from Butch Songin in their 35-0 shutout of the LA Chargers
        on 10-08-60
Caught a 6 yard TD pass from Butch Songin in their 31-24 loss to the Denver Broncos on 10-23-60
Longest run was 13 yards in their 38-21 victory over the New York Titans on 11-11-60
Longest return of a kickoff was 33 yards in their 38-21 win over the NY Titans on 11-11-60
Longest return of a punt was 19 yards from a Charlie Milstead punt in their 37-21 loss to Houston on 12-18-60
12 games/4 started
Michigan State Spartan

WENDELL, Ryan (#62)
Born on March 4, 1986 in Ponoma, TX
6'2" and 275 pounds
Lineman (LS)　　　　　2009-15
79 Regular Season Games/49 started and 12 Playoff Games/7 started
Long snapper for Tom Brady's 32 yard punt in their 34-20 win over the Buffalo Bills on 12-29-13
Member of the 2014 World Championship Team
Fresno State Bulldog

WEST, Melvin "Mel" (#24)
Born on January 14, 1939 in Columbia, MO
5'9" and 190 pounds
HB/KR　　　　　1961
26 carries for 90 yards, 5 receptions for 42 yards and 7 kickoff returns for 191 yards
Longest reception was an 18 yard pass from Butch Songin in their 45-17 win over Denver on 09-16-61
Longest run was 31 yards in their 23-21 win over the Buffalo Bills on 09-23-61
Longest was a 37 yard return of a kickoff by Curley Johnson in their 37-30 loss to the NY Titans on 10-01-61
4 games/2 started
11th Round Draft Pick in 1961
Missouri Tiger

WESTBROOK JR., Donald "Don" (#83) *"Westy"*
Born on November 1, 1953 in Cheyenne, WY
5'10" and 185 pounds
WR/KR (PR)　　　　　1977-81
23 receptions for 393 yards + 3 TDs, 3 carries for 6 yards, 2 completions for 52 yards and blocked a punt
19 kickoff returns for 290 yards, 2 punt returns for 5 yards and 1 recovery of a Patriots onside kick
Recovered fumbles by Joe Washington, Vaughn Lusby and Mike Haynes
Caught 1 TD pass from Matt Cavanaugh and 2 TD passes from Tom Owen
Recovered an onside kick by Patriots Kicker John Smith in their 34-27 loss to the Colts on 09-18-78
Longest was a 33 yard return of a kickoff by Rafael Septien in their 17-10 loss to Dallas on 12-03-78
Blocked a punt by Chuck Ramsey in their 56-3 rout of the New York Jets on 09-09-79
Longest was a 5 yard return of a punt by Chuck Ramsey in their 56-3 rout of the Jets on 09-09-79
Tossed a 28 yard left handed pass to Russ Francis in their 24-17 win over the Lions on 10-07-79
Longest run was 4 yards in their 31-26 loss to the Baltimore Colts on 10-28-79
Longest reception was a 38 yard pass from Steve Grogan in their 26-6 win over Buffalo on 11-04-79
Tackled Brent McClanahan for a 1 yard loss on a fake punt play in their 27-23 win over the Vikings on 12-16-79
Threw a 24 yard left handed pass to Don Hasselbeck in their 27-23 win over the Vikings on 12-16-79
71 Regular Season Games/1 started (on 12-20-81) and 1 Playoff Game (on 12-31-78)
Recovered Mike Haynes' fumbled punt return in their 31-14 Divisional loss to Houston on 12-31-78
Nebraska Cornhusker

WHALEN JR., James "Jim" (#82)
Born on May 20, 1943 in Cambridge, MA
6'2" and 210 pounds
Tight End/LS   1965-69
153 receptions for 2,487 yards + 17 TDs, 1 carry for no gain and 1 fumble recovery
Caught 1 TD pass from Don Trull, 4 TDs from Mike Taliaferro and Tom Sherman and 8 TDs from Babe Parilli
Long Snapper for Kicker Gino Cappelletti and Punter Tom Yewcic
Recovered Speedy Duncan's fumbled punt return in their 13-13 Tie with San Diego on 10-17-65
Caught a 3 TD passes from Babe Parilli in their 41-10 rout of Miami at Boston College on 10-15-67
Had a career long 87 yard TD reception of a pass from Tom Sherman in their 48-14 loss to the Jets on 10-27-68
Took a lateral from Tom Sherman but ran for no gain in their 33-14 win over the Bengals on 12-01-68
First Team All Pro Tight End in 1968
70 games/48 started
3rd Round Draft Pick in 1965
Boston College Eagle

WHEATLEY, Terrence (#22)
Born on May 5, 1985 in Walnut Creek, CA
5'10" and 187 pounds
Cornerback   2008-09
11 games/1 started (on 11-02-08)
Colorado Buffalo

WHEELER, Dwight (#62) *"Whimpy"*
Born on January 13, 1955 in Memphis, TN
6'3" and 269 pounds
Tackle/LS/Center   1978-83
Recovered Mark Moseley's squibbed kickoff in their 16-14 loss to the Redskins on 09-03-78
Long Snapper for Kicker Fred Steinfort in their 26-3 loss to the Jets on 11-27-83
Long Snapper for Kicker Joaquin Zendejas in their 21-7 win over the LA Rams on 12-11-83
Long Snapper for Punter Rich Camarillo for 3 games in 1983
72 Regular Season Games/40 started and 1 Playoff Game (on 01-08-83)
#102 pick in the 1978 NFL Draft
Tennessee State Tiger

WHEELER, Mark (#97)
Born on April 1, 1970 in San Marcos, TX
6'3" and 285 pounds
DT/NT   1996-98
5 sacks and 1 fumble recovery
Had 2 sacks of Stan Humphries and 3 sacks of Neil O'Donnell and recovered a fumble by Dan Marino
40 Regular Season Games/31 started and 6 Playoff Games/5 started
Texas A & M Aggie

WHIGHAM, Larry (#25) *"Hollywood"*
Born on June 23, 1972 in Hattiesburg, MS
6'2" and 205 pounds
DB/ST(KR)　　　　　　1994-2000
4 interceptions for 81 yards + 1 TD, 5 sacks, 2 fumble recoveries and 1 kickoff return for no gain
2 blocked punts and 2 deflected punts
Intercepted Frank Reich and had 3 interceptions of Dan Marino
Recovered fumbles by Dave Meggett and Aaron Bailey
Sacked Kent Graham, Damon Huard, Troy Aikman and had 2 sacks of Rick Mirer
Caught a punt by Patriots Punter Pat O'Neill on the 3 yard line in their 23-17 win vs San Diego on 11-20-94
Deflected a 17 yard punt by Jeff Feagles in their 31-0 shutout of the Arizona Cardinals on 09-15-96
Blocked a punt by Greg Montgomery, that Tedy Bruschi returned for a TD, in their 46-38 win vs Balt.
　　　on 10-06-96
Downed Tom Tupa's punt on 1 yard line and 2 plays later PATS got a safety, in 28-25 win vs Buffalo on 10-27-96
Downed Tom Tupa's punt on 3 yard line and next play PATS got a safety in their 24-19 loss to the Jets
　　　on 10-19-97
Had a career long 60 yard TD return of a pass by Dan Marino in their 27-24 win over Miami on 11-23-97
Deflected a 13 yard punt by Mark Royals in their 30-27 win over the Saints on 10-04-98
Recovered a short kickoff by Louie Aguiar in their 40-10 win over the Kansas City Chiefs on 10-11-98
Blocked a punt by Sean Landeta in their 24-9 loss to the Philadelphia Eagles on 12-19-99
Recovered a blocked field goal in their 13-10 Overtime win vs the Bills on 12-17-00
AFC Defensive Player of the Week in their 27-24 win over Miami on 11-23-97
AFC Special Team Player of the Week in their 20-6 Championship win vs Jacksonville on 01-12-97
AFC Pro Bowl Special Team Player in 1997
106 Regular Season Games/5 started and 7 Playoff Games
Tackled Punter Bryan Barker on the 4 yard line in their 20-6 Championship win over the Jaguars on 01-12-97
NE Louisiana Indian

WHITE, Adrian (#38)
Born on April 6, 1964 in Orange Park, FL
6'0" and 200 pounds
Defensive Back　　　　1993
5 games/4 started
Florida Gator

WHITE, Chris (#59)
Born on January 15, 1989 in Mobile, AL
6'2" and 241 pounds
Linebacker　　　　　　2013-14
29 Regular Season Games and 5 Playoff Games
Member of the 2014 World Championship Team
Mississippi State Bulldog

WHITE, David (#51)
Born on February 27, 1970 in Oak Ridge, TN
6'2" and 235 pounds
Linebacker   1993
6 games
Nebraska Cornhusker

WHITE, Harvey (#10)
Born on March 3, 1938 in Greenwood, SC
6'1" and 191 pounds
QB/RB/TE   1960
3 completions for 44 yards, 5 carries for 7 yards and 2 receptions for 24 yards
Longest run was 5 yards in their 35-0 shutout of the Los Angeles Chargers on 10-08-60
Longest reception was a 13 yard pass from Butch Songin in their 31-24 loss to Denver on 10-23-60
Longest completion was a 23 yard pass to Tom Stephens in their 45-16 loss to the LA Chargers on 10-28-60
9 games/2 started
1st Round Draft Pick in 1960
Clemson Tiger

WHITE, James (#28) *"Sweet Feet"*
Born on February 3, 1992 in Ft. Lauderdale, FL
5'10" and 205 pounds
Running Back   2014-19
274 carries for 1,119 yards + 8 TDs, 320 receptions for 2,809 yards + 24 TDs
1 completion of 35 yards and 4 kickoff returns for 69 yards
Caught 24 Regular Season TD passes and 3 Post Season TD passes from Tom Brady
Longest reception was a 68 yard pass from Tom Brady in their 20-10 loss to Miami on 01-03-16
Longest run was 32 yards in their 28-22 loss to the Houston Texans on 12-01-19
Longest was a 21 yard return of a kickoff by Harrison Butler in their 23-16 loss to the Chiefs on 12-8-19
Completed a 35 yard pass to Jakobi Meyers in their 23-16 loss to the Chiefs on 12-08-19
78 Regular Season Games/13 started and 12 Playoff Games/3 started
36 carries for 146 yards + 5 TDs, 59 receptions for 506 yards + 3 TDs and one 2 point run in the playoffs
Caught a 19 yard TD pass from Tom Brady in their 34-16 Divisional win over the Houston Texans on 01-14-17
Caught a 5 yard TD pass from Tom Brady in their Epic Super Bowl 34-28 OT win vs the Falcons on 02-05-17
Ran for a 2 point conversion in their Super Bowl 34-28 OT win vs the Falcons on 02-05-17
Ran for a 1 yard TD in their 34-28 OT Super Bowl win vs the Atlanta Falcons on 02-05-17
Ran for a 2 yard TD to defeat the Atlanta Falcons 34-28 in Overtime in the Super Bowl on 02-05-17
Scored 20 points in their Epic Super Bowl 34-28 OT win over the Atlanta Falcons on 02-05-17
Ran for a 6 yard TD in their 35-14 Divisional rout of the Tennessee Titans on 01-13-18
Caught a 5 yard TD pass from Tom Brady in their 35-14 Divisional win over the Tennessee Titans on 01-13-18
Ran for a 1 yard TD in their 24-20 Championship win over the Jacksonville Jaguars on 01-21-18
Dashed 26 yards for a TD in their 41-33 Super Bowl loss to the Philadelphia Eagles on 02-04-18
Member of the 2014, 2016 and 2018 World Championship Teams
#130 pick in the 2014 NFL Draft
Wisconsin Badger

WHITE, Jeffrey "Jeff" (#2)
Born on June 10, 1948 in Bronxville NY
5'10" and 170 pounds
Kicker/Punter　　　　1973
Kicked 14 field goals and 21 extra points and 6 punts for 163 yards
Longest punt was 51 yards in their 30-14 loss to the Miami Dolphins on 10-28-73
His onside kick was recovered by his teammate Claxton Welch in their 33-13 loss to the Jets on 11-11-73
Had a career long 48 yard field goal in their 32-0 shutout of the Houston Oilers on 11-25-73
11 games
Texas El Paso Miner

WHITE, James "Jim" (#87)
Born on September 5, 1948 in Chicago, IL
6'4" and 256 pounds
Defensive End　　　　1972
Sacked Dennis Shaw in their 27-24 loss to the Buffalo Bills on 11-19-72
13 games/6 started
#73 pick in the 1972 NFL Draft
Colorado State Ram

WHITE, Reginald "Reggie" (#90) *"The Other"*
Born on March 22, 1970 in Baltimore, MD
6'4" and 296 pounds
Defensive Tackle　　　　1995
1.5 sacks
Shared in a sack of Vinny Testaverde and sacked Glenn Foley
16 games/7 started
North Carolina A & T Aggie

WHITE, Tracy (#58)
Born on April 14, 1981 in Charleston, SC
6'0" and 235 pounds
LB/Special Team　　　　2010-12
42 Regular Season Games/2 started and 6 Playoff Games
Howard Bison

WHITTEN, Phillip "Todd" (#15)
Born on February 16, 1965 in Dallas, TX
6'0" and 185 pounds
Quarterback　　　　1987
Only game played was on 10-18-87
Knelt on the last 2 plays in their 21-7 victory over the Houston Oilers on 10-18-87
Stephen F. Austin State Lumberjack

WHITTINGHAM, Fred (#53)
Born on February 4, 1939 in Boston, MA
6'1" and 240 pounds
Linebacker (KR)   1970
Had a 24 yard return of a kickoff by Mike Mercer in their 16-14 loss to San Diego on 11-15-70
13 games
California Polytechnic Mustang

WICHARD, Murray (#90)
Born on November 16, 1963 in New York, NY
6'2" and 260 pounds
Defensive Lineman   1987
1 sack and 2 fumble recoveries
Shared in a strip sack of Jeff Christensen and Willie Totten
Recovered fumbles by Jeff Christensen and Willie Totten
3 games
Frostburg State Bobcat

WIGGINS, Jermaine (#49 and #85) *"Our Snow Plow"*
Born on January 18, 1975 in East Boston, MA
6'2" and 255 pounds
Tight End   2000-01
Wore # 49 for 1 game on 12-04-00 and then #85 from 2000-01
30 receptions for 336 yards + 5 TDs
Caught 2 TD passes from Drew Bledsoe and 3 TD passes from Tom Brady
Cradled a 1 yard TD pass, on 4th + 1, from Drew Bledsoe in their 30-24 win over the Chiefs on 12-04-00
Longest reception was a 59 yard pass from Drew Bledsoe in their 27-24 loss to the Dolphins on 12-24-00
Grabbed a 3 yard TD pass, with 36 ticks left, from Tom Brady, in their 29-26 OT win vs SD on 10-14-01
20 Regular Season Games/8 started and 3 Playoff Games/1 started (on 02-03-02)
Member of the 2001 World Championship Team
Georgia Bulldog

WILBURN, Steve (#99)
Born on February 25, 1961 in Chicago, IL
6'4" and 266 pounds
Defensive End   1987
Shared in a sack of Jeff Christensen and Willie Totten
3 games/3 started
Illinois State Redbird

WILFORK, Vince (#75) *"Air"*
Born on November 4, 1981 in Boynton Beach, FL
6'2" and 325 pounds
Nose Tackle   2004-14
Nicknamed *"Air"* after his leaping block of Nick Folk's 52 yard field goal attempt
16 sacks, 3 interceptions for 48 yards, 12 fumble recoveries for 1 TD
Blocked an extra point and a field goal attempt
Shared in a sack of Jake Delhomme and had 2 ½ sacks of Chad Henne
Sacked Drew Bledsoe, Jay Fiedler, Derek Anderson, Brett Favre, Dan Orlovsky and Matt Moore
Sacked Ryan Fitzpatrick, Matt Schaub and Ryan Tannehill,
Recorded 2 sacks of Ben Roethlisberger and Chad Pennington
Intercepted Philip Rivers, Jason Campbell and David Carr
Recovered fumbles by Edgerrin James, Chris Chambers, Kerry Collins, J.P. Losman and Philip Rivers
Recovered fumbles by Matt Flynn, Rex Grossman, Marlon Moore, Ryan Williams and C. J. Spiller
Recovered fumbles by Petyon Manning and Ryan Tannehill
Blocked an extra point attempt by Sebastian Janikowski in their 49-26 win over the Oakland Raiders
          on 12-14-08
Recovered Matt Flynn's fumble on the last play of their 31-27 win over the Packers on 12-19-10
Had a career long 28 yard return of a pass by Philip Rivers in their 35-21 win over San Diego on 09-18-11
Had a 19 yard return of a pass by Jason Campbell in their 31-19 win over the Oakland Raiders on 10-02-11
Recovered Rex Grossman's fumble in the end zone for a TD in their 34-27 win over the Redskins on 12-11-11
Forced Jets Center Brandon Moore backwards which caused the Mark Sanchez "butt fumble" on 11-22-12
Had a 1 yard return of a pass by David Carr in their 16-9 victory over the Oakland Raiders on 09-21-14
Tipped Nick Folk's 52 yard field goal attempt in their 17-16 victory over the NY Jets on 12-21-14
AFC Pro Bowl Nose Tackle in 2007, 2009-12
First Team All Pro Nose Tackle in 2012
158 Regular Season Games/148 started and 21 Playoff Games/19 started
3 sacks in the playoffs and 1 fumble return of 31 yards
Shared in a sack of Jake Plummer in their 27-13 Divisional loss to the Denver Broncos on 01-14-06
Returned Chad Pennington's backwards lateral 31 yards in their 37-16 Wild Card win over the Jets on 01-07-07
Sacked Tim Tebow in their 45-10 Divisional rout of the Denver Broncos on 01-14-12
Shared in another sack of Tim Tebow in their 45-10 Divisional win over Denver on 01-14-12
Sacked Joe Flacco in their 23-20 AFC Championship win over the Ravens on 01-22-12
Member of the 2004 and 2014 Championship Teams
Ron Burton Community Service Award on 2010
21ˢᵗ pick in the 2004 NFL Draft
Miami Hurricane

WILHITE, Jonathan (#24)
Born on February 23, 1984 in Monroe, LA
5'9" and 183 pounds
Defensive Back   2008-10
3 interceptions for 33 yards and 1 fumble recovery
Intercepted JaMarcus Russell, Peyton Manning and Ryan Fitzpatrick and recovered a fumble by Lendale White
Had a 17 yard return of a pass by Peyton Manning in their 35-34 loss to the Colts on 11-15-09
39 Regular Season Games/3 started and 1 Playoff Game (on 01-10-10)
#129 pick in the 2008 NFL Draft
Auburn Tiger

WILLIAMS, Brent (#96)
Born on October 23, 1964 in Flint, MI
6'4" and 283 pounds
DE (NT)   1986-93
43.5 sacks, 10 fumble recoveries for 92 yards and 2 TDs and blocked a field goal
Shared in a sack of Bernie Kosar, Mike Tomczak, Browning Nagle, Steve DeBerg and Scott Mitchell
Sacked Gary Hogenboom, Dan Marino, Pat Ryan, Bubby Brister, Rusty Hilger and John Elway
Sacked Cody Carlson, Chris Chandler, Don Majkowski, Dave Krieg, Gary Kubiak and Warren Moon
Sacked Jack Trudeau, Timm Rosenbach, Boomer Esiason, Jim Everett, Billy Joe Tolliver and Donald Hollas
Had 1 ½ sacks of Jeff George and Randall Cunningham and 2 sacks of Vinny Tesataverde and Chris Miller
Had 6 ½ sacks of Ken O'Brien and 9 sacks of Jim Kelly
Recovered fumbles by Tony Paige, Dave Krieg, Jim Kelly, Freeman McNeil, Barry Foster and Brad Baxter
Returned fumbles by Rueben Mayes, Dave Wilson, Dan Marino and Dave Krieg
Returned Ray Donaldson's bad snap to Gary Hogenboom 26 yards in their 33-3 rout of the Colts on 09-07-86
Had a 21 yard Game Winning TD return of a fumble by Dave Wilson in their 21-20 win vs the Saints
   on 11-30-86
Recovered Dave Krieg's fumble, on Seattle's 6 yard line, in their 13-7 win over Seattle on 12-04-88
Recovered his strip sack of Jim Kelly in their 33-24 victory over the Buffalo Bills on 11-19-89
Had a 45 yard TD return of a fumble by Dave Krieg in their 33-20 loss to the Seahawks on 10-07-90
Blocked a 48 yard field goal attempt by Dean Biasucci in their 16-7 win over the Colts on 09-01-91
AFC Defensive Player of the Week in their 33-24 win over Buffalo on 11-19-89
121 Regular Season Games/101 started and 1 Playoff Game (on 01-04-87)
#193 pick in the 1986 NFL Draft
Toledo Rocket

WILLIAMS, Brian (#49)
Born on October 14, 1957 in New Orleans, LA
6'3" and 240 pounds
Tight End   1982
Only game played was on 11-21-82
Southern Jaguar

WILLIAMS JR., David "D.J." (#45)
Born on September 10, 1988 in Fort Worth, TX
6'2" and 236 pounds
Tight End   2013
2 games (on Dec. 1st and Dec.29th)
Arkansas Razorback

WILLIAMS, Derwin (#82)
Born on May 6, 1961 in Brownwood, TX
6'0" and 180 pounds
Wide Receiver   1985-87
14 receptions for 228 yards and 1 fumble recovery
Longest reception was a 30 yard pass from Tony Eason in their 26-20 win over Green Bay on 09-08-85
Recovered Darryl Clack's fumbled kickoff return in their 23-17 OT loss to the Cowboys on 11-15-87
42 Regular Season Games/1 started (on 09-15-85) and 2 Playoff Games
#192 pick in the 1984 NFL Draft
New Mexico Lobo

WILLIAMS, Edwin "Ed" (#54)
Born on September 8, 1961 in Odessa, TX
6'4" and 244 pounds
Linebacker   1984-87 and 1990
2 sacks, 3 fumble recoveries and 1 interception return of 51 yards
Recovered a fumble by J.J. Birden and 2 fumbles by Sammy Winder
Recovered a punt that hit Gary Padjen, on the Colts 6 yard line, in their 16-10 win over Indy on 12-16-84
Had a 51 yard return of a pass by Danny White pass in their 23-17 OT loss to the Cowboys on 11-15-87
Recovered a fumble by Sammy Winder and lateraled it to Jim Bowman in their 31-20 loss to Denver on 12-06-87
Sacked Boomer Esiason and Todd Philcox in their 41-7 loss to the Cincinnati Bengals on 09-23-90
62 Regular Season Games/10 started and 4 Playoff Games
#43 pick in the 1984 NFL Draft
Texas Longhorn

WILLIAMS, Grant (#76)
Born on May 10, 1974 in Hattiesburg, MS
6'7" and 320 pounds
Tackle   2000-01
29 Regular Season Games/12 started and 3 Playoff Games
Member of the 2001 World Championship Team
Louisiana Tech Bulldog

WILLIAMS, Joejuan (#33)
Born on December 6, 1997 in Nashville, TN
6'3" and 212 pounds
DB/Special Team   2019--
9 Regular Season Games and 1 Playoff Game (on 01-04-20)
#45 pick in the 2019 NFL Draft
Vanderbilt Commodore

WILLIAMS, Jonathan "Jon" (#44)
Born on June 1, 1961 in Somerville, NJ
5'9" and 205 pounds
Kickoff Returnman   1984
23 kickoff returns for 461 yards
Had a career long 29 yard return of a kickoff by Joe Danelo in their 21-17 win over the Bills on 09-02-84
Had another 29 yard return of a kickoff by Jim Breech in their 20-14 win over the Bengals on 10-14-84
9 games
#70 pick in the 1984 NFL Draft
Penn State Nittany Lion

WILLIAMS, Kim "Brooks" (#80)
Born on December 7, 1954 in Baltimore, MD
6'4" and 226 pounds
Tight End   1983
Caught a pass for no gain from Steve Grogan in their 31-0 shutout of the Bills on 10-23-83
13 games
North Carolina Tar Heel

WILLIAMS II, Lawrence "Larry" (#75)
Born on July 3, 1963 inn Orange, CA
6'5" and 292 pounds
Guard   1992
Pounced on Jeff Carlson's fumble in their 20-10 loss to the Cincinnati Bengals on 12-20-92
13 games/9 started
Notre Dame Fighting Irish

WILLIAMS, Lester (#72)
Born on January 19, 1959 in Miami, FL
6'3" and 275 pounds
Nose Tackle   1982-85
5 sacks, 2 fumble recoveries and 1 blocked field goal attempt
Shared in a sack of Archie Manning and Joe Ferguson
Sacked Richard Todd, Cliff Stoudt, Joe Theismann and Eric Hipple
Recovered fumbles by Theotis Brown and Dave Krieg
Blocked a 52 yard field goal attempt by Norm Johnson in their 16-0 shutout of Seattle on 12-19-82
40 Regular Season Games/13 started and 5 Playoff Games/5 started
Recovered Dan Marino's fumble in their 31-14 AFC Championship win vs Miami on 01-12-86
#27 pick in the 1982 NFL Draft
Miami Hurricane

WILLIAMS, Malcolm (#41)
Born on November 22, 1987 in Grand Prairie, TX
5'11" and 200 pounds
Special Team   2011-12
4 Regular Season Games and 3 Playoff Games
Texas Christian Horned Frog

WILLIAMS, Michael (#85)
Born on September 8, 1990 in Reform, AL
6'6" and 269 pounds
Tight End   2015
3 receptions for 26 yards and 3 kickoff returns for 18 yards
Longest reception was a 15 yard pass from Tom Brady in their 40-32 win over the Bills on 09-20-15
Had a 10 yard return of a kickoff by Jordan Gay in their 20-13 win over the Bills on 11-23-15
15 Regular Season Games/9 started and 2 Playoff Games/1 started (on 01-24-16)
Alabama Crimson Tide

WILLIAMS, Perry (#38)
Born on April 12, 1964 in Cartersville, GA
6'1" and 200 pounds
Defensive Back   1987
Picked off a pass by Willie Totten pass in their 14-7 victory over the Buffalo Bills on 10-11-87
3 games
Clemson Tiger

WILLIAMS, Tobias "Toby" (#90)
Born on November 19, 1959 in Washington, DC
6'3" and 264 pounds
Nose Tackle　　　　　1983-88
14.5 sacks and 1 fumble recovery
Shared in a sack of Pat Ryan, Paul McDonald, Dave Archer and Rusty Hilger
Sacked David Woodley, Brian Sipe, Joe Ferguson, Joe Pisarcik, Randall Cunningham and Jim Kelly
Had 2 sacks of Jim McMahon and Ken O'Brien and 2 ½ sacks of Art Schlichter
Recovered Boomer Esiason's fumble in their 20-14 win over the Bengals on 10-14-84
80 Regular Season Games/56 started and 1 Playoff Game/1 started (on 01-04-87)
#265 pick in the 1983 NFL Draft
Nebraska Cornhusker

WILLIAMSON, John "J.R" (#55)
Born on October 9, 1941 in El Dorado, AR
6'2" and 220 pounds
LB/Center　　　　　1968-71
2 fumble recoveries and 1 interception return of 2 yards
Recovered fumbles by Dick Christy and Gene Foster
Had a 2 yard return of a pass by Bob Griese in their 27-14 victory over Miami on 09-20-70
39 games/1 started (on 09-21-69)
Louisiana Tech Bulldog

WILSON, Darrell (#47)
Born on July 28, 1958 in Camden, NJ
5'11" and 180 pounds
Special Team　　　　　1981
Only game played was on 11-08-81
UCONN Husky

WILSON, Darryal (#48)
Born on September 19, 1960 in Florence, AL
6'0" and 182 pounds
Wide Receiver　　　　　1983
9 games
#47 pick in the 1983 NFL Draft
Tennessee Volunteer

WILSON, David (#26)
Born on June 10, 1970 in Los Angeles, CA
5'10" and 192 pounds
Special Team　　　　　1992
Only game played was on 10-25-92
California Golden Bear

WILSON, Edward "Eddie" (#12)
Born on August 14, 1940 in Redding, CA
6'0" and 190 pounds
QB (P)   1965
20 completions for 257 yards + 1 TD, 8 carries for 4 yards and 6 punts for 194 yards
Had 6 punts for 194 yards (longest was 49 yards) in their 13-13 tie with the San Diego Chargers on 10-17-65
Longest completion was a 30 yard pass to Jim Whalen in their 30-21 loss to the Raiders on 10-24-65
Longest run was 17 yards in their 30-21 loss to the Oakland Raiders on 10-24-65
Threw an 8 yard TD pass to Jim Colclough in their 27-23 win over the Jets on 11-28-65
14 games/1 started (on 10-17-65)
Arizona Wildcat

WILSON II, Eugene (#26)
Born on August 17, 1980 in Maywood, IL
5'10" and 195 pounds
Defensive Back   2003-07
10 interceptions for 74 yards + 1 TD and 4 fumble recoveries for 4 yards
Intercepted Kerry Collins, Jay Fiedler Aaron Brooks and Kellen Clemens
Had 2 interceptions of Drew Bledsoe, Chad Pennington and Josh McCown
Recovered fumbles by Edgerrin James, Steve Heiden, Antwann Randle El and Chris Baker
Had a career long 24 yard return of a pass by Chad Pennington in their 23-7 win over the Jets on 12-26-04
Recovered Antwann Randle El's attempted lateral to Hines Ward in their 23-20 win over the Steelers on 09-25-05
Picked off Aaron Brooks, in the end zone, on the last play, in their 24-17 win over the Saints on 11-20-05
Had a 4 yard return of a fumble by Chris Baker in their 20-10 win over the New York Jets on 12-16-07
Had a 5 yard TD return of a pass by Kellen Clemens in their 20-10 win over the Jets on 12-16-07
AFC Defensive Player of the Month in September 2004
62 Regular Season Games/55 started and 10 Playoff Games/8 started
Intercepted Ben Roethlisberger *twice* in their 41-27 Championship win over the Steelers on 01-23-05
Member of the 2003 and 2004 World Championship Teams
#36 pick in the 2003 NFL Draft
Illinois Fighting Illini

WILSON, Jerrel (#4)
Born on October 4, 1941 in New Orleans, LA
6'2" and 222 pounds
Punter   1978
54 punts for 1,921 yards
Longest punt was 57 yards in their 17-10 loss to the Dallas Cowboys on 12-03-78
14 Regular Season Games and 1 Playoff Game (on 12-31-78)
4 punts for 173 yards in their 31-14 Divisional Game loss to the Houston Oilers on 12-31-78
Southern Mississippi Golden Eagle

WILSON, Joseph "Joe" (#23)
Born on August 11, 1950 in Raeford, NC
5'10" and 210 pounds
RB (KR)   1974
15 carries for 57 yards, 3 receptions for 38 yards and 2 kickoff returns for 33 yards
Longest return was an 18 yard return of a kickoff by John Leypoldt in their 29-28 loss to Buffalo on 11-03-74
Longest run was 12 yards in their 34-27 loss to the Miami Dolphins on 12-15-74
Longest reception was a 23 yard pass from Jim Plunkett in their 34-27 loss to Miami on 12-15-74
12 games
Holy Cross Crusader

WILSON, Marc (#15)
Born on February 15, 1957 in Bremerton, WA
6'6" and 205 pounds
Quarterback   1989-90
214 completions for 2,631 yards + 9 TDs and 12 carries for 49 yards
Threw 1 TD pass to George Adams and 2 TDs to Cedric Jones, Hart Lee Dykes, Marv Cook and Irving Fryar
Longest completion was a 65 yard TD pass to Cedric Jones in their 27-26 loss to the Jets on 11-05-89
Longest run was 11 yards in their 28-10 loss to the Steelers on 12-17-89
Holder for Jason Staurovsky and Greg Davis
30 games/10 started
BYU Cougar

WILSON, Tavon (#27)
Born on March 19, 1990 in Washington, DC
6'0" and 212 pounds
Defensive Back   2012-15
5 interceptions for 161 yards + 1 TD and 2 fumble recoveries
Intercepted Jake Locker, Ryan Fitzpatrick, Kellen Clemens, Andrew Luck and Tyrod Taylor
Recovered fumbles by Kevin Kolb and Fred Jackson
Had a career long 74 yard TD return of a pass by Tyrod Taylor in their 41-7 rout of the Ravens on 12-22-13
54 Regular Season Games/4 started and 7 Playoff Games
Member of the 2014 World Championship Team
#48 pick in the 2012 NFL Draft
Illinois Fighting Illini

WINDSOR, Robert "Bob" (#86) *"Schooner"*
Born on December 19, 1942 in Washington, DC
6'4" and 220 pounds
Tight End   1972-75
74 receptions for 915 yards + 6 TDs, 1 recovery of an onside and 1 fumble recovery
Caught 6 TD passes from Jim Plunkett
Recovered an onside kick by George Hunt in their 24-16 win over the Baltimore Colts on 10-07-73
Longest reception was a 36 yard pass from Jim Plunkett in their 13-10 win over the Bears on 10-21-73
Caught a 10 yard TD pass from Jim Plunkett, on the last play, in their 17-14 win over the Vikings on 10-27-74
Recovered Sam Cunningham's fumble in their 33-19 win over San Diego on 11-09-75
48 games/33 started
Kentucky Wildcat

WINOVICH, Chase (#50) *"Thor"*
Born on April 19, 1995 in Jefferson Hills, PA
6'3" and 250 pounds
LB/DE   2019--
5.5 sacks and 1 return of a blocked punt for a 6 yard TD
Shared in a sack of Ryan Fitzpatrick, Luke Falk and Baker Mayfield
Sacked Josh Rosen, Colt McCoy, Josh Allen and Deshaun Watson
Had a 6 yard TD return of a blocked punt in their 35-14 rout of the Giants on 10-10-19
16 Regular Season Games and 1 Playoff Game
#77 Pick in the 2019 NFL Draft
Michigan Wolverine

WINSLOW II, Kellen (#82)
Born on July 21, 1983 in San Diego, CA
6'4" and 240 pounds
Tight End   2012
Caught a 12 yard pass from Tom Brady in their 31-30 loss to the Baltimore Ravens on 09-23-12
Only game played was on 09-23-12
Miami Hurricane

WIRGOWSKI, Dennis (#85 and #70) *"Wirgo"*
Born on September 20, 1947 in Bay City, MI
6'5" and 257 pounds
DE (K/LS)   1970-72
Wore #85 for the Boston Patriots in 1970 and #70 for the New England Patriots from 1971-72
5 sacks and 2 fumble recoveries
Sacked Greg Landry, Al Woodhall, Dan Pastorini, Dennis Shaw and Archie Manning
Recovered fumbles by Pete Banaszak and Dennis Shaw
Kicked off in the games played on September 27, 1970 and on October 4, 1970
Long Snapper for Punter Pat Studstill and Kicker Mike Walker in their 31-7 loss to the Bengals on 09-17-72
37 games/26 started
#212 pick in the 1970 NFL Draft
Purdue Boilermaker

WISE JR., Deatrich (#91)
Born on July 24, 1994 in St. Petersburg, FL
6'5" and 275 pounds
Defensive Lineman   2017-19
11.5 sacks
Sacked Alex Smith, Drew Brees, Jameison Winston, Matthew Stafford, Mitchell Trubisky and Josh McCown
Sacked Patrick Mahomes and had 1 ½ sacks of Tyrod Taylor, Ben Roethlisberger and Deshaun Watson
46 Regular Season Games/11 started and 5 Playoff Games/2 started
Sacked Marcus Mariota *twice* in their 35-14 Divisional Playoff Game win over Tennessee on 01-13-18
Member of the 2018 World Championship Team
#131 pick in the 2017 NFL Draft
Arkansas Razorback

WITT, Hillery "Mel" (#70 and #71) *"Marvelous Mel"*
Born on November 23, 1946 in Fort Worth, TX
6'3" and 250 pounds
DE/DT   1967-70
Wore #70 from 1967-69 and #71 in 1970
Had a 4 yard TD return of a pass by Joe Namath in their 47-31 loss to the Jets on 09-22-68
35 games/13 started
#128 pick in the 1967 NFL Draft
Arlington State Maverick

WOHLABAUGH, Dave (#64)
Born on April 13, 1972 in Hamburg, NY
6'3" and 296 pounds
Center   1995-98
Recovered 3 fumbles by Drew Bledsoe
57 Regular Season Games/57 started and 6 Playoff Games/6 started
#112 pick in the 1995 NFL Draft
Syracuse Orangeman

WONSLEY, George (#35)
Born on November 23, 1960 in Moss Point, MS
5'10" and 218 pounds
RB/KR   1989
3 kickoff returns for 69 yards
Longest was a 40 yard return of a kickoff by Mike Lansford in their 24-20 loss to the LA Rams on 12-24-89
5 games
Mississippi State Bulldog

WOODHEAD, Danny (#39)
Born on January 25, 1985 in North Platte, NE
5'9" and 200 pounds
RB/KR   2010-12
250 carries for 1,199 yards + 10 TDs and ran for Two 2 point conversions
92 receptions for 982 yards + 4 TDs and 22 kickoff returns for 480 yards
Caught 4 Regular Season TD passes and 1 Post Season TD pass from Tom Brady
Longest reception was a 50 yard pass from Tom Brady in their 45-3 rout of the NY Jets on 12-06-10
Ran for a 2 point conversion in their 35-21 win over the San Diego Chargers on 09-18-11
Longest was a 37 yard return of a kickoff by Dan Carpenter in their 27-24 win over Miami on 12-24-11
Ran for a 2 point conversion in their 49-21 rout of the Buffalo Bills on 01-01-12
Longest run was 19 yards in their 31-21 win over the Denver Broncos on 10-07-12
45 Regular Season Games/9 started and 6 Playoff Games/3 started
Caught a 4 yard TD pass from Tom Brady in their 21-17 Super Bowl loss to the NY Giants on 02-05-12
Chadron State Eagle

WOODS, Carl (#34)
Born on October 22, 1964 in Gallatin, TN
5'11" and 200 pounds
Running Back   1987
4 carries for 20 yards + 1 TD
Ran for a 4 yard TD in their 14-7 victory over the Bills on 10-11-87
Longest run was 13 yards in their 14-7 win over Buffalo on 10-11-87
2 games (on Oct. 4th and Oct. 11th)
Vanderbilt Commodore

WOODS, Pierre (#58)
Born on January 6, 1982 in Cleveland, OH
6'5" and 255 pounds
Linebacker   2006-10
Sacked Brett Favre and Shaun Hill
54 Regular Season Games and 7 Playoff Games
Michigan Wolverine

WOODY, Damien (#65)
Born on November 3, 1977 in Beaverdam, VA
6'3" and 330 pounds
Center/Guard   1999-2003
Recovered fumbles by Terry Allen, Tom Brady and Joe Andruzzi
Fell on Joe Andruzzi's deflected pass reception fumble in their 38-34 win vs the Colts on 11-30-03
AFC Pro Bowl Center in 2002
78 Regular Season Games/76 started and 4 Playoff Games/4 started
Member of the 2001 and 2003 World Championship Teams
#17 pick in the 1999 NFL Draft
Boston College Eagle

WOOTEN, Ron (#61) *"Rootin-Tootin"*
Born on June 28, 1959 in Bourne, MA
6'4" and 274 pounds
Guard   1982-88
Recovered a fumble by Craig James in their 22-19 victory over the Buffalo Bills on 11-23-86
98 Regular Season Games/96 started and 6 Playoff Games/6 started
#157 pick in the 1981 NFL Draft
North Carolina Tar Heel

WREN, Darryl (#27)
Born on January 25, 1967 in Tulsa, OK
6'1" and 188 pounds
Defensive Back   1993-94
3 interceptions and 1 recovery of a Patriots onside kick
Intercepted 2 passes by Rodney Peete and lost 9 yards trying to return a pass by Steve Beuerlein
Recovered an onside kick by Patriots Kicker Scott Sisson in their 28-14 loss to the Houston Oilers on 10-17-93
20 games/5 started
Pittsburg State Gorilla

WRIGHT, Elmo (#17)
Born on July 3, 1949 in Matagorda County, TX
6'0" and 190 pounds
Wide Receiver   1975
4 receptions for 46 yards
Longest reception was a 20 yard pass from Steve Grogan in their 45-31 loss to the Bills on 11-23-75
4 games
Houston Cougar

WRIGHT, Michael "Mike" (#99)
Born on March 1, 1982 in Cincinnati, OH
6'4" and 295 pounds
Defensive Lineman   2005-11
15 sacks, 3 fumble recoveries and blocked a field goal
Sacked David Carr, Josh Freeman, Ryan Fitzpatrick, Tarvaris Jackson and Philip Rivers
Shared in a sack of Kurt Warner and strip sacked Patrick Ramsey, JaMarcus Russell and Mark Sanchez
Had 1 ½ sacks of Chad Henne, 2 sacks of Ben Roethlisberger and 3 sacks of Joe Flacco
Recovered fumbles by Aaron Rodgers, Jon Kitna and Kerry Collins
Blocked a 40 yard field goal attempt by Olindo Mare in their 20-10 win over the Dolphins on 10-08-06
Tackled Punter Donnie Jones before he was able to punt in their 20-10 win over Miami on 10-08-06
Recovered Roosevelt Colvin's strip sack of Jon Kitna in their 28-21 victory over the Lions on 12-03-06
81 Regular Season Games/22 started and 4 Playoff Games
Cincinnati Bearcat

WRIGHT, Timothy "Tim" (#81)
Born on April 7, 1990 in Wall Township, NJ
6'4" and 245 pounds
Tight End   2014
26 receptions for 259 yards + 6 TDs
Caught 6 TD passes from Tom Brady
Longest reception was a 30 yard pass from Tom Brady in their 43-17 win over the Bengals on 10-05-14
16 Regular Season Games/2 started and 3 Playoff Games
Member of the 2014 World Championship Team
Rutgers Scarlet Knight

WYMAN, Devin (#72) "De-Vo"
Born on August 29, 1973 in Lynwood, CA
6'7" and 290 pounds
Defensive Tackle   1996-97
Sacked Mark Brunell in their 28-25 Overtime win vs the Jacksonville Jaguars on 09-22-96
15 games/4 started
#206 pick in the 1996 NFL Draft
Kentucky State Thorobred

WYNN, Isaiah (#76)
Born on December 10, 1996 in St. Petersburg, FL
6'2" and 310 pounds
Offensive Tackle   2019--
8 Regular Season Games/8 started and 1 Playoff Game/1 started
#23 pick in the 2018 NFL Draft
Georgia Bulldog

YANCY, Carlos (#40)
Born June 26, 1970 in Sarasota, FL
6'0" and 185 pounds
Cornerback   1995
4 games
#234 pick in the 1995 NFL Draft
Georgia Bulldog

YATES, Billy (#74)

Born on April 15, 1980 in Fort Worth, TX
6'2" and 305 pounds
Offensive Lineman   2005-08
22 Regular Season Games/11 started and 1 Playoff Game
Texas A & M Aggie

YATES, Robert "Bob" (#50)

Born on November 20, 1938 in Montpelier, VT
6'1" and 240 pounds
OL/Kicker   1960-65
Kicked off in 55 games over the 1961-65 seasons
3 kickoff returns (lateralled 2 of them to Bob Suci) and 1 fumble recovery
Caught Jim Norton's free kick and lateraled it to Bob Suci in their 46-28 win over Houston on 12-08-63
Received a kickoff by Jack Spikes and lateraled it to Bob Suci in their 35-3 loss to the Chiefs on 12-14-63
Recovered Larry Garron's fumble in their 26-17 loss to the San Diego Chargers on 10-09-64
Recovered Mike Mercer's squibbed kickoff in their 43-43 tie with the Oakland Raiders on 10-16-64
68 Regular Season Games/26 started and 2 Playoff Games
Kicked off 10 times in 2 playoff games
Had a 5 yard return of a kickoff by George Blair in their 51-10 Championship loss to SD on 01-05-64
Syracuse Orangeman

YEWCIC, Tom (#14) *"Comrade"*

Born on May 9, 1932 in Comemaugh, PA
5'11" and 185 pounds
Punter (QB/RB)   1961-66
377 punts for 14,553 yards and 87 completions for 1,374 yards + 12 TDs
72 carries for 424 yards + 4 TDs and 7 receptions for 69 yards
Tossed 1 TD pass to Jim Crawford and Gino Cappelletti and 2 TD passes to Ron Burton
Completed 3 TD passes to Jim Crawford and 5 TD passes to Jim Colclough
Threw an 18 yard HB Option TD pass to Jim Colclough in their 45-17 rout of the Broncos on 09-16-61
Longest reception was a 46 yard pass from Babe Parilli in their 45-17 rout of the Broncos on 09-16-61
Ran for a 20 yard gain, on 4th + 4, as the Punter in their 26-16 win over the Raiders on 10-26-62
Lofted a 69 yard TD pass to Ron Burton in their 21-17 loss to the Houston Oilers on 11-18-62
Spun from the rush & tossed a 69 yard TD pass to Ron Burton in their 21-10 win over Buffalo on 11-23-62
Heaved career long 78 yard TD pass to Jim Colclough in their 24-17 win over the NY Titans on 11-30-62
Advanced his own QB fumble 3 yards in their 20-14 win vs the San Diego Chargers on 12-09-62
Longest run as a QB for 46 yards in their 14-10 loss to the Denver Broncos on 09-29-63
Longest punt was 70 yards in their 27-23 win over the Jets on 11-28-65
Holder for Gino Cappellettti in 1962
77 Regular Season Games/6 started at QB and 2 Playoff Games
14 punts for 523 yards and 3 completions for 39 yards in the playoffs
Holds the Playoff Team Record with his 68 yard punt in their AFL Championship Game loss on 01-05-64
Ran for a 14 yard gain in their AFL Championship Game loss to the San Diego Chargers on 01-05-64
Michigan State Spartan

ZABEL, Steve (#54)
Born on March 20, 1948 in Minneapolis, MN
6'4" and 235 pounds
Linebacker (K)   1975-78
10 sacks, 8 fumble recoveries for 8 yards, 1 interception and 1 recovery of an onside kick
Sacked Dan Fouts, Joe Ferguson, Earl Morrall, Bob Griese, Joe Namath and Steve Ramsey
Sacked Bobby Douglass, Steve Bartkowski, Jim Hart and Richard Todd
Recovered fumbles by Lydell Mitchell, Clarence Davis, Mark van Eeghen, Ron Lee and Joe Namath
Recovered fumbles by Johnny Rodgers and Curtis Brown and had an 8 yard return of a fumble
       by Mike Livingston
Snatched an airborn fumble by Lydell Mitchell in their 21-10 win over the Colts on 10-19-75
Kicked an extra point, after Steve Grogan's record setting TD, in their 31-14 win over Tampa on 12-12-76
Had an 8 yard return of a fumble by Mike Livingston in their 21-17 win over the Kansas City Chiefs
       on 09-18-77
Recovered Bill Troup's lateral that was juggled by Ron Lee in their 34-27 loss to the Colts on 09-18-78
Picked off a pass by Ken Anderson in their 10-7 win over the Cincinnati Bengals on 10-15-78
Recovered Tom Dempsey's onside kick in their 14-10 win over the Bills on 11-05-78
49 Regular Season Games/44 started and 2 Playoff Games/2 started
Shared in a 1/3 of a sack of Dan Pastorini in their 31-14 Divisional loss to Houston on 12-31-78
Oklahoma Sooner

ZACKERY, Anthony "Tony" (#25)
Born on November 20, 1966 in Seattle, WA
6'2" and 195 pounds
Special Team   1990-91
Harry Newsome's 30 yard punt deflected off him in their 26-23 OT win vs the Vikings on 10-20-91
Downed Shawn McCarthy's 93 yard punt, on the Bills 1 yard line, in their 22-17 loss to Buffalo on 11-03-91
18 games
#223 pick in the 1989 NFL Draft
Washington Husky

ZAMBERLIN, John (#54)
Born on February 13, 1956 in Tacoma, WA
6'2" and 230 pounds
Linebacker   1979-82
3.5 sacks, 1 interception return of 11 yards and 2 fumble recoveries
Shared in a sack of Jim Zorn and sacked Ken Stabler, Archie Manning and Jim McMahon
Recovered a blocked FGA and lateraled to Mike Haynes in their 21-11 win vs the Jets on 10-05-80
Recovered Mike Augustyniak's fumble in their 28-24 loss to the New York Jets on 10-11-81
Had an 11 yard return of a pass by Ken Stabler in their 38-10 rout of the Houston Oilers on 10-18-81
56 Regular Season Games/15 started and 1 Playoff Game
#135 pick in the 1979 NFL Draft
Pacific Lutheran Lute

ZENDEJAS JR., Joaquin (#2)
Born on January 14, 1960 in Curimeo, Mexico
5'11" and 176 pounds
Kicker   1983
3 extra points kicked
2 games (on Dec. 11th and Dec. 18th)
Laverne Tiger

ZEREOUE, Amos (#31)
Born on October 8, 1976 in the Ivory Coast
5'8" and 212 pounds
Running Back   2005
7 carries for 14 yards and 1 reception for 5 yards
Longest run was 12 yards in their 28-20 loss to the Denver Broncos on 10-16-05
Caught a 5 yard pass from Tom Brady in their 28-20 loss to the Denver Broncos on 10-16-05
3 games
West Virginia Mountaineer

ZOLAK, Scott (#16) "Zo"
Born on December 12, 1967 in Pittsburgh, PA
6'5" and 230 pounds
Quarterback   1992-98
124 completions for 1,314 yards + 8 TDs and 36 carries for 85 yards
Threw 1 TD pass to Ben Coates, Greg McMurty, Sam Gash, Robert Edwards and Shawn Jefferson
Tossed 1 TD pass to Tony Simmons and 2 TD passes to Lovett Purnell
Longest run was 19 yards in their 6-0 loss to the Indianapolis Colts on 12-06-92
Longest completion was a 72 yard pass to Vincent Brisby in their 30-17 loss to the Falcons on 10-01-95
Ran for 8 yards, on 4th and 2, on a fake field goal attempt in their 31-17 loss to the Saints on 12-03-95
AFC Offensive Player of the Week in their 37-34 OT win vs the Colts on 11-15-92
Holder for Matt Bahr
54 Regular Season Games/7 started and 3 Playoff Games/1 started (on 01-03-99)
22 completions for 193 yards in the playoffs
#84 pick in the 1991 NFL Draft
Maryland Terrapin

CHAPTER 8

YEARLY POSITIONAL ROSTER
AND RECORD OF EVERY TEAM

1960 Boston Patriots Roster   Team Record 5-9

QB: Tom Dimitroff, Tom Greene, Butch Songin and Harvey White

RB: Walter Beach, Ron Burton, Dick Christy, Jim Crawford, Jake Crouthamel, Larry Garron, Tom Greene, Bill Larson, Walt Livingston, Alan Miller, Gerhardt Schwedes, Billy Wells and Harvey White

WR: Jack Atchason, Joe Biscaha, Gino Cappelletti and Jim Colclough

TE: Jerry Green, Joe Johnson, Oscar Lofton, Mike Long, Tom Stephens and Harvey White

OL: Abe Cohen, Bobby Cross, Walt Cudzik, Jack Davis, Tony Discenzo, Art Hauser, Harry Jagielski Bob Lee, Charlie Leo, George McGee, Tony Sardisco and Bill Striegel

DL: Al Crow, Bill Danenhauer, Bob Dee, Art Hauser, Jim Lee Hunt, Harry Jacobs, Harry Jagielski Don McComb, Al Richardson, Tony Sardisco and Hal Smith

LB: Tom Addison, Phil Bennett, Bill Brown, Walt Cudzik, Harry Jacobs and Jack Rudolph

DB: Walter Beach, Fred Bruney, Gino Cappelletti, Larry Garron, Ross O'Hanley, Leroy Phelps, Chuck Shonta, Bob Soltis and Clyde Washington

K: Gino Cappelletti, Walt Cudzik and Tony Discenzo

P: Tom Greene and Clyde Washington

1961 Boston Patriots Roster   Team Record 9-4-1

1961 Associated Press All Pro 1st Team Offensive Guard Charlie Leo

QB: Babe Parilli, Butch Songin and Tom Yewcic

RB: Walter Beach, Ron Burton, Jim Crawford, Larry Garron, Billy Lott, Ger Schwedes, Clyde Washington, Billy West and Tom Yewcic

WR: Gino Cappelletti, Jim Cloclough and Chuck Shonta

TE: Joe Johnson, Bill Kimber and Tom Stephens

OL: Houston Antwine, Walt Cudzik, Jerry DeLucca, Milt Graham, Harry Jagielski, ***Charlie Leo,*** Willis Perkins, Tony Sardisco, John Simerson and Bob Yates

DL: Houston Antwine, Bob Dee, Larry Eisenhauer, Milt Graham, Jim Lee Hunt, Harry Jagielski, Dick Klein, Paul Lindquist, LeRoy Moore and Tony Sardisco

LB: Harry Jacobs, Rommie Loudd, Frank Robotti and Jack Rudolph

DB: Walter Beach, Ron Hall, Ross O'Hanley, Al Romine, Chuck Shonta, Bob Soltis, Tom Stephens Bobby Towns, Clyde Washington, and Don Webb

K: Gino Cappelletti and Bob Yates

P: Tom Yewcic

Special Team Kickoff Returnman Ray Ratkowski

1962 Boston Patriots Roster   Team Record 9-4-1

1962 Associated Press All Pro 1st Team Defensive End Larry Eisenhauer

QB: Don Allard, Babe Parilli and Tom Yewcic

RB: Ron Burton, Jim Crawford, Larry Garron, Claude King and Billy Lott

WR: Gino Cappelletti, Jim Colclough, Art Graham and Don Webb

TE: Tony Romeo and Tom Stephens

OL: Walt Cudzik, Milt Graham, Dick Klein, Charlie Leo, Charlie Long, Billy Neighbors Tony Sardisco and Bob Yates

DL: Houston Antwine, Bob Dee, *Larry Eisenhauer,* Jim Lee Hunt, Dick Klein, LeRoy Moore and Jesse Richardson

LB: Tom Addison, Nick Buoniconti, Rommie Loudd and Jack Rudolph

DB: Fred Bruney, Dick Felt, Ron Hall, Ross O'Hanley, Chuck Shonta and Don Webb

K: Gino Cappelletti and Bob Yates

P: Tom Yewcic

1963 Boston Patriots Roster   Team Record 8-7-1   AFL Eastern Division Champions

1963 Associated Press All Pro 1st Team DT Houston Antwine and DE Larry Eisenhauer

QB: Babe Parilli and Tom Yewcic

RB: Ron Burton, Harry Crump, Larry Garron, Billy Lott and Tom Neumann

WR: Gino Cappelletti, Jim Colclough and Art Graham

TE: Tony Romeo

OL: Walt Cudzik, Jerry DeLucca, Milt Graham, Charlie Long, Don Oakes, Dave Watson + Bob Yates

DL: *Houston Antwine,* Bob Dee, *Larry Eisenhauer,* Bill Hudson, Jim Lee Hunt, Jesse Richardson

LB: Tom Addison, Nick Buoniconti, Don McKinnon and Jack Rudolph

DB: Dick Felt, Ron Hall, Ross O'Hanley, Chuck Shonta, Tom Stephens, Bob Suci and Don Webb

K: Gino Cappelletti and Bob Yates

P: Tom Yewcic

1964 Boston Patriots Roster   Team Record 10-3-1

1964 Associated Press AFL MVP Gino Cappelletti

1964 AP All Pro Defensive 1st Team LB Nick Bouniconti, DE Larry Eisenhauer and DB Ron Hall

1964 AP All Pro Offensive 1st Team Offensive Guard Billy Neighbors and QB Babe Parilli

QB: *Babe Parilli* and Tom Yewcic

RB: Ron Burton, Jim Crawford, J.D. Garrett and Larry Garron

WR: *Gino Cappelletti,* Jim Colclough, Art Graham and Al Snyder

TE: Tony Romeo

OL: Jerry DeLucca, Charlie Long, Jon Morris, *Billy Neighbors,* Don Oakes, Bob Schmidt, Lennie St. Jean, Dave Watson and Bob Yates

DL: Houston Antwine, Bob Dee, *Larry Eisenhauer,* Jim Lee Hunt, Jesse Richardson and Lennie St. Jean

LB: Tom Addison, *Nick Bouniconti,* Mike Dukes, Lonnie Farmer, Don McKinnon and Jack Rudolph

DB: Dick Felt, *Ron Hall,* Ross O'Hanley, Chuck Shonta, Tom Stephens and Don Webb

K: *Gino Cappelletti* and Bob Yates

P: Babe Parilli and Tom Yewcic

Special Team Returnman Dave Cloutier

1965 Boston Patriots Roster   Team Record 4-8-2

1965 Associated Press All Pro 1st Team LB Nick Bouniconti

QB: Babe Parilli and Eddie Wilson

RB: Joe Bellino, Ron Burton, J.D. Garrett, Larry Garron, Ellis Johnson, Jim Nance and Tom Yewcic

WR: Joe Bellino, Gino Cappelletti, Jim Colclough and Art Graham

TE: Bill Dawson, Tony Romeo and Jim Whalen

OL: Justin Canale, Charlie Long, Jon Morris, Billy Neighbors, Tom Neville, Lennie St. Jean and Bob Yates

DL: Houston Antwine, Bob Dee, Larry Eisenhauer, Jim Lee Hunt, Tom Neville, George Pyne and Lennie St. Jean

LB: Tom Addison, *Nick Bouniconti,* Mike Dukes, Ed Meixler, Jack Rudolph

DB: Jay Cunningham, Dick Felt, White Graves, Tom Hennessey, Ross O'Hanley, Chuck Shonta and Don Webb

K: Justin Canale, Gino Cappelletti and Bob Yates

P: Eddie Wilson and Tom Yewcic

1966 Boston Patriots Roster   Team Record 8-4-2

1966 Associated Press American Football League MVP Jim Nance

1966 AP All Pro 1ˢᵗ Team LB Nick Bouniconti, Center Jon Morris and RB Jim Nance

QB: John Huarte and Babe Parilli

RB: Joe Bellino, Bob Cappadona, J.D. Garrett, Larry Garron, Ellis Johnson and *Jim Nance*

WR: Joe Bellino, Gino Cappelletti, Jim Colclough, Art Graham and Vic Purvis

TE: Tony Romeo and Jim Whalen

OL: Joe Avezzano, Jim Boudreaux, Justin Canale, Charlie Long, *Jon Morris,* Tom Neville,
      Don Oakes, Karl Singer, Lennie St. Jean and Long Snapper Jim Whalen

DL: Houston Antwine, Bob Dee, Larry Eisenhauer, Jim Lee Hunt, Ed Khayat and John Mangum

LB: Tom Addison, *Nick Bouniconti,* Lonnie Farmer, Jim Fraser and Doug Satcher

DB: Jay Cunningham, Dick Felt, White Graves, Ron Hall, Tom Hennessey, Billy Johnson, Vic Purvis
      Chuck Shonta and Don Webb

K: Gino Cappelletti

P: Jim Fraser and Tom Yewcic

1967 Boston Patriots Roster   Team Record 3-10-1

1967 Associated Press All Pro 1ˢᵗ Team LB Nick Bouniconti and RB Jim Nance

QB: John Huarte, Babe Parilli and Don Trull

RB: Joe Bellino, Bob Cappadona, J.D. Garrett, Larry Garron and *Jim Nance*

WR: Joe Bellino, Gino Cappelletti, Jim Colclough, Art Graham and Bobby Leo

TE: Bobby Nichols, Tony Romeo and Jim Whalen

OL: Jim Boudreaux, Justin Canale, Charlie Long, Jon Morris, Tom Neville, Don Oakes
      Karl Singer, Lennie St. Jean and Long Snapper Jim Whalen

DL: Houston Antwine, Bob Dee, Larry Eisenhauer, Tom Fussell, Jim Lee Hunt, John Mangum,
      Ed Toner and Mel Witt

LB: *Nick Bouniconti,* Ray Ilg, Ed Philpott and Doug Satcher

DB: John Charles, Jay Cunningham, White Graves, Ron Hall, Billy Johnson, Leroy Mitchell
      Vic Purvis and Don Webb

K: Justin Canale and Gino Cappelletti

P: Terry Swanson

1968 Boston Patriots Roster   Team Record 4-10

QB: King Corcoran, Tom Sherman and Mike Taliaferro

RB: R.C. Gamble, Larry Garron, Preston Johnson, Jim Nance, Gene Thomas and Gino Cappelletti

WR: Gino Cappelletti, Jim Colclough, Art Graham, Aaron Marsh, Bill Murphy and Bob Scarpitto

TE: Bobby Nichols and Jim Whalen

OL: Jim Boudreaux, Justin Canale, Paul Feldhausen, Tom Funchess, Charlie Long, Jon Morris Tom Neville, Don Oakes, Karl Singer and Lennie St. Jean

DL: Houston Antwine, Jim Boudreaux, Dennis Byrd, Whit Canale, Larry Eisenhauer, Jim Lee Hunt, Ed Toner and Mel Witt

LB: Nick Bouniconti, Jim Cheyunski, Ray Ilg, Ed Koontz, Ed Philpott, Doug Stacher and J.R. Williamson

DB: John Charles, Billy Johnson, Daryl Johnson, Art McMahon, Leroy Mitchell, Willie Porter and Don Webb

K: Gino Cappelletti

P: Bob Scarpitto and Terry Swanson

1969 Boston Patriots Roster   Team Record 4-10

QB: Kim Hammond, Tom Sherman and Mike Taliaferro

RB: Teddy Bailey, Sid Blanks, R.C. Gamble, Carl Garrett, Bob Gladieux and Jim Nance

WR: Gino Cappelletti, Charley Frazier, Aaron Marsh, Bill Rademacher, Tom Richardson and Ron Sellers

TE: Barry Brown and Jim Whalen

OL: Tom Funchess, Ezell Jones, Charlie Long, Mike Montler, Jon Morris, Tom Neville and Lennie St. Jean

DL: Houston Antwine, Ron Berger, Johnny Cagle, Larry Eisenhauer, Karl Henke, Jim Lee Hunt Ray Jacobs, Ezell Jones, Ed Toner and Mel Witt

LB: Barry Brown, John Bramlett, Johnny Cagle, Jim Cheyunski, Ken Herock, Ed Philpott, Marty Schottenheimer and J.R. Williamson

DB: Larry Carwell, John Charles, Tom Janik, Daryl Johnson, John Outlaw, Clarence Scott and Don Webb

K: Gino Cappelletti

P: Tom Janik

1970 Boston Patriots Roster   Team Record 2-12

QB: Joe Kapp and Mike Taliaferro

RB: Sid Blanks, Carl Garrett, Bob Gladieux, Odell Lawson, Jim Nance and Eddie Ray

WR: Charley Frazier, Gayle Knief, Bill Rademacher, Tom Richardson, Ron Sellers and Bake Turner

TE: Tom Beer, Barry Brown and Eddie Ray

OL: Gary Bugenhagen, Tom Funchess, Ezell Jones, Angelo Loukas, Mike Montler, Jon Morris
Tom Neville and Lennie St. Jean

DL: Houston Antwine, Ron Berger, Tom Funchess, Jim Lee Hunt, Ezell Jones, Ike Lassiter,
Rex Mirich, Dennis Wirgowski and Mel Witt

LB: Mike Ballou, John Bramlett, Jim Cheyunski, Dan Kecman, Ed Philpott, Marty Schottenheimer,
Fred Whittingham and J.R. Williamson

DB: Randy Beverly, Larry Carwell, Daryl Johnson, Art McMahon, John Outlaw, Clarence Scott
and Don Webb

K: Gino Cappelletti, Charlie Gogolak and Dennis Wirgowski

P: Tom Janik

1971 New England Patriots Roster   Team Record 6-8

QB: Jim Plunkett

RB: Carl Garrett, Bob Gladieux, Odell Lawson, Jack Maitland and Jim Nance

WR: Hubie Bryant, Eric Crabtree, Reggie Rucker, Al Sykes and Randy Vataha

TE: Tom Beer and Roland Moss

OL: Halvor Hagen, Mike Haggerty, Bill Lenkaitis, Mike Montler, Jon Morris, Tom Neville
and Lennie St. Jean

DL: Julius Adams, Houston Antwine, Bill Atessis, Ron Berger, Mike Haggerty, Ike Lassiter, Art May,
Dave Rowe and Dennis Wirgowski

LB: Jim Cheyunski, Dennis Coleman, Randy Edmunds, Steve Kiner, Ed Philpott, Kenny Price
and Ed Weisacosky

DB: Randy Beverly, Larry Carwell, Phil Clark, Rickie Harris, Irvin Mallory, John Outlaw,
Perry Pruett, Clarence Scott and Don Webb

K: Charlie Gogolak

P: Tom Janik

Special Team Returnman Ron Gardin

1972 New England Patriots Roster   Team Record 3-11

QB: Brian Dowling and Jim Plunkett

RB: Josh Ashton, Carl Garrett, Bob Gladieux, Jack Maitland, Henry Matthews and John Tarver

WR: Hubie Bryant, Tom Reynolds, Reggie Rucker and Randy Vataha

TE: Tom Beer and Bob Windsor

OL: Sam Adams, Halvor Hagen, Bill Lenkaitis, Wayne Mass, Mike Montler, Jon Morris, Tom Neville Bob Reynolds, Lennie St. Jean and Long Snapper Dennis Wirgowski

DL: Julius Adams, Ron Berger, Rick Cash, Halvor Hagen, Dave Rowe, Jim White and Dennis Wirgowski

LB: Ron Acks, Dick Blanchard, Jim Cheyunski, Ralph Cindrich, Ron Kadziel and Ed Weisacosky

DB: Ron Bolton, Larry Carwell, Rickie Harris, George Hoey, Honor Jackson, Art McMahon John Outlaw and Clarence Scott

K: Charlie Gogolak and Mike Walker

P: Pat Studstill

1973 New England Patriots Roster   Team Record 5-9

QB: Brian Dowling, Jim Plunkett and Dick Shiner

RB: Josh Ashton, Sam Cunningham, Paul Gipson, Mack Herron, Bob McCall, John Tarver and Claxton Welch

WR: Reggie Rucker, Darryl Stingley and Randy Vataha

TE: Bob Adams and Bob Windsor

OL: Sam Adams, Willie Banks, Leon Gray, John Hannah, Kevin Hunt, Bill Lenkaitis, Jon Morris, Tom Neville, Bob Reynolds and Lennie St. Jean

DL: Julius Adams, Nate Dorsey, Ray Hamilton, Mel Lunsford, Art Moore, Dave Rowe, and Donnell Smith

LB: Ron Acks, Edgar Chandler, Doug Dumler, Will Foster, Bob Geddes, Steve Kiner, Steve King, Brian Stenger and John Tanner

DB: Ralph Anderson, Ron Bolton, Greg Boyd, Sandy Durko, George Hoey, Honor Jackson, Don Martin and Dave Mason

K: Bill Bell and Jeff White

Ps: Bruce Barnes and Jeff White

1974 New England Patriots Roster   Team Record 7-7

QB: Neal Graff, Jim Plunkett and Dick Shiner

RB: Josh Ashton, Sam Cunningham, Noe Gonzalez, Mack Herron, Ed Jenkins, Andy Johnson, John Tarver and Joe Wilson

WR: Eddie Hinton, Al Marshall, Reggie Rucker, Steve Schubert, Darryl Stingley, Joe Sweet and Randy Vataha

TE: Bob Adams and Bob Windsor

OL: Sam Adams, Bill DuLac, Allen Gallaher, Leon Gray, John Hannah, Bill Lenkaitis, Jon Morris and Tom Neville

DL: Julius Adams, Ray Hamilton, Craig Hanneman, Mel Lunsford, Tony McGee, Art Moore, and Donnell Smith

LB: Rodrigo Barnes, Kent Carter, Gail Clark, Maury Damkroger, Will Foster, Sam Hunt, Steve King, Steve Nelson, John Tanner and George Webster

DB: Ron Bolton, Sandy Durko, Jim Massey, Prentice McCray, Dave McCurry, Jack Mildren, Willie Osley, Ken Pope and John Sanders

K: John Smith

P: Bruce Barnes and Dave Chapple

1975 New England Patriots Roster   Team Record 3-11

QB: Neil Graff, Steve Grogan and Jim Plunkett

RB: Bobby Anderson, Don Calhoun, Allen Carter, Sam Cunningham, Doug Dressler, Mack Herron Andy Johnson and Leon McQuay

WR: Mel Baker, Steve Burks, Darryl Stingley, Randy Vataha and Elmo Wright

TE: Russ Francis and Bob Windsor

OL: Sam Adams, Steve Corbett, Bill Dulac, Doug Dumler, Leon Gray, John Hannah, Shelby Jordan, and Bill Lenkaitis

DL: Julius Adams, Pete Cusick, Ray Hamilton, Craig Hanneman, Martin Imhoff, Mel Lunsford, Tony McGee, Art Moore, Jerry Patton and Dave Tipton

LB: Rodrigo Barnes, Maury Damkroger, Bob Geddes, Sam Hunt, Steve King, Steve Nelson, Kevin Reilly, Rod Shoate, George Webster and Steve Zabel

DB: Ron Bolton, Dick Conn, Bob Howard, Durwood Keeton, Jim Massey, Prentice McCray and John Sanders

K: John Smith

P: Mike Patrick

1976 New England Patriots Roster   Team Record 11-3

1976 Associated Press All Pro 1st Team Offensive Guard John Hannah

QB: Steve Grogan and Tom Owen

RB: Don Calhoun, Allen Carter, Sam Cunningham, Ike Forte, Andy Johnson and Jess Phillips

WR: Marlin Briscoe, Steve Burks, Ricky Feacher, Darryl Stingley and Randy Vataha

TE: Pete Brock, Al Chandler and Russ Francis

OL: Sam Adams, Pete Brock, Leon Gray, *John Hannah,* Bill Lenkaitis, Bob McKay, Tom Neville and Fred Sturt

DL: Julius Adams, Richard Bishop, Ray Hamilton, Mel Lunsford, Tony McGee, Art Moore and Dave Tipton

LB: Pete Barnes, Sam Hunt, Steve King, Steve Nelson, Jim Romaniszyn, Donnie Thomas, George Webster and Steve Zabel

DB: Doug Beaudoin, Joe Blahak, Dick Conn, Tim Fox, Willie Germany, Mike Haynes, Bob Howard, Prentice McCray, John Sanders and Randy Vataha

K: John Smith and Steve Zabel

P: Mike Patrick

1977 New England Patriots Roster   Team Record 9-5

QB: Steve Grogan

RB: Don Calhoun, Sam Cunningham, Ike Forte, Horace Ivory and Jess Phillips

WR: Steve Burks, Stanley Morgan, Darryl Stingley and Don Westbrook

TE: Al Chandler, Russ Francis and Don Hasselbeck

OL: Sam Adams, Pete Brock, Leon Gray, John Hannah, Bob Hyland, Shelby Jordan, Bill Lenkaitis, Bob McKay, Tom Neville and Fred Sturt

DL: Julius Adams, Richard Bishop, Greg Boyd, Ray Hamilton, Mel Lunsford, Tony McGee and Art Moore

LB: Pete Barnes, Ray Costict, Sam Hunt, Steve King, Steve Nelson, Rod Shoate and Steve Zabel

DB: Doug Beaudoin, Raymond Clayborn, Dick Conn, Tim Fox, Mike Haynes, Bob Howard and Prentice McCray

K: John Smith

P: Mike Patrick

1978 New England Patriots Roster   Team Record 11-5   AFC East Champions

1978 AP All Pro 1st Team Offensive Tackle Leon Gray and Offensive Guard Leon Gray

QB: Steve Grogan and Tom Owen

RB: Don Calhoun, Sam Cunningham, Horace Ivory, Andy Johnson, James McAlister and Mosi Tatupu

WR: Harold Jackson, Stanley Morgan, Carlos Pennywell and Don Westbrook

TE: Al Chandler, Russ Francis and Don Hasselbeck

OL: Sam Adams, Pete Brock, Bob Cryder, Terry Falcon, *Leon Gray, John Hannah,* Shelby Jordan, Bill Lenkaitis, Bob McKay, Fred Sturt and Dwight Wheeler

DL: Julius Adams, Richard Bishop, Greg Boyd, Ray Hamilton, Ernie Holmes, Mel Lunsford, Tony McGee, and Greg Schaum

LB: Ray Costict, Mike Hawkins, Sam Hunt, Steve King, Merv Krakau, Steve Nelson, Rod Shoate and Steve Zabel

DB: Doug Beaudoin, Sidney Brown, Raymond Clayborn, Dick Conn, Tim Fox, Mike Haynes and Prentice McCray

K: Nick Lowery, David Posey and John Smith

P: Mike Patrick and Jerrel Wilson

1979 New England Patriots Roster   Team Record 9-5

1979 Associated Press All Pro 1st Team Offensive Guard John Hannah

QB: Matt Cavanaugh, Steve Grogan and Tom Owen

RB: Don Calhoun, Allan Clark, Sam Cunningham, Horace Ivory, Andy Johnson and Mosi Tatupu

WR: Harold Jackson, Ray Jacobs, Stanley Morgan and Don Westbrook

TE: Al Chandler, Russ Francis and Don Hasselbeck

OL: Sam Adams, Pete Brock, Bob Cryder, Terry Falcon, *John Hannah,* Shelby Jordan, Bill Lenkaitis, Garry Puetz and Dwight Wheeler

DL: Julius Adams, Richard Bishop, Mark Buben, Bob Golic, Ray Hamilton, Mel Lunsford and Tony McGee

LB: Ray Costict, Bob Golic, Mike Hawkins, Sam Hunt, Steve King, Bill Matthews, Steve Nelson, Rod Shoate and John Zamberlin

DB: Doug Beaudoin, Raymond Clayborn, Dick Conn, Tim Fox, Mike Haynes, Prentice McCray, Rick Sanford and Mark Washington

K: John Smith

P: Eddie Hare

1980 New England Patriots Roster   Team Record 10-6

1980 Associated Press All Pro 1st Team Offensive Guard John Hannah

QB: Matt Cavanaugh and Steve Grogan

RB: Don Calhoun, Allan Clark, Vagas Ferguson, Chuck Foreman, Horace Ivory, Andy Johnson and Mosi Tatupu

WR: Preston Brown, Harold Jackson, Stanley Morgan, Carlos Pennywell and Don Westbrook

TE: Russ Francis and Don Hasselbeck

OL: Sam Adams, Pete Brock, Bob Cryder, *John Hannah,* Shelby Jordan, Bill Lenkaitis, Garry Puetz and Dwight Wheeler

DL: Julius Adams, Richard Bishop, Ray Hamilton, Mel Lunsford, Doug McDougald, Tony McGee and Steve McMichael

LB: Bob Golic, Mike Hawkins, Steve King, Bill Matthews, Larry McGrew, Steve Nelson, Rod Shoate and John Zamberlin

DB: Raymond Clayborn, Bill Currier, Tim Fox, Mike Haynes, Roland James, Prentice McCray and Rick Sanford

K: Mike Hubach and John Smith

P: Mike Hubach

1981 New England Patriots Roster   Team Record 2-14

1981 Associated Press All Pro 1st Team Offensive Guard John Hannah

QB: Matt Cavanaugh, Steve Grogan and Tom Owen

RB: Don Calhoun, Tony Collins, Sam Cunningham, Vagas Ferguson, Horace Ivory, Andy Johnson and Mosi Tatupu

WR: Harold Jackson, Stanley Morgan, Carlos Pennywell, Ken Toler and Don Westbrook

TE: Lin Dawson and Don Hasselbeck

OL: Pete Brock, Bob Cryder, *John Hannah,* Brian Holloway, Shelby Jordan, Bill Lenkaitis, Garry Puetz and Dwight Wheeler

DL: Julius Adams, Richard Bishop, Mark Buben, Steve Clark, Ray Hamilton, John Lee and Tony McGee

LB: Don Blackmon, Bob Golic, Mike Hawkins, Steve King, Bill Matthews, Steve Nelson, Rod Shoate and John Zamberlin

DB: Raymond Claynborn, Paul Dombroski, Kevin Donnalley, Tim Fox, Mike Haynes, Roland James, Keith Lee, Rick Sanford and Darrell Wilson

K: Mike Hubach and John Smith

P: Rich Camarillo, Ken Hartley and Mike Hubach

1982 New England Patriots Roster   Team Record 5-4   Lost 1st Round Playoff Game

QB: Matt Cavanaugh, Tom Flick and Steve Grogan

RB: Tony Collins, Larry Cowan, Sam Cunningham, Vagas Ferguson, Mosi Tatupu, Mark van Eeghen and Robert Weathers

WR: Morris Bradshaw, Preston Brown, Cedric Jones, Stanley Morgan and Ken Toler

TE: Lin Dawson, Don Hasselbeck and Brian Williams

OL: Pete Brock, Bob Cryder, Darryl Haley, John Hannah, Brian Holloway, Shelby Jordan, Dwight Wheeler and Ron Wooten

DL: Julius Adams, George Crump, Luther Henson, Dennis Owens, Ken Sims, Ron Spears, and Lester Williams

LB: Don Blackmon, Tim Golden, Brian Ingram, Larry McGrew, Steve Nelson, Andre Tippett, Clayton Weishuhn and John Zamberlin

DB: Raymond Clayborn, Paul Dombroski, Mike Haynes, Roland James, Keith Lee, Fred Marion, Rick Sanford and Ricky Smith

K: Danny Miller, Rex Robinson and John Smith

P: Rich Camarillo

Special Team Kickoff Returnman Greg Taylor

1983 New England Patriots Roster   Team Record 8-8

1983 Associated Press All Pro 1st Team Offensive Guard John Hannah

QB: Tony Eason, Steve Grogan and Mike Kerrigan

RB: Tony Collins, George Peoples, Mosi Tatupu, Mark van Eeghen and Robert Weathers

WR: Cedric Jones, Stanley Morgan, Stephen Starring, Clarence Weathers and Darral Wilson

TE: Lin Dawson, Don Hasselbeck, Derrick Ramsey and Brooks Williams

OL: Pete Brock, Bob Cryder, Darryl Haley, *John Hannah,* Brian Holloway, Art Kuehn, Steve Moore, Dwight Wheeler and Ron Wooten

DL: Julius Adams, Dave Browning, Marshall Harris, Luther Henson, Dennis Owens, Doug Rodgers, Ken Sims, Ron Spears and Lester Williams

LB: Don Blackmon, John Gillen, Tim Golden, Brian Ingram, Larry McGrew, Steve Nelson, Johnny Rembert, Ed Reynolds, Andre Tippett and Clayton Weishuhn

DB: Raymond Clayborn, Paul Dombrowski, Roland James, Keith Lee, Ronnie Lippett, Fred Marion, Rick Sanford and Ricky Smith

K: John Smith, Fred Steinfort and Joaquin Zendejas

P: Rich Camarillo

<u>1984 New England Patriots Roster</u>   <u>Team Record 9-7</u>

QB: Tony Eason, Steve Grogan and Mike Kerrigan

RB: Tony Collins, Greg Hawthorne, Craig James, Bo Robinson, Mosi Tatupu, Robert Weathers
      and Jon Williams

WR: Irving Fryar, Cedric Jones, Stanley Morgan, Stephen Starring and Clarence Weathers

TE: Lin Dawson, Derrick Ramsey and Bo Robinson

OL: Pete Brock, Paul Fairchild, Darryl Haley, John Hannah, Brian Holloway, Steve Moore,
      Guy Morriss and Ron Wooten

DL: Julius Adams, Smiley Creswell, Luther Henson, Dennis Owens, Doug Rogers, Ken Sims,
      Scott Virkus, Lester Williams, and Toby Williams

LB: Don Blackmon, Tim Golden, Brian Ingram, Larry McGrew, Steve Nelson, Johnny Rembert,
      Ed Reynolds, Andre Tippett and Clayton Weishuhn

DB: Paul Dombroski, Ernest Gibson, Roland James, Keith Lee, Ronnie Lippett, Fred Marion,
      Rod McSwain, Rick Sanford and Ricky Smith

K: Tony Franklin

P: Rich Camarillo and Luke Prestridge

<u>1985 New England Patriots Roster</u>   <u>Team Record 14-6</u>   <u>Lost to Chicago in Super Bowl</u>

1985 Associated Press All Pro 1st Team Offensive Guard John Hannah and LB Andre Tippett

QB: Tony Eason, Steve Grogan and Stephen Starring (took direct snap)

RB: Tony Collins, Craig James, Mosi Tatupu and Robert Weathers

WR: Irving Fryar, Greg Hawthorne, Cedric Jones, Stanley Morgan, Stephen Starring
      and Derwin Williams

TE: Lin Dawson and Derrick Ramsey

OL: Pete Brock, Tom Condon, Paul Fairchild, *John Hannah,* Brian Holloway, Trevor Matich,
      Steve Moore, Guy Morriss, Art Plunkett and Ron Wooten

DL: Julius Adams, Dennis Owens, Ken Sims, Ben Thomas, Garin Veris, Lester + Toby Williams

LB: Don Blackmon, Brian Ingram, Larry McGrew, Steve Nelson, Johnny Rembert, Ed Reynolds,
      Andre Tippett and Ed Williams

DB: Jim Bowman, Raymond Clayborn, Ernest Gibson, Roland James, Ronnie Lippett, Fred Marion
      and Rod McSwain

K: Tony Franklin

P: Rich Camarillo

1986 New England Patriots Roster   Record 11-6   Lost to Denver in Divisional Game

QB: Tony Eason, Steve Grogan and Tom Ramsey

RB: Tony Collins, Reggie Dupard, Craig James, Mosi Tatupu and Robert Weathers

WR: Irving Fryar, Cedric Jones, Stanley Morgan, Stephen Starring and Derwin Williams

TE: Greg Baty, Greg Hawthorne and Willie Scott

OL: Bill Bain, Pete Brock, Paul Fairchild, Darryl Haley, Brian Holloway, Trevor Matich, Steve Moore, Guy Morriss and Ron Wooten

DL: Milford Hodge, Dennis Owens, Mike Ruth, Ken Sims, Ben Thomas, Garin Veris, Brent Williams and Toby Williams

LB: Mel Black, Don Blackmon, Steve Doig, Larry McGrew, Steve Nelson, Johnny Rembert, Ed Reynolds, Andre Tippett, Clayton Weishuhn and Ed Williams

DB: Jim Bowman, Raymond Clayborn, Ernest Gibson, Vencie Glenn, Roland James, Ronnie Lippett, Fred Marion, Rod McSwain and Gene Profit

K: Tony Franklin

P: Rich Camarillo

1987 New England Patriots *NFL Roster*   Total Record 8-7 (including strike games)

1987 Associated Press All Pro 1st Team LB Andre Tippett

QB: Tony Eason, Doug Flutie and Steve Grogan

RB: Tony Collins, Elgin Davis, Reggie Dupard, Bruce Hanson, Craig James, Michael LeBlanc, Robert Perryman and Mosi Tatupu

WR: Irving Fryar, Cedric Jones, Stanley Morgan, Stephen Starring and Derwin Williams

TE: Greg Baty, Lin Dawson, Russ Francis and Willie Scott

OL: Bruce Armstrong, Pete Brock, Paul Fairchild, Sean Farrell, Trevor Matich, Steve Moore, Guy Morriss, Art Plunkett, Danny Villa and Ron Wooten

DL: Julius Adams, Milford Hodge, Mike Ruth, Ken Sims, Garin Veris, Brent and Toby Williams

LB: Mel Black, Don Blackmon, Steve Doig, Tim Jordan, Larry McGrew, Steve Nelson, Johnny Rembert, Ed Reynolds, *Andre Tippett* and Ed Williams

DB: Jim Bowman, Raymond Clayborn, Ernest Gibson, Darryl Holmes, Roland James, Ronnie Lippett, Fred Marion, Rod McSwain and Eugene Profit

K: Tony Franklin

P: Rich Camarillo

1987 New England Patriots *Strike Team* Roster   *Record 2-1*

QB: Bob Bleier, Doug Flutie and Todd Whitten

RB: Frank Bianchini, Tony Collins, Bruce Hansen, Michael LeBlanc, Chuck McSwain + Carl Woods

WR: Brian Carey, Wayne Coffey, Dennis Gadbois, Larry Linne and Clay Pickering

TE: Todd Frain and Arnold Franklin

OL: George Colton, Sean Farrell, Guy Morriss, Greg Robinson, Todd Sandham, Eric Stokes, Bill Turner, Darren Twombly and Ron Wooten

DL: John Guzik, Dino Mangiero, Tom Porell, Ben Reed, Murray Wichard and Steve Wilburn

LB: Rogers Alexander, Mel Black, Rico Corsetti, Steve Doig, Jerry McCabe, Joe McHale, Greg Moore, Frank Sacco, Randy Sealby and Andre Tippett

DB: Ricky Atkinson, Raymond Clayborn, Duffy Cobbs, David Hendley, Darryl Holmes, Joe Peterson, Jon Sawyer, Ron Shegog and Perry Williams

K: Tony Franklin and Eric Schubert

P: Alan Herline

1988 New England Patriots Roster   Team Record 9-7

QB: Tony Eason, Doug Flutie, Steve Grogan and Tom Ramsey

RB: Marvin Allen, Elgin Davis, Reggie Dupard, Craig James, Robert Perryman, John Stephens and Mosi Tatupu

WR: Irving Fryar, Dennis Gadbois, Cedric Jones, Sammy Martin and Stanley Morgan

TE: Lin Dawson, Russ Francis, Steve Johnson and Willie Scott

OL: Bruce Armstrong, Mike Babb, Paul Fairchild, Sean Farrell, Trevor Matich, Tom Rehder, Danny Villa and Ron Wooten

DL: Tim Goad, Milford Hodge, Edmund Nelson, Ken Sims, Garin Veris, Brent + Toby Williams

LB: Thomas Benson, Vincent Brown, Tim Jordan, Larry McGrew, Eric Naposki, Johnny Rembert, Ed Reynolds and Andre Tippett

DB: Jim Bowman, Raymond Clayborn, Ernest Gibson, Darryl Holmes, Roland James, Ronnie Lippett, Fred Marion, Rod McSwain and Eugene Profit

K: Teddy Garcia and Jason Staurovsky

P: Jeff Feagles

1989 New England Patriots Roster   Team Record 5-11

QB: Tony Eason, Doug Flutie, Steve Grogan and Marc Wilson

RB: Marvin Allen, Reggie Dupard, Patrick Egu, Robert Perryman, John Stephens, Mosi Tatupu
       and George Wonsley

WR: Glenn Antrum, Hart Lee Dykes, Irving Fryar, Cedric Jones, Sammy Martin, Stanley Morgan,
       and Michael Timpson

TE: Marv Cook, Lin Dawson and Eric Sievers

OL: Bruce Armstrong, Mike Babb, David Douglas, Paul Fairchild, Sean Farrell, Mike Morris,
       Tom Rehder, David Viane, Danny Villa and Long Snapper Marv Cook

DL: Tim Goad, Milford Hodge, Gary Jeter, Emanuel McNeil, Peter Shorts, Ken Sims
       and Brent Williams

LB: Vincent Brown, Terrance Cooks, Tim Jordan, Orlando Lowry, Larry McGrew, Eric Naposki,
       Johnny Rembert, Ed Reynolds, Bruce Sholtz and David Ward

DB: Jim Bowman, Raymond Clayborn, Eric Coleman, Howard Feggins, Darryl Holmes,
       Maurice Hurst, Roland James, Fred Marion, Rod McSwain, Rodney Price and Erroll Tucker

K: Greg Davis and Jason Staurovksy

P: Jeff Feagles

Special Team Kickoff Returnman Kitrick Taylor

1990 New England Patriots Roster   Team Record 1-15

QB: Steve Grogan, Tommy Hodson and Marc Wilson

RB: George Adams, Marvin Allen, Jamie Morris, Robert Perryman, John Stephens + Mosi Tatupu

WR: Hart Lee Dykes, Irving Fryar, Cedric Jones, Sammy Martin, Greg McMurtry + Michael Timpson

TE: Marv Cook, Lin Dawson, Zeke Mowatt and Eric Sievers

OL: Bruce Armstrong, Gene Chilton, Stan Clayton, Elbert Crawford, David Douglas, Paul Fairchild,
       Chris Gambol, Damian Johnson, David Viane, Danny Villa and LS's Marv Cook + Tim Goad

DL: Ray Agnew, Fred DeRiggi, Tim Goad, Marion Hobby, Sean Smith, Garin Veris + Brent Williams

LB: Vincent Brown, Richard Harvey, Ilia Jarostchuk, Johnny Rembert, Ed Reynolds, Chris Singleton,
       Richard Tarditts, Andre Tippett and Ed Williams

DB: Eric Coleman, Tim Hauck, Maurice Hurst, Brian Hutson, Roland James, Jamie Lawson,
       Ronnie Lippett, Fred Marion, Rod McSwain, Ron Overton, Junior Robinson,
       Mickey Washington and Tony Zackery

K: Jason Staurovsky

P: Brian Hansen

Special Team Kickoff Returnman Pat Coleman

1991 New England Patriots Roster   Team Record 6-10

1991 All Pro 1st Team Tight End Marv Cook

QB: Tommy Hodson and Hugh Millen

RB: George Adams, Marvin Allen, Robert Perryman, Ivy Joe Hunter, Leonard Russell,
John Stephens and Jon Vaughn

WR: Rob Carpenter, Irving Fryar, Sammy Martin, Greg McMurtry, Gene Taylor + Michael Timpson

TE: Ben Coates and *Marv Cook*

OL: Bruce Armstrong, Freddie Childress, Gene Chilton, Elbert Crawford, Pat Harlow, Jon Melander,
Gregg Rakoczy, Danny Villa and Long Snapper Marv Cook

DL: Ray Agnew, Chris Gannon, Tim Goad, Marion Hobby, Sean Smith, Fred Smerlas, Garin Veris
and Brent Williams

LB: Vincent Brown, Richard Harvey, David Howard, Johnny Rembert, Ed Reynolds, Chris Singleton,
Richard Tarditts and Andre Tippett

DB: Harry Colon, Darrell Fullington, Tim Gordon, Jerome Henderson, Maurice Hurst, David Key,
Ronnie Lippett, Fred Marion, David Pool, Mickey Washington and Tony Zackery

K: Charlie Baumann and Jason Staurovsky

P: Shawn McCarthy and Bryan Wagner

1992 New England Patriots Roster   Team Record 2-14

QB: Jeff Carlson, Tommy Hodson, Hugh Millen and Scott Zolak

RB: Sam Gash, Scott Lockwood, Leonard Russell, John Stephens, Kevin Turner and Jon Vaughn

WR: Irving Fryar, Greg McMurtry, Walter Stanley and Michael Timpson

TE: Ben Coates and Marv Cook

OL: Bruce Armstrong, Gene Chilton, Eugene Chung, Pat Harlow, Gregg Rakoczy, Reggie Redding,
Larry Williams and Long Snappers Marv Cook + Tim Goad

DL: Ray Agnew, Tim Edwards, Chris Gannon, Tim Goad, Marion Hobby, Fred Smerlas
and Brent Williams

LB: Vincent Brown, Todd Collins, David Howard, Gene Lockhart, Rob McGovern, Johnny Rembert,
Dwayne Sabb, Chris Singleton, Richard Tarditts and Andre Tippett

DB: Darren Anderson, Roger Brown, Tim Gordon, Jerome Henderson, Maurice Hurst, Dion Lambert,
David Pool, Randy Robbins, Rod Smith and David Wilson

K: Charlie Baumann

P: Shawn McCarthy

1993 New England Patriots Roster   Team Record 5-11

QB: Drew Bledsoe, Scott Secules and Scott Zolak

RB: Corey Croom, Sam Gash, Burnie Legette, Scott Lockwood, Leonard Russell and Kevin Turner

WR: Vincent Brisby, Ray Crittenden, Ronnie Harris, Greg McMurtry and Michael Timpson

TE: Ben Coates, Marv Cook and Rich Griffith

OL: Bruce Armstrong, Mike Arthur, Rich Baldinger, Eugene Chung, Mike Gisler, Pat Harlow, Todd Jones, Bill Lewis, Brandon Moore, Todd Rucci and Long Snapper's Marv Cook and Tim Goad

DL: Ray Agnew, Chris Gannon, Tim Goad, Mario Johnson, Aaron Jones, Mike Pitts, John Washington and Brent Williams

LB: David Bavarro, Jason Carthen, Todd Collins, Dwayne Sabb, Chris Singleton, Chris Slade, Andre Tippett and David White

DB: Harlon Barnett, Jerome Henderson, Maurice Hurst, Dion Lambert, Vernon Lewis, Terry Ray, Rod Smith, Renya Thompson, Adrian White and Darryl Wren

K: Matt Bahr and Scott Sisson

P: Mike Saxon

1994 New England Patriots Roster   Team Record 10-7   Lost Wild Card Game to Cleveland

1994 All Pro 1st Team Tight End Ben Coates

QB: Drew Bledsoe and Scott Zolak

RB: Marion Butts, Corey Croom, Sam Gash, Burnie Legette, Blair Thompson, Leroy Thompson and Kevin Turner

WR: Vincent Brisby, Troy Brown, Ray Crittenden, Ronnie Harris, Steve Hawkins + Michael Timpson

TE: John Burke and ***Ben Coates***

OL: Bruce Armstrong, Mike Arthur, Eugene Chung, Mike Gisler, Pat Harlow, Bob Kratch, Max Lane, Todd Rucci and Doug Skene and Long Snapper Steve DeOssie

DL: Ray Agnew, Troy Barnett, Tim Goad, Aaron Jones, Mike Jones, Mike Pitts + Sylvester Stanley

LB: David Bavarro, Vincent Brown, Jason Carthen, Todd Collins, Steve DeOssie, Willie MGinest, Marty Moore, Dwayne Sabb and Chris Slade

DB: Harlon Barnett, Corwin Brown, Myron Guyton, Maurice Hurst, Vernon Lewis, Terry Ray, Ricky Reynolds, Rod Smith. Larry Whigham and Darryl Wren

K: Matt Bahr and Pat O'Neill

P: Pat O'Neill

1995 New England Patriots Roster   Team Record 6-10

1995 All Pro 1ˢᵗ Team Tight End Ben Coates

QB: Drew Bledsoe and Scott Zolak

RB: Corey Croom, Sam Gash, Rupert Grant, David Green, Curtis Martin and Dave Meggett

WR: Vincent Brisby, Troy Brown, Hason Graham, Ray Lucas and Will Moore

TE: John Burke, **Ben Coates,** David Frisch and Lovett Purnell

OL: Bruce Armstrong, Jeff Dellenbach, Mike Gisler, Pat Harlow, Bob Kratch, Max Lane, David Richards, William Roberts, Todd Rucci, Dave Wohlabaugh and LS Steve DeOssie

DL: Troy Barnett, Ferric Collons, Aaron Jones, Mike Jones, Pio Sagapolutele, Walter Scott, Chris Sullivan, Mark Wheeler and Devin Wyman

LB: Bobby Abrams, Vincent Brown, Alcides Catanho, Ted Johnson, Willie McGinest, Marty Moore, Dwayne Sabb and Chris Slade

DB: Corwin Brown, Eddie Cade, Myron Guyton, Jimmy Hitchcock, Maurice Hurst, Ty Law, Vernon Lewis, Mike McGruder, Lawyer Milloy, Terry Ray and Ricky Reynolds. Otis Smith and Larry Whigham

K: Matt Bahr, Pat O'Neill, Adam Vinatieri and Bryan Wagner

P: Matt Bahr, Pat O'Neill and Bryan Wagner

1996 New England Patriots Roster   Team Record 13-6   Lost Super Bowl to Green Bay

QB: Drew Bledsoe and Scott Zolak

RB: Keith Byars, Sam Gash, Marrio Grier, Curtis Martin and Dave Meggett

WR: Vincent Brisby, Troy Brown, Terry Glenn, Hason Graham, Shawn Jefferson, Dietrich Jells, Ray Lucas and Will Moore

TE: Mike Bartrum, John Burke, Keith Byars, Ben Coates and Lovett Purnell

OL: Bruce Armstrong, Jeff Dellenbach, Mike Gisler, Bob Kratch, Max Lane, David Richards, William Roberts, Todd Rucci, Dave Wohlabaugh and Long Snapper Mike Bartrum

DL: Troy Barnett, Ferric Collons, Chad Eaton, Mike Jones, Pio Sagapolutele, Walter Scott, Chris Sullivan, Mark Wheeler and Devin Wyman

LB: Monty Brown, Tedy Bruschi, Todd Collins, Ted Johnson, Willie McGinest, Marty Moore, Dwayne Sabb and Chris Slade

DB: Corwin Brown, Willie Clay, Jerome Henderson, Jimmy Hitchcock, Ty Law, Vernon Lewis, Mike McGruder, Lawyer Milloy, Terry Ray, Ricky Reynolds, Otis Smith + Larry Whigham

K: Adam Vinatieri

P: Tom Tupa and Adam Vinatieri

1997 New England Patriots Roster   Team Record 11-7   Lost Divisional to Pittsburgh

QB: Drew Bledsoe and Scott Zolak

RB: Keith Byars, Derrick Cullors, Sam Gash, Marrio Grier, Curtis Martin, Dave Meggett
and Sedrick Shaw

WR: Vincent Brisby, Troy Brown, Tony Gaiter, Terry Glenn, Shawn Jefferson and Dietrich Jells

TE: Mike Bartrum, Ben Coates and Lovett Purnell

OL: Bruce Armstrong, Damon Denson, Ed Ellis, Mike Gisler, Heath Irwin, Max Lane, Scott Rehberg,
Todd Rucci, Danny Villa, Dave Wohlabaugh and Long Snapper Mike Bartrum

DL: Ferric Collons, Chad Eaton, Mike Jones, Brandon Mitchell, Zefross Moss, Chris Sullivan,
Henry Thomas, Mark Wheeler and Devin Wyman

LB: Tedy Bruschi, Todd Collins, Vernon Crawford, Ted Johnson, Willie McGinest, Marty Moore,
Bernard Russ and Chris Slade

DB: Chris Canty, Chris Carter, Willie Clay, Jimmy Hitchcock, Steve Israel, Ty Law, Steve Lofton,
Mike McGruder, Lawyer Milloy and Larry Whigham

K: Adam Vinatieri

P: Tom Tupa

1998 New England Patriots Roster   Team Record 9-8   Lost Wild Card to Jacksonville

1998 All Pro 1st Team Cornerback Ty Law

QB: Drew Bledsoe and Scott Zolak

RB: Tony Carter, Derrick Cullors, Robert Edwards, Chris Floyd, Harold Shaw and Sedrick Shaw

WR: Vincent Brisby, Troy Brown, Henry Ellard, Terry Glenn, Shawn Jefferson, Anthony Ladd
and Tony Simmons

TE: Mike Bartrum, Ben Coates, Lovett Purnell and Rod Rutledge

OL: Bruce Armstrong, Mike Bartrum, Damon Denson, Ed Ellis, Heath Irwin, Max Lane
and Zefross Moss

DL: Ferric Collons, Chad Eaton, Willie McGinest, Brandon Mitchell, Leonta Rheams, Greg Spires,
Chris Sullivan, Henry Thomas and Mark Wheeler

LB: Tedy Bruschi, Todd Collins, Dana Cotrell, Vernon Crawford, Ted Johnson, Willie McGinest,
Marty Moore, Bernard Russ, Chris Slade and Shawn Stuckey

DB: Chris Canty, Willie Clay, Steve Israel, Tebucky Jones, *Ty Law,* Steve Lofton, Lawyer Milloy,
and Larry Whigham

K: Adam Vinatieri

P: Tom Tupa

1999 New England Patriots Roster   Team Record 8-8

1999 All Pro 1st Team Safety Lawyer Milloy

QB: Drew Bledsoe and John Friesz

RB: Terry Allen, Tony Carter, Jerry Ellison, Kevin Faulk, Chris Floyd, Harold Shaw
and Lamont Warren

WR: Vincent Brisby, Troy Brown, Terry Glenn, Shawn Jefferson, Sean Morey and Tony Simmons

TE: Mike Bartrum, Ben Coates and Rod Rutledge

OL: Jason Anderson, Bruce Armstrong, Mike Bartrum, Damon Denson, Ed Ellis, Health Irwin,
Max Lane, Zefross Moss, Todd Rucci and Damien Woody

DL: Ferric Collons, Chad Eaton, Bob Kuberski, Willie McGinest, Brandon Mitchell, Greg Spires,
Chris Sullivan and Henry Thomas

LB: Tedy Bruschi, Vernon Crawford, Ted Johnson, Andy Katzenmoyer, Jeff Kopp, Marty Moore,
Bernard Russ and Chris Slade

DB: Terry Billups, Chris Carter, Rico Clark, Tony George, Steve Israel, Tebucky Jones, Ty Law,
Lawyer Milloy, Kato Serwanga and Larry Whigham

K: Adam Vinatieri

P: Lee Johnson

2000 New England Patriots Roster   Team Record 5-11

QB: Michael Bishop, Drew Bledsoe, Tom Brady, Kevin Faulk (took direct snap) and John Friesz

RB: Tony Carter, Kevin Faulk, Chris Floyd, Raymont Harris, Patrick Pass, Jeff Paulk,
J.R. Redmond and Harold Shaw

WR: Troy Brown, Chris Calloway, Shockmain Davis, Terry Glenn, Curtis Jackson, Tony Simmons

TE: Eric Bjornson, Chris Eitzmann, Rod Rutledge and Jermaine Wiggins

OL: Jason Andersen, Joe Andruzzi, Bruce Armstrong, Derrick Fletcher, Sale Isaia, Adrian Klemm,
Max Lane, Lonie Paxton, Greg Robinson-Randall, Grey Ruegamer, Grant Williams
and Damien Woody

DL: Chad Eaton, Reggie Grimes, Bobby Hamilton, Garrett Johnson, David Nugent,
Brandon Mitchell, Greg Spires and Henry Thomas

LB: Tedy Bruschi, Matt Chatham, Antico Dalton, Rob Holmberg, Olrick Johnson, Ted Johnson,
Andy Katzenmoyer, Willie McGinest, Marc Megna, Chris Slade and Maugaula Tuitele

DB: Tony George, Antwan Harris, Tebucky Jones, Antonio Langham, Ty Law, Lawyer Milloy,
Kato Serwanga, Otis Smith, Matt Stevens and Larry Whigham

K: Adam Vinatieri

P: Lee Johnson

2001 New England Patriots Roster   Team Record 14-5   Beat the Rams in the Super Bowl

QB: Drew Bledsoe, Tom Brady and Kevin Faulk (took direct snap)

RB: Marc Edwards, Kevin Faulk, Patrick Pass, JR Redmond, Antowain Smith and Bryan Cox

WR: Troy Brown, Fred Coleman, Bert Emanuel, Terry Glenn, Curtis Jackson, Charles Johnson, David Patten and Torrance Small and Terrell Buckley

TE: Rod Rutledge and Jermaine Wiggins

OL: Joe Andruzzi, Mike Compton, Kenyatta Jones, Matt Light, Lonie Paxton, Greg Robinson-Randall, Grey Ruegamer, Grant Williams and Damien Woody

DL: Bobby Hamilton, Brandon Mitchell, David Nugent, Riddick Parker, Anthony Pleasant, Jace Sayler and Richard Seymour

LB: Kole Ayi, Tedy Bruschi, Matt Chatham, Bryan Cox, Rob Holmberg, Larry Izzo, Ted Johnson, Willie McGinest, Marty Moore, Roman Phifer, Maugaula Tuitele, TJ Turner and Mike Vrabel

DB: Hakin Akbar, Terrell Buckley, Je'Rod Cherry, Antwan Harris, Tebucky Jones, Ben Kelly, Ty Law, Lawyer Milloy, Leonard Myers, Terrence Shaw, Otis Smith and Matt Stevens

K: Adam Vinatieri

P: Lee Johnson, Adam Vinatieri and Ken Walter

2002 New England Patriots Roster   Team Record 9-7

2002 All Pro 1st Team Kicker Adam Vinatieri

QB: Tom Brady, Rohan Davey and Damon Huard

RB: Marc Edwards, Kevin Faulk, Patrick Pass, J.R. Redmond and Antowain Smith

WR: Deion Branch, Troy Brown, Fred Coleman, David Givens, Donald Hayes and David Patten

TE: Fred Baxter, Cam Cleeland, Christian Fauria, Daniel Graham and Mike Vrabel

OL: Joe Andruzzi, Tom Ashworth, Mike Compton, Russ Hochstein, Kenyatta Jones, Adrian Klemm, Matt Light, Stephen Neal, Lonie Paxton, Greg Robinson-Randall, Grey Ruegamer and Damien Woody

DL: Jarvis Green, Bobby Hamilton, Bernard Holsey, Rick Lyle, Steve Martin, Anthony Pleasant and Richard Seymour

LB: OJ Brigance, Tedy Bruschi, Matt Chatham, Larry Izzo, Ted Johnson, Willie McGinest, Roman Phifer, Maugaula Tuitele and Mike Vrabel

DB: Terrell Buckley, Je'Rod Cherry, Victor Green, Antwan Harris, Chris Hayes, Jimmy Hitchcock, Tebucky Jones, Ben Kelly, Ty Law, Leonard Myers and Otis Smith

K: *Adam Vinatieri*

P: Ken Walter

2003 New England Patriots Roster   Team Record 17-2   Beat Panthers in the Super Bowl

2003 All Pro 1ˢᵗ Team Safety Rodney Harrison, CB Ty Law and DL Richard Seymour

QB: Tom Brady, Rohan Davey, Kevin Faulk (took direct snap) and Damon Huard

RB: Larry Centers, Mike Cloud, Kevin Faulk, Fred McCrary, Patrick Pass, Antowain Smith
        and Dan Klecko

WR: Deion Branch, Troy Brown, David Givens, Bethel Johnson, David Patten, JJ Stokes
        and Dedric Ward

TE: Fred Baxter, Christian Fauria and Daniel Graham

OL: Joe Andruzzi, Wilbert Brown, Mike Compton, Brandon Gorin, Russ Hochstein, Brian Kinchen,
        Lonie Paxton, Adrian Klemm, Dan Koppen, Matt Light, Sean McDermott and Damien Woody

DL: Jarvis Green, Bobby Hamilton, Dan Klecko, Rick Lyle, Anthony Pleasant, *Richard Seymour,*
        Ty Warren and Ted Washington

LB: Tully Banta Cain, Tedy Bruschi, Matt Chatham, Rosevelt Colvin, Larry Izzo, Ted Johnson,
        Willie McGinest, Roman Phifer and Mike Vrabel

DB: Chris Akins, Je'Rod Cherry, Don Davis, Antwan Harris, *Rodney Harrison, Ty Law,*
        Shawn Mayer, Aric Morris, Tyrone Poole, Asante Samuel and Eugene Wilson

K: Adam Vinatieri

P: Brooks Barnard, Tom Brady and Ken Walter

2004 New England Patriots Roster   Team Record 17-2   Beat the Eagles in Super Bowl

2004 All Pro 1ˢᵗ Team Defensive Lineman Richard Seymour

QB: Tom Brady, Rohan Davey and Adam Vinatieri (took direct snap)

RB: Rabih Abdullak, Cedric Cobbs, Corey Dillon, Kevin Faulk, Patrick Pass and Dan Klecko

WR: Deion Branch, Troy Brown, David Givens, Bethel Johnson, Kevin Kasper, David Patten
        and P.K. Sam

TE: Christian Fauria, Daniel Graham, Benjamin Watson, Jed Weaver and Mike Vrabel

OL: Joe Andruzzi, Tom Ashworth, Brandon Gorin, Russ Hochstein, Adrian Klemm, Dan Koppen,
        Matt Light, Gene Mruczkowski, Stephen Neal and Lonie Paxton

DL: Jarvis Green, Marquise Hill, Ethan Kelley, Dan Klecko, *Richard Seymour,* Keith Traylor,
        Ty Warren and Vince Wilfork

LB: Eric Alexander, Tully Banta Cain, Tedy Bruschi, Matt Chatham, Rosevelt Colvin, Larry Izzo,
        Ted Johnson, Justin Kurpeikis, Willie McGinest, Roman Phifer and Mike Vrabel

DB: Je'Rod Cherry, Don Davis, Randall Gay, Rodney Harrison, Ty Law, Omare Lowe,
        Shawn Mayer, Earthwind Moreland, Tyrone Poole, Hank Poteat, Dexter Reid, Asante Samuel,
        Eugene Wilson and Troy Brown

K: Adam Vinatieri

P: Josh Miller

2005 New England Patriots Roster   Team Record 11-7   Lost Divisional to Denver

2005 All Pro 1ˢᵗ Team Defensive Lineman Richard Seymour

QB: Tom Brady, Matt Cassel and Doug Flutie

RB: Mike Cloud, Corey Dillon, Heath Evans, Kevin Faulk, Patrick Pass and Amos Zereoue

WR: Deion Branch, Troy Brown, Bam Childress, Andre' Davis, Tim Dwight, David Givens and Bethel Johnson

TE: Tom Ashworth, Christian Fauria, Daniel Graham, Benjamin Watson and Mike Vrabel

OL: Tom Ashworth, Brandon Gorin, Russ Hochstein, Nick Kaczur, Dan Koppen, Matt Light, Logan Mankins, Gene Mruczkowski, Stephen Neal, Lonie Paxton, Ross Tucker + Billy Yates

DL: Jarvis Green, Marquise Hill, Dan Klecko, *Richard Seymour,* Ty Warren, Vince Wilfork and Mike Wright

LB: Eric Alexander, Tully Banta Cain, Monty Beisel, Chad Brown, Tedy Bruschi, Rosevelt Colvin, Larry Izzo, Wesley Mallard, Willie McGinest and Mike Vrabel

DB: Bam Childress, Don Davis, Arturo Freeman, Randall Gay, Rodney Harrison, Artrell Hawkins, Ellis Hobbs, Tyrone Poole, Hank Poteat, Asante Samuel, James Sanders, Chad + Guss Scott, Duane Starks, Michael Stone and Eugene Wilson

K: Adam Vinatieri

P: Josh Miller

2006 New England Patriots Roster   Team Record 14-5   Lost AFC Champ to Colts

QB: Tom Brady, Matt Cassel and Vinny Testaverde

RB: Corey Dillon, Heath Evans, Kevin Faulk, Lawrence Maroney and Patrick Pass

WR: Troy Brown, Reche Caldwell, Doug Gabriel, Jabar Gaffney, Chad Jackson, Kelvin Kight and Jonathan Smith

TE: David Thomas and Benjamin Watson

OL: Wesley Britt, Russ Hochstein, Nick Kaczur, Dan Koppen, Matt Light, Logan Mankins, Lonie Paxton, Gene Mruczkowski, Stephen Neal, Ryan O'Callaghan and Billy Yates

DL: Jarvis Green, Marquise Hill, Richard Seymour, Le Kevin Smith, Ty Warren, Vince Wilfork, and Mike Wright

LB: Eric Alexander, Tully Banta Cain, Tedy Bruschi, Rosevelt Colvin, Larry Izzo, Junior Seau, Mike Vrabel and Pierre Woods

DB: Willie Andrews, Rashad Baker, Bam Childress, Don Davis, Randall Gay, Rodney Harrison, Artrell Hawkins, Ellis Hobbs, Chidi Iwuoma, Corey Mays and Ray Mickens

K: Stephen Gostkowski

P: Josh Miller, Todd Sauerbrun and Ken Walter

<u>2007 New England Patriots Roster</u>   <u>Team Record 18-1</u>   <u>Lost to Giants in Super Bowl</u>

2007 League MVP Tom Brady

2007 All Pro 1ˢᵗ Team: Tom Brady, Matt Light, Randy Moss, Asante Samuel and Mike Vrabel

QB: *Tom Brady,* Matt Cassel and Matt Gutierrez

RB: Kyle Eckel, Heath Evans, Kevin Faulk, Laurence Maroney and Sammy Morris

WR: Troy Brown, Jabar Gaffney, Chad Jackson, *Randy Moss,* Donte' Stallworth, Kelley Washington, and Wes Welker

TE: Marcellus Rivers, David Thomas, Benjamin Watson and Mike Vrabel

OL: Wesley Britt, Russ Hochstein, Nick Kaczur, Dan Koppen, *Matt Light,* Logan Mankins, Stephen Neal, Ryan O'Callaghan, Lonie Paxton and Billy Yates

DL: Jarvis Green, Rashad Moore, Richard Seymour, Le Kevin Smith, Santonio Thomas, Ty Warren, Vince Wilfork and Mike Wright

LB: Eric Alexander, Chad Brown, Tedy Bruschi, Rosevelt Colvin, Larry Izzo, Corey Mays, Junior Seau, Adalius Thomas, *Mike Vrabel* and Pierre Woods

DB: Willie Andrews, Rashad Baker, Randall Gay, Rodney Harrison, Ellis Hobbs, Eddie Jackson, Brandon Meriweather, Mel Mitchell, *Asante Samuel,* James Sanders, Antwain Spann, Ray Ventrone and Eugene Wilson

K: Stephen Gostkowski

P: Chris Hanson

<u>2008 New England Patriots Roster</u>   <u>Team Record 11-5</u>

2008 All Pro 1ˢᵗ Team Kicker Stephen Gostkowski

QB: Tom Brady, Matt Cassel and Kevin O'Connell

RB: Heath Evans, Kevin Faulk, BenJarvus Green-Ellis, Lamont Jordan, Laurence Maroney, and Sammy Morris

WR: Sam Aiken, Jabar Gaffney, Randy Moss, Matthew Slater, Stephen Spach, Kelley Washington, and Wes Welker

TE: Tyson DeVree, David Thomas and Benjamin Watson

OL: Wesley Britt, Dan Connolly, Russ Hochstein, Nick Kaczur, Dan Koppen, Mark LeVoir, Matt Light, Logan Mankins, Stephen Neal, Lonie Paxton and Billy Yates

DL: Jarvis Green, Richard Seymour, Le Kevin Smith, Ty Warren, Vince Wilfork and Mike Wright

LB: Eric Alexander, Tedy Bruschi, Rosevelt Colvin, Gary Guyton, Larry Izzo, Jerod Mayo, Vince Redd, Junior Seau, Adalius Thomas, Mike Vrabel and Pierre Woods

DB: Rodney Harrison, Ellis Hobbs, Brandon Meriweather, Deltha O'Neal, Mike Richardson, James Sanders, Lewis Sanders, Antwan Spann, Ray Ventrone, Jason Webster, Terrence Wheatley and Jonathan Wilhite

K: *Stephen Gostkowski*

P: Matt Cassel and Chris Hanson

2009 New England Patriots Roster   **Team Record 10-7**   **Lost Wild Card to Ravens**

2009 All Pro 1ˢᵗ Team WR Wes Welker

QB: Tom Brady and Brian Hoyer

RB: Kevin Faulk, BenJarvus Green-Ellis, Laurence Maroney, Sammy Morris and Fred Taylor

WR: Sam Aiken, Julian Edelman, Joey Galloway, Randy Moss, Matthew Slater, Isaiah Stanback, Brandon Tate and *Wes Welker*

TE: Chris Baker, Michael Matthews and Benjamin Watson

OL: Dan Connolly, Jake Ingram, Nick Kaczur, Dan Koppen, Mark LeVoir, Matt Light, Logan Mankins, Stephen Neal, Rich Ohrnberger, Kendall Simmons, Sebastian Vollmer, and Ryan Wendell

DL: Titus Adams, Ron Brace, Jarvis Green, Rob Ninkovich, Myron Pryor, Terdell Sands, Ty Warren, Vince Wilfork and Mike Wright

LB: Eric Alexander, Tully Banta-Cain, Derrick Burgess, Gary Guyton, Jerod Mayo, Junior Seau, Adalius Thomas and Pierre Woods

DB: Kyle Arrington, Leigh Bodden, Darius Butler, Patrick Chung, Bret Lockett, Brandon McGowan, James Sanders, Shawn Springs, Terrence Wheatley, Jonathan Wilhite and Randy Moss

K: Stephen Gostkowski

P: Chris Hanson

2010 New England Patriots Roster   **Team Record 14-3**   **Lost Divisional to Jets**

2010 League MVP Tom Brady

2010 All Pro 1ˢᵗ Team QB Tom Brady, Guard Logan Mankins and LB Jerod Mayo

QB: *Tom Brady* and Brian Hoyer

RB: Thomas Clayton, BenJarvus Green-Ellis, Kevin Faulk, Sammy Morris and Danny Woodhead

WR: Deion Branch, Julian Edelman, Randy Moss, Taylor Price, Brandon Tate and Wes Welker

TE: Alge Cumpler, Rob Gronkowski and Aaron Hernandez

OL: Dan Connolly, Jake Ingram, Matt Katula, Dan Koppen, Mark LeVoir, Matt Light, *Logan Mankins,* Stephen Neal, Rich Ohrnberger, Sebastian Vollmer and Ryan Wendell

DL: Ron Brace, Landon Cohen, Brandon Deaderick, Louis Leonard, Kyle Love, Eric Moore, Quinn Ojinnaka, Myron Pryor, Gerard Warren, Ty Warren, Vince Wilfork and Mike Wright

LB: Jermaine Cunningham, Tully Banta-Cain, Shawn Crable, Dane Fletcher, Gary Guyton, Rob Ninkovich, *Jerod Mayo,* Marques Murrell, Brandon Spikes, Tracy White and Pierre Woods

DB: Kyle Arrington, Darius Butler, Sergio Brown, Tony Carter, Patrick Chung, Brandon Meriweather, Devin McCourty, Jarrad Page, James Sanders and Jonathan Wilhite

K: Stephen Gostkowski, Shayne Graham and Wes Welker

P: Zoltan Mesko

<u>**2011 New England Patriots Roster**</u>   <u>**Team Record 15-4**</u>   <u>**Lost Super Bowl to Giants**</u>

2011 All Pro 1ˢᵗ Team TE Rob Gronkowski and WR Wes Welker

QB: Tom Brady and Brian Hoyer

RB: Kevin Faulk, BenJarvus Green-Ellis, Stevan Ridley, Shane Vereen and Danny Woodhead

WR: Deion Branch, Julian Edelman, Chad Johnson, Taylor Price, Matthew Slater, Tiquan Underwood and *Wes Welker*

TE: Dan Gronkowski, *Rob Gronkowski,* Aaron Hernandez and Thomas Welch

OL: Danny Aiken, Marcus Cannon, Dan Connolly, Dan Koppen, Matt Light, Logan Mankins, Nick McDonald, Nate Solder, Donald Thomas, Sebastian Vollmer, Brian Waters + Ryan Wendell

DL: Mark Anderson, Ron Brace, Andre Carter, Landon Cohen, Jermaine Cunningham, Brandon Deaderick, Shaun Ellis, Albert Haynesworth, Kyle Love, Eric Moore, Myron Pryor, Alex Silvestro, Gerard Warren, Vince Wilfork and Mike Wright

LB: A.J. Edds, Dane Fletcher, Gary Guyton, Niko Koutouvides, Jerod Mayo, Rob Ninkovich, Brandon Spikes, Jeff Tarpinian and Tracy White

DB: Phillip Adams, Kyle Arrington, Josh Barrett, Leigh Bodden, Sergio Brown, Patrick Chung, Ras-I Dowling, James Ihedigbo, Nate Jones, Devin McCourty, Antwaun Molden, Sterling Moore, Lousaka Polite, Ross Ventrone, Malcolm Williams, Julian Edelman, Rob Gronkowski and Matthew Slater

K: Stephen Gostkowski

P: Zoltan Mesko

<u>**2012 New England Patriots Roster**</u>   <u>**Team Record 13-5**</u>   <u>**Lost Championship to Ravens**</u>

2012 All Pro 1ˢᵗ Team Defensive Lineman Vince Wilfork

QB: Tom Brady and Ryan Mallett

RB: Brandon Bolden, Deion Branch, James Develin, Lex Hilliard, Stevan Ridley, Shane Vereen and Danny Woodhead

WR: Kamar Aiken, Julian Edelman, Brandon Lloyd, Greg Salas, Matthew Slater, Donte' Stallworth and Wes Welker

TE: Daniel Fells, Rob Gronkowski, Aaron Hernandez, Michael Hoomanawanui, Visanthe Shiancoe and Kellen Winslow

OL: Danny Aiken, Marcus Cannon, Dan Connolly, Logan Mankins, Nick McDonald, Mitch Petrus, Nate Solder, Donald Thomas, Sebastian Vollmer and Ryan Wendell

DL: Jake Bequette, Ron Brace, Jermaine Cunningham, Brandon Deaderick, Marcus Forston, Justin Francis, Chandler Jones, Kyle Love, Terrell McClain, Trevor Scott and *Vince Wilfork*

LB: Bobby Carpenter, Dont'a Hightower, Niko Koutouvides, Jerod Mayo, Rob Ninkovich, Mike Rivera, Brandon Spikes, Jeff Tarpinian and Tracy White

DB: Kyle Arrington, Patrick Chung, Marquice Cole, Alfonzo Dennard, Ras-I Dowling, Nate Ebner, Steve Gregory, Derrick Martin, Devin McCourty, Sterling Moore, Aqib Talib, Malcolm Williams, and Tavon Wilson

K: Stephen Gostkowski

P: Zoltan Mesko

2013 New England Patriots Roster   Team Record 13-5   Lost Championship to Denver

QB: Tom Brady

RB: LaGarrette Blount, James Develin, Stevan Ridley, Shane Vereen and Leon Washington

WR: Danny Amendola, Josh Boyce, Austin Collie, Aaron Dobson, Julian Edelman, Matthew Slater, and Kenbrell Thompkins

TE: Chris Baker, Rob Gronkowski, Michael Hoomanawanui, Matthew Mulligan, Zach Sudfeld and D.J. Williams

OL: Danny Aiken, Marcus Cannon, Dan Connolly, Josh Kline, Logan Mankins, Nate Solder, Will Svitek, Sebastian Vollmer and Ryan Wendell

DL: Jake Bequette, Michael Buchanan, Andre Carter, Marcus Forston, Chandler Jones, Chris Jones, Tommy Kelly, Andre Neblett, Sealver Siliga, Isaac Sopoaga, Joe Vellano and Vince Wilfork

LB: Steve Beauharnais, Jamie Collins, Ja'Gared Davis, Dane Fletcher, Dont'a Hightower, Jerod Mayo, Rob Ninkovich, Brandon Spikes and Chris White

DB: Kyle Arrington, Marquis Cole, Kanorris Davis, Alfonzo Denard, Nate Ebner, Justin Green, Steve Gregory, Duron Harmon, Devin McCourty, Logan Ryan, Aqib Talib and Tavon Wilson

K: Stephen Gostkowski

P: Ryan Allen and Tom Brady

2014 New England Patriots Roster   Team Record 15-4   Beat Seattle in Super Bowl

2014 All Pro 1st Team TE Rob Gronkowski and CB Darrelle Revis

QB: Tom Brady and Jimmy Garoppolo

RB: LaGarrette Blount, Brandon Bolden, James Devlin, Jonas Gray, Stevan Ridley, Shane Vereen, and James White

WR: Danny Amendola, Josh Boyce, Aaron Dobson, Julian Edelman, Brandon LaFell, Matthew Slater, Kenbrell Thompkins, Bryan Tyms and Wes Welker

TE: *Rob Gronkowski,* Michael Hoomanawanui, Steve Maneri, Tim Wright and Nate Solder

OL: Danny Aiken, Chris Barker, Marcus Cannon, Dan Connolly, Jordan Devey, Cameron Fleming, Josh Kline, Nate Solder, Bryan Stork, Shane Vereen, Sebastian Vollmer, Ryan Wendell and Long Snapper Rob Ninkovich

DL: Alan Branch, Michael Buchanan, Dominique Easley, Chandler Jones, Chris Jones, Zach Moore, Sealver Siliga, Joe Vellano and Vince Wilfork

LB: Akeem Ayers, Jonathan Casillas, Jamie Collins, Ja'Gared Davis, Darius Fleming, Jerod Mayo, Rob Ninkovich, Deontae Skinner and Chris White

DB: Kyle Arrington, Brandon Browner, Malcolm Butler, Patrick Chung, Alfonzo Denard, Nate Ebner, Devin McCourty, *Darrelle Revis,* Logan Ryan and Tavon Wilson

K: Stephen Gostkowski

P: Ryan Allen

2015 New England Patriots Roster   **Team Record 13-5**   **Lost Championship to Denver**

2015 All Pro 1ˢᵗ Team K Stephen Gostkowski and TE Rob Gronkowski

QB: Danny Amendola (took direct snap), Tom Brady and Jimmy Garoppolo

RB: LaGarette Blount, Brandon Bolden, Travaris Cadet, Joey Iosefa, Steven Jackson, Dion Lewis and James White

WR: Danny Amendola, Aaron Dobson, Julian Edelman, Leonard Hankerson, Chris Harper, Damaris Johnson, Brandon LaFell and Keshawn Martin

TE: Scott Chandler, Asante Cleveland, *Rob Gronkowski,* Michael Hoomanawanui and Michael Williams

OL: David Andrews, Chris Barker, Marcus Cannon, Joe Cardona, Cameron Fleming, Tre' Jackson, Josh Kline, Shaq Mason, Nate Solder, Bryan Stork, Sebastian Vollmer, LaAdrian Waddle and Ryan Wendell

DL: Alan Branch, Malcom Brown, Dominque Easley, Trey Flowers, Geneo Grissom, Akiem Hicks, Chandler Jones, Ishmaa'ily Kitchen, Jabaal Sheard and Sealver Siliga,

LB: Jonathan Bostic, Jamie Collins, Darius Fleming, Jonathan Freeny, Dont'a Hightower, Rufus Johnson, Eric Martin, Jerod Mayo, Rob Ninkovich and Dekoda Watson

DB: Tarell Brown, Malcolm Butler, Patrick Chung, Justin Coleman, Nate Ebner, Bradley Fletcher, Duron Harmon, Leonard Johnson, Brandon King, Devin McCourty, Dewey McDonald, Rashaan Melvin, Jordan Richards, Logan Ryan and Tavon Wilson

K: Nate Ebner and *Stephen Gostkowski*

P: Ryan Allen

Special Team Gunner Matthew Slater

2016 New England Patriots Roster   **Team Record 15-4**   **Beat Falcons in Super Bowl**

2016 All Pro 1ˢᵗ Team Special Team Matthew Slater

QB: Tom Brady, Jacoby Brissett and Jimmy Garoppolo

RB: LeGarrette Blount, Brandon Bolden, James Develin, D.J. Foster, Dion Lewis and James White

WR: Danny Amendola, Julian Edelman, Michael Floyd, Chris Hogan, Malcolm Mitchell, Matt Slater

TE: Martellus Bennett, A.J. Derby, Rob Gronkowski, Clay Harbor and Matt Lengel

OL: David Andrews, Marcus Cannon, Joe Cardona, Cameron Fleming, Ted Karras, Shaq Mason, Nate Solder, Joe Thuney and LaAdrian Waddle

DL: Alan Branch, Malcom Brown, Trey Flowers, Woodrow Hamilton, Anthony Johnson, Chris Long, Jabaal Sheard and Vincent Valentine

LB: Jamie Collins, Jonathan Freeny, Geneo Grissom, Dont'a Hightower, Shea McClellin, Barkevious Mingo, Rob Ninkovich, Elandon Roberts and Kyle Van Noy

DB: Patrick Chung, Justin Coleman, Nate Ebner, Duron Harmon, Cyrus Jones, Jonathon Jones, Brandon King, Devin McCourty, Jordan Richards, Eric Rowe and Logan Ryan

K: Stephen Gostkowski

P: Ryan Allen

Special Team Gunner *Matthew Slater*

2017 New England Patriots Roster   Team Record 15-4   Lost Super Bowl to Eagles

2017 League MVP Tom Brady

2017 All Pro 1st Team QB Tom Brady and TE Rob Gronkowski

QB: ***Tom Brady*** and Brian Hoyer

RB: Brandon Bolden, Rex Burkhead, James Develin, Mike Gillislee, Dion Lewis and James White

WR: Danny Amendola, Kenny Britt, Brandin Cooks, Phillip Dorsett, Chris Hogan and Bernard Reedy

TE: Dwayne Allen, Martellus Bennett, ***Rob Gronkowski*** and Jacob Hollister

OL: David Andrews, Marcus Cannon, Joe Cardona, Cole Croston, Cameron Fleming,
        Ted Karras, Shaq Mason, Nate Solder, Joe Thuney and LaAdrian Waddle

DL: Alan Branch, Malcom Brown, Adam Butler, Trey Flowers, Ricky Jean Francois, James Harrison,
        and Deatrich Wise

LB: Marquis Flowers, Jonathan Freeny, Nicholas Grisby, Geneo Grissom, Lawrence Guy,
        David Harris, James Harrison, Dont'a Hightower, Harvey Langi, Eric Lee, Cassius Marsh,
        Trevor Reilly, Elandon Roberts and Kyle Van Noy

DB: Johnson Bademosi, Malcolm Butler, Patrick Chung, Nate Ebner, Stephon Gilmore,
        Duron Harmon, Jonathan Jones, Brandon King, Devin McCourty, Jordan Richards, Eric Rowe
        and Rob Gronkowski

K: Stephen Gostkowski

P: Ryan Allen

Special Team Gunner Matthew Slater

2018 New England Patriots Roster   Team Record 14-5   Beat Rams in Super Bowl

2018 All Pro 1st Team CB Stephon Gilmore

QB: Tom Brady, Julian Edelman (took direct snap on 11-11-18) and Brian Hoyer

RB: Kenjon Barner, Rex Burkhead, James Develin, Jeremy Hill, Sony Michel, James White
        and Cordarrelle Patterson

WR: Phillip Dorsett, Julian Edelman, Josh Gordon, Chris Hogan, Riley McCarron,
        and Cordarrelle Patterson

TE: Dwayne Allen, Rob Gronkowski and Jacob Hollister

OL: David Andrews, Trent Brown, Marcus Cannon, Joe Cardona, Cole Croston, James Ferentz,
        Ted Karras, Shaq Mason, Brian Schwenke, Joe Thuney and LaAdrian Waddle

DL: Malcom Brown, Adam Butler, Adrian Clayborn, Trey Flowers, Lawrence Guy, Derek Rivers,
        Danny Shelton and Deatrich Wise

LB: Ja'Whaun Bentley, Keionta Davis, Nicholas Grisby, Geneo Grissom, Dont'a Hightower,
        Ramon Humber, Ufomba Kamalu, Albert McClellan, Elandon Roberts, John Simon
        and Kyle Van Noy

DB: Patrick Chung, Keion Crossen, Nate Ebner, ***Stephon Gilmore,*** Duron Harmon, J.C. Jackson,
        Cyrus Jones, Jonathan Jones, Brandon King, Devin McCourty, Jason McCourty, Obi Melifonwu,
        Eric Rowe, Josh Gordon and Rob Gronkowski

K: Stephen Gostkowski

P: Ryan Allen

Special Team Gunner Matthew Slater

2019 New England Patriots Roster   Team Record 12-5   Lost to Tenn in Wild Card

2019 All Pro 1st Team CB / 2019 NFL Defensive Player of the Year Stephon Gilmore

QB: Tom Brady and Jarrett Stidham

RB: Brandon Bolden, Rex Burkhead, James Develin, Damien Harris, Sony Michel, Elandon Roberts and James White

FB: James Develin, James Ferentz, Jakob Johnson, Elandon Roberts and Eric Tomlinson

WR: Antonio Brown, Phillip Dorsett, Julian Edelman, Josh Gordon, N'Keal Harry, Jakobi Myers, Gunner Olszewsi and Mohamed Sanu

TE: Ryan Izzo, Matt LaCosse, Eric Tomlinson and Benjamin Watson

OL: Marcus Cannon, Joe Cardona, Korey Cunningham, Jermaine Eluemunor, James Ferentz, Ted Karras, Shaq Mason, Marshall Newhouse, Joe Thuney and Isiah Wynn

DL: Michael Bennett, Adam Butler, Shilique Calhoun, Byron Cowart, Lawrence Guy, Danny Shelton, John Simon, Chase Winovich and Deatrich Wise

LB: Ja'Whaun Bentley, Shilique Calhoun, Jamie Collins, Dont'a Hightower, Elandon Roberts, John Simon and Kyle Van Noy

DB: Justin Bethel, Terrence Brooks, Patrick Chung, Nate Ebner, *Stephon Gilmore*, Duron Harmon, J.C. Jackson, Jonathan Jones, Devin McCourty, Jason McCourty, Obi Melifonwu, Jordan Richards and Joejuan Williams

P: Jake Bailey

K: Jake Bailey, Nick Folk, Kai Forbath, Stephen Gostkowski and Mike Nugent

Special Team Gunner Matthew Slater

TOP 3 MOST MEMORABLE PLAYERS BY POSITION

Quarterback	**Running Back**	**Wide Receiver**	**Tight End**
Tom Brady	James White	Julian Edelman	Rob Gronkowski
Drew Bledsoe	Jim Nance	Troy Brown	Ben Coates
Steve Grogan	Sam Cunningham	Stanley Morgan	Russ Francis

Center	**Guard**	**Offensive Tackle**	**Nose Tackle**
Jon Morris	John Hannah	Bruce Armstrong	Vince Wilfork
Dan Koppen	Logan Mankins	Matt Light	Ray Hamilton
Pete Brock	Joe Andruzzi	Leon Gray	Tim Goad

Defensive Tackle	**Defensive End**	**Inside Linebacker**	**Outside Linebacker**
Richard Seymour	Willie McGinest	Dont'a Hightower	Andre Tippett
Vince Wilfork	Rob Ninkovich	Tedy Bruschi	Willie McGinest
Houston Antwine	Trey Flowers	Steve Nelson	Mike Vrabel

Cornerback	**Safety**	**Punter**	**Kicker**
Ty Law	Rodney Harrison	Ryan Allen	Adam Vinatieri
Stephon Gilmore	Devin McCourty	Rich Camarillo	Stephen Gostkowski
Mike Haynes	Patrick Chung	Jake Bailey	Gino Cappelletti

Long Snapper	**Holder**	**Punt Returner**	**Kickoff Returner**
Lonie Paxton	Ken Walter	Julian Edelman	Raymond Clayborn
Jon Morris	Babe Parilli	Mack Herron	Ellis Hobbs
Pete Brock	Lee Johnson	Mike Haynes	Kevin Faulk

Special Team Gunner	**Both Offense / Defense**	**Unheralded Performer**
Matthew Slater	Troy Brown	Danny Amendola
Mosi Tatupu	Mike Vrabel	Larry Garron
Larry Izzo	Gino Cappelletti	Ron Hall

Offensive One Game Wonder	**Defensive One Game Wonder**	**Special Team One Game Wonder**
David Patten	Malcolm Butler	Bob Gladieux
Jonas Gray	Lester Williams	Dan Connolly
Shane Vereen	Prentice McCray	Patrick Chung

SOURCES AND ADDENDUM

Archives from: *The Boston Globe, Boston Herald, Patriot Ledger, Washington Post* and *The New York Times*

Websites: RemembertheAFL.com, Gridiron-uniforms.com, PATSFANS.com, IMDB.com and TV.com

God Rest the Soul of these great people who I had the distinct pleasure of hearing their stories:
Houston Antwine, Joe Bellino, Ron Burton, Nick Bouniconti, Larry Eisenhauer, Larry Garron, Ron Hobson, Bill Lenkaitis, Will McDonough, Babe Parilli, Jack Rudolph, Tom Stephens and Mosi Tatupu.

Appreciated the time I spent with: Joe Andruzzi, Tully Banta-Cain, Michael Bishop, Drew Bledsoe, Jim Boudreaux, Jim Bowman, Greg Boyd, Jacoby Brissett, Pete Brock, Malcom Brown, Troy Brown, Reche Caldwell, Bob Cappadona, Gino Cappelletti, Rick Cash, Matt Cassel, Matt Chatham, Jim Cheyunski, Patrick Chung, Ralph Cindrich, Raymond Clayborn, Thomas Clayton, Tony Collins, Vernon Crawford, Sam Cunningham, Steve DeOssie, Aaron Dobson, Ed Ellis, Kevin Faulk, Christian Fauria, Doug Flutie, Tim Fox, Russ Francis, Bob Golic, Art Graham, Jarvis Green, Steve Grogan, Rob Gronkowski, Ron Hall, John Hannah, Antwan Harris, Rodney Harrison, Dont'a Hightower, Brian Hoyer, Larry Izzo, Craig James, Roland James, Ilia Jaroschtuk, Billy Johnson, Daryl Johnson, Ted Johnson, Steve King, Dan Koppen, Max Lane, Harvey Langi, Ty Law, Bobby Leo, Matt Light, Ronnie Lippett, Curtis Martin, Bill Matthews, Prentice McCray, Willie McGinest, Lawyer Milloy, Stanley Morgan, Jon Morris, Sammy Morris, Stephen Neal, Steve Nelson, Tom Neville, Rob Ninkovich, Patrick Pass, Tom Porell, Grey Ruegamer, Mike Ruth, Logan Ryan, Rick Sanford, Harold Shaw, Tom Sherman, Chris Slade, Matthew Slater, Fred Smerlas, Otis Smith, Lenny St. Jean, Chris Sullivan, Andre Tippett, Darren Twombly, Mark van Eeghen, Kyle Van Noy, Randy Vataha, Garin Veris, Adam Vinatieri, Sebastian Vollmer, Mike Walker, Clayton Weishuhn, Jermaine Wiggins, Jon Williams, Tom Yewcic, Steve Zabel, and Scott Zolak.

Some of these stats were verified by the Elias Sports Bureau and Pro-Football Reference.com.

Some of this research has been acknowledged in the following books:

Moving the Chains! Tom Brady and the Pursuit of Everything
Charles P. Pierce, ISBN 978-0374299231. Published by Farrar, Straus and Giroux.

Game Changers: The Greatest Plays in New England Patriots History
Sean Glennon, ISBN 1600784003. Published by Triumph Books.

Bill Belichick vs the NFL: The Case for the NFL's Greatest Coach
Erik Frenz, ISBN 162937117. Published by Triumph Books.

The New England Patriots Playbook: Inside the Huddle for the Greatest Plays in Patriots History
Sean Glennon, ISBN 16293711254. Published by Triumph Books.

The PATS: An Illustrated History of the New England Patriots
Glenn Stout and Richard Johnson, ISBN 1328917401. Published by Houghton Mifflin Harcourt

From Darkness to Dynasty! The First 40 years of the New England Patriots Football Team
Jerry Thornton, ISBN 1611689740. Published by ForeEdge.

Tom Brady vs the NFL: The Case for Football's Greatest Quarterback
Sean Glennon, ISBN 1629373249. Published by Triumph Books.

Total Patriots: The Definitive Encyclopedia of the World Class Franchise
Bob Hyldburg, ISBN 9781600780998. Published by Triump Books.

FINAL THOUGHTS

On July 4, 1994, while watching the Woburn fireworks display, I kept myself busy between each launch until the finale trying to come up with the best player to wear every uniform # of the Patriots. Only until I reached #41 did I have trouble remembering the names of players. So, the next day I called my friend Gil Santos and he suggested that I get a Patriots Media Guide. I noticed that some of the players listed in that media guide were NA (not available). Gil also suggested that I contact Richard Johnson at the Sports Museum and he gave me access to a ton of material from the early years of the Patriots.

As I was researching the uniform #s from old media guides, game programs, and reports, etc., I noticed many fascinating items that I wanted to catalog as well. Over a few years I would stop by the Sports Museum Archives Facility and collect the stats on every blocked punt, blocked field goal attempt, onside kick recovery, lateral return, and many other bits of information.

Along the journey I met Patriots reporters Ron Hobson and Will McDonough and they introduced me to former Patriots Chief Statisticians Denny Lynch, Ed Brickley and Pete Palmer. These guys were extremely helpful as they kept a ton of their personal notes and game reports while they worked for the Patriots. They gladly shared their valuable information with me as it was not available on the internet.

Now it became a challenge to collect and verify the football related information of every player who has played for the Patriots. My quest became an obsession and eventually I was given access to the files at Foxboro Stadium. Stacey James, the Patriots Vice President of Media Relations, allowed me to review every line of every game during the off season and occasionally during off days during the season for the Patriots. After numerous 10-12-hour daily visits, the Patriots put this information on a disc for me so that I wouldn't need to work around their schedule.

Over the years, I would be an in-studio guest on various sports radio shows and that is where I met Steve Burton, Nick Cafardo, and Ron Borges.

I shared with Steve that I was in the process of writing a book and his dad Ron was the first former player that I interviewed. Steve shared with me that he had never spent time reminiscing with his dad about his career with the Patriots. Not many of the Boston Patriots Games in the early 1960s were televised and most of the game reports were not available.

When I found out that Steve's dad was diagnosed with terminal cancer in 2003, I wrote a few pages regarding the highlights of Ron's career for both of them. Steve had the chance a few months before Ron's death to share these memories with his dad in the Intensive Care Unit at the hospital. Ron was very weak but was able to acknowledge what his son was reading to him. In fact, Steve said that Ron asked in a soft voice, "Why are you reading this? and "I wasn't that good." It was a glorious, emotional connection that Steve continues to cherish.

By 2004, the Patriots had already won two World Championships and I still had a ton of missing information. After receiving tremendous feedback and encouragement from Steve Burton and his family, along with other players and their families, I knew that I had to finish the job.

Former *Boston Globe* reporter Nick Cafardo mentioned to me that once I was done with my extensive research he would put me in touch with a publisher. In 2008 I signed a publishing contact with Triumph Books. They had hoped to release *Total Patriots* after the Patriots beat the Giants to win the Super Bowl and go undefeated in the 2007 Season. Unfortunately, the Patriots lost that game and the book was published in September 2009 as part of the 50th Anniversary of the Patriots.

In August of 2016, I was approached by Bryan Morry, the Executive Director of the Patriots Hall of Fame, (where my *Total Patriots* book is displayed) and he asked me if I could provide the football-related bios of every Patriots player in an excel spreadsheet. He thought it would be a fabulous idea to have an interactive computer display of this information for the fans who visit the Patriots Hall of Fame. With the help of my computer wizard friend and fraternity brother Jack McGee we completed that process earlier this year. Thanks to Bryan's great idea I compiled all of this updated information in this book for every Die Hard Patriots Fan as well. We hope this interactive display will be available for everyone at the Patriots Hall of Fame next year.

Throughout my fascinating journey, I have discovered so many interesting lessons about life. Some of these thoughts I have shared at various speaking engagements. "Passion, Persistency and Faith" was the theme of one of my talks. I have also developed a "Do Your Job" workshop that captures the many modules of what it takes to have an invincible world champion mindset and commitment to win.

I now offer my services and vast knowledge of the Patriots as a lecturer, guest speaker, leadership coach, and mindset mentor for sales and training events. I am also available to serve as a Master of Ceremonies for annual client appreciation dinners, charity, or other public events. My passion is to share these stories and lessons so that we all have a purposeful driven and happy life.

Thanks, and God bless you and your family!

Bob Hyldburg
HistorianBob@hotmail.com